Also from Westphalia Press
westphaliapress.org

Friends in the Seventeenth Century

by Charles Evans

WESTPHALIA PRESS
An imprint of Policy Studies Organization

Westphalia Press
An imprint of Policy Studies Organization
1527 New Hampshire Ave., NW
Washington, D.C. 20036
info@ipsonet.org

ISBN-13: 978-1-63391-870-2
ISBN-10: 1-63391-870-X

Cover design by Jeffrey Barnes:
jbarnesbook.design

Daniel Gutierrez-Sandoval, Executive Director
PSO and Westphalia Press

Updated material and comments on this edition
can be found at the Westphalia Press website:
www.westphaliapress.org

FRIENDS

SEVENTEENTH CENTURY.

BY

CHARLES EVANS, M.D.

New and Revised Edition.

PHILADELPHIA:

FOR SALE AT FRIENDS' BOOK-STORE,

No. 304 ARCH STREET.

1885.

PREFACE.

THE motive that has prompted the preparation of the present work, has been the hope that, by thus bringing the substance of the principal parts of the narratives of other writers into a more condensed form, the members of the religious Society of Friends — especially the young — may be induced to make themselves familiar with its rise, and the severe trials that attended its early progress: that thus they may become better acquainted with the character of the instruments employed by the Head of the Church to gather Friends into a distinct body, the manner in which He prepared them for the service, and the consistent system of Scriptural doctrine they inculcated, under the teaching and help of his Holy Spirit.

Want of correct information on these points, has led some to slight or undervalue the religious attainments and Christian standing of those extraordinary men and women, who, amid contumely and suffering, of which few now have an adequate conception, reasserted the simplicity and spirituality of the Gospel, proclaimed anew some of its cardinal truths, that had been long obscured or disregarded, demonstrated the inconsistency therewith of the man-made ordinances and will-worship, existing in the professing Church, and exemplified, in life and conversation, the self-denying requirements of the divine law written in the heart.

They were bold and uncompromising witnesses for the truth as it is in Jesus; and if, occasionally, one rose up among them, who, from an untempered zeal, and the peculiar spirit of the time, was betrayed into extravagances, of which the body did not approve, it in nowise derogates from the religious principles, labors, or character of the devoted band that, in obedience to the commands of their Divine Leader, contended for the faith once delivered to the saints, and for the enjoyment of the right of liberty of conscience. By suffering and constancy, they laid the foundation of the religious freedom and privileges we now enjoy, and gave an impetus to civil liberty and moral reform, from which the professed Christian world has reaped no little benefit.

The literature approved by the Society is extensive and instructive. No fear need be entertained that it will teach unscriptural doctrine, or bias the reader towards evil or improper practices. Well would it be for the Society, were it more generally studied by its members. Should the following pages prove a means of inducing more of them to read and rightly estimate it, a principal object in the production of this work will have been attained.

It has not been thought needful to specify, on all occasions, the author from whom the respective facts are taken; but the following works have been consulted; and great care has been given to have the accounts correct:

Sewel's History, Gough's History, Barclay's Friends in Scotland, Rutty's Friends in Ireland, Bowden's Friends in America, Besse's Sufferings, The London Friends' Meetings, The Fells of Swarthmoor, The Penns and Peningtons of the Seventeenth Century, Proud's History of Pennsylvania, Neal's History of the Puritans, Bancroft's History of America, and the Journals or Memoirs of over twenty Friends; to most of whom frequent reference is made in the work.

C. E.

PHILADELPHIA, 1875.

CONTENTS.

CHAPTER I.

CHAPTER II.

CHAPTER III.

CHAPTER IV.

CHAPTER V.

CHAPTER VI.

CHAPTER VII.

CHAPTER XI.

CHAPTER XII.

CHAPTER XIII.

CHAPTER XIV.

CHAPTER XV.

CHAPTER XVI.

CHAPTER XVII.

CHAPTER XVIII.

CHAPTER XIX.

CHAPTER XX.

CHAPTER XXI.

CHAPTER XXII.

CHAPTER XXIII.

CHAPTER XXIV.

CHAPTER XXV.

CHAPTER XXVI.

CHAPTER XXVII.

CHAPTER XXVIII.

CHAPTER XXIX.

FRIENDS

IN THE

SEVENTEENTH CENTURY.

CHAPTER I.

Reformation under Henry VIII. — Edward VI. — Mary — Elizabeth —
Manner in which the Doctrines, Organization, &c., of the Church of Eng-
land were determined — Prerogative of the Crown to decide in Spiritual
Matters — No Liberty of Conscience — Witnesses to Truth — John Wycliffe
—Translation of the Bible — Progress of Inquiry and Doctrinal Differences
— Puritans — Intolerance of the Government and the Church — Presbyte-
rians — Independents — Baptists — Numerous Sects — Development of
Principles of Civil Liberty — Growth of the Contest between the Church
and Dissenters — Justice by Law defeated — Origin of the Pilgrim Fathers
— They found what was to be an Asylum for the Oppressed — Course pur-
sued by Charles I. — Resistance of the Scots to Prelacy, &c. — The Long
Parliament — Civil War — Cromwell — Attention of the People kept directed to Modes and Professions of Religion — Claims of the High Church
Party — Their views of Dissenters — Opinions and Feeling of Dissenters
towards that Party — Barbarous Laws enacted by the Presbyterians when
in Power — Summary Extinguishment of their Power by Cromwell —
General and loud Professions of Religion.

THE reformation of the national religion introduced into England
by Henry VIII. was effected by the exercise of arbitrary power,
rather to gratify evil passions roused by papal opposition, and for
self-aggrandizement, than from any desire to promote clearer views
of Christianity. The change was such as was required to shift the
title of "Supreme Head of the Church," and divert ecclesiastical
revenues from the Pope at Rome to the bluff but royal layman, who
was accustomed to use the sword or axe and block, to rid himself of
whoever or whatever stood opposed to his will. It was, however, a
means for largely extending access to sources of religious knowledge,

9

and rousing the people, in measure, from the superstitious ignorance and apathy, which it was the policy of Rome to keep undisturbed.

The crude reform of Henry was relieved in some of its more hard and rugged features, and brought nearer into conformity with the purer profession of Christianity, promulgated by the greater reformers on the continent, by Edward VI. Mild, scrupulous and devotional as he is represented to have been, though he established Protestantism in his kingdom, he was hardly fitted to detect and successfully oppose the selfishness and craft, actuating some engaged in prescribing what should be the doctrines and organization of "The Church;" so that the laws governing its action, constituting its hierarchy, defining the powers and privileges its dignitaries should enjoy, and restricting the people in the exercise of religious duties, all manifest the leaven of the same assumed priestly authority, the same will-worship, the same superstitious reverence for the functions and powers of the clergy, in the "Church" established by act of Parliament, as had characterized the religion that had been discarded.

The fires of Smithfield, kindled at the bidding of the bigoted and cruel Mary, while they inspired terror of the spirit and policy of the upholders of Romanism, at the same time warmed many among the thoughtful and religious into more effective zeal, and implanted more deeply in the minds of others, sympathizing with suffering humanity, an interest in the success of some reformation, which would, at least, free the nation from the sanguinary and unsparing tyranny of the priestly despots at Rome.

Queen Elizabeth found herself surrounded with dangers and difficulties that threatened to set aside her questionable right to the throne. Her numerous subjects who clung to the papal religion, while they loudly rejected her as their rightful sovereign, yet demanded of her protection in the exercise of their worship, inseparably connected with fealty to the Pope. Many Puritans who had left their country during the persecution of Queen Mary, had imbibed the more enlightened opinions and principles of the Protestants in France or Geneva, and they now sought a modification of the liturgy, the church powers and ceremonials, as established by Edward VI. Elizabeth, however, equally regardless of the complaints of the one, and the remonstrance of the other, took counsel of her own stubborn will, declared that "Supreme Head of the Church" was no meaningless title, and that she would regulate the religion of her realm, according to her own standard of what was right and necessary, and would have all her subjects to conform to it.

History discloses that the dissensions about religion among the different professors, and the exigencies of the civil government, furnished plausible reasons why the Crown and council, or the Parliament, should decide upon the doctrines and system of church government that should be recognized as established by law. Those who had drunk deeply of the spirit of Protestantism, were strongly bent upon discarding from the polity and ritual of the legally constituted church, everything that signally marked the papal system. They were eager to imitate the sweeping reformation exhibited at Geneva. Others who feared, lest by too great changes, there would not be left in the hands of the clergy the power they desired, and who were willing to take advantage of the natural tendency in the human mind to be influenced by show and ceremony, even in connection with the "services of religion," were strenuous for continuing many of the different orders of priests, with whatever dogmas and practices in the old time faith, would cherish their authority, and make their services indispensable. These were anxious that the robes and trappings that had distinguished their papistical predecessors should be retained. Yet the ceremonies of "consecration," were repulsive even to some who were entitled to the office of bishop, and some of them refused to wear the vestments thought necessary by others for prelates or clergy. The controversy was long and bitter, and consequently compromises had to be extorted or voluntarily made; and the resulting articles of belief, liturgy, order of priests, and ritual, prescribed by secular authority, were incorporated in what has long been known as "The Church of England."

During the reign of Queen Mary, Parliament, from deference to the Pope, had repealed the Act by which the Sovereign was made the Supreme Head of the church; but it was now restored, and the king or queen of the realm was clothed with authority to decide in all matters of faith and practice; to prescribe what doctrines should be preached, and to amend or redress all heresies; awarding the punishment that should be suffered by those who disobeyed whatever, on this subject, had received the royal sanction: the punishment varying from fines to imprisonment, and even death. Thus it became a prerogative of the crown, either with or without the advice of the council, to judge for and direct the whole nation what form of religion it should profess and uphold; utterly depriving each and all of the enjoyment of the right of liberty of conscience.

Notwithstanding the lapse that long existed from the purity and

simplicity of primitive Christianity, it had pleased the merciful
Head of the church, at various times and in different places, during
the dark ages of the apostacy, to raise up men — one here and
another there — who, through the operation of Divine Grace, or the
Light of Christ on their minds, were brought to see in part through
the darkness and corruption that surrounded them, and were enabled
to protest against the superstition and idolatry that had crept into
the professing church, perverting the worship which is required to
be in spirit and in truth, blinding the people to the liberty and
privileges the gospel of salvation was intended to confer, and subjecting them to the oppressive impositions of a self-constituted body,
claiming to be clothed with power and functions, incompatible with
the constitution of the church of Christ.   These witnesses for the
truth had promulgated it, so far as it had been opened to their
understandings; thereby bringing on themselves opposition and
persecution.   But the general purity of their lives, their faith and
patience in tribulation, and the Christian fortitude and peace with
which several of them had confirmed their testimony at the stake,
had commended the doctrines they preached to many who heard
them; and who, though afraid to avow them openly, treasured them
in their hearts, and often declared them to others around, or transmitted them to those who came after them.

In England, John Wycliffe, as early as 1375, had denounced the
Pope as anti-Christ, and used the influence he had acquired by his
learning and religious character, to disseminate opinions entirely
opposed to some of the cherished articles in the Popish creed.
Above all, he succeeded in producing a version of the Holy Scriptures in English; supposed to be the first translation into a modern
language ever made.   He was condemned and branded as a heretic
by a council of bishops, and his translated Bible was proscribed.
But many were convinced of the truths he promulgated; the converts being subsequently called Lollards, after a martyr for the
same truths advocated by Wycliffe, named Lolhard, who was burnt
at Cologne.

From the time of Wycliffe to the period when a formal separation from the Romish church was effected by the reformation under
Henry VIII., the attention of not a few among the people was kept
turned, more or less, to the perversions of Christian doctrine taught
by the priests, and to the corruptions which they practised or sanctioned, by devoted individuals, made willing to attempt stemming
the superstitious ignorance and irreligion of the times.   In 1534,

William Tyndale, who had been long laboring in the work, published his improved translation of the Scriptures; which being eagerly sought after, and copies distributed among many who could read, a knowledge of the Sacred truths contained therein was widely spread, and proved a powerful means of diffusing light and improved feeling; thereby convincing many of the errors of the religion in which they had been educated, and emboldening them to teach doctrines at variance with those enforced by the national church.

The different eminent men made use of, to point out the errors and corruptions in the professing church, and bring the attention of its members back to the cardinal truths of Christianity, were lights in the respective periods in which they lived and could not be hid; but most of them got but partial views of the truths revealed in the gospel; though like the voice of one crying in the wilderness, their labors tended to prepare the way of the Lord; and the numbers attracted to them, served, in measure, to disintegrate the great body of professors, and to draw zealous worshippers into some organic cohesion.

After the Reformation in England was fully established, in the reign of Elizabeth, there were those who saw, more or less clearly, the many Popish errors that had been retained in the doctrines and constitution of the " Episcopal church," and who, being sincerely desirous that the people should be taught " in the way of God more perfectly," testified boldly against the disputed points in the creed, the man-made hierarchy, and many of the ceremonies still enjoined and practised. Some of these promulgated their opinions with so much zeal and success, that being denounced by prelates high in ecclesiastical authority, strenuous efforts were made to silence them, and a few were arrested, tried, condemned, and, by order of the queen, burned at the stake. But the spirit of free inquiry and religious liberty had obtained sufficient hold on the minds of large numbers, not to be expelled or silenced by this barbarous persecution. Many withdrew from attending at the authorized places of public worship, and as they came to recognize and understand one another, in relation to their dissent from the national religion, and the work of Grace in their hearts, they were drawn into outward fellowship and covenanted to keep together.

Those who thus essayed a purer form of worship and discipline, received, from others who affected to contemn them, the name of Puritans, and as there were among them, some who held benefices, and yet refused to use the Episcopal liturgy in their " churches," they thus incurred the censure, and soon the bitter hatred of the bishops, headed by Whitgift, bent on protecting and extending their own ill-gotten power; and also the interference of the Government, determined that all should bow unresistingly to its "Act of Uniformity," which forbade, under severe penalties, any other mode of worship, or any other form of prayer or praise than those prescribed by the Queen and Parliament. The two were not long in inflicting punishment on all whom they could bring within reach of their power, who refused to comply with their arbitrary and unchristian requisitions; and many suffered severely. Driven into more intimate relations by the means taken to destroy them, and finding they could no longer remain in membership with the "Established church," which they had all along desired, a large portion of these Puritans formed themselves into a separate religious Society; and substituting for bishops and other high ecclesiastics, experienced men as rulers, whom they called Presbyters, they received, from this, the name of Presbyterians.

Another party of Puritans, which had adopted the sentiments of a popular preacher, named Robert Brown, and from him had been called Brownists, went further than the Presbyterians in protesting against the assumptions, and the corruptions of the national church. They held that these accepted errors destroyed her right to be considered a true church, and that her ministers, with the position, the titles and the power they assumed, were not rightly qualified ministers of Christ. They also insisted that every congregation constituted a church of itself, with full power to choose its own pastor, and exercise control over its own members, without the interference of any other congregation or body claiming superior authority; and from this peculiarity in their church government, they obtained the name of Independents.

Although the doctrine of the necessity of arriving at the age of religious understanding before baptism was administered, and that it must be done by immersion, had been entertained, and frequently preached by some from the time of Wycliffe, and many who held it, under the name of Anabaptists, suffered greatly, some even unto death at the stake, it was not until near the beginning of the seventeenth century, that the Baptists formed a distinct religious body. Its early members appear to have attained more clear and spiritual views of the Christian religion than most others of the time, and consequently were greatly inveighed against. They boldly asserted the right of all professors to enjoy liberty of conscience; that as

Christ was the alone Head of the church, He only could qualify for preaching his gospel, and that school learning was not necessary to fit a man for a minister. They denied the right to demand pay for preaching, and some of them alleged that both war and taking an oath were opposed to the precepts and spirit of the New Testament. It was not many years, however, before some of these truths were lost sight of by them.

As inquiry and disputation upon points of faith and practice spread, especially during the civil war, the division and subdivision of religious professors multiplied. Their names were too numerous to be here recited; but there were Seekers, who, William Penn says, "At their outset were very diligent, plain, and serious; strong in Scripture and bold in profession, bearing much reproach and contradiction;" Levellers, Waiters, Familists, Perfectionists, Ranters, and Muggletonians, the last two being distinguished by their blasphemous notions, and wild, anarchical discourses.

It was a natural consequence of entertaining religious opinions more in accordance with the Headship of Christ in the church, with the equality of its members, and the brotherhood of man, as set forth in the New Testament, that the political principles of the different bodies into which the Puritans had been divided, should be modified thereby. These associations therefore, without any avowed antagonism to the civil authority of the State, were an element in the community more or less opposed to the commonly received belief in the divine right of kings, and to the right of the government to regulate the creed, the organization, or the discipline of the church. They constituted a body unconsciously under the influence of the leaven of republicanism; gradually working on all brought within the reach of its action, preparing them to appreciate and seek for civil as well as religious liberty, and at last to resist successfully the usurpations of the Sovereign and the high church party.

While the fear of the machinations of the Pope, his emissaries and adherents, had pressed upon them, Conformists and Non-conformists united in repelling them, and in endeavoring to punish, and, if possible, to drive them from the realm. But as those professing Romanism diminished in number, and in their efforts to embarrass and weaken the government, and the Episcopal church party felt itself securely entrenched in power, it became less hostile towards them, and more zealous for an indisputable supremacy of the king in council, the divine origin of its own constitution and dignities, and the duty of unquestioning submission of each and all subjects to whatever was enacted by either church or State. Opposition to its *dicta* or measures met with no toleration, and the clergy cherished an animosity towards Dissenters, as they called them, which increased in proportion as they found them determined to maintain their own convictions of right, and resist encroachments on their liberties. On both sides the passions became too much inflamed to allow the voice of reason to be heeded; religious controversy ripened into civil strife; carried on by the king and his coadjutors, the high church party, in support or defence of measures adopted by the Sovereign, under the authority of his assumed prerogative and by a portion of the Parliament and the people, in disputing illegal exactions, and refusing to comply with arbitrary and unconstitutional edicts.

Appeal was made to the Courts, but the subserviency of the Judges to the expressed wishes or the menaces of the crown, prevented the administration of laws, long before enacted for the preservation of the rights of the subjects; thus defeating the demands of justice and equity, and subjecting to close imprisonment and other severe punishments, some of the noblest and most distinguished men that adorn that period of England's history. The national hierarchy were implacable in the enforcement of other laws provided to compel to uniformity; using them and ecclesiastical courts, as a means to harass and crush the Dissenters; so that many of the Presbyterians, Independents, and others, in order to escape the cruel persecution that often stripped them of the means of subsistence, by heavy fines, &c., while it prevented the exercise of their forms of worship, fled to Holland, and other places on the continent.

Among those thus driven from their native country, and who had taken up their abode in Holland, was a congregation of Independents, whose pastor was John Robinson. In addition to the depressing feeling accompanying exile, these persecuted religionists had to endure many hardships in their new home, arising from their poverty, and the uncertainty of finding a fixed dwelling place. There also grew up a feud between them and other congregations of separatists, and, in course of time, finding their number decreasing, they resolved to seek another asylum where, with unrestricted liberty of conscience, they might still be within the jurisdiction of England's sovereign power. After carefully considering the advantages of different places of refuge proposed, they resolved to remove to America. Accordingly in the Seventh month of 1620, about four years before the death of King James I., a portion of them embarked at Delfthaven in two vessels, sailing first for Southampton, England, intending to make the necessary arrangements there for obtaining the right of settlement and establishing a colony. Many obstacles and vexations detained them in that port, and after getting away, one of the vessels had to return. The other — the Mayflower — after a voyage of two months, arrived on the shores of New England, and surmounting many difficulties, finally landed on what subsequently received the name of Plymouth Rock. These bold adventurers have become world renowned as "The Pilgrim Fathers."

They founded a colony, which was understood to be a refuge for those persecuted for their religion, where such should find safety and peace. They appear to have been religious-minded men, disciplined in the school of adversity, and doubtless, under the feeling awakened by the suffering they had passed through, they were sincere in the feeling of toleration and charity; but, as will be seen in succeeding pages, these virtues were incompatible with principles otherwhere avowed, and their successors either forgot, or grievously disregarded the disposition of their forefathers. For three years they endured almost incredible hardships.

James, while he occupied the Scottish throne, manifested a strong disposition to favor the national Kirk, but he had hardly crossed the border on his way to take possession of the throne of England, before he gave evidence how little he was governed by fixed principles of religion or conduct, by siding with the high church party he there found in the ascendant; and with the motto "No bishop, no king," he used the power he could command, to make all professors subservient to prelacy. Nevertheless he bestowed a priceless boon upon his country, by the celebrated translation of the Scriptures, which was undertaken and published under his patronage.

Charles I., who ascended the throne on the death of James I., pursued the same policy as his father, but with more directness and determination. It was during his reign, that the widening of the breach between the established church and different classes of Puritans, of which notice has been taken, took place most rapidly and irreparably; the feelings of both parties becoming so embittered towards each other, that the whole nation was in a state of excitement and contention. As one step after another was taken by the royal party, to enforce their measures and punish opposition, calling forth more determined resistance, it became evident that a crisis was approaching, wherein the people would see the liberties of their country fatally sacrificed, or the monarch and the Episcopal Church, of which he was the head, deprived of much of their power for evil.

In his infatuated obstinacy to have his own way, and rule by what he called his divine right, notwithstanding the wide-spread disaffection throughout England, arising from the high-handed efforts to drive all into the observance of the formula prescribed by the "Church," Charles resolved to force prelacy and the liturgy on the Scots. Under the tuition of John Knox and his coadjutors, that portion of his subjects had become fully indoctrinated with Calvinism, and such was their attachment to its dogmas and their own system of church government, that the announcement of an intention to introduce Episcopacy as the national religion, at once roused their passion and called forth open and determined opposition. They broke out into riots; threatened to take the lives of any bishops who might come among them, and by force prevented the reading of the "stated services" in the places of worship. This was followed by the adoption of the "Solemn League and Covenant," sworn to by most of the nobles, the ministers and the people; by which they bound themselves to resist to the uttermost the introduction among them of the Episcopal Church, and to preserve their own form of religion — Presbyterianism — intact.

The king having resolved to resort to the sword to settle his quarrel with the Scots, into which he had so recklessly plunged, found it necessary to convene a parliament — none having been called together for eleven years — in order to obtain the means to carry on the war. But though this was supplied, he was disappointed in his attempts at coercion, and was obliged to forego his project of fastening prelacy and the liturgy on his rebellious subjects. The parliament, which at first had manifested a strong desire to act favorably towards its sovereign, having afterwards proceeded to inquire into some of the more glaring abuses that had existed for a long time, was at once dissolved by the king.

It soon became apparent that, under the pressure of feelings called forth by the presence of an army more powerful than his own, Charles had dissembled in his concessions to the Scots; and it was not long before he sought and found an occasion for disregarding the stipulations into which he had entered, and to carry out his own perverse will. To strike a blow that would be felt, required extra funds, and the public mind was in no temper to submit patiently to an attempt made to raise the sum required by the exclusive action of the House of Lords, which the king had assembled at York.

Finding there was no alternative between submission to the demands of the insurgent and incensed Presbyterians in the north, and facing another parliament, the king issued the writs, and when assembled once more applied to it for assistance.

Having convened in the Ninth month of 1640,* it at once became apparent that a large majority of the members represented a constituency determined to have their grievances heard and redressed. The Commons speedily entered on the performance of this duty. Finding the power was in their hands, they resolved to make thorough work, and, in order to prevent the king cutting short the reforming measures contemplated, by again suddenly dismissing the legislature of the nation, they began by enacting a law requiring that at no time should more than three years elapse between the dissolution of one parliament and the meeting of another; and afterwards they passed a resolution for their own unlimited continuance.

This Parliament became famous as the Long Parliament. It claimed to speak and act for the nation in opposition to the encroachments of the king and his party on the rights of the people, and their disregard of the people's clearly expressed will. The contention between the two became more and more acrimonious and irreconcilable; accusations and recriminations were freely exchanged as well as demands made and refused. Each party prepared for the desperate struggle all saw was impending, and in 1642, the sword was unsheathed, and blood first shed in the sanguinary civil war carried on under the banners of Cavaliers and Roundheads. After varying fortunes on both sides, the contest resulted in the overthrow of the Royalist armies and power; the king, after being made prisoner, was brought to the block; the whole government and polity of the realm were reconstructed, and finally, Oliver Cromwell, having risen above all competitors, was appointed Lord Protector of England.

It will have been seen that from the introduction of the Reformation into England by Henry VIII., in addition to the necessity of keeping the papists from again obtaining ascendency, and reducing the kingdom to dependence on the Pope, which at the outset was a primary object, doctrines and forms of religion had been, more or less, forced on the attention of the people, by the struggle kept up between the high church party in power, to maintain the principles and the ecclesiastical organization adopted by it, and other religious professors bent on asserting liberty of conscience, and

* The dates in this work are according to the old style.

escaping the penalties of worshipping in conformity with what they recognized as the requirements of the gospel. It was not likely to be diverted from the momentous subject when "the bloody queen" Mary, ascended the throne, and re-delivered the Kingdom to the will of the See of Rome, and the "tender mercies" of Legates and Cardinals. The many martyrs who, during her short reign, perished at the stake, as witnesses for the truths of the gospel, so far as they understood them, challenged the attention of all, and awakened in the minds of the more sober part of the people, a feeling of reverence for themselves, and for the cause for which they laid down their lives; thus bringing home to the hearts of those who reflected on the startling events of the time, the conviction that religion was of higher importance than the ordinary affairs of secular life.

During the long period of civil commotion, or military conflict, that intervened from the death of King James to the establishment of the Commonwealth, religious faith and church government were subjects that largely occupied the minds of thinking men. The war was waged as much on account of theological differences as civil rights. Even where conformity was professed, many were convinced of the unrighteousness of the church system, under which so many in the nation groaned. Controversy and persecution spread abroad a knowledge of some truths long concealed or obscured ; and men who were sincerely desirous to know and to do their Heavenly Father's will, were drawn by sympathy into union, one with another, for the purpose of edifying each other in the religion they held most dear.

The Anglican Church party, of which the king was the spiritual and the political head, though numbering among its " clergy " and " laity " many who were exemplary for their piety, was yet, as a head and body, determined to force on all the notions,—That there could be no church where there were no bishops ; that there could be no bishops unless they were " consecrated " by those having apostolical succession, and that *its* priests alone could availingly administer what were called the " sacraments ;" viz., baptism or sprinkling, working regeneration ; and the " eucharist ; in which they alleged the bread and wine, after the prescribed action of the priest, underwent some inexplicable change, so that they who partook of them, derived spiritual sustenance from the body and blood of Christ. Ignoring that their own " church " was but a disowned offspring of rebellion from its mother at Rome, who denounced it as altogether heretical, they stigmatized all Dissenters as schismatics, and scoffed at their respective pretensions to be a part of the church of

Christ; denied their organizations to be sanctioned by scriptural or traditional authority, and rejected the claims of their ministers to be called to the work, or to be capable of performing any ministerial service. But among the men attached to the Episcopal party, with extensive learning and large acquaintance with the claims and interests of the established church there were some, such as Hales, Chillingworth and Jeremy Taylor, whose theories of doctrinal differences and the right of church government, were far more liberal than those of the dignitaries, whose bigotry and narrow thought urged the court and church into the oppressive and exasperating measures that finally wrecked the whole party.

On the other hand, the Dissenters denounced, with equal fervor, the close approximation of the "Church established by law" to some of the unscriptural dogmas, and many of the idolatrous rites and ceremonies of the hated papists, from whom they had copied them; while they fiercely resented the arrogant assumptions of its hierarchy, and claimed for themselves to be the champions of an open Bible, an unfettered ministry, and a free church. They justly charged many of those holding ministerial offices in the "Establishment," with leading irreligious lives, and, by precept and example, encouraging vain and corrupt practices among the people; while they claimed that with them, religion was the primary object in life, and that they were prepared, should the power be conferred upon them, to bring about not only a change of religious profession, but a real reformation in the morals of the people.

Although there were among those who stood high in the different sects, men who put on the profession of religion for some sinister purpose, and practised not a little cant and hypocrisy; and among the undissembling, many with a fanatical zeal that led them far beyond the bounds of Christian charity, yet, scattered throughout nearly all, were numerous persons of undoubted piety; the uppermost desire of whose hearts, was to live in love with all men, and to be found in the proper discharge of their civil and religious duties.

When the war resulted in the "Roundheads" destroying or scattering their opponents, the Presbyterians, who had a large majority in the parliament, obtained for a time control of the nation. They had been fighting long and fiercely against the Cavaliers, ostensibly for the enjoyment of the right of liberty of conscience, and that all Christians should worship the Almighty in accordance therewith; but when they believed the power to be securely in their hands, they at once began to enforce conformity to their own religious views.

They asserted the plenary and infallible inspiration of the Scriptures, but declared that theirs was the only true interpretation of them, and made no secret that their principles were opposed to toleration, and that they were prepared to visit with the severest punishments, all who would not assent to what they required. Accordingly, while the army under Cromwell was in the north, subduing the Scots, who had risen in favor of Charles, they enacted a law, by which a persistent refusal to acknowledge the truth of any one of eight specified articles of faith, incurred the penalty of death; and a similar rejection of either of sixteen other points of belief, subjected the "heretic" to imprisonment, &c., until he should agree not to maintain his errors any longer. They also passed an ordinance entitled "A Form of Church Government to be used in the Churches of England and Ireland." These measures at last brought them into conflict with the Independents, who were neither so bigoted nor so intolerant. The latter sought to effect a change to a milder policy. The Presbyterians refused any abatement or compromise, and Cromwell, who was connected with the Independents, brought his invincible legions to his aid, took the reins of government into his own hands, and purged the House of his opponents.

The Episcopal Church was no longer recognized; those of its clergy who refused to conform to the new order of things, were expelled from their "livings;" which were taken possession of by some of those who had previously been called Dissenters, and who now availed themselves of the laws for collecting tithes, which were unrepealed. "Religion," says Orme, "was now the language and garb of the Court; prayer and fasting were fashionable exercises; a profession was the road to preferment." The soldiers professed to unite the military and spiritual vocations, so that in their camps preaching and praying alternated with their drills; they sang psalms or hymns as they charged their enemies, and when occasion offered, officers or privates, who supposed themselves gifted for the work, entered the pulpit or mounted a gun-carriage, and worked on the feelings of their audience by long sermons, or by prayers nearly equally extended.

CHAPTER II.

Review of Points in the Preceding Chapter — Truths of the Gospel lost Sight of — Birth and Youth of George Fox — Early religious Character — Travels from Home — Deep Mental Conflicts and Exercises — Gospel Truths opened to his Understanding — Full belief in the Divinity and Atonement of Christ — Extracts from his Journal descriptive of his State and the knowledge Attained — First Appearance as a Minister — Political and Religious State of England at that time — Continued inward exercises — Doctrines Preached and his Commission from the Lord — Progress of Truth — Gospel Testimonies Revived, Promulgated and Maintained by G. Fox—Plainness in Speech, Behavior and Apparel — The Sacred Truths of the Scriptures to be understood by the aid of the Holy Spirit — Call and Qualification of a Gospel Minister—Perfection—Imprisonments—Attempt to induce G. F. to join the Army—Origin of the name Quaker—Prison Reform—Women's Preaching.

IN the preceding chapter, a glance has been taken of the political and religious condition of England during the time that elapsed between the enforcement of the Reformation by Henry VIII., and the inauguration of the Commonwealth under Cromwell. It has been seen that the antagonism between different parties embracing the new faith, had extended from those in power in State and Church, to different classes of the people: that it first developed passionate controversy between the "Established Church," and those who could not accept all its teachings, nor admit the arrogant claims of its dignitaries: that this led to cruel persecution, in an unsuccessful attempt to extinguish opposition to what were believed by many to be an unscriptural creed, and an oppressive and domineering priesthood: that the dissatisfaction terminated in a general outbreak of a spirit, determined to obtain more free exercise of civil and religious liberty; which, after a sanguinary conflict, wrested the government out of the control of the king and the high church party. Cromwell, who was the master mind of the Captains of his age, seized the reins of government, and directed military and political power to enforce, if not conformity to his own creed, subjection to his personal authority. He professed to desire that liberty of conscience should be enjoyed; but self-interest and the love of place, often induced him to wink at the intolerant conduct of others, who made use of the position they occupied by his appointment, to inflict penalties for religious opinions, or modes of worship, differing from their own.

During the eventful period reviewed, men had become accustomed to think upon and discuss the points of religious belief, on which there long had been differences of opinion; and as the state of the professing church, as well as that of the nation at large, had been throughout such as to demand the attention of those who had capacity to think and to act, very many within different classes of society, took deep interest in the subjects brought into dispute; which thus acquired a dignity and importance previously withheld from them.

Nevertheless, there were certain great and fundamental truths or principles of the gospel, underlying the whole system of Christianity, which though they may have been admitted in theory or written creeds, had long been very much lost sight of, denied or perverted, in the self-seeking teaching of the overbearing clergy, and the heated and blinding controversies of sects or parties, struggling for liberty or power. Although the doctrine of the influence of the Holy Spirit was thus admitted, his indwelling with men, or that "The Grace of God which bringeth salvation had appeared unto all men, teaching them" how to become partakers of the salvation purchased by Christ, was unacknowledged or denied.

It was claimed by the "Church,"—said to be organized in accordance with the Divine will, that to it belonged exclusively all the authority and right which a commission from Christ could convey, — that it was collectively inspired by the Holy Spirit, and its individual members participated in the influence of that Spirit through the external "means of grace" possessed and administered by the "Church;" as baptism, the eucharist, preaching, praying, and instruction in the Scriptures.

The Bible was received as the complete and final revelation of the Divine will, in relation to everything connected with the salvation of the soul, and consequently was considered the primary rule of faith and practice; but the authoritative interpretation of the text, was virtually claimed and made binding by the "Church;" or in other words, by the "clergy;" who, as a body, were not disposed to give any exegesis that would curtail their power, or otherwise injuriously affect their interest. The Headship of Christ in the church, and that equality among believers set forth in his declaration, "One is your master, even Christ, and all ye are brethren," were generally disallowed or perverted, by denying the bestowal of Spiritual gifts on any but such as had undergone a prescribed course of study, and been *ordained* by men. These formed a distinct *class*, with peculiar titles, power, and privileges; exercising their ministerial functions as a profession, and claiming the right to demand pecuniary compensation for their services. That Christ's kingdom is not of this world, and therefore his disciples are forbidden to fight, though so clearly set forth in his teaching, and so fully confirmed by the whole spirit of the gospel, was altogether ignored; and consequently the constitution and working of the predominant church, were complicated with the character and action of the political government, and none appeared to comprehend its organization and the execution of its duties, without connection with and dependence on the Legislature or the administration of the State, and without holding that as these were often brought into collision with opponents, Christians were therefore warranted in engaging in war.

But He who watches over his Church by night as well as by day, as He had preserved witnesses to the truth throughout the ages of almost universal darkness, so was He now at work in the hearts of individuals, preparing them to detect and reject the many errors in doctrine, and the many rites and ceremonies by which man in his own will and wisdom, had overlaid and obscured the truth, and to turn away from them ; also from those who claimed to be ministers of Christ, while their lives bore witness that they knew not what it was to be subjected to his heart-changing baptism, or to cease from serving the spirit of the world. Thus there were those in different portions of the professing Church, who were longing after a more spiritual religion than could be found while it maintained such a mechanical routine of ceremony, between the worshipper and the Father of Spirits ; who were seeking a more full exemplification of the transforming power and purity of the gospel, and were earnestly looking for a clearer light to shine upon the path of the just.

That light came not by any sudden outburst of religious illumination within any one of the various sections into which the visible Church was divided ; but by the inshining of the Day Spring from on high, in the hearts of different members attached to them, who were hungering and thirsting after righteousness, and waiting to be taught the way of the Lord more perfectly. The work had been and was going on secretly and with slow progress, hidden in the hearts of many, like seed in the warm earth, awaiting the time and the means by which it would be more powerfully quickened, and enabled to push forth the blade, form the ear and perfect the full corn in the ear.

George Fox was born in Drayton-in-the-Clay, in Leicestershire, in the year 1624, about one year before the death of King James I. He was the son of Christopher and Mary Fox, the maiden name of the latter being Lago, said to be of the stock of the martyrs. They were members of the Episcopal Church, and were highly esteemed for their piety; the father being called by his neighbors " Righteous Christer," on account of his honesty and uprightness.

George Fox was remarkable, when a child, for his gravity and sedateness, and he states that when but eleven years of age, he " knew pureness and righteousness ; " and that "The Lord taught [him] to be faithful in all things, and to act faithfully in two ways ; viz., inwardly to God, and outwardly to man, and to keep to yea and nay in all things."

Seeing the seriousness of his youthful character, his relatives at first thought to have him educated for becoming a priest ; but that being abandoned, he was placed with a shoemaker, who also dealt in cattle and wool ; and in the latter George was employed. It does not appear that he received any further school education than enabled him to read and write and cast accounts, with facility. Conscientiously just and exact in all his dealings, it became a common saying among those who knew him, that " If George says verily — a word he often used — there is no altering him."

When about nineteen years of age [1642], being at a fair, he was much grieved by two of his acquaintances, who were professors of religion, with whom he had gone to an inn, for some refreshment — drinking healths, and urging him to join them therein. He refused, and left them. That night he was sleepless, being brought under great exercise of mind ; and having cried fervently unto the Lord, he states, He said unto me, " Thou seest how young people go together into vanity, and old people into the earth ; thou must forsake all, young and old, keep out of all, and be as a stranger unto all." This appears to have been the beginning of " The various exercises, trials and troubles," through which the Lord led him, in order, as he observes, " To prepare and fit him for the work, unto which He had appointed him."

Believing it required of him, he left home in the Seventh month of 1643, and tarrying a shorter or longer time at different places, but not forming intimate acquaintance with any, he arrived in London, where he had an uncle residing, who was a Baptist. Here, as elsewhere, he was a close observer of the doctrines and practices of different professors, but they corresponded not with the standard he saw held up in the Scriptures, and learning that his relatives were uneasy at his prolonged absence from home, he returned into Leicester, where he remained for a time. Continuing under great sorrow and exercise of mind, not only on account of the sense given him of his own condition, as a fallen child of Adam, and his entire inability by any means at his own command to extricate himself therefrom, and also of the superficiality of the religion of those with whom he was brought into contact — many of whom, though they made much profession, appeared to know little or nothing of that transforming Grace, which, as it is obeyed, makes man a new creature—he passed some years without coming to that full settlement and peace which his soul longed for.

At this time the Episcopal Church was yet in power, and to remove his doubts and receive instruction in the way of righteousness, he often resorted to priests who had acquired high character; but, he says, "I found no comfort in them." He, however, became noted among many, of different religious denominations, as a young man of remarkable experience and discerning of spirits. Although his conflicts were many, and his sorrow, at times, great, yet he was favored, through the Light of Christ shining in his soul, with many revelations respecting subjects connected with the spirituality of the gospel of Christ, and the many corruptions that had crept into and marred the professing church, but which were accepted by the people as being all right. Thus he saw, that although the members of the different denominations claimed to be believers, yet that none were *true* believers but those who were born of God, and had passed from death unto life; also, that "being bred at Oxford or Cambridge was not enough to fit and qualify men to be ministers of Christ." That Christ, as the Head of his own church, could alone call and qualify those whom He ordains to preach the gospel of life and salvation; He first, by the transforming operation of his Grace, and the baptisms of the Holy Ghost and fire, making them practically acquainted with the gospel, as the power of God unto salvation, and thus fitting them to receive the gift. That "God, who made the world, did not dwell in temples made with hands." As these things were so at variance with the opinions formed by his education, and generally believed, they at first almost staggered him, but he soon became convinced they were incontrovertible truths which he was bound to maintain.

His firm belief in the deity and atonement of Christ is fully set forth in his reply to a question put to him by the priest of Drayton. He says, this priest asked me, "Why Christ cried out upon the cross, 'My God, my God, why hast thou forsaken me?'

And why, He said, 'If it be possible, let this cup pass from me; yet not my will, but thine be done?' I told him; at that time the sins of all mankind were upon him, and their iniquities and transgressions, with which He was wounded; which He was to bear and to be an offering for, as He was man, but died not as He was God; so in that He died for all men, tasting death for every man, He was an offering for the sins of the whole world. This I spoke, being at that time, in a measure, sensible of Christ's sufferings." [1645.]

As George Fox was the first and the principal instrument made use of by the Head of the Church, in gathering and founding the Society of Friends, it seems right to give a more detailed account of his religious exercises, and the gradual unfolding to his understanding, by the same Spirit that dictated the Scriptures, of the doctrines and testimonies of the gospel as believed in and held by Friends, than can be expected of others, in this account of the rise of the Society. The following passages are therefore taken from his journal:

1646. "Though I had great openings, yet great trouble and temptations came many times upon me, so that when it was day I wished for night, and when it was night I wished for day; and by reason of the openings I had in my troubles, I could say as David said, 'Day unto day uttereth speech, and night unto night showeth knowledge.' When I had openings they answered one another, and answered the Scriptures; for I had great openings of the Scriptures: and when I was in troubles, one trouble also answered to another."

.   .   .   .

1647. "I fasted much, walked abroad in solitary places many days, and often took my Bible and sat in hollow trees and lonesome places till night came on; and frequently in the night walked mournfully about by myself: for I was a man of sorrows in the time of the first workings of the Lord in me.

"During all this time I was never joined in profession of religion with any, but gave up myself to the Lord, having forsaken all evil company, taken leave of father and mother, and all other relations, and travelled up and down as a stranger in the earth, which way the Lord inclined my heart; tarrying sometimes more, sometimes less in a place: for I durst not stay long in a place, being afraid both of professor and profane, lest, being a tender young man, I should be hurt by conversing much with either. For which reason I kept much as a stranger, seeking heavenly wisdom and getting knowledge from the Lord; and was brought off from outward things, to rely on the Lord alone. Though my exercises and troubles were very great, yet were they not so continual but that I had some intermissions, and was sometimes brought into such an heavenly joy, that I thought I had been in Abraham's bosom. As I cannot declare the misery I was in, it was so great and heavy upon me, so neither can I set forth the mercies of God unto me in all my misery. O the everlasting love of God to my soul, when I was in great distress! when my troubles and torments were great, then was his love exceeding great."

.   .   .   .

"But as I had forsaken the priests, so I left the separate preachers also, and those called the most experienced, for I saw there was none among them all that could speak to my condition. And when all my hopes in them and in all men were gone, so that I had nothing outwardly, to help me, nor could tell what to do, then, O then, I heard a voice which said, 'There is one, even Christ Jesus, that can speak to thy condition.' When I heard it, my heart did leap for joy. Then the Lord let me see why there was none upon the earth that could speak to my condition, namely, that I might give Him all the glory."

.   .   .   .

"My desires after the Lord grew stronger, and zeal in the pure knowledge of God, and of Christ alone, without the help of any man, book, or writing. For though I read the Scriptures that spake of Christ and of God, yet I knew Him not but by revelation, as He who hath the key did open, and as the Father of life drew me to his Son by his Spirit. Then the Lord gently led me along, and let me see his love, which was endless and eternal, surpassing all the knowledge that men have in the natural state, or can get by history or books."

"One day, when I had been walking solitarily abroad, and was come home, I was taken up in the love of God, so that I could not but admire the greatness of His love; and while I was in that condition, it was opened unto me by the eternal light and power, and I therein clearly saw, That all was done and to be done in and by Christ; and how He conquers and destroys this tempter the devil, and all his works, and is atop of him; and that all these troubles were good for me, and temptations for the trial of my faith, which Christ had given me. The Lord opened me, that I saw through all these troubles and temptations. My living faith was raised, that I saw all was done by Christ the life, and my belief was in Him."

.   .   .   .

"As the Light appeared, all appeared that is out of the Light; darkness, death, temptations, the unrighteous, the ungodly; all was manifest and seen in the Light. After this, a pure fire appeared in me: then I saw how He sat as a refiner's fire, and as the fuller's soap. Then the spiritual discerning came into me; by which I discerned my own thoughts, groans, and sighs; and what it was that veiled me, and what it was that opened me. That which could not abide in the patience, nor endure the fire, in the Light I found to be the groans of the flesh, that could not give up to the will of God; which had so veiled me, that I could not be patient in all trials, troubles, anguishes, and perplexities; could not give up self to die by the cross, the power of God, that the living and quickened might follow Him, and that that which would cloud and veil from the presence of Christ, that which the sword of the Spirit cuts down, and which must die, might not be kept alive. I discerned the groans of the Spirit, which opened me, and made intercession to God: in which Spirit is the true waiting upon God, for the redemption of the body, and of the whole creation. By this true Spirit, in which the true sighing is, I saw over the false sighings and groanings."

.   .   .   .

"The Lord God opened to me by his invisible power, how 'Every man was enlightened by the divine light of Christ.' I saw it shine through all, and that they that believed in it came out of condemnation to the Light of life, and became the children of it; but they that hated it, and did not believe in it, were condemned by it, though they made a profession of Christ. This I saw in the pure openings of the Light without the help of any man; neither did I then know where to find it in the Scriptures; though afterwards, searching the Scriptures, I found it. For I saw in that Light and Spirit which were before the Scriptures were given forth, and which led the holy men of God to give them forth, that all must come to that Spirit, if they would know God or Christ, or the Scriptures aright, which they that gave them forth were led and taught by."

These exercises and openings appear to have been experienced by George Fox, when between the twentieth and twenty-fourth years of his age. Having been thus prepared by the baptism of the Holy Ghost and fire, and received a call from his divine Master to enter upon the work of the ministry, his first recorded appearance as a preacher of the Gospel, was in 1647, at Duckenfield and Manchester; where, he says, "Some were convinced, who received the Lord's teaching, by which they were confirmed and stood their ground."

The state of England at that time (1647) was most sad and per-
plexing. The civil war had been attended with great destruction of
human life and devastation of property in all parts of the Kingdom.
Three factions had been long struggling for pre-eminence. The King
though a prisoner had not yet been brought to trial. It was uncertain whether Presbyterians or Independents would finally succeed in retaining the civil and ecclesiastical authority. The former
gave evidence by the sanguinary laws passed by their party in Parliament, that the possessions and life of no man would be safe who
would not conform his belief to certain articles prescribed by them ;
which were not to be openly discredited upon pain of death. The
latter professed to favor liberty of conscience, but their whole course
made it evident that they were determined to obtain and secure
power by every means within their reach. The bloody conflict for
supremacy, so long waged with the cruelty of jealousy and the
blood-thirstiness of sectarian hate, employing the sword to decide
between rival theories of religion and church government, appeared
to be ended ; but there was still much confusion in reference to
ecclesiastical differences, and embittered discord between the parties
striving for mastery ; leading many to fear that the sword would
never be sheathed if to it was to be left the adjustment of spiritual
interests. Men of thoughtful minds had come to see that though
the war had been undertaken ostensibly to redress both civil and
religious grievances, there was little prospect of attaining either end ;
and witnessing the deplorable losses and calamities attending it, and
that their hopes of settlement and domestic comfort were disappointed, many of them had become earnest in seeking for more dura-
ble riches, and to find some solid foundation to rest on, amid the fluc-
tuations of doctrines and ecclesiastical domination that surrounded
them. Others than George Fox, wearied and disgusted with the
self-seeking and hypocritical profession of many who made themselves conspicuous as spiritual guides, withdrew from the ordinary
places of worship, and in retirement, self-examination and study of the
Scriptures, sought to ascertain and to perform their religious duties.

No party was so assured of retaining power as to deem it expedient to attempt to enforce laws for the repression of religious inquiry; so that the places for worship throughout the country were
often occupied by teachers of different denominations, and discussions on theological subjects between persons of differing opinions
were not uncommon.

William Penn referring to this period and to the work assigned to

George Fox, says, "It was about that time that the eternal, wise and good God, was pleased, in his infinite love, to honor and visit this benighted and bewildered nation with his glorious Day Spring from on high; yea, with a most sure and certain sound of the word of Light and Life, through the testimony of a chosen vessel, to an effectual and blessed purpose, can many thousands say; glory be to the name of the Lord forever!"

George Fox, as he went through various places in 1647, continued to preach to the people, and to dispute with some who opposed the doctrine he promulgated. By this means, he brought many to see how far they had fallen short of the truth as it is in Jesus, and by directing them to the Light of Christ in the heart, or the gift of Divine Grace, which Christ had purchased for every man, and instructing them in the alone means whereby they could know their salvation wrought out, many were convinced, and brought to unite with him; and several meetings of Friends were set up. This success of his ministry, and the fame of his piety and zeal brought many to see him, and a man of the name of Brown, when on his death-bed, prophesied that he would be an eminent instrument in the Lord's hand to convert the people. But George was fearful of being drawn aside from the strait and narrow way by these things, and though he declined not to declare the truth to the people, yet he was careful not to be influenced by the applause of men. Nevertheless Satan suggested to him that he had sinned against the Holy Ghost; but as he could not see wherein that sin had been committed, he escaped the temptation.

Seeing that the same work of the Lord was being carried on in others, his own sorrows and troubles were assuaged, and he says, "Tears of joy dropped from me, so that I could have wept night and day with tears of joy to the Lord, in humility and brokenness of heart."

Being in the early part of 1648, at a great meeting of professors, at Mansfield, he was moved to pray, and so great was the power attending, that the house seemed to be shaken, and the people observed, "That it was as in the days of the Apostles, when the house was shaken where they were met."

1648. Speaking of the commission he had received, he says: "I was sent to turn people from darkness to the light, that they might receive Christ Jesus; for to as many as should receive Him in his light, I saw He would give power to become the sons of God; which I had obtained by receiving Christ. I was to direct people to the Spirit, that gave forth the Scriptures, by which they might be led into·all truth, and so up to Christ and God, as those had been who gave them forth. I was to turn them to the Grace of God, and to the truth in the heart; which came by Jesus; that by this grace they might be taught, which would bring them salvation, that their hearts might be established by it, their words might be seasoned, and all might come to know their salvation nigh. I saw Christ died for all men, was a propitiation for all, and enlightened all men and women with his divine and saving light; and that none could be true believers, but those who believed therein. I saw that the Grace of God, which brings salvation, had appeared to all men, and that the manifestation of the Spirit of God was given to every man, to profit withal."

.   .   .   .

"When the Lord God and his Son Jesus Christ sent me forth into the world to preach his everlasting gospel and kingdom, I was glad that I was commanded to turn people to that inward Light, Spirit and Grace, by which all might know their salvation and their way to God; even that Divine Spirit which would lead them into all truth, and which I infallibly knew would never deceive any. But with and by this divine power and Spirit of God, and the light of Jesus, I was to bring people off from all their own ways, to Christ the new and living way; from their churches, which men had made and gathered, to the church in God, the general assembly written in heaven, which Christ is the head of; and off from the world's teachers made by men, to learn of Christ, who is the way, the truth, and the life, of whom the Father said, 'This is my beloved Son, hear ye him;' and off from all the world's worships, to know the Spirit of Truth in the inward parts, and to be led thereby, that in it they might worship the Father of spirits, who seeks such to worship him; which Spirit they that worshipped not in, knew not what they worshipped."

The public ministry of George Fox was now fairly begun, and from this time until his death, when out of prison, and not prevented by sickness, his travels, and other services for the Truth were continued almost uninterruptedly. In a "Narrative of the Spreading of Truth," &c., written by him, in 1676, he says:

"The Truth sprang up first to us, so as to be a people to the Lord, in Leicestershire in 1644, in Warwickshire in 1645, in Nottinghamshire in 1646, in Derbyshire in 1647, and in the adjacent counties in 1648, 1649, and 1650; in Yorkshire in 1651, in Lancashire and Westmoreland in 1652, in Cumberland, Durham, and Northumberland, in 1653, in London and most of the other parts of England, Scotland and Ireland, in 1654.

" In 1655, many went beyond sea, where Truth also sprang up, and in 1656 it broke forth in America and many other places."

Having, by obedience to the manifestations of Divine Grace learned to distinguish between the voice of the true Shepherd and that of the stranger, he was made quick of discerning, in the Lord's holy fear, those things in common observance in the professing church, and in the different ranks of society, which had been contrived by man to promote his self-interest or minister to the pride of the human heart. He thus found it enjoined upon him to keep strictly to the use of the Scriptural language of thou and thee to a single person; to refrain from the customary modes of salutation, as uncovering the head or bowing the body; also giving flattering titles to any. As he was convinced that the common use of the pronoun *you* to a single individual, was not only ungrammatical, but had originated from a corrupt source, and like the customary complimentary salutations and titles was untruthful and fostered the honor that men seek one from another, he felt required to bear testimony against them all. He saw that as all were required to speak the truth on all occasions, and as Christ and his Apostle James had positively forbidden swearing of any kind, so it was unlawful for a Christian to take an oath. And as Christ was the Prince of Peace, and had commanded his followers to love their enemies, to do good to all, to forgive all who trespassed against them, and to resist not evil, so his disciples could not fight, nor take part in war, let it be waged under what plea it might. He believed it right to banish from use the ordinary heathen names of the days of the week, and the similar names given to the months of the year, and in lieu thereof to name both numerically.

Seeing the vanity and folly connected with dress, and how people were brought into bondage by fashion, and thereby betrayed into things destructive of a religious life, he practised great simplicity therein himself, and bore a decided testimony against ornamentation or changing with the fashions.

Fully believing in the fundamental truths of the Gospel held in common by what were called the evangelical churches, he saw that the truths recorded in the Holy Scriptures were often mutilated or rendered nugatory by the construction put upon them by the unlearned in the school of Christ. He therefore constantly taught that the Scriptures could not be rightly understood or interpreted, except by the Spirit which dictated them, and, that it was thus and thus only, that the *man of God* may be perfect, thoroughly furnished unto all good works. The necessary deduction from this was, that the Spirit itself was superior to the Scriptures which had been written under its inspiration, and by which alone their sacred contents could be rightly interpreted and applied; and as Christ had enlightened every man that cometh into the world with a measure of this Spirit, or Divine Grace, so *it* was the primary rule of faith and practice; which, however, the Scriptures would never contradict.

Christ being the glorified Head who alone could prepare for, ordain, and commission ministers in His church, so the ministers made by studying divinity and ordained by men alone, were not true ministers of the Gospel; that as men and women were one in Christ Jesus, He conferred the gift for the ministry upon both alike, whether learned or unlearned, and both could exercise it in the assemblies of the people, or wherever He called them thereto; and that when so exercised, it must be under the immediate inspiration of Him who alone knows the states of those addressed, and what is the spiritual food convenient for them. That the Gospel must be preached without money and without price, in accordance with the commandment of Christ to his disciples, "Freely ye have received, freely give." The several testimonies here enumerated, have been maintained by the members of the Society of Friends, who were led by the same Spirit as George Fox and his fellow laborers, ever since their day, and are felt to be as binding on them now, as they were on them.

There were few of the testimonies which Friends were called to bear that caused them more cruel persecution and suffering than that relative to the use of the Scripture language of *thou* and *thee*, and the refusal to bow or take off the hat, or to give the ordinary flattering salutations. Alluding to this, George Fox says: "Oh! the blows, punchings, beatings, and imprisonments we underwent, for not putting off our hats to men. For that soon tried all men's patience and sobriety what it was. . . . The bad language and evil usage we received on this account is hard to be expressed, besides the danger we were sometimes in of losing our lives for this matter; and that by the great professors of Christianity, who thereby discovered that they were not true believers." [1648.]

The doctrine promulgated respecting the true character of Gospel ministry, and the testimony borne against receiving pecuniary compensation for preaching, as it struck at the trade of the priests, and of all who made merchandise of what they called the Gospel, natu-rally roused their opposition and animosity; and consequently there was no class from whom Friends encountered more determined hos-tility, or at whose hands they underwent more bitter and prolonged persecution than the clergy.

As the whole tenor of the principles inculcated by G. Fox and the early Friends was calculated to draw people off from the ob-servance of forms and ceremonies, or a dependence on the teaching of men, and to centre their attention on the work of regeneration through the aid of the Holy Spirit in the heart, and also to lead to the attainment of a state of perfection or holiness, through its sanctifying power and influence; these also drew forth much contradiction and resistance from those who wished not to be disturbed in the belief, that Christ having paid the penalty for sin, and purchased salvation for them, there was no repentance, no suffering for sin, no cross-bearing and self-denial necessary on their part; and from those who contended that man could not escape from sinning in this life.

Besides preaching repentance and amendment of life, G. Fox, found a duty laid upon him to go to the courts, or to write to the Judges, inciting them to avoid oppression, and to administer justice in all their doings; and also in warning those who kept ale houses and other places of entertainment, not to allow of drinking to ex-cess, nor any immoral conduct; and to declare against all deceit or untruthfulness in buying or selling, likewise against stage plays, gaming, &c.

Being at Nottingham on a First-day of the week, he went into the "great steeple house" of the town, and hearing the priest give an incoherent explanation of the text which he took, he testified against it, and explained what he believed to be the true meaning. Whereupon the officers put him into a filthy, offensive prison, where he was kept for some time. Afterwards he was removed to the sheriff's house, who, with his wife, was "much changed by the power of the Lord;" and allowed him to hold meetings at their house. There seems to have been a wonderful evidence of divine power attending these gatherings, and many were convinced. The magis-trates having neglected to bring their prisoner before the court when it was sitting, he was detained there "a pretty long time," and then set at liberty; this was his first imprisonment, and it occurred in 1649. At Mansfield Woodhouse, for speaking to the priest and people in their place of worship, they knocked him down, and he "was cruelly beaten and bruised with their fists, Bibles and sticks."

They then hauled him away and set him in the stocks, where he was kept for some hours. But, he says, " The Lord's power soon healed me, and that day some were convinced of the Lord's truth, and turned to his teaching."

Travelling from place to place his ministry was so powerful that multitudes were convinced, and regular meetings of Friends were established in many places.

1650. Being at Derby, and learning there was to be a great " lecture " delivered there that day, at which many officers, priests, and preachers were to be in attendance, he felt it his duty to go to it; where, after the "service " was through, he spoke to the congregation what he believed to be required of him. Although the people were quiet, he was taken before the magistrates. In the course of the examination, G. Fox was asked whether he was sanctified? he answered, Yes: then they asked if he had no sin? to which he answered, " Christ my Saviour has taken away my sin, and in Him is no sin." Being asked how he knew that Christ did abide in us? G. F. said, "By his Spirit that He hath given us." It was then temptingly queried, " If any of us were Christ"? G. F. answered, " Nay, we are nothing, Christ is all."

These magistrates, nevertheless, committed George Fox and a man of the name of John Fretwell to the " House of Correction " for six months, as blasphemers. J. Fretwell proved unfaithful to the truth and so got released; but G. Fox, refusing the offer of his relatives to the magistrates, to be bound that he would not come any more there, was kept to the end of the six months in his first place of confinement, and nearly six months longer in the common jail. The change in the place of imprisonment took place in consequence of the Commissioners of Parliament, who were recruiting for the army, sending for George, when they knew that the time for which he was committed was nearly expired, and offered to make him a captain in the army, urging him to accept it, and said the soldiers were desirous to have him for their commander. But George says, " I told them I knew from whence all wars arose, even from the lusts, according to James' doctrine; and that I lived in the virtue of that life and power that took away the occasion of all wars. Yet they courted me to accept of their offer, and thought I did but compliment them. But I told them I was come into the covenant of peace which was before wars and strifes were. They said, they offered it in love and kindness to me, because of my virtue; and such like flattering words they used. But I told them, If that was their love

and kindness, I trampled it under my feet.   Then their rage got up
and they said, "Take him away, jailer, and put him into the
prison amongst the rogues and felons."   So I was put into a lousy,
stinking place, without any bed, amongst thirty felons, where I was
kept almost half a year; yet at times they would let me walk to
the garden, believing I would not go away."

Notwithstanding the vileness of the inmates of the prison, he was
preserved from contamination, and was often engaged in reproving
their wickedness and striving to reform them.   There being a young
woman there who was condemned to be hanged for stealing, George
wrote to the Judges, showing how wrong it was to take human life
for such crimes; that it was contrary even to the Mosaic law, and
altogether irreconcilable with the religion of Christ; and moving
them to have mercy on her.   She was taken to the gallows and
there reprieved; and being returned to the prison, she afterwards
became convinced of the truth and joined Friends.

Seeing the pernicious effects resulting from keeping the prisoners
so that they could mingle together promiscuously, and the older and
more hardened convicts thus have opportunities to teach the younger
offenders lessons of vice, and spread and increase wickedness, he
thought it his duty to write out his observations and the conclusions
to which they had led him, and communicate them to the Judges;
that they might adopt some measures to arrest an evil so detrimental
to the safety of society.   This is the first essay at prison reform of
which we have account.

George Fox and those who had joined in fellowship with him,
called themselves " Friends of Truth," while others, owing to their
so frequently speaking of the Light of Christ, had named them
" Children of Light ;" but at one of the interviews between G. Fox
and Gervas Bennet— one of the magistrates who had committed him
at Derby — the former bade the latter " Tremble at the word of the
Lord ;" whereupon Bennet called him a Quaker.   This epithet
of scorn well suited the tastes and prejudices of the people, and it
soon became the common appellation bestowed on Friends.

In the forepart of this imprisonment the jailer treated G. Fox
with much harshness, but he became greatly changed, and told his
wife "He had seen the day of Judgment, and George was there, and
he was afraid of him, because he had done him so much wrong and
spoken so much against him."   He became convinced of the Truth,
and very loving towards George.   Many came to visit him while
in confinement and to discourse about religion, some of whom were

thus convinced of the truth of the doctrines he held. Being thus prevented from travelling and so spreading the glad tidings of the Gospel of life and salvation, George Fox did not neglect the use of his pen, to endeavor to bring the magistrates who had sent him to prison, to a sense of the iniquity of their conduct; also to warn and reprove the priests of the town. He likewise sent forth a paper " To be spread among Friends, and other tender people, for the opening of their understandings in the way of truth, and directing them to the true Teacher in themselves." Understanding that some who had been convinced were falling away, and that Friends were undergoing great persecution, he addressed an epistle to the latter, showing his sympathy with them, and encouraging them to take patiently the suffering they were undergoing.

It was in 1650 that we have the first account of a woman preaching among Friends; Elizabeth Hooten, whom George Fox had met in 1647, and in the course of their interview had so spoken as to convince her, and she became a Friend.

With a knowledge of the spiritual nature of the gospel, and that male and female are both one in Christ Jesus, Friends at once recognized in its dispensation, the fulfilment of the prediction of the prophet Joel, " And it shall come to pass in the last days, I will pour out my Spirit upon all flesh, and your sons and your *daughters* shall prophesy." The Apostle Paul defines prophesying as speaking to others to edification and exhortation and comfort. He also gives his view as to the manner to be observed, when a person of either sex is engaged in this service. Thus, " Every man praying or prophesying having his head covered, dishonoreth his head ; but every woman that prayeth or prophesieth with her head uncovered, dishonoreth her head." The apostle here gives instruction, as to what is to be observed, in the exercise of the same gift by both sexes, and as it is directed equally to men and women, it is evident he recognized the bestowal of the gift on both sons and daughters. There is no contradiction to this, in his saying in another place, " Let your women keep silence in the churches ; for it is not permitted unto them to speak : " . . . . " for it is a shame for women to speak in the church : " the whole context showing, that when he makes use of that language, he refers exclusively to asking questions in the place of worship, or attempting to argue and dispute there; instead of which, the women were to ask their husbands at home.

CHAPTER III.

Friends despised and condemned by all Professors — Reasons why — Convince-
ments — Occurrence at Beverly — G. Fox accused of saying he was Christ —
William Dewsbury — Steeple Houses — Friends increasing and forming into
a Society — Cruel treatment Received — Instances of the abuse of G. F. —
Convincement of two Priests — Francis Howgil — John Audland — Edward
Burrough — Extract from a Letter — Swarthmore Hall — Judge Fell and
Wife — Margaret Fell's account of G. Fox's services there — Priest Lampit
— M. Fell joins with Friends.

CHARLES I. had been beheaded in the early part of 1649, and
Cromwell was succeeding in concentrating the power of the government in his own hands, not intending to share it with any but such
as were willing to be subservient to his will. As the Independents,
of whom he professed to be one, had clamored loudly for liberty of
conscience, it was to have been expected that no denomination of
Christians would be oppressed on account of their religious belief;
and it is probable, that if Cromwell could have had his own way in
this matter, without endangering his popularity, such would have
been the case. But though the peaceable principles which Friends
boldly avowed, restrained them from any attempt to interfere with
the government, and their constant assurance that, while conscientiously bound to adhere to their own religious views, they were
equally bound to maintain Christian charity towards all, they were
nevertheless objects of hatred or scorn to very many of their fellow
countrymen, perhaps of dread to some.

The high, but loose, professors in the different religious Societies,
could not bear the requirement of strict self-denial and godly living in every day life, which the doctrines Friends preached enjoined;
nor the destruction of priestcraft and hireling ministry which followed embracing those doctrines; as was repeatedly manifested by
the desertion of the "Churches" and priests, among congregations
into which their preachers had found admittance, and declared those
doctrines with power. They were therefore branded as fanatics,
bent on disturbance of the public peace, and the doctrines they
held and taught were denounced as absurd or blasphemous.

The great fundamental truths, so earnestly insisted on by the
early Friends, that Christ, by that most acceptable sacrifice which
He made of himself, had not only atoned for sin, but had purchased a
measure or manifestation of his Spirit, whereby he enlightens every

man that cometh into the world; and that all who would become children of God by adoption, must be led and governed by this measure of Divine Grace, or Holy Spirit, notwithstanding it is so plainly set forth by Christ and his apostles, was ridiculed by some, and represented by others as blasphemous. Their belief that " communion," or partaking of the flesh and blood of Christ, was only to be known as the heart was opened to receive Him, and consisted in the soul being permitted to feed on Him spiritually; in accordance with his declaration, " Behold I stand at the door and knock, if any man hear my voice and open unto me, I will come in and sup with him and he with me; " and that the " one baptism," spoken of by the apostle, was not that which can only put away the filth of the flesh, but that which is administered by Christ alone, described as with the Holy Ghost and fire; these two articles of their faith were asserted to exclude them from the visible Church, and render them justly liable to punishment by the secular power.

Thus Episcopalians, Presbyterians, Independents and Baptists, widely as they differed in belief one from the other, and generally as they disliked each other, united in denouncing, and when they had the opportunity, in harassing and sorely abusing the Quakers. The ignorant populace, accustomed to be led on by those to whom they looked as spiritual guides, were easily incited to violence against them, when they heard them stigmatized by their priests as deceivers, menaced with punishment or actually fined and imprisoned: hence the frequency with which the Quaker ministers were stoned, and beaten by the rabble, when they had been engaged in preaching the gospel to them.

1651. After being set at liberty, George Fox travelled through the north of England, preaching the way of life with such power that very many were brought to the acknowledgment of the truth, and joined the Society; among whom were William Dewsbury, Richard Farnsworth, Thomas Aldam and James Naylor; all of whom in the course of a short time became fully approved ministers of the gospel.

Being at Beverly in the " east riding " of Yorkshire, at the house of Justice Hotham, the latter told G. Fox that he had known the principle of the Light within, which he was promulgating, for ten years; and he manifested great friendliness towards him, saying, " My house is your house." He also informed George that " a great woman " of Beverly had called on him, and in the course of conversation, told him " That the last Sabbath day — as she called it — there was an angel or spirit came into the church at Beverly, and spoke the wonderful things of God, and when it had done, it passed away, they not knowing whence it came or whither it went; but it astonished all, both priests and professors and the magistrates of the town." It was George who was at the "church," and her account shows the clearness and authority with which he spoke, as well as the superstitious notions of the people respecting spirits or ghosts.

A certain Scotch priest who met with G. Fox, and asked him many questions, all of which he answered, afterwards declared, that if ever he met with him again, he would have his life: adding that he would give his head, if G. Fox was not knocked down within a month. But notwithstanding his murderous feelings towards one who had never done him harm, in the course of time he became convinced of the principles of Friends, joined the Society, and was glad to entertain G. Fox at his house.

1652. Coming into Gainsborough, in Lincolnshire, G. Fox found the town in an uproar on account of the preaching of a Friend in the market; and a man asserting that he had heard G. Fox say that he was Christ, the people rushed into the house where George was; and he stepping on a table explained to them, that he had said that Christ was in them unless they were reprobates, and that it was by the power of Christ within that he then spoke to them, not that he was Christ: this satisfied and quieted the people. Then turning to his accuser, he told him that the word of the Lord to him was, that Judas' end would be his; and shortly after this poor man hanged himself.

William Dewsbury, who, as has been mentioned, was convinced by George Fox, when the latter was holding meetings at Balby (1651), was a native of Yorkshire, being born at Allerthorpe in the forepart of the seventeenth century. He lost his father when about eight years of age, and so deep was the impression made on his naturally serious and reflective mind by this bereavement, that he began to spend many of the hours usually devoted by children to play, in retirement, prayer and solemn meditation. He says, "The word of the Lord came to me, saying, 'I created thee for my glory; an account thou must give me of all thy words and actions.'" Convicted by the Monitor within, that by nature he was prone to sin, and that he was living in a state not conformable to the law of God, he was brought under condemnation and sorrow therefor, and commenced striving to lead an altered course of life.

His first occupation was that of a shepherd-boy, the quiet and retiredness of which were congenial with his serious and contemplative disposition; but when nearly fourteen years of age he was placed apprentice with a cloth-weaver near Leeds; he requesting to go there because he had heard there were people in that neighborhood who were more strict in religious observances than most others. But he was disappointed by finding that attendance at their places of worship and converse with some who made high profession, did not satisfy the longings of his soul to enjoy peace and communion with God.

When about twenty-one years of age, his mental conflicts continuing, he was caught with the spirit then so generally prevailing, and entered the parliamentary army, under the plea of "going up to the help of the Lord against the mighty," and fighting for the Gospel. But though there were much talk about religion, and no little preaching and praying among both men and officers, he gained no real settlement or satisfaction; he, like others, being too much engaged in looking without for that which is to be found only within. Still in pursuit of that which would bring him peace, he journeyed into Scotland searching for some whom he could recognize as walking in the fear of the Lord. Returning from there, he associated for some time with Independents and Baptists; among the latter of whom were some tender-hearted people. But, he says, the Lord discovered to me that, "In all these turnings in my carnal wisdom while seeking the kingdom of God without, thither the flaming sword turned to keep the way of the tree of life, fenced me from it, cut me down, rent all my coverings, and destroyed that mind which thus looked out to find the kingdom of heaven. Then my mind was turned within by the power of the Lord to wait his counsel. And the word of the Lord came to me and said, 'Put up thy sword into its scabbard; if my Kingdom were of this world, then would my children fight.'"

He now found there were enemies of his own house, against which he was called to fight, not with carnal weapons, but with the sword of the Spirit; the word of God inwardly revealed. As he gave heed to this discerner of the thoughts and intents of the heart, he clearly saw that he could no longer have anything to do with military affairs; so he left the army altogether and returned to his former occupation. He now grew in grace and in the saving knowledge of our Lord and Saviour Jesus Christ, and felt a strong prompting to declare to others what the Lord had done for his soul. But the Lord showed him that the time for this had not yet come, and he says he received a distinct command to refrain until the

year 1652, when there would be a greater hungering and thirsting
for the knowledge of the right way of the Lord, in the hearts of the
people, than was then the case.   He married a young woman who
had passed, like himself, through many deep baptisms and trials ;
their marriage taking place at a Baptists' meeting.

It was at an evening meeting that W. Dewsbury first heard
George Fox preach, and he owned the doctrines he proclaimed, and
soon after joined the Society.   George Fox says, "After the meet-
ing, it being moonlight, I walked out into the field, and William
Dewsbury and his wife came to me in the field, and confessed to the·
Truth, and received it, and after some time he did testify to it."
In 1652, according as it had been before revealed to him, he was
called into the ministry, often suffering greatly for the testimony of
Jesus.   He says the command to him on this occasion was, "The
leaders of my people cause them to err, in drawing them from the
Light in their consciences.   Freely thou hast received, freely give
and minister ; and what I have made known to thee in secret declare
thou openly."   With this commission, and under a sense of duty to
go forth, and preach the everlasting gospel, he left his home, and
travelled through Lancashire, Cumberland and Westmoreland.

Although George Fox felt himself often moved to go to the
"steeple houses," as he called them, to speak to both priest and congregation, generally waiting quietly until the priest had got through
with his usual services, and then declaring the doctrines set forth in
the Holy Scriptures, yet, unless where Friends had their own meeting
houses, he mostly held his meetings either in private houses or in the
open fields.   Occasionally both priest and people desiring to hear
him, invited him to come into their "church," which, however, he
almost always refused on account of the superstitious notions then
entertained that the "church" was a holy place, and that it was in
such "consecrated houses" only that the Gospel could be properly
preached.   He says, "The steeple houses and pulpits were offensive
to my mind, because both priests and people called them the house
of God, and idolized them ; reckoning that God dwelt in the outward
house.   Whereas they should have looked for God and Christ to
dwell in their hearts, and their bodies to be made the temples of
God ; for the apostle said, 'God dwelleth not in temples made with
hands:' but by reason of the people idolizing those places, it was
counted a heinous thing to declare against them."

Going from place to place in the northern shires disseminating
the truths of the Gospel, as they had been opened to his under-

standing by the Spirit, he met with much success in bringing people, in the various ranks of life, to receive his doctrines, and to be willing to enter upon the truly religious life which they required; so that many were added to the Society, which now began to take form, and many meetings were established, and many zealous ministers sent forth by the Lord of the harvest to labor in his vineyard.

He also, in common with his brethren, met with much abuse and cruel treatment: and it may be truly said, they went forth with their lives, as it were, in their hands; often escaping death only by the providential interference of the Master whom they served.

It would swell this account to too great size to narrate a tithe of the instances recorded of the cruel treatment endured by this valiant soldier of Jesus Christ, while laboring to turn the people from darkness to light, and from the power of Satan unto God. The following may serve to show what was the character of the abuse and suffering he passed through; and also how greatly the people were excited against him and his friends; so that oftentimes, besides the personal injury they endured, it was difficult for them to procure food and lodging for their money.

1652. "The next day, Friends and friendly people having left me, I travelled alone, declaring the day of the Lord amongst people in the towns where I came, and warning them to repent. I came towards night into a town called Patrington. As I walked along the town, I warned both priests and people (for the priest was in the street), to repent and turn to the Lord. It grew dark before I came to the end of the town, and a multitude of people gathered about me, to whom I declared the word of life.

"When I had cleared myself I went to an inn, and desired them to let me have a lodging; but they would not. I desired a little meat or milk, and I would pay for it; but they refused. So I walked out of the town, and a company of fellows followed, and asked me, What news? I bid them repent, and fear the Lord. After I was gone a pretty way, I came to another house, and desired the people to let me have a little meat, drink, and lodging for my money; but they denied me. I went to another house, and desired the same; but they refused me also. By this time it was grown so dark that I could not see the highway; but I discerned a ditch, and got a little water and refreshed myself. Then I got over the ditch, and, being weary with travelling, I sat down amongst the furze bushes till it was day. About break of day I got up, and passed on the fields. A man came after me with a great pikestaff, and went along with me to a town, and he raised the town upon me, with the constable and chief constable before the sun was up. I declared God's everlasting truth amongst them, warning them of the day of the Lord, that was coming upon all sin and wickedness; and exhorted them to repent. But they seized me, and had me back to Patrington, about three miles, guarding me with watch-bills, pikes, staves, and halberds. When I was come to Patrington, all the town was in an uproar, and the priest and constables were consulting together; so I had another opportunity to declare the word of life amongst them, and warn them to repent. At last a professor, a tender man, called me into his house, and there I took a little milk and bread, having not eaten for some days before. Then they guarded me about nine miles to a justice." This justice after examining into his case released him and he returned again to the village, where he held a great meeting and many were convinced.

" I went to Balby, and Doncaster, where I had formerly preached repentance on the market-day: which had made a noise and alarm in the country. On First-day I went to the steeple house, and after the priest had done, I spoke to him and the people what the Lord commanded me; and they were in a great rage, hurried me out, threw me down, and haled me before the magistrates. A long examination they made of me, and much work I had with them. They threatened my life if ever I came there again; and that they would leave me to the mercy of the people. Nevertheless, I declared truth amongst them, and directed them to the light of Christ in them; testifying unto them, 'That God was come to teach his people himself, whether they would hear or forbear.' After awhile they put us out (for some Friends were with me) among the rude multitude, and they stoned us down the streets. An innkeeper, a bailiff, came and took us into his house; and they broke his head, so that the blood ran down his face, with the stones that they threw at us. We stayed awhile in his house, and showed the more sober people the priest's fruits. Then we went away to Balby about a mile off. The rude people laid wait for us, and stoned us down the lane; but, blessed be the Lord, we did not receive much hurt."

" The next First-day I went to Tickhill, whither the Friends of that side gathered together, and a mighty brokenness by the power of God there was amongst the people. I went out of the meeting, being moved of God to go to the steeple house. When I came there, I found the priest and most of the chief of the parish together in the chancel. I went up to them, and began to speak; but they immediately fell upon me; the clerk up with his Bible, as I was speaking, and 'struck me on the face with it, so that my face gushed out with blood; and I bled exceedingly in the steeple house.' The people cried, 'Let us have him out of the church.' When they had got me out, they beat me exceedingly, threw me down, and turned me over a hedge. They afterwards dragged me through a house into the street, stoning and beating me as they dragged me along; so that I was all over besmeared with blood and dirt. They got my hat from me, which I never had again. Yet when I was got upon my legs, I declared the word of life, showed them the fruits of their teacher, and how they dishonored Christianity. After awhile I got into the meeting again amongst Friends, and the priest and people coming by the house, I went with Friends into the yard, and there spoke to the priest and people. The priest scoffed at us, and called us Quakers. But the Lord's power was so over them, and the word of life was declared in such authority and dread to them, that the priest fell a trembling himself; and one of the people said, 'Look how the priest trembles and shakes, he is turned a Quaker also.' When the meeting was over, Friends departed; and I went without my hat to Balby about seven or eight miles. Friends were much abused that day by the priest and his people: insomuch that some moderate justices hearing of it, two or three of them came and sat at the town to examine the business. He that had shed my blood was afraid of having his hand cut off, for striking me in the church, as they called it; but I forgave him, and would not appear against him."

1652. Francis Howgil who, with several other priests, had heard George Fox preach at Sedbergh, was so deeply affected by the truths he declared, that when a certain captain found fault with George for not being willing to go into the chapel to hold the meeting, he replied to him, saying, "This man speaks with authority, and not as the Scribes." On the next First-day, F. Howgil was himself preaching in the chapel at Firbank, when, as he afterwards said, he thought George Fox looked in as he passed by the house, and his spirit was ready to fail him. He soon brought his sermon to an end, as did John Audland, another priest who was officiating there. In the afternoon G. Fox held a meeting near to a chapel, at which there were a thousand people; among whom were F. Howgil and John Audland. Both were now fully convinced of the truth of the doctrines proclaimed, and freely gave up to unite in fellowship with Friends.

F. Howgil had received a liberal education at the University, in order to fit him to become a priest in the "Episcopal Church;" for which he received ordination. Becoming dissatisfied with the burdensome ceremonies and superstitious observances retained in that establishment, he left it, and in pursuit of a more spiritual worship than that he had forsaken, he joined the Independents, among whom he became a preacher. But notwithstanding his training in divinity, and his zealous engagement in what he thought were good works, fasting, praying and exhorting, he continued sensible that he did not obtain the victory over his evil propensities and the assaults of Satan. With all his profession of religion, his conscience convinced him of the truth of the declaration of the apostle, " Know ye not that to whom ye yield yourselves servants to obey, his servants ye are to whom ye obey ; whether of sin unto death, or of obedience unto righteousness," and he could not obtain the peace he sought, by the belief of the doctrine he taught, that Christ had taken the guilt of sin upon himself.

He was in this state of mind, when he heard George Fox declare that the Light of Christ, or a measure of his Holy Spirit, was given to every man, and that it was to this Light or Spirit that every one must have their thoughts, words and deeds brought, to be by it judged, if they would enter and walk in the narrow way of salvation. He saw that, with all his learning and high profession, he had been ignorant of the first principles of the gospel, and that the work of religion was to be known in the heart, and salvation to be wrought out with fear and trembling, the Holy Spirit working on the soul according to his good pleasure. He at once resigned himself to this transforming power, and under its convictions for sin, he experienced the gift of true repentance, and was enabled to look with an eye of living faith to the Lamb of God that taketh away the sin of the world, and to know forgiveness through his atoning blood. He gave himself up to serve the Lord, who bestowed on him a gift in the ministry, which he exercised without money and without price.

John Audland was quite a young man, and like Howgil, was a preacher among the Independents, with whom, from his fluency, he was very popular. He had been married about two years, and had his wife with him when they heard G. Fox speak at Firbank Chapel. Such was the power and religious fervor with which the word of life was declared by that eminent servant of Christ, that it came home to the hearts of both with convincing force, and they embraced it and conformed their lives to its requirements, casting their lot with the despised Quakers. [1652.] Both in time became ministers.

As Howgil and Audland, while holding their benefices, had received tithes from their flocks, they now felt that duty required them to return the money they had received for preaching, which they accordingly did.

At Kendal George Fox had a meeting in the town hall, in which he says he showed the people " How they might come to the saving knowledge of Christ, and to have a right understanding of the Holy Scriptures; opening to them what it was that would lead them into the way of reconciliation with God; and what would be their condemnation." Going thence to the house of Miles Bateman, at Underbarrow, he there met with Edward Burrough, a young man of about seventeen years of age, who, with many others, had followed him from Kendal, and they entering into disputation, Edward, though a lad of superior intellectual power, with a good education, and determined withal to maintain the high religious notions he entertained, was overthrown in argument and convinced of the truth of the doctrine he had heard George preach. [1652.]

E. Burrough's parents were members of the " Episcopal Church," and had trained him in its doctrines and practices. He had been a serious-minded child, inclined to religious thoughtfulness, and not disposed to take upon trust, without investigation, such an important matter as religious belief. F. Howgil, who in after years became his intimate friend and close companion, says, " He had the spirit of a man when he was but a child. His delight was always among good people, and to be reading the Scriptures, and his very strength was bent, towards God." Not finding what he longed for among Episcopalians, he joined the Presbyterians. He says, " When I was about seventeen years of age, it pleased God to show himself a little to me, and something struck me with terror. When I had been praying, I often heard the voice, ' Thou art ignorant of God; thou knowest not where He is; to what purpose is thy prayer?' So, much fear came upon me, and broke me off from praying many times; troubles came thick into my mind, and fearfulness fell upon me. I was struck off from my delights, and what I had gathered in as of God, died." Whilst in this unsettled state, he says, " It pleased the Lord to send into these parts his faithful servant and messenger, George Fox. He spoke the language which I knew not, notwithstanding all my high talking." His heart was softened; he remarks the Lord was pleased to show him that he was in the prodigal state, above the cross of Christ, out of the pure fear of the Lord, and not worthy to be called a son. He now passed through a dispensation of condemnation and repentance, while the axe was being laid to the root of the corrupt tree, the Lord's fan purging the floor of his heart, and the chaff being burnt up with unquenchable fire. Thus he came into a state of acceptance, and by continued obedience to the divine will revealed in his heart, he attained to the stature of a man in Christ Jesus, and was made an eminent instrument in the Lord's hand to contend with spiritual wickedness in high places, and to build up the church on the most holy faith.

His parents were much displeased at him for joining the Quakers, whom they looked upon as heretics, and tried to induce him to leave them; but when they found that he was fully convinced of the truth of their principles and resolved to continue in fellowship with them, they turned him out of doors; and though he besought them, that though they disowned him as a son, they would let him remain with them as a hired servant, they refused, and he was obliged to go forth, giving up father and mother with home and all its comforts for Christ's sake; whom he found a rich rewarder of all them that diligently seek him.

It was not very long after this that E. Burrough and J. Audland went forth as fellow-laborers in the gospel, and to share in the reproaches and afflictions, the beatings, stonings, halings and other cruelties practised at that time on the promulgators of the truths of the gospel as held by Friends. In a letter describing the religious labor in which they had been and still were engaged, and the success attending it, J. Audland says, "Dear Friends, the work of the Lord is great, and I see that the Lord will raise up to himself a pure and large people, to serve and worship him in Spirit and in Truth. My dear brother and fellow laborer, E. Burrough, salutes you in the Lord."

George Fox, having gone through the dales of Yorkshire, in which hundreds had been convinced, and known the work of regeneration begun and carried on in them, by a practical belief in the doctrines he taught, came again into Lancashire and stopped at Ulverstone, where a priest of the name of Lampit — a truckler to the times — held the living. George soon had a sense of the character of this man, whom he met at Swarthmoor, the residence of Judge Fell, and to whom, in the course of conversation, he told some plain truths, which the priest was far from relishing.

Swarthmoor Hall stands about a mile from Ulverstone, and not far from Morecamb bay. Thomas Fell, who owned it and resided in it, had been a successful barrister, before being raised to the bench. He had been in Parliament, but retired therefrom in the early part of Cromwell's administration.

In 1632, when thirty-two years of age, he married Margaret Askew, then in the nineteenth year of her age. She was a daughter of John Askew, and was a descendant of Anne Askew the martyr. She had received as good an education as it was then common to give to females of her rank in life. Their wealth and the salary he received as Judge, enabled them to keep open house, and among the numerous guests resorting there, were often to be found those in the station of ministers, or teachers of religion. It appears that both the Judge and his wife partook of the spirit of the times, were earnest inquirers on the subject of religion, and, with their household, strict in the observances of the "church" to which they belonged.

The differing reports respecting George Fox, which were widely circulated; some representing him as a wizard and wicked man, and some extolling him as an unimpeachable character and extraordinary preacher, who was unsparing in his attacks upon the hireling priests, turning multitudes from following them, and to the teaching of Christ himself by his Spirit in the heart, had no doubt excited no little curiosity to see and hear him in the mistress of Swarthmoor and in her family.

1652. Margaret Fell was from home when G. Fox arrived at her house. On her return the children told her what had passed between him and the priest; at which she was troubled, as Lampit was the minister of the "church" where she attended. In the evening George preached to the family. The next day Lampit came there again, and they entered into a long discourse, from which Margaret got an insight of the priest's true condition. There being a day appointed for "humiliation" soon after, M. Fell desired G. Fox to be present at the "steeple house," at Ulverstone, but he told her that must be as the Lord directed him. When the time arrived he felt moved to go, and on arriving, found the priest and congregation singing. But the words sung, G. Fox says, were "So unsuitable to their states, that after they had done singing I was moved of the Lord to speak to him and the people."

Margaret Fell thus narrates what occurred afterward: " And when they were singing before the sermon he came in, and when they had done singing he stood up upon a seat or form, and desired 'that he might have liberty to speak;' and he that was in the pulpit said he might. And the first words that he spoke were as followeth : 'He is not a Jew that is one outward, neither is that circumcision which is outward ; but he is a Jew that is one inward, and that is circumcision which is of the heart.' And so he went on and said 'that Christ was the light of the world, and lighteth every man that cometh into the world, and that by this light they might be gathered to God,' &c. I stood up in my pew, and wondered at his doctrine; for I had never heard such before. And then he went on, and opened the Scriptures and said, ' The Scriptures were the prophets' words, and Christ's and the apostles' words, and what, as they spoke, they enjoyed and possessed, and had it from the Lord :' and said, ' Then what had any to do with the Scriptures, but as they came to the Spirit that gave them forth. You will say, Christ saith this, and the apostles say this ; but what canst thou say ? Art thou a child of light, and hast walked in the light, and what thou speakest, is it inwardly from God ?' &c. This opened me so, that it cut me to the heart; and then I saw clearly, we were all wrong. So I sat down in my pew again, and cried bitterly ; and I cried in my spirit to the Lord, ' We are all thieves, we are all thieves, we have taken the Scriptures in words, and know nothing of them in ourselves.' So that served me, that I cannot well tell what he spoke afterwards ; but he went on in declaring against the false prophets, priests and deceivers of the people. And there was one John Sawrey, a justice of peace, and a professor, that bid the churchwarden take him away : and he laid his hands on him several times, and took them off again, and let him alone; and then after a while he gave over, and came to our house again that night. And he spoke in the family amongst the servants, and they were all generally convinced ; as William Caton, Thomas Salthouse, Mary Askew, Anne Clayton, and several other servants. And I was struck into such a sadness, I knew not what to do, my husband being from home. I saw it was the truth, and I could not deny it ; and I did, as the apostle saith, ' I received the truth in the love of it ;' and it was opened to me so clear, that I had never a tittle in my heart against it; but I desired the Lord that I might be kept in it, and then I desired no greater portion."

.   .   .   .

"About three weeks' end my husband came home; and many were in a mighty rage, and a deal of the captains and great ones of the country went to meet my then husband as he was coming home, and informed him, 'That a great disaster was befallen amongst his family, and that they were witches; and that they had taken us out of our religion; and that he must either set them away, or all the country would be undone.' But no weapons formed against the Lord shall prosper, as you may see hereafter.

"So my husband came home greatly offended; and any may think what a condition I was like to be in, that either I must displease my husband or offend God; for he was very much troubled with us all in the house and family, they had so prepossessed him against us. But James Naylor and Richard Farnsworth were both then at our house, and I desired them to come and speak to him, and so they did, very moderately and wisely; but he was at first displeased with them, till they told him 'They came in love and goodwill to his house.' After that he had heard them speak awhile he was better satisfied, and they offered as if they would go away; but I desired them to stay and not go away yet, for George Fox will come this evening. . . . And then my husband was pretty moderate and quiet, and his dinner being ready he went to it, and I went in and sat me down by him. And while I was sitting, the power of the Lord seized upon me, and he was struck with amazement and knew not what to think, but was quiet and still. And the children were all quiet and still, and grown sober, and could not play on their music that they were learning; and all these things made him quiet and still."

"At night Geo. Fox came, and after supper my husband was sitting in the parlor, and I asked him if Geo. Fox might come in? and he said yes. So George came in without any compliment, and walked into the room, and began to speak presently; and the family and James Naylor and Richard Farnsworth all came in; and he spoke very excellently as ever I heard him, and opened Christ's and the apostles' practices, which they were in, in their day. And he opened the night of apostacy since the apostles' days, and laid open the priests and their practices in the apostacy; that if all England had been there, I thought they could not have denied the truth of those things. So my husband came to see clearly the truth of what he spoke, was very quiet that night, said no more and went to bed.

"The next morning came Lampit, priest of Ulverstone, and got my husband into the garden, and spoke much to him there; but my husband had seen so much the night before, that the priest got little entrance upon him. When the priest Lampit was come into the house, George spoke sharply to him, and asked him 'When God spake to him and called him to go and preach to the people?' But after awhile the priest went away: this was on the sixth day of the week, about the Fifth month, 1652. And at our house divers Friends were speaking one to another, how there were several convinced here-aways, and we could not tell where to get a meeting; my husband also being present, he overheard, and said of his own accord, 'You may meet here if you will:' and that was the first meeting we had that he offered of his own accord. And then notice was given that day and the next to Friends, and there was a good large meeting the first day, which was the first meeting that was at Swarthmoor, and so continued there a meeting from 1652 to 1690."

" After a few weeks George went to Ulverstone steeple-house again, and the said justice Sawrey, with others, set the rude rabble upon him, and they beat him so that he fell down as in a swoon, and was sore bruised and blackened in his body, and on his head and arms. Then my husband was not at home; but when he came home, he was displeased that they should do so, and spoke to justice Sawrey, and said, ' It was against law to make riots.' After that he was sore beat and stoned at Walney till he fell down, and also at Dalton was he sore beat and abused ; so that he had very hard usage in divers places in these parts. And then when a meeting was settled here [1652] he went again into Westmoreland, and settled meetings there ; and there was a great convincement, and abundance of brave ministers came out there-aways ; as John Camm, John Audland, Francis Howgil, Edward Burrough, Miles Halhead, and John Blaykling, with divers others. He also went over the sands to Lancaster, and Yelland, and Kellet, where Robert Widders, Richard Hubberthorn and John Lawson, with many others, were convinced. And about that time he was in those parts, many priests and professors rose up, and falsely accused him for blasphemy, and did endeavor to take away his life, and got people to swear at a sessions at Lancaster that he had spoken blasphemy. But my then husband and Colonel West, having had some sight and knowledge of the truth, withstood the two persecuting justices, John Sawrey and Thompson, and brought him off, and cleared him ; for indeed he was innocent."

Judge Fell appears not to have adopted all the principles of Friends ; but being convinced of the right of every one to enjoy liberty of conscience where it did not interfere with the rights of others, he was conspicuous in that day of intolerance and persecution, for making use of power and influence that were at his command, in protecting the oppressed and in striving to moderate the unrighteous zeal and cruel prejudice of his times. He lived about six years after his wife's convincement, during which time he left off attendance on the ministry of the priest Lampit, and having given permission to Friends to hold their meetings at his house, he often sat in his study with the door open to hear the preaching that might take place in the meeting held in his great hall.

Margaret Fell was so thoroughly convinced at the time referred to in her account, that she never wavered; but keeping close to the manifestations of the light of Christ to her soul, she became established in the truth; took an active part in succóring Friends under suffering; and as a mother in Israel, enjoyed until her death, the confidence and correspondence of most Friends of note throughout the kingdom. She, in the course of time, became the wife of Geo. Fox. At the time of Judge Fell's decease, they had one son and seven daughters living; the oldest of the latter being then twenty-five years of age, and the youngest five. All the daughters appear to have adopted the faith of Friends, with their mother, who was left, in her widowhood, to bear as well as she could, the cruel impositions which were sure to be inflicted on her, if she lived in accordance with her religious convictions.

CHAPTER IV.

Justification of Friends' Speaking in the " Churches "—George Whitehead — Early Friends' Love for the Scriptures — Effectual Preaching of George Whitehead —Wm. Barber imprisoned for twenty years — Imprisonment of G. Whitehead — Injustice of Magistrates encourages the violence of the people — Persecution of Wm. Dewsbury at Tholthorpe — At Derby — Change in Priests who had become Friends — Some reasons why the Priests opposed Friends — Their efforts to excite prejudice against Friends, and their Inconsistency—Cromwell's ordinances of Toleration —Not observed towards Friends — Old Laws revived, for the punishment of Friends—Priests accuse G. Fox of Blasphemy—Cruel usage of G. F. at Walney Island—Trial of G. F. at Lancaster — Cleared of the charges, and writes Addresses to some of the Justices.

IN palliation of the dreadful cruelty inflicted on Friends who visited and spoke at the so-called churches, often instigated or promoted by the priests, the charge has been brought against them, that in so doing, their conduct was rude and partook of fanatical insolence.

But in judging of their actions in this matter, due consideration must be given to the circumstances, the temper and the custom of the time in which they came forth. The places of worship had been provided by and belonged to the government. After the Presbyterians obtained power in the Long Parliament, the clergy of the " Episcopal Church," were no longer authorized to have exclusive possession of them. The Presbyterians, however, though they openly declared that they abhorred toleration, were too much in awe of the Independents and Baptists, to attempt installing their own preachers in the "national churches," to the exclusion of all others. True, many of them sought and obtained the benefices from which their predecessors had been driven, and were glad to get hold of the revenues attached to them. Not a few of those who had professed to be Episcopalians, while that party was in power and had the "livings" to bestow, changed their profession of religion to suit the mutations of the times, and eagerly sought to secure the revenues connected with their former parishes.

During the progress of the civil war, as has been before observed —the strife respecting different points of faith was constantly kept up; and Presbyterians, Baptists, Independents, and members of other sects, often resorted to the different places of worship, to expound the principles they held, or to dispute on points of faith and practice; and it was no unusual circumstance for word to be given out from the pulpit, that if any one present had aught to say, he might speak. Oliver Cromwell, who was attached to the Independents, rebuked the Presbyterians of Scotland, when they entered complaint to him that "the pulpit doors were open to all intruders;" reminding them that He who ascended up on high, gave his gifts to whom He would; and demanding of them whether they had become envious because Eldad and Medad prophesied? Besides, it was well known that many of the parish priests, though exceedingly avaricious, not unfrequently neglected their flocks, and often indulged in immoralities. George Fox declared that in thus doing, Friends followed the example of Christ and his apostles, who went into the synagogues of the Jews to preach to and to teach the people.

Sewel, in allusion to this subject, has the following:

"Perhaps some will think it was very indecent that they went so frequently to the steeple-houses, and there spoke to the priests; but whatsoever any may judge concerning this, it is certain that those teachers generally did not bring forth the fruits of godliness, as was well known to those who themselves had been priests and

freely resigned their ministry, thenceforth to follow Christ in the
way of his cross; and these were none of the least zealous against
that society among whom they formerly had ministered with an
upright zeal. Yet they were not for using sharp language against
such teachers, who, according to their knowledge, feared God; but
they levelled their aim chiefly against those, who were only rich in
words, without bringing forth true Christian fruits, and works of
justice.

"None therefore need think it strange, that those called Quakers
did look upon such teachers as hirelings. And that there were not
a few of that sort, appeared plainly when King Charles II. was restored; for those who had formerly cried out against Episcopacy, and
its liturgy, as false and idolatrous, then became turn-coats, and put
on the surplice, to keep in the possession of their livings and benefices. But by so doing, these hypocrites lost not a few of their
auditors, for this opened the eyes of many, who began to inquire
into the doctrine of the denounced Quakers, and saw that they had a
more sure foundation, and that this it was which made them stand
unshaken against the fury of persecution."

So notorious was the profligacy and hypocrisy of not a few of
those who held the "livings," that Oliver Cromwell appointed a
Commission of laymen, called "Triers," to take the subject under
their special care, receive complaints, examine witnesses, &c., and
displace those found guilty of the charges brought against them,
and several were so dismissed.

When Friends felt it required of them to go to these "churches,"
if they had anything to say, it was very seldom uttered until after
the "service" was gone through; and George Whitehead, in one
of the papers he published, draws attention to the fact, that when
Friends had established meetings for themselves, it was not an uncommon thing for ministers and teachers of other religious Societies,
to come into them, put questions respecting the doctrines preached,
and enter into disputes thereon.

George Whitehead, of whom mention has just been made, was a
man who became a pillar in the Church, and conspicuous for his
many sufferings, and his important services in and for the infant
Society, of which he early became a member. From the memoir of
himself which he wrote, it appears that from his boyhood he was of
a serious turn of mind, and observant of the religious profession and
corresponding lives of those with whom he associated. His parents
thinking that he might become an ordained minister in the estab-

lished "Church," gave him so good an education that he afterwards became a tutor, and followed that occupation for years. Not liking the "Church," he consorted for a while with the Presbyterians; but he saw that they fell short of what he believed the Christian is called to. In order to satisfy the strong desires which the Lord, even in his early days, had raised in his heart, after a knowledge of his truth and a life consistent therewith, he went among the most highly esteemed of different religious denominations.

But he states that his longing after true repentance and amendment of life, was often quenched by indulgence in music and other vain pursuits. But as the Lord was pleased, by the secret reproofs of his Spirit, to bring him under condemnation for the vanity in which he took delight, he was preserved from running far into folly, and from continuing content with the outside religion in which he saw so many were resting.

Having heard of a people called Quakers, who were said to tremble at the word of the Lord, and were reviled by wicked people, he made inquiry concerning them, and learning there were a few of them at Sedbergh, near Kendal, in Westmoreland, not far from where he was born, he concluded to go to their meeting. That which impressed him most at this meeting, was what appeared to him to be "A great work or power of the Lord breaking the hearts of divers into great sorrow, weeping and contrition of spirit," which, he says, "I believed to be a godly sorrow for sin, in order for unfeigned repentance." Observing a young woman go out of the meeting he followed her, and seeing her "mourning bitterly," and hearing her cry out "Lord make me clean, make me clean," he says, "This far more tenderly and deeply affected my heart, than what I had heard spoken [in the meeting] and more than all the preaching I had ever heard."

Being convinced by the testimony of Grace to his soul, that there was a divine power at work among this people, causing both godly sorrow and contrition, in order to bring them to true repentance and amendment of life, so as really to experience regeneration and sanctification, he resolved to leave all dead and empty forms, and to resort constantly to the meetings of the reviled Quakers. This was in the seventeenth year of his age. His judgment was confirmed in the full belief that the doctrines of Friends were in exact accordance with those taught by Christ and his apostles; so that he says he was fully convinced before he met with George Fox, whom he first heard preach in an evening meeting held at the house of Captain Ward, Sunnybank, Westmoreland. [1652.]

Being sure that without being converted as well as convinced, and without being regenerated and sanctified, he could not enter into the Kingdom of heaven, he says, " I saw it was my place to retire inwardly to the Light, to the Grace of God, the immortal, incorruptible Seed, the ingrafted Word, which is our principle; frequently testified of among the said people, according to Holy Scripture." . . . " I was persuaded to wait in the light, in the way of his [the Lord's] judgments, and to bear and submit to his fatherly chastisements and reproofs of instruction; believing that Zion must be redeemed through judgment and her converts with righteousness." . . . " I had a spiritual warfare to go through, a body of sin to be put off and destroyed; though [I was] not grown to that maturity, as many of riper years who [have been] guilty of many gross evils by their longer continuance and custom of sinning. Nevertheless I knew a real necessity of the work of sanctification, inward cleansing from sin, and being born again. That is the new birth, that is born from above, which only is entitled to the Kingdom of Christ and of God, which no unclean person can inherit."

" In waiting upon God and sincerely seeking after him, with my mind inwardly retired, and my soul breathing after his name and power, He was graciously pleased often to renew his merciful visitations to my poor soul, and in the midst of judgment and chastisements to remember mercy, that He might be feared." " His eternal word by judgment, caused fear and trembling in his presence, and by showing mercy, brokenness and true tenderness of heart, which I often felt. In the lively remembrance thereof I find still great cause to ascribe praise and glory to his excellent name, power and goodness, through his dear Son, even the Son of his love, our blessed Lord and Saviour Jesus Christ."

Speaking of the meetings which he attended during this time of his being engrafted into Christ, the living Vine, and his early growth in Him, he says he was " Much inwardly exercised in waiting upon the Lord among them [Friends] where *we had little preaching,* but our meetings *were kept much and often in silence,* or but few words declared; the Lord was pleased sometimes, by his power and word of life, to tender and open my heart and understanding; so that He gave me, among some others, now and then, a few words livingly to utter, to their and my own comfort." " It was out of these and such *frequently silent meetings,* the Lord was pleased to raise up,

and bring forth living witnesses, faithful ministers and true prophets in early days." " We also waiting in true silence upon Him,
and eyeing his inward appearance in Spirit, and the work of his
power in us, came truly to see and feel our strength renewed, in
living faith, true love and holy zeal for his name and power; insomuch that the Lord gradually brought us to experience what He
said of old by his holy prophet, 'Keep silence before me, O islands!
and let the people renew their strength : let them come near ; then
let them speak ; let us come near together to judgment.' Thus
keeping silence before the Lord and drawing near to Him in a true
silent frame of spirit, to hear first what the Lord speaks to us,
before we speak to others, whether it be of judgment or mercy, is
the way for renewing our strength, and to be his ministers, to speak
to others only what He first speaks to us.   O ! that the people truly
minded this ; that they would seriously consider hereof: then would
they not run after, or follow such of their ministers, priests or prophets who run and God never sent them ; who say, 'Thus sayeth
the Lord,' when God hath not spoken to them, and who shall not
profit the people at all."

Our Saviour declared that "God is a Spirit, and they that
worship him must worship him in spirit and in truth, for the Father
seeketh such to worship him."   Hence Friends from the beginning
have believed that acceptable worship cannot be performed by man
in his own time and will ; but it is a duty that must be discharged
under the immediate prompting and aid of the Holy Spirit, and is
not limited to set times, places or persons.   That nevertheless it is
obligatory on Christians to meet at set times and places, to bear an
outward testimony to their dependence on and allegiance to the
Author of their lives and of all their sure mercies, and in a visible
fellowship to strive for ability to offer unto Him that worship which
He seeks.   To be enabled thus to worship it is necessary to wait in
the silence of all flesh on the gift of Divine Grace bestowed, that so
through its assistance an offering may be prepared — of whatever
kind it may be — that will be accepted by the Father, through the
mediation of the great High Priest of the new covenant.   " The
preparation of the heart in man, and the answer of the tongue is of
the Lord."   This is equally necessary for those who minister as for
any other member of a congregation.   Their worship, if acceptable,
must be performed in the same way, and if called to minister, they
must wait on the great Head of the church to know when and
what to speak.   He alone knows the various conditions of those

present, and what food is convenient for the states addressed. "For what man knoweth the things of a man save the spirit of man which is in him? even so the things of God knoweth no man, but the Spirit of God." . . . . "Which things also we speak, not in the words which man's wisdom teacheth, but which the Holy Ghost teacheth; comparing spiritual things with spiritual." "Likewise the Spirit also helpeth our infirmities, for we know not what we should pray for as we ought." "I will pray with the Spirit and I will pray with the understanding also. I will sing with the Spirit and with the understanding also."

A blessing is promised on those who thus wait and watch, though silence may not be broken by preaching, prayer or praise; for our Saviour declares, speaking of those servants who are found watching: "Verily I say unto you, that He will make them sit down to meat, and will come forth and serve them;" and they can bear testimony that they who wait upon the Lord do renew their spiritual strength.

The early Friends were remarkable for their diligent reading of the Holy Scriptures, as their memoirs or journals show, and their belief was firm that they would never be found contradicting the revelations of the Holy Spirit to the soul. George Whitehead says, "I always had a love for the Bible and to reading therein, from my childhood; yet did not truly understand, nor experience those doctrines essential to salvation, nor the new covenant dispensation, until my mind was turned to the Light of Christ, the living eternal Word, the entrance whereof giveth light and understanding to the simple." Nevertheless he found the knowledge of the Scriptures which he had obtained prior to his understanding being illuminated by the inshinings of the Holy Spirit, of much advantage to him. He therefore advises, "I would not have Christian parents remiss in educating and causing their children to read the Holy Scriptures; but to induce them both to learn, and frequently to read therein, *i. e.* the Bible."

This will be found the care and advice of the early Friends generally; while they set their faces like a flint against any undertaking to expound or apply them, unless they knew what it was to be brought into the same Spirit that inspired the holy men who wrote them.

The memorial of Devonshire Monthly Meeting concerning George Whitehead, declares that "He was one whom the Lord had fitly qualified and prepared by his divine power and Holy Spirit, for the work whereunto he was called, and whereby he was made one of the most able ministers of the gospel in our day."

"He went forth, travelling on foot to preach the Truth in several of the midland counties, and on one occasion, nearly all the persons composing the meeting which he was addressing were convinced through his lively testimony and prayer." He travelled through Norfolk and Suffolk when in the nineteenth year of his age, holding meetings, at which many were convinced of the truth of the princi- ples held by Friends and joined the Society. When at Norwich he was opposed by an Antinomian, who "pleaded for sin to continue even in the best of saints." G. Whitehead says, "By the Lord's help I stood over him and his perverse gainsayings, to his confusion."

In 1654 he was at a place called Diss, in Norfolk, where, with others, William Barber was convinced by him; of whom he long after speaks as "our ancient and faithful Friend William Barber," and at the same time alluding to his wife says, "I observed the Lord endued her with much patience, considering the great and long suffering her husband endured, by imprisonment in Norwich Castle *for the space of twenty years or more;* chiefly for non-pay- ment of tithes to an old priest of the parish ; who appeared implaca- bly malicious in his prosecution, or rather persecution and revenge."

Believing it was required of him by his divine Master to go to what was called Peter's church in Norwich, after the priest had got through, G. Whitehead began to speak, but was soon stopped, and greatly abused by the congregation, who, endeavoring to pull him in different directions at the same time, so strained him that he suffered great pain; but he says he was healed in a few days. The mayor after questioning him in relation to water baptism, committed him to prison, though there was no charge against him. In the jail he found two other ministering Friends who had been committed a few days before, because of their having preached repentance and amendment of life in the market-place, and through the country around. The jailer was avaricious and cruel, and because the Friends would not comply with his extortionate demands, they were obliged "To lodge upon the bare boards of the floor, in our wearing clothes, and little covering besides; and thus we lodged for eight weeks together in the cold winter, and though we endured much cold, yet were we through the Lord's mercy generally preserved in health." To estimate the cruelty which could inflict such suffering, it must be remembered that G. Whitehead was then but a lad, and naturally of a weakly constitution.

When brought before Judge Cock at the evening session of the court, he was so much incensed at the Friends for coming in his presence with their hats on, that though they plead having not broken any law, and that wearing their hats was not out of disrespect, but because they were restrained by their religious principles from uncovering their heads as a token of reverence, except to Almighty God, he positively refused to give them relief. John Bolton, who had made profession with Friends but shortly before, commiserating the condition of the two Friends, and standing just behind them, allowed his kind feelings to overcome his sense of right, and suddenly pulled off their hats, hoping thereby to pacify the Judge; nevertheless the latter remanded them to their cold and comfortless prison. But J. Bolton was soon sorely troubled for what he had done, and though off his guard for the moment, being sincere and conscientious, he could not rest until he had gone back into the court, openly confessed how wrong he had acted in taking off the Friends' hats, and severely condemned himself therefor. To this the Judge replied thus, " He thought what John had done, would not hold with the Quakers' principle;" thus showing he was fully aware that the not uncovering the head was from a conscientious motive.

The Judge however, without further trial, discharged the two Friends, but the jailer, under pretence of having commenced an action for debt due for lodging, still kept them in the same way as before, for eight weeks longer, when he dying, they were allowed to go free, and G. Whitehead remarks, " So the Lord delivered us by removing our unmerciful oppressor." [1654.]

When Magistrates and Judges, who were sworn to dispense justice and equity without partiality, were so utterly regardless of the common rights of their fellow countrymen as to refuse to hear their cause, to give them a knowledge of the law which they were told had been broken, or to bring their accusers face to face with them, and often fined and imprisoned them for not complying with their own illegal demands, it was to be expected that their inferior officers and the jailers, like the one who imprisoned G. Whitehead and companions of his own will, would follow the example set them, and often practice on their prisoners such unrestrained cruelty as their persecuting spirits prompted them to. Hence it was a frequent occurrence that Friends were kept in jail to gratify the malice of the jailers, and while within their power, were beaten by them unmercifully without any redress being within reach.

William Dewsbury being at York in 1654, was charged with

being a seducer of the people, and with being *suspected* of blasphemy, and breaking the peace of the nation by promulgating principles contrary to the Gospel; Judge Wyndham having issued the warrant for his apprehension while sitting on the bench. William had gone to Tholthrope and was sitting quietly in a meeting there, when a constable rushed in and thrust at him twice with an iron fork, evidently with the intention of maiming or killing him. William says, " The Lord by his power chained him and hindered his bloody intent ;" and by some means he failed to execute the warrant. Another however was procured, and the house wherein William and his friends were staying, was surrounded after midnight by the people of the town with the high constable at their head, and the doors and windows attacked with great fury; they being determined to have their own way with this innocent servant of the Lord. Having dragged him out they " Urged him along the street, shouting, from one ale house to another, until they found one open," where he was placed under the guard of two men, and in the morning, without anything being proved against him, was committed by Justice Dickenson to York castle. Here, without trial, he was kept close prisoner four months. At the time of the general assizes he was brought before Judge Wyndham, when his friends " anxiously interceded " that he might be allowed to have his accusers brought face to face with him ; telling the court that if it was found he had broken any just law, they were willing he should suffer for it. The Judge promised that William should have a fair trial; but broke his word; for without any examination, though accused of crimes which if true would have endangered his life, and though arrested as a criminal in such a violent manner, after proclamation being made that if any one had any thing against him, to speak, he was set at liberty.

About a month after, while preaching to a large congregation at Derby, he was seized and carried before the General Sessions of the town, which was then sitting. One of the Justices said to him haughtily, " In whose presence dost thou now stand?" William replied seriously, " In the presence of the everlasting God :" when the jailer was at once ordered to put him in prison for disturbing the court. Towards night the mayor sent for him to inquire what he came to do ! He answered, " To declare the word of the Lord to the consciences of the inhabitants of Derby." The mayor then asked, " If he would go out of the town?" William replied, " When the Lord orders me to go forth, then I shall go; till then, I shall stay." Being told that if he would go, promising not to return, the prison doors should be open, and he might go, he replied, " He would not go until the man who said he had authority to put him in, came by the same authority and took him out." He was sent back to prison; but not long after, the man under whose charge he was sent to prison, came and took him out. This man took him out of the town, and threatening him greatly should he ever return, bade him go. But William, not feeling clear of the place, disregarded the command and threatening, and returned at once, staying until he felt easy to leave.

From among the multitudes that had been convinced throughout the northern shires of England, there were now a goodly number, both men and women, come forth in the work of the ministry, qualified and willing to preach the gospel freely, and to bear the testimony the Lord gave them against all false doctrines, and all those who sought to make merchandise of what they called the gospel, by preaching for hire. As several of those, now ministers among Friends, had once been hireling ministers themselves, who had given up their "livings," and where they could, returned the money received for their services, they knew, by experience, the difference between their former commission and that they had now received; between their former motives for preaching and the spirit that now inspired them, as well as the difference between the compensation they once obtained for their "service," and that which was now given them by their Lord and Master. These had great influence among those who knew them, and by their and others' unwearied labor and patient suffering, many were turned to the Lord. [1654.]

Finding such large numbers were turning " Quakers," to the great diminution of their flocks, the priests began to preach vehemently against them, and to bring many false charges against them and the doctrines they said they held; particularly for what they alleged was a blasphemous assumption, of being led or guided by the Spirit of Christ dwelling within them. As Friends declined the baptism of water, and the eating of bread and drinking of wine at the Lord's supper, they were declared to be no part of the Church of Christ, and a strong effort was made to associate them with the Ranters, whose notorious impiety, with the open blasphemy of some of their members, made them objects of aversion to most. The uncompromising faithfulness with which Friends bore testimony to free, unpaid gospel ministry; to the equality of the members of the Church of Christ, He being the alone Head and High Priest therein, and all the members truly baptized by the Holy Ghost and fire, equally "A chosen generation, a royal priesthood, a holy nation, a peculiar people," and that the Church should never be under the control of the secular power; striking, as it did, at the distinction between clergy and laity, and cutting away the foundation on which the punishing power of the hierarchy rested, induced the clergy to look upon them as enemies; who, if allowed to go on propagating their doctrines and converting the people to them, would finally destroy their craft, and take away the means for maintaining their "Churches."

They, therefore, not only spoke most bitterly against them, but many of them spared not whatever means was in their power, to exaggerate the prejudice existing in the community towards them, and to excite the populace to acts of violence, if thought necessary, to drive them from, or prevent them coming into their respective neighborhoods. Yet these were the people who had fanned the spirit of war into a flame throughout the kingdom; waged ostensibly to secure liberty of conscience, and, as they said, to break up the power of an usurping priesthood, bent upon punishing all who would not conform to what they prescribed as the true religion, or who were seeking to worship God in another manner than they thought right. Profession of religion was then the fashion of the Court, and what were considered religious exercises occupied the attention of priests and people, in much sincerity doubtless by some; but often as a cloak to cover the hypocrisy of others, and to open the way to preferment.

They longed to extirpate what they branded as heresy, and to stop the mouths of all who presumed to call in question the doctrines they preached, or to deny the validity of their claims, rightly to possess the power and functions they exercised. But Cromwell and his council had ordained, " That none be compelled to conform to the public religion by penalties or otherwise, but that endeavors be used to win them by sound doctrine and the example of a good conversation." "That such as profess faith in God by Jesus Christ, though differing in judgment from the doctrine and discipline publicly held forth, shall not be restrained from, but shall be protected in the profession of their faith, and the exercise of their religion; so as they abuse not this liberty to the civil injury of others, and to the actual disturbance of the public peace on their parts." Popery, Prelacy, and licentiousness under profession of religion, were excluded from the benefit of these provisions.

This should have tied the hands of those who were prepared and anxious to punish Friends for their religious faith; but as has been already shown, and as will be further seen, provisions of law were altogether powerless to restrain either justices or priests, when their passions and prejudices urged them to inflict penalties of the severest kind on the hated "Quakers;" who would persist in acting according to the dictates of the Monitor within, and stood as unyielding witnesses to what they believed to be the truth as it is in Jesus.

There were, however, three enactments standing on the statute book, which furnished means whereby Friends might be made to suffer under color of law, if courts could be found pliant enough to disregard equity in carrying out the letter. ·

One was imposing severe penalties against blasphemy; but not defining exactly what was to be considered blasphemous. Another was making every suspicious person liable to have the oath of allegiance to the Government tendered him, and to be punished severely if he refused to take it; and the third, continuing the imposition of tithes and the laws for collecting them, until the government should provide some other means of support for the ministers.

These old statutes were largely employed by the persecutors of Friends, before Parliament enacted any laws directed specially against the Quakers.

1652. It was determined by a number of priests, if possible, to bring George Fox under the punishment imposed by the first of these laws. He and James Naylor had been at a meeting in Cockan, where a man had tried to shoot the former, snapping a pistol at him; which, however, he could not get to go off. After the meeting they crossed to Walney Island, lying between Morecambe bay and the estuary of the little river Duddon in Lancashire. The next morning going in a boat to James Lancaster's, so soon as George Fox landed, about forty men attacked him, with staves, clubs, and fishing-poles, beating him, and endeavoring to force him into the water; but as he pressed on to pass through them, they knocked him down insensible. James Lancaster, who had been convinced by him, threw himself over George's body to shield him from the blows; but his wife, who had been persuaded to believe that George had bewitched her husband, was busily engaged in throwing stones at his face. After regaining consciousness he attempted to rise, but was beaten down again and thrust into the boat; which J. Lancaster seeing, got in likewise and rowed to the other side.

Landing at the little town again, the people here made a furious attack upon him with "pitchforks, flails, and staves," determined that he should not stay in the town; crying out " Kill him; knock him on the head; bring a cart and carry him away to the church-yard." Thus they drove him out of the town; when, J. Lancaster having left him to go after J. Naylor, who had also been dreadfully beaten, George went to a ditch and washed himself, and made out to walk to the house of a priest, who had been convinced of the truth as held by Friends. Margaret Fell hearing of his being there and that he was so badly bruised he could hardly speak, sent a horse for him to ride on to Swarthmoor; which he made out to ac-complish, though not without suffering great pain. Judge Fell on coming home, and hearing what had befallen George on the island and in the town, issued warrants for the apprehension of the rioters; many of whom fled that part of the country, and George Fox, de-clining to give information against any, because, as he told the Judge, their cruel conduct was the legitimate fruit of their priest's teaching, the matter was dropped.

1652. A large number of priests having combined together for the purpose of having G. Fox tried on the charge of blasphemy, he went voluntarily to the session of the court at Lancaster, where the indict-ment was found against him. There were on the bench Judge Fell, Justices Benson, Sawrey, and Thompson, and one Colonel West. About forty priests appeared as his prosecutors, who had chosen one of their number named Marshal to be their spokesman. A young priest and two sons of priests were the witnesses, who had all sworn to having heard G. Fox utter blasphemy. After the case was opened, the witnesses were examined, Marshal conducting the taking of evidence, and giving his explanation of their testimony.

But the witnesses were so confused and contradictory to their state-ments, that it became evident they were not keeping to the truth. One having been examined, when another was giving his evidence, he became so at a loss that he could not go on, and said "The other could say it." The Judges said to him, "Have you sworn it, and given it already upon oath, and now say that ' he can say it.' It seems you did not hear those words spoken yourself, though you have sworn it."

The following is taken from the journal of George Fox: " There were then in court several who had been at that meeting, wherein the witnesses swore I spoke those blasphemous words which the priest accused me of; and these being men of integrity and reputa-tion in the country, did declare and affirm in court, that the oath,

which the witnesses had taken against me, was altogether false; and
that no such words as they had sworn against me were spoken by
me at that meeting. Indeed, most of the serious men of that side
of the country, then at the sessions, had been at that meeting, and
had heard me both at that and other meetings also. This was taken
notice of by Colonel West, who being a justice of the peace, was then
upon the bench; and having long been weak in body, blessed the
Lord, and said, the Lord had healed him that day; adding, that
he never saw so many sober people and good faces together in all
his life. Then turning himself to me, he said in the open sessions,
"'George, if thou hast anything to say to the people, thou mayest
freely declare it.' I was moved of the Lord to speak: and as soon
as I began, priest Marshal, the orator for the rest of the priests,
went his way. That which I was moved to declare, was this: "That
the Holy Scriptures were given forth by the Spirit of God; and all
people must first come to the Spirit of God in themselves, by which
they might know God and Christ, of whom the prophets and apostles learnt, and by the same Spirit know the Holy Scriptures; for
as the Spirit of God was in them that gave forth the Scriptures,
so the same Spirit must be in all them that come to understand the
Scriptures. By which Spirit they might have fellowship with the
Father, with the Son, with the Scriptures, and with one another: and
without this Spirit they can know neither God, Christ, nor the Scriptures, nor have a right fellowship one with another.' I had no sooner
spoken these words, but about half a dozen priests, that stood behind
me, burst into a passion. One of them, whose name was Jackus,
amongst other things that he spake against the truth, said, that
the Spirit and the letter were inseparable. I replied, 'Then every
one that hath the letter, hath the Spirit; and they might buy the
Spirit with the letter of the Scriptures.' This plain discovery of
darkness in the priest moved Judge Fell and Colonel West to reprove them openly, and tell them, that according to that position,
they might carry the Spirit in their pockets as they did the Scriptures. Upon this, the priests, being confounded and put to silence,
rushed out in a rage against the justices, because they could not
have their bloody ends upon me. The justices, seeing the witnesses
did not agree, and perceiving they were brought to answer the priests'
envy, and finding that all their evidences were not sufficient in law
to make good their charges against me, discharged me. And after
Judge Fell had spoken to Justice Sawrey and Justice Thompson
concerning the warrant they had given forth against me, and showing

them the errors thereof, he and Colonel West granted a *supersedeas* to stop the execution of it. Thus I was cleared in open sessions of those lying accusations which the malicious priests had laid to my charge; and multitudes of people praised God that day, for it was a joyful day to many. Justice Benson, of Westmoreland, was convinced; and Major Ripan, mayor of the town of Lancaster, also."

Under a sense of the wickedness of some of the justices who were most active in persecuting Friends, and of those priests who incited them and the people to treat them with such barbarity as took place on some occasions, George Fox addressed them individually, by letters containing serious exhortations to a different course, and solemn warnings of the consequences, if they persisted in the same evil way they had been pursuing. He also published a warning to the people of Ulverstone, and the neighborhood of Swarthmoor. This was in 1652.

CHAPTER V.

NOTWITHSTANDING the persecution and suffering almost continually attending membership with Friends, throughout the northern parts of England, large numbers continued to be added to them. There were many foolish stories, intended to operate on the superstitious notions of the ignorant, widely circulated, relative to George Fox; as that he was seen at two different places many miles asunder at nearly the same time, sometimes on a great black horse, and sometimes without any apparent means of locomotion; that he never laid down on a bed; that it was impossible to draw blood from him; and that those who came about him were bewitched by him. From all this it was asserted to be evident that he was a wizard, and that those who joined with him would come to nought in the course of a short time. Still the people flocked to hear him and his faithful coadjutors, and it was rarely a meeting was held, whether of their own, or among others, that some were not brought to confess that the power of the Lord was manifestly among them, and to be willing to take part with them in their afflictions, if they might also share with them in the blessed assurance that they were building on Christ Jesus, the foundation of many generations of the righteous.

Many books and pamphlets denouncing Friends were written and published, containing grievous charges against them, and false representations of the doctrines they were said to have preached; but as these were at once replied to by some one or more of their number, and the untruth or unfairness of what was alleged, exposed, while their religious belief and their Christian practices were fully and fairly stated, these attacks proved a means of informing the unprejudiced and propagating the principles held by Friends.

The northern parts of England had by this time been thoroughly visited, by those who felt themselves called to preach what they believed to be primitive Christianity; and the feet of several of those zealous preachers were turned towards other parts of the nation. In 1654, John Audland and Thomas Airey went to Bristol, where they were soon joined by John Camm. The latter was born in Westmoreland, was of a good family, and had been religiously inclined from his youth. He was one of Geo. Fox's converts, and having embraced the truth from heartfelt conviction, and been made willing to yield obedience to its requirings, he grew therein, and became an eminent minister of the gospel. They had many meetings among the Baptists and Independents living in the town, and also preached to large gatherings of people in the immediate neighborhood. Many were convinced of the truth of the doctrines they declared; among whom were Josiah Cole, George Bishop, Charles Marshall and Barbara Blaugdone, who afterwards became distinguished members in the Society.

Charles Marshall, speaking of the great exercise the converts in Bristol passed through, when aroused to a sense of their lost condition by this effectual preaching, and setting in earnest to experience reconciliation and regeneration, says: "Oh! the tears, sighs and groans, tremblings and mournings, at the sight of the middle wall of partition that we then saw, in our awakened states, that stood between us and the Lord; and in the sight and sense of our spiritual wants and necessities. . . . . Oh! the strippings of all needless apparel,

and the forsaking of superfluities in meats and drinks; for we walked
in a plain, self-denying path; having the fear and dread of God on
our souls, and being afraid of offending in word or deed. Our words
were few and savory, our apparel and houses plain, being stripped
of superfluities; our countenances grave, and deportment weighty
among those we had to do with."

F. Howgill and E. Burrough, having come into Bristol, the magistrates commanded them to leave the city; but when brought
before them they replied, that as they were free-born Englishmen,
and had broken no law, they intended to remain until the same
sense of duty that had brought them there, called them away. Finding they could not be legally expelled, some of the magistrates and
priests incited the populace to drive the Friends away by violence. J.
Audland and J. Camm, intending to have a meeting at Brislington,
two miles from Bristol, started to go there; but were met at the
bridge by an infuriated rabble, who, crying out " kill them, knock
them down, or hang them," made a violent assault upon them; so
that they narrowly escaped with their lives, and were forced to go
back into the city. The mob strove to get possession of the two
Friends, in order to execute their murderous designs upon them;
but, by the courageous efforts of one of those who had been convinced
by them, they were got into his house, and thus protected from the
attempted violence, though the infuriated multitude threatened to
pull the house down. Several of those who had been convinced and
joined Friends, were thrown into jail. Elizabeth Marshall having
spoken to the priest after he had dismissed the congregation, the
magistrates encouraged the people to assault her, which they did,
giving her many blows with their canes and cudgels.

Great hatred and distrust of the Roman Catholics existed at that
time in the minds of the common people, and the magistrates of
Bristol, hoping to make these feelings contribute towards discredit-
ing the Quakers, issued a warrant, in which they said, " Forasmuch
as information hath been given us upon oath, that certain persons of
the Franciscan order in Rome, have of late come over into England.
and under the notion of Quakers, drawn together several multitudes
of people in London; and whereas, certain strangers going under
the names of John Camm, John Audland, George Fox, James Naylor, Francis Howgill, and Edward Burrough, and others unknown,
have lately resorted to this city, and in like manner, under the notion of Quakers, drawn multitudes of people after them, and occasioned very great disturbances amongst us; and forasmuch as by

the said information it appeareth to us to be very probable, and much to be suspected, that the said persons so lately come hither, are some of those that came from Rome, as aforesaid; these are therefore, in the name of his highness, the Lord Protector, to will and require you to make diligent search through your ward for the aforesaid strangers, or any of them, and all other suspected persons, and to apprehend and bring them before us, or some of us, to be examined and dealt with according to law; hereof fail you not." [1654.]

This spirit of persecution prevailed in Bristol for many years, inflicting grievous wrongs and sufferings on the peaceable and inoffensive Friends; who, however, amid it all, kept steadily to their meetings and their profession, and had the satisfaction of seeing their number increase, and the testimony they bore to the truth gain more and more place with the religiously minded people.

Barbara Blaugdone, who was one of the early converts at Bristol, was a school-mistress; but when she became a plain Friend, her pupils were taken from her, and shortly after, for speaking in one of the "churches" against the formalities practised, she was imprisoned for three months. Sometime after, at Marlborough, for exhorting the people to fear God, she was again imprisoned for six weeks. On being released, she went to the magistrate who had committed her and so spoke to him that, he afterwards confessed to her, he was convinced her doctrines were true, though he flinched from taking up the cross and openly adhering to them.

Feeling it laid upon her to go to the house of the Earl of Bath, where she had often spent much time with his family in vain amusements, and warn them against such indulgences, the servant, who knew her, sent her to the back of the house, where a mastiff dog was set on her. The savage beast came bounding towards her, but suddenly turned away, yelping, and did her no harm; which Barbara ascribed to the immediate interposition of Divine Providence. The wife of the Earl came to her, listened to her exhortation and thanked her, but asked her not into the house, though they had once been on intimate terms.

At Great Torrington, having spoken to the people in their "church," she was arrested and taken before the mayor, who seemed very loth to send her to prison. But the priest was bent on having her punished, saying she ought to be whipped as a vagabond. She bid him prove that she had ever asked for bread. As he could not do this, he insisted that she had broken the law by speaking in the "church," and so urged the mayor, that finally he committed her to Exeter jail, which was twenty miles off. When the assizes came round, she was not brought to trial ; but when the session was over the sheriff came with a beadle, took her into another room, and there whipped her until the blood ran down her back. She never winced as the blows fell on her, but sang aloud, rejoicing that she was counted worthy to suffer in the Lord's cause. The sheriff exclaimed, " Do you sing ? I 'll make you cry by and by ! " He then laid on with increased violence ; at which Ann Speed, who was with her, began to weep ; but Barbara still bore the torture without complaint, and afterwards said, such was the Divine support she felt, that she believed if they had whipped her to death, she would not have felt dismayed. The sheriff seeing that the wrath and cruelty of man could not move her, bid the beadle cease striking her, and allowed Ann to dress her lacerated back. The next day she was put with a company of Gypsies and turned out of the town ; the sheriff following them for two miles, and forbidding her to come back. When he had gone, however, Barbara returned and went to the prison to visit the Friends who were kept there. After being with them for some time she returned to Bristol.

It would extend the narrative too greatly to mention even a few of the many cases of personal suffering inflicted on Friends in Bristol ; those, however, of Temperance Hignell and George Harrison may be noticed ; the former of whom was knocked insensible for speaking reprovingly to a priest, and while in that condition so grievously beaten, that after being shut up in jail, she had to be carried out in a basket, and in two days died. The latter was kept in jail until he died.

In 1654, two women Friends, the name of one of whom was Isabel Buttery, went up to London from the North of England ; carrying with them an address written and printed by George Fox, with the following long title, " To all that would know the way to the Kingdom, whether they be in forms, without forms, or got above all forms, a direction to turn your minds within, where the voice of God is to be heard, whom you ignorantly worship as afar off ; and to wait upon him for true wisdom. That you may know truth from error, the Word from the letter, the power from the form, and the true prophets from the false : given forth by one of those whom the World in scorn calls Quakers." Without seeing the contents of the pamphlet, the title will give a good idea of the doctrines inculcated in it.

This pamphlet was distributed by the two women Friends, assisted by two brothers, Simon and Robert Dring ; who lived in the city, and who appear to have been convinced of the doctrine thus promulgated, as they opened their respective houses for holding meetings, for all who inclined to assemble there for the purpose of Divine worship. Although I. Buttery is said to have occasionally spoken a few words in these meetings, yet they were generally held in silence. For distributing the pamphlet in "St. Paul's churchyard," on a First-day evening, I. Buttery and a maid-servant of R. Dring's were arrested, carried before the Lord Mayor, and under pretence of having broken the "Sabbath," were committed to the common jail, where vagabonds and common street-walkers were usually sent. How long they were kept there is not known.

In the summer of this year, F. Howgil, E. Burrough and Anthony Pearson—the latter of whom had been a justice of the peace—came to London, and at once entered on the religious service which they believed required of them ; occasionally preaching at the meetings of Friends already established, but more frequently, at meetings held at different places ; sometimes in churches, sometimes elsewhere, for the purpose of religious inquiry and dispute, to which all who chose might go.

London, at that time (1654), was a walled city, with no entrances but through embattled gates ; having few wide or large streets, and few stately edifices ; the most of the houses being of wood. It was a common practice among the tradesmen and apprentices, after the labors of the day were pretty much over, to go out into the fields that surrounded the city and engage in games of various kinds. On one occasion of the kind there was a contest in wrestling, and a strong, well-trained man, who had already been victorious over three opponents, stood resting, in the ring formed by the admiring crowd, waiting to see if any other would be so bold as to confront him, and wrestle for the prize. No one appeared to dispute his prowess. E. Burrough, who happened to be passing at the time, and had stopped among the spectators, stepped into the ring as though he was intending to engage in the contest. The crowd, as well as the wrestler, were taken by surprise at seeing a young man of such plain appearance and serious countenance, place himself in such a position, and stood wondering what would be the issue. But Edward had a far different kind of wrestling in view than that in which they were interested ; even to wrestle against "The rulers of the darkness of this world, against spiritual wickedness in high places." So he began at once to address the motley audience, thundering against sin and all unrighteousness, and striving to turn his hearers from darkness to the light of Christ Jesus the Saviour, and from the power of Satan unto God. Such was the engaging manner of his address, and the convincing power accompanying the doctrine he preached, that he was heard by that mixed multitude with becoming quiet and admiration, and some were convinced.

Edward was so noted, even in that day of dauntless Christian courage, for righteous zeal and supernatural energy, when engaged in the exercise of the gift with which his Master had entrusted him, that he was designated " A son of thunder."

William Crouch, who was a resident in London, speaking of E. Burrough says, " He was a man, though but young, of undaunted courage; the Lord set him above the fear of his enemies, and I have beheld him filled with power by the spirit of the Lord; for instance at the Bull-and-Mouth; when the room, which was very large, hath been filled with people, many of whom had been in uproars, contending one with another; some exclaiming against the Quakers, accusing and charging them with heresy, blasphemy, sedition and what not; that they were deceivers and deluded the people ; that they denied the holy Scriptures and the resurrection. Others endeavoring to vindicate them, and speaking of them more favorably. In the midst of all which noise and contention, this servant of the Lord hath stood upon a bench, with his Bible in his hand—for he generally carried one about him—speaking to the people with great authority from the words of John vii. 12: ' And there was much murmuring among the people concerning him (viz. Jesus) for some said he is a good man ; others said nay, but he deceiveth the people.' And so suitable to the present debate amongst them, that the whole multitude were overcome thereby, and became exceedingly calm and attentive, and departed peaceably, and with seeming satisfaction.

While diligently pursuing the great work that engaged them in London, F. Howgil and E. Burrough occasionally addressed letters to Margaret Fell, some extracts from which will give a little insight of the manner in which the cause prospered in their hands.

In one, dated Fifth mo. 29th, 1654, speaking of the deep religious solicitude they constantly feel, under a sense of the magnitude and serious character of the work assigned them, and their fervent desire to be kept faithful and bold, with wisdom to discern what to spare and what to destroy ; they say, " We have three meetings or more every week, very large, more than any place will contain, and which we can conveniently meet in. Many of all sorts come to us, and many of all sects are convinced; yea, hundreds do believe; and by the power of the gospel declared among them is the witness of God raised, which shall never die. There are some brought under the power exceedingly, which strikes terror into the hearts of many; and many lie under true judgment, and a true love is raised up in many, and the time of redemption to many is drawing nigh." . . . "Our dear brethren, John Audland and John Camm, went from us the last Sixth-day out of this city towards Oxford, to be there the last First-day: our hearts were broken in separating one from another, for our lives were bound up in one, and we partake of one another's sufferings and of one another's joy. We received letters every week from the prisoners at Chester; the work of the Lord goes on gloriously in that county; there is a precious seed; and Anthony Pearson writes to us of the like in the county of Durham. It is even our reward to hear that the Lord is raising that up in power which was sown in weakness." . . . "Our chiefest care is that we may be preserved in obedience, in power and in wisdom; that the Lord may be glorified by us."

The sufferings of Friends at Chester were often very severe. The authorities made use for torture of an excavation in a rock, called "Little Ease," of which the following description is given in Besse's Collection of Sufferings. "It was an hole hewed out in a rock; the breadth, and cross from side to side was seventeen inches; from the back to the side of the great door at the top, seven inches; at the shoulders, eight inches; at the breast, nine inches and a half; from the top to the bottom, one yard and a half; with a device to lessen the height, as they are minded to torment the person put in, by draw-boards, which shoot over the two sides to a yard in height or thereabouts."

Into this stone case prisoners were thrust, and there kept for hours, or until their tormentors thought they had suffered as much as they could endure and live. Friends, both men and women, were repeatedly subjected to this barbarous punishment, and a minister, named Richard Sale, who was so corpulent a man that it took four men to force his body into the hole, was so greatly injured thereby that he soon after died in consequence.

In a letter from F. Howgil to Robert Widders, dated about a month later than the former, he says, "We have been in great service continually since we came into this filthy place: here is the trimmed harlot, the mystery of witchcraft; and the devil rules and is head in all sorts. We have been at the most eminent Societies in the city, and we have had strong fightings with them over and over, and at some steeple-houses; and but that they have our persons in contempt, they say none speak like us; but the devil will not stoop so low. We have two or three meetings in a week, and no place large enough; so that we are much put to it. And we have been guided in much wisdom, so that all them that hate us have nothing to accuse us of, as of tumults or disorder in the least. Some wait to entrap us, but in wisdom we are guided."

From the journals and letters of Friends active at that time, the character of the labors undergone by the Friends in London can be in part ascertained. E. Burrough and R. Hubberthorn being at a meeting of Baptists held in the "Glasshouse," the former was allowed to speak until he had relieved himself of the exercise that had lain upon him; but Richard addressing the congregation, they became excited and turned him out of the house. He then in company with John Camm went to a meeting of a sect called "Lockers," where they largely declared the truths of the gospel. Anthony Pearson and F. Howgil on the same day repaired to a meeting of those called "Waiters." The man who was addressing the audience stopped when he saw the Friends enter, and F. H. began to preach; opening the doctrine of the indwelling of the Holy Spirit in the heart of man, and its work in the salvation of the soul. A person present, who said he acknowledged the truth of the doctrine, drew wrong conclusions from it; which afforded A. P. opportunity to illustrate the doctrine still more clearly and convincingly; and E. Burrough coming in, he also set it forth in its scriptural clearness and fulness. On another day the Friends met with their brethren in their own meeting houses; then some of them went to a large meeting held in a place called Ely-House, under control of a man styled the Governor. In the company were some "Ranters," one of whom was speaking. Edward broke in on his unsavory discourse and preached so powerfully that he convinced several. The Ranter followed him, and when he stopped, F. Howgil addressed the assembly, under a similar anointing as had attended E. B. The Ranter again replied, and in the conclusion desired the audience to say whether he had not spoken to their consciences as convincingly as the two Friends? to which the people with one consent answered, No. At an appointed meeting held in a meeting house of Anabaptists, where many who usually met there attended, the gospel labors of the Friends proved so effectual, that a large portion of the members seceded from the congregation.

So greatly did the Lord bless his word, preached in the demonstration of the Spirit and of power, that in about four months the Friends of London found it almost impracticable to hold their own meetings in the houses they then had, so great were the crowds of noisy and rude persons who came to them. To obviate this difficulty, a large meeting house was provided, — known as the Bull-and-Mouth, — which would hold about a thousand persons. [1654.] This was used for public meetings, where all who chose might attend; while the body of Friends continued to hold their meetings for worship in private houses, many of which were offered by members for the purpose.

It is probable, this was found necessary in other places beside London, and it explains a passage in one of George Fox's epistles, where he says, "And when there are any meetings in *unbroken* places, ye that go to minister to the world, take not *the whole meeting* of Friends thither, to suffer with and by the world's spirit; but let Friends keep together, and wait *in their own meeting-place;* so will the life in the Truth be preserved and grow. And let three, or four, or six, *that are grown up and are strong in the Truth,* go to such *unbroken* places, and *thresh the heathenish nature,* and there is true service for the Lord." This shows how careful and how desirous he was, that those, newly converted, who were as yet but babes in Christ, or had not attained to that stability in the Truth which would enable them to contend for its doctrines and testimonies, should be kept retired in Friends' comparatively quiet meetings; there to wait upon the Lord, in the silence of all flesh, to experience their spiritual strength increased.

While in London at this time, F. Howgil went to see Oliver Cromwell at the Court, and spoke so convincingly to him and those about him, that two who heard him, afterwards embraced the faith of Friends, and joined the Society.

The Robert Widders, to whom the last letter quoted from was addressed, had been convinced in the early part of Geo. Fox's ministry, and like his brethren, had suffered much for his integrity and faithfulness to his conscientious convictions. At one time he was so unmercifully beaten in a "church" yard, that he lay on the ground for some time as dead; but recovering, he went seven miles that day to another steeple-house; where he told the priest that "the hand of the Lord was against him." He was arrested, and before the justice, he told the priest he was in the spirit of persecution, which he denied; but directly after accused Robert of having stolen the horse he rode on, and said, "He could find it in his heart to be his executioner with his own hands." The justice having made out the warrant to commit him to prison and given it to the constable, asked Robert, by what authority or power he came to seduce and bewitch the people? To which he replied, " I came not to seduce and bewitch the people; but I came in that power which shall make thee, and all the powers of the earth, bend and bow before it — the mighty power of God." While Robert thus spoke, the power alluded to seemed to seize upon the justice, so that he took the warrant out of the constable's hand, and permitted Robert to go on his way [1653].

Active and zealous a minister of the gospel as Richard Hubberthorn must have been, and highly as he was esteemed by Friends in his day, there appears to be but little recorded that gives information relative to his early days. He was a native of Lancashire, born of pious and respectable parents, and from his youth was serious and disposed to a religious life. Like many others of the early Friends, he had been an officer in the parliamentary army, and, in his zeal for religion, was occasionally engaged in preaching to the soldiers. It is probable that he was one of the many convinced by Geo. Fox, at the meetings held by him at Sedberg and Firbank chapel, in the early part of 1652. Coming under the converting power of Divine Grace, he was brought through deep and mortifying exercises of mind, and made willing to sell all, in order to become possessed of the pearl of great price. When prepared by the blessed Head of the Church to receive it, He bestowed upon him a gift in the ministry; and he went forth to preach Jesus Christ and him crucified, and to take his share of the cruel abuse practised on the faithful men and women who were instrumental in gathering and establishing the Society of Friends. He is represented to have been a man of small stature, weakly, and slow of speech. He was possessed of deep knowledge in the mysteries of religion, of sound judgment, and fervent and effective in the exercise of his ministerial gift.

Not long after he had joined the then infant Society, he was dragged out of a meeting, with others, carried some distance into the fields, there bound hand and foot, and left to pass a winter night without the means to shelter or relieve themselves. Accompanying George Whitehead, he went to Norwich in 1654, and for speaking to a priest, and not taking off his hat when brought before the magistrates, he was cast into prison, and confined there nearly a year. During his imprisonment, he addressed several epistles to Friends, for their encouragement and edification.

Oxford, long renowned as a seat of learning, where so many had been trained in its schools of Divinity, was not behindhand in pre-judging the Quakers, and decrying their principles; nor in follow-ing the example set in other parts of the country, to treat them with indecent scorn and barbarous cruelty.

In 1654, two women, named Elizabeth Heavens and Elizabeth Fletcher, the latter quite young in years, having preached to the people in the streets and spoken to the students at the college, the latter made an attack upon them, pushed E. Fletcher first against a gravestone, and then into an open ·grave. Not satisfied with this, they tied the two women together, put them under a pump, and after drenching them there, threw them into a ditch ; through which they finally dragged E. Fletcher, and so cruelly abused her, that she never recovered from the injuries then received, and did not live long after.

Notwithstanding this inhuman treatment, these two innocent women, shortly afterward, under 'a sense of duty, went into a " church," and after the " service" was over began to exhort the people to godliness, but were immediately arrested and sent to the common prison by two magistrates who were present. The mayor refused to have anything to do with punishing them ; saying he would provide them with food, clothing or money, if they required either, but that those who had committed them, might deal with them if they had broken any law. The magistrates agreed that they should be whipped as vagrants ; and having drawn up an order to that effect presented it to the mayor ; but he refused to sign it, or to allow the corporate seal to be affixed to the order.

The magistrates and Vice-Chancellor of the University then re-solved to take the responsibility themselves, and accordingly the next morning, these two unoffending women were ordered to be " soundly whipped ;" which was done, though the executioner man-ifested his unwillingness to be engaged in such work.

After George Fox had been cleared in open court, of the charge of blasphemy preferred against him by about forty priests [1652] he continued his gospel labors, travelling still in the northern parts of England. On one occasion, being at Swarthmoor Hall, and hearing the judge and Justice Bennet conversing on the news of the day, and of the " Long Parliament," which was then sitting, George says, " I was moved to tell them, before that day two weeks the parliament should be broken up and the speaker plucked out of his chair; and that day two weeks Justice Benson told Judge Fell, that now he saw George was a true prophet; for Oliver had broken up the parliament." In 1653 he went into Cumberland, though he had previously heard it had been declared, that if ever he came there his life would be taken.

On the first day of the week, in the afternoon, being in the " church," at a place called Bootles, after the priest had got through, he began to speak, when the priest ordered him to stop, as he had no right to speak there. But George told him that he (the priest) had his hour-glass, and having preached by that and finished, now "The time was as free for him (George) as it was for him (the priest);" who himself was a stranger in the place. So George preached to the people, who were quiet. When they came into the yard, the priest, who was greatly excited, addressed the bystanders, saying: "This man hath gotten all the honest men and women in Lancashire to him, and now he comes here to do the same." Then, said George to him, " What wilt thou have left? And what have the priests left them, but such as themselves? For if they be the honest that receive the truth and are turned to Christ, then they must be the dishonest that follow thee, and such as thou art." Some also of the priest's people began to plead for their priests, and for tithes. George told them, " It were better for them to plead for Christ, who had ended the tything priesthood with the tythes, and had sent forth his ministers to give freely, as they had received freely." So the Lord's power came over, put to silence, and restrained the rude people, that they could not do the mischief they intended.

Having moved on, preaching from day to day, until he arrived at Carlisle, on the first of the week he went into the " steeple-house," and after the priest had finished, spoke to the congregation. The priest left, and the magistrates ordered George out of the house, but he went on " declaring the word of the Lord." The people becoming tumultuous, the governor sent a file of musketeers to stop the outbreak. George retired to the house of a lieutenant, who was convinced, and there a meeting was held of Friends and some Baptists. The next day the magistrates issued a warrant; which when George heard of he went to them, and had a long disputation with them. They committed him to the jail as a blasphemer, a heretic, and a seducer. He was, as usual, cruelly treated by the upper jailer.

1653. When the assizes came on it was generally reported that George was to be hung. The high sheriff did what he could to have him convicted of some capital offence, saying, "He would guard him to execution himself." They would not allow his friends to visit him, nor any one to go to him except to carry necessary things. While the judge, justices and sheriff appeared to be managing so as to have him sentenced to death, the clerk of the court started a question which brought them to see that they lacked the authority to do as they proposed ; and being thus defeated in their intention, they resolved that George should not be brought to trial, but to leave him in the hands of the magistrates of the town.

Anthony Pearson, a justice of the peace, who had been convinced of the truth in a conversation he had with G. Fox on one occasion, at Swarthmoor Hall, sent a communication to the judges of the court, pointing out the illegal and oppressive course pursued towards George; that he had not been examined, knew not who were his accusers, no witnesses had been brought forward, and no sentence passed on him ; and yet he was kept in the strictest confinement, and none of his friends allowed to visit him. But it was without effect. The judges left the town, and then the magistrates ordered the jailer to put George down into a prison among "moss-troopers, thieves, murderers," and abandoned women. "A filthy, nasty place it was," where men and women were huddled in a most indecent manner, and so lousy, that one woman was almost eaten to death by lice. George says, "Yet as bad as the place was, the prisoners were all made very loving and subject to me, and some of them were convinced of the truth, as the publicans and harlots were of old ; so that they were able to confound any priest that might come to the grates to dispute. But the jailer was cruel, and the under-jailer very abusive both to me and to Friends that came to see me ; for he would beat Friends with a great cudgel, who did but come to the window to look in upon me. I could get up to the grate, where sometimes I took in my meat; at which the jailer was often offended. Once he came in a great rage, and beat me with his cudgel, though I was not at the grate at that time ; and as he beat me, he cried, Come out of the window, though I was then far from it While he struck me I was moved to sing in the Lord's power, which made him rage the more. Then he fetched a fiddler, and set him to play, thinking to vex me ; but while he played, I was moved in the everlasting power of the Lord God to sing ; and my voice drowned the noise of the fiddle, struck and confounded them, and made them give over fiddling and go their way."

Singing of psalms or hymns was not practised among Friends in their meetings for worship; though they believed that where an individual was moved thereto by the Holy Spirit, to sing that which was applicable to his or her present condition, it was an accepted service; as was divinely inspired preaching or praying. But as it was liable to great abuse, by performers being induced thus to use expressions altogether untrue as applied to themselves, and there was a great snare in the pleasurable emotions excited by the harmony of sweet sounds, they rejected " sacred " singing and music, as it was ordinarily practised.

The report that had been raised at Carlisle that George Fox was to lose his life, spread so as finally to reach the ears of some members of Parliament; who reported to that body that a young man was in prison at Carlisle who it was expected would be sentenced to death for his religion; whereupon a letter was sent to the sheriff and magistrates in relation to it.

The Governor of the Castle, accompanied by Anthony Pearson, went to the prison to inspect it, and inquire into the treatment of the prisoner. They found the place so bad, and the smell so offensive, that they blamed the magistrates severely for thrusting George into such an abominable prison. Calling the jailers before them, the governor obliged the head jailer to find surety for his future good behavior, and the under jailer, for his barbarous treatment of the prisoners, he put into confinement in the same apartment with George Fox. The magistrates now becoming uneasy, set George at liberty without ever bringing him to trial.

While George Fox was in Carlisle prison, a little lad about sixteen years of age came to see him. He was then and there convinced of the truths of the gospel, and though so young, G. Fox says, " The Lord quickly made him a powerful minister of the word of Life, and many were turned to Christ by him, though he lived not long;" his name was James Parnel.

This youthful martyr for the testimony of Jesus was born at Retford, in Nottinghamshire, in 1638, and was educated in the schools of the neighborhood, attending at the place of worship where his kindred resorted. Early made sensible of the corruption of his heart by nature, and anxious to know a thorough redemption from sin, of which the Holy Spirit convicted him; but ignorant where to find the light and power which could redeem and change him, he again and again formed resolutions to abstain from what he knew to be wrong, and to lead a godly life. But his good intentions and his determined will, were not sufficient to resist the power of his

corrupt appetites and the temptations of Satan. He repeatedly
gave way, and so made work for repentance. Nevertheless his
Heavenly Father followed him, in mercy, with the reproofs of instruction, showed him the emptiness and deadness of the forms of
worship that were generally practised, and kept alive in his soul a
thirst after Himself and to become his disciple. What passed
between him and George Fox in Carlisle jail is not known ; but
whatever George may have said reached the witness for Truth in
James Parnel's heart, and a willingness was wrought to deny himself, take up his daily cross and follow Christ in the regeneration,
by waiting upon and obeying the light of his Holy Spirit shining in
the dark recesses of his soul. [1653.]

After the conference, he appears to have returned to his own
home, and to have patiently borne the winnowing of the Lord's
fan, thoroughly purging the floor of his heart. His refusal longer
to comply with the vain customs of the world, his plain appearance
and language, and his frequenting the meetings of Friends, offended
his relatives, who despised and rejected him. When called to the
work of the ministry, he went forth without " purse or scrip," fully
given up to do or to suffer in the precious cause of Him who had
brought him up out of an horrible pit, and out of the miry clay, set
his feet upon a Rock, established his goings, and put a new song
into his mouth. He was low in stature, but boy as he was, was endued with Christian courage; which prevented his flinching from
preaching repentance and amendment of life to high and low, to
rebuke hypocrisy, and boldly to proclaim the revelation of Christ's
spirit in the heart, to be the power of God unto salvation.

Having, in the course of his travels, gone to Cambridge and testified against the corruption existing among priests and people, he
was sent to prison, and kept there a considerable length of time.
But as there was no legal authority for this treatment, he was set at
liberty and driven out of the town as a vagabond.

In 1655, having heard that a fast had been proclaimed at Colchester, to take place on a specified day, when prayers were to be
offered up against "the errors of the Quakers," James felt himself
required to go there, which he did. He remained quietly in the
"church," until the priest had got through with his charges and
invectives against the Quakers; after which he observed, " That it
is the order of the true church, that all may speak one by one; and
if anything be revealed to him that stands by, let the first hold his
peace." After he had spoken a short time, he was asked, " What

church he owned?" to which he replied, "The church in God."
The priest said he spoke nonsense. James bade him point out
wherein he had spoken nonsense. The priest said, "In saying the
church in God." James pulling out his Bible, read where the
Apostle addresses the Thessalonians as the church in God, and told
his antagonist that it was blasphemous to say that expression was
nonsense. The priest then accused him of lies and slander, and in
order to prevent his replying, went back into the pulpit and began
to pray. The magistrates ordered James to take off his hat, but
rather than obey them he went out of the meeting house.

A little time after, one of the magistrates arrested him, and some
of his friends engaged that he should appear before them when they
had got through with their service. He accordingly went before
them—four justices and six priests. One of the justices pulled his
hat off his head and threw it away. They asked him many questions and then committed him to the common jail.

As the session of the court was to be held at Chelmsford, eighteen
miles from Colchester, when the time arrived for its sitting, James
was fastened to a chain with murderers and other felons, and thus
led through the country ; being kept chained night and day. He
was brought to the bar of the court handcuffed, but this barbarity
roused the feelings of the people so greatly, that at the next sitting his manacles were removed. He was accused of entering the
"church" riotously; of telling the minister that he blasphemed ;
of using reproachful words against him ; and that he could give no
good account of himself, as to where he lived, but appeared to be
an idle person, &c.

James plead his own cause, showing that so far from entering the
"church" riotously, he went in quietly by himself ; that he did not
deny telling the priest he thought it blasphemous in him to say the
expression "Church in God" was nonsense, and that it was not
indecent or improper to call a justice who had acted so unjustly
towards him, unrighteous or a persecutor, &c.. That his former life
and conversation would speak for him that he was not an idle or
disorderly person, but was lawfully engaged in the work to which
he had been called. The judge betrayed the determination he had
come to, by telling the jury that if they did not find the prisoner
guilty, the sin would lie upon their own heads. James desired to
address the jury in his own defence, but the judge would not allow
him. The jury on consultation, declared him guilty of having
written an answer to the mittimus issued for him ; and though the
court strove hard to get them to alter their verdict, they did not

consent. Ja nes was sent out of the court room, and when brought back, the judge said the Lord Protector had charged him to punish those who contemned either magistracy or ministry, and he therefore fined him (about forty pounds), and he was to be kept in prison until it was paid. He was sent to a ruinous old castle used as a prison, and the jailer was charged not to allow any " giddy-headed people "—meaning Friends—to come to him.

The jailer and his wife were more than willing to carry out the evident wishes of the court. They allowed none to see James, but such as would abuse him. The wife swore she would " have his blood." She set on the man to beat him, and several times laid violent hands on him herself. She instigated other prisoners to take the victuals brought for him by his friends. She refused to allow him to have the use of a trundle bed brought for him, but forced him to lie on the damp stones. The walls of Colchester castle were of great thickness—about twelve feet—and in one part of them were two rows of small vaulted chambers, probably intended, and certainly well fitted, to destroy the health of whoever might be confined in them. Into one of these, this innocent young man — then in his nineteenth year — was obliged to go. It was about twelve feet from the ground, and a ladder six feet long was provided, from the top of which, the prisoner must climb up by a rope to the entrance of the damp and cramped apartment. For all needful purposes, he was required to descend and ascend this dangerous passage, to his dismal abode; and in order to oblige him to run the risk of falling the oftener, his cruel jailers refused to allow him the use of a basket and cord, which his friends had provided, to draw up his food and drink.

Confinement, under these circumstances, produced the effect that could hardly have been unforeseen, if it was not desired. He began to lose his muscular power, and his limbs became benumbed. In this condition, as he was one day endeavoring to reach his wretched room, when having got to the top of the ladder, with his food in one hand, he missed catching the rope as he clutched at it with the other, and fell on the rough stones below; cutting his head, and was so jarred and bruised, that he was taken up as one dead. So far were his sufferings from in anywise softening the hearts of his merciless jailers, that they put him into the cell below that he had occupied; which was so small that it was called the oven, and when the door was shut, there was no opening for the admission of light or air.*

* Thomas Scattergood, in his journal, has the following: " After tea I took a walk with G. Gibson and John Kendall to the castle, and went over the old

Here they immured him so closely, that he appeared likely to die from suffocation; they not permitting him to go into the yard below, to breathe the fresh air. And now was witnessed one of those striking evidences of Christian fellowship and sympathy, that drew from some of that day the exclamation, "See how the Quakers love one another." Three of his friends, William Talcot, Edward Grant and Thomas Shortland, went to the justice and offered to be bound under a penalty of forty pounds, if they did not comply, to enter that dismal hole and lie, body for body, while James was allowed to go to the house of one of them until recovered from his illness.

But it was in vain; so implacable was the enmity of those to whom he had done no wrong, but who had the power in their own hands, that they would not consent even to his walking occasionally in the yard. Once the door of his stifling cell being open, James stepped out and walked between the high walls that shut in the narrow passage below; which the jailer seeing, went and locked the door of his cell; and though it was in the depth of winter, kept him in the yard, unsheltered, all night.

But He who, in his inscrutable wisdom, permitted wicked men thus to persecute this youthful and devoted servant, was watching over him in mercy, and when He saw it was enough, and the end designed had been accomplished, sent his pale messenger to free him from his bonds, and the inhumanity of man. His imprisonment had lasted nearly a year, when his persecutors seeing that death was near, permitted two of his friends — Thomas Shortland and Ann Langley — to visit him. James was sensible that his release was approaching, and remarked to one of them, "Here I die innocently." To T. Shortland he said, "This death must I die, Thomas; I have seen great things; don't hold me, but let me go. Will you hold me?" To which A. Langley replied, "No, dear heart, we will not hold thee." He observed that "one hour's sleep would cure him of all." The last words he uttered were, "Now I go;" and stretching himself out, he slept about an hour, and then breathed his last; leaving the pent-up cell where his suffering body had been so long shut in, to enter the glorious courts of heaven; where the wicked cease from troubling, the weary are at rest, and the songs of the redeemed are forever heard. During his confinement he addressed several epistles to his fellow believers. [1655.]

ruins, where I was shown the hole in the wall, from which, it is supposed, dear James Parnell fell when confined in this place; and also his apartment below, which looks like a baker's oven; the thickness of the wall being about four times the length of my walking stick." — Friends' Library, Vol. 8, page 105.

CHAPTER VI.

Evidence of the Seeking State of the People — Large Assemblages to hear G. Fox — G. F. visits his native place — Treatment by the Priests — Colonel Hacker — G. Fox and Cromwell — Visitation to Capt. Drury — G. Fox in London — Alexander Parker — Extracts from Letter — Humphrey Bache — John Crook — Extract from another Letter — Imprisonment of William Dewsbury — Trial before Judge Hale — Same before Judge Atkins — Reflections on the causes that kept Friends from having justice done them — General views of Religion, and of those of Friends — Miles Halhead — Interesting interview with a Justice's Wife — Extraordinary incidents in M. Halhead's course — Misrepresentations of Friends' belief in Christ.

IT must be considered strong evidence of the long unsettled condition of the minds of the people, on the subject of religious belief, and of the uneasiness produced by the want of certainty as to what was true, and what could be relied on to stand unmoved amid the various jarring parties, which were crying, " Lo here is Christ! or, lo He is there!" that they flocked so numerously to hear what were the doctrines preached by Friends, and what the character of the religion that drew upon them the hatred and abuse of so many, both high professors and the ignorant, yet enabled them to speak undoubtingly of what they had experienced in the way of salvation, and made them willing to endure the unmeasured scorn and unrelenting persecution meted them in all places.

1653. George Fox, speaking of the multitude that came to a meeting which he had appointed to be held near Cockermouth, in Cumberland, says, "The country people came in like as it had been to a fair." "I looked about for a place to stand upon, to speak to the people; for they lay all up and down, like people at a leaguer." Again, of another meeting, "We had a general meeting of thousands of people, atop of a hill near Langland. There were as many people as one could well speak over, the multitude was so great." Then as to the character of the preaching and its effect upon the audience: "A glorious and heavenly meeting it was; for the glory of the Lord did shine over all. Their eyes were turned to Christ their teacher; and they came to sit under their own vine; insomuch that Francis Howgil, coming afterwards to visit them, found *they had no need of words;* for they were sitting under their teacher Christ Jesus; in the sense whereof he sat down amongst them, without speaking anything. A great convincement there was in Cumberland, Bishoprick, Northumberland, Westmoreland, Lancashire and Yorkshire, and the plants of God grew and flourished, the heavenly rain descending, and God's glory shining upon them : many mouths were opened by the Lord to his praise; yea, to babes and sucklings He ordained strength." Finding the Society increasing in numbers so rapidly, and "divers young convinced ones coming daily" among Friends, George Fox addressed an epistle to them "For stirring up the pure mind, and raising an holy care and watchfulness in them over themselves and one another, for the honor of Truth."

In the early part of 1654, George Fox went to Drayton, in Leicestershire, to visit his relations. Here he again met with priest Stevens, who had been pastor over him in his youth. They soon got into a dispute, the priest having invited the people to be present. Stevens finding that he could not obtain advantage by argument, said to the people, "This is the business; George Fox is come to the light of the sun, and now he thinks to put out my star-light." George told him, he would not quench the least measure in any, if it was from the "bright and morning Star; but that he must speak the truth freely, and that no minister of Christ could take tithes." Their dispute ended for the present, but George returning to the place in about two weeks, Stevens had associated with himself seven other of his clerical brethren, and the dispute was renewed. George refused to go into the steeple-house, and having James Parnel, Thos. Taylor, and other Friends with him, they went a little distance to the top of a hill. The priests soon gave over arguing, and the people began to be rude. Several men suddenly seized George, and lifting him up, bore him off to the porch of the "church," intending to carry him in; but the door was fastened, and in their eagerness they all fell down together, George being underneath. Having extricated himself he returned to his friends, and as the priests kept aloof, he preached to the people; showing why he denied those priests and all hirelings, and declaring the spiritual nature of the Christian dispensation. Many were convinced that day, and George's father was so well satisfied, that he said, "Truly, I see he that will stand to the truth, it will bear him out."

The priests, baffled in their efforts to get the better of George by disputation, resolved to bring the secular power to their aid. They arranged to have soldiers present at his meetings, who should take the names of the Friends present, and have them sent to their homes. The first attempt failed; but George being at Whetstone, and about to hold a meeting, there came seventeen troopers with a marshal of Col. Hacker's regiment, and took him; leaving the other Friends at George's request, who said he would answer for them all, and at night brought him before Col. Hacker, his major and captains. After some reasoning about the priests and the meetings, the Colonel told George he might go home, if he would stay at home and not go abroad to meetings. This George refused to do, as he said he had done nothing for which he should make his home his prison, and that he must attend meetings as the Lord should order him. The Colonel's son said, "Father, this man has reigned too long, it is time to have him cut off." George replied, "For what? What have I done, or whom have I wronged, from a child? I was born and bred in this country, and who could accuse me of any evil from a child?" As George would not comply with the conditions proposed, the Colonel said, "Well, then I will send you to-morrow morning, by six o'clock, to my Lord Protector, by Capt. Drury, one of his life-guard."

That night George was kept prisoner, and the next morning, when Captain Drury was about to start with him, he desired that he might first speak with the Colonel. Colonel Hacker had not yet risen, and George being taken to his bedside, the Colonel began at once to bid him go home and hold no more meetings. George again refusing to comply, the Colonel said, "Then you must go before the Protector." Whereupon George knelt at the bedside, and "Besought the Lord to forgive him; for he was like Pilate, though he would wash his hands;" and he bid him, "When the day of his misery and trial should come upon him, then remember what he had said to him." [1654.]

Colonel Hacker was afterwards tried and condemned to death for having acted as one of the judges that sat in judgment upon Charles I., and the day before his execution, on being reminded of what he had done to G. Fox, he confessed that he had trouble for it.

Captain Drury behaved courteously to G. Fox on their way to London, allowing him to go and visit Wm. Dewsbury and Marmaduke Storr, who were in prison at Northampton, but tried to persuade him to comply with the proposal to go home and hold no meetings. Arrived in London, Captain Drury reported to the Protector that he had George Fox in custody. The Protector bid the Captain tell George that he required him to promise he would not take up sword or other carnal weapon against the government. The next morning, George says, "I was moved of the Lord to write a paper to the

Protector, by the name of Oliver Cromwell; wherein I did in the presence of the Lord God declare, that I did deny the wearing or drawing of a carnal sword, or any other outward weapon, against him or any man. And that I was sent of God to stand a witness against all violence, and against the works of darkness; and to turn people from darkness to light; to bring them from the occasion of war and fighting to the peaceable gospel, and from being evil-doers, which the magistrate's sword should be a terror to,"

In the course of a short time he was taken before the Protector, and he gives this account of their interview: "It was in the morning, before he was dressed; and one Harvey, who had come a little among Friends, but was disobedient, waited upon him. When I came in, I was moved to say, 'Peace be in this house:' and I exhorted him 'to keep in the fear of God, that he might receive wisdom from Him; that by it he might be ordered, and with it might order all things under his hand unto God's glory.' I spoke much to him of truth; and a great deal of discourse I had with him about religion: wherein he carried himself very moderately. But he said, We quarrelled with the priests, whom he called ministers. I told him, 'I did not quarrel with them, they quarrelled with me and my friends. But, said I, if we own the prophets, Christ, and the apostles, we cannot hold up such teachers, prophets and shepherds, as the prophets, Christ, and the apostles declared against; but we must declare against them by the same power and Spirit. Then I showed him, That the prophets, Christ, and the apostles declared freely, and declared against them that did not declare freely; such as preached for filthy lucre, divined for money, and preached for hire, and were covetous and greedy, like the dumb dogs that could never have enough; and that they, who have the same Spirit that Christ and the prophets, and the apostles had, could not but declare against all such now, as they did then.' As I spoke he several times said, It was very good, and it was truth. 'I told him, That all Christendom (so called) had the Scriptures, but they wanted the power and Spirit that those had who gave forth the Scriptures; and that was the reason they were not in fellowship with the Son, nor with the Father, nor with the Scriptures, nor one with another.' Many more words I had with him; but people coming in, I drew a little back. As I was turning, he catched me by the hand, and with tears in his eyes, said, 'Come again to my house; for if thou and I were but an hour of a day together, we should be nearer one to the other;' adding, 'That he wished me no more ill than he did to his own soul.' I told him, 'If he did, he wronged his own soul; and admonished him to hearken to God's voice, that he might stand in his counsel, and obey it; and if he did so, that would keep him from hardness of heart; but if he did not hear God's voice, his heart would be hardened.' He said, it was true. Then I went out; and when Captain Drury came out after me, he told me, His Lord Protector said, I was at liberty, and might go whither I would. Then I was brought into a great hall, where the Protector's gentlemen were to dine. I asked them, What they brought me thither for? They said, It was by the Protector's order, that I might dine with them. I bid them let the Protector know, I would not eat of his bread, nor drink of his drink. When he heard this, he said, 'Now I see there is a people risen, that I cannot win either with gifts, honors, offices, or places; but all other sects and people I can.' It was told him again, 'That we had forsook our own, and were not like to look for such things from him.'

"Being set at liberty, I went to the inn where Captain Drury at first lodged me. This captain, though he sometimes carried it fairly, was an enemy to me and to truth, and opposed it. When professors came to me, while I was under his custody, and he was by, he would scoff at trembling, and call us Quakers; as the Independents and Presbyterians had nicknamed us before. But afterwards he came and told me, That, as he was lying on his bed to rest himself in the daytime, a sudden trembling seized on him, that his joints knocked together; and his body shook so that he could not rise from his bed: he was so shaken, that he had not strength enough left to rise. But he felt the power of the Lord was upon him; and he tumbled off his bed, and cried to the Lord, and said, he would never speak against the Quakers more, such as trembled at the word of God."

George Fox remained in London during the succeeding months of that year [1654]; busily engaged in attending the meetings of Friends, preaching to the multitudes that thronged them, and also making use of the pen to express his opinions and feelings on many points. He put forth an address, "To all professors of Christianity;" another to "All that follow the World's fashions." He also wrote an address to the Commissioners whom Cromwell had appointed to be "Triers of Ministers," and an exhortation and warning to the Pope, and the Rulers of Europe. He went a second time to Whitehall, where the court was; and to those of the family whom he saw, to the officers, and those that "were called Oliver's gentlemen, who were of his guard," he " Declared the word of the Lord, and that the Lord was come to teach his people himself." Some in the family were convinced ; and George tried to have another interview with Oliver, but failed.

E. Burrough, F. Howgil, and several other ministers of note, had been laboring assiduously, and, as has been before stated, large numbers had been gathered to the principles of Friends, and many meetings were held in different parts of the city. George says, "So great were the throngs of people, that I could scarcely get to and from the meetings for the crowds, and the truth spread exceedingly."

Among others in London brought under the convincing, converting power of the Spirit of Truth, and prepared to accept the self-denying doctrines promulgated by Friends, was Humphrey Bache. He had been a goldsmith, but finding his business diminished and much interfered with after the breaking out of the civil war, he relinquished it, and engaging in the service of the Parliament, he was appointed to oversee a company of men employed in throwing up fortifications around the city. He appears to have been a man of good character, well-intentioned, and up to that time strictly honest.

Having discovered that others in similar station as that he held, were in the habit of defrauding their employers, either by charging for more men than they had at work, or by adding a few pence to their daily wages, with or without their knowledge, and pocketing the surplus, he was strongly tempted to follow their example. He saw the wrong that was thus done, and for a time was restrained by his sense of obligation to refrain from the evil; but by tampering with the temptation, his perception of right and wrong became confused, and after a hard struggle with his convictions, he yielded, and sacrificed his integrity and peace of mind, by robbing the government that had made him one of its officers.

The satisfaction he had once had in his honest efforts to obtain a livelihood, was now destroyed by the reproofs of instruction ; which, had he submissively yielded to them, would have proved the way to renewed spiritual life; but he turned away from them, and strove to satisfy himself with reasoning — suggested by Satan, who was a liar from the beginning — that as the money taken belonged to no one in particular, there was but little harm in what he had done, and that it was a common practice with others.

Being afterwards employed in the custom-house, he there found that a system for robbing the treasury was pursued by many of the officers, by taking bribes to make false returns, &c. Though he had never thoroughly repented of the sin into which his evil covetousness had before betrayed him, yet he remembered the bitterness of the remorse that had, at times, harrowed up his soul for taking that which did not belong to him, and for a time he steadily turned away from the temptations presented. But the grand adversary of man's happiness knows, not only when and where to lay his baits, but also how to employ those whom he has induced to yield to his wicked suggestions, as emissaries for beguiling others into his service; and he prompted some of Humphrey's fellow officers, who were increasing their incomes by illicit practices, to ply him with plausible arguments, why he should not hesitate to conform to what was so customary.

Instead of turning a deaf ear to the voice of the tempter, and seeking strength by prayer to Him who is a present help in every needful time, resolutely to withstand the covetousness of his own heart, and the wiles of the deceiver, he again listened to the pleadings of the worldly-wise charmers, and fell into the snare set for his feet; concluding it was not worth while for him to attempt being better than those around him. Having once more yielded to brave the guilt of robbery in order to increase his means, he found he had not strength of himself to stop in his criminal career, and he joined hands with those who were defrauding the revenue. Nevertheless his long-suffering omniscient Creator left him not without the convictions and pleadings of his Holy Spirit; often bringing him under a sense of the wickedness of the course he was pursuing, and filling his heart with anguish and fear as to the final consequences. But instead of closing in with these visitations of light and mercy, he strove stoutly against them, and allowed his internal strife and dread, to sour his temper, and make him a source of unhappiness to his wife, and in his whole domestic circle. Such, however, became the distress under which a sense of guilt caused him to pass much of his time, that he resolved no longer to partake of the unrighteous gains; and for a year before he left the custom-house he scrupulously adhered to his determination.

It was about the time of his coming to this resolution, that he was induced by curiosity to attend a meeting held in London by Francis Howgil and Edward Burrough. It does not appear that anything then said took hold of him; but he inclined to see and hear more of the much talked of Quakers. Not long after he was at a meeting held in the Bull-and-Mouth meeting house, where George Fox,

E. Burrough, and F. Howgil were present. One of these Friends, in the course of his sermon, speaking of the necessity for every disciple of Christ to take up his daily cross and follow Him, said, "The carnal mind is enmity against God. As any one comes to stand in the cross, which is the power of God, this enmity is broken down and reconciliation is witnessed. The enmity is slain by the power of God; by that which crosseth the carnal mind — the Light of Christ." This proved to be an arrow that struck between the joints of Humphrey's harness, and the swift witness for God in the secret of his soul, testified to its truth. He was conscious that light had repeatedly shone into his dark heart — though the darkness comprehended it not—showing him his sin, and reproving him for following his carnal inclinations. He was now convinced that this was the Light of Christ, and that his salvation depended on his obeying its discoveries and requirements, however much these might be in the cross to his natural propensities; which stood opposed to the government of Christ, and must be crucified and slain before that government could be established over his soul.

Aroused to a sense of his lost condition, brought to realize, in measure, the exceeding sinfulness of his manifold sins, and his own incapacity to extricate himself from the thraldom into which he had been brought, he was happily made willing to keep his attention fixed on the measure of Divine Grace vouchsafed to his soul; to wait upon that as the only means of obtaining a *saving* knowledge of God, and of the things that belong to his everlasting well-being, and patiently to abide under the transforming power of Him, whose right it was, to will and to do according to his own good pleasure. As his sins were set in order before him in the light of Christ Jesus the Saviour, he saw with anguish how deeply he had violated the divine law, by taking that which did not belong to him; and also that he could not hope for peace, unless he restored all that he had unjustly obtained. This plunged him into additional conflict and distress. He shrunk from the exposure of his former dishonesty, and he knew that to make complete restitution, would require a half of all he possessed, and leave but little for the support of his wife and children.

It was a remarkable circumstance, that while Humphrey Bache was struggling under these deep and conflicting exercises of mind, clearly seeing what was required of him, by Him who alone could grant forgiveness of his sins, but held back by the pleadings of pride and the fears relative to future ability to provide for his family,

George Fox — who does not appear to have had previous acquaintance with him — felt it required to make him a visit. Humphrey soon began to disclose his condition to George, when the latter said to him, " He that confesseth and forsaketh his sins, shall find mercy." The poor man, sensible that G. Fox was greatly exercised on his account, says, " The Lord reached down his right arm of power, touched my heart with his grace, and made me willing to submit to his will, and give up the sum of money I had received unjustly. Waiting in the Light this was made plain to me to be near one hundred and fifty pounds. But it lay on my heart to restore more than less. So I was made free by the power of the Lord, and did give back at the excise office in London, one hundred and sixty pounds. Then I felt the truth of the words George Fox spake to me : ' He that confesseth and forsaketh his sins, shall find mercy ; ' for much ease, peace and refreshment I received into my soul."

Humphrey Bache now left the custom-house and returned to his former business of a goldsmith. As he kept upon the watch, and continued to walk in obedience to the requirements of Divine Grace, he found that his growth in the truth depended on his obedience in what many called small and foolish things ; as using the plain language of thou and thee to a single person, discarding compliments, whether in speech or manner, and refusing to conform to the vain fashions and customs of the world. This cost him much, and he often felt the power of temptation to turn his feet out of the straight and narrow way. Faltering or turning aside, as he sometimes did, always marred his peace, and had to be retraced with heartfelt repentance ; but as he kept steadily under the yoke of Christ, walking in the light, he became established on the immutable foundation of prophets and apostles, and prepared for usefulness in the Church. He joined in membership with Friends, and in 1656 a meeting was regularly held at his house.

In carrying on his business, he found himself restrained from making or selling rings or trinkets, as he was made conscious that they merely ministered to the pride of the human heart.

When, in 1662, the storm of persecution beat so vehemently on the defenseless heads of Friends, because they would keep up their meetings for divine worship, H. Bache shared—as he had repeatedly before — in the cruel punishments inflicted, and was thrust into a prison already overcrowded with his fellow sufferers. Here close confinement in a depraved atmosphere, so preyed upon his vital energies, that he did not long survive his liberation ; but shortly after laid down his life for the testimony of a good conscience, and entered upon the enjoyment of the things which eye hath not seen nor ear heard, neither have entered into the heart of man, but which God hath prepared for them that love him.

Alexander Parker had accompanied G. Fox, when he was sent up by Col. Hacker, and remained with him for some time. In a letter to Margaret Fell, dated First month, 1655, he says, " So we are yet in this city, and for a while continue in it. There are many Friends come up, as F. Howgil and E. Burrough, Thomas Salthouse, Miles Halhead, William Caton, John Stubbs, and many others; but I believe we shall disperse abroad after to-morrow. We do not want for any thing : here are many precious Friends in the city, who would do anything for us, or let us have anything ; but George is not very free, but rather keeps clear. Our horses are at the inn where we lay; but so many coming to see George, they (innkeepers) rather grow weary, and wish us to take another place."

George and Alexander took a turn out into Bedfordshire, where resided John Crook, a justice, at whose house they held a meeting, and the people were generally convinced. J. Crook, himself, embraced the principles of Friends, and became an approved minister, suffering much for the truth he had espoused.

Returning to London, they again entered into the multiplied and successful labors which Friends were engaged in there. Another letter from A. Parker to M. Fell, will give the reader some idea of the state of things in that city at the time, and the field of service in which other Friends were engaged. " Our dearly beloved George Fox is yet in this city (Third month, 1655), and I know little at present of his removing. The work is great, and many are daily convinced. We have seven or eight meetings on First-day, and all are pretty quiet. F. Howgil and E. Burrough had a great dispute with the chief of the Baptists on the Third-day of this week, and on Fourth-day, another with two of the chief of the Water Baptists. Many of their hearers who are not satisfied, came, and some Friends, and the power of the Lord was over them; though they are a very wise and subtle generation, yet the Lord, by his wisdom in weak ones, confounds and overturns them. *A great shatter* is among all the forms and gathered Churches—as they are called—and many are inquiring after truth." "Concerning our Friends in Northampton, they all continue in prison, as far as I know; Yorkshire Friends have lately been with them, and have supplied their necessities. Those in Bedford, likewise continue [in prison].* And for Friends at Norwich, they are all released but Christopher Atkinson. John Stubbs and William Caton were with us last week. They are sweetly carried on in the work of the Lord, and are much strengthened; they went back again towards Dover. John Slee and Thomas Lawson went into Sussex. John Wilkinson and John Story are going westward. Thomas Salthouse and Miles Malhead are about Bristol, and lack nothing; nor any Friends; for as they come up here, if any want, our friends Francis and Edward supply them. The charge truly is great, but our desire is to make it as easy as possibly we can. Here are in this city many precious Friends, and they begin to know George; though at the first he was strange to them, and one thing they all take notice of: *that if George be in the company, all the rest are, for the most part, silent;* which they did much wonder at."

"Our brethren Thomas Aldam and Anthony Pearson came into the city yesternight. They are now with George. Francis and Edward, and Gervase Benson are all here," &c.

Among the Friends alluded to as being in prison in Northampton, was William Dewsbury, who, in that year (1655), had been made a prisoner on complaint of a priest, who had publicly accused him of things which he could not prove. William called on him to show the people wherein he had deceived them, but he could not; so the high constable seized him and conducted him as a criminal to the market place, threatening to bring a charge of blasphemy against him. Nothing, however, was proved against him, and he went to the house of a person named Ellington, from the upper window of which, he preached to the people collected below. Many were effectually convinced, among whom was Francis Ellington, who afterwards suffered imprisonment with William Dewsbury.

William was arrested the next day on the charge of "being one who is commonly called a Quaker;" but was sent to prison with a mittimus that stated, among other things, that he had spoken blasphemy. He and a Friend named Joseph Storr — who was charged with nothing but being present at the examination of William—were put into a dungeon, twelve steps under ground, among thieves and murderers, to be there kept until the assizes; which was a month off. They were refused a copy of the mittimus, and when the assizes came on, their cases were passed by without trial to the next session,

* J. Lancaster, T. Stubbs, and A. Patrickson, imprisoned for not taking off their hats.

which was not for two months. Two more Friends, F. Ellington and Henry Williams, were thrust into the dismal hole with them, the latter having been dreadfully beaten previously.

1655. When the assizes came round again, they were all brought to the bar, before Judges Matthew Hale and H. Wyndham. William Dewsbury in his journal gives an interesting account of what took place during their examination. Matthew Hale was known to be a religious minded man, but it was evident that, though he knew really nothing about the principles of Friends, he allowed himself to be strongly influenced by the common prejudice against them. Wyndham had before shown himself inimical to them.

The account of the trial is too long to be given here. The fore part of it was occupied by questions and answers between Judge Hale and William Dewsbury; the latter on behalf of himself and his fellow sufferers demanding to be informed what law they had broken; and defending the doctrines inculcated by Friends. The prisoners were set aside, but recalled before the court broke up. Some one ordered their hats to be taken off, but when about to take off Dewsbury's, Judge Hale bade him keep it on, and those of the other Friends returned to them. Afterwards he accused W. D. of "not being the man he pretended to be," and commanded him as a prisoner to take off his hat.

Judge Hale.—"Art thou judge, that thou standest covered, and will not uncover, as other prisoners do?

W. D. — What I do, God is my witness, I do it not in contempt to any; but in obedience to the power of God, for conscience' sake.

Judge.—If you will not stand as prisoners, I will not do anything concerning you; but here I found you and here I shall leave you.

W. D.—We have been above ten weeks in the low jail, and no breach of any law found against us. We stand subject to the power of God, whatever He suffers thee to do with us.

Judge Wyndham. — If thou and Fox had it in your power, you would soon have your hands imbrued in blood.

W. D.—It is not so. The Spirit of Truth which we witness in us is peaceable, and neither doth violence nor sheds blood; and the hands of all that are guided by the Spirit of Truth, the Light and power of Christ, are bound from offering violence or shedding blood."

As all the Friends declined to give sureties to appear at the next session of the court, unless they were told what law they had broken, they were sent back to the offensive low dungeon where they had already lain so long.

At the next sessions they, and other Friends who had been imprisoned with them, were brought before Judge.Atkins. No indictment was found against them. So frivolous were the charges made in court by their enemies, that the judge said to the clerk of the court, " Why do you trouble me with that which there is no matter of fact in ? I much wonder you should trouble the judge of the assize with such small things, and not end them in your own sessions, for we come hither to determine greater matters." Nevertheless, the Friends were not allowed to plead in their own defence, but were told they showed contempt of authority in not taking off their hats; and as they would not give surety for their good behavior, or to appear voluntarily, unless they were told for what they were to answer, they were remanded to their former filthy place of confinement, where they lay six months longer, until discharged by an order from Oliver Cromwell.

In this day of enlightened public opinion and civil freedom, it seems almost incredible that the rights and liberty of reputable men could have been so sported with by officials sworn to execute the laws justly and impartially. But while it is impossible to reconcile the treatment received by Friends from the hands of the judiciary, with the principles of justice and equity, which always coincide with Christian charity, it would not be right to judge them by the recognized standard of the present day. It is evident, that much as had been done and suffered throughout the nation in the cause of civil and religious liberty, neither was properly understood nor rightly estimated. Frequent change of government and of religious profession, had unsettled law and undermined its force. At the close of the long and sanguinary contentions that had shaken down the throne and immolated its incumbent, the minds of the rulers in State and church, were too much engrossed with efforts to use the power they had grasped, for securing their own authority, to pay much regard to individual rights, which lie at the foundation of all free government.

Cromwell and his party had spoken fairly on liberty of conscience; but they were conscious that the power they held was usurped, and that stealthy and embittered enemies were constantly on the watch, to embrace the first opportunity presented, that promised a successful challenge of their authority and effort to hurl them from the position they occupied. Nothing but the genius and iron will of the Protector, kept down the discontent and rebellious hate that laid smouldering under various guises, ever ready to break the peace, could his vigilant and piercing eye be blinded or deceived long enough to allow of a hopeful insurrection.

When the army was called on to swear allegiance to the new government, many among the officers declined doing so. Some of these, it was known, were partially convinced of the truth of the principles held by Friends, and scrupled to take an oath ; —of these most afterwards became members of the Society. This excited the jealousy and perhaps the fears of those in power.

As regards correctness of religious belief, there had undoubtedly no little advance been made since the dawn of the Reformation. The elements of reform had gone on removing abuses and simplifying the abstruseness of dogma, and complication of ritual. The people, nevertheless, were too ignorant of the simplicity of the faith taught in the New Testament, and too much in the dark respecting the spirituality of the Gospel dispensation, the headship of Christ in his church, and the brotherhood of all its true members to escape from the specious show, and the selfish, grasping, subtle spirit of priestcraft. The distinction between clergy and laity, was so wide, and so jealously preserved, that any interference of the latter in ecclesiastical matters, was looked upon by the former as an impertinent interference. In the popular mind, the "ministry" was so immediately and inseparably associated with the "church," that they looked on them as identical ; and as the "church" had long been, and still was considered a part of the State, attacks upon the "ministers" were resented by the government, as being made upon itself.

Friends, as has been seen, were called on to stand as witnesses of the great truths that there was but one Head in the church and all true believers stood on the same footing ; that none should attempt to lord it over the heritage, but should be ensamples to the flock ; that Christ alone made the ministers in his church, and dispensed other gifts for the edification of the body ; that as He died for all, so He also had given to every one a measure of his Spirit ; which was for a guide and rule, and which, as it was obeyed, would bring salvation to the soul ; that the Scriptures were the words of God, but not the Word ; that the true knowledge and application of them was to be known only through the Spirit which dictated them ; and that the Gospel must be freely preached, as it was freely received ; therefore, that tithes, and all exactions for religious services, were unlawful, and unauthorized by Christ. These Gospel truths struck at the root of all State authority and all exclusive superiority of any class in the church militant; destroying the wide distinction men had.made between clergy and laity.

In those days of religious disputation and latitudinarian assumption, many sects had sprung up; some of which avowed licentious principles, and manifested great turbulence and disregard of civil government; claiming to be restrained by nothing but their own will and wishes. These differed altogether from Friends, who, while they taught that all should be led by the Spirit of God in order to become the sons of God, always maintained that that Spirit would never sanction either doctrines or practices that were contrary to the Holy Scriptures; and that it was a duty to yield obedience to civil government in everything that did not interfere with the allegiance which man owes to his Creator.

But their principles were not understood, nor yet the religious origin of their testimony against the ordinary mode of salutation, the refusal to take off the hat as a mark of respect to man, and the use of the Scriptural language of thou and thee to a single person. Therefore it is not to be wondered at, that many goodly men, such as Judge Hale, should have classed them, at first, with other sectaries which were really inimical to the government, and willing to promote disorder throughout the country. Judge Hale afterwards came to know them better, and to esteem them very differently; and Justice Hotham, who was no Friend, but who knew how many were running into extravagance and almost unbridled license in their religious professions, declared emphatically, that "If God had not raised up this principle of Light and Life, which George Fox preached, the nation had been overrun with Ranterism, and all the justices in the nation, could not have stopped it, with all their laws:" because, said he, "They would have said as we said, and done as we commanded, and yet have kept their old principle still; but this principle of Truth overthrows that principle, and the root and ground thereof."

Although there is no memoir of Miles Halhead extant, and the accounts of his religious labors incidentally given in the histories of the times, and the journals of other Friends, are but meagre, yet sufficient has been preserved, to show that he was little, if any, behind the chiefest of the band of zealous preachers, who during the rise of the Society of Friends, went forth with their lives in their hands, to proclaim the glad tidings of salvation through a crucified Saviour, by obedience to the revelations of his Spirit to the soul.

The place of his nativity was probably Underbarrow, in West-moreland, and he appears to have been convinced of the doctrines and testimonies of the gospel as held by Friends through the ministry of George Fox, in the commencement of his travels to spread them. The first circumstance related concerning him, is that being on his way to attend the meeting then just established at Swarthmoor (1653), he met on the road the wife of a justice of the peace, and not knowing her, he passed by without greeting her in any way, which so displeased her, that she sent her servant-man to beat him, which he did. Whereupon Miles, turning back to her, said, " Thou Jeze-bel! thou proud Jezebel! couldst thou not suffer the servant of the Lord to pass by thee quietly ? " She put forth her hand as though intending to strike him, and spit in his face, saying, " I scorn to fall down at thy words." Miles replied, "Thou proud Jezebel! thou that hardenest thy heart and brazenest thy face against the Lord and his servant, the Lord will plead with thee in his own time, and set in order before thee the things that thou hast done this day to his servant." He then went on his way.

About three months after this occurrence, Miles believed it required of him to go to this same woman at her own house, and went. Arriving at Houlker Hall — the place of her residence — and she being at the door and not recognizing her, he asked her if she was the mistress of the house? She replied, " No, but if you would speak with Mrs. Preston, I will entreat her to come to you." Going in she returned with another woman and said, " Here is Mrs. Preston." But he, immediately becoming sensible of the deception, said, " Woman, how dar'st thou lie before the Lord and his servant? Thou art the woman I came to speak to." She being silent, he proceeded, " Woman, hear what the Lord's servant hath to say unto thee : O ! woman, harden not thy heart against the Lord ; for if thou dost He will cut thee off in sore displeasure ; therefore take warning in time, and fear the Lord God of heaven and earth, that thou may'st end thy days in peace."• Having delivered his message he went away.

Some three years after, being in the same neighborhood, Miles met a man on the road who accosted him and said, " Friend, I have something to say to you which hath lain upon me this long time. I am the man that, about three years ago, at the command of my mistress, did beat you very sorely ; for which I have been very much troubled, more than for anything I ever did in all my life ; for truly, night and day it hath been often in my heart that I did not well in beating an innocent man that never did me any hurt or harm.

I pray you forgive me, and pray the Lord to forgive me, that I may be at peace and quiet in my mind." Miles answered, "Truly, friend, from that time to this day I never had anything in my heart against thee nor thy mistress but love. The Lord forgive you both. I desire that it may never be laid to your charge; for ye knew not what ye did."

Believing it to be his religious duty at different times to go to places of worship to declare the word of Truth given to him, he often met with grievous abuse, more than once being beaten until nearly deprived of life. At Stanley chapel, the doors being ·closed against him, he waited patiently in the yard until the congregation came out, intending to address them, but some of them immediately fell upon him in a great rage, and after abusing him, one took him by the shoulders and another by the legs and tossed him over the wall. So exceedingly bruised was he by the fall, that he could scarcely get home. But his Lord and Master had promised him that he should be healed of all his injuries if he was faithful to his requirings, and his promise was fulfilled in a remarkable manner. [1653.]

Besides several other circumstances in which this valiant servant was called upon to do and to suffer, Sewel narrates the following: "He came to Furneiss, in Lancashire, to the house of Captain Adam Sands, where he found a great number of professors gathered, and priest Lampit preaching. But as soon as Miles entered, Lampit was silent, which continuing a pretty while, Captain Sands said to him, 'Sir, what is the matter: are you not well?' to which the priest answered, 'I am well, but I shall speak no more as long as this dumb devil is in the house.' 'A dumb devil,' said the Captain, 'where is he?' 'This is he,' said the priest, pointing with his hand, 'that standeth there.' Then the Captain said, 'This man is quiet and saith nothing to you: I pray you, sir, go on in the name of the Lord; and if he trouble or molest you in my house, I will send him to Lancaster castle.' But the priest said again, 'I shall not preach as long as this dumb devil is in the house.' Then the Captain said to one Camelford, a priest also, 'I pray you, sir, stand up and exercise your gift, and I will see that you be not disturbed.' But this priest answered as the other, 'I shall not speak as long as this dumb devil is in the house.' Then the people cried, 'Lord rebuke thee, Satan; Lord rebuke thee, Satan; what manner of Spirit is this that stops our ministers' mouths?' Then the Captain came to Miles, and taking him by the hand, led him out of the house. In all that time he had not spoken a word, and saw now the accomplishment of what he had been persuaded of before, viz., that an invisible power would confound by him the wisdom of the priests, when he spoke never a word.

"Lampit and Camelford had been active in the barbarous treatment of George Fox at Ulverstone and Cockan.

1653. "This year Miles Halhead came to Berwick in Northumberland, and went to the Mayor of that town, and spoke to him in his shop thus: 'Friend, hear what the servant of the Lord hath to say unto thee. Give over persecuting the Lord's servants, whom He doth send in love to this town of Berwick, to show you the way that leads to life eternal. I charge thee, O man, touch not the Lord's anointed, nor do his prophets any harm, lest thou procure the anger of the living eternal God against thee.' This bold language so offended the Mayor, that he sent Miles to prison, where he was about ten weeks, and then was brought to the sessions, where a bill drawn up against him, was read in open court: but he denied the contents thereof, yet said, 'But what I said to the Mayor of this town, I will not deny.' And then he related the aforesaid words he spoke to the Mayor. Whereupon the Recorder said, 'Sirs, as I understand by his own words, if he cannot prove the Mayor of this town a persecutor, in my judgment he hath wronged him.' To this Miles answered, 'If the Mayor of this town of Berwick, dare say in the presence of the Lord, whose presence is here, that he is no persecutor, but the persecuting nature is slain in him, I will be willing to abide the judgment of the court.' Then the clerk of the court said, 'Mr. Mayor, if you will say that you are no persecutor, but the persecuting nature is slain in you, he is willing to abide the judgment of the court.' To this the Mayor answered, 'I know not what to do; I would I had never seen him; I pray you, let him go, and let us be no more troubled with him.' Then Miles said that he would prove this Mayor of Berwick the greatest persecutor in town or country. 'I was once [thus he went on], committed to prison in this town before, by some of the Justices that are now in this court; but thou, O man, hast exceeded them all; thou hast committed me, and kept me in close prison, for about ten weeks, for speaking to thy own person, in thy own shop. Now I make my appeal to the Recorder of this town of Berwick, as I am a free-born Englishman, whether my imprisonment be legal, according to the law of this nation, or not?' Then the Recorder of the town stood up and said, 'It is not very legal for any minister of the law to imprison any man in his own cause.' Then the court cried, 'Take him away.'

The chief priest of the town then stood, and desired the court that he might ask Miles one question ; to this Miles said, 'The Lord knows thy heart, O man, and at this present has revealed thy thoughts to his servant ; and therefore, now I know thy heart also, thou high priest, and the question thou wouldst ask me ; and if thou wilt promise me before the court, that if I tell thee the question thou wouldst ask me, thou wilt deal plainly with me, I will not only tell thee thy query, but I will answer it.' Then the priest said he would. Then Miles proceeded : 'Thy question is this : thou wouldst know whether I own that Christ that died at Jerusalem, or not?' To this the priest wondering said, 'Truly, that is the question.' Then Miles said, 'According to my promise, I will answer it before this court; in the presence of the Lord God of heaven, I own no other Christ than He who died at Jerusalem, and made a good confession before Pontius Pilate, to be the Light and Way that leads fallen man out of sin and evil up to God eternal, blessed forever more.' More questions were not asked him, but the jailer was commanded to take him away. Yet within a short time the court gave orders to release him.''

There were frequent efforts made to give currency to the statement that the only Christ which Friends believed in was what they claimed to be the Spirit of Christ in themselves, and therefore that they rejected Jesus Christ who died at Jerusalem, as the Saviour of the world. Friends again and again refuted this slander, and set forth as plainly as words could express, their full belief in the Lord Jesus Christ; his eternal Divinity, his propitiatory sacrifice for the sins of the whole world, his resurrection and ascension into heaven, his now appearing there as the Mediator between God and man, and his coming the second time, without a sin offering, unto salvation, by his Holy Spirit; which the apostle designates as "Christ within the hope of glory." But it suited the persecuting feelings and views of those who, in that day, desired their suppression as living witnesses to the truth, as it has suited the Socinian belief of some in the present day, to disregard their clear declarations of the contrary, and to endeavor to fasten upon them sentiments they repudiated and abhorred.

In a work designed to be limited, as this is, room cannot be spared to give many extracts from the declarations of faith frequently made by Friends, nor from the journals of the more noted members, both in the early days of the Society and since, wherein is plainly set forth their full and unequivocal belief in the Deity of

Christ, and the Atonement made by him for sin.*   George Fox's
journal, like that of other Friends, bears frequent and unmistakable testimony to this; a few extracts will be incidentally given
hereafter.

CHAPTER VII.

Introduction of Quakerism into Scotland — Friends travelling there in 1654 —
John Stubbs — William Caton — Dover — Luke Howard — Samuel Fisher—
L. Howard convinces S. Fisher of the general impropriety of Psalm Sing-
ing — J. Stubbs and W. Caton at Maidstone — Ireland — William Edmund-
son — Religious Convincement and Progress — Travels with J. Tiffin — W.
Edmundson visits G. Fox — E. Burrough and F. Howgil in Ireland — Other
Ministers in Ireland — A Bishop and his Wife — Priests' petition against
Friends — Order issued against them — E. Burrough and F. Howgil banished
the Island — B. Blaugdone in Ireland — Identity of Religious Principles and
Practices embraced by Friends everywhere—Instance of trial of W. Edmundson's faith in Divine Revelation — W. E. takes up land in order to bear
testimony against tithes — Suffering endured by Friends in Ireland.

THERE are no particulars preserved of the labors of the ministers among Friends who first travelled into Scotland in order
to spread a knowledge of the glad tidings of the gospel.   Early in
the year 1654, Christopher Fell, George Wilson and John Grave
were drawn to visit Scotland and to labor there, but how long they
stayed, and how extensively they travelled does not appear.   Prior,
however, to any Friends arriving in Scotland, several earnest seekers
after truth through the inshining of the Holy Spirit on their understandings, had become burdened with the formality and will-worship
which prevailed in that country among the professors of religion,
and engaged to search for more substantial good, so as to know
their souls more fully redeemed from the world, and more given up
to serve the Creator of all things.   These had withdrawn from the
public preachers, and assembled together to seek after ability to
worship God in spirit and in truth.   As they felt the refreshing,
strengthening effect of thus waiting on the Lord, they were anxious
that their friends should partake with them ; and as the number

* Full evidence of this, may be seen in a work entitled, "An Exposition of the Faith of the Religious Society of Friends, commonly called
Quakers," by Thomas Evans.

enlarged, two meetings were set up, and held as was the practice among Friends. John Barclay states there were at least two such meetings; one held at Drumbowy and one at Heads. It also appears that there had been ministers raised up among them who spoke to edification: their names were William Osborne, a Colonel in the army; Richard Rae and Alexander Hamilton. These meetings had been held for a year before any Friends from England visited them.

Besides those whose names are already mentioned, Miles Halhead and James Lancaster went into Scotland in 1654, and also Catharine Evans and Sarah Chevers. When at Dumfries, the last named men Friends, went to a place of worship where the people were making much lamentation on account of their sins. They stayed quietly until their worship was over, when Miles began to deliver the message he believed called for by his Master. The hearers soon became enraged, and drove both Friends out of the town, intending to stone them when they got to the near river side; but they waded through the water and so escaped. From there they went to Edinburgh and Leith, calling the people to repentance, and obedience to the convictions of Divine Grace in the secret of their hearts. They also visited the garrisons, preaching to the officers and soldiers. In his communication, on one occasion, Miles told the officers and soldiers, who appeared to be much affected, " That the anger of the Lord was kindled against them, because they had not performed their promises, which they had made Him in the day of their distress; when their enemies encompassed them on every side; for then the Lord delivered them, and gave them victory : but they had returned Him evil for good, and committed violence against those He sent to declare his word among them." He afterwards went to Glasgow and Stirling, but tarried not long, returning to England.

It does not appear that the labors of any of the Friends then in Scotland were attended with much convincement. In 1655 William Caton and John Stubbs arrived at Edinburgh, where they found that some disorder had crept in among the little company of Friends, in consequence of the unfaithfulness of some who had been convinced. Their gospel labors were blessed to the restoring of good order, and to the edification of the church. W. Caton went to the principal place of worship in the city, but was not allowed to say much; the multitude attacking him and carrying him into the street. Here he was rescued by a guard of soldiers, who conducted him with

drawn swords to the place he desired to reach. He had an interview with General Monk, who at that time had command of the
army in Scotland.

John Stubbs has been mentioned already. He was convinced by
George Fox while George was confined in Carlisle jail [1653]. He
had been an officer in the army, and when Cromwell required all of
them to take the oath of allegiance to the government, he felt it
wrong to swear, and so he left the army. He was a learned man,
and a linguist, being well versed in Latin, Greek, and Hebrew, and
having likewise considerable knowledge of several of the Oriental
languages. Embracing the doctrines of the gospel as preached by
G. Fox, and coming under the searching, cleansing operation of
the measure of the Holy Spirit vouchsafed to him, his conduct
and conversation soon became consistent with the principles he professed, and it was not long before he was entrusted with a gift in
the ministry, and he became an able minister of the new covenant.
He and Wm. Caton travelled much together.

Wm. Caton had been taken into Judge Fell's family to reside
when he was about fourteen years of age; being companion to the
Judge's son, and receiving the same school instruction as he. He
appears to have been a favorite with the Judge, his wife and
daughters. The singular plainness of George Fox's address and
manners when on his first visit to Swarthmoor [1652], attracted the
lad's attention to him, and when he heard him declare the truths of
the gospel, in the family circle and at their place of worship, they sank
deep into his mind. The doctrine of the inward Light or measure
of Divine Grace appealed to his own consciousness, for he had often
been reproved by it for evil, and being convinced, he resolved to
regulate his future life thereby. Hence he soon found himself, young
as he was, obliged to deny himself of many things he had before
thought allowable, if not commendable; to take up his daily cross and
follow the leadings of Him who now became his Lord and Master. In
all these exercises and close trials, he found Margaret Fell a wise
adviser and nursing mother. He was then about seventeen years
of age. As he gained one victory after another, over his spiritual
enemies, his heart was often filled with joy and gratitude to the
Lord on high, who had shown him his mercy and loving-kindness,
and brought him to enjoy the liberty of the sons of God.

As he became more firmly established in the right way of the
Lord, the duty was laid upon him to go to places of worship
and to market-places, to preach repentance to the people, by turn-

ing to the light of Christ in their breasts, and being willing to obey its manifestations. For this he soon had to endure scorn, beating, and other ill treatment, which he endured with meekness and patience. Believing that he was called to go forth into the harvest-field of the world and labor, he became anxious to be released from his engagement with Judge Fell. At first the Judge was unwilling to part with him, but his wife, being sensible that a gift in the ministry had been conferred on William, and that his Master was calling him to service abroad, persuaded her husband, and he at last consented to his going. He left the family near the close of the year 1654; being then in the nineteenth year of his age.

After travelling through several different shires in the northern and middle sections of England, he arrived in London, where he joined John Stubbs. When clear of their religious service in that city, they went together to Dover. Here they separately attended places of worship resorted to by Baptists and Independents. Their awakening ministry produced such effect, that they were haled before the magistrates, who having questioned them, ordered, under a penalty, that no one should entertain them. A shoemaker of the name of Luke Howard, however, took them into his house, where they held a meeting. The Mayor sent four constables to the house, with an order that Luke should deliver them up, that they might be sent out of the town. But the doors being shut, he refused to allow the officers to enter his house, or to obey the order, as it was not lawful. They continued some days as his guests, during which time he became convinced of the doctrines they preached, and soon joined the Society. At a place called Lydd they were instrumental in bringing Samuel Fisher to see more clearly the error in which he had long been involved, and to introduce him into communion with Friends. He had been educated at the University, ordained a priest in the "Church of England;" and obtained a "living" at Lydd. It was a singular circumstance that Luke Howard, sometime before he knew anything about Friends, became dissatisfied with singing psalms in public worship, and Samuel Fisher, as a learned minister, was requested to visit him, and try to convince him of the error he was under. In the course of the conversation between them, Luke said, "That God was a spirit, and must be worshipped in spirit and in truth; and that it was contrary to truth for a proud man to sing, 'He was not puffed up in mind; he had no scornful eye, and did not exercise himself in things too high,' when he lived in pride, wherein God beheld him afar off; or, for him to sing, 'Rivers of tears run down my eyes, because other men keep not thy laws;' when he never knew true sorrow or repentance for his own sins."

The conversation resulted in convincing 'S. Fisher that Luke was right, and so he ceased having the psalms given out to his congregation to sing. Becoming more and more uneasy with the ceremonies and practices used in his " church," he gave up his " living," and resigned his commission as a priest to the bishop. He then joined the Baptists, and became a preacher among them. When J. Stubbs and W. Caton came to Lydd, he received them into his family, and also received the truth and lived up to it.

1654. Continuing their gospel labors, J. S. and W. C. arrived at Maidstone, and entered on the service assigned them. " J. Stubbs was taken at the steeple-house, and W. Caton, the day following, from his inn, and both were sent to the house of correction, where they were searched, and their money, ink-horns, and Bibles, &c., taken from them. Afterwards they were stripped, and their necks and arms put in the stocks, and in that condition were desperately whipped. A hard encounter indeed, especially for such a young man as W. Caton was; but they were supported by an invisible hand. Afterwards means were used to compel them to work; and it was told them, he that would not work should not eat. But they were not free to consent thereto, because they esteemed this demand unjust, not being guilty of the breach of any law. Thus they were kept without victuals for some days, only a little water once a day was allowed them. In the meanwhile the malefactors that were there, would have given them of their bread; yea, the women of the house being moved with compassion, would have given them something privately; but they were not free to accept of either. Now the report of this cruelty being spread in the town, many began to be offended at it; so that an officer was sent to make restitution of some of their things, which had been taken from them, and then they bought victuals with their own money. Not long after they were parted, and with officers conveyed out of the town, one at the one end of it, and the other at the other."

Some time after, Wm. Caton went over to Calais, in France, where he had an opportunity to speak to a number of the chief men of that city; a Scotch lord who was there, acting as interpreter for him. Returning thence, he again met with J. Stubbs, and they embarked for Holland, where they were engaged in religious service for some time, and coming back to England, travelled into Scotland, as has been already mentioned.

There is no account of Ireland having been visited by any Friend, prior to Wm. Edmundson going there for the purpose of trade; and as he afterward became a principal instrument in the Lord's hand, to raise up and settle meetings of Friends in that island, some account of him may be interesting.

He was born in Westmoreland, in 1627, being the son of John and Grace Edmundson. He became an orphan when eight years of age, and was unkindly used by his uncle, to whose care he was confided, having to endure many hardships. When of suitable age, he was placed apprentice to a carpenter, with whom he lived several years. He states that from early life, he was sensible of the strivings of the Lord's holy Spirit with him, bringing him under a sense of his sins, and creating longing desires after salvation. But he knew not what it was that was thus visiting him, nor how to find the way to the Physician of value. When of age, he entered the Parliament army, and after the overthrow of the royal troops, marched, under Cromwell, into Scotland. He records that in his many dangers and narrow escapes from death, he was repeatedly brought under great condemnation for his wickedness, and fear seized on him, at the thought of what would become of his soul, if cut off; and he made many resolutions to turn to the Lord by repentance; but as they were in his own will, they were forgotten when temptation again presented.

He was in the sanguinary battle at Worcester, where the Scotch army was routed. After being quartered in Derbyshire, he says, "The common discourse was of the Quakers, and various reports were of them;" strange stories were told of them, "but the more I heard the more I loved them, yet had not an opportunity to speak with any of them." Having charge of some recruits for the army, he marched with them into Scotland; soon after which, he left military life altogether. On returning to England, he married, and having a brother in the army in Ireland, he and his wife concluded to go there and open a store. Accordingly they went, taking the goods with them. They were, however, disappointed in getting to the place where they had expected to settle; but went with his brother to the north of the island and settled at Antrim.

Having sold the merchandise he had taken with him, he returned

to England to renew his stock, and being in the north, when George
Fox and some other Friends were in the neighborhood where his
relations resided, he heard that James Naylor was to have a meeting near by. To this meeting he went, with his elder brother and
another kinsman, and they were all convinced of the truth by the
powerful preaching of J. N. This was in 1653.

Describing the mental conflicts through which he passed, after he
had come fully to realize the truth of what he had heard, and the
inshining of the measure of the Lord's Spirit to his soul, he says,
"I knew it was the Truth which led into all truth, agreeably to the
Holy Scriptures of the Law and Prophets, Christ and his apostles, and I thought all that heard it declared must own it, it was
so plain to me. A few days after I was thus far convinced of the
blessed truth, the Lord's power seized on me, through his Spirit;
whereby I was brought under great exercise of mind, yea, all my
parts came under this exercise; for the Lord's hand was mighty upon
me, in judgments mixed with mercy, so that my former ways were
hedged up. But I loved the Lord's judgments, for I knew I had
sinned against Him, and must be purged through judgment. And
though under this exercise of conscience towards God, yet I did my
business in England, and shipped my goods to be landed at Belfast
or Carrickfergus."

Embarking with his goods, he was strongly tempted to take advantage of his brother's troop being at Belfast, and by their aid to
land his merchandise without paying duty. He successfully resisted
this, and on meeting his brother after landing, he found himself
obliged to omit all the customary forms of complimentary address,
and use nothing but the plain language of thou and thee. When
about to land his goods, the officers required the ordinary oath respecting the bills of lading, and William telling them he could not
violate Christ's command by swearing, they refused to allow them
to come ashore. The great change in his manner, the singularity
of his language and demeanor, and the unheard of scrupulousness
about taking an oath, excited the wonder of all with whom he came
in contact, causing much talk about the Quakers, and about William
in particular. After some time, however, he was allowed to bring
his parcels to the custom-house.

He continued to pass through many deep baptisms. "The Lord's
hand," he says, "was heavy upon me day and night, so that I tra-
vailed under great conflict between flesh and Spirit, and was much
cast down with sorrow and trouble of mind; but none there under-

stood the cause of any sorrow and trouble, or gave a word of comfort to ease me." The people thought he was bewitched, or going crazy. While in this state, a Major Bousfield came to his house, but he was absent from home. On hearing on his return that the Major had been there, and that he professed to hold Friend's principles, and was acquainted with G. Fox, who had been at his house; so ardently did William thirst for some advice and consolation, that might get him out of his struggling condition, that he immediately mounted horse and rode twelve miles to meet with him. When together, the Major talked much of his religious experience; of his unity with G. Fox and J. Naylor; and then advised William to be cheerful and merry, and not look at those inward troubles that bowed him down, and would, if he gave way to them, lead him to despair. He told him it was evident that God loved him, to make of him a chosen vessel, and He would love him to the end, as nothing could frustrate his will.

William says, "This doctrine healed me without the cross of Christ, which answered my will and carnal desires; for I loved the truth I was convinced of, and would have had it, with my carnalities, fleshly liberties, worldly pleasures and profits. So when the Lord's power would arise to bow me down under his cross, I would reason against it with the arguments afore mentioned, and thereby would get from under judgment." But his gracious Lord in mercy to his soul, did not leave him to perish in this false rest. Again, he says, "The Lord would not leave me so, praised be his Name forever; whose merciful hand preserved me, and his power took fresh hold of my heart and inward parts; which bowed me under his judgments, and opened the eye of my understanding; plainly showing me there was that still alive in me, which must be crucified, which opposed the will of God." Giving himself up to the thorough heart-cleansing, transforming baptisms of the Holy Ghost and fire, in due time he experienced what it was to be brought up out of the horrible pit, and out of the miry clay; to have his feet placed firmly on the Rock, Christ Jesus; to have his goings established, and a new song put into his mouth, even praises unto his God.

Having removed to Lurgan in the county of Armagh, he kept a store, and also followed grazing. His plain appearance and language, and refusing to take off his hat as a token of respect, attracted much attention, so that he became "the talk and gazing stock of the people;" while, he says, "Professors watched me narrowly, to find occasion against me and the principles of Truth."

But, although he was at times subjected to scorn, invectives, and blows, the Lord preserved him; and though at first people did not understand why he always kept to one price in selling his goods, they were not long in being convinced of its justice; and his trade increased so much, that he became uneasy with it, fearing lest he would become rich; .he therefore declined entering as largely into it as the many opportunities presented invited him to.

1654. It was at his house in Lurgan, that the first meeting of Friends was established in Ireland. William, his wife and brother met for some time together,.for the purpose of waiting on and worshipping the Most High, and ere long four more converts joined them. Their meetings were long held in silence, but such was the evidence of the presence of the Head of the church in their midst, that their numbers went on increasing, and in course of time William had a few words to offer. A gift in the ministry having been conferred upon him, and a Friend of the name of John Tiffin coming over from England on religious service, William joined him, and they travelled in the north of Ireland, holding meetings where they could. Such were the false and fearful stories spread abroad throughout the country respecting the Quakers, that it was with difficulty these two Friends could find any willing to receive them into their houses. At one place where they had been promised they should have a house to hold a meeting in, on coming to it they were refused; so the three, J. Tiffin, William, and his brother, seated themselves where three lanes met, and held their meeting. Though it does not appear there was much preaching, yet much inquiry was excited, and opportunity afforded to spread a knowledge of the truths of the Gospel as held by Friends.

Feeling drawn to visit George Fox, William crossed to England, and going into Leicestershire he met him at Badley, where a great meeting of Friends from several parts was held. After the meeting, George and William walked into an orchard together; the former kneeled down and prayed, and "The Lord's heavenly power and presence were there," and George "was tender over" this thoroughly converted, but comparatively inexperienced minister. George wrote an epistle to those in Ireland who had joined the Society; which William on his return read to them, and he says, "The power of the Lord seized on us, whereby we were mightily shaken and broken into tears and weeping."

In the fourth month of this year (1655), E. Burrough and F. Howgil arrived in Dublin. Though separated by religious service for a short time while in England, each without the other knowing it, had felt it required of him to go to Ireland. They met in London, and from there started for this new field of labor. Their first meeting in Dublin was at the house of a Captain Rich, and the next at the residence of a Captain Alan. They had a number of pretty full meetings in succession, but though several were caught in the gospel net, the convincement was not extensive. After laboring together for about three weeks, F. Howgil felt himself called to travel towards Cork, leaving E. B. in the city. The separation was a severe trial to both, but believing it to be in the will of their Divine Master, they sought for resignation. In a letter to Margaret Fell, Edward says, " With heaviness of spirit I write unto thee, yea, and with my eyes filled with tears; for I am separated outwardly from my dear beloved brother F. Howgil."

F. Howgil had a companion when he left Dublin, named Edward Cook, who was a cornet in the Protector's own troop, but who, with others, had adopted the peaceable principles of the gospel, and determined to cast in his lot with the Quakers.

Elizabeth Fletcher and Elizabeth Smith, two ministers from England had gone over to Ireland in the year preceding that in which F. Howgil and E. Burrough arrived there, and the former was probably the first Friend who held a meeting in Dublin.

Miles Halhead, James Lancaster, and Miles Bateman had also travelled pretty extensively through several of the Provinces, holding meetings and embracing every opportunity to promulgate the truths of the gospel; with great success in many places. This was in 1654.

E. Burrough remained several weeks in Dublin and then went to the North, laboring among the people generally as he passed along. He was arrested and tried as a vagabond and again as a Jesuit, but was not detained long either time. In the Eleventh month of 1655, he went southward and joined his friend F. Howgil, at Cork. The latter had been industriously engaged in the work assigned to him, and many had been converted by his ministry. They went together to Limerick, but were not allowed to have any meeting there, and were ordered out of the city. E. Burrough preached to the people from the horse's back, as he rode out; and when they had passed the gate, they both addressed the multitude that had followed them. At Kinsale, the wife of a priest named Edward Worth was convinced, and her husband being afterward made bishop, she suffered much at his hands, because she would not give up her conscientious convictions. The priests in different parts of the country, finding that many from among their congregations were leaving them and joining with Friends, became alarmed for their revenues and authority, and deputized a pretty large number of their craft to go up to Dublin and obtain some action from the Lord Deputy and council, by which a stop would be put to the labors of Friends. Accordingly the Lord Deputy — who was Cromwell's son Henry — and his council issued an order to the magistrates to send " All that were called Quakers," to Dublin. This order was delivered to the governors of Cork and Kinsale, but the former refused to be instrumental in executing it, and said openly, that the Friends who had been there, had done more good, " than all the priests in the country had done for a hundred years."

E. Burrough and F. Howgil returning to Cork, the high Sheriff arrested them, and placing them under a guard of soldiers, they were forwarded from garrison to garrison until they arrived in Dublin; the soldiers behaving very civilly to them, and allowing them to speak to the people as they passed along. Being brought before the council they were examined, but no charge was made against them; nevertheless they were kept closely in prison until they were banished from the island. [1655.]

The day on which these two Friends were sent away, Barbara Blaugdone arrived at Dublin, and went directly to the Lord Deputy's mansion, and with some difficulty obtained admittance to his apartments. While in the outer drawing-room, an attempt was made to impose upon her. As they knew she had never seen the Lord Deputy, a number of his attendants went into the room where she was sitting, all of them bare-headed but one, who wore his hat. She looked at them, and an internal intimation was given her, that no one present was the person for whom she had a message. One of the attendants said to her, " Why do you not speak to our Lord?" She replied, " When I see your lord, I shall deliver my message to him." Soon after a person came in and took a seat. Barbara immediately arose and addressed him, warning him against fighting against God and persecuting his servants, and advising him to take the advice given by Gamaliel, &c., &c. She was not molested, and leaving the city, she went to Cork. During her stay in Ireland, she was repeatedly imprisoned; but her preaching was attended by so much power, that many were convinced by her.

Meetings were now settled in many parts of the island, and several ministers were raised up from among the members. The doctrine of the indwelling of Divine Grace in the heart of man, and its sufficiency, if obeyed, to bring salvation, began to be more generally understood, and many were found willing to receive it, to come under its regenerating power, and to endure the self-denial and weaning from the world and its spirit, into which it led; being made willing to suffer affliction with the people of God, rather than to enjoy the pleasures of sin for a season. The sufferings of Friends, however, increased greatly, very many being put in wretched prisons, on account of not paying tithes.

In Ireland, as in England and Scotland, those who joined the Society by convincement, found themselves called on to walk in the same strait and narrow way. As they came individually to yield obedience to the inspeaking word of Divine Grace in their souls, they learned day by day to distinguish between the voice of the true Shepherd and that of the stranger, and thus came to know of the doctrine; and they all spoke the same language. They saw that the friendship of the world was enmity with God, and as witnesses of the purity and spirituality of the religion of Christ, they dare not shrink from open, unyielding opposition to the corrupt principles and practices that prevailed in civil society, and in the so-called Church. They could not comply with the changeable fashions, the language, or the complimentary address of the community around them. Knowing the origin of all true gospel ministry, and that it was freely received through the immediate inspiration of the Head of the Church, they declared there could be no compulsory compensation for its exercise, nor could it ever be made merchandise of, or a means for obtaining a livelihood.

Having experienced that the "one baptism" which saveth, was not the putting away the filth of the flesh, but that administered by Christ himself; whereby the soul itself is washed and made clean — the effectual washing of regeneration and renewing of the Holy Ghost — and that partaking of the flesh and blood of Christ, was inward and spiritual, when He condescended to come into the soul and sup with it, and allowed it to feed on Him, the living bread, they dare not substitute any ceremonials therefor, and felt bound to bear testimony against them, as shadows which drew away the attention from the substance, that alone administered life. Hence here, as in England, they were continually brought into collision with the hireling priests; and on account of their promulgating these truths, of their refusing to pay tithes, and because, in obeying the command of Christ, they could not swear, they were often consigned to noisome prisons or dungeons, where great cruelty was habitually practised on them. As their sufferings increased on account of their faithfulness, and the malice of their enemies urged them on to make their persecution more barbarous, so the arm of the Holy one of Israel was made bare for their support and consolation; and in the midst of their afflictions, they could adopt the language of the Psalmist, "Oh! how great is thy goodness, which thou hast laid up for them that fear thee; which thou hast wrought for them that trust in thee before the sons of men."

William Edmundson, who had been assiduously attending to the work whereunto his Master called him, met with divers circumstances — as he travelled from place to place preaching the word, and laboring to strengthen his brethren and build them up on the most holy faith — which confirmed the truth and reality of the doctrine of the gift to man of a measure of the Holy Spirit, designed to guide him into all truth, and preserve him from all error. On one occasion, as he was travelling towards his home, it was clearly made known to him that on the night of that day an effort would be made to rob his house. As he prepared to hasten on, he felt himself stopped from going, and a clear intimation that he must return to Clough, a town which he had left far behind; though the service he was to perform there was not made known. After a severe conflict, lest he might be deluded, he was enabled to resign himself, his wife, children and property into the Lord's hand, and in simple obedience, to turn about and go towards the little town in which he felt his presence was required; his gracious Master assuring him that He would protect his house and family. Arriving there the next day, he found two women Friends, lately come from England, who, having been travelling from place to place, on foot, owing to the depth of the mud through which they had to wade during their last day's journey, had become so exhausted that one of them was taken to her bed, and losing faith, had given way to despair; consequently plunging the other into great distress. William was made the instrument of administering to their spiritual needs, and so effectual was the word given him to communicate to them, that the next day they were able to leave the place, and he, placing them both on his horse, walked beside them to Carrickfergus; where leaving them, he went home. Here he learned, that on the night of the day in which it had been revealed to him that an effort would be made to rob his house, some persons attempted to get in through the window; but the window fell into the room, with so much noise, that it alarmed the family, and the robbers were frightened away. Thus the word of the Lord unto him was confirmed, and he enabled to rejoice that he had been willing to walk by faith and not by sight.

In 1656, feeling it laid on him to take up land in order that he might bear a more practical testimony against the unchristian imposition of tithes, William Edmundson gave up his store, and removed into the county of Cavan, where in a little time a meeting of Friends was settled, and their numbers continued to increase. Spoiling of goods, and painful imprisonments were the lot of many who appeared to be the most likely instruments to spread abroad a knowledge of the principles of truth and righteousness; but the Word of God could not be bound, and W. Edmundson says, "Truth was much spread and meetings settled in several places ; and many being convinced and brought to a knowledge of God, were added to Friends."

A mere profession among Friends of the spiritual religion which belongs to the Christian dispensation, was then of little or no account. They were known wherever they appeared by the fruits produced by their transforming religion, and their sincerity was tested by the fire of persecution. Despised and rejected as they were by the men of this world, the life derived from the inexhaustible Fountain of light and life circulated freely among them ; and the love that bound them together as children of one Father, was, if possible, strengthened and deepened by the fellowship of suffering. W. E. says, "In those days the world and the things of it, were not near our hearts; but the love of God, his truth and testimonies, lived in our hearts. We were glad of one another's company, though sometimes our outward fare was very mean, and our lodging on straw. We did not mind high things, but were glad of one another's welfare in the Lord, and his love dwelt in us."

Gough in his history, speaking of Ireland about the close of 1656, says, "By a general account published about this time, it appears that for speaking the truth in steeple-houses, markets, and other places, ninety-four persons of this [Friends'] Society had been sufferers by fines, whipping, putting in stocks, imprisonment, and loss of goods. That nineteen persons had been imprisoned for meeting to worship God in their own houses; and that twelve had been stopped as they were passing along the streets or highways on their lawful occasions, and committed to prison."

CHAPTER VIII.

E. Burrough writes to Cromwell — Friends increase in London — Anne Downer —Gilbert Latey — Rebecca Travers and James Naylor—G. Fox arrested by order of Major Ceely — Committed to Jail for not taking the oath of Abjuration — Trial — False charge brought by Major Ceely — G. Fox's Defence — A second charge from Ceely — Injustice on the Bench — Character of the Prisons and Jailers — Prisoners in " Doomsdale " — Suffering — Friends increase in Number — G. Fox and others kept shut up without Trial — Released without Trial — The cruel Jailer's Recompense — James Naylor — Convincement — An account of his Preaching — Charged with denying the Manhood of Christ — Cleared but Imprisoned — Personal Appearance and Eloquence of J. Naylor — Circumstances connected with his Fall — G. Fox's interview with J. N. — His Trial and Punishment — His Repentance — Acknowledgment — Restoration — Death.

IN this year [1655] E. Burrough being in London, and seeing how Cromwell winked at the persecution of Friends by those who, having got possession of the benefices and places formerly occupied by the Episcopal clergy, were determined, if possible, to put down all opposition to their ministry and exactions, — addressed a letter to him, in which he told him plainly, That he had given himself up to pride and vain glory; had broken or disregarded the vows he had made to the Lord in the days of his humility and distress, and was allowing his subordinates to commit grievous oppression and cruelty, in his name, on the Lord's people ; and therefore if he did not repent and change his course, the judgments of the Lord would come upon him. Cromwell had just before got the Parliament, — composed of his own picked men,— to sanction the oath of abjuration against Charles Stuart, the son of Charles I.; and it was made much use of to harass Friends and send them to prison.

The number of Friends in London continued to increase, and among those who joined the Society were several who became highly valued and useful members. Anne Downer was the first woman Friend convinced there, who had a gift in the ministry conferred on her. She travelled much, not only when called forth to preach the everlasting Gospel, but often in going from place to place to succor the afflicted brethren or sisters who were in bonds and suffering. Her gospel labors were blessed to the convincement of many. She was first married to a Friend named Greenwell, but he did not live long, and sometime after being left a widow she became the wife of

George Whitehead. The testimonies and memorial respecting her, speak of her as not only adorning the doctrines she preached, by her life and conversation, but that she often suffered severely and cheerfully for the blessed cause she had espoused.

Gilbert Latey who, when young, had come to London from Cornwall to reside, had followed his business with great success. He was a tailor, and acquiring a high reputation, he was employed by the fashionable, and by others of the first rank in the nation. But in his prosperity he was not unmindful of the things that belonged to his everlasting peace. He was a seeker after a knowledge of the truth ; going to hear all who were considered eminent as teachers of the way of salvation ; but, as he afterwards testified, " it was like seeking the living among the dead." Hearing that some men who had come out of the north, were to have a meeting at the house of a widow who lived in Whitecross street, he went thither. It so happened that E. Burrough was there at that time, and such was the baptizing power with which he preached the truths of the Gospel, and to the states of the audience, that Gilbert was fully convinced thereby ; and not consulting with flesh and blood, he at once gave up to the operation of the Grace of God on his soul ; to which he had been directed. Dwelling under the convicting, converting power of this heavenly gift, he became regenerated and gradually grew in the Truth, from the state of a child to that of a strong man, and was endowed with a quick discerning, and sound judgment ; which made him very serviceable in settling the church in good order and purity.

When he had enlisted under the banner of the cross, and been made willing to practise self-denial and to stand in opposition to the spirit of the world, he found himself brought under close trial on account of his business. His best customers were men of rank, and others who were accustomed to have their clothes made in the fashion, with much cost for lace and other superfluities. He felt that he could no longer be an instrument for thus gratifying their pride and vanity. He therefore decided that, let the consequences be what they might, he could work for such no more, nor yet allow any of those employed by him to do that which he clearly saw was wrong. Some who had heretofore patronized him, now said he was deranged ; and his parents were so displeased, that they banished him from their house, while his brothers and sisters derided him. His customers left him, and he was obliged to discharge his workingmen ; so that it looked probable, he would himself have to hire out as a journeyman, to do such work as he was easy with. Severe as the trial was he bore it contentedly, esteeming the reproach of Christ greater riches than the treasures of Egypt; and preferring to give up outward gain and comfort, rather than lose the enjoyment of that peace with which the Lord replenished His soul. His divine Master was round about and protected him, enabling him to bear all He permitted to come upon him, with meekness and resignation, and proved himself to be a rich rewarder for obedience to his requirings. Soon after the time in which he passed through this trial, he was commissioned by his Master to proclaim the glad tidings of salvation to the people; and it was not long before he found himself sharing with his fellow believers in the abuse and suffering heaped upon those valiant sons and daughters of the morning. He, with fifteen or sixteen other Friends, were on one occasion committed to Gate-house prison, in Westminster, for having met together for the purpose of Divine worship. The whole sixteen were thrust into a dungeon or hole, which was about ten feet wide and eleven feet long, and so dark that at mid-day they could see but little better than at mid-night. The walls were constantly wet, and the space being so small, in order to take rest or sleep, a few only could lie on the cold ground, while the others were forced to stand: and such was the cruelty of the jailer, that he would not allow the straw that was brought for their use to be given to them. But the Lord supported them under all the suffering which He permitted to be inflicted on them, for the trial of their faith and patience, and in course of time delivered them out of the hands of their oppressors.

Rebecca Travers was a gentlewoman who was thought of account in that day of religious excitement and high profession. She had received a good, religiously guarded education, and was a zealous professor among the Baptists. The many reports that had reached her of the Quakers in the north, had prejudiced her strongly against them. She looked upon them as worthless, uncivil fanatics, who were very uncomely in their appearance, their manners and carriage; with whom those who stood fair in church or State could wish to have little or nothing to do.

James Naylor having come to London in 1655, preached with so much eloquence that many of the higher rank flocked to hear him, and some of the Baptist pastors challenged him to dispute with them. A time and place was agreed on, and there was no little interest excited among very many. Rebecca Travers having been invited by one of her friends to accompany her to hear this dispute, consented to go, fully prepared — as she afterwards said — to witness the defeat of the rustic Quaker by the learned ministers of her own Society. But greatly was she surprised and confounded, when the "countryman," rising on a platform opposite to the ministers, after they had spoken, poured out such a stream of Scriptural argument as overturned all the objections that had been brought forward against the principles of Friends, and showed that those principles were based on the immutable foundation of truth. Two of the Baptist ministers said they were sick, and went away, while the other failed to show how the texts he quoted sanctioned the opinions he advanced.

Though mortified at the result of the dispute, Rebecca was curious to hear J. Naylor preach, and the next First-day went to the Bull-and-Mouth meeting, where he spoke so convincingly, that she remarked, " She could not but declare, that if she had lived in the apostles' days, she could not have heard truth more plainly, nor in greater power and demonstration of the Spirit, than she had that day." From that time she became a constant attender at the meetings of Friends; but still she found it a hard matter fully to act up to the doctrines she knew to be true. There were many things to be given up hard to part with, and her former habits of religious profession prompted to seek for that knowledge in divine things, which could be obtained by the natural understanding alone. Some time after, having been invited to dine in company with J. Naylor, a person present who was a high professor, put many curious questions to him. James answered him with wisdom, but with great caution; but not so as to gratify the strong desire she felt to hear him discourse of these sacred mysteries. Presently J. Naylor, reaching across the table, took her by the hand and addressing her, said, " Feed not on knowledge; it is as truly forbidden to thee, as ever it was to Eve: it is good to look upon; but not to feed on; for who feeds on knowledge, dies to the innocent life." This was spoken with power, and carried conviction to her soul. She gave up her own willing, and searching into hidden mysteries, became emptied of her self knowledge, and taking up the daily cross, she found that as a babe in Christ, all that was necessary for her to know of those things hidden from the wise and prudent, was revealed to her by the Spirit of her Father in heaven. She became an acceptable minister in the Society; suffered much for witnessing to the truth, and died beloved, in a good old age.

In the early part of 1656, George Fox wrote an address to the inhabitants of England, in order to show, that in this last dispensation, Christ by his Holy Spirit was come to teach the people himself. &c.   A copy of this paper accidentally coming into the hands of Peter Ceely, a major in the army, and justice of the peace, who lived at St. Ives, in Cornwall county, when George Fox, who was travelling in that neighborhood, with Edward Pyot and William Salt, came there, he had them arrested and brought before him.   The Major producing the address, asked George whether he wrote it? to which he replied in the affirmative.   He then tendered the three Friends the oath of abjuration.   George handed to him the answer which he had written to that oath, showing the reason why Friends could not take it, nor any other oath; and which answer George told him had been given to the Protector himself.   But the Major committed them to Launceston jail, sending them there under a guard of horsemen.   The mittimus stated that they pretended their habitations were at Bristol, Drayton and London; but "They were going under the notion of Quakers, and acknowledged themselves to be such," that they had spread papers tending to disturb the peace, and refused to give sureties for their good behavior, &c.

They were kept in close confinement for nine weeks before the court sat, at which they were to be tried.   Such was the excitement and curiosity aroused by the rumors spread abroad concerning them, that many from far and near came to see the prisoners while in jail.   This afforded them an opportunity to speak to their visitors respecting the doctrines they held, and occasionally to preach to the people generally; so that many were convinced by them.

1656.   When the assizes came on, the crowd that came to see them and hear the trial was so great, that it was with difficulty the soldiers and sheriff's officers could get them through the streets and into the court room.   The expectation was that they would be hanged. Chief Justice Glyn was on the bench, and when they entered G. Fox said, "Peace be amongst you."   The Judge ordered them to take off their hats, but G. F. asked him where was the law that commanded prisoners to take off their hats; and where was there any instance mentioned in the Scripture of persons being commanded to take off their hats.   The Judge growing angry, said, "Take him away — prevaricator — I'll ferk him."   They were then thrust into the dock with the thieves.   Presently the Judge ordered them brought up again; which being done, "Come," said the Judge, addressing G. Fox, "where had any hats, from Moses to Daniel? Come, answer me; I have you fast now."   G. Fox replied, "Thou may'st read in the third of Daniel, that the three children were cast into the fiery furnace, by Nebuchadnezzar's command, with their coats, their hose and their *hats* on." The Judge finding no reply that he could make, cried out, "Take them away, jailer;" and so they were kept a while among the thieves, and then taken back to prison. In the afternoon, being brought up again, G. Fox handed a paper which he had written against swearing, to the jurymen. The Judge getting the paper, asked George whether he had written that seditious paper? George requested it might be read in open court, and then he could say whether he wrote it or not. The Judge objected, but George insisting, the clerk read it aloud, and George owned it was his production; and as it was very much in the language of Scripture, he did not see how they could deny its truth. That subject was then dropped, and the jailer was ordered to take off the prisoners' hats. The prisoners then asked the court why they had been kept in prison nine weeks, and now there was nothing alleged against them but not taking off their hats. They desired the Judge to do them justice for their false imprisonment.

Instead of righting them, an indictment was read against them for "coming into court by force of arms and in an hostile manner." They denied it being true, and demanded to have justice done them for imprisonment without cause shown.

Then Major Ceely — who had committed them, and was sitting on the bench as a justice — rose, and addressing the judge, said, "May it please you, my Lord, this man — pointing to George Fox — went aside with me and told me how serviceable I might be for his design; that he could raise forty thousand men at an hour's warning, and involve the nation in blood, and so bring in King Charles; and I would have aided him out of the country but he would not go. And if it please you, my Lord, I have a witness to swear to it." The Judge perceiving that this was a lie, was not forward to examine the witness. G. Fox then desired that his mittimus should be read, that he might know of what he was accused: "For," said he, "if I have done anything worthy of death or of bonds, let all the country know it." The Judge would not permit it to be read, and sent George away.

On being again brought into court G. Fox repeatedly requested that the mittimus should be read, and as the people were very desirous to hear it, one of his fellow prisoners read it. George Fox then addressed the Judge and Justices thus, "Thou that sayest thou art Chief Justice of England, and you that be Justices, ye know that if I had put in sureties I might have gone whither I pleased, and have carried on the design, if I had one, which Major Ceely has charged me with. And if I had spoken those words to him, which he hath declared here, then judge ye, whether bail or main-prize could have been taken in that case." Then addressing himself to Major Ceely, he said, "When or where did I take thee aside? Was not thy house full of rude people, and thou as rude as any of them, at our examination, so that I asked for a constable, or other officer to keep the people civil? But if thou art my accuser, why sittest thou on the bench? That is not the place for thee to sit in; for accusers do not use to sit with judges: thou ought to come down and stand by me, and look me in the face. Besides I would ask the Judge and Justices this question: whether or not Major Ceely is not guilty of the treason which he charges against me, in concealing it so long as he hath done? Doth he understand his place, either as a soldier or a justice of the peace? For he tells you here, that I went aside with him, and told him what a design I had in hand; and how serviceable he might be for it: that I could raise forty thousand men in an hour's time, and bring in King Charles, and involve the nation in blood. Moreover, that he would have aided me out of the country, but I would not go; and therefore he committed me to prison for want of sureties for good behavior, as the mittimus declares. Now do not ye see plainly, that Major Ceely is guilty of this plot and treason that he talks of, and hath made himself a party to it, by desiring me to go out of the country, and demanding bail of me; and not charging me with this pretended treason till now, nor discovering it? But I deny and abhor his words, and am innocent of his devilish design."

· "The Judge by this, seeing clearly that Ceely, instead of ensnaring G. Fox, had ensnared himself, let fall that business. But then Ceely got up again, and said to the Judge, 'If it please you, my Lord, to hear me; this man struck me, and gave me such a blow, as I never had in my life.' G. Fox smiling at this, said, 'Major Ceely, art thou a justice of peace, and a Major of a troop of horse, and tells the Judge here, in the face of the court and country, that I, who am a prisoner, struck thee; and gave thee such a blow, as thou never hadst the like in thy life? What! art thou not ashamed? Prithee, Major Ceely, where did I strike thee; and who is thy witness for that? Who was by?' To this Ceely said it was in the castle-green, and that Captain Bradden was standing by when G. Fox struck him; who then desired the Judge to let him produce his witness for that: and he called again upon Ceely, to come down from off the bench; telling him it was not fit that the accuser should sit as judge over the accused. Ceely then said, Captain Bradden was his witness: which made G. Fox say to Captain Bradden, who was present there, 'Didst thou see me give him such a blow, and strike him as he saith?' Bradden made no answer, but bowed his head. G. Fox then desired him to speak up, if he knew any such thing: but he only bowed his head again. 'Nay,' said G. Fox, 'speak up, and let the court and country hear, and let not bowing of the head serve the turn. If I have done so, let the law be inflicted on me. I fear not sufferings, nor death itself; for I am an innocent man concerning all his charge.' But Bradden would not testify to it. And the Judge, finding those snares would not hold, cried, 'Take him away, jailer;' and fined the prisoners twenty marks apiece, for not putting off their hats, and to be kept in prison till they paid the fine: and so they were brought back to jail again.

"At night Captain Bradden came, with seven or eight justices, to see them; and they being very civil, said, they did not believe that either the Judge, or any in the court, believed those charges which Major Ceely had made upon G. Fox. And Bradden said, Major Ceely had an intent to have taken away G. Fox's life, if he could have got another witness. 'But,' said G. Fox, 'Captain Bradden, why didst not thou witness for me or against me, seeing Major Ceely produced thee for a witness, that thou sawest me strike him? And when I desired thee to speak either for me, or against me, according to what thou sawest or knewest, thou wouldst not speak.' 'Why,' said he, 'when Major Ceely and I came by you, as you were walking in the castle-green, he put off his hat to you, and said, "How do you do, Mr. Fox? Your servant, sir." Then you said to him, Major Ceely, take heed of hypocrisy, and of a rotten heart; for when came I to be thy master, or thou my servant? Do servants use to cast their masters into prison? This was the great blow he meant that you gave him.' G. Fox hearing this, called to mind that as they were walking by, Ceely had spoken the aforesaid words, and that he himself indeed made such an answer, as is mentioned; and he thought he said nothing amiss, since Ceely so openly had manifested his hypocrisy and rotten-heartedness, when he complained of this to the Judge in open court, and would have made all believe that G. Fox gave him a stroke outwardly with his hand. A report of this trial being spread abroad, divers people, of whom some were of account in the world, came far and near to see him and his friends in prison, which tended to the convincement of some."

This account of the trial is taken from Sewel, and is of interest as showing the character of the charges often preferred against Friends, and how grossly violating all the principles of justice and law, was the treatment received by them from Judges and Courts.

It remains to be seen what was the measure of punishment inflicted on these innocent men, because under a sense of religious duty, they could not take off their hats as a token of reverence or honor to the Judge and Justices. Truly, as William Penn saith, these testimonies against the pride of the human heart, which some make light of as being of no worth, were " a close and distinguishing test upon the spirits of those whom they [Friends] came among; showing their insides, and what predominated, notwithstanding their high and great profession of religion."

It is one of the curious evidences of the laxity in that day, of care or oversight of the prisons so much used, and the prison discipline exercised therein, that the one in which these Friends had been confined, and were now sent back to, without any prospect of release, belonged to a Baptist preacher who was a Colonel in the army ; and having purchased it, placed in it as jailer whomsoever he chose. The present incumbent of the office had been burnt in the hand and on the shoulder for theft; the under jailer, as well as the wives of both, had also been branded as thieves ; so that there was little ground for hope that the prisoners would escape the brutal treatment usually bestowed on those who were placed in the power of such wicked custodians. In prospect of their long detention, the three Friends informed the jailer they could no longer pay him board for themselves and horses, but must have a free prison. Exasperated at the loss of the opportunity to fleece them, he resolved to make them suffer for it as severely as he could. He therefore put them into a dungeon, called Doomsdale, where convicts awaiting execution were usually kept. It was " a nasty, stinking place, so noisome that, it was observed, few that went into it, ever came out again in health." It had not been cleaned out for a long time, and the filth covering its floor was nearly ankle-deep. Although the effluvia arising from it was so abominable as to sicken nearly every one at first going into it, yet the wicked jailer would not allow the Friends to clean it out, nor to spread straw over the bottom. In the evening, some friendly person brought them a little straw and a candle, and they, hoping to diminish the sickening smell, set fire to the straw. But the room directly over their heads was occupied by prisoners and the head jailer, and the smoke found its way through the wide cracks of the floor; whereupon the jailer, in a rage, poured down upon them through the cracks whatever filth he could collect, "Till we were so bespattered that we could not touch ourselves, nor one another." In this condition they were obliged to stand all night; for such was the condition of the bottom of the dungeon, they could not sit down. George Fox says, "A great while he kept us after this manner before he would let us cleanse the place, or suffer us to have any victuals brought in, but what we got through the grate."

But all this cruelty failed to break the spirit or weaken the hands of these "good soldiers of Jesus Christ," in the work whereunto He had called them. He supplied them with a strength which their adversaries could neither weary out nor comprehend. He was with them, as with the three children in the fiery furnace, and when reviled and abused for his name's sake, He spread a table for them in the presence of their enemies, which the latter could neither withhold from them nor partake of themselves.

Hoping to frighten the Friends, the jailer told them that Doomsdale was haunted by the spirits of those who had died within its walls. But "I told them," says George Fox, " that if all the spirits and devils in hell were there, I was over them in the power of God, and feared no such thing; for Christ, our Priest, would sanctify the walls of the house to us, He who bruised the head of the devil. The priest was to cleanse the plague out of the walls of the house under the law, which Christ, our Priest, ended ; who sanctifies both inwardly and outwardly the walls of the house, the walls of the heart, and all things to his people."

Many came to visit the Friends in their dungeon, and the word of the Lord went forth from them to the convincing of not a few, some of whom were persons of note in the parts of the country whence they came. So that one of the Lord Protector's chaplains told him, "They could not do George Fox a greater service for the spreading of his principles in Cornwall, than to imprison him there." The assizes coming round again, the three Friends sent a statement of their suffering condition to the court; whereupon an order was issued that "Doomsdale door should be opened, and that they should have liberty to cleanse it, and to buy their meat in the town." A full recital of their case, and of the cruelties practised on them, was also sent to Cromwell, who, after perusing it, sent an order to the

Governor of Pendennis Castle, to make inquiry whether any of the military officers or the soldiers had been accessory to the abuse of Friends. The Governor instituted the inquiry, and two or three being brought before him who had treated G. Fox with inhumanity, they were severely reprimanded and threatened; so that the fear caused by this interference tended.to lessen the great imposition practised on Friends.

Although a large number of the ministers, both men and women, were now shut up in jails in different parts of the country, yet the Society continued to increase rapidly, and its principles spread through Cornwall, Devonshire, Dorsetshire and Somersetshire, as they had done in most other parts of·England. In some parts of the country the magistrates appointed " Watchers," who watched the roads, pretending to be looking for beggars and tramps, but in reality to stop any Friends who might be travelling abroad. Many instances occurred of highly respectable men and women, well off as to this world's goods, but who, being Friends, were taken up and severely whipped as vagabonds.

Another assizes came round and passed by, without George Fox and his companions being brought to trial, who, though let out of Doomsdale, were kept close prisoners. Several other Friends were sent to prison by the Justices, for not taking off their hats in obeisance to them; and a general warrant was issued from the court at Exon "·For apprehending all Quakers."

In the meantime the prisoners were not idle. Edward Pyot, who had been a captain in the army, and was well acquainted with law, prepared and sent to the Chief Justice Glynne, a closely reasoned presentment of their case; showing how grievously they were oppressed and deprived of the rights of every Englishman, by the course pursued towards them, under his cognizance and authority, and asking for a fair trial; but it was all in vain. George Fox wrote and had printed an examination and reply to the warrant issued at Exon, showing its injustice and unchristian character. He wrote a warning to the priests and professors of Christianity in England; also an Exhortation to Friends in the ministry; and several other papers, addressed to different classes, calling upon them to turn from the evil of their ways and to practise the religion they professed. Large numbers of people continued to visit the prisoners, some from evil and some from good motives, and not a few were reached by their ministry, were convinced of the truth of the doctrines for which they suffered, and joined the Society.

It was no doubt a close trial to many of the members of the recently gathered Society, that so highly gifted and favored a minister and leader as George Fox, should be imprisoned for so long a time, and several used every means in their power to have him, and the Friends committed with him, either discharged, or brought before a court for trial. One Friend went to Oliver Cromwell, and offered himself — body for body — to lie in Doomsdale in place of George Fox, if he could thereby be released. Cromwell refused to accept the offer; but turning to the officers of the Council, who were around him, he asked, "Which of you would do so much for me, if I were in the same condition?" and though he did not then attempt to interfere, he was much affected with this evidence of self-sacrifice and love existing among Friends. Sometime after, he commissioned General Desborough to examine into the case, and if Friends "would go home and preach no more," to set them at liberty.

Desborough took but little interest in their hard case, and when he found that the prisoners would not make the promise which he endeavored to exact, he betook himself to different kinds of recreation, and left the whole matter in the hands of Major Bennet, the Baptist preacher and owner of the jail. Bennet sent for the Friends to meet him at an Inn, and there offered to release them if they would pay the jailer the fees he demanded. But they refused, on the ground that they had been imprisoned illegally, and most barbarously maltreated during great part of their incarceration, and neither the jailer nor any one else had any just claim on them: they were still detained. "At last" — to use the words of G. Fox— "the power of the Lord came so over him [Bennet] that on the 13th of the Seventh month, 1656, we were set at liberty." They had been closely immured in that dreadful dungeon for six months. The wicked jailer, who had treated them with so great cruelty, having perpetrated some fresh crime, for which the law took hold of him, was shut up in Doomsdale, the same dungeon wherein, of his own will, he had kept George Fox and his fellow prisoners closely confined; was ironed and beaten by the man who succeeded him in office, and bid remember how he had treated those "good men," whom without any just cause he had thrust into that vile hole: here he died.

But in this year [1656], Friends met with a trial that grieved them much more deeply than all the bodily suffering inflicted by imprisonment, whipping, or other means of torture could do. This was the fall of one, who had been an eminently gifted minister and much loved fellow-laborer in the great work which the Lord had begun, and was carrying on, in the nation. James Naylor came out of Yorkshire, being born at Ardesley, near Wakefield, about the year 1616. His parents were of good repute and possessed of a competent estate. He appears to have received a fair English education, and his writings show that he profited by it. When about twenty-two years of age he married and removed to Wakefield; where he continued to reside until 1641, when he entered the Parliamentary army, in which he continued for eight or nine years, and was promoted, first under Fairfax and afterwards under Lambert, becoming Quartermaster under the latter. His health failing, he left the army and returned home. He professed with the Independents, and there is reason to believe that his mind was early much enlightened in regard to the spiritual nature of the Christian religion.

George Fox coming to Wakefield, in 1651, James Naylor, in company with others, went to see him, and from the conversation that ensued, James was fully convinced of the truth of the doctrine which George preached. This was near the time when William Dewsbury and wife, R. Farnsworth, Thomas Aldam and others, were convinced by George Fox. In 1652, while following the plough, James believed that it was clearly made known to him, by divine revelation, that he must leave all, and go forth in the service of his Master, depending entirely on Him to supply all his needs; with the promise that he should lack nothing. At first he rejoiced that the Almighty had condescended thus to communicate his will to him, and he prepared to go; but the cross was so great, to leave his home and kindred, that he held back, and at last concluded to remain where he was. He now was brought under great condemnation and distress for his disobedience, so that it seemed for awhile that his life would be taken from him. After a time he was made willing to submit to the divine will concerning him, and started on foot, travelling to the West. As he travelled from place to place, it soon became manifest that he had received an extraordinary gift in the ministry, and marvellous was the effect often produced by his preaching.

That faithful minister of the Gospel, James Wilson, received the following account from an officer under Cromwell. "After the battle of Dunbar, as I was riding in Scotland, at the head of my troop, I observed at some distance from the road, a crowd of people and one higher than the rest; upon which I sent one of my men to see, and bring me word what was the meaning of this gathering. Seeing him ride up and stay there, without returning according to my order, I sent a second who stayed in like manner, and then I determined to go myself. When I came thither I found it was James Naylor preaching to the people, but with such power and reaching energy, as I had not, until then, been witness of. I could not help staying a little, although I was afraid to stay; *for I was made a Quaker; being forced to tremble at the sight of myself.* I was struck with more terror by the preaching of James Naylor, than I was at the battle of Dunbar, when we had nothing else to expect, but to fall a prey to the swords of our enemies, without being able to help ourselves. I clearly saw the cross to be submitted to ; so I durst stay no longer, but got off, and carried condemnation for it in my own breast. The people there, in the clear and powerful opening of their states, cried out against themselves, imploring mercy, a thorough change, and the whole work of salvation to be effected in them." George Fox frequently mentions James Naylor in the first part of his journal, as being united with him in religious labor, and the service he rendered in promoting the good cause they both had so deeply at heart. He was a frequent sufferer for the testimony of Jesus, and while he kept humble, and little in his own eyes, his Master clothed him with divine authority and a discerning spirit; teaching his hands to war, and his fingers to fight with the weapons that are mighty, through God, to the pulling down of strongholds.

In 1652, when holding a meeting at Orton, or Overton, a small town in Westmoreland, he was set upon by five priests, who, after he had retired to a Friend's house, sent for him to come to them in a field ; where they pressed him with many questions ; which he replied to so wisely, that they could not find ground for the arrest and punishment they desired to inflict on him. They, however, followed him, and subsequently drew up three petitions against him, to be presented to the Justices ; accusing him of denying the manhood of Christ, of saying that Christ was in him, and that there was but one Word of God. There was a long examination by the four Justices, in which one of them asked him — " Is Christ in thee ? "

J. N.—" I witness him in me, and if I should deny him before men, He would deny me before my Father, who is in heaven.

Justice.— Spiritual, you mean ? J. N.— Yea, spiritual.

Justice.— By faith, or how ? J. N.— By faith."

He was examined on the other points, and such were his answers,

that at the close, Justice Pearson, who was on the bench, declared
that the words spoken by J. Naylor, " Were neither within the Act
against blasphemy, nor against any law." Nevertheless, two of the
Justices succeeded in having him committed to the jail at Appleby,
where he was kept prisoner for twenty weeks. Two of the Justices
who examined him were Anthony Pearson and Gervase Benson;
both of whom afterwards joined Friends.

After being released from prison in 1653, James Naylor travelled
through different parts of England, diligently exercising his gift,
and meeting with the like fare as his brethren and sisters in the
household of faith. Near the close of 1654, or the beginning of
1655, he arrived in London, which, he afterwards said, he entered
with a presentiment that some ill awaited him there.

He is represented as being a man of fine personal appearance,
with a remarkably placid and sweet countenance, gifted with an
extraordinary silvery, melodious voice, and an eloquence that not
only clothed the deep and solemn truths he wished to impress, in
appropriate and fluent language, but enabled him to arrest and
captivate the attention of the learned, as well as of those of rank
and fashion. How far the popularity which these characteristics
had already obtained, had drawn him off from that close watchfulness and humble dependence upon the Shepherd of the sheep, in
which alone is safety, before coming into London, cannot be known.
As has been already related, F. Howgil, E. Burrough, and other
ministers, had been successfully laboring within the walls of that
city, and had gathered very many into the fold; so that a considerable number of meetings of Friends, were regularly held in
houses situated in various sections.

In the short account of Rebecca Travers, mention has been made
of some of the services rendered to the good cause by J. Naylor, in
London; and Sewel says, " He preached in such an eminent manner,
that many admiring his great gift, began to esteem him much above
his brethren; which as it brought him no benefit, so it gave occasion for some difference in the Society; and this ran so high, that
some forward and inconsiderate women, assumed the boldness to
dispute with F. Howgil and E. Burrough openly, in their preaching. Whereupon they, who were truly excellent ministers, did not
fail, according to their duty, to reprove this indiscretion." Stung
by this deserved reproof, these forward and weak-minded women,
determined to seek support in their pernicious course; and one of
them, named Martha Simmons, went to J. Naylor and strove to set

him against his two brethren, and thus make a party in their favor. James, however, had not yet lost his power of discernment, nor allowed his feelings of love and respect for his worthy companions and fellow sufferers, to be blunted, so as to desire to draw a party to himself at their expense; and he declined giving a judgment against them. Disappointed in producing the effect she desired, M. Simmons gave way to a kind of hysterical moaning and weeping, which so affected James, that he became dejected and disconsolate. It is probable that the conflicting emotions called forth by the circumstances and people with which he was surrounded, so preyed upon him, as to deprive him measurably of the right use of his reason. Be that as it may, from that time he became greatly changed; estranged himself from his true and judicious friends, and listening to the flatteries of the shallow and flighty women and men who gathered around him, allowed spiritual pride to take possession of his heart, to puff him up above the restraining power of the Witness for Truth, and finally to betray him into assumptions or expressions that amounted to blasphemy.

How long J. Naylor continued in London does not clearly appear, but during the time, the infatuation of his followers increased, and his own spiritual understanding became more darkened. Letters were sent to him by some of the former, in which he was addressed as the " Everlasting Son of Righteousness;" the " Prince of Peace;" the "only begotton Son of God;" the "Fairest among Ten Thousand," and abounding with other extravagant and impious expressions. Towards the middle of the year 1656, he left London, professedly for the purpose of visiting George Fox, who was then in Launceston. He appears to have been accompanied by several of his deluded votaries. At Exeter they were arrested by the "watchers" as vagrants, and the magistrates sent them to the common prison, where many Friends were already incarcerated; Naylor being fined twenty marks for not taking off his hat. While shut up here, the women who were of Naylor's company, ran into great extravagances; kneeling before him and kissing his feet.

George Fox, as already mentioned, had been liberated from Launceston jail in the Seventh month of this year [1656], and had again entered on his arduous labors as a gospel minister. Coming to Exeter he went to the prison to visit his friends, who were there under bonds. Here he met with J. Naylor, and he gives the following account of what passed:

"The night that we came to Exeter, I spoke with James Naylor:

for I saw he was out, and wrong, and so was his company. The next day, being First-day, we went to visit the prisoners, and had a meeting with them in the prison; but James Naylor, and some of them, could not stay the meeting. There came a corporal of horse into the meeting, who was convinced, and remained a very good Friend. The next day I spoke to James Naylor again; and he slighted what I said, was dark, and much out; yet he would have come and kissed me. But I said, 'Since he had turned against the power of God, I could not receive his show of kindness.' The Lord moved me to slight him, and to 'set the power of God over him.' So after I had been warring with the world, there was now a wicked spirit risen among Friends to war against. I admonished him and his company."

J. Naylor and his company having been liberated by order of the Council, after they had been imprisoned about three months, travelled on towards Bristol, and during their progress their fanaticism reached its greatest height of absurdity and impiety. They entered Bristol, J. N. on horseback, his horse led by one of the women, and a man bareheaded walking before, while others of the company spread scarfs, handkerchiefs, &c., in the way, which was deep with mud, and the whole company sang, "Holy, holy, holy is the Lord God of Hosts! Hosannah in the highest." Thus they proceeded as far as the high cross in the city, when they were stopped and taken before the Mayor, who committed them to prison.

J. Naylor having been sent up to London, and his case reported to the Parliament, then sitting, a committee was appointed by it to examine into the circumstances of the case, and report their judgment thereon. After three days this committee reported the charges against him proved. This report was received on the 5th of the Twelfth month [1656], and Parliament debated upon the case for thirteen days, and then convicted James Naylor guilty of blasphemy, and declared him to be an impostor. Upon a motion that his punishment should be death, the votes stood eighty-two yeas and ninety-six nays. On the 17th of the month the following sentence was carried, and ordered to be executed:

"That James Naylor be set on the pillory, with his head in the pillory, in the Palace-yard, Westminster, during the space of two hours, on Thursday next, and be whipped by the hangman through the streets, from Westminster to the Old Exchange, London; and there likewise be set on the pillory, with his head in the pillory, for the space of two hours, between the hours of eleven and one, on

Saturday next, in each place wearing a paper containing an inscription of his crimes; and that at the Old Exchange his tongue be bored through with a hot iron, and that he be there also stigmatized in the forehead with the letter B; and that he be afterwards sent to Bristol, and be conveyed into, and through the said* city on horseback, with his face backward, and there also publicly whipped the next market-day after he comes thither; and that thence he be committed to prison in Bridewell, London, and there restrained from the society of all people, and there to labor hard till he shall be released by Parliament; and during that time he be debarred the use of pen, ink and paper, and shall have no relief but what he earns by his daily labor."

This sentence breathes of that fierce spirit of cruelty and intolerance which, in that day, actuated many who professed to be disciples of the meek and holy Redeemer, who laid down his life for the sins of the world. It overshot the mark aimed at; for while it was hoped that it would inspire the people with a salutary dread of the crime of which J. Naylor was adjudged to be guilty, and tend to prevent them from giving countenance to the "Quakers," on whom it was hoped to reflect the guilt and opprobrium, its barbarity excited commiseration for the victim, and led men to reflect rather on the character of the religion which could allow its professors to so far violate all the best feelings of humanity, to gratify their vindictiveness.

The Speaker being authorized to issue his warrant to the several officers to carry the sentence into effect, James Naylor was brought to the bar of the House, and as the Speaker was about to pronounce the sentence, James observed, that he did not know what was his offence; to which the Speaker replied, he should know his offence by his punishment. At the close of the sentence, James was about to speak, but was prevented; when he said, "I pray God, He may not lay it to your charge."

"The 18th of December, J. Naylor suffered part of the sentence; and after having stood full two hours with his head in the pillory, was stripped, and whipped at a cart's tail, from Palace-yard to the Old Exchange, and received three hundred and ten stripes; and the executioner would have given him one more, (as he confessed to the Sheriff,) there being three hundred and eleven kennels, but his foot slipping, the stroke fell upon his own hand, which hurt him much. All this Naylor bore with so much patience and quietness, that it astonished many of the beholders, though his body was in a most pitiful condition: he was also much hurt with horses treading on his feet, whereon the print of the nails was seen. R. Travis,* a grave person, who washed his wounds, in a certificate which was presented to the Parliament, and afterwards printed, says, 'There was not the space of a man's nail free from stripes and blood, from his shoulders, near to his waist, his right arm sorely striped, his hands much hurt with cords, that they bled, and were swelled; the blood and wounds of his back did very little appear at first sight, by reason of abundance of dirt that covered them, till it was washed off.' Nay, his punishment was so severe, that some judged his sentence would have been more mild, if it had been present death: and it seemed indeed that there was a party, who not being able to prevail so far in Parliament as to have him sentenced to death, yet strove to the utmost of their power to make him sink under the weight of his punishment; for the 20th of December was the time appointed for executing the other part of the sentence, viz., boring through his tongue, and stigmatizing in his forehead; but by reason of the most cruel whipping, he was brought to such a low ebb, that many persons of note, moved with compassion, presented petitions to the Parliament on his behalf, who respited his further punishment for one week." †

Several hundred persons of different religious denominations now petitioned Parliament to remit the remaining part of the sentence; but it was soon apparent that no mercy was to be extended from its members. Application was then made to the Lord Protector, who sent a communication to the House, and the subject was debated; but as the time for carrying out the other part of the sentence was close at hand, the "ministers," who were particularly active in the case, succeeded in baffling every effort to save the victim.

On the 27th, James stood on the pillory and had his tongue bored with a hot iron. Neal, in the Appendix to his History of the Puritans, inserts an account of this cruel infliction, as given in Sayer's History of Bristol; from which the following is taken: " He having stood till two (in the pillory), the executioner took him out, and having bound his arms with cords to the pillory, and he having put forth his tongue, which he freely did, the executioner, with a red hot iron, about the bigness of a quill, bored the same, and by order from the Sheriff, held it in a small space, to the end that the beholders might see and bear witness that the sentence was thoroughly executed.

* She who was convinced by him in London.   † Sewel.

Then, having taken it out and pulled the cap off that covered his face, he put a handkerchief over his eyes, and putting his left hand to the back part of his head, and taking the red hot iron letter in his other hand, put it to his forehead 'till it smoked: all which time James never so much as winced; but bore it with astonishing and heart-melting patience." . . . . "This also was very remarkable, that notwithstanding there might be many thousands of people, yet they were very quiet, few being heard to revile him, or seen to throw anything at him. And when he was burning, all the people before him and behind, and on both sides of him, with one consent, stood bare-headed."

When able to be moved he was taken to Bristol, to be there whipped through the streets at the cart tail; which was done; though the executioner, it was said by command, used but very little force in applying the lash, respecting which Sayer remarks, "A trait of mercy, in the midst of such brutality, which ought to be recorded to the credit of the magistracy of Bristol."

Great was the glorifying of the enemies of Friends at the fall of poor James Naylor. He was known to have been an eminent instrument among them, and it was hoped that after what had occurred, Friends would no longer dare to propagate their doctrines, and the Society would soon disappear. No effort was spared to make Friends responsible for the wrong doing of those infatuated professors; but Friends — knowing that it sprung, not from the truth of the Gospel as professed by them, but from a wide departure therefrom; and instead of giving heed to the warning, preserving manifestations of the Holy Spirit to the soul, allowing the affections to be captivated by that which ministers to the gratification of the carnal mind, and the judgment to become perverted by self-exaltation — kept on in the even tenor of their way, and while they mourned over the loss of their fallen brother, and bore an unequivocal testimony against his errors, they suffered it not to shut up their hearts against him, nor to induce them faithlessly to relax in godly zeal for the promotion of truth and righteousness.

In the course of the two years' confinement of J. Naylor in Bridewell, it pleased the Lord again to visit him with the Day-spring from on high, by which the darkness that had shrouded his spiritual vision was dispelled, and he brought to see how grievously he had departed from the way of the Lord, and involved himself and others in guilt and wretchedness. The gift of that repentance not to be repented of, was mercifully vouchsafed to him, and in abased-

ness and sincerity, he was enabled to confess his sin and receive forgiveness.　He wrote many acknowledgments of his departure from
the truth, which he had once known, deploring the dishonor his
conduct had brought upon it, and upon the Society to which he belonged, and condemning in the strongest terms the course he had
pursued.

The following from one of those affecting documents, is very instructive; as showing that the most eminent gifts are held in frail
earthen vessels; and that there is no safety, even for the most favored
instrument, unless the injunction of Christ is continually observed,
" What I say unto you, I say unto all, Watch, watch and pray lest
ye enter into temptation." " Not minding in all things to stand single
and low to the motions of that endless life, by it to be led in all
things within and without; but giving away to the reasoning part,
as to some things which in themselves had no seeming evil, by little
and little it drew out my mind after trifles, vanities and persons,
which took the affectionate part, by which my mind was drawn out
from the constant watch, and pure fear, into which I once was begotten.　Thus having in a great measure lost my own guide, and
darkness being come upon me, I sought a place where I might have
been alone to weep and cry before the Lord, that his face I might
find, and my condition recover.　But then my adversary, who had
long waited his opportunity, had got in and bestirred himself every
way, so that I could not be hid; and divers messages came to me,
some true, some false, as I have seen since.　So I, knowing some to
be true, to wit, how I had lost my condition, with this I let in the
false message also; and so letting go that little of the true light
which I had yet remaining in myself, I gave up myself wholly to
be led by others; whose work was then to divide me from the children of light, which was done: though much was done by divers of
them to prevent it, and in bowels of tender love many labored to
have stayed me with them.　And after I was led out from them,
the Lord God of my life sent divers of his servants with his word
after me, for my return; all which was rejected; yea, the provoca-
tion of that time of temptation was exceeding great against the pure
love of God; yet He left me not; for after I had given myself under
that power, and darkness was above, my adversary so prevailed,
that all things were turned and perverted against my right seeing,
hearing, or understanding; only a secret hope and faith I had in
my God, whom I had served, that He would bring me through it,
and to the end of it, and that I should again see the day of my re-

demption from under it all; and this quieted my soul in my greatest tribulation."

To Friends whom he had so deeply grieved, on account of the reproach he had brought on the precious truth they professed, he wrote: — "Dear brethren: My heart is broken this day, for the offence that I have occasioned to God's truth and people, and especially to you, who in dear love followed me, seeking me in faithfulness to God, which I rejected; being bound wherein I could not come forth, till God's hand brought me, to whose love I now confess: and I beseech you, forgive wherein I evilly requited your love in that day. God knows my sorrow for it, since I see it, that ever I should offend that of God in any, or reject his counsel; and now that paper you have seen lies much upon me, and I greatly fear further to offend, or do amiss, whereby the innocent truth, or people of God should suffer, or that I should disobey therein.

"Unless the Lord himself keep you from me, I beseech you let nothing else hinder your coming to me, that I might have your help in the Lord: in the mercies of Christ Jesus this I beg of you, as if it was your own case; let me not be forgotten of you.

"And I entreat you, speak to Henry Clarke, or whoever else I have most offended; and by the power of God, and in the Spirit of Christ Jesus, I am willing to confess the offence, that God's love may arise in all hearts, as before, if it be his will, who only can remove what stands in the way; and nothing thereof do I intend to cover: God is witness herein."

He also sent an address to Parliament, declaring that Christ Jesus — the Immanuel, of whose sufferings the Scriptures declare — was Him alone whom he confessed before men; "and that to ascribe this name, power, or virtue to James Naylor, or for that to be exalted or worshipped, to me is great idolatry, and with the Spirit of Christ Jesus in me, it is condemned; which Spirit leads to lowliness, meekness and long suffering."

Sayer, in his history of Bristol, says, that after J. Naylor's discharge from Bridewell, he returned to that city, and in a meeting with his friends there, made a recantation of his errors in so affecting a manner, that they were convinced of the sincerity of his repentance. Sewel also records, "This is certain, that James Naylor came to very great sorrow, and deep humiliation of mind; and therefore, because God forgives the transgressions of the penitent, and blotteth them out, and remembereth them no more, so could James Naylor's friends do no other than forgive his crime, and thus take back the lost sheep into their Society. He having afterwards obtained his liberty, behaved himself as became a Christian, honest and blameless in conversation; and patiently bore the reproach of his former crimes."

How long he remained in Bristol does not appear, but, probably, not long. He returned to London, and while there, wrote and had printed a reply to "The Fanatic History;" a work published by one Richard Blorne, but generally understood to have been put forth under the patronage of a number of ministers; the drift of which was, to bring Friends and their principles into disrepute; to effect which, J. Naylor's case was referred to.

In the Eighth month of 1660, he left London on foot for the North, intending to go to his native place in the neighborhood of Wakefield. After getting a few miles beyond Huntingdon, he was taken sick; and was found near evening in a field, bound; having been robbed. Being taken to the house of a Friend at Holm, he received medical advice and attention, for which, and the kindness of those about him, he expressed his gratitude, saying, "You have refreshed my body, the Lord refresh your souls." He lived not many days; dying in the forty-fourth year of his age. A few hours before his death, he uttered the following beautiful language, in the presence of several who were waiting upon him:

"There is a spirit which I feel, that delights to do no evil, nor to revenge any wrong, but delights to endure all things in hope to enjoy its own in the end. Its hope is to outlive all wrath and contention, and to weary out all exaltation and cruelty, or whatever is of a nature contrary to itself. It sees to the end of all temptations. As it bears no evil in itself, so it conceives none in thought to any other: if it be betrayed, it bears it; for its ground and spring are the mercies and forgiveness of God. Its crown is meekness, its life is everlasting love unfeigned, and takes its kingdom with entreaty, and not with contention, and keeps it by lowliness of mind. In God alone it can rejoice, though none else regard it, or can own its life. It is conceived in sorrow, and brought forth without any to pity it; nor doth it murmur at grief and oppression. It never rejoiceth but through sufferings; for with the world's joy it is murdered. I found it alone, being forsaken. I have fellowship therein with them who lived in dens, and desolate places of the earth, who through death obtained this resurrection, and eternal holy life."

CHAPTER IX.

G. Fox and O. Cromwell — E. Burrough and O. Cromwell — Wales — George
Fox in Scotland — Curses — Persecution in Scotland — Visits to the Continent —West Indies — Mary Fisher — First instance of Whipping a Friend
—Anne Austin — Colony of Massachusetts —Roger Williams —Anne Hutchinson — M. Fisher and A. Austin land at Boston — Witches — Mary Fisher
and the Sultan — Eight more Friends at Boston — Imprisonment — Laws
passed against Quakers — Curiosity Excited—Nicholas Upshal—Mary Dyer
and Ann Burden in Boston — Embarkation of Eleven Friends for America
— John Copeland and Christopher Holder in Massachusetts — Whippings
—Misrepresentations — First Declaration of Friends' Faith published in
America — A new Law against Quakers — Murmurs of the People.

AFTER being released from Launceston jail in 1656, Geo. Fox
found it laid upon him to travel throughout England ; not only
to continue to spread a knowledge of the truth, but also to confirm
those who had been converted thereto, in obedience to the manifestations of Divine Grace, and in faithfulness to the several duties
required of them.   Coming up to London, when near Hyde Park,
observing a crowd, he rode up and found that the Lord Protector
was passing by.   George guided his horse along side of him, Cromwell ordering the guard not to keep him away.   They entered into
conversation, and he embraced the opportunity to speak to the Protector respecting the sufferings Friends were undergoing ; to bring
home to him the responsibility resting on him, for what was being
done in his name, and to exhort him to put a stop to that which was
so contrary to the spirit of Christ and to Christianity.

Shortly after G. Fox and E. Pyot had an interview with Cromwell and some of his Council at Whitehall; in which the sufferings
of Friends were again laid before him, and the doctrine of the
Light of Christ in the soul fully explained and enforced.   But
Cromwell said it was but a natural light, and behaved in a light
and trifling manner.   But George reproved him, and says, " The
power of the Lord God arose in me, and in it I was moved to bid
him to lay down his crown at the feet of Jesus."

George Fox, who had observed with much sorrow, that not only
were Friends cruelly persecuted for their adherence to the religion
of Christ, but that indulgence in the spirit of intolerance and malice
was hardening the hearts of the people, and rendering them more
and more irreligious and ripe for licentious indulgence, was con-

vinced that the government would not be allowed to stand. He says, in 1658, " I had a sight and sense of the king's return a good while before, and so had some others. I wrote to Oliver several times; and let him know, that while he was persecuting God's people, they whom he accounted his enemies were preparing to come upon him. When some forward spirits, that came among us, would have bought Somerset-house, that we might have meetings in it, I forbade them to do so: for I then foresaw the king's coming in again. Besides, there came a woman to me in the Strand, who had a proph- ecy concerning King Charles's coming in, three years before he came; and she told me, she must go to him to declare it. I advised her to wait upon the Lord, and keep it to herself; for if it should be known that she went on such a message, they would look upon it to be treason; but she said, she must go and tell him, that he should be brought into England again. I saw her prophecy was true, and that a great stroke must come upon those in power: for they that had then got possession were so exceeding high, and such great persecution was acted by them who called themselves saints, that they would take from Friends their copyhold lands, because they could not swear in their courts. Sometimes, when we laid these sufferings before Oliver Cromwell, he would not be- lieve it. Wherefore Thomas Aldam and Anthony Pearson were moved to go through all the gaols in England, and to get copies of Friends' commitments under the gaolers' hands, that they might lay the weight of their sufferings upon Oliver Cromwell. And when he refused to give order for the releasing of them, Thomas Aldam was moved to take his cap off his head, and rend it in pieces before him, and to say unto him, ' So shall thy government be rent from thee and thy house.' "

Having proceeded and visited those parts of England where he had not been already, G. Fox returned to London [1656], and while there, prepared and had published, an answer to the several objections that had been made public to the doctrines held and promulgated by Friends. Finding that party spirit had spread among the mem- bers of the Society in and about London, arising from the case of James Naylor, he addressed a short epistle to them, warning against " party heats," and exhorting to live in that power which would deliver them therefrom. He also addressed another epistle to all Friends, encouraging them to keep up their meetings in the Lord's power; and yet another to those who had come, or were coming forth in the ministry, to beware that no disorder should be brought into the meetings by those who sometimes uttered a few words of praise or thanksgiving. Many other productions of his pen, all in defence of the truth, or to spread it more widely, were published by him.

Both he and E. Burrough addressed O. Cromwell, earnestly expostulating with him for allowing the persecution of Friends to go on, when he had the power at any-time to arrest it. Finding their remonstrance produced no change, E. Burrough sought and obtained an interview with the Protector; during which the sufferings that Friends were undergoing were particularly stated, and what were the offences alleged against them. Cromwell heard him respectfully, and assured him that he disapproved of persecution and cruelty, and that he was not guilty of them, nor personally responsible for them. But E. Burrough brought the matter home to him; and told him he made himself responsible for these evil doings, by connivance, and refusing to use the power he possessed to prevent them. Cromwell, however, at that time was too deeply involved in intrigue to raise himself to the throne and wear a crown, and too anxious to secure the devotion of the intolerant but supple Parliament, to be willing to give protection to the hated Quakers, at the expense of offending those rigid Independents and Presbyterians, who were seeking their destruction; and who still held the authority of the national Council in their hands.

In the fore part of 1657, George Fox travelled through Wales; being accompanied by John ap John, a Welchman, who when Friends were first heard of in Wales — had been sent by Morgan Watkins — a noted minister—to see and inquire what kind of people they were; and coming where George Fox then was, and hearing him preach, was convinced of the truth of his doctrines, and soon after joined the Society. They had large meetings and many were convinced. In the latter part of this year G. Fox travelled throughout the northern shires of England, and found that in several places, such had been the effect of Friends' preaching, that many of the "steeple-houses" were shut up, the congregations having generally joined their Society. Keeping on north he entered Scotland, and went from town to town until he had traversed nearly the whole of it. He met with much opposition, especially from the State ministers, who railed against Friends because they preached against the foreordained election and reprobation of individuals, from the foundation of the world. A great cry was raised against Friends, and against George Fox in particular; who, it was said, had seduced the honest men in England and was now come into Scotland to do the same thing there. A large assembly of the "ministers" was therefore convened, which had drawn up a number of curses, that were to be read in their "churches," and all the people were to respond, Amen.

One was, " Cursed is he that sayeth, Every man hath a light within him, sufficient to lead him to salvation : And let all the people say, Amen."

Another. " Cursed is he who saith, Faith is without sin : And let all the people say, Amen."

Another. " Cursed is he that denieth the Sabbath day : And let all the people say, Amen."

There were several ministering Friends travelling in Scotland, at that time, and many of the inhabitants embraced the doctrine of the Universal Saving Light of the Holy Spirit, mercifully vouchsafed to every man to profit withal ; in opposition to the dark dogma of unconditional election and reprobation. This naturally excited the rigid Presbyterians, and determined them to use every means in their power to put a stop to what they deemed so great a heresy.

The second time G. Fox came into Edinburgh, he was summoned to appear before the Council of the city. He says, " When the time came I appeared, and was had into a great room, where many persons came and looked at me. After awhile the doorkeeper had me into the council chamber : and as I was going, he took off my hat. I asked him, ' Why he did so ? and who was there, that I might not go in with my hat on ? I told him, I had been before the Protector with my hat on.' But he hung up my hat and had me in before them. When I had stood awhile, and they said nothing to me, I was moved of the Lord to say, ' Peace be amongst you. Wait in the fear of God, that ye may receive his wisdom from above, by which all things were made and created ; that by it ye may all be ordered, and may order all things under your hands to God's glory.' "

After questioning him as to his object in coming into Scotland, and how long he expected to stay, &c., he was put out of the room, and when brought back was told, " He must depart out of Scotland by the end of a week." When he asked why ? what transgression had he committed ? they replied they would not dispute with him, but he must go. George, however, remained in the city, and did not fail to address and send to the Council an expostulation against their illegal and unchristian judgment concerning him ; showing that such conduct could only be the result of hearts still in the darkness of unbelief and disobedience to the Light of Christ.

Friends in many parts of that nation were now brought under great suffering in consequence of the State ministers, who publicly excommunicated them; and playing on the superstitious fears of the people, strictly forbade any person of either sex, under penalty of being cursed, to buy anything from or sell anything to those who professed to be Quakers. For a time, in some places, it seemed as though Friends might perish for want of the necessaries of life; but some of the magistrates interfered, and put a stop to the inhuman course of the priests.

Feeling released for the present from Edinburgh, G. Fox went to Sterling, Glasgow, and through other towns, accompanied by Robert Widders, James Lancaster, and Alexander Parker. They were evilly treated in many places, but fainted not in their labor of love, and patience of hope, and their good Master sustained them. "The people — says G. Fox — were turned to the Lord Jesus Christ who died for them and had enlightened them, that with his light they might see their evil deeds; be saved from their sins by Him; and might come to know Him to be their teacher. But if they would not receive Christ and own Him, it was told them that this Light, which came from Him, would be their condemnation."

Hearing that the council of Edinburgh had granted warrants for his apprehension, because he had not left Scotland as they had ordered, George returned to that city, and was present at a large meeting, to which many officers and soldiers came. No one meddled with him; and he says, "The everlasting power of God was set over the nation, and his Son reigned in his glorious power." He now returned into England. Again, speaking of the doctrine he preached as he went from once place to another, he says, "I opened to the people where they might find Christ Jesus; turned them to that Light He had enlightened them withal, that in the light they might see Christ who died for them, turn to Him, and know Him to be their Saviour and teacher." . . . . "I turned them to the Spirit of God, which led the holy men of God to give forth the Scriptures, and showed them that they must also come to receive and be led by the same Spirit, in themselves — a measure of which was given to every one of them — if ever they came to know God and Christ and the Scriptures aright." After visiting Friends in many parts of the north of England, sometimes tarrying at places where he felt specially called to labor or to write on some particular subject, he arrived in London again in the early part of 1658.

During the years 1657 and 1658, several Friends labored in the love of the gospel, in different parts of the continent. William Ames and William Caton visited different towns in Holland; Christopher Birkhead was at Rochelle, in France, whence he went into Holland; where he was imprisoned for a considerable length of time, but was finally released through the intercession of the Ambassador of the States General, in England. In 1657, George Bailey, believing himself called to go into France, in order to bear witness to the spirituality of the religion of Christ, went over from England; and in the course of his mission, having testified against the superstition and idolatry of the people, in their worship and practices, as enjoined by the popish religion, he was shut up in prison, and kept there until he died. There had also a number of Friends sailed at different times for the British West Indies, among whom were John Rouse, Henry Fell and Peter Head, also Mary Fisher and Anne Austin. Henry Fell was a relative of Judge Fell, and lived in Lancashire. At what time he was convinced does not appear, but he was eminently gifted in the ministry of the Gospel, and labored abundantly in his own country.

Mary Fisher was a native of the north of England, being born there in 1623. She was a woman with high intellectual endowments, and was among the early converts to the principles of the gospel as held by Friends. In the year 1652, she gave up to forego the comforts and endearments of home, in order to render obedience to the call of her heavenly Father, to go forth and labor for the gathering of souls to Christ. Having delivered a message to a congregation at Selby, at the close of the public worship, she was arrested and committed to prison in York Castle, where she was closely kept for sixteen months. Soon after her release from this confinement, in company with Elizabeth Williams, another minister, she travelled through various counties, preaching the word to very many, who were surprised that two such defenceless females had the courage and Divine support, to undergo so many hardships in order to perform what they felt to be a duty, and to bring people to a more practical knowledge of the blessing of the gospel of Christ. At Cambridge, the collegians took great offence at their doctrine relative to the qualifications of a gospel minister, and the uselessness of ceremonies and stated services under profession of worship. They, therefore, derided and reviled them, and the Mayor of the city, in his zeal to support the students' cause, had them whipped at the market-cross, until the blood ran down their bodies. Being released from the whipping-post, in the presence of the multitude that had collected to see their punishment, they kneeled down and petitioned their Heavenly Father, who had marvellously supported them, to grant forgiveness to their persecutors. This was the first time that punishment with the lash was publicly inflicted on a Friend. Near the close of 1653, Mary Fisher was again imprisoned six months within the walls of York Castle, because of declaring the truth in the " steeple-house " at Pontefract, where she had her residence; and shortly after her release, she was once more sent back to the prison, because she had not repented of her aforesaid religious service, and was not willing to give surety for her future good behavior. The last incarceration lasted three months.

In 1655, she found it required of her to visit, in the love of the gospel, the West India Islands belonging to Great Britain, and with Anne Austin she embarked therefor; and they had much religious service among the inhabitants, especially in Barbadoes.

Anne Austin appears to have lived in London, and to have been brought to a knowledge of the Truth, so far as instrumental means were concerned, by the ministry of some one of those Friends employed by the Head of the Church to preach the gospel in that city. There is but little left on record respecting her, but it appears that she was an approved minister, and after her return to England from the West Indies, she was imprisoned for a long time in one of the dismal jails of London, for having been found engaged in the exercise of her gift as a minister in one of Friends' meetings in that city. She died during the awful " plague " which visited London in 1665.

Before noticing the reception given to Mary Fisher and Anne Austin, at Boston, it may be well to precede it, and the account of the persecution of Friends in Massachusetts, by a glance at the religious condition of that colony.

It must have been seen, from what has been narrated already, that notwithstanding all that had been said and done under the plea of securing or defending liberty of conscience, that liberty was either very imperfectly understood, or the party speaking or contending for it, thought when it was obtained for themselves, they would be justified in obliging all others to conform to their views. The Puritans, who, as is mentioned in the first chapter, fled from their own country to Holland, because they were not allowed in England to worship the Most High according to the dictates of their own consciences [1620], afterwards left Holland for America, and landed on the inhospitable shores of New England, to found and build up amid its trackless wilds, a home for themselves, and an asylum for all who were persecuted because of their religious belief.

They had been allowed to occupy the territory of which they had taken possession as subjects of the Crown of Great Britain, for some years before any legal title thereto was conferred upon them. The patent for "The Governor and Company of Massachusetts Bay," was granted by Charles I. in 1629. Under it, a large number of emigrants came out and settled at Salem. These, though while in England they professed to be in sympathy with the "Church of England," were dissenters, or non-conformists, holding the Puritan faith; and when deciding upon the character of the "church," its government and powers, in their new home, they threw off all subordination to the "established church" of their mother country.

By the charter, the administration of the affairs of the colony was vested in a Governor, a Deputy and eighteen Assistants, and the ordinances and regulations were to be enacted by that portion of the corporators who continued to reside in England. As the association was looked upon more in the light of a trading company than a civil power, it was allowed to regulate its own affairs. It was, however, specially provided in the charter, that no laws or ordinances should be passed that were contrary to the laws of England.

Episcopacy at that time was enforcing its iron rule in Great Britain; but the broad Atlantic intervened between the seat of its power and the unyielding religionists, settled here and there on the rugged shores of New England, and the intolerant prelates had no tool among the latter to attempt carrying out their commands. The church therefore was independent, self-constituted and congregational in form; holding the Calvinistic faith in its simplest and most pitiless dogmas, and no more tolerant than that, to escape whose oppression the members had exiled themselves from their native soil. So rigid were they in maintaining its doctrines and discipline, and so determined that episcopacy should obtain no foothold among them, that at Salem, when it was found that two members of the council, who had come out with the first colonists under the charter, were dissatisfied with the omission of every part of the Church of England service from the religious exercises, Governor Endicott told them, "New England was no place for them," and they were sent back.

Before the end of 1629 the charter was secretly—without the knowledge of the king—transferred from that part of the company which was to remain in England and enact the laws, to the freedmen living in the colony who were, or should become members of the corporation. This transfer, of course, conferred no new political power; but by putting the choice of officers, and the enactment of the laws, in the hands of the settlers, they were placed in a situation to assume, and soon did assume, the functions of an independent provincial government. Large privileges were conferred on the corporation to promote the interest of the colonies, but it acquired no right to any territory within the dominion of the Crown, that clothed it with authority to exclude other subjects of their Sovereign from entering or settling within its boundaries.

It may be freely admitted these Puritan colonists were sincere believers in the purity of the religion they professed, and zealous that nothing should mar that purity; but the source whence their political existence and power were drawn, had bestowed on them neither right nor privilege to constitute a new State church; conformity to which was to be a *sine qua non*, in order to live or mingle among them. But fanatical zeal prompted them to seize upon that which did not belong to them, and so soon as they had gained possession of their extended territory, and had brought their form of government into action, it was resolved that all who were or should come among them, must conform to the form of religion and religious practices which they had adopted, or suffer the punishment prescribed for heresy and contumacy. Laws were enacted requiring every freeman to pay a tax for building and keeping in repair the place of worship, and to provide the salary of the minister; also imposing a fine on those who persistently absented themselves from the " stated services."

This intolerant policy was soon applied in the punishment of Roger Williams. He had come over to settle in the colony in 1631, and was engaged as a preacher or teacher; first at Salem and afterwards at Plymouth. Too much enlightened to approve of the narrow and bigoted course pursued by the civil and church authorities, he had the integrity and boldness to declare publicly, that punishment for obeying the dictates of conscience in regard to religion was persecution, and contrary to the precepts of Christ, and that it was an unjustifiable violation of the guaranteed rights of Englishmen, to force them to attend at those places of worship only that were approved by the rulers of the colony. He was cited before the court in 1635, and being convicted of holding these opinions, he was banished from the colony.

Two years after this despotic and illegal act (1637), a party of religious professors, headed by a highly intelligent and virtuous woman, named Anne Hutchinson, which differed from the rulers on the subject of justification by works, was driven out of Massachusetts, and had likewise to take refuge among the natives. Williams and his friends having settled on Narraganset Bay, and the last exiles at Providence, the two succeeded in purchasing from the Indians a considerable extent of country, and having applied to the home Government, they obtained a charter for the colony of Rhode Island.

The spirit of bigotry and persecution in Massachusetts was not weakened nor allayed by the intolerant treatment of those who had dared to exercise a sober judgment in order to keep a conscience void of offence; but subsequently, when it was found that some of their colonists had adopted the views of the Baptists respecting immersion and the disapproval of infant baptism, the rulers manifested their uncharitableness by fines, whippings, and finally by banishment, until they had driven them out of the boundaries of their colony.

With such a spirit as this prevailing, it was hardly to be wondered at, that when intelligence reached Boston, in the Fifth month of 1656, that a ship had arrived in the bay, having on board two women who were Quakers, consternation was apparent wherever the news reached. These Friends were Mary Fisher and Anne Austin. Governor Endicott was absent from the city; but the Deputy Governor, Bellingham, immediately dispatched orders not to allow the two women to land; to search their luggage, and if any books or writings were found, to have them at once delivered to an officer to be brought on shore. A council of magistrates was convened, which issued an order, stating, that although a law existed "against heretics and erroneous persons," yet the Master of the ship Swallow, had brought within their jurisdiction two women "of that sort of people commonly known by the name of Quakers," who are found to hold "very dangerous, heretical and blasphemous opinions," and to have books inculcating those opinions, &c., &c. Therefore, to preserve the peace and truth enjoyed "among the churches of Christ in this country," their books (about one hundred) were to be burned by the common hangman; that they — the two women — be committed to prison, and no one be allowed to speak to or communicate with them, unless by order of some one in authority, and to be so kept until they can be sent away. That the master of the ship who brought them give security by a bond for £100 that he will cause them to be transported to Barbadoes at his own expense. M. Fisher and A. Austin were brought ashore and put into the prison; pens, ink and paper were taken from them, and to prevent any one speaking to them, the only window in their prison room was boarded up, and it was ordered that a fine of £5 be imposed on every one detected holding converse with them.

Among a people so infatuated, and with minds so open to the delusions that accompany a superstitious fear of everything not in accordance with their accustomed notions of what is right and true, it was to be expected that the hallucination respecting witchcraft, should find ready place. It had begun its fatal career among the Puritans in Massachusetts, some having already been put to death as witches, and it afterwards scourged the colony in so awful a manner, that none knew when they were safe. To bring odium and perhaps death upon the two innocent and helpless women they now had in their power, it was given out that most likely they were witches; and they were closely examined on that point. But nothing could be drawn from them that gave supposable ground for such a charge. Foiled in their interrogatories, the magistrates went on to outrage all decency, by ordering them to be stripped, and examination made, if the mark of the devil's seal or signature could be found on their skin. This shameful outrage failed, however, to furnish the coveted evidence, and then another order was issued, forbidding any person to provide them with food; and they would certainly have perished by starvation, had not a citizen, whose humanity was touched by their sufferings, bribed the jailer to allow him secretly to administer to their necessities. For five weeks they were thus kept shut up, and then were sent on board the ship that brought them, and transported to Barbadoes; the jailer having been allowed to take possession of their beds and their Bibles, for his fees. After a short stay in the West Indies, Mary Fisher returned to England; but again visited some of the islands in 1658, and having finished her work there, once more returned home.

In 1660, under an apprehension that it was required of her to deliver a message from the Lord to Sultan Mahomet IV., M. Fisher set out for Adrianople, in European Turkey, near which city the army of the Sultan was encamped. Having arrived at Smyrna, the English Consul there stopped her, and sent her back to Venice;

hoping thus to frustrate her design. But she, not finding herself clear of the burden that lay upon her, took another route, and when she reached Adrianople, sent a messenger to the Grand Vizier, requesting him to inform the Sultan, there had an English woman come from her own country, to deliver to him a message from the great God. The next day the Sultan had her brought before him, while surrounded by his officers of rank. He treated her with marked respect, and told her, by interpreters, that if she had a message from the Lord God to him, to deliver it without fear, saying neither more nor less than she was commissioned, for their hearts were open to receive it. After a short pause she communicated what she believed had been given her by her Master. Having finished, the Sultan asked her if she had anything further to say? She replied, No, and then asked him if he had fully understood what she had delivered? He answered, Yes, every word, and it was the truth. The interview being concluded, the Sultan tried to persuade her to remain in that country; observing, that he had great respect for a woman who had taken so much trouble to deliver him such a message. Finding she could not be induced to remain, he offered her a guard of soldiers, to see her safe to Constantinople, whither she wished to go; saying he would not for any consideration, that she should come to the least hurt in his dominions. This kind offer she declined, and after answering the queries of some of the officers, relative to her opinion of Mahomet as a prophet, she left; arrived safely at Constantinople, without receiving the slightest ill treatment in word or act, and from there returned home. Subsequently, she was twice married, and with her second husband, whose name was John Cross, she emigrated to America, and settled in Charleston, South Carolina; where, there is reason to believe, she closed her long and eventful life; though there is no record of her death.

1656. Little more than a month had elapsed since the arrival of the two women Friends just mentioned, at Boston, and the vessel which was bearing them away had barely left the bay, when another ship, with eight Friends — four men and four women — on board, cast anchor in that port. The Captain having reported his passengers to the Governor, as soon as it was known that eight of them were Quakers, officers were sent on board the vessel to seize their boxes, chests and trunks, and search if there were any " erroneous books and hellish pamphlets " in them, and to bring the Friends before the Court then sitting. The examination turned on belief in the character of the Almighty, and on the Scriptures. As there were several of the "stated ministers" present, and the scriptural arguments of the Friends proved difficult of refutation, the ministers and magistrates fell out among themselves. Sending the Friends to prison for the night, the court had them brought before it again the next morning. The prisoners demanded why they had been arrested and imprisoned. Instead of informing them, Governor Endicott replied, "Take heed ye break not our *ecclesiastical laws*, for then ye are sure to stretch by a halter."

The Court sentenced them to be banished; to be closely imprisoned until the ship in which they came was ready to sail, then to be put on board, and carried back whence they came. The Captain was required to give bond in £500 that he would comply with this order to carry them away. He at first refused; inasmuch, as he alleged, every Englishman who had not broken the law had the right to go where he pleased, within the kingdom; but after four days' confinement in the wretched prison in Boston, he submitted and signed the bond. The Friends, deprived of pen, ink and paper, were kept closely immured for more than two months, and were then sent on board the vessel; the jailer being first authorized to seize all their bedding, and whatever other goods they had, for his fees. As the ship was bound for England, and the voyage might be tedious, some of the citizens, commiserating the Friends thus exposed to further suffering, redeemed the bedding and goods, and allowed them to take them with them, in order that they might not be altogether unprovided with the comforts of life.

This arbitrary and intolerant course pursued towards Friends by the Governor and Council of Massachusetts, was not only in contravention of the laws of England, but there was no law for it in the Colony. In order, therefore, to give whatever measures they might hereafter think proper to pursue in similar cases the form of law, the Governor and Council addressed "The Commissioners of the United Provinces," recommending that some general rules should be adopted to prevent "such notorious heretics as Quakers, Ranters," &c., coming among them. Of this the Commissioners approved; and it was proposed by them to the several Courts that they should make provision for keeping such "heretics" away, or for sending them away on their arrival.

In 1643 the several towns or colonies of Plymouth and Boston, in Massachusetts, and others in Connecticut and New Haven, had entered into a confederacy, designated the "New England Confederacy," for mutual defence, to promote unanimity and the general welfare. The "Commissioners of the United Provinces " were appointed by them severally, and these Commissioners had the right to propose to the governments of the respective colonies, such measures as they deemed advisable for the good of the whole. The " General Court " at Boston, eager to avail itself of that recommendation, on the 14th of the 10th month, 1656, approved and enacted an order, imposing fine or imprisonment on any master of a vessel of any size or kind, who knowingly should land anywhere within the precincts of the colony, any of that " cursed sect of heretics, commonly called Quakers : " " That any or all of that sect who shall come into the Colony from foreign parts, or from neighboring colonies, shall forthwith be sent to the House of Correction, and on their entrance there, shall be severely whipped ; then be kept constantly at work during the time that may elapse before they are sent out of the Colony, and that no one be allowed to hold converse with them." To import, possess, pay for, spread or conceal any book or writing containing any of the " devilish opinions " of the Quakers, incurred a fine of £5. To express approbation of or defend the " devilish opinions " of the Quakers, incurred the fine of £2 for the first offence ; for the second £4 ; and for the third, imprisonment until opportunity presented for banishing the offender. The Court of Plymouth passed a similar ordinance.*

This law was proclaimed at Boston, with beat of drum throughout the town. But alas for the persecutors ! their unchristian course aroused the indignation of some, and excited the curiosity of many more, to know what the " devilish opinions " of " that cursed sect of heretics, commonly called Quakers," were ; and upon investigation, several were convinced of their truth and accordance with Scripture. Nicholas Upshal, a man who stood high in both the church and the Colony, having expressed disapprobation of the laws just enacted, was summoned before the court, and having there plead with the Governor and Magistrates not to attempt to carry the law into effect, lest they should be found fighting against God, he was fined £20, imprisoned, and banished; thirty days only being allowed him to make the needful arrangements respecting his family and property.

Among those attached to Anne Hutchinson, who, as has been

* See " The Blue Laws of Connecticut; Quaker Laws; Blue Laws of Plymouth and Massachusetts," &c.; published at Hartford, Connecticut, 1838, page 14.

previously stated, were banished from Massachusetts for their Anti-nomian opinions [1637], were Mary Dyer and her husband, who settled in Rhode Island. Mary, having for some purpose gone on a visit to England, while there, was convinced of the principles held by Friends, joined the Society, and became an approved minister among them. Having embarked to return to her husband, she had a fellow passenger named Ann Burden, who, with her husband, had been a resident of Boston for many years; but having been banished for the same cause and at the same time as M. Dyer, they had gone to England, where her husband died. The widow was returning to Boston, to collect some considerable debts, due her deceased husband's estate. Immediately on their arrival they were seized by order of the magistrates, and placed in close confinement, to prevent any speaking with them. In their examination, A. Burden plead the lawfulness of the object for which she had come; but the only answer given to this was, that "*as she was a plain Quaker,* she must abide their laws." After lying in prison three months, to the great injury of her health, Ann was sent on board a ship to be taken back to England. Some kind-hearted citizens of Boston, pitying the persecuted widow, who had children depending on her, exerted themselves, and got several of her debtors to pay what they owed her, in goods, to the amount of £40. But the magistrates, after finding that the captain of the ship on board which Ann was sent, was too humane to seize any portion of these goods for passage money, levied on them themselves to the amount of £6 10s., and then forbid any of the remainder to be put on board the ship; so that the poor prisoner lost all, and was carried back to England to contend with her poverty as she could. After M. Dyer had been imprisoned for some time, her husband, who was not a Friend, came to Boston for her; but before he could obtain her release, the Court extorted a promise from him, and bound him in a heavy penalty if not performed, that he would not allow his wife to lodge in any town in the colony, nor to speak to any person while on her journey.

The law of Massachusetts, imposing a severe penalty on the captain of any vessel in which any of the dreaded Quakers should be brought to her shores, made it very difficult, if not impossible, for such Friends as felt it to be their religious duty to go to that colony, to procure passage thereto; owners and captains being afraid of the consequences of carrying them. But a seafaring Friend, in England, named Robert Fowler, having a small vessel built, felt it required of him to offer to take such Friends as were under religious bonds to go; and accordingly, eleven embarked in the Fourth month, 1657, and were landed, some at New Amsterdam, and some at Providence, Rhode Island.   Two of these Friends, John Copeland and Christopher Holder, having visited Martha's Vineyard, were ordered away by the Governor, who directed some of the Indians to carry them over to the mainland.   These savage natives, however, were not willing forcibly to expel the strangers, and allowed them to remain among them several days; when the Friends feeling prepared to depart, they took them in their canoes and landed them on the coast, whence they proceeded to Sandwich.   Here they succeeded in holding meetings, at which several were convinced of the truth of the doctrines preached by them.   Going thence to Plymouth, and there preaching, the whole community was soon in an uproar.   Though arraigned before the magistrates, at both Sandwich and Plymouth, there being nothing illegal proved against them, they were discharged; with an order to depart at once out of the colony.   But as the fruits of their ministry were becoming apparent, in the conversion of several to the truths of the gospel as held by them, the ministers of the colonial Church stirred up the Commissioners — one of whom had like to have choked C. Holder, by thrusting a glove into his mouth, to prevent him from speaking — to send them as prisoners to Boston.   Here, after being separately examined, they were sentenced to receive each thirty lashes; which was executed in the most barbarous manner with a three-corded knotted whip; the executioner measuring his distance from the victim, so that he might make the stroke with the greatest force.   With their flesh cut and torn they were then thrust into the vile prison, and without bed or straw to lie on, were left for three days, without food or drink; and continued to be kept closely incarcerated in the damp and cold, without fire or warmth for nine weeks.   These two sufferers were shortly joined by Richard Dowdney, another Friend; who having landed at New Amsterdam, and engaged in religious service there and in its vicinity, had travelled north, and reaching Dedham, in Massachusetts, was at once recognized as a Quaker, by his plain speech and appearance.   He was forthwith apprehended and sent to Boston, and three hours after his arrival, was subjected to similar torture of the lash as his brethren had undergone, and then to share with them in the sufferings, endured in their pent-up cell.

1657. As it was necessary, in order to reconcile many who were dissatisfied with the course pursued towards the Quakers by the rulers, to represent them in the most odious and repulsive light, especially as to what was said to be their unbelief in the holy Scriptures, and the doctrines of the gospel therein recorded, slanders of this description were industriously manufactured and propagated throughout the community. To counteract these misrepresentations, to cause the truth to be known, and to take from the persecutors of Friends any such unfounded excuse for their unchristian acts, these three Friends found means to draw up and send forth a document; which, as it is the first declaration of faith published by Friends in America, is given here.

It is entitled : " A Declaration of Faith and an Exhortation to obedience thereto, Issued by Christopher Holder, John Copeland, and Richard Dowdney, while in Prison, at Boston, in New England, 1657.

"Whereas it is reported by them that have not a bridle to their tongues, that we who are by the world called Quakers, are blasphemers, heretics and deceivers, and that we do deny the Scriptures, and the truths therein contained : therefore, We who are here in prison, shall in a few words, in 'truth and plainness, declare unto all people that may see this, the ground of our religion and the faith that we contend for, and the cause wherefor we suffer. Therefore, when you read our words, let the meek spirit bear rule, and weigh them in the equal balance, and stand out of prejudice, in the Light that judgeth all things, and measureth and manifesteth all things.

" We do believe in the only true and living God, the Father of our Lord Jesus Christ; who hath made the heavens and the earth, the sea and all things in them contained, and doth uphold all things that He hath created by the word of his power. Who at sundry times and in divers manners spake in times past to our fathers by the prophets; but in these last days He hath spoken unto us by his Son, whom He hath made heir of all things, and by whom He made the world. The which Son is that Jesus Christ that was born of the Virgin ; who suffered for our offences, and is risen again for our justification, and is ascended into the highest heavens, and sitteth at the right hand of God the Father. Even in Him do we believe; who is the only begotten Son of the Father, full of Grace and Truth. And in Him alone do we trust for salvation ; by whose blood we are washed from sin; through whom we have access to the Father with boldness; being justified by faith in believing in his name. Who hath sent forth the Holy Ghost, to wit, the Spirit of Truth, that proceedeth from the Father and the Son ; by which we are sealed

and adopted sons and heirs of the Kingdom of heaven. From the
which Spirit the Scriptures of truth were given forth, as sayeth the
Apostle Peter. 'Holy men of God spake as they were moved of
the Holy Ghost.' The which were written for our admonition, on
whom the ends of the world are come; and are profitable for the
man of God, to reprove, and to exhort, and to admonish, as the Spirit
of God bringeth them unto him, and openeth them in him, and
giveth him the understanding of them.

"So that before all [men] we do declare that we do believe in
God the Father, Son and Holy Spirit, according as they are declared of in the Scriptures; and the Scriptures we own to be a
true declaration of the Father, Son and Spirit, in [which] is
declared what was in the beginning, what was present, and was to
come.

"Therefore all people in whom honesty is, stand still and consider.
Believe not them that say, Report, and we will report it — that say,
come let us smite them with the tongue; but try all things, and hold
fast that which is good. Again we say, take heed of believing and
giving credit to reports: for know [ye] that the truth in all ages
was spoken against, and they that lived in it, were, in all ages of the
world hated, persecuted and imprisoned, under the name of heretics,
blasphemers," &c. [Here part of the original document is torn
away. Then supposed to be speaking of the Light of Christ, it goes
on] "that showeth you the secrets of your hearts, and the deeds
that are not good. Therefore while you have light, believe in the
light, that you may be the children of the Light. For as you love
it and obey it, it will lead you to repentance, bring you to know
Him in whom is remission of sins; in whom God is well pleased;
who will give you an entrance into the kingdom of God, an inheritance among them that are sanctified. For this is the desire of our
souls for all that have the least breathings after God; that they
may come to know Him in deed and in truth, and find his power
in and with them, to keep them from falling, and to present them
faultless before the throne of his glory: who is the strength and
life of all those who put their trust in Him; who upholdeth all
things by the word of his power; who is God over all, blessed forever, Amen.

"Thus we remain friends to all who fear the Lord; who are sufferers, not for evil doing, but for bearing testimony for the truth, in
obedience to the Lord God of Life; unto whom we commit our
cause; who is risen to plead the cause of the innocent, and to help him

that hath no help on the earth; who will be avenged of all his enemies, and will repay the proud doers.

CHRISTOPHER HOLDER.
JOHN COPELAND.
RICHARD DOWDNEY.

From the House of Correction, in Boston, 1st of 8th month, 1657."

A protest against persecution having been put forth by these Friends, the Ministers and Magistrates were so enraged at it, and at finding that many of their own people were becoming converts to the doctrines of the "cursed sect," that they ordered all Quakers then in prison to be whipped severely twice a week, to begin with fifteen lashes, and to increase three every time the scourge was applied. Finding that their already cruel law against the Quakers, did not prevent their coming into the Colony, when they believed they were required to go there by their divine Master, they in 1658 enacted another; which besides the penalties imposed by the former, made it a penal offence for any one to harbor or conceal a Quaker; for which there was to be exacted £2 for every hour of such concealment or harboring, with imprisonment until it was paid; and every Quaker coming within their jurisdiction, if a man, was for the first offence to have one of his ears cut off, and to be kept in the House of Correction until sent out of the country; and for the second offence to have the other ear taken off, and to be kept closely confined until banished. If a woman, to be severely whipped and kept in prison until sent away; the same to be repeated if she came again. For the third offence—as coming into the country was called—he or she was to have the tongue bored through with a hot iron, and to be imprisoned until sent away. Every one living in the Colony who should become a Quaker, was to be punished in the same manner.*

But notwithstanding the sectarian prejudice and unreasoning opposition that prevailed in many throughout that community, there were not a few who were alarmed for the consequences of the course pursued, and ashamed that such barbarity should be practised among them; while others were affected with compassion for those who suffered so meekly and patiently. The murmurs and complaints became more and more distinctly heard, until at last the Governor and Magistrates thought it prudent to put an end to the scourging, by banishing the three men Friends, and Mary Clark, who had recently come into Boston.

* Blue Laws, Quaker Laws, &c., pages 14, 15.

CHAPTER X.

Connecticut—Humphrey Norton—His Sufferings at New Haven—Unsuccessful Efforts of Massachusetts to induce Rhode Island to follow her Example
— Death of Oliver Cromwell — His Character and Course.— Sufferings of
Friends under the Commonwealth — Statement of G. Fox respecting
Friends — Richard Cromwell — Increased Suffering — Friends offer to lie
in Prison as Substitutes for those there — Address of E. Burrough to the
Rulers — New Netherlands — Robert Hodshone — His dreadful Sufferings
at New Amsterdam — His Release — Remonstrance of Some of the Inhabitants of Long Island — Their Punishment — Friends increase in Number — Meetings Settled — Case of John Bowne — Stop of Persecution in
New Netherlands — Friends in Virginia — Josiah Cole and Thomas Thurston — Course of Episcopalians in Virginia — George Wilson's Sufferings
and Death — Other Ministers Sent —Whipping — Maryland — Persecution
in that Colony — Convincements — Disunity.

THE Colony of Connecticut was an off-shoot of the Pilgrims of
Massachusetts, and they gave ample evidence that they largely
participated in the same spirit that actuated their fellow professors.
Humphrey Norton, a Friend who had spent some months travelling
in Rhode Island, and had also visited Plymouth in the Bay Colony,
whence he was banished, was taken up at Southhold and carried to
New Haven, where he was heavily ironed and imprisoned, without
light or fire, though the weather was cold [1657]. When brought
before the Court one of their ministers charged him with heresy, and
when Humphrey attempted to answer him, a large iron key was
forced into and fastened in his mouth so that he could not speak. He
was then told that when the priest* was finished, he might answer.
But the priest, so soon as he had concluded his charges, went away.
The Court then interrogated him, and remanded him to prison. At
the end of ten days, he was again brought before the Court, which
at once proceeded to sentence him. He was to be first whipped,
then have the letter H burned into his hand, to signify *Heretic*, and
to be banished from the Colony of New Haven. All which was
carried into effect. Thirty-six lashes were applied to his bare back
as he was held fast in the stocks, and the brand burnt deeply. All
this he bore without a complaint, and when he was loosed from the
stocks, he raised his voice in prayer and praise, to the affecting as-
tonishment of the beholders; many of whom expressed their disgust

---

* The title of Priest was then very commonly given to all "regularly
ordained preachers."

at the inhuman treatment and exhibition. The magistrates strove to induce him to pay his fine and the jail expenses, which he refused. A Dutch settler in the Colony, deeply affected with the sufferings of this innocent man, went to the Magistrates, and offered to pay them twenty Nobles if they would let him go, which they gladly accepted. He was sent into Rhode Island.

The Commissioners of the United Colonies in Massachusetts, were incensed at finding that the neighboring Colony of Rhode Island allowed the Quakers to come within and freely travel through it, and forgetting that their intolerance had banished the founders of Rhode Island colony from their own soil, they resolved to apply to it to follow their example, and to pass laws of the same unchristian character as their own, against the Quakers. Accordingly, at their session in 1657, they addressed the Governor of Rhode Island, urging him and the Assembly to proceed in accordance with their wishes. But, to the honor of the latter, they refused; stating that they considered liberty of conscience one of the dearest rights they possessed, and they were unwilling to restrict it in the manner proposed; but if, at any time, they found the Quakers violating the civil law, they would hold them accountable, and punish them the same as others.

In 1658, Oliver Cromwell was suddenly called from works to rewards; after having exercised the high office of Lord Protector of the Commonwealth about ten years. As a military man and a statesman, he certainly was the most remarkable personage of his age and country. Without the title and trappings of royalty, he exercised more absolute power than many kings had dared to assume; and had he pursued the dictates of his conscience, uninfluenced by the intolerant spirit of the mixed party which he used as tools to work his own exaltation, there is little doubt but he would have effected as great and beneficial changes in the ecclesiastical policy of the government, as he did in its civil administration, and its foreign relations. That he was convinced every man had the right to worship according to the dictates of his conscience, he again and again declared; but his ambition betrayed him into the double crime of violating his own sense of right, and of permitting his authority to be used in punishing others, because they could not follow his example, and go contrary to what they believed to be their religious duty. To this he was instigated by many of the popular preachers of the day, who he well knew, wielded a power that could stir up the people to resistance to his usurped government; and who, actuated by lust of place and influence, entertained ill-will against those that questioned their pretensions, or boldly denied their fitness for the duties of the office they assumed. Hence their hatred of Friends, whose religious principles struck at the foundation of ecclesiastical power, and the lawfulness of tithes; and who declared that the gospel should be preached without money and without price. Cromwell feared to offend the priests; and he was aware that the principles of Friends did and would restrain them from any attempt to unsettle his government; and brave as he had been on the battle field, he had not courage to defend or relieve the innocent and non-resistant sufferers, at the expense of offending the clergy. So, while disclaiming wish or right to meddle with the exercise of religious faith, so long as the civil law was not infringed, he allowed cruel persecution to be inflicted in his name for conscientious belief, by men whom he knew made religion but a cloak for the promotion of their own sinister ends.

At the time of Cromwell's death, there were about one hundred and fifty Friends incarcerated in the jails and dungeons of the Commonwealth; many of them put there without trial, and none of them charged with any greater offence than not being willing to swear; not paying tithes; meeting together for the purpose of Divine worship; or some other occasion " concerning the law of their God." Nearly two thousand had grievously suffered prior to the death of Cromwell; of whom twenty-one had died in prison, either from the aggravated abuse inflicted on them, or from long continued confinement in the poisonous atmosphere of those dismal abodes. Beside this, Friends were often despoiled of great portion of their worldly possessions by heavy fines, imposed under one plea or another, and on account of the demands for tithes, which the installed ministers exacted with great severity. But notwithstanding the absence of all legal protection, and the persevering efforts of their adversaries to destroy them as a religious Society, they continued to increase and to become more firmly established; sadly disappointing some of their oppressors, who had predicted their extermination in the course of one or two years.

It must have been a source of heartfelt thankfulness to George Fox, in looking over the comparatively few years that had elapsed since he was first sent forth as a preacher of righteousness, that notwithstanding all the opposition the word of Truth had met with, and the severe ordeal through which those who embraced it had to pass, so many thousands had already been convinced and converted; and that the Lord on high was showing that his protecting arm was underneath and round about them; that He was not only bearing them up above the raging waves of men's passion and oppression, but was causing their uprightness and conscientiousness to receive a reward even in this life. George says [1653], "At the first con- vincement, when Friends could not put off their hats to people, nor say You to a single person, but Thou and Thee, or could not bow, nor use flattering words in salutations, nor go into the fashions and customs of the world, many Friends, that were tradesmen, lost their customers; for the people were shy of them, and would not trade with them; so that for a time some could hardly get money enough to buy bread. But afterwards, when people came to have experience of Friends' honesty and faithfulness, and found that their Yea was Yea, and their Nay was Nay; that they kept to a word in their deal- ings, and that they would not cozen and cheat them; but that if they sent a child to their shops for anything, they were as well used as if they had come themselves; the lives and conversations of Friends did preach, and reached to the witness of God in the people. Then things altered so, that all the inquiry was, 'Where was a draper, or shop-keeper, or tailor, or shoemaker, or any other tradesman, that was a Quaker?' Insomuch that Friends had more business than many of their neighbors; and if there was any trading, they had a great part of it. Then the envious professors altered their note, and began to cry out, 'If we let these Quakers alone, they will take the trade of the nation out of our hands.' This hath been the Lord's doings to and for his people! which my desire is, that all who pro- fess his holy truth may be truly kept sensible of; and that all may be preserved in and by his power and Spirit, faithful to God and man: first to God, in obeying him in all things; and then in doing unto all men that which is just and righteous, in all things that they have to do or deal with them in: that the Lord God may be glorified in their practising truth, holiness, godliness, and righteous- ness amongst people, in their lives and conversations."

Parliament had conferred on Cromwell the power to name his successor, and shortly before his death he had nominated his son Richard; who accordingly was installed as Protector, and the gov- ernment seemed but little disturbed by the change. It soon became apparent, however, that the son possessed neither the talents, the energy, nor the influence, which had enabled his father to play one party against another, and to keep the army ever ready to enforce the will and policy of its favorite head and leader. Party animosity manifested itself with a violence that before had been kept in check; and Generals, Republicans and Royalists respectively, eagerly sought the opportunity to effect the establishment of their own power; and it soon became apparent that some revolution must ere long take place, that would put the reins of government into more competent hands.

In the meantime the sufferings of Friends were continually on the increase, and though R. Cromwell expressed his unwillingness that it should be so, and his desire to afford relief, the power of the intolerant Parliament was too great to allow him to carry out his wishes. Friends in London were indefatigable in their efforts to obtain relief for their brethren, who were shut up in prison throughout the country. They petitioned the Parliament, presenting a statement of the several cases of suffering, which were then crying for relief, and the alleged causes of complaint against them. Finding that the hearts of the members were too greatly hardened, by bigotry and prejudice, to be moved by their representations or their importunity, they gave an affecting proof of their Christian love for their brethren, and the unselfish motives that prompted the solicitation for their release from the jails where they were held in bondage, by presenting to Parliament a printed paper, signed by one hundred and sixty-four Friends, offering themselves as substitutes, body for body, to take the places of their brethren or sisters, in different places of confinement, who were sick or in danger of losing their lives, from being so long subjected to prison life and fare. This, however, was equally unsuccessful, and three of the petitioners being brought before the House, the Speaker reprimanded them for the " scandal " their statements cast on magistracy, and bid them go home, mind their business, and submit themselves to the laws of the nation and its magistrates [1659].

E. Burrough now wrote a long and plain-spoken address to the "Rulers of the Nation," whoever they were; in which, after pointing out the unchristian course that had been pursued by those who had borne rule in England for a long course of years, the dishonor that had been brought on truth and righteousness thereby, the superstition and idolatry of the people, and the calamities that had overtaken the nation therefor; the persecution of the righteous now going on, and their unpitied sufferings, he boldly tells them, that unless they stop in their career and repent of their doings, "Your estates shall not be spared from the spoiler, nor your necks from the axe: your enemies shall charge treason upon you, and if you seek to stop the Lord's work, you will not cumber the earth very long:" which was not long in being fulfilled.

Before any further recitation of the sufferings of Friends in the Colonies of Massachusetts and Connecticut, it may be well to refer to an instance of like suffering in the Dutch settlement of New Amsterdam. Cases of unmitigated cruelty in the two forementioned Colonies are too numerous, for reference to be made within this limited narrative, to any but some of the more conspicuous; brought forward rather to exhibit the religious constancy of the sufferers, than to expose the persecuting spirit of the rulers and ministers.

In 1657, a Friend named Robert Hodshone, being at Hamstead, in the settlement of New Netherlands, had a meeting with some of the English living there. He was arrested, and taken before a mag-. istrate, who committed him to prison; his knife, Bible and papers being taken away from him, and he pinioned. On the day but one after, two women who had entertained him were arrested and put into a cart, to the tail of which Robert, still pinioned, was fastened, and thus drawn through the woods in the dark to New Amsterdam, the chief town, where he arrived much bruised and torn. Loosed from the cart, he was led by the rope to a filthy dungeon, into which he was thrust. Being brought before Stuyvesant the Governor, without being allowed to make a defence or explanation, his sentence was read to him in Dutch; which was, That he should work two years at the wheel-barrow, with a negro, or pay a fine of six hundred dollars. He was then put back into the dungeon; where none were allowed to come to him who could speak English. The next day, on being brought out of the dungeon, he was chained to a wheel-barrow, and commanded to work in repairing the walls of the town. Feeling himself restrained from this, he declined; whereupon a negro slave was ordered to beat him with a tarred rope. This was done; the fellow beating him until he fainted and fell to the ground. The Sheriff, who superintended the horrid work, bid the negro to raise him up and renew the flogging, which he did; continuing the blows until he again fainted and fell. Failing thus to make him work, the Sheriff conducted him to the Governor, who was in the fort, and complained of Robert's obstinacy. He was kept in the sun throughout the remainder of the day, the burning heat of which acting on his lacerated and bruised body, which had received no sustenance for many hours, caused him again to faint away; but he says, that his mind was "stayed upon the Lord," who sweetly refreshed him. He was closely confined in the dungeon for about a week, when the Governor, who was greatly incensed at his not submitting to his will, had him brought out, and ordered him to be stripped to the waist, to be drawn up by the hands from the ground and weights attached to his feet, and as thus suspended to be severely beaten with rods. This• unmerciful sentence having been executed, he was again thrust into the dungeon, and kept two days and nights without food, when it was demanded of him to pay his fine; which he refused. The urgent petition of the poor sufferer, that some of his own country people might be allowed to come to him, was at last granted, and a kind-hearted English woman came, who dressed his wounds and administered to his wants; though she thought he could hardly survive many hours. Having informed her husband of the deplorable condition of the prisoner, he went to the Governor and offered him a fatted ox if he would allow him to bring Robert to his house, that he might be properly nursed. The hard-hearted Governor refused to permit any change, unless the whole sum of six hundred dollars was raised. When the people learned this unfeeling decision, they at once set about raising the money, which, however, Robert declined accepting, though sensible of their kindness. He believed that the Lord would heal his mangled body, and restore his strength, so that he could work enough in the prison to pay for his board.

It being discovered that one Captain Willett, from Massachusetts, had instigated the cruel treatment of R. Hodshone, the people gave him to understand they greatly disapproved of his conduct. Finding how he had discredited himself, in the hope of removing the odium, he applied to the Governor to forego further punishment, and let the prisoner go. This application was seconded by Stuyvesant's sister, whose feelings had been deeply touched by the torture inflicted on the patient sufferer, and moved by the representations of the two, and the known disapprobation by many of the people of the intolerance manifested, he finally consented to Robert's release, without his paying any portion of the fine. He was discharged about the middle of the Seventh month; and then pursued his religious labors in Rhode Island.

Many of the settlers on Long Island having become favorable to the principles of Friends, one of them was fined £12 upon a charge of having assisted R. Hodshone in holding a religious meeting. This, together with a law enacted, imposing a fine of £50 on any one receiving a Quaker into his house, so offended the inhabitants of the island, that they forwarded to the Governor a remonstrance against it, signed by the Sheriff, town clerk, and a number of citizens convened at a town meeting. On this being presented, Stuyvesant was highly indignant, and the Council being convened, warrants were issued for the Sheriff and town clerk, who were brought to New Amsterdam and thrown into prison; where they were kept for a considerable time, and then allowed to leave the jail, but not the town. Several others were arrested and fined heavily, especially those who were thought to favor " the abominable sect of Quakers." Thomas Tilton was one of those fined £12 for "having dared to provide a Quaker woman with lodging, who had been banished out of the province."

But the testimony borne by Friends to the spirituality of the Christian religion; to the perceptible inward manifestation of the Spirit of Christ, and its transforming work in the soul; to the necessity of taking up the cross daily, and walking in the straight and narrow way of self-denial; to the disuse of forms and ceremonies, and against the unauthorized assumption of the priesthood in things pertaining to the church of Christ, and the meek and unresisting spirit in which they bore the indignities and cruel abuses heaped upon them, appealed too forcibly to the Witness for Truth in the breasts of hearers and beholders, to fail of convincing many tender-hearted people that they were preachers of righteousness; commissioned by the Head of the church to proclaim the word of reconciliation to those who were sitting in darkness and the shadow of death. Notwithstanding the anathemas hurled against the Quakers, and the certainty of suffering if numbered with them, many joined the Society in Long Island, and in the years 1658 and 1659, several meetings were settled along the western part of the island.

The persecution of Friends in New Amsterdam was put an end to by the home government. John Bowne having become convinced of the truth of Friends' principles, not only openly avowed his religious belief, but opened his house for holding a meeting. For this he was fined £25. Refusing to pay, he was thrown into the dungeon in the town, and there kept without food or water until nearly famished; but as his constancy failed not, and the Master whom he served, upheld him above the malice of his enemies, the Governor resolved to banish him. He was told that unless he paid the fine within three months, he should be torn from his wife and children and sent to Holland. As he could not be brought to deny his religion, he was, in the 10th month of 1663, put on board a vessel, which conveyed him to Holland; a statement of his case being also forwarded. Upon hearing the circumstances of his conduct and treatment from the sufferer himself, the home Government, which was altogether tolerant in regard to religious belief, at once reversed his sentence, and wrote to the Governor and Council, ordering them to allow all such to be unmolested.

The first visit made by a Friend to Virginia appears to have been in 1656, when Elizabeth Harris arrived there, and as there was, at the time, no obstruction thrown in the way of her gospel labors, she was instrumental in convincing several, of the sound scriptural doctrines she preached, and of the necessity to conform in life and conversation thereto. One of her converts, named Robert Clarkson, was a man of superior character and influence, and on him devolved much of the religious exercise and care connected with the little community of Friends planted in Virginia.

Josiah Cole and Thomas Thurston, who had long been engaged in religious service in their own country (England), felt themselves called to go into Virginia, in order to spread among the people there a knowledge of what they believed to be the truth as it is in Jesus, in its simplicity and spirituality. They accordingly embarked and arrived there in 1658. But that Colony had been settled principally by Episcopalians, in whose hands the power of the government was lodged. Finding that some of the settlers had adopted the principles of Friends, and fearing that their peculiar doctrines and testimonies would spread, and their own religious forms and ceremonies thereby be called in question and perhaps abandoned, the dominant sect resolved to imitate the persecutors in New England, to pass a law for the banishment of Friends, and to make it felony for any thus sent away to return. This was done in 1658. The rulers had, prior to the deposition of Charles I., prohibited any minister to preach or teach within their limits, unless in conformity with the rites and belief of the church of England. This was to prevent any of the Puritans settling among them. But during the time of the Commonwealth this law was not regarded, and toleration of differences in religious profession was observed, until the action taken against Friends.

It is not certain whether Josiah Cole and Thomas Thurston, while in Virginia, on their first visit, met with much opposition or not, but after they left, and had travelled through the wilderness from that colony to Rhode Island, suffering many hardships in their perilous journey, T. Thurston believed it right for him to return to Virginia. He had not been there long, before he was imprisoned and kept confined for a considerable length of time. The Governor finally released him, and allowed him to hold some meetings, at which there were many convinced.

After the restoration of Charles II. to the throne, the Episcopalians revived their intolerant policy, and George Wilson, of Cumberland, having gone to Virginia in 1661, he was thrust into a loathsome dungeon at Jamestown, was most mercilessly scourged, and then put in irons. He was thus kept, without light or fresh air, until his flesh actually rotted off the bones, and he laid down his life, a martyr for Christ and the testimony of His truth. While suffering this lingering death, he penned several "precious writings," which manifested the lamb-like spirit he cherished; so that he declared, when speaking of his persecutors, "For all their cruelty, I can truly say, Father, forgive them, they know not what they do."

Previous to this hostile attitude being generally adopted, the feet of several gospel messengers had been turned towards that province; among whom were Christopher Holder, Robert Hodshone and William Robinson, who visited there in 1658. In 1660, Josiah Cole was laboriously engaged there during a second visit; and in 1661, George Rolfe, Elizabeth Hooten — who was the first woman minister in the Society — with Joan Brocksoppe, were engaged as gospel ministers among the settlers, and do not appear to have been arrested. The effectual preaching of these dedicated servants, as well as of some others who arrived in the country near the close of that year, was blessed to a considerable number; who were convinced of the truth of the doctrine they set forth, and became prepared to join in membership with the Society.

Unrestrained by the deplorable consequences which they saw had before resulted from their unchristian policy, the Governor and Council of Virginia, in 1662, imposed heavy fines on all who should be "So filled with the newfangled conceits of their own heretical inventions, as to refuse to have their children baptized," and all ship-masters were forbidden, on pain of banishment, to bring any non-conformists into the colony. John Porter, one of the representatives, was expelled from the Assembly, in 1663, "because he was well affected to the Quakers."

In 1663, Mary Tomkins and Alice Ambrose, having come into

the Colony and entered upon the religious service required of them, strengthening the hands of those who professed with Friends, and spreading a knowledge of their doctrines, were after some time arrested, and subjected to the infliction of "Thirty-two stripes" with a "nine-corded whip." Afterwards their goods were seized, and they expelled beyond the limits of the Colony.

It has been before mentioned, that when Josiah Cole and Thomas Thurston set out, after their first visit to Virginia, for Rhode Island, they travelled through the intervening wilderness; in which journey they necessarily passed through Maryland; where the settlers were very sparsely located. Their association was principally with the Indians; but this was the first visit of any Friend to that province. Towards the close of 1658, Thomas Thurston returned into Maryland in order to discharge a duty he felt laid upon him, to hold religious meetings among those who were residing there, and bring them to a knowledge of the practical effects of believing in and obeying the Light of Christ manifested to the soul.

Reports respecting Friends and the doctrines they held, had reached the inhabitants of that colony, and as usual, they were grossly misrepresented; so that notwithstanding the unsectarian policy of Lord Baltimore, so strong a prejudice had been excited against them, that when it was known T. Thurston was a minister among the dreaded Quakers, and that he was there to propagate their doctrines and testimonies, it produced no small excitement; and the Court, moved by the clamor and apprehension, lent its aid to the persecuting spirit of the time, had him arrested, and sentenced him to imprisonment "for a year and a day." Those in authority also passed a law imposing fines on any who received or entertained Quakers. Under this law four Friends were fined, and another was cruelly whipped "for not assisting to apprehend" T. Thurston.

But the authorities in Maryland, as in other places, soon learned, that wherever a belief of religious duty called Friends, they dare not flinch from its performance, let the consequences be what they might. In 1659 William Robinson, Christopher Holder, and Robert Hodshone came into the province. Among the scattered settlers — none of whom then resided in towns — there were many who, having long had their attention turned to the subject of religion, and not deriving much benefit from the little teaching or preaching to which they had access, were in measure prepared to receive the truths of primitive Christianity, as they heard them set forth in convincing power, by these gospel messengers. There were, therefore, a considerable number who joined in the religious profession with Friends.

Political disturbances having occurred, during which the power of Lord Baltimore was set aside, there was no further effort made during that time to enforce the law against Friends. When, however, after the restoration of Charles II., Lord Baltimore's authority over the province was again established, a trial of a different kind came upon the Friends. A strict militia law was enacted, with heavy fines imposed on those who did not serve, and on those who would not take the oaths enjoined. The accounts preserved, instance thirty Friends from whom property to the amount of £172 4s. 9d. was taken in 1658 and 1659, on account of militia fines; and from twelve who were fined for not swearing, £80.

It is probable that the suffering thus inflicted on persons who had recently settled in the wilderness country, had proved more than the faith of some in their newly adopted principles enabled them to bear; for J. Cole, who was there in 1660 on his second visit, writes, that he found the harmony that ought to exist among Friends had been interrupted, by some who " run into words without life," and others who "judged rashly." This breach in harmony he was greatly instrumental in healing. In 1662 twenty-three Friends, who during the two previous years had allowed their names to be enrolled among the militia, being now fully convinced that all war was contrary to the gospel of Christ, declined to sanction the proceeding any longer, and each was fined 500 lbs. of tobacco.

Religious intolerance now manifested itself again, and Josiah Cole was banished the province. But he had not been long expelled, before five other ministering Friends arrived; and the more enlightened views of Lord Baltimore and his counsellors in England, were in course of time brought to bear on the colonial rulers, and all traces of persecution on account of religious belief ceased to be found on their records.

The first planting and spread of Friends and their principles in New Jersey, Pennsylvania and North Carolina did not occur until some years after their introduction in the other provinces mentioned, and reference will be made to those colonies when further on.

CHAPTER XI.

Dread in New England of the Spread of Quakerism — Action of Court of Plymouth — Sarah Gibbons and Dorothy Waugh — William Leddra—William Brend's Dreadful Suffering—Fear of Endicott—Excuse of the Minister —Cutting off Ears—State of things in New Plymouth—Meetings — Spread of Friends' principles—Transportation ordered—Banishment on pain of Death —A few frightened by it.— William Robinson and Marmaduke Stevenson — Patience Scott—Mary Dyer— Trial for Life —Execution of two Friends—Reprieve of M. Dyer—Return, Trial and Execution of M. Dyer —J. Nicholson and Wife.

CIRCUMSTANCES of a tragical character connected with Friends, having taken place in Massachusetts prior to the restoration of Charles II., notice will be taken of them before returning to affairs in Great Britain

The alarming evidence of the spread of "The Quaker Contagion," —as the Puritans of New England designated the reception of the principles of Friends—among the inhabitants of Massachusetts, induced the Court, at Plymouth, in 1657, as has been already mentioned, to imitate that of Boston, by enacting a law to prevent any one entertaining a Quaker, under a penalty of £5; for default in the payment of which fine, the offender was to be whipped.

There were now fifteen ministering Friends within the limits of New England, exclusive of those in Rhode Island, and the number of converts had so greatly increased, that it was said the greater part of the town of Sandwich had joined with Friends. Sarah Gibbons and Dorothy Waugh, who were engaged in a religious service in Rhode Island, feeling it required of them to visit the town of Salem, in Massachusetts, although it was winter, and snow on the ground, started on foot, and walked the whole distance of ninety miles; carrying what was needful with them, and lodging under such shelter as they could procure in the wilderness. Having, by the providence of their almighty Preserver, arrived and delivered their message, it was gladly received by many. When clear there, they went to Boston, where they were soon thrust into its jail, and shortly after dreadfully whipped, in public, with a three-corded knotted scourge, which mangled their backs deeply. When this was over, their tormentors and the people around, were astonished to hear them vocally offer thanksgiving and praise to their heavenly Father, for the help of His sustaining presence in the midst of their sufferings. They were again thrust into the prison, where, as the jailer told them, he should keep them for his fees, it is uncertain how long they would have been kept, had not a kind-hearted person from Rhode Island paid the jailer's demand, and thus set them at liberty.

1658. William Leddra and William Brend having been arrested at Newburyport, were examined by the magistrates there, who, after close interrogation and the clear unequivocal answers of the Friends, honestly confessed they could not detect anything unsound or heretical in their opinions; but as they were Quakers it was required they should be sent to Boston, which was accordingly done. Here they were separated and each put into a cell, the window of which was closely shut up so as to exclude both light and air. As they declined complying with the jailer's terms for food, he starved them for five days, and then brought a little food for them to see, hoping the cravings of appetite would induce them to comply. Finding this did not move them, they were subjected to severe whipping, and told they might liberate themselves by paying the fees and the expenses of a Marshal to accompany them out of the colony. William Brend was then about seventy years of age, but not regarding this additional claim against cruelty, the jailer fastened an iron ring around his neck and a fetter to each ankle, and by main strength drew his feet and neck so close together as to admit only the lock that fastened the two shackles together to be between them, and left him lying in this dreadfully painful condition for sixteen hours. On releasing the old man on the following morning the jailer ordered him to work, with which, William not feeling it would be right for him to comply, the infuriated man commenced beating him with a tarred rope, an inch in thickness, " over his back and arms, with all his strength," and again thrust his bruised and torn body into his dismal cell. In the afternoon of the same day, the jailer again ordered him to work; which he could not have done had he been willing, but as he declined, the enraged man again began beating him with a similar rope, and continued his barbarous labor until his own strength gave out, inflicting on him at that time ninety-seven blows, and then left him with a threat that he would return in the morning to give him as many more. William had now been five days without food, his body had been racked by the unnatural position into which it had been dragged and thus kept for sixteen hours, and his flesh had been torn and beaten into a jelly by the repeated scourgings he had received from the hands of his tormentor. When, therefore, the jailer came to his unventilated cell in the morning, he found him cold, and apparently sinking into death. Alarmed lest he might be charged with having murdered his prisoner, he informed Endicott, the Governor, of his condition, and a physician was sent to see whether anything could be done to prevent their poor victim from dying on their hands. After examining him the physician reported it was impossible to restore him and that he must die, for his flesh was so torn and bruised it would rot from the bones. When this came to be known by the citizens their indignation was aroused, and it appeared probable there would be a tumult. Endicott, with the meanness that often attends a cruel disposition, now endeavored to extricate himself from blame, by shifting it all on to the jailer; and to appease the people he issued a hand-bill, declaring that this official should be summoned to the next Court to answer for his conduct.

But John Norton, the principal "minister of the gospel" in Boston, was not willing to admit there had any wrong been done, and he publicly declared he would defend the jailer; for he said, as William Brend had "endeavored to beat the gospel ordinances black and blue, it was but just to beat him black and blue;" logic that was worthy of the man and the occasion. He also threatened that if "they dealt with him [the jailer] he would leave them." But the Lord dealt marvellously with his dedicated servant, and contrary to all expectation restored him to health and soundness, so that he was enabled, without yielding to the demands of his persecutors, to go forth, and again engage in publishing the glad tidings of salvation to the people.

John Rouse, Christopher Holder and John Copeland, after having been repeatedly whipped in the Boston prison, because they were Friends, and would not stay away from that town when they believed themselves called by their divine Master to go there, were, on the 7th of the Seventh month, 1658, brought into the Court, and sentenced, each to have his right ear cut off. This savage sentence was executed privately in the prison. Sewel gives the following account of it: —"Then they were carried to the prison, and on the 16th of September, the Marshal's deputy came thither, letting as many come in as he thought meet; and when the doors were made fast, the Marshal read the following order:

" To the Marshal-general, or to his deputy : You are to take with you the executioner, and repair to the house of correction, and there see him cut off the right ears of John Copeland, Christopher Holder and John Rouse, Quakers; in execution of the sentence of the Court of Assistants, for the breach of the law entitled Quakers.

EDWARD RAWSON, Secretary."

" Then the prisoners were brought into another room, where John Rouse said to the Marshal, ' We have appealed to the chief magis- trate of England.' To which he answered, he had nothing to do with that. Holder said, " Such execution as this should be done publicly, and not in private: for this was contrary to the law of England.' But Captain Oliver replied, ' We do it in private to keep you from tattling.' Then the executioner took Holder, and when he had turned aside his hair, and was going to cut off his ear, the Marshal turned his back on him, which made Rouse say, ' Turn about and see it; for so was his order.' The Marshal then, though filled with fear, turned and said, ' Yes, yes, let us look on it.' Rouse, who was more undaunted than his persecutor, suffered the like, as did also the third, and they said, ' Those that do it ignorantly, we desire from our hearts the Lord to forgive them ; but for them that do it maliciously, let our blood be upon their heads ; and such shall know in the day of account, that every drop of our blood shall be as heavy upon them as a millstone.' " They were afterwards whipped and sent out of the colony.

"JOHN ROUSE TO MARGARET FELL.

" Dearly Beloved Sister, M. F.—About the last of the Sixth month, 1657, I came from Barbadoes with another Friend, an inhabitant of the island ; and, according to the appointment of the Father, landed on Rhode Island in the beginning of the Eighth month, on an out part of the island ; and being come thither, I heard of the arrival of Friends from England ; which was no small refreshment to me. After I had been there a little while, I passed out of the island into Plymouth Patent, to Sandwich, and several other towns thereabouts ; where, in the winter time, more service was done than was expected. Some time after, I was in Connecticut with John Copeland, where the Lord gave us no small dominion, for there we met with one of the greatest disputers of New England, who is priest of Hartford, who was much confounded, to the glory of truth and to his shame. After some stay there, we returned to Rhode Island, where Hum- phrey Norton was, and after some time, he and I went into Plymouth Patent, and they having a Court while we were there, we went to the place where it was; having sent before to the Governor the grounds of our coming; but we were straightway put in prison, and after twice being before them, where we were much railed at, they judged us to be whipped. Humphrey Norton received twenty-three stripes, and I fifteen with rods, which did prove much for the advantage of truth and their disadvantage; for Friends did with much boldness own us openly in it, and it did work deeply with many. After we were let forth thence, we returned to Rhode Island, and after some stay there we went to Providence, and from thence to Boston, to bear witness in a few words in their meeting-house, against their worship, till they haled us forth and had us to their house of correction, and that evening we were examined and committed to prison. On the Seventh-day, in the evening, they whipped us with ten stripes each, with a three-fold whip, to conclude a wicked week's work, which was this: on the Second-day, they whipped six Friends; on the Third-day, the jailer laid William Brend (a Friend that came from London), neck and heels, as they call it, in irons for sixteen hours; on the Fourth-day, the jailer gave William Brend one hundred and seventeen strokes with a pitched rope; on the Fifthday, they imprisoned us; and on the Seventh-day we suffered. The beating of William Brend did work much in the town, and for a time much liberty was granted; for several people came to us in the prison; but the enemies, seeing the forwardness and love in the people toward us, plotted, and a warrant was given forth that, if we would not work, we should be whipped once in every three days, and the first time have fifteen stripes, the second eighteen, and the third time twenty-one. So on the Second-day after our first whipping, four of us received fifteen stripes each; the which did so work with the people, that on the Fourth-day after we were released. We returned to Rhode Island, and continued there awhile, and after some time, Humphrey Norton went into Plymouth Patent to Friends there, and I was moved to come to Boston; so that, that day five weeks [after], I was released; at night I was put in again. There were Christopher Holder and John Copeland, two of the Friends which came from England; and we do lie here, according to their law, to have each of us an ear cut off; but we are kept in the dominion of God, and our enemies are under our feet. It is reported that we shall be tried at a Court that is to be held next week, and if the ship do not go away from hence before then, thou shalt hear further how it is ordered for us (if God permit). There was a great lamenting for me by many when I came again, but they were not minded by me; I was much tempted to say, I came to the town to take shipping to go to Barbadoes, but I could not deny Him who moved me to come hither, nor his service, to avoid sufferings. This relation, in short, I have given thee, that thou might know how it hath fared with me since I came into this land. About five weeks since, six Friends,* having done their service here, took shipping for Barbadoes; two whereof were to go to Virginia and Maryland, two for London, and the other two were inhabitants of Barbadoes; so that there are only four of us in the land.

" Dear Sister, truth is spread here above two hundred miles, and many are in fine conditions, and very sensible of the power of God, and walk honestly in their measures. Some of the inhabitants of the land who are Friends have been forth in the service, and they do more grieve the enemy than we; for they have hoped to be rid of us, but they have no hope to be rid of them. .. . . . One of the inhabitants of Salem was whipped three times in five days, once to fulfil their law, and twice for refusing to work; after eleven days' imprisonment he was let forth, and hath gotten much strength by his sufferings. Great have been the sufferings of Friends in this land, but generally they suffer with much boldness and courage, both the spoiling of their goods, and the abusing of their bodies. There are Friends, few or more, almost from one end of the land to the other, that is inhabited by the English. A firm foundation there is laid in this land, such an one as the devil will never get broken up. If thou art free to write to me, thou may direct thy letter to be sent to Barbadoes for me; so in that which is eternal do I remain, thy brother, in my measure, who suffers for the Seed's sake, earnestly thirsting for the prosperity and peace of Zion, the City of the living God.   JOHN ROUSE.

From a Lion's Den called Boston Prison,
      this 3d day of the Seventh month, 1658.

" My dear fellow-prisoners, John Copeland and Christopher Holder, do dearly salute thee. Salute me dearly in the Lord to thy children, and the rest of thy family who are in the truth."

As has been mentioned each suffered the loss of an ear.
John Rouse was the son of a rich planter in Barbadoes; both

* These doubtless were William Leddra, and Thomas Harris, of Barbadoes, and William Brend, Richard Hodgson, Dorothy Waugh, and Sarah Gibbons. The four left in New England being Humphrey Norton, John Copeland, Christopher Holder, and John Rouse.

father and son having joined Friends from convincement. He appears to have been entrusted with a gift in the ministry very early in life, and was evidently quite young when travelling and suffering in New England. He afterwards married a daughter of Margaret Fell, and settled in London, carrying on the business of a merchant and trading to Barbadoes. John Copeland was likewise a young and unmarried man, a native of Yorkshire. He spent between two and three years in America, and sometime after returning home, he married and was settled in London. Christopher Holder came out of Gloucester. He twice crossed the Atlantic to America, having suffered imprisonment in his native land on account of his religious principles. He, like the others of that band of the Lord's missionaries, continued faithful, notwithstanding the persecution he had to endure.

That the same intolerance and cruel persecution as was manifested by the Court of Boston, was closely copied by the colony at New Plymouth, the following extracts from a letter, written by James Cudworth, who had been a Magistrate of that settlement, and a Captain or commissioned officer in the military, will serve to show. It is given in Gough's History.

1659. " As for the state and condition of things amongst us it is sad and like so to continue; the antichristian, persecuting spirit is very active. He that will not whip, persecute and punish men that differ in matters of religion, must not sit on the bench, nor sustain any office in the Commonwealth. Last election Mr. Hatherly and myself were left off the bench, and I was discharged of my captainship because I had entertained some of the Quakers at my house, that I might be the better acquainted with their principles. I thought it better to do so, than with the blind world to censure, condemn, rail at, and revile them, when they neither saw their persons nor knew any of their principles; but the Quakers and myself cannot close in divers things; and so I signified to the Court I was no Quaker—but withal told them, that as I was no Quaker, so I would be no persecutor. This spirit did work the two years that I was in the magistracy; during which time I was on sundry occasions forced to declare my dissent in sundry actings of that nature, which though done with all moderation and due respect, yet wrought great disaffection and prejudice in them against me, and produced a petition to the Court against me, signed with nineteen hands; which was followed by another in my favor signed with fifty-four hands. The Court returned in answer to the last petition that they acknowledged my parts and gifts, and professed they had nothing against me, only in the thing of my giving entertainment to the Quakers; though I broke no law in so doing, for our law then was, *If any entertain a Quaker, and keep him after he is warned by a magistrate to depart, he shall pay* 20s. *a week for entertaining him.* But since that a law hath been made, *That if any entertain a* Quaker, *though but a quarter of an hour, he shall forfeit* £5. Another, *That if any see a* Quaker, *he is bound, though he lives six miles or more from a constable, to give immediate notice to him, or else be subject to the censure of the Court.* Another, *That if the Constable know or hear of any* Quaker *in his precincts, he is presently to apprehend him, and if he will not presently depart the town, to whip and send him away.* Divers have been whipped within our patent; and truly, to tell you plainly, the whipping of them with that cruelty, as some of them have been whipped, and their patience under it, hath sometimes been the occasion of gaining more adherents to them, than if they had suffered them openly to have preached a sermon.

"Another law made against the *Quakers* is, That if there be a Quakers' meeting any where in this Colony, the party in whose house or on whose ground it is, shall pay 40s., the preacher 40s., and every hearer 40s. Our last law is — That the Quakers are to be apprehended, and carried before a Magistrate, and by him committed to close prison till they will promise to depart, and never come again, and will also pay their fees (neither of which they will ever do), and they must be kept only with the country allowance (which is coarse bread and water). No friend may bring them any thing, nor be permitted to speak to them; nay, if they have money of their own, they may not make use of it to relieve themselves.

"All these carnal and antichristian ways being not of God's appointment, effect nothing as to the obstructing or hindering them in their way or course. It is only the word and spirit of the Lord that is able to convince gainsayers; these are the mighty weapons of a Christian's warfare, by which mighty things are done and accomplished.

"The Quakers have many meetings and many adherents, almost the whole town of Sandwich is adhering to them. The sufferings are grievous to, and sadden the hearts of, most of the pious and virtuous part of this Commonwealth; it lies down and rises up with them, and they cannot put it out of their minds. The Massachusetts have banished six on pain of death, and I wish that blood may not be shed. Our poor people are pillaged and plundered of their goods, and haply when they have no more to satisfy the insatiable desire of their persecutors, may be forced to fly, and glad to have their lives for a prey.

"The means whereby they are impoverished, are their scrupling an oath, and for their meetings. It being found that they had a conscientious scruple against swearing, all were called upon to take the oath of fidelity; which they refusing, a clause was added, That if any man refused or neglected to take it by such a time, he should pay £5 or depart the Colony. They are required to take the oath again at every successive Court, and as they cannot, they are distrained over and over again. On this account thirty-five head of cattle, as I have been credibly informed, have been by the authority of our Court taken from them the latter part of this summer.

"The last Court of Assistants — the Court was pleased to determine fines on Sandwich men for meetings £150, whereof William Newland is charged £24 for himself and wife; William Allen £46, and a poor weaver £20. Brother Cook told me, one of the brethren was in the house, when the Marshal came to demand the money, when all that he was worth did not amount to £10. What will be the end of such courses or practices the Lord only knows!

"Our civil powers are so exercised in matters of religion and conscience, that we have no time to do anything that tends to promote the civil prosperity of the place. We must now have a State religion, such as the powers of this world will allow, and no other; a State ministry and a State way of maintenance, and we must worship and serve the Lord Jesus as the world shall appoint us; we must all go to the public place of meeting in the parish where we dwell, or be presented. I am informed of three or four score last Court, presented for not coming to public meetings, at ten shillings a time.

"We are wrapped up in a labyrinth of confused laws, that the freemen's power is quite gone. Sandwich men may not go to the bay, lest they be taken up for Quakers. William Newland was there about his occasions ten days ago, and they put him in prison twenty-four hours, and sent for divers to witness against him, but had not proof enough to make him a Quaker, which if they had, he should have been whipped; nay, they may not go about their occasions in other towns in our colony, but warrants lie in ambush to apprehend and bring them before a Magistrate, to give an account of their business.

JAMES CUDWORTH."

The faithful labors and exemplary suffering of these messengers of glad tidings, continued to be not in vain; a large number in the different provinces were gathered into the Society, and meetings were settled at different points. In Rhode Island, where the spirit of Christianity was manifested by the absence of persecution, there were two large meetings, one at Newport and one at Providence; the Governor, William Coddington, having joined with Friends, likewise Nicholas Easton, who also had filled that office; there were also Friends in places more interior. In Salem, Massachusetts, at least eighteen families had become members. At Sandwich most of the inhabitants were convinced of the principles of the gospel as held by Friends, and openly professed them. At Scituate and at Hampton, both small settlements, their principles had found entrance to the hearts of not a few of the inhabitants, who were thus prepared to manifest kindness to and approbation of those gospel ministers who were sent among them. Those who joined Friends, in those places where the ruling powers were determined, if possible, to destroy them, or at least to prevent the introduction of their doctrines and testimonies within their jurisdiction, soon had the sincerity of their profession put to the test. Fines, imprisonment and stripes were lavishly employed to punish those who dared avow the religion their consciences approved, and to deter others from following their example. But still the work went on; strength and courage were given to bear afflictions for Christ's sake; and He also raised up and qualified ministers among them, who strengthened the faith of the believers, and preaching righteousness by life and conversation, as well as by word of mouth, drew others to come and have fellowship with them. The Courts at Boston and Plymouth condemned several who absented themselves from the "stated meetings," and assembled together to worship after the manner of Friends, to be transported to Virginia or one of the West India islands, and be sold for slaves; but to the honor of the captains of the vessels, be it recorded, there was no one then found willing to be instrumental in carrying out the barbarous edict; and so it had to be given up.

Doubtless it was a source of great mortification to the self-esteem, as well as provocative of the jealousy of the Magistrates, and others in authority at Boston, to find their imperious award of such severe punishment for the Quakers coming or springing up among them, had had the effect rather to excite commiseration in the hearts of the people, and thus to open the door for the reception of their principles, than to keep them out of the Colony. It was specially grating

to the " ministers," to find many of the people calling their authority
and religious standing in question, and siding with a people whom
they denounced as a " cursed sect."

The different classes of Puritans were noted for the submission
and reverence they showed towards their ministers; prompting
reliance on them not only in spiritual matters and the government
of the church, but to employ and depend on them in many secular
affairs. Their character and standing were thought to be intimately
interwoven with the authority and stability of the State. Besides
this, in the New England colonies, no one was admitted to the
" freedom of the body politic " and the right to vote, but members
of the " church;" and as the minister had a controlling voice in the
admission of members into the " church," the power to shape and
direct the government was thus placed almost directly in their
hands. Hence there was a close connection between the Courts and
the church council; the former being ever liable to be influenced
by the latter. The ministers did not fail to use this power to promote their own interest, and the views entertained by them relative
to the demands of the rigid religion they professed : and drawing
their theories of government and the application of law from the
Mosaic model, overlooking the wide difference between that dispensation and the Christian, the penal code they were instrumental in
having framed for the Colonies was deeply stained with blood.

They were now determined to put a stop to what they professed
to believe to be a great evil, by connecting its advocacy and the
presence of its confessors, with sacrifice of human life. Accordingly
they drew up, and presented to the Magistrates, a petition that a
law should be made to banish the Quakers *on pain of death.* Thus
urged and sanctioned by their spiritual guides, the General Court in
Boston resolved to take this last step in the merciless and fearful
course they had heretofore pursued ; a step which, however palliated
by considerations of the blind zeal and cruel temper of the times,
has placed an indelible stigma on their religious character.

The " Assistants," who were chiefly Magistrates, and formed a
kind of upper house, assented to the ordinance without hesitation ;
but it met with decided opposition in the House of Deputies. The
ground was there taken, that as the Act proposed to put human life
in jeopardy, without trial by jury, it was not only unjust, but directly contrary to the law in England. The Ministers and Magistrates, however, were bent on having the power sought put into their
hands, and they spared no pains, by persuasion and the influence

attached to their stations, to induce those opposed to the measure to change their votes. In two instances they were successful, and another of the former opponents being kept away by sickness, the law was finally passed by a majority of one vote.

On the 21st of Tenth month, 1658, the Act was proclaimed; by which it was provided, "That every person or persons, *of the cursed sect of the Quakers*, who is not an inhabitant of, but is found within, this jurisdiction, shall be apprehended without warrant, where no Magistrate is at hand, by any constable, commissioner or selectman, and conveyed from constable to constable to the next Magistrate, who shall commit the said person to close prison, there to remain without bail until the next Court of Assistants, where they shall have a legal trial : and being convicted *to be of the sect of the Quakers* shall be sentenced to be banished *upon pain of death.* And that every inhabitant of this jurisdiction, being convicted to be of the aforesaid sect, either by taking up, publishing, or defending *the horrid opinions of the Quakers*, or the stirring up mutiny, sedition or rebellion against the government, or by taking up their absurd and destructive practices, viz.: Denying civil respect to equals and superiors, and withdrawing from our church assemblies, and instead thereof frequenting meetings of their own, in opposition to our church order : or by adhering to, or approving of any known Quaker, and the tenets and practices of the Quakers, that are opposite to the orthodox received opinions of the godly, and endeavoring to disaffect others to civil government, and church orders, *or condemning the practice and proceedings of this Court against the Quakers*, manifesting thereby their complying with those, whose design is to overthrow the order established in church and State; every such person, upon conviction before the said Court of Assistants, in manner as aforesaid, shall be committed to close prison for one month, and then, unless they choose voluntarily to depart this jurisdiction, shall give bond for their good behavior, and appear at the next Court, where continuing obstinate, and refusing to retract and reform the aforesaid opinions, they shall be sentenced to banishment upon pain of death."

It will thus be seen that the crime for which the death penalty was to be inflicted, was simply being a Quaker; the previous proceedings were the preliminary steps to this fatal consummation. The introduction of the charges against Friends in relation to mutiny, sedition or rebellion, or opposition to civil government, was to induce the belief that they were guilty of those crimes; which was altogether untrue, as they had again and again declared, both by published documents and by word of mouth; asserting that while they could not recognize the right of government to interfere with liberty of conscience, or to dictate what a man *should* or *should not* believe; they fully yielded to it active obedience in all things which did not contravene the law of God, and where they thought it did, passive submission by non-resistance to the penalty. It appears from a letter written by William Robinson to George Fox, dated the 12th of the Fifth month, 1659, that the severity of this law was too much for the·fortitude and constancy of some of those who had recently united with Friends, and had before suffered more or less on behalf of the good confession made by them. Six, upon being banished upon pain of death, left the Colony to take up their abode permanently in other places.

The first of those who offered up their lives for the testimony of Jesus, were William Robinson and Marmaduke Stevenson; the former a merchant of London, and the latter a Yorkshireman. These two Friends, together with Mary Dyer, Nicolas Davis, and Patience Scott, were in the prison in Boston. Nicolas Davis had gone to that town for no other purpose than to collect and pay some debts. Patience Scott, who was a daughter of Richard and Katharine Scott, was a child of but eleven years of age, who, believing that it was required of her by her Saviour to see the Governor and Councils in Boston, and plead with them not to attempt to execute their unrighteous laws against Friends, had left her home, more than a hundred miles distant, and travelled to that town; where she was speedily arrested as a Quaker and put into prison, where she was kept more than three months on prisoner's fare.

When brought before the Court, the three men and M. Dyer were sentenced to banishment on pain of death; but it seemed too absurd, even to those Magistrates, to banish such a child under that penalty, and her case perplexed them. She was closely examined, and her answers were so far beyond what could have been expected from one so young in years, that the Governor remarked there was a spirit in her above that of a woman, and that it must be the devil. They made the following record of her case, "The Court duly considering the malice of Satan and his instruments, by all means and ways to propagate error, and disturb the truth and bring in error and confusion among us; that Satan is put to his shifts to make use of such a child, not being of the years of discretion, nor understanding the principles of religion, judge meet so far to slight her as a Quaker, as only to admonish and instruct her according to her capacity, and so discharge her; Captain Hutchinson undertaking to send her home." The following order respecting the others was issued to the jailer:

"You are required by these, presently to set at liberty William Robinson, Marmaduke Stevenson, Mary Dyer, and Nicholas Davis, who by an order of the Court and Council, had been imprisoned, because it appeared by their own confession, words, and actions, that they are Quakers; wherefore a sentence was pronounced against them, to depart this jurisdiction on pain of death, and that they must answer it at their peril, if they, or any of them after the 14th of this present month, September, are found within this jurisdiction, or any part thereof. EDWARD RAWSON."

Boston, September 12, 1659.

N. Davis, who had come to Boston on secular business only, returned home; and Mary Dyer also left the Colony for the present. Before William Robinson was sent away, as he was a minister of note, it was thought best to subject him to scourging. He was therefore fastened to a gun-carriage, stripped, and twenty lashes with a three-corded whip were given him.

The two men Friends went as far as Salem, where, feeling themselves called to endeavor to strengthen the faith of their brethren, they tarried and attended their meetings. They were soon arrested and sent back to the prison at Boston, where each was chained by the leg. In the next month, Mary Dyer having returned, as she was speaking to Christopher Holder, who was then in Boston, inquiring for a ship in which to embark for England, she was arrested and sent to prison.

Sewel gives a full account of the trial and execution of these three Friends, from which the following is extracted:

"On the 20th of October these three were brought into the court, where John Endicott and others were assembled. And being called to the bar, Endicott commanded the keeper to pull off their hats: and then said that they had made several laws to keep the Quakers from amongst them; and neither whipping, nor imprisoning, nor cutting off ears, nor banishing upon pain of death, would keep them from amongst them. And further he said, that he or they desired not the death of any of them. Yet notwithstanding, his following words without more ado, were, 'Give ear, and hearken to

your sentence of death.'   W. Robinson then desired that he might
be permitted to read a paper, giving an account of the reason why
he had not departed that jurisdiction.   But Endicott would not
suffer it to be read, and said in a rage, ' You shall not read it, nor
will the Court hear it read.'   Then Robinson laid it on the table.
He had written this paper the day before, and some of the contents,
were that he being in Rhode Island, the Lord had commanded him
to go to Boston and to lay down his life there.   That he also had
felt an assurance that his soul was to enter into everlasting peace
and eternal rest.   That he durst not but obey, without inquiring
further concerning it ; believing that it became him as a child, to
show obedience to the Lord, without any unwillingness.   That this
was the cause, why after banishment on pain of death, he stayed in
their jurisdiction : and that now with sincerity of heart he could
say, ' Blessed be the Lord, the God of my life, who hath called me
hereunto, and counted me worthy to testify against wicked and
unjust men,' &c.   W. Robinson desiring again that the paper might
be read, that so all that were present might hear it, it was denied
him, and Endicott said, ' William Robinson, hearken to your sentence of death ; you shall be had back to the place whence you
came, and thence to the place of execution, to be hanged on the gallows till you are dead.'   This sentence was not altogether unexpected to W. Robinson ; for it was four months now that he had
believed this would be his share.

" Robinson being taken away, M. Stevenson was called, and Endicott said to him, ' If you have any thing to say, you may speak.'
He knowing how they dealt with his companion, was silent ; though
he had also written in prison a paper, containing the cause of his
being come there ; but he kept it with him, and found afterwards
occasion to deliver it to somebody.   Then Endicott pronounced
sentence of death against him, saying, ' Marmaduke Stevenson, you
shall be had to the place whence you came, and thence to the gallows,
and there be hanged till you are dead.'   Whereupon M. Stevenson
spoke thus : ' Give ear, ye Magistrates, and all who are guilty ; for
this the Lord hath said concerning you, and will perform his word
upon you, that the same day ye put his servants to death, shall the
day of your visitation pass over your heads, and you shall be cursed
for evermore.   The mouth of the Lord of hosts hath spoken it.   Therefore in love to you all, I exhort you to take warning before it be too
late, that so the curse may be removed.   For assuredly, if you put

us to death, you will bring innocent blood upon your own heads, and swift destruction will come unto you.'

"After he had spoken this, he was taken away, and Mary Dyer was called, to whom Endicott spoke thus : 'Mary Dyer, you shall go to the place whence you came, (to wit, the prison,) and thence to the place of execution, and be hanged there until you are dead.' To which she replied, 'The will of the Lord be done.' Then Endicott said, 'Take her away, Marshal.' To which she returned, 'Yea, joyfully I go.' And in her going to the prison, she often uttered speeches of praise to the Lord ; and being full of joy, she said to the Marshal, he might let her alone, for she would go to the prison without him. To which he answered, 'I believe you, Mrs. Dyer : but I must do what I am commanded.' Thus she was led to prison, where she was kept a week, with the two others, her companions, that were also condemned to die."

The account which M. Stevenson had drawn up, narrated the different steps by which he had been prepared for and drawn to offer himself up for the work and service in which he was then engaged ; and after speaking of his gospel labors in Rhode Island, ends as follows :— "So, after a little time that I had been there, visiting the seed which the Lord hath blessed, the word of the Lord came unto me saying, 'Go to Boston with thy brother, William Robinson.' And at this command I was obedient, and gave up myself to do his will, that so his work and service may be accomplished ; for He hath said unto me, that He hath a great work for me to do ; which is now come to pass ; and for yielding obedience to and obeying the voice and command of the ever-living God, who created heaven and earth, and the fountains of waters, do I, with my dear brother, suffer outward bonds near unto death ; and this is given forth to be upon record, that all people may know, who hear it, that we came not in our own wills, but in the will of God."

Mary Dyer likewise sent a paper to the Court, in which she declared, that although she was charged with bringing her own blood on her head, such was not the case. That she came among them out of love to them, to persuade them not to bring the guilt of shedding innocent blood upon their souls : and she assured them, that if they refused to obey the law of the Lord, or to listen to the voice of his servants, all their laws and punishments would be of no avail, for He will send more of his servants whom they called "Cursed Quakers," among them, to preach to the seed that was yet preserved in this place, &c., &c.

On the day appointed for the execution — 27th of Tenth month, 1659 — the prisoners were escorted to the gallows by a company of about two hundred men. Wilson, the "minister," of course was present; for when the Court was deliberating on the sentence to be passed on the Quakers, he prompted them by saying, "Hang them, or else," — and he drew his finger across his own throat — indicating, Cut their throats. Drums were kept beaten, to prevent the crowd hearing what the Friends might have to say. The three walked hand in hand, and the Marshal having asked Mary Dyer, "Are you not ashamed to walk thus, hand in hand, between two young men?" she replied: "No, this is to me an hour of the greatest joy I could enjoy in this world. No eye can see, no ear can hear, no tongue can utter, and no heart can undertand the sweet incomes or influences, and the refreshings of the Spirit of the Lord which now I feel."

"Thus going along, W. Robinson said, ' This is your hour, and the power of darkness.' But presently the drums were beaten; yet shortly after the drummers leaving off beating, Marmaduke Stevenson said, 'This is the day of your visitation, wherein the Lord hath visited you.' More he spoke, but could not be understood, by reason of the drums being beaten again. Yet they went on with great cheerfulness, as going to an everlasting wedding feast, and rejoicing that the Lord had counted them worthy to suffer death for his name's sake.

"When they were come near the gallows, the priest said in a taunting way to W. Robinson, 'Shall such jacks as you come in before authority with their hats on?' To which Robinson replied, ' Mind you, mind you, it is for the not putting off the hat we are put to death?' Now being come to the ladder, they took leave of each other with tender embraces, and then Robinson went cheerfully up the ladder, and being got up, said to the people, 'This is the day of your visitation, wherein the Lord hath visited you: this is the day the Lord is risen in his mighty power, to be avenged on all his adversaries.' He also signified, that he suffered not as an evil-doer: and desired the spectators to mind the light that was in them; to wit, the Light of Christ, of which he testified, and was now going to seal it with his blood. This so incensed the envious priest, that he said, 'Hold thy tongue; be silent; thou art going to die with a lie in thy mouth.' The rope being now about his neck, the executioner bound his hands and legs, and tied his neckcloth about his face: which being done, Robinson said, 'Now ye are made manifest;' and the executioner being about turning him off, he said, ' I suffer for Christ, in whom I live, and for whom I die.' He being turned off, Marmaduke Stevenson stepped up the ladder, and said, ' Be it known unto all this day, that we suffer not as evil-doers, but for conscience' sake.' And when the hangman was about to turn him off, he said, ' This day shall we be at rest with the Lord ; ' and so he was turned off.

" Mary Dyer seeing her companions hanging dead before her, also stepped up the ladder ; but after her coats were tied about her feet, the halter put about her neck, and her face covered with a handkerchief, which the priest Wilson lent the hangman, just as she was to be turned off, a cry was heard, 'Stop, for she is reprieved.' Her feet being then loosed, they bade her come down. But she whose mind was as it were already in heaven, stood still, and said, she was there willing to suffer as her brethren did, unless they would annul their wicked law. Little heed was given to what she said, but they pulled her down, and the Marshal and others taking her by the arms, carried her to prison again. That she thus was freed from the gallows, this time, was at the intercession of her son, to whom it seems they could not then resolve to deny that favor."

M. Dyer was now started for home under the care of four horsemen, who, after going about fifteen miles with her, left her with a man and horse to pursue the remainder of the journey. She soon sent the man and horse back, and took her own way to her residence. Having passed the winter in Rhode Island and on Long Island, she believed it required of her to go again to Boston, and without consulting with flesh and blood, she gave up to go, and arrived in Boston on the 21st of the Third month, 1660 ; and on the 31st she was ordered before the Court. " Being come, the Governor, John Endicott, said, ' Are you the same Mary Dyer that was here before ?' And it seems he was preparing an evasion for her, there having been another of that name returned from Old England. But she was so far from disguising, that she answered undauntedly, ' I am the same Mary Dyer that was here the last General Court.' Then Endicott said, 'You will own yourself a Quaker, will you not ?' To which Mary Dyer said, ' I own my self to be reproachfully called so.' Then the jailer (who would also say something), said, ' She is a vagabond.' And Endicott said, the sentence was passed upon her the last General Court, and now likewise : ' You must return to the prison, and there remain till to-morrow at nine o'clock ; then, thence you must go to the gallows, and there be hanged till you are dead.' To which Mary Dyer said, ' This is no more than what thou saidst before.' And Endicott returned, ' But now it is to be executed ; therefore prepare yourself to-morrow at nine o'clock.' She then spoke thus : ' I came in obedience to the will of God the last General Court, desiring you to repeal your unrighteous laws of banishment on pain of death; and that same is my work now, and earnest request; although I told you, that if you refused to repeal them, the Lord would send others of his servants to witness against them.' Hereupon Endicott asked her, whether she was a prophetess ? And she answered, she spoke the words that the Lord spoke to her ; and now the thing was come to pass.   And beginning to speak of her call, Endicott cried, ' Away with her; away with her.'   So she was brought to the prison-house where she was before, and kept close shut up until the next day.

"About the appointed time the Marshal, Michaelson, came, and called for her to come hastily ; and coming into the room where she was, she desired him to stay a little ; and speaking mildly, said, she should be ready presently.   But he being of a rough temper, said he could not wait upon her, but she should now wait upon him.   Then Mary Dyer was brought forth, and with a band of soldiers led through the town, the drums being beaten before and behind her, and so continued, that none might hear her speak all the way to the place of execution, which was about a mile.   With this guard she came to the gallows, and being gone up the ladder, some said to her, that if she would return she might come down and save her life.   To which she replied, ' Nay, I cannot, for in obedience to the will of the Lord I came, and in his will I abide faithful to the death.'   Then Captain John Webb said, that she had been there before, and had the sentence of banishment upon pain of death, and had broken the law in coming again now : and therefore she was guilty of her own blood.   To which she returned, ' Nay, I came to keep blood-guiltiness from you, desiring you to repeal the unrighteous and unjust law of banishment upon pain of death, made against the innocent servants of the Lord ; therefore my blood will be required at your hands, who wilfully do it ; but for those that do it in the simplicity of their hearts, I desire the Lord to forgive them.   I came to do the will of my Father, and in obedience to his will, I stand even to death.'   Then priest Wilson said, ' Mary Dyer, O repent, O repent, and be not so deluded, and carried away by the deceit of the devil.' To this Mary Dyer answered, ' Nay, man, I am not now to repent.' And being asked by some, whether she would have the elders pray for her, she said, ' I know never an elder here.'   Being further asked, whether she would have any of the people to pray for her? She answered. she desired the prayers of all the people of God. Thereupon some scoffingly said, 'It may be she thinks there is none here.' She looking about said, ' I know but few here ' Then they spoke to her again, that one of the elders might pray for her. To which she replied, 'Nay, first a child, then a young man, then a strong man, before an elder in Christ Jesus.' After this she was charged with something which was not understood what it was, but she seemed to hear it; for she said, 'It is false, it is false; I never spoke those words.' Then one mentioned that she should have said, she had been in paradise. To which she answered, 'Yea, I have been in paradise several days.' And more she spoke of the eternal happiness into which she was now to enter. In this well-disposed condition she was turned off, and died a martyr for Christ, being twice led to death; which the first time she expected with undaunted courage, and now suffered with Christian fortitude.

" Thus this honest, valiant woman finished her days; but so hardened were these persecutors, that one of the Court said scoffingly, ' She did hang as a flag for others to take example by.' "

Her husband, who never professed with Friends, presented a touching appeal to Governor Endicott, President of the Court that condemned her, pleading that her life might be spared. No notice appears to have been taken of it.

There were several Friends still confined in Boston jail, of whom four were inhabitants of Salem — sent there on account of having embraced the principles of Friends; — and two, Joseph Nicholson and wife, from Cumberland, England. The latter were shortly brought before the Court and sentenced to banishment on pain of death; to depart within nine days. This was on the 7th of First month, 1660. Three other Friends had similar sentences passed on them, and were sent out of the jurisdiction of the Court; among whom were William Leddra and Wenlock Christison.

Joseph Nicholson's wife being sick, could not leave the prison until the expiration of the time allowed. They went to Salem, and on the 20th, were again arrested and committed to prison. The Court, whether intimidated by the murmured dissatisfaction of many, with its sanguinary proceedings, or moved by the fact that J. Nicholson. and wife had come to New England to settle and follow their occupation, instead of carrying out their former sentence, by ordering their execution, had them sent to Rhode Island.

By the accounts preserved of the meetings of Friends in New

England, it appears that at least two Monthly Meetings had been established for transacting the affairs of the Church, viz., Sandwich, which was the first set up in America, and Pembroke—held at Scituate—prior to 1660: and there is a minute of the "Court of Plymouth," directing two of its officers to endeavor to hinder Friends from holding "a constant Monthly Meeting," at Duxburrow.

It is fair to state, as showing some disposition to try other means than punishment, to *reclaim* the Quakers, that this same Court granted permission to four persons "to frequent Quaker meetings," to "endeavor to *reduce* them from the error of their ways."

CHAPTER XII.

Failure of R. Cromwell — General Monk — Persecution of Friends by the Soldiers — Restoration — King Charles' Promises —Friends discharged from Jail — G. Fox, Jr., and R. Grassingham — Imprisonment of George Fox — M. Fell and Anne Curtis apply to the King — G. Fox sent up to London — R. Hubberthorn and the King — Anglican Church — Fifth Monarchy Men — Persecution renewed — Events in London — Thousands of Friends Imprisoned — Remonstrances and Redress — Persecution under old Laws —Act of Uniformity — Act against Quakers for not Swearing — Friends before Parliament — Storm Impending — Richard Brown and John Robinson.

THE feeble hands of Richard Cromwell were not fitted, under the circumstances which surrounded him, to retain the emblems of power that had fallen into them because of his near relationship to the great Captain, who had seized and wielded them with such striking effect. The ambitious and disaffected members of the Parliament, and the self-seeking officers of the army, were constantly intriguing to promote their own private interests, and as the Protector was not likely to be of much use to either party, and unable to form a party of his own, he was hustled out of the way, and retired to private life. Dissatisfaction spread throughout the nation. Richard had dissolved the Parliament sitting when he came into office, and recalled that portion of the Long Parliament called the "Rump;" but its standing and authority were generally despised, and when it undertook to act in opposition to the wishes of the army, a band of soldiers again forcibly dismissed it, and closed the doors. For a while military power was supreme, and had the different sections of the army and its officers remained united, they might have fastened a despotism on the people which they could not have shaken off. But they were jealous one of another, and thus paralyzed their strength. General Monk began to march that part of the army over which he held command, from Edinburg towards London. He refused to acknowledge the authority of the military Junto, and as the greater part of the people sided with him, it was forced to yield, and the "Rump" once more entered the legislative halls. On arriving in London, Monk dissembled as to the course he intended to pursue, until he felt assured there was no other officer with sufficient military force to oppose him : then he declared for a free Parliament, which was joyfully accepted by the nation. When it was fully installed, with the House of Lords, it took the necessary precautionary steps, and the way being prepared, it invited Charles Stuart to fill the vacant throne; which he hastened to accept. [1660.]

Directly upon the arrival of Monk, and while his soldiers had unrestricted possession of London, they treated Friends with much severity, and, it was currently reported, by his orders. Edward Billing, who was one of the Friends who had offered to take the place of any one of their brethren suffering in prison, gives the following account in a letter to a Friend.

" . . . . Since General Monk's coming to London with his army, we have been very much abused in our meetings ; as in the Palace-yard, where we were pulled out by the hair of the head, kicked and knocked down, both men and women, in a manner not here to be expressed. Many were the knocks and kicks and blows myself and wife received. And this was done by General Monk's foot, who came into the meeting with sword and pistol, being, as they said, bound by an oath to leave never a sectarian in England; saying that they had orders from Lord Monk to pull us out of our meeting ; which, with inexpressible cruelty, they did. The meeting in the Palace-yard I suppose thou knowest.

" After they had beaten us in the house with their swords in the scabbards, and with whips, out they drag us, and kick us into the kennel, where many a blow I received, being knocked and kicked through the Palace-yard, even to the hall door. Being got within the hall, after a little recovery I was moved to write a little note to the Speaker in the House,— Parliament being then sitting. As soon as I got into the lobby I sent into the House for Serjeant Chedleton, who came to me, and I gave him the note, laying it upon him to give it to the Speaker, which he did, and it was forthwith read in the House, when an enemy stands up and says, ' The multi-

tude is appeased,' &c., &c. I passed through them back again to
the meeting-house, when they fell upon me the second time, as before. In my passing back to my own lodging they ceased not, but
kept crying, 'Kill him, kill him!'

"We afterwards met Colonel Rich, who was much affected to see
and hear of our usage. With him I passed through the Palace-
yard again, the soldiers and multitude being just then beating a
woman of the house at the door, and plundering the house, notwithstanding it had been said that the tumult was appeased. At last I
got to Whitehall, where General Monk was, with whom I had present audience. In a few words I laid the whole matter before him,.
and told him that the soldiers said they had his order for it. [He
said] he might say they had not. I answered, that since he and his
army had come to town we could not pass the streets without much
abuse; not having been so much abused these many years — nay, I
say, *never by soldiers*."

Upon this representation and that of R. Hubberthorn, who also
had an interview with him, General Monk issued this order, which
is still preserved among the Swarthmoor documents in London: "I
do require all officers and soldiers to forbear to disturb the peaceable meetings of the Quakers, they doing nothing prejudicial to the
Parliament or Commonwealth of England.—GEORGE MONK."

1660. The restoration of Monarchy, the return of the long exiled
King, the sudden relaxation of the sumptuary laws and ascetic
practices of the Puritans, and the free scope given by royal permission and example, to all kinds of sensual indulgence, threw the
thoughtless people into wild delirium: they gave loose rein to their
passions, and in the reaction, there seemed danger of great part of
the nation plunging into senseless riot or gross licentiousness.

At first it appeared as though Friends might rejoice, in common
with others, at the return of the Monarchy. The King, who was
good-natured and careless about religion in any form, before he
was assured of being recalled, and with the hope of opening the
way for his unopposed return, had given forth, from Breda, in the
Fourth month of 1660, a declaration of the policy he would pursue
when once seated on the throne of his father. In this declaration
he had emphatically stated, as one of the stipulations voluntarily
made, and for the exact performance of which he solemnly pledged
the word of a king, that "Because the passion and uncharitableness
of the times have produced several opinions in religion; by which
men are engaged in parties and animosities against each other,

which, when they shall hereafter unite, in a freedom of conversation, will be composed, or better understood; *we do declare a liberty to tender consciences, and that no man shall be disquieted, or called in question, for differences of opinion in matters of religion, which do not disturb the peace of the kingdom;* and that we shall be ready to consent to such an act of Parliament, as, upon mature deliberation, shall be offered to us for the full granting of that indulgence."

Soon after entering on his royal duties the King issued a Proclamation, setting free all who were confined in any part of the kingdom, on account of their conscientious opinions or religious belief; by which about seven hundred Friends were restored to liberty; of which they had been deprived,—some for a long time,—by their intolerant and persecuting adversaries.

Notwithstanding this fair show of moderation and enlightened policy in ecclesiastical affairs, there were those about the Court who were only biding their time, in order again to inaugurate a forced conformity in religious profession, and mode of worship. There were also in many parts of the country, Magistrates whose previous history did not afford a very safe foundation on which to rest their hopes of future preferment, and who were therefore desirous, by embracing any opportunity that presented for displaying their newly fledged loyalty, to draw a veil over their past course, and show how ready they were to do anything they thought might commend them to royal favor.

Among the latter was the Mayor of Harwich, who had shown himself an implacable enemy of Friends, and was greatly incensed on finding that a considerable number in the town had embraced their principles and established a meeting in the place. Hearing that George Fox the younger, was to be at the meeting, he first arrested several who were on their way to it, and then went there himself with a constable, and took G. Fox, Jr., into custody, and without letting him know of what he was accused, sent him to prison. R. Gressingham, shipwright for the Admiralty in that port, being at the meeting and convinced of the truth of the doctrines declared, voluntarily went to prison with George.

G. Fox, Jr., having in the course of his sermon, in allusion to the prevailing wickedness, used the expression, " Woe unto the rulers and teachers of this nation, who suffer such ungodliness as this, and do not seek to suppress it," the Mayor and Magistrates sent up to Parliament an account of the arrest they had made, and charging the two prisoners with speaking against the government and nearly causing a mutiny. Whereupon Parliament ordered that they be at once sent to London and put under charge of the Sergeant-at-arms. They were imprisoned in Lambeth gate-house, and kept week after week without any notice being taken of their case. They addressed Parliament, stating they knew not with what offence they were charged, desired to be brought face to face with their accusers, and expressed willingness to suffer punishment if they had broken any law. The Speaker refused to lay their communication before the House, because it was not addressed to him as "Right Honorable." They then had their address printed and a copy presented to each member. At the end of fourteen weeks from the time they were committed to Lambeth gate-house, without any examination or any official action in the case, an order passed the House, for their discharge on bail, to appear when required. The Sergeant-at-arms, however, detained them for his fees, a long time, but finally they were set at liberty by order of the Privy Council. George Fox the Younger, as he styled himself, was convinced in an interview he had with George Fox in 1651; and though an older man than the latter, yet as he said he had not witnessed the second birth until long after his namesake, he took the title of the younger, by way of distinction. While in Lambeth prison he wrote "A noble Salutation of Charles Stuart," wherein he reviewed the affairs of the nation for many years, pointing out to the King wherein his father's government had committed evil, and brought punishment upon themselves; also, the wrong doing of the party in power that succeeded him, and the destruction that had come upon it. He then warned the King not to countenance pride or oppression, neither to seek revenge on his former enemies: "For I plainly declare unto thee, that this kingdom, and all the kingdoms of the earth, are properly the Lord's. And this know, that it was the just hand of God, in taking away the kingdom from thy father and thee, and giving it unto others; and that also it is the just hand of the Lord to take it again from them, and bring them under thee, though I shall not say, but that some of them went beyond their commission against thy father, when they were brought as a rod over you: and well will it be for thee, if thou becomest not guilty of the same trangressions."

1660. George Fox (the elder) being at the house of Margaret Fell—who was now a widow—was arrested by a constable with a warrant from a Magistrate named Porter, who had been a violent partisan of the Parliament, but was now officiously loud and intermeddling for the King. They carried George to Ulverstone, where they kept him all night, putting sixteen men to keep guard over him, three of whom sat in the chimney-place all night, for fear he might escape up the flue without their knowing it. So strange were their superstitious notions about him, that one of his keepers said, he had supposed that a thousand men could not have taken him. They abused him much the next day as they were conveying him to Lancaster. When brought before Porter, he asked for what he had been apprehended, and complained of the abuse he had received. But the magistrate refused to take any notice of his complaints, and also to let him know what was the charge against him, saying, he must keep the King's secrets. He made out a mittimus and sent him to prison, to be there kept until delivered by order of the King and Parliament. Some of George's friends applied to the jailer for a copy of the mittimus, which he refused to give; but finally was prevailed on to allow them to read it. They found that it charged George Fox with being a principal leader among the Quakers, and that he, with others, had recently endeavored to raise an insurrection in that part of the country, intending to embroil the whole kingdom in blood.

Being thus made acquainted with the charges against him, Geo. Fox sent his defence to the King and Parliament; showing how untrue the charges were; that the principles held by him and by Friends, were opposed to all violence and war, and that there was no ground for any of the accusations made by Porter. Margaret Fell also had published an account of the illegal manner in which her domicile had been invaded, and her guest arrested and taken from there, without authority or order, &c.

As G. Fox was kept close prisoner, M. Fell resolved to go to London and seek an interview with the King, to give him a truthful statement of the case. Porter, hearing of this, started for London also. When he arrived there, several about the Court, who saw and recognized him as formerly a furious Parliament officer, reminded him of his doings, and of his having been active in ruining their estates; at which he became alarmed, and hastily returned home.

Anne Curtis, a daughter of a former Sheriff of Bristol, who had been hanged near his own door for having been engaged in an effort to bring back King Charles, having gone to Lancaster jail to see G. Fox, and heard a statement of the unjust proceedings against him, resolved also to go to London, and seek an opportunity to speak to the King on his behalf. Accordingly on reaching the city, she and M. Fell went to the palace, and obtained admittance to the King; who, when he heard whose daughter Anne was, received them kindly, and upon hearing their statement, and the request that G. Fox should be brought to London that the King might hear his cause himself, commanded his secretary to send such an order down. It being necessary, however, that a writ of "*habeas corpus*" should be issued from one of the Judges of the Court of the King's Bench, that was procured.

But Porter, who feared lest George Fox might take steps to bring him to punishment for his illegal and cruel treatment, resorted to every shift and evasion to delay compliance with the writ. George steadily refused to pay any fees, to give any bond, or to do any thing more than promise that if released he would go up to London of his own accord. At first it was proposed to send a troop of horse with him, and then the jailer and some bailiffs, but it was found either would involve more expense than the county could afford. At last they were obliged to accede to George's terms, and so, the man charged with being "engaged in promoting insurrection to involve the whole kingdom in blood," was allowed to start off from his close prison, on his simple promise that, if the Lord permit, he would be in London sometime during the term of the Supreme Court. Richard Hubberthorn and Robert Widders accompanied him, and after spending two or three days at Swarthmoor, and holding meetings in different places, they arrived in London on the day that some of the Judges who condemned Charles I. were hanged and quartered.

Having gone before two of the Judges in their chambers, who took George's word to appear in Court, instead of requiring bail, he, the next day, fulfilled his promise and plead his own cause. No accuser being found to appear against him, he was at the instance of the King, through Esquire Marsh, honorably discharged, after having been a prisoner over twenty weeks. [1660.]

Sewel narrates the substance of a conversation that passed between the King with some of the Lords of the privy council, and Richard Hubberthorn; who, about this time, had sought and obtained an interview with Charles for the purpose of giving him correct information relative to Friends, and the great persecution and suffering they had endured, and were still exposed to. It is as follows:

"R. H.—Since the Lord hath called us, and gathered us to be a people, to walk in his fear, and in his truth, we have always suffered and been persecuted by the powers that have ruled, and been made a prey of, for departing from iniquity, and when the breach of no just law could be charged against us, then they made laws on purpose to ensnare us; and so our sufferings were unjustly continued.

King. — It is true, those who have ruled over you have been cruel, and have professed much which they have not done.

R. H. — And likewise the same sufferings do now abound in more cruelty against us in many parts of this nation: as for instance, one at Thetford in Norfolk, where Henry Fell, (ministering unto the people,) was taken out of the meeting and whipped, and sent out of the town, from parish to parish, towards Lancashire; and the chief ground of his accusation in his pass, (which was shown to the King,) was because he denied to take the oath of allegiance and supremacy; and so because that for conscience' sake we cannot swear, but have learned obedience to the doctrine of Christ, which saith, 'Swear not at all;' hereby an occasion is taken against us to persecute us: and it is well known that we have not sworn for any, nor against any, but have kept to the truth, and our yea hath been yea, and our nay, nay, in all things, which is more than the oath of those that are out of the truth.

King. — But why can you not swear? for an oath is a common thing amongst men to any engagement.

R. H. — Yes, it is manifest, and we have seen it by experience; and it is so common amongst men to swear, and engage either for or against things, that there is no regard taken to them, nor fear of an oath; that therefore, which we speak of in the truth of our hearts, is more than what they swear.

King. — But can you not promise before the Lord, which is the substance of the oath?

R. H. — Yes, what we do affirm, we can promise before the Lord, and take Him to our witness in it; but our so promising hath not been accepted, but the ceremony of an oath they have stood for, without which all other things were accounted of no effect.

King. — But how may we know from your words that you will perform?

R. H. — By proving us; for they that swear are not known to be faithful, but by proving them; and so we, by those that have tried us, are found to be truer in our promises, than others by their oaths; and to those that do yet prove us, we shall appear the same.

King. — Pray, what is your principle?

R. H. — Our principle is this, 'That Jesus Christ is the true Light, which enlighteneth every one that cometh into the world, that all

men through Him might believe; and that they were to obey and
follow this Light as they have received it, whereby they may be led
unto God, and unto righteousness, and the knowledge of the truth,
that they may be saved.

King. — This do all Christians confess to be truth; and he is not
a Christian that will deny it.

R. H. — But many have denied it both in words and writings,
and opposed us in it; and above a hundred books are put forth in
opposition unto this principle.

Then some of the lords standing by the King, said, that none
would deny that every one is enlightened.

And one of the lords asked, how long we had been called Quakers,
or did we own that name?

R. H. — That name was given to us in scorn and derision, about
twelve years since; but there were some that lived in this truth
before we had that name given unto us.

King. — How long is it since you owned this judgment and way?

R. H. — It is near twelve years since I owned this truth, according to the manifestation of it.

King. —Do you own the sacrament?

R. H. — As for the word sacrament, I do not read of it in the
Scripture; but as for the body and blood of Christ I own, and that
there is no remission without blood.

King. — Well, that is it; but do you not believe that every one
is commanded to receive it?

R. H. — This we do believe, that according as it is written in the
Scripture, that Christ at his last supper took bread and brake it;
and gave to his disciples, and also took the cup and blessed it, and
said unto them, 'And as often as ye do this, (that is, as often as
they brake bread,) you show forth the Lord's death till He come;'
and this we believe they did, ' and they did eat their bread in singleness of heart from house to house;' and Christ did come again to
them according to his promise; after which they said, 'We being
many are one bread, for we are all partakers of this one bread.'

Then one of the King's friends said, 'It is true; for as many
grains make one bread, so they being many members, were one body.'

Another of them said, 'If they be the bread, then they must be
broken.'

R. H. — There is a difference between that bread which He brake
at his last supper, wherein they were to show forth, as in a sign,.
his death until He came, and this whereof they spake, they being

many are one bread; for herein they were come more into the substance, and to speak more mystically, as they knew it in the Spirit.

King's friends. — Then they said, it is true, and he had spoken nothing but truth.

King. — How know you that you are inspired by the Lord?

R. H. — According as we read in the Scriptures, that, 'The inspiration of the Almighty giveth them understanding;' so by his inspiration is an understanding given us of the things of God.

Then one of the lords said, How do you know that you are led by the true Spirit?

R. H. — This we know, because the Spirit of Truth reproves the world of sin, and by it we were reproved of sin, and also are led from sin, unto righteousness, and obedience of truth, by which effects we know it is the true Spirit; for the spirit of the wicked one doth not lead into such things.

Then the King and his lords said it was truth.

King.— Well of this you may be assured, that you shall none of you suffer for your opinions or religion, so long as you live peaceably, and you have the word of a King for it; and I have also given forth a declaration to the same purpose, that none shall wrong you or abuse you.

King. — How do you own Magistrates, or magistracy?

R. H. — Thus we do own Magistrates: whosoever is set up by God, whether King as supreme, or any set in authority by him, who are for the punishment of evil-doers, and the praise of them that do well, such we shall submit unto, and assist in righteous and civil things, both by body and estate: and if any Magistrates do that which is unrighteous, we must declare against it; only submit under it by a patient suffering, and not rebel against any by insurrections, plots, and contrivances.

King. — That is enough.

Then one of the lords asked, Why do you meet together, seeing every one of you have the church in yourselves?

R. H. — According as it is written in the Scriptures, the church is in God, Thess. i. 1. 'And they that feared the Lord, did meet often together in the fear of the Lord,' and to us it is profitable, and herein we are edified and strengthened in the life of Truth.

King. — How did you first come to believe the Scriptures were truth.

R. H. — I have believed the Scriptures from a child to be a decla-

ration of truth, when I had but a literal knowledge, natural education, and tradition; but now I know the Scriptures to be true, by
the manifestation and operation of the Spirit of God fulfilling them
in me.

King. — In what manner do you meet, and what is the order in
your meetings?

R. H.— We do meet in the same order as the people of God did,
waiting upon Him: and if any have a word of exhortation from
the Lord, he may speak it; or if any have a word of reproof or admonition, and as every one hath received the gift, so they may minister one unto another, and may be edified one by another; whereby
a growth into the knowledge of the Truth is administered to one
another.

One of the lords. — Then you know not so much as you may
know, but there is a growth then to be admitted of.

R. H. — Yes, we do grow daily into the knowledge of the Truth,
in our exercise and obedience to it.

King. — Are any of your friends gone to Rome?

R. H. — Yes, there is one in prison in Rome.

King. — Why did you send him thither?

R. H. — We did not send him thither, but he found something
upon his spirit from the Lord, whereby he was called to go to declare against superstition and idolatry, which is contrary to the will
of God.

King's friend said, There were two of them at Rome, but one was
dead.

King. — Have any of your friends been with the great Turk?

R. H. — Some of our friends have been in that country.

Other things were spoken concerning the liberty of the servants
of the Lord, who were called of Him into his service, that to them
there was no limitation to parishes or places, but as the Lord did
guide them in his work and service by his Spirit.

So the King promised that we should not any ways suffer for our
opinion or religion: and so in love passed away.

The King having promised Richard Hubberthorn over and again,
that his friends should not suffer for their opinion, or religion, they
parted in love. But though the King seemed a good-natured prince,
yet he was so misled, that in process of time he seemed to have forgotten what he so solemnly promised " on the word of a King."

There is reason to believe that Charles II. was, at this time, sincere in his promise of protection to Friends in the enjoyment of

their religious belief and mode of worship; for so little hold had religious principles upon him, that every profession of them was alike indifferent to him, so that it did not interfere with his safety and self-gratification. But the same want of religious principle rendered his "*word of a king*" no more reliable than the word of any other time-server in his profligate Court.

Under the fair-seeming show put on by the lords and the Episcopal clergy, there was lurking hatred of all that was opposed to the Anglican Church, as it was formally established by law, with its forms and ceremonials, and a burning desire for revenge on those who, in years just passed by, when contending for liberty in matters of religious belief, had placed their feet on the necks of the Royalists, and made them keenly feel that, whatever their rank or station, they were no better than other men. For nearly twenty years they had had to submit to the powerful hand that held them in its grasp, and to feel the sharpness of the blood-stained sword wielded by those whom they hated and despised, and in their lack of Christian virtue they longed to retaliate.

The King's promise of the enjoyment of liberty of conscience made at Breda, and his proclamation concerning the concessions to be made in ecclesiastical regulations, put forth in the Tenth month of 1660, appeared to set the subject of freedom in religious belief and practice, on a basis that would screen the different professors of Christianity from interference or persecution, provided their conduct was peaceable. But though the Puritan Parliament, while in power, had passed ordinances establishing their particular form of church belief and regulation, it had never repealed the old laws that made episcopacy the national form of church constitution and government. Prelacy, therefore, with its unchristian power and privileges, was re-established; the bishops were again admitted to the House of Lords, and places of profit and honor were monopolized by Episcopalians, and by those who, having little or no religion, were free to profess any that opened the way to preferment.

Edward Hyde, Earl of Clarendon, was the Premier, and he used his talents and high position to advance the pretensions of the Anglican Church, and to make the most of every opportunity that presented, to distress and punish the deserters from its doctrines and ritual. It was evident there was a determination on the part of the episcopacy, as speedily as possible, to appropriate for their own emolument, for the teaching of their own creed, and for the promotion of their own policy, all the endowments accumulated within what was designated by the State "the church ;" which they claimed to constitute the nation; and that those who were not willing to rank themselves among its members, should be considered outside of national protection.

Although both houses of Parliament at first returned thanks to the King for his "most gracious proclamation" in reference to a modified toleration of dissent, yet when they found that the people in their excess of loyalty and licentious indulgence were in no wise disposed to heed, or take offence at changes made in religious profession or church control, they refused to give it the sanction of a law, and thereby prevented its moderate provisions from going into effect. The doctrine of passive, unconditional submission to what was sanctioned by the King was insisted on. Every Episcopal minister who had been ejected from his "living"—if he had not at any time expressed approbation of the "murder" of Charles I., or declared against infant baptism—was at once restored to his benefice; the present incumbent being commanded to give it up peaceably. Many other measures indicated that nothing but a plausible pretext was wanted, to let loose the pent-up malignant passions, and sweep away every barrier designed to obstruct their gratification, and, if possible, drive all dissenters into a common ruin.

That pretext was given by the fanatical outbreak of the "Fifth Monarchy Men." These deluded enthusiasts had adopted a wild notion that Cromwell was anti-Christ, and that as he was gone, the time had come for setting up what they designated as the Fifth Monarchy; in which "King Jesus" was to reign and govern. Under the leading of one Venner, a wine cooper, they sallied from their meeting-house, in the evening of the first day of the week, in the first month of 1661, being about fifty men, well armed, and determined to put down the newly installed King and Court, and inaugurate the government of "King Jesus," — who was to appear in person—and of the saints. Though they fought desperately, the whole party was soon killed or captured, and eleven of those who surrendered were hanged.

Although this insane rebellion —if rebellion it may be called— did not extend beyond the comparatively few Millenarians in London, and was completely ended in three or four days, it gave the returned loyalists and church party an excuse for setting at naught the promise of the King, at Breda, and his more recent declaration of indulgence; and for adopting measures to gratify their thirst for vengeance on their former conquerors, and their hatred of all who dissented from their ecclesiastical domination. Taking advantage of the impression left on men's minds, by the events of the recent civil war, their present revolt from the moral strictness of former Puritan rule, and their infatuated delight at the restoration of the monarchy, the religious phrensy of the Fifth Monarchy Men was represented by some of those in power, as but the natural result of dissent from the " Church ; " and the opinion was industriously promulgated that all dissenters — schismatics, as they were called—were hostile to the government, were plotting against it, and unless crushed out, would on the first favorable opportunity essay to overturn it. Under the plea of preventing treason, at first an order from the King in Council was proclaimed, forbidding the meetings of " sectaries," in great numbers. This was quickly followed by another, in which the Anabaptists, Quakers, and Fifth Monarchy Men, are specially named, and forbidden to assemble together under profession of worshipping God, unless it be in the parish church or chapel, or a family meeting to worship in its own house. All other meetings were declared riotous and illegal. The different civil officers were enjoined to search out any such illegal meetings, arrest those found therein, and bind them over to appear at the next session of the proper Court.

The Anglican Church, while rejecting and denouncing the Church of Rome, as apostate and corrupt, yet claimed Divine authority for its own constitution and prelatic incumbents, as being transmitted from the commencement of the Christian Church, through the papal hierarchy, notwithstanding the unbelief and wickedness that had confessedly prevailed among so many of the order. By this figment of apostolic succession, it continued to delude the people, and perhaps deceive some of its own ministers into the belief that its organization, functions and authority, came down from, and were in accordance with, those of the primitive believers. As the kingdom of its acknowledged head, was far more of this world than of any other, its servants considered themselves bound to fight for its support and defence, and hence the secular power was freely employed to enforce its decrees, and destroy those it considered its enemies.

Although from their first rise, Friends had declared that they believed all war and fighting to .be contrary to the commands of Christ and the spirit of his gospel, and therefore they could not participate therein, nor in any wise give countenance thereto ; and their quiet, peaceable behavior, under severe persecution, had given evidence that this belief governed their whole conduct; and although the leaders of the Fifth Monarchy Men had borne testimony, just prior to their execution, that Friends knew nothing of their intentions, nor were in any way connected with them ; yet it suited the present policy, to class them with these insurgents, and another not numerous nor popular body of professors, apparently with the design, that if these were first put down or destroyed, the way would be more fully open to make a direct attack upon the Presbyterians and Independents.   The flood-gates of cruel abuse and persecution were at once opened ; and, with the proclamation, the arbitrary and intolerant course authorized by it, began to be put in force throughout all parts of the country.

George Fox was in London at the time the insurrection broke out, and on the night of the Seventh-day following it, a company of troopers came to the house where he was staying, seized him, and were about taking him to prison, when Esquire Marsh, who, out of friendship for him, had come to lodge in the same house with him, spoke to their commander, and promising to be responsible for his appearance in the morning, obtained his release.   On First-day morning another company of soldiers came to the house, before the troopers arrived, and took George away.   The soldiers were " exceeding rude," and when they had brought him to Whitehall, where many were gathered, he began to preach to them.   Some courtiers hearing him thus engaged, said to the soldiers, Why do you let him preach ?   Put him where he cannot stir : whereupon they put him in prison.   But he had not been shut up many hours, before Esquire Marsh, by speaking to one of the lords, had him set free.   But many Friends, who were on their way to one or another of the meeting-houses, were greatly abused, and thrust into prison.

1660. After the proclamation, imprisonment and abuse were the common lot of Friends in all parts of the country.   They were seized while on the road attending to their necessary business, dragged out of their houses, beaten, and shut up in prisons, so foul and so crowded that several sickened and died.   George Fox says, " We heard of several thousands of our Friends that were cast into prisons in several parts of the nation, and Margaret Fell carried an account of them to the King and Council.   The next week we had an account of several thousands more that were cast into prison, and she went and laid them also before the King and Council.   They wondered how we could have such intelligence, seeing they had given such strict charge for the intercepting of all letters : but the Lord did so order it, that we had an account notwithstanding all their stoppings."

Friends in London prepared and had presented to the King an address, in which they set forth their peaceable principles, denied being concerned in any plots against the government, and answered every objection raised against them, as being disaffected or insubordinate to the powers that be.   They also set forth the cruel treatment they received, from officers and the people, while they were harmless and unresisting; and warned those in power of what would be the consequences, if they persisted in persecuting innocent people, who were striving to serve the Lord in simplicity and sincerity, and who were dear to Him as the apple of his eye.

George Fox also issued an epistle to Friends, consoling and encouraging them under their afflictions, exhorting them to steadfastness, in view of the glorious reward that awaited them in a world where the wicked cease from troubling, and the weary are forever at rest.   He also advised that accounts of all sufferings endured by Friends be sent up to London.

The unremitting efforts of Friends to move those in authority to give heed to their declarations of unresisting obedience to the laws; either actively where they did not contravene their religious principles, or passively by suffering whatever penalties were inflicted where active compliance could not be yielded; the accumulated evidence that they were in no way cognizant of or connected with the Fifth Monarchy Men, or any other plotters against the government, and the strong appeals made by M. Fell and some other Friends, to the King and Council on behalf of their suffering brethren, at length were crowned with success, and the King issued a proclamation, ordering all those Friends who had been imprisoned in consequence of the measures taken in reference to the recent insurrection, to be discharged, without being obliged to pay any fees.

But though Friends were thus exonerated from all complicity with those who rebelled against the King, and the prisons were freed from the thousands that had crowded them — in some nigh unto suffocation — yet many were still deprived of liberty on account of refusing to pay tithes, or to take an oath of allegiance. The common people continued greatly prejudiced against them, and incited thereto by wicked and designing men, they joined with the soldiers in violently disturbing their meetings for worship, and in often harassing and maltreating both men and women, engaged in the discharge of their religious duties.

Some old laws, enacted in the reigns of Henry VIII., Elizabeth, and James I., against the Papists, inflicting severe penalties for non-compliance with certain requisitions of the government in church matters, were now revived, and distorted so as to apply them to Friends, and under the influence of the malignant feeling prevailing against them, proved a means for subjecting many to unjust and severe punishment. The Act passed in the reign of Henry VIII., empowered any two Magistrates, upon complaint made against a defendant for not paying tithes, or for any contumacy committed in any suit for tithes, to commit said defendant to jail; there to remain until he obeys the law and satisfies the claim; or gives surety for his compliance.

An Act passed in the reign of Elizabeth, imposed a fine of one shilling on every person over sixteen years of age, " for each Sunday or Holiday," that he absented himself from the parish church.

By another Act, a fine of twenty pounds per month was imposed on every one, over the age mentioned, who committed the same offence.

By a third Act, persons convicted of similar wilful absence from church were made liable to have all their goods, and two-thirds of their lands seized, and sold to pay the said fine of twenty pounds per month ; the same to be repeated every year, so long as they may forbear to be present at the church.

By another Act, passed in the same reign, persons so absenting themselves more than a month, without lawful cause; attending a conventicle, or persuading another to do so, " under pretence of religion," are made liable to be committed to prison, and be there kept until they conform. And if they do not so conform within three months,— being so required by a Magistrate in open Assize,— they abjure the realm. If they refuse to abjure the realm, or if they return without the Queen's license, they shall be deemed felons, and be executed without benefit of clergy.

The law made in the reign of James I., made it imperative on all to swear allegiance to the King, denying any right of the Pope to interfere with the kingdom, or any power in him to excommunicate or depose the King, &c.

There were few of the testimonies of the gospel, for maintaining which Friends suffered more in person and estate, than that against swearing. Founded on the plain and emphatic commands of Christ, and his Apostle James, it allowed of no compromise or subterfuge, in those who believed those commands comprehended oaths of all descriptions, and who acted in accordance with the conviction that they must obey God rather than man. During those days of civil commotion, when the reins of government were repeatedly shifted from one hand to another, the party in power sought to obtain security, by enlisting men's consciences in its support, through what was considered the sacredness of an oath. Though as each came into place and power, the same form was gone through as had been observed at the inauguration of that which went out; showing that an oath added nothing to correct principles where they existed, and afforded no reliable substitute where they were lacking; yet swearing was insisted on by those who, from want of proper enlightenment, and in obedience to long-established custom, disregarded the teachings of experience, and considered it necessary to bind effectually, not only men believing like themselves, but others, whose tender consciences would not allow them to swerve from the allegiance they owed to Christ. Hundreds of Friends languished long in jails, and many suffered the extreme penalty of the law, because they could not take an oath, and yet none of them was ever known to plot against the government under which they were living, or refuse to comply with any law that did not interfere with their religious principles.

One instance is recorded of a Friend who, when he found he was about to be premunired, gave way, stifled the dictates of the Holy Spirit to his soul, and took the required oath of allegiance. But this poor man was mercifully brought to a sense of his fall, and favored with the gift of repentance. In this humble condition, he wrote the following letter to those with whom he had been in prison, and who remained there:

"My dear Friends.— I desire to lay before you this my condition in this my fall, that my fall may be no cause for you to stumble, but that you by it may be the more encouraged to stand; for I have yielded to the betrayer, and so betrayed the innocent seed in me; for I forsook the counsel of the Lord, and consulted with flesh and blood, and so I fell into the snare of the world, and yielded to the covenant; and so I rested satisfied in what I had done, for some certain hours; but when the Lord in his power looked back upon me, then I remembered what I had done; then I remembered that I had denied truth which once I had professed, though once I thought I should have stood when others fell. So the terrors of the Lord have taken hold on me, and I lie under the judgments of the Lord.

"And now I feel the truth of the words that were spoken by Christ, 'That he that faileth in one tittle, is guilty of all;' and now

I feel the truth of that, ' That it is better to forsake wife and child; en, and all that a man hath, even life itself, for Christ and the truth's sake, than to break one tittle of the law of God written in the heart.' So I hope that, by mercy and judgment, the Lord will redeem me to himself again.   The Lord may suffer some to fall, that the standing of them that stand faithful may seem to be the more glorious, and for them to take heed lest they fall.

" Now I know and feel, that it is better to part with any thing of this world, though it be as dear to one as the right hand, or the eye, than to break our peace with God.

" Pray for me ; for my bonds are greater than yours.

EDWARD CHILTON."

Windsor, the 22d of the Eleventh month, 1660.

The Parliament, most of the members of which gave little evidence of devotion to anything but monarchy and vice, in its determination to enforce unqualified obedience to the King and the Anglican hierarchy, endeavored to degrade religion into a mere affair of State, and so in 1662, took upon itself to enact laws which prescribed the avowal of certain religious opinions as essential to holding or exercising the duties of any civil office under the government.   Thus all magistrates, members of corporations, town clerks, &c., must make declaration, that the "Solemn League and Covenant," was unlawful and not binding on any ; and they must, within one year prior to being elected or appointed to any such office, have taken " the sacrament of the Lord's Supper," according to the rites of the " Church of England."   This was to get rid of the Dissenters who were in, or might wish to hold such office.

1661. The famous Savoy Conference — in which a number of Presbyterian ministers met a Commission of Episcopal clergy to attempt so to modify the Liturgy, &c., as to enable the former and those they represented to continue to hold the "livings" they occupied — having failed ; and the minds of the people being kept constantly excited with reports of plots and insurrections concocted and about to be set in action by the Dissenters; which reports were got up and sent on their travels by persons about the Court, the way was believed to be prepared for taking the final step of demanding of all ministers, lecturers, or teachers of religion, conformity to the established " Church," under pains and penalties for refusing; by which, if it was not hoped to induce many to comply, they would·at least offer the means for bringing the obnoxious Dissenters under suffering.   Accordingly the Act of·Uniformity, as it was called, was passed, and being signed by the King, was carried into effect in a very short time. About two thousand "ministers" were thus obliged to give up their "livings" to others who were prepared to comply with the course required. Although the Bishop of London had said, after learning the views of the Presbyterians at the Savoy Conference, "Now we know their views, we will make them all knaves if they conform;" yet many did not scruple to comply; and Neal says, that "Some who persuaded their brethren to dissent, complied themselves and got the others' 'livings.'"

It was not to be expected at such a time, and while such a spirit prevailed among those in power, that Friends should escape, without another effort being made to stop their bold and faithful declarations of the simple, spiritual religion of Christ, and the order and service in his militant church. Those who had now got possession of the rich and high places in the so-called church, and were determined to lord it over the whole heritage, were resolved, if possible, to stop the mouths of the zealous and indefatigable Quakers, who bore an uncompromising testimony against the hierarchy, and priestcraft in all its guises, and its insatiable greed of place and profit. They were an unresisting people, who sought neither civil offices nor lucrative livings, and though they might not be driven into submission to what they delared to be wrong, if heavy fines and imprisonments were imposed for not complying with the laws enacted, their estates might be made a source of income to those who were legally, however unjustly, authorized to inflict punishment on them.

Accordingly a Bill was prepared, and while it was in the hands of the Committee appointed by Parliament, George Whitehead, Richard Hubberthorn and Edward Burrough, obtained interviews with the members, and plead the cause of their suffering brethren with earnestness and truthfulness. G. Whitehead gives an account in his journal of the substance of what was urged against the false charges contained in the Bill, respecting Friends, and the principles they held; also against the unchristian spirit it betrayed, and the cruel measures it enjoined upon a people, whose whole course had showed they were orderly, inoffensive and practically religious. They declared that Friends "Met together in the name and fear of the Lord God, and in obedience to Him, as the saints of old did; so that they might as well go about to make a law, that we should not pray in the name of Christ Jesus, as to make one to hinder or suppress our meetings, which are in his name, and from which we may no more refrain, than Daniel could forbear praying to the true God, though it was contrary to King Darius' decree."

The Bill being reported to the House, a motion was made and carried — Friends having petitioned therefor — that the Quakers be heard at the bar. The aforementioned Friends, together with Edward Pyott, entered, and in turn addressed the Commons; the members being nearly all present. E. Burrough dwelt on the fact that the meetings of Friends did not endanger the public safety, and were not, as alleged in the Preamble — a terror to the people, but were peaceable, and for the worship and service of the Almighty, which was in accordance with the command of God; and that no human law should contravene his commands; if it did, it was *ipso facto*, null and void, and men were not bound to obey it. R. Hubberthorn argued, that whereas the Preamble charged that Friends maintained a secret and strict correspondence among themselves, implying there was, therefore, danger of plotting in their meetings, the very fact of their being open and public, from which none were excluded, proved that no such purpose could be designed; and that if such a fear existed, or Friends entertained any such evil intent, the restricting their meetings to five was the way to promote such secret plotting. He entreated Parliament not to punish a Christian people, entertaining no disorderly principles, on causeless suspicion of danger, nor hinder them in the performance of their religious duty. G. Whitehead reviewed the history of Friends from their rise; showing that though they had been cruelly persecuted under different rulers, they had never rebelled nor sought revenge. That if the King and Parliament should now pass this Bill into a law, and thus endeavor to trample an innocent, conscientious people under foot, it would in no wise tend to their honor, nor add to their security. That the King had solemnly promised liberty of conscience to those who were peaceable; that nothing had occurred, and nothing had been proven against Friends to deprive them of the benefit of that promise, and they were prepared, at any time, to show that their principles were founded on the righteous law of God, and were in accordance with the doctrines and precepts of Christ. Edward Pyott urged upon them the rule laid down by Christ, "Whatsoever ye would that men should do unto you, do ye even so unto them." He reminded them that this was commanded *them* as well as all others, by Christ himself, and begged them to consider what they would have done, were they in the same situation as Friends.

Friends had previously given at length in print the reasons for their conscientious refusal to swear; that it was in consequence of the express command of Christ and his Apostle James, and from no hesitation about owing allegiance to the King, or obedience to the laws which did not interfere with the rights of conscience. They also pointed out how the proposed law would open a wide door for all low and wicked people to maltreat and spoil them.

Several of the members seemed affected by what was said, and some, curious to know the speakers better, pulled G. Whitehead by the arm as they were passing out. He asked what was wanted? they replied, " Nothing, but to look upon you." George was then but twenty-six years of age.

The Bill, however, was passed [1662], and although the King had told the Parliament at its opening, that " He valued himself much upon keeping his word, and upon making good whatsoever he had promised to his subjects;" and although he had sufficient knowledge of what Friends were as Christian professors, as explained to him by R. Hubberthorn in the interview wherein he promised, *on the word of a king*, Friends should not suffer for their religion or opinions, while peaceable, yet he signed it and it became a law. So worthless is " the word of a king" who is devoid of religious principles. The law was as follows:

" An Act for preventing mischiefs and dangers that may arise by certain persons called Quakers, and others refusing to take lawful oaths.

" Whereas of late times, certain persons under the name of Quakers, and other names of separation, have taken up, and maintained sundry dangerous opinions and tenets, and among others, that the taking of an oath, in any case whatsoever, although before a lawful Magistrate, is altogether unlawful, and contrary to the word of God ; and the said persons do daily refuse to take an oath, though lawfully tendered, whereby it often happens that the truth is wholly suppressed, and the administration of justice much obstructed : and whereas the said persons, under a pretence of religious worship, do often assemble themselves in great numbers in several parts of this realm, to the great endangering of the public peace and safety, and to the terror of the people, by maintaining a secret and strict correspondence amongst themselves, and in the meantime separating and dividing themselves from the rest of his majesty's good and loyal subjects, and from the public congregations, and usual places of divine worship :

" II. For the redressing therefore, and better preventing the many mischiefs and dangers that do, and may arise by such dangerous tenets, and such unlawful assemblies, (2) Be it enacted by the King's most excellent majesty, by and with the advice and consent of the lords spiritual and temporal, and commons assembled in Parliament, and by authority of the same, that if any person or persons, who maintain that the taking of an oath, in any case soever (although before a lawful Magistrate), is altogether unlawful, and contrary to the word of God, from and after the four-and-twentieth day of March, in this present year of our Lord, one thousand six hundred and sixty-one, shall wilfully and obstinately refuse to take an oath, where, by the laws of the realm, he or she is, or shall be bound to take the same, being lawfully and duly tendered, (3) or shall endeavor to persuade any other person, to whom any such oath shall in like manner be duly and lawfully tendered, to refuse and forbear the taking of the same, (4) or shall by printing, writing, or otherwise go about to maintain and defend that the taking of an oath in any case whatsoever, is altogether unlawful; (5) and if the said persons, commonly called Quakers, shall at any time after the said four-and-twentieth day of March, depart from the places of their several habitations, and assemble themselves to the number of five or more, of the age of sixteen years or upwards, at any one time, in any place under pretence of joining in a religious worship not authorized by the laws of this realm, that then in all and every such case the party so offending, being thereof lawfully convicted by verdict of twelve men, or by his own confession, or by notorious evidence of the fact," &c. The penalty for the first offence was a fine not exceeding £5, and in case of its non-payment, three months, imprisonment: for a second offence a fine of £10, and in default of payment an imprisonment of six months at hard labor, and for a similar offence a third time, to be transported beyond the sea to some of his majesty's possessions.

The regular meetings of Friends were at this time scattered throughout England, Scotland and Ireland, and in some neighborhoods they were numerous and large. In the "London Friends' Meetings," it is stated there were in that city at that time two of what were called *public* meeting-houses; where some ministering Friends resorted, to meet with the mixed multitude that usually flocked to them, with the expectation of hearing the doctrines of the gospel as held by Friends, declared and elucidated, under the authority of the Head of the Church, by some of his anointed servants. Beside these, there were in the city and its suburbs twenty houses, in which meetings of Friends for Divine worship were regularly held.

Other dissenters were, under other laws, liable to be harassed and suffer, if they continued to assemble for public worship; but it was evident, from the provisions of this special law, that a fearful storm was gathering over Friends, which would try the foundation on which they were built, and bring those who were faithful to their Divine Master into great suffering. The civic officers in London were specially inimical to Friends. The Lord Mayor was Richard Brown, who, having been a Puritan and a Republican in the days of the Commonwealth, thought it the more necessary to make an unwonted display of his present loyalty to the King, by persecuting and mercilessly beating and abusing the unresisting Quakers. He had commanded the "train bands," when the Fifth Monarchy Men were put down, and had received knighthood for his subserviency. He had a congenial associate in John Robinson, who for his services to the royal party, had been made Governor of the Tower. Armed with the authority of law, unrestricted by the few mutilated rights yet accorded to Englishmen not in harmony with the Court and Church, and devoid of those principles of mercy and justice that would have restrained their evil passions, these two men became conspicuous as tools, for carrying out the designs of those who hoped, by unflagging oppression and pitiless distress, to wear out the constancy of Friends; to force them to betray their principles, and bow their necks to the galling yoke of the established Church.

CHAPTER XIII.

E. Burrough — John Burnyeat — Scotland — A. Jaffray — Converts — Patrick Livingstone — Misrepresentation — Excommunication — Visits to Ireland — Wm. Edmundson's Account of things in Ireland — Persecution — Friends on the Continent — Wm. Ames in Germany — E. Burrough and S. Fisher at Dunkirk — Friends at Rome — John Perrot — Catharine Evans and Sarah Cheevers at Malta.

E. BURROUGH, when before the Committee of Parliament, in relation to the then pending Bill, had told them plainly, that if it became a law, he should feel it his duty to exhort his brethren still to continue to attend their meetings. He was at Bristol when information reached him that the law was passed, and would soon go into operation. He felt that he must hasten back to London, to strengthen and encourage Friends there, by his example, and by sharing with them whatever affliction might be permitted to come upon them. When taking leave of his beloved fellow members, he uttered, what the event proved to be, a prophetic declaration : " I go up to London again, to lay down my life for a testimony to that truth I have declared, through the power of the Spirit of God."

Before entering upon the brief account that may be given of the general suffering among Friends that ensued, when the threatening storm burst in full force upon the Society, it may be well to glance at the progress made by Friends in other parts, where the seed had been sown.

Scotland had partaken of the fervent, indefatigable labors of John Burnyeat. This Friend was born in Cumberland, and had been convinced of the truth of Friends' doctrines, under the ministry of George Fox, in 1653, being at the time in the twenty-third year of his age. He remarks that he had been a high professor of religion, and was greatly esteemed by others, who, like himself, could talk much about their belief in Christ, and what He had done for them as a Saviour, in offering himself as a sacrifice for their sins ; but who knew little or nothing about Him as a Light in their consciences, and a Refiner and Sanctifier. But when he heard G. Fox, in the power of the everlasting gospel, direct " his hearers unto the light and appearance of Christ Jesus their Saviour in their own hearts, that they might come really to know Him," the witness for Truth in his breast, convinced him that this was glad tidings of salvation to him, and to all who were willing thus to have Christ revealed in them, and to obey his blessed voice.

The account given in his journal of his own experience and that of his companions, is so descriptive of the thorough, heart-cleansing, transforming process through which they passed, before they knew what it was to be truly grafted into Christ as fruit-bearing branches, and which, all who are really born again, and know what it is to enter the kingdom of God, have to undergo, that it may be properly introduced here, and profitably pondered by the reader. It shows what kind of Christian believers the early Friends were, and how they were made such.

Speaking of the work of regeneration, as it was begun and carried on in his soul, and in the souls of his fellow believers, as they were made willing to wait upon the Light, or Grace of God, and yield obedience to its requisitions upon them — he says :

"Through which deep judgment did spring in my soul, and great affliction did grow in my heart; by which I was brought into tribulation and sorrow, such as I had never known before in all my profession of religion; so that I might say, in spirit, it was the day of Jacob's troubles; for the God of heaven by the light of his blessed Son, which shined in my heart, let me see the body of death and power of sin which reigned in me, and brought me to feel the guilt of it upon my conscience; so that I could say, He made me, even as it were, to possess the sins of my youth. And notwithstanding all my high profession of an imputative righteousness, and that though I lived in the act of sin, the guilt of it should not be charged upon me, but imputed to Christ, and his righteousness imputed to me, yet I found it otherwise when I was turned unto the Light which did manifest all reprovable things. . . . Then I saw there was need of a Saviour to save *from* sin, as well as of the blood of a sacrificed Christ to blot out sin, and of faith in his name for the remission of sins passed. . . . Then when the war was truly begun, all my high conceit in my invented notional faith, and my pretence and hopes of justification thereby, were overthrown; so that all I had builded for several years in my profession, after the days of my mouth — in which tender stirrings were in me after acquaintance with the Lord, and the knowledge of and peace with him—was seen to be but a Babel tower; upon which God brought confusion." . . . . "I saw I had been feeding with all the carnal professors of religion [on the tree of knowledge], and how we had made a profession of that which we had no possession of; but our souls were in the death, feeding upon the talk of that which the saints of old did enjoy; and wherein I saw there was no getting to the tree of life, that our souls might be healed by the leaves of it, and so feed upon the fruit thereof, that we might live forever, but as there was a coming under the wounding, slaying sword that Christ brings; by which the life of the old man comes to be destroyed—who would still live in sin and serve it, and yet profess faith in Christ and to be his servant — which is impossible. I saw there was no remedy [alternative], either I must be buried, by that fiery baptism of Christ, with Him into death, or there could be no rising with Him into newness of life; there might be a rising into newness of profession, notion and words; but that would not do; it was newness of life I must come to; the other I had tried over and over. I saw that I must die with Him, or be planted with Him in the likeness of his death; that is die unto sin, if ever I came to be planted with Him, in the likeness of his resurrection, and so live unto God; according to Romans, vi." .... "Then we began to mourn after a Saviour and to cry for a deliverer and helper; for the day of the Lord that made desolate had overtaken us, and the fire and sword that Christ brings upon the earth, by which He takes away peace, had reached unto us, and yet we knew not from whence it came, though the burning and the judgment thereby were begun, by which the filth was to be taken away. . . . . . . In that distress and vale of tears wherein we walked, our hearts became quite dead to the world, and all its pleasures and glory, and also to all our former dead profession; for we saw there was no life in it, nor help nor salvation from it; though some of us had tried it thoroughly. . . . . And as we had been turned to the light, so were our understandings informed, and we got to some degree of staidness in our minds ✦ which before had been as the troubled sea — and a hope began to appear in us, and we met together often, and waited to see the salvation of God, which we had heard of that He would work by his own power. And after we had met together for some time, ... the wonderful power from on high was revealed amongst us; and many hearts were reached therewith, and broken and melted before the God of the whole earth; and great dread and trembling fell upon many, and the very chains of death were broken thereby, the bonds loosed, and many souls eased and set at liberty; and the prisoners of hope began to come forth, and they that had sat in darkness to show themselves. And the promises of the Lord came to be fulfilled unto many, as spoken of by Isaiah, xlix. 9, and lxii. 7, and lxi. 23. .... Thus being gathered by the Lord Jesus Christ, the great Shepherd and Bishop of our souls, we became his sheep, and did learn to know his voice and to follow Him; and He gave unto us eternal life, and manifested the riches of his grace in our hearts, by which we were saved, through faith, and delivered from that wrath, fear and terror which had been so weighty upon our souls, and, in measure, from the power of that death, which had reigned and made us miserable and wretched; and we came to partake of that life wherein the blessedness doth consist. . . . . . O! the joy and the great delight with which our hearts were overcome at many times in our reverent and holy assemblies. . . . . And now unto them that had known the night of sorrow, was the joyful morning come, according to that ancient experience of David, Psalm, xxx. 5, and such as had been in the foregoing deep afflictions, tossings and distresses, came to witness the fulfilling of that great gospel promise; 'O! thou afflicted, tossed with tempests and not comforted; behold I will lay thy stones with fair colors, and lay thy foundations with sapphires: and I will make thy windows of agates, and thy gates of carbuncles, and all thy borders of pleasant stones. And all thy children shall be taught of the Lord, and great shall be the peace of thy children. In righteousness shalt thou be established, thou shalt be far from oppression, for thou shalt not fear, and from terror, for it shall not come near thee.' "

John Burnyeat came forth in the ministry in a little more than three years after his convincement, but did not travel much out of his own county for some time after. He was imprisoned twenty-three weeks in Carlisle jail, after being beaten and otherwise maltreated, for speaking to priest Denton. In 1658 he travelled into Scotland, where his ministry was effectual to the convincement of several. He was engaged there about three months, and travelled as far north as Aberdeen, back to Edinburg, and west to Port Patrick, preaching in the "steeple-houses and markets," and other places where the people congregated.

In 1662, William Dewsbury was drawn in the love of the Gospel, to visit Scotland a second time. His labors appear to have been more immediately productive of numerous convincements in and about Aberdeen, than those of the Friends who preceded him at that place. No doubt, many had been previously preparing to receive the glad tidings which he proclaimed among them. J. Barclay, in reference to the religious engagements of the different ministers who had been sent into Scotland, and the effect resulting from their loving labors, says, "The gospel messages of these and other zealous witnesses, reached the consciences of many who heard them. Yet with regard to Aberdeen and the district thereabout, no open espousal of the tenets peculiar to the people called Quakers took place until towards the end of the year 1662; when William Dewsbury was drawn in love to these prepared and panting souls, to proclaim among them 'The acceptable year of the Lord;' even deliverance from the bondage of corruption, by the law of the Spirit of life in Christ Jesus. Thus was the remarkable work of convincement — which had been secretly going on in some hearts for several years, through many deep conflicts of spirit — helped forward to such a point, that they were made willing even in all things, to take up the daily cross, *though in various respects as bitter as death*, and to follow the guidance of Christ by his Spirit within them, whithersoever He should be pleased to lead."

Among the converts made then and there [1662], was Alexander Jaffray. He had been in religious profession with the Scotch Presbyterians, and had held the rank of Chief Magistrate of the city of Aberdeen. By giving heed to the manifestations of Divine Grace to his soul, he had long before become dissatisfied with many of the opinions and practices to which his education had led him to attach much importance, had been enabled to put them away, and, in great humiliation of self, and close watchfulness unto prayer, had been kept striving for " A state of pure and full reliance upon the Lord's direction; of simple, quiet resignation unto the Lord's disposal in all things, according as his will and power should be made known in the secret of the heart."

Not long after his convincement, A. Jaffray went to reside at Inverary, where a meeting of Friends was soon established, a considerable number of the more respectable citizens adopting the principles preached by them. After the Episcopal clergy had got the power into their hands, they easily persuaded Archbishop Sharp to sanction their persecution of Friends, and having summoned A. Jaffray to appear before the High Commission Court, they sentenced him " To be confined to his own dwelling-house, and keep no meetings therein, nor go anywhere without the bishop's license, under the penalty of a fine of six hundred marks."

Some other persons, both men and women, well known and highly respected, having joined with Friends in and about Aberdeen, the usual misrepresentation and gross slander of them and their principles, were industriously spread abroad; especially from the pulpits of the "ordained ministers." Thus R. Barclay says they were described, " As demented, distracted, bodily possessed of the devil; as practising abominations under color of being led to them by the Spirit." As to their principles, they were branded with being " Blasphemous deniers of the true Christ; of heaven, of hell, angels, the resurrection of the body, and day of judgment; inconsistent with magistracy; nothing better than John of Leyden, and his accomplices."

For a time these calumnies were received by the generality of the people as truths; but it was not long before sober-minded individuals began to investigate for themselves, and finding that these charges were untrue, and originated in prejudice and malice, many were led to embrace the doctrines promulgated by Friends, and to be willing to bear the testimonies of the Gospel maintained by them. Among these converts were George Gray and Nancy Sim, both unlearned and in humble life, yet held in such high repute, for their blameless lives and religious experience, that the "minister" of the parish in which they lived said, boastingly, "That he had a weaver and a poor woman, whom he would defy any of the Quakers to equalize, either for knowledge or good life." When, therefore, he found they had left his teachings and were joined with Friends, he was greatly incensed; but his anger availed not, for George Gray continued steadfast in the faith, and became an acceptable minister, a scribe well instructed unto the Kingdom of heaven, bringing forth out of his treasury things new and old. Nancy Sim opened her house for Friends to hold their meetings, and in a short time the people flocked to them in such numbers, there was not room to accommodate them, so that it was frequently necessary to adjourn to the fields.

One of the most extraordinary ministers of the gospel raised up in Scotland in those early days of the Society, was Patrick Livingstone, who was a native of Montrose, and in 1659, when twenty-five years of age, was thoroughly convinced of the accordance of the doctrines and testimonies of the gospel, as promulgated by Friends, with the truths recorded in the holy Scriptures, and the revelations of the Holy Spirit in the hearts of true believers. After having been some time settled and grounded in the Truth, with his strong will so subjected to that of his Divine master, that he was willing to suffer reproach and persecution for his name's sake, he was entrusted with a large gift in the ministry, and became a zealous messenger of the glad tidings of the gospel to his own nation, and to the people of England and Ireland. He was a valiant soldier in the Lamb's army, not turning his back in the day of battle and suffering, but, freed from the fear of man, strove fervently for the honor of his glorified Captain, and the promotion of his cause. His services among his own countrymen were eminently blessed, so that through his means the number of members in Scotland was multiplied; and he was instrumental in settling a meeting at Kinmuck, which continued to increase until it became the largest in that nation.

Persecution soon began to show itself; the rabble, prompted thereto by the "leaders of the people," often abused Friends greatly when they appeared in the streets of the towns, stoning them, beating them, and sometimes pulling out their hair. Many were subjected to long imprisonment; when, as in England, they had to bear the barbarous treatment of cruel and implacable jailers. Yet here, as in other places, the patient, unresisting endurance of the sufferers, preached louder than words; so that while the peace that passeth all understanding rewarded those who endured hardness as good soldiers of Jesus Christ, others were thereby drawn into the communion of Friends, and made willing to share in their bonds and afflictions.

The misrepresentation and denunciation of the ministers were accompanied by the published censure of the presbytery, and the excommunication of not a few of those whom they had once esteemed as ornaments of their " church." Among others, James Urquhart was excommunicated, and the " minister " of the parish where he resided, named Wm. Forbes, was directed to publish it from the pulpit. Knowing Urquhart to be an honest, good man, the minister was very loth to be the instrument of thus publicly branding him as a heretic and disbeliever. But finding that unless he obeyed, he would be likely to lose his stipend, he stifled his convictions, and thus publicly denounced him. No sooner had he performed the service laid upon him by the presbytery, than he fell into great distress of mind, and could no longer officiate in his parish, until at length he was brought to a willingness publicly to confess, " That his discomposure was a just judgment upon him for cursing with his tongue a person whom he believed in his conscience to be a very honest man."

But alas! his own daughter, Jane Forbes, having forsaken the vanities of the world, and also the endearing associations of her domestic relations and associations, to obtain peace of mind by joining the Quakers, she was excommunicated, and her father was required publicly to pronounce the sentence. The poor man again struggled to overcome his convictions that the whole proceeding was wrong, or to escape from the repulsive service required of him, but being threatened with ejection from his living unless he did as he was bid, he determined to obey; but when about to read the excommunication he was suddenly struck with death.

In Ireland many faithful laborers were continually travelling to and fro throughout most parts of the country. William Edmundson speaks of Thomas Loe, John Burnyeat and Robert Lodge, as laboring abundantly in the gospel of Christ Jesus, and whose exercises were often crowned with much success. He, himself, was indefatigable in his efforts to promote the cause of truth and right-eousness, and often suffered deeply and resignedly in its behalf. Resolute and undaunted, he was always ready to face any danger when duty called; while such was the purity of his life, the fervency of his spirit, the firmness of his faith, and the disinterested compre-hensiveness of his Christian love for the souls of his fellow men, that he often won the admiration of even his persecutors, and ob-tained great influence with many of those in power.

Referring to the state of things among Friends in Ireland, about the end of the Commonwealth [1660], he says, "Many people were convinced and meetings increased mightily; yet some who were con-vinced and professed truth in words, did not walk answerably in their conversations, but were careless and loose; from under the cross of Christ, both in words and deeds; which gave occasion to our adversaries to reproach us, and speak evil of the way of truth, and was a stumbling-block to others, in whom were desires after the knowledge of God and the way of life. The concern of this came weightily upon me, and sunk my spirit into a deep exercise for Truth, which was discernible in my face and body, to those who knew me; and I was made a threshing instrument in the hand of the Lord, to thresh sharply, and to reprove and rebuke such as walked loosely in the liberty of their own will and flesh, and held the profession of truth in unrighteousness."

Again, in reference to the troubles brought upon Friends by the proclamation issued by the King, soon after his restoration, he ob-serves, "King Charles coming in, the nation was in heaps of con-fusion, and people ran upon us, as if they would destroy us at once or swallow us up; breaking up our meetings, taking us up on the highways and haling us to prison; so that there was a general im-prisonment of Friends in this nation. I was prisoner at Mary-borough with many more Friends; yet the Lord supported and bore up our spirits above sufferings and men's cruelties. Friends were fresh and lively in the Lord's goodness and covenant of light and life; contented in the will of God: for we had many heavenly, blessed meetings in prison, and the Lord's presence was with us, to our great comfort and consolation in Him, who wrought liberty for us in his own time."

Feeling it laid upon him as a religious duty, to make an effort to have Friends set free, Wm. Edmundson, prisoner though he was, applied to the Sheriff, who granted him leave of absence for twenty days. Hastening to Dublin he presented a petition to the Earls of

Orrery and Mountrath, who at that time were the Lord Justices, and to Sir Morris Eustace, the Chancellor; asking that, as Friends were guilty of no breach of law, nor any disloyalty to the government, they should be liberated from imprisonment. He says, " I was closely exercised in that service, but the Lord's power gave me courage, opened my way to proceed, and gave success to it, so that I got an order for Friends' liberty throughout the nation; though they were full of business, and abundance of all sorts attending." Several copies of this order having been made out, he got them all signed and dispatched to the Sheriffs of the respective counties. Finding on his return to the prison at Maryborough that his fellow prisoners were still kept there, though the Government's order had been received, he made inquiry for the cause, and learned that it was for the fees charged, and the Sheriff said they should lie there until they rotted, unless the fees were paid. William now applied to the Justices of the county for a statement of the cause for which the Friends were still detained, and having obtained it, he at once set off again for Dublin. He arrived at the residence of the Earl of Mountrath, just as he had entered his coach to go to the Council, and the Earl seeing him coming, stopped the coach to inquire his business. William told him the cause of his present journey and handed him the statement of the Justices. Being invited to follow to the Council chamber, he went; where he was furnished with another order to the Sheriffs to release Friends without their being required to pay any fees. He now returned again to the prison and saw his friends set free: the Sheriff telling him he was a devil. But when the Episcopal bishops were reinstated in their dioceses, and Parliament had passed the law against the Quakers, Friends in Ireland participated in the suffering which their fellow members had to endure throughout the kingdom.

A number of Friends had been engaged in endeavoring to spread the principles held by them, in different parts of the Continent of Europe, but the three who labored more abundantly there, and met with the most success, were William Ames, William Caton, and John Stubbs. Under the ministry of the two first named, there had been several of the citizens of Amsterdam convinced in the year 1657, (among whom were the parents of William Sewel, the historian,) and a meeting was established there, though the magistrates were very unfriendly. As those Friends, in consequence of being called to other fields of labor, could not remain long with those who were newly gathered, few of whom had much religious experience, their meeting soon became a resort for persons holding extravagant opinions, whose conduct tended to bring Friends into disrepute. In order to clear the truth of reproach, Friends testified against the unsound and fantastical sentiments of those who had intruded into their meetings, and printed an exposition of the doctrines they held, and the mode of worship approved by them. This tended to counteract in measure the evil consequences that had followed the conduct of those not belonging to the Society; and in course of a few years, there were several Friends residing in different parts of Holland.

In 1659, William Caton was again in Holland, when he found that Friends' meeting in Amsterdam was still occasionally much disturbed by disorderly persons, who sometimes behaved in a riotous manner; calculated, if not intended, to excite displeasure in the Magistrates, and to lead to the interference of the civil authority. In order to escape this annoyance, he advised Friends to change the place for meeting frequently, one week in one house, the next week in another; which was done to some advantage.

William Ames travelled through parts of Germany, visiting serious-minded people where he heard of them, and declaring the message with which he was entrusted, wherever he found an opening to receive it. At Heidelberg [1660] he was admitted to the Court of Charles Lodowick, Elector Palatinate, who treated him kindly, entertaining him at his own table, and allowing him to have free intercourse with his subjects. At the town of Kriesheim, not far from Worms, he met with a company of Baptists, and a considerable number of them were convinced of the truth by his preaching, and made open profession of it for many years in that country. After William Penn had got possession of Pennsylvania, these German Friends removed there, and, settling not far from Philadelphia, gave the place of their abode the name of Germantown.

The effect produced by the ministerial labors of William Ames, stirred up some of those in power, to enact a law imposing a fine on whoever should entertain him; but the Elector remitted the fine, and when the Consistory sent Ames word to appear before it, the Prince forbade their meddling with him. William also travelled into Bohemia and Poland, but it does not appear that the people in those countries were prepared to receive the doctrines he preached.

In 1659, E. Burrough and Samuel Fisher went over to Dunkirk, which, though a French town, contained an English garrison, and

was held by the British Crown. On arriving they were sent for by
the deputy Governor, who, with the council of officers, questioned
them as to their principles, and the business on which they had come.
The Friends informed them they had come under a sense of duty,
to endeavor to show the Jesuits, Friars, and Priests, the error of
their ways, and to preach the everlasting gospel to them and the
people. The Council wished to persuade them to give up their design, and to depart from the place, treating them, however, with
courtesy. They told the officers they could not take their advice,
as they believed they had come in the will of God, and they must
strive to perform the duty He had laid upon them. The next day
they managed to obtain an interview with the Capuchin friars, in
which they declared unto them the gospel truth, that every man has
received a measure of Divine Grace or Light of Christ, which was
intended to enlighten and lead him in the way of salvation ; and
that the Lord was about to search and try them, and bring their
idolatrous worship and ways to an end. They afterwards addressed
a number of Queries to them, written in Latin. They then sought
and obtained interviews with Friars of other orders, and with the
chief of the Jesuits. But none of them were willing to accept the
doctrine inculcated by the Friends, and when they essayed to speak
with the nuns, the latter asked them if they were of *the order* of the
Quakers? and on their replying they were of those called Quakers,
the nuns said they were forbidden to hear them, and left them.

Hearing that after they had left, one of the Chaplains had spoken
against them, they prepared and sent to him six Propositions, which
they informed him, they were prepared to defend and prove to be
true, viz. :

"1st. That Christ hath enlightened *all* men with a light sufficient
to bring them to salvation if they follow it.

2d. That God hath given Christ to be the Saviour of *all* men.

3d. That none are justified by Christ and his righteousness without them, but as they have received Christ and his righteousness,
and witnessed them revealed in themselves.

4th. That the saints of God may be perfectly free from sin in this
life, so as no more to commit it.

5th. That the national ministers and churches, not only of papists,
but of the protestants also, as they now stand, are not true ministers
and churches of Christ.

6th. That the Scriptures are a true declaration, given forth from
the Spirit of God, by holy men of God, moved by it to write them;

and are profitable; but are not the foundation, nor the most perfect rule of faith and life to the saints."

The Chaplain, however, was not disposed to enter into a disputation with them, and sent them word "The Governor was not willing." After this the Friends had several meetings with the soldiers of the garrison, and having performed the service required of them, after another interview with the Governor and Council, in which they had much religious discourse, they returned to England.

John Stubbs and Samuel Fisher visited Rome in 1660, and obtained an opportunity to speak to some of the Cardinals and others of the Romish hierarchy; testifying against their superstition and idolatry, and the dark condition of the papists generally. They also circulated some works setting forth the truths of the gospel; which some of the monks confessed were true, but said that if they should make such an acknowledgment openly, they might expect to be burnt. It does not appear that these two Friends were molested while in the Pope's dominions, and when they had got through with the work in which they were engaged, they came safely to their homes.

About this same time John Perrot and John Love went to Rome. On their way, at Leghorn, they were arrested and brought before some of the officers of the Inquisition, who interrogated them; but their answers were such, that no charge could be laid against them, and they were dismissed. At Venice, John Perrot obtained an interview with the Doge, and after free conversation with him, presented him with some of the writings of Friends. At Rome they bore such open testimony against the idolatry of the people as to give offence, and they were apprehended and lodged in the Inquisition. J. Love died in this fearful prison, and though it was given out at the time that he starved himself to death, it was afterwards divulged that he maintained his integrity to the last, and that there was reason to believe he was assassinated in the night, to prevent his giving trouble in Rome. Perrot was detained a long time in the Inquisition, and would seem to have given place to no little spiritual pride on account of his suffering for the truth. After he was released, he wrote some letters to Friends in England couched in language strongly savoring of spiritual assumption and self-exaltation; which letters he signed with his given name only — John, in imitation of the Apostle. He appears to have been a man of considerable intellectual ability, and to have come in measure under the power of true religion; but for want of keeping in humility and on the watch, he lost his first estate, and ran into opposition to the truth; finally becoming an open apostate, violating and setting at naught the testimonies of Truth which he once had maintained and contended for. His subsequent doings will be mentioned in another place.

In 1658, Catharine Evans and Sarah Chevers, of whom mention has already been made, embarked for Leghorn, intending to journey to Alexandria. After spending some days in religious service in Leghorn, they set sail for Alexandria. The captain of the vessel in which they were, concluded to stop at Malta with another ship in company with him. The women Friends had a presentiment when arrived there, that much suffering awaited them, though of what kind they did not see. Having met the English Consul in the street, the day after their arrival, he stopped and inquired for what purpose they had come there. On their informing him how it happened they were there, and presenting him with some books, he kindly invited them to make his house their home while they stayed. Accepting his invitation, they remained in his family about three months; during which time many came to see them. Having called on the Governor, he told them he had a sister in the nunnery who was desirous to see them. They accordingly went to the place and had free conversation — so far as they could understand each other's language — with the nuns, among whom they distributed some books. While on this visit, one of the monks took them into the chapel, and insisted on their bowing to the high altar, which they as firmly refused, letting him know they considered it would be idolatry. On one occasion they went into one of the places of worship while they were engaged in the service, and Catharine, turning her back to the high altar, kneeled down and offered up praise and supplication to the Most High. The priest who was officiating, putting off his robes, came and kneeled by her, so remaining until she was done. He then offered her something he had in his hand, which she refusing to take, he handed it to Sarah, but she returned it to him again. He asked them if they were Lutherans or Calvinists? to which they replying, No; he asked them if they would be willing to go to Rome? They said, No. Having inquired if they were not Catholics? they told him they were servants of the living God. The people around looked on with wonder, but they were allowed to depart in peace.

They now had a sense that there was some plotting for their hurt, of which they told the Consul, and their suspicion that he was, in some way, accessory to it. He did not deny it, and said that he wanted some sign that they were messengers of God. A few days afterwards, they were sent for by the Inquisition. They were taken before the chief Inquisitor, who, after questioning them and hearing their replies, told them, that if they would change their mind, and do as they commanded them, to let him know, otherwise he would use them as he pleased. They replied, " the will of the Lord be done," and they were shut up in an inner room, with only two small holes in it for the admission of light and air. As the weather was extremely hot, they thought there was an intention to suffocate them. Again and again they were brought before the Inquisitor, sometimes together and sometimes separate, and various means were resorted to, to induce them to acknowledge the Catholic religion, and the authority of the Pope and his subordinates, but they steadily refused; adhering to their first declaration, that they had been brought there innocently on their part; that they were servants of Jesus Christ, and that they could not acknowledge any authority that was contrary to his, nor any religion but that which was in accordance with the Holy Scriptures, and the testimony of the Holy Spirit in their hearts. Efforts were repeatedly made to compel them to swear that they would speak the truth, when they were questioned about George Fox, what induced them to leave their own country and travel abroad, and what they expected to do if they were ever set at liberty. But while they affirmed they would always speak the truth, they quoted the command of Christ and of his Apostle James, not to swear, as being imperative to them, and therefore they could not conscientiously take an oath. On being asked what Christ it was they owned? they replied Jesus Christ, who died at Jerusalem.

The friars tried, in many ways, to entrap them in their talk, and the Chief Inquisitor had them brought before him time after time; sometimes threatening them with death, and sometimes with imprisonment for life, if they did not bow to his authority, recant their religion, and become members of the Catholic Church. But they remained firm and unyielding; declaring they were in the true faith, and were resigned to leave the event of their release from the persecution and suffering they endured, to Him who was able to uphold them under all that He might permit to come upon them, and who would, if He saw fit, release them in his own time, either by taking them to himself, or by opening their prison doors and letting them go free. At times, as they felt qualified, they spoke boldly against the idolatry and superstition they witnessed around them, and with Divine authority rebuked the hypocrisy and duplicity of the friars.

The room in which they were long kept, was not only small, hot, and without proper ventilation, but it was infested with a cloud of gnats, which were incessantly stinging and annoying them; so that it seemed probable, the intention of their persecutors was to wear out life by these combined causes. All desire for food left them; they fasted for days, their strength failed, and an eruption broke out over all parts of their bodies. Faint, and deprived of every outward thing necessary to administer relief or refreshment, these devoted women looked for death from day to day, if not by the slow torture they were undergoing, by being burnt at the stake, with which they were repeatedly threatened. But they were resigned to whatever might be permitted to come upon them, and amid all their afflictions were permitted to enjoy that peace which passeth all understanding, and which He whom they served, alone could give.

On more than one occasion a physician was brought to see them, but they declined to take the medicine he prescribed, asking the monk who accompanied him, if their object was to try to lengthen out their lives, in order to keep them in suffering? He attempted to strike Catharine on the mouth with his crucifix, which he held up before her. She asked him, if he thought that was the kind of cross which Paul said crucified him to the world and the world unto him? He said it was, which she denying, he again attempted to strike her on the mouth. She told him the apostles were no strikers; when he declared she should be first whipped, then quartered and her body burnt. She replied, she did not fear him, for the Lord was on their side. That evening there was a proclamation made at the gate of the Inquisition, drums were beaten, and there seemed to be great commotion among the people. The Friends, who could hear the tumult, supposed their burning, which had often been threatened, was now about to be executed. It turned out, however, that all the noise and apparent preparation for some great event, had been got up to frighten them, with a hope they would thereby be induced to comply with the commands of the Inquisitor; but they were enabled to resign themselves into the Lord's keeping, and patiently abide the issue.

They were now parted, and shut up in rooms distant one from another, so that they could hold no intercourse with each other, unless occasionally they persuaded some one to carry a note. Then their pens, ink and paper, were taken away, and no one was per- mitted to receive or deliver a message from or to either of them. This separation was felt by them to be the greatest affliction they had to endure, and it was continued a whole year.

For more than three years they were thus closely imprisoned, ex- cept when one or the other was so ill that it became necessary, in order to preserve life, she should be removed to where there was a more free circulation of air. During all this time, there was no re- laxation of artifice and effort, to induce them to yield obedience to the Church of Rome, or to acknowledge its ministers, its ceremo- nials and its discipline, to belong to the Church of Christ. Threats of being put in chains, of whipping, and of death by various forms, were freely employed to drive them to bow to a crucifix, or to a painting of a saint, or to partake of bread and wine, which the monks affirmed had been transformed into the flesh and blood of Christ, by their consecration; or to do anything, however small, that might be taken as an evidence of their submission to the papal hierarchy; but by keeping constantly on the watch, they were kept in the Lord's holy fear, and it preserved them from the snares of death. Thus they were kept from betraying the cause of their Divine Master, and occasionally, when persons came to their rooms to look at them, or for other purposes, as they were enabled, they preached the gospel to them, and instructed them in the way of salvation.

It was proposed, at one time, to send Catharine to Rome, and then to send both, but the Inquisitors were not able to agree about it. One of the friars was, therefore, dispatched there, to lay the charges that had been drawn up against them, before the high officers; but though there seemed to be preparations made for some more deci- sive measures in their case, nothing came of it. The English Consul came to see them, bringing with him a piece of money sent them by an English Captain then in the port; but they were not easy to re- ceive it. The Consul was much affected with seeing the condition they were in. Catharine reminded him of their having told him, he was conniving at their being brought under the power of the Inquisition, and that he had said he wanted a sign that they were servants of God, and she asked him, whether what they then told him was not true, viz., " Thou art a condemned person, and standest guilty before God; yet nevertheless repent, if thou canst find a place." He trembled, and was so overcome he could hardly stand. Not long after he died.

Two Englishmen who arrived at Malta, hearing of their imprisonment in the Inquisition, made great efforts to obtain their release, and though they were not successful in that, yet it is probable their declarations, and the interest they manifested in their welfare, had a good effect; for the Magistrates had them brought before them, inquired whether they were in want of anything, and directed their pens, ink and paper to be restored, and they allowed to write to England. The newly appointed Consul and Francis Steward, an English captain, made further efforts to have them set free, but the Magistrates informed them it could not be done without an order from the Pope. Yet the two Friends were brought into the court chamber, and had an opportunity of speaking to their countrymen. "The captain of the ship, who also was there, spoke to them with tears in his eyes, and told them what he had done in their behalf, but in vain. 'It is the Inquisitor,' said he, 'who will not let you go free: you have preached among these people.' To which they said, that they had witnessed the truth, which they were willing to maintain with their blood. He replied, if they could be set free, he would freely give them their passage, and provide for them. And they returned, his love was as well accepted of the Lord, as if he did carry them. He also offered them money, but they refused to take any. They then gave him a relation of their imprisonment and sufferings, and said they could not change their minds, though they were to be burnt to ashes, or chopped in small pieces. In the meanwhile it grieved the captain that he could not obtain their liberty; and going away, he prayed God to comfort them; and they besought the Lord to bless and preserve him unto everlasting life, and never to let him, nor his, go without a blessing from Him, for his love. For he ventured himself exceedingly in that place, by laboring to get their freedom."

These outside attempts to procure the release of the Friends, irritated the Inquisitors, friars and monks greatly; but though they strongly declared they would take away their lives rather than let them go, unless they would own their religion, they yet feared to proceed so far with two subjects of Great Britain, who were known to be in their keeping. They, however, were shut up as closely as possible, the doors of their rooms not being opened for weeks, and the system of abuse and annoyance heretofore practised, being kept up by those who passed in their food, and other ways waited on them. They refused to work for the friars, but when able employed part of their time in knitting stockings for the poor, and in mending the clothing of other prisoners, when it was brought to them.

Daniel Baker, a minister among Friends, who had left England intending to go to Constantinople, was stopped at Smyrna by the English Consul, who sent him to Zante, from whence he went to Leghorn. While here he felt strongly drawn to go to Malta and see if he could extend any succor to Catharine Evans and Sarah Chevers, who he knew had been prisoners for three years in the Inquisition there. Accordingly he took shipping for that island, and on his arrival there obtained an audience with the grand Inquisitor. As he spoke the Italian language, he addressed him in it, with these words, "I am come to demand the just liberty of my innocent friends, the English women, in prison in the Inquisition." The Inquisitor asked whether he was related to them, or whether he had come out of England for the purpose of delivering that message. Finding that neither was the case, he told him the women should remain where they were until they died, unless some of the English merchants would be bound in the sum of four thousand dollars, that if allowed to go, they would never return to that place. Neither he nor the two women were willing that this should be done; so his demand was fruitless. He then proposed to the Inquisitor to be imprisoned for them, if they might go free; and finding that would not be accepted, he offered that his own life should be taken, if by that means he could purchase their discharge. Such unselfish, Christian love struck the priests with admiration; but they were inexorable, and some of them, fearing the influence such a man might have, the Pope's deputy threatened him with the Inquisition, and wished to have him bound not to speak to any one while he stayed on the island, but himself and the British. Daniel refused to comply, and they were afraid to push the matter further. He remained in the town three weeks, during which time he managed to send the Friends some letters and receive replies from them. He also got to see them at a distance, and to address a few words of loving encouragement to them.

Some time after Daniel's departure, the Friends were told that if they would only kiss the cross, they would be set free, and might stay at the Consul's house until they obtained a passage to England; but they refused, declaring they would never purchase their liberty at any such price. After they had been imprisoned about six months more than three years, Catharine Evans was impressed with a sense that the time for them to go forth was come, and that their application for liberty would now be granted. Soon after having heard that the Inquisitor was in the Inquisition Court chamber, they desired to be allowed to go and speak to him. Being admitted to his presence, they told him, though they had committed no wrong, they had been suffering nearly four years for conscience' sake, and they desired that an end should be put to their imprisonment. He spoke courteously to them, and said he would apply to the Pope to release them without their entering into any obligation. A few days after, he came to them attended by the Chancellor, and a Lieutenant, and asked them if they would return to their families, if he set them free? They replied, that if it were the will of the Almighty, such was their intent; whereupon the Inquisitor told them they were discharged, and he and the Magistrates and other officers took leave of them respectfully, saying they wished them a prosperous journey home. Catharine and Sarah then kneeled down and prayed that nothing might be laid to their [the officers] charge, as they knew not what they had done. They were detained eleven weeks longer at the Consul's house, when an English frigate came into the port, on which they embarked, and stopping a short time at Leghorn, they arrived safe in England. Friends in England had not been unmindful of them while in their bondage, but had used every means at their command to obtain their liberation, and it was thought that the intercession of George Fox and Gilbert Latey, with the Lord d'Aubigny, the Spanish Ambassador in London, who at their instance wrote to those in Malta, was a cause of their release.

CHAPTER XIV.

Apology of the New England Persecutors — William Leddra — Wenlock Christison — Edward Wharton — Trouble of the Court — Trial of W. Christison — A new Law — Friends travel into Maine—Severe Scourging—Mary Tompkins — Alice Ambrose — Ann Coleman — Elizabeth Hooten — Her Sufferings in Massachusetts — King's Mandamus — It is taken to Boston — G. Fox and two Representatives from Boston — The Severity of Persecution abates — Last instance of Woman-Whipping in Boston.

BEFORE noticing the continued sanguinary persecution of Friends in New England, it will be right to give the reader some account of a declaration put forth by the Governor and Magistrates of Boston, in justification of the course they had pursued towards Friends, and especially in regard to taking away the lives of

William Robinson and Marmaduke Stevenson. This apology appears to have been prepared and published between the time when those two Friends were executed, and the subsequent hanging of Mary Dyer. [1659.]

After stating their conviction, that their care for the support of the law of the land and the law of God, entitled them to the commendation of all prudent and pious men, yet as weaker men out of pity, and for want of full information, may be induced to blame them as bloody persecutors, they think it requisite to rehearse the gradual steps taken. They then say that *having heard* of the "pernicious principles and practices" of the Quakers, they had thought it right and for the good of the people, to send those away who arrived at their shores, in order to secure the peace and order which was established, and prevent their destructive opinions from undermining the same. They then proceed as follows :

"And accordingly a law was made and published, prohibiting all masters of ships to bring any Quakers into this jurisdiction, and themselves from coming in on a penalty of the house of correction, till they should be sent away. Notwithstanding which, by a back door they found entrance, and the penalty inflicted on themselves proving insufficient to restrain their impudent and insolent obtrusions, was increased by the loss of the ears of those who offended the second time ; which also being too weak a defence against their impetuous frantic fury, necessitated us to endeavor our security ; and upon serious consideration, after the former experiments by their incessant assaults, a law was made, that such persons should be banished upon pain of death, according to the example of England, in their provision against Jesuits ; which sentence being regularly pronounced at the last Court of Assistants, against the parties above named, and they either returning, or continuing presumptuously in this jurisdiction after the time limited, were apprehended, and owning themselves to be the persons banished, were sentenced by the Court to death, according to the law aforesaid, which hath been executed upon two of them. Mary Dyer (upon petition of her son, and the mercy and clemency of this Court,) had liberty to depart within two days ; which she hath accepted of. The consideration of our gradual proceeding will vindicate us from the clamorous accusations of severity, our own just and necessary defence calling upon us, (other means failing,) to offer the point, which these persons have violently and wilfully rushed upon, and thereby become felons *de se ;* which, might it have been prevented, and the sov-

ereign law, *salus populi*, been preserved, our former proceedings, as
well as the sparing Mary Dyer upon an inconsiderable intercession,
will manifestly evince, that we desire their lives absent, rather than
their deaths present."

Those who have attempted to excuse the unchristian course of the
authorities in New England, in their treatment of Friends, have
asserted they *believed* that the principles held by Friends were calculated to overturn civil government, as well as to uproot the
cardinal doctrines of Christianity. Such may have been the case
with some, who had no means for ascertaining the truth. In this
supposed justification, sent forth to the world by the active members of the government, they state they *had heard* that their (the
Quakers) "principles and practices," were destructive of good order,
&c. Or, as Governor Endicott stated in an address to King Charles,
after the judicial murder of Mary Dyer, that the Quakers " were
open blasphemers, seducers from the glorious trinity, from the Lord
Jesus Christ and the blessed gospel ; open enemies to the government itself, and malignant promoters of doctrines directly tending
to subvert both Church and State." Upon all these points Friends
had made clear and specific statements; denying the truths of all
such charges, and emphatically declaring the principle of Christianity firmly held by them in common with all other orthodox professors, and the obedient, non-resisting practices those principles led
them into, under whatever form of government they were placed.
These declarations were not made in a corner. They were openly
avowed and published abroad to the world. What apology then
can be made for men in power, who hastily and hotly condemned
innocent men and women to death upon mere *hearsay* evidence of
the religious opinions they held ; refusing to examine into the truth
or falsity of the allegations, vague and trivial as those allegations
were, and sternly and persistently forbidding their victims to plead
on their own behalf? The same kind of reasoning as is used in the
Magistrates' apology, would justify every " *auto da fe* " lighted by
the Inquisition.

That civil government is a Divine ordinance has always been
acknowledged by Friends, to be executed for the encouragement
and protection of those who do well, and for the terror and punishment of those who do evil. But no government can change the
intrinsic character of right and wrong. It may make this or that
lawful or unlawful ; but it cannot make that right by law which is
morally wrong in itself. The almighty Ruler of the universe, in

sanctioning civil government, conferred no power on it to contravene his will, or to take from his creature man the obligation to reverence and obey Him in all things. The duty of subjects to render obedience to law, therefore runs parallel with the obligation on rulers to require nothing contrary to the known will of the Supreme Lawgiver. Where this parallelism is broken, by those in authority enacting and enforcing laws that come in conflict with the teaching of the New Testament, or with the immediate disclosure of the Divine will to the soul, obedience to the higher law is a duty that cannot be set aside by human authority, although that authority may wickedly extend the power it usurps, to inflict punishment for not conforming to its unrighteous behests.

The course of the Massachusetts Governor and Courts was in accordance with the principles on which the Puritans had before acted, a determined attempt to crush out all liberty of conscience, which nevertheless they claimed for themselves. For in the aforementioned address to King Charles, they say, they " Had chosen rather the pure Scripture worship, with a good conscience, in that remote wilderness among the heathen, than the pleasures of England, with subjection to the imposition of the then so disposed, and so far prevailing hierarchy; which they could not do without *an 'evil conscience.*" It has been already seen how determined they were that others, not of the same faith with themselves, should not enjoy the same rights as they possessed ; and it will be further exemplified by the continuance of the narrative of the transactions in New England, in relation to Friends.

It was before mentioned, when giving some account of the persecution of Friends, at Boston, that William Leddra and Wenlock Christison, had been banished from that Colony on pain of death. The former, whose home was in Barbadoes, where he had lived for some years, had suffered grievously, while, in obedience to what he believed to be his religious duty, he was travelling from place to place in the Colonies, preaching the glad tidings of salvation to the people. But stripes and imprisonment could not turn him aside from obeying the requirings of his Lord and Master, and so, though knowing that obedience would probably cost him his life, when it was made known to him he must return to Boston, he freely gave up and went there. This was in the Tenth month of 1660. He was at once arrested and committed to jail, where he was chained fast to a large log of wood, and kept in that condition, without fire, for several months, though the weather was cold. On the ninth of the First month, 1661, he was again brought before the Court, still chained to the log, and on his asking the jailer, when he intended to take the irons from his legs? he replied, "When thou art going' to be hanged."

Sewel, who took great pains to obtain correct information, gives the following account of the trial and execution:—" W. Leddra then being brought to the bar, it was told him by the rulers, speaking of their law, that he was found guilty, and so that he was to die. He said, 'What evil have I done?' The answer was, his own confession was as good as a thousand witnesses. He asked, what that was? To which they answered, that he owned those Quakers that were put to death, and that they were innocent. Besides, that he would not put off his hat in Court, and that he said *thee* and *thou*. Then said William to them. 'You will put me to death for speaking English, and for not putting off my clothes?' To this Major-General Denison returned, 'A man may speak treason in English.' And William replied, 'Is it treason to say *thee* and *thou* to a single person?' But none answered, only Simon Broadstreet, one of the Court, asked him whether he would go for England? To which he answered, 'I have no business there.' Hereupon Broadstreet, pointing to the gallows, said, 'Then you shall go that way.' To which William returned, 'What! will ye put me to death for breathing in the air in your jurisdiction? And for what you have against me, I appeal to the laws of England for my trial; and if by them I am guilty, I refuse not to die.' Of this no notice was taken, but instead thereof, they endeavored to persuade him to recant of his error, (as they styled it,) and to conform; to which, with a grave magnanimity, he answered, 'What! to join with such murderers as you are? Then let every man that meets me say, Lo, this is the man that hath forsaken the God of his salvation.'

. "Whilst the trial of W. Leddra was thus going on, Wenlock Christison, who was already banished upon pain of death, came into the Court. This struck a damp upon them, insomuch that for some space of time there was silence in the Court.

"It having been told W. Leddra, that at the last General Court he had liberty given him to go for England, or to go out of their jurisdiction, and that promising to do so, and come there no more, he might save his life; he answered, 'I stand not in my own will, but in the will of the Lord: if I may have my freedom, I shall go, but to make you a promise, I cannot.' But this was so far from giving content, that they proceeded to pronounce sentence of death again:

him; which being done, he was led from the Court to prison again. The day before his death, he wrote a letter to his friends; from which the following extracts are taken:

"'Most dear and inwardly beloved,—The sweet influences of the morning star, like a flood distilling into my innocent habitation, hath so filled me with the joy of the Lord in the beauty of holiness, that my spirit is as if it did not inhabit a tabernacle of clay, but is wholly swallowed up in the bosom of eternity, from whence it had its being.

"'Alas, alas, what can the wrath and spirit of man, that lusteth to envy, aggravated by the heat and strength of the king of the locusts, which came out of the pit, do unto one that is hid in the secret places of the Almighty, or unto them that are gathered under the healing wings of the Prince of Peace? under whose armor of light they shall be able to stand in the day of trial, having on the breast-plate of righteousness, and the sword of the Spirit, which is their weapon of war against spiritual wickedness, principalities and powers, and the rulers of the darkness of this world, both within and without. Oh, my beloved! I have waited as a dove at the windows of the ark, and have stood still in that watch, which the Master, (without whom I could do nothing,) did at his coming reward with fulness of his love; wherein my heart did rejoice, that I might in the love and life of God speak a few words to you, sealed with the spirit of promise, that the taste thereof might be a savor of life to your life, and a testimony in you of my innocent death: and if I had been altogether silent, and the Lord had not opened my mouth unto you, yet He would have opened your hearts, and there have sealed my innocency with the streams of life, by which we are all baptized into that body which is in God, in whom and in whose presence there is life: in which, as you abide, you stand upon the pillar and ground of truth. . . . .

"'As the flowing of the ocean doth fill every creek and branch thereof, and then retires again towards his own being and fulness, and leaves a savor behind it, so doth the life and virtue of God flow into every one of your hearts, whom He hath made partakers of his divine nature; and when it withdraws but a little, it leaves a sweet savor behind it, that many can say, they are made clean through the word that He hath spoken to them: in which innocent condition you may see what you are in the presence of God, and what you are without Him. . . . . And although you know these things, and many of you, much more than I can say; yet, for the love and zeal I bear to the truth and honor of God, and tender desire of my soul to those that are young; that they may read me in that from which I write, to strengthen them against the wiles of the subtile serpent that beguiled Eve, I say, stand in the watch within, in the fear of the Lord, which is the very entrance of wisdom, and the state where you are ready to receive the secrets of the Lord: hunger and thirst patiently, be not weary, neither doubt. Stand still, and cease from thy own working, and in due time thou shalt enter into the rest, and thy eyes shall behold his salvation, whose testimonies are sure and righteous altogether: let them be as a seal upon thine arm, and as jewels about thy neck, that others may see what the Lord hath done for your souls. Confess Him before men, yea, before his greatest enemies; fear not what they can do unto you: greater is He that is in you, than he that is in the world: for He will clothe you with humility, and in the power of his meekness you shall reign over the rage of all your enemies in the favor of God; wherein as you stand in faith, ye are the salt of the earth; for many seeing your good works may glorify God in the day of their visitation.

.   .   .   .

Your Brother,

WILLIAM LEDDRA.'

Boston Jail, First month 13th, 1661.

"The next day after this letter was written, the execution of W. Leddra was performed, which was on the 14th of the First month. After the lecture was ended, the Governor, John Endicott, came with a guard of soldiers to the prison, where W. Leddra's irons were taken off, with which he had been chained to a log both night and day during the cold winter; and now they were knocked off, according to what the jailer once said, as hath been related before. William then having taken his leave of Wenlock Christison, and others then in bonds, when called, went forth to the slaughter, encompassed with a guard to prevent his speaking to his friends; which Edward Wharton, an inhabitant of Salem, and also banished on pain of death, seeing, and speaking against, one amongst the company said, 'O Edward, it will be your turn next!' To which Captain Oliver added, 'If you speak a word, I'll stop your mouth.' Then W. Leddra being brought to the foot of the ladder, was pinioned, and as he was about to ascend the same, he took leave of his friend, E. Wharton, to whom he said, 'All that will be Christ's disciples, must take up the cross.' He standing upon the ladder, somebody said, 'William, have you anything to say to the people?' Thereupon he spoke thus, 'For the testimony of Jesus, and for testifying against deceivers and the deceived, I am brought here to suffer.' This took so much with the people, that it wrought a tenderness in many. But to quench this, priest Allen said to the spectators, 'People, I would not have you think it strange to see a man so willing to die, for that's no new thing. And you may read how the apostle said, that some should be given up to strong delusions, and even dare to die for it.' But he did not say where the apostle speaks so. As the executioner was putting the halter about his neck, he was heard to say, 'I commit my righteous cause unto thee, O God.' The executioner then being charged to make haste, W. Leddra, at the turning of the ladder, cried, 'Lord Jesus, receive my spirit;' and so he was turned off, and finished his days. The hangman cut down the dead body, and lest it should be as barbarously used as those of William Robinson and Marmaduke Stevenson, (which none holding when cut down, fell to the ground to the breaking of W. Robinson's skull,) Edward Wharton, John Chamberlain, and others, caught the body in their arms and laid it on the ground, till the hangman had stripped it of its clothes. The body being stripped, William's friends took it, laid it in a coffin, and buried it. For further confirmation of what hath been related, the following letter of one of the spectators, that was there accidentally, may be added:

"'BOSTON, March 26, 1661.

"'On the 14th of this instant, there was one William Leddra, who was put to death. The people of the town told me, he might go away if he would; but when I made further inquiry, I heard the Marshal say, that he was chained in prison, from the time he was condemned, to the day of his execution. I am not of his opinion: but yet truly methought the Lord did mightily appear in the man. I went to one of the Magistrates of Cambridge, who had been of the jury that condemned him, (as he told me himself,) and I asked him by what rule he did it? He answered me that he was a rogue, a very rogue. But what is this to the question, (I said,) where is your rule? He said, he had abused authority. Then I goes after the man, (W. Leddra,) and asked him, whether he did not look on it as a breach of rule to slight and undervalue authority? And I said that Paul gave Festus the title of honor, though he was a heathen. "I do not say that these Magistrates are heathens," I said. Then when the man was on the ladder, he looked on me, and called me friend, and said, " Know that this day I am willing to offer up my life for the witness of Jesus." Then I desired leave of the officers to speak, and said, Gentlemen, I am a stranger both to your persons and country, and yet a friend to both, and I cried aloud, for the Lord's sake, take not away the man's life; but remember Gamaliel's counsel to the Jews. If this be of man it will come to nought, but if it be of God, ye cannot overthrow it: but be careful ye be not found fighters against God. And the captain said, Why had you not come to the prison? The reason was, because I heard the man might go if he would; and therefore I called him down from the tree, and said, Come down, William, you may go if you will. Then Captain Oliver said, it was no such matter; and asked, what I had to do with it? And besides, bade me begone: and I told them, I was willing: for I cannot endure to see this, I said. And when I was in the town, some did seem to sympathize with me in my grief. But I told them they had no warrant from the word of God, nor precedent from our country, nor power from his majesty, to hang the man. I rest your friend,

THOMAS WILKIE.' "

To Mr. George Ladd, master of the
"America," now at Barbadoes.

Edward Wharton, who, though under sentence of banishment on pain of death, had striven to keep as near to his dear friend Wm. Leddra, as the blood-stained executioners of his sentence would permit, was an inhabitant of Salem, and had been convinced of the principles of Friends early after they were first promulgated in that Colony. He had been kept close prisoner in Boston for nearly a year prior to his being brought before the Court to receive sentence. While before them he inquired of Governor Endicott what he had to lay to his charge? Who replied, his not taking off his hat. E. Wharton observed, that wearing his hat was no ground for perse-cuting him, and he repeated his request to be informed what was the specific charge against him. But he could obtain no other re-ply to this, than "You shall know that afterwards:" he was then sent back and confined in the same cell with Wm. Leddra. When again brought before the Court he again asked, "For what he was treated as an evil-doer?"

"The Court.— Your hair is too long, and you have disobeyed the commandment which sayeth, ' Honor thy father and mother.'

E. W.— Wherein?

Court.— In that you will not put off your hat to magistrates.

E. W.— I own and love all magistrates and rulers, who are for the punishment of evil-doers, and for the praise of them that do well.

.   .   .   .

Rawson.— Hold up your hand.

E. W.— I will not. Thou hast no evil to charge me with.

Rawson.— Hear your sentence of banishment.

E. W.— Have a care what you do; for if you murder me, my blood will lie heavy upon you.

Rawson.— Edward Wharton, attend to your sentence of banishment. You are, upon pain of death, to depart this jurisdiction; it · being the eleventh of this instant, March [1661], by the one and twentieth of the same, on pain of death."

E. Wharton told the Court, he had no intention to go away, and then addressing the persons assembled on the injustice and inhumanity of the proceedings, told them he had been taken from his home where he was following his lawful calling, and led through the country like a culprit, without being able to find out of what he was accused, and now he bid them take notice, there had been nothing alleged against him, but the length of his hair, and wearing his hat.

As E. Wharton was a man of good repute and influence among his fellow-citizens, many of whom had expressed their indignation at the imprisonments, and cruel scourgings already inflicted upon him, on account of his religious belief and the kindness shown by him to his suffering brethren and sisters in the same household of faith, his case gave great uneasiness to his persecutors, and they were anxious to get rid of him as speedily as possible.

The Court of Boston found it had entered upon a course the end of which it could not discern; but which, as it dyed the hands of its members more and more deeply with blood, multiplied the number who were liable to become its victims, while it was exciting more strongly the opposition of their own people, and calling forth the condemnation of its fellow colonists. Fears, lest the home government — now restored to a monarchy, with the episcopal hierarchy re-established in power — might call it to account for its illegal and inhuman proceedings, began to shake its arrogant assumption of power, and to lead its members to doubt the policy of continuing the execution of their murderous laws, even under the pretext of maintaining their rigid religious belief and discipline intact. There were many within its jurisdiction, who had already committed what the law designated an offence incurring the penalty of banishment on pain of death, and there were several who had been sent away after receiving that sentence. These latter, both men and women, had left their homes and gone forth at their Master's bidding, to do his work, with their lives in their hands; and the experience acquired within the short time since the punishment of death had been prescribed for Quakers, once banished and again found within the limits of its power, convinced the Court, that however much it hated and despised them, they counted not their lives dear unto themselves, and so soon as they believed duty required it, they would return to warn its members of the wickedness of the course they were pursuing, and meekly suffer whatever might be permitted to come upon them. But it appeared to have determined that one already within their grasp, should not escape the doom they had prepared for such incorrigible Quakers.

Sewel in his account of the trial of Wm. Leddra mentions, that while it was going on, Wenlock Christison walked into the Court. He was a man naturally of resolute and independent spirit, which, having been brought under the yoke and government of Christ, left him firm in purpose and unflinching in manner, when engaged in his Master's service, and required to stand in opposition to the unrighteous exactions of his fellow-men.

The Court was about to pass sentence of death on Wm. Leddra, when Wenlock entered. He had before suffered under sentence of the Court, and knew well the spirit and temper of its members. His unexpected appearance, boldly facing the men who had declared he should die, should he again be found within their jurisdiction, struck them with such surprise and fear, that it was some time before they could proceed with their business. At length one of the Magistrates said, " Here is another, fetch him to the bar.

Rawson.— Is not your name Wenlock Christison ?

W. C.— Yes.

Endicott.— Wast thou not banished on pain of death ?

W. C.— Yea, I was.

Endicott.— What dost thou here then ?

W. C.— I am come to warn you that you shed no more innocent blood ; for the blood that you have shed already cries to the Lord for vengeance."

He was then sent to the prison. On the day of Wm. Leddra's execution he was again brought before the Court.

" Member of the Court.— Unless you renounce your religion you shall surely die.

W. C.— Nay, I will not change my religion nor seek to save my life; neither do I intend to deny my Master; but if I lose my life for Christ's sake, and the preaching of the gospel, I shall save my life."

Some of the members refusing to condemn him at that time, he was remanded to the prison, and a person afterwards saying to him that William Leddra was dead, and " O! thy turn is next," he replied, " The will of the Lord be done."

At the next General Court in the Fourth month, 1661, he was again arraigned, and Governor Endicott asked him, " What he had to say why he should not die?

W. C.— I have done nothing worthy of death; if I had, I refuse not to die.

Endicott.— Thou art come in amongst us in rebellion, which is the sin of witchcraft, and ought to be punished.

W. C.— I came not in among you in rebellion, but in obedience to the God of heaven, not in contempt of any one of you, but in love to your souls and bodies; and *that* you shall know one day, when you and all men must give an account of the deeds done in the body. Take heed, for you cannot escape the righteous judgments of God.

Major-General Adderton.— You pronounce woes and judgments, and those that are gone before you, pronounced woes and judgments, but the judgments of the Lord are not come upon us yet.

W. C.— Be not proud, neither let your spirits be lifted up. God doth but wait until the measure of iniquity is filled up, and you have run your ungodly race; then will the wrath of God come upon you to the uttermost. And as for thy part, it hangs over thy head, and is near to be poured down upon thee, and shall come as a thief in the night, suddenly, when thou thinkest not of it.* By what law will you put me to death?

Court.— We have a law, and by our law, you are to die.

W. C.— So said the Jews of Christ, we have a law, and by our law he ought to die. Who empowered you to make that law?

Court.— We have a patent and are patentees; judge whether we have not power to make laws?

* It was certainly a remarkable coincidence, if we call it nothing more, that not long after, General Adderton, when returning from reviewing some soldiers, was suddenly thrown from his horse and killed instantly.

W. C.— What! have you power to make laws repugnant to the laws of England?

Endicott.— Nay.

W. C.— Then you are gone beyond your bounds, and have forfeited your patent; and this is more than you can answer. Are you subjects to the King; yea or nay?

Rawson.— What will you infer from that, what good will that do you?

W. C.— If you are, say so: for in your petition to the King, you desire that he will protect you, and that you may be worthy to kneel among his loyal subjects.

Court.— Yes: we are so.

W. C.—Well, so am I; and for anything I know, am as good as you, if not better; for if the King did but know your hearts as God knows them, he would see they are as rotten towards him as they are toward God. Therefore, seeing that you and I are subjects to the King, I demand to be tried by the laws of my own nation.

Court.— You shall be tried by a bench and jury."

[Heretofore the Court had, itself, exercised the powers of accuser, judge and jury, but as taking of life without trial by jury was in opposition to the law of England, it began to fear the consequences if it persevered in the practice.]

" W. C.— That is not the law, but the manner of it: for if you will be as good as your word, you must set me at liberty; for I never heard or read of any law that was in England to hang Quakers.

Endicott.— There is a law to hang Jesuits.

W. C.— If you put me to death, it is not because I go under the name of a Jesuit, but a Quaker; therefore I appeal to the laws of my own nation.

Court.— You are in our hands, and have broken our laws, and we will try you.

W. C.— Your *will* is your law, and what you have power to do *that* you will do, and seeing that the jury must go forth on my life, this I say to them, in the fear of the living God: Jury, take heed what you do, for you have sworn by the living God, that you will true trial make, and just verdict give according to the evidence. What have I done to deserve death? Keep your hands out of innocent blood."

The jury being charged by the Court, went out and quickly returned with a verdict of guilty.

" Secretary.— Wenlock Christison, hold up your hand.

W. C.— I will not. I am here and can hear thee.

Secretary.— Guilty or not guilty?

W. C —I deny all guilt, for my conscience is clear in the sight of God.

Endicott.— The jury hath condemned thee.

W. C.— The Lord doth justify me; who art thou that condemnest?"

" Then they voted as to the sentence of death, but were in a manner confounded, for several could not vote him guilty of death. The Governor seeing this division, said, ' I could find in my heart to go home :' being in such a rage, that he flung something furiously on the table; which made Wenlock say, 'It were better for thee to be at home than here, for thou art about a bloody piece of work.' Then the Governor put the Court to vote again; but this was done confusedly, which so incensed the Governor, that he stood up and said, ' You that will not consent, record it : I thank God I am not afraid to give judgment.' ' Wenlock Christison, hearken to your sentence: you must return to the place whence you came, and thence to the place of execution, and there you must be hanged until you are dead, dead, dead.'

W. C.—' The will of the Lord be done, in whose will I came amongst you, and in whose counsel I stand, feeling his eternal power, that will uphold me unto the last gasp.' Moreover, ' Known be it•unto you all, that if ye have power to take my life from me, my soul shall enter into everlasting rest and peace with God, where you yourselves shall never come. And if ye have power to take my life from me, which I do question, I do believe you shall never more take Quakers' lives from them; note my words: do not think to weary out the living God, by taking away the lives of his servants. What do you gain by it? for the last man that you have put to death, here are five come in his room. And if ye have power to take my life from me, God can raise up the same principle of life in ten of his servants, and send them among you in my room, that you may have torment upon torment, which is your portion; for there is no peace to the wicked, saith my God.'

Endicott.— Take him away."

Wenlock was conducted back to prison, where were upwards of twenty Friends incarcerated; five of whom had been banished on pain of death.

George Bishop having published a work, giving an account of the sufferings of Friends in some of the New England Colonies, inflicted under the sanction of laws enacted there, also narrating the doings of the Courts, and the sentiments avowed by some of their members, it had come to the King's knowledge, who said he would put a stop to it. It is probable, that by some means this had reached the ears of Governor Endicott and his coadjutors; for in five days after they had sentenced W. Christison to be hung, the day before that appointed for his execution the Marshal and Constable came to the prison, and informed him and his companions in tribulation, they were sent by the Court to acquaint them with their new law.

"W. C.— What means this : have ye a *new law ?*

Marshal.— Yes.

W. C.— Then ye have deceived most people.

Marshal.— Why ?

W. C.— Because they did think the gallows had been your last weapon. Your Magistrates said that your law was a good and wholesome law, made for your peace and the safeguard of your courtry. What! are your hands now become weak ? The power of God is over you all."

Thus the prison-doors were opened, and twenty-seven men and women Friends ; some of whom had been long pent up in its cramped and unventilated cells, were set at liberty ; two of them however, Peter Pearson and Judith Brown, to undergo the penalty prescribed by the " new law ; " which was whipping at the cart's tail, through the different towns, as the victims were thus driven out of the limits of the Colony. [1661.]

This was not a *new law*, having been enacted by the authorities in Boston, in 1658. It authorized any person, to apprehend a "vagabond Quaker," who did not give respect " *by the usual gestures thereof;* " to take him or her before a Magistrate, who shall grant a warrant " to the constable or other *meet* person," who shall " have him or her stripped naked from the middle upward, and tied to a cart's tail," and whipped through the town ; then transfer him or her to the constable of the next town, and so on until out of the jurisdiction of the Court. In case of the return of a " vagabond Quaker," who had been thus punished, he or she was to be placed in jail, and, unless the Court ordered otherwise, he or she was to be branded on the left shoulder with the letter R, then severely whipped and sent away as before.*

The two Friends, P. Pearson and J. Brown, were strangers in the country. They were stripped to the waist, tied to the cart, and lashed through the streets of Boston : where they further suffered is

* " Blue Laws of Connecticut, Quaker Laws," &c.

not mentioned. The Friends liberated, began, at once, to preach boldly to the people, and with such effect, that the Magistrates, at their wits' end how to stop the spread of Quaker principles, called out the soldiers, and ordered a company of them to drive all the Quakers out of the Colony, and into the wilderness; which was done. But notwithstanding the torture of the lash that awaited them, they all returned; those who were residents, to their homes, and those who had come to the place under a sense of religious duty, to enter again on the service required of them.

The plea now resorted to for inflicting punishment on Friends was, that they were " *vagabonds* ;" though those who were residents in the Colony, both men and women, were known to be honest and industrious persons, some of them with families which they supported reputably by their respective callings; and those who came from other places were of good families, were amply able to bear their own expenses, and were engaged in the performance of what they believed to be a religious duty.

Scourging in the severest manner was now the common lot of those who publicly preached the doctrines of Friends, or who allowed meetings for worship to be held by them, in their houses. Space cannot be allowed for narrating the many cases of barbarous whipping inflicted. It may, however, be noticed, that in 1662, three women Friends, viz., Mary Tomkins, Alice Ambrose and Ann Coleman, from England, accompanied by Edward Wharton, of whom mention has been already made, travelled north into Maine, declaring the doctrines of the gospel to the people. At Dover, where they had an opportunity to satisfy many who resorted to the inn where they put up, to inquire what their hope and belief were, the minister of the town, in order to prejudice his hearers against them, declared that they denied " magistracy, ministers, the churches of Christ, and the three persons in the trinity." To which they replied, " Take notice, people, this man falsely accuseth us, for godly magistrates and the ministers of Christ we own, and the churches of Christ we own, and that there are three that bear record in heaven, which three are the Father, Word and Spirit, we own." The priest went away in a rage, and many were convinced of the truth.

Major Shapleigh, a Magistrate in Maine, invited them to his house, — where he had a priest residing with him, who went away — and allowing a meeting to be held there, he and his wife were convinced, dismissed their minister, and had a meeting of Friends held regularly under their roof. In the Tenth month of the same year

the same women Friends returned to Maine, to visit and strengthen
the new converts; and when at Dover, the minister who had opposed them, when there before, instigated the Magistrates to arrest
and punish them. Accordingly they were brought before one of
them, who issued a warrant, drawn up by the minister, who acted
as his clerk, and addressed to the constables of eleven towns, as
follows, "You and every of you are required, in the King's majesty's name, to take these vagabond Quakers, Ann Coleman, Mary
Tomkins and Alice Ambrose, and make them fast to the cart's tail;
and driving your cart through your several towns, to whip them
on their backs, not exceeding ten stripes apiece on each of them, in
each town, and so convey them from constable to constable, till they
come out of this jurisdiction. as you will answer it at your peril."
While this inhuman punishment was being inflicted at Dover, two
of the spectators, who rebuked the "minister" for laughing, as he
witnessed the application of the knotted scourge to the bare bodies
of his feeble victims, were placed in the stocks for this manifestation of sympathy. At the third town through which they were
lashed, their "torn bodies and weary steps" so deeply affected the
inhabitants, that one of them persuaded the constable to make him
his deputy, and upon obtaining the warrant, he at once set them at
liberty, and they went on into Maine to the house of Major Shapleigh.

1662. After finishing their work in that section of country, they
believed it required of them to return to Dover. Arriving there they
went to Friends' meeting on the First-day of the week. While Alice
Ambrose was engaged in prayer, two constables, who were brothers,
entered, and seizing her, dragged her out of the house, and through
deep snow and over stumps and trees for the distance of a mile.
Mary Tomkins was then subjected to similar cruelty, and they were
locked up. The next morning, a canoe being procured, they were
told they were to be taken down to the mouth of the harbor, and
there put in the water; so that they should not trouble them any
more. On their refusing to go voluntarily, M. Tomkins was seized,
thrown on her back, and thus dragged down the hill in such a
violent manner, that she repeatedly fainted. Alice Ambrose was
brought down with the same ferocious cruelty, forced into the water
and kept floating alongside the canoe until she was nearly drowned.
But before their murderous purpose could be accomplished, there suddenly arose so violent a storm that the constables and an "elder,"
named Hate-evil Nutwel, who was with them, were obliged to seek
shelter. Afterwards the three women Friends—Ann Coleman shar-

ing in the same persecution — were taken back to the house, and at midnight were driven out into the wilderness to perish, unsheltered, from the cold and snow ; Alice Ambrose's clothes being frozen stiff upon her. But the Master whom they served, and who numbered the very hairs of their heads, supported and cheered them by his invisible presence, healed them of their many injuries, and enabled them to pursue their gospel labors in different places, notwithstanding their portion repeatedly was whipping or being kept in the stocks.

Before leaving the New England persecution of Friends, it may be well to notice the case of Elizabeth Hooten, who, after having been engaged in religious service in Virginia, as before mentioned, had come into Boston, and with Joan Brocksoppe — a woman Friend as old as herself — was imprisoned there for a considerable length of time. [1661.] When liberated, they were carried many miles into the wilderness and there left, without food or means of shelter. Nevertheless they travelled through the woods until they reached Rhode Island, where they were kindly entertained. Thence they sailed for the West Indies, and after being engaged there in religious service, believing it required of them, they returned to Boston. On their arrival they were immediately arrested, and carried on board the ship that brought them; which going to Virginia, landed them there. Thence Elizabeth sailed for England and remained there for some time. Still feeling it required of her to go again to Boston, she made preparation therefor, and having obtained·a license from the King to settle in any of the colonies of the kingdom, and " To buy a house for herself to live in, for Friends to meet in, and ground to bury their dead in," she, with her daughter Elizabeth, then a young woman, set sail and shortly reached the place of destination.

Directly after arriving, E. Hooten endeavored to purchase a house and lot, but the Magistrates, though they paid so much respect to the King's license as not to fine the captain of the ship who brought her over, steadily refused to allow her to purchase property within their jurisdiction. Finding her efforts to establish a home there, fruitless, she proceeded to accomplish the mission of gospel love she had long believed herself called to, towards the inhabitants of the northern part of Massachusetts. In the course of this service, she endured much suffering. [1662.] At Hampton, she was imprisoned for some time. At Dover, she was kept in the stocks, and then thrust into prison, where she remained four days. At Cambridge, she was shut up in a " noisome dungeon " two days and nights, " without food or drink, and with nothing to sit or lie on but the damp floor."

As the weather was cold, her suffering was great, and a Friend having brought her some milk, to keep her from sinking, he was summarily brought before the authorities, who fined him £5, and committed him likewise to prison. The next day Elizabeth was ordered before the same Court, which sentenced her to be whipped through three towns and expelled the Colony. She was then fastened to the whipping-post, and had ten lashes laid on her bare back. At Watertown, she again received ten lashes, and at Dedham, being tied to a cart's tail, ten lashes more were laid on with great severity. Torn and bruised as she was, she was placed on horseback, and without allowing her to take her clothing, carried many miles into the wilderness, and left there near night, with nothing to protect her from the inclement cold, or to defend her from the wolves, which were numerous. There was no doubt but her persecutors thought she must perish. But if so, their design was frustrated: the eternal God was her refuge, and underneath were the everlasting arms, which bore her up, and enabled her to reach a town called Rehoboth in the morning; whence she travelled into Rhode Island, and coming among Friends there, she gave thanks to God who had counted her worthy to suffer for his great name sake, and signally supported her through so many and grievous cruelties.

As her clothing, and some other articles belonging to her, were at Cambridge, Elizabeth and her daughter went there, and having obtained her goods, they started to return to Rhode Island, and in the forest met Sarah Coleman, an aged Friend living at Scituate. Soon after, they were all arrested and carried back to Cambridge, where they were shut up in the prison. When brought before the authorities, they were sentenced to be whipped through three towns, and expelled the Colony. This was executed in the same barbarous manner as before, and they then carried over the line into Rhode Island. [1662.]

Undeterred by the severities practised upon her, this dedicated woman did not hesitate to obey the requirings of her Divine Master, and at two different times in 1662, after her expulsion, as before narrated, she returned to Boston, and each time was treated in the same merciless manner, with imprisonment and severe scourging through various towns. Again, in 1665, she was in Boston, and spoke to the people attending the funeral of Governor Endicott, calling their attention to the miserable condition in which he died. For this she was imprisoned; as she was afterwards at Braintree and Salem. Her peaceful end will be noticed hereafter.

It has been previously stated, t' at in consequence of the dissatisfaction and complaint among many of the inhabitants of the Colony
in Massachusetts, arising from the execution of William Robinson,
Marmaduke Stevenson and Mary Dyer, those in authority at Boston,
had issued a defence of, or rather an apology for, their infliction of
the penalty of death on account of religious belief; a copy of which
apology had been forwarded to the rulers in England. [1659.] So
soon as it became known there, some Friends, especially Edward
Burrough, reviewed it, and exposed its weakness and absurdity;
which review was presented to the King, who expressed his disapprobation of the action of the Colonial Government. Upon intelligence of the hanging of William Leddra reaching the mother country, it moved Friends there deeply, and E. Burrough sought and
obtained an interview with the King, in which he told him, that
" A vein of innocent blood was opened in his kingdom, which, if not
stopped, would overrun all;" to which the King replied, " But I
will stop that vein." E. Burrough then said, it should be done
speedily, "for we know not how many may soon be put to death."
" As speedily as you will," said the King, and ordering his secretary to be called, a mandamus was forthwith drawn up and signed.

A day or two after, E. Burrough again waited on the King, and
asked him if he would be willing to depute one called a Quaker, to
carry his mandamus to New England. The King replying favorably, Samuel Shattock was named, and he was duly empowered to
take the mandamus and deliver it to the Governor. S. Shattock
had been banished from Boston, on pain of death, and it was peculiarly appropriate that such an one should be the messenger of the
King's determination, to stop the further effusion of blood, for holding the religious principles of Friends. The mandamus was as
follows :

" Charles R.— Trusty and well-beloved, we greet you well. —
Having been informed that several of our subjects amongst you,
called Quakers, have been, and are imprisoned by you, whereof
some have been executed, and others, (as hath been represented
unto us,) are in danger to undergo the like; we have thought fit to
signify our pleasure in that behalf for the future; and do hereby
require, that if there be any of those people called Quakers amongst
you, now already condemned to suffer death, or other corporeal punishment, or that are imprisoned, and obnoxious to the like condemnation, you are to forbear to proceed any further therein; but that
you forthwith send the said persons, (whether condemned or impris-

oned,) over into this our kingdom of England, together with the
respective crimes or offences laid to their charge; to the end that
such course may be taken with them here, as shall be agreeable to
our laws, and their demerits. And for so doing, these our letters
shall be your sufficient warrant and discharge.

"Given at our Court at Whitehall, the 9th day of September,
1661, in the thirteenth year of our reign.

"By his majesty's command,

"WILLIAM MORRIS."

The superscription was:

"To our trusty and well-beloved John Endicott, Esq., and to all
and every other the Governor, or Governors of our Plantations of
New England, and of all the Colonies thereunto belonging; that
now are, or hereafter shall be; and to all and every the ministers
and officers of our said Plantations and Colonies whatsoever, within
the continent of New England."

Having so far succeeded in their efforts to protect and aid their
beloved and suffering brethren in New England, there being no
vessel in port likely to sail soon for Boston, Friends at once offered
Ralph Goldsmith, who was master of a good ship, £300 if he would
sail within ten days — with or without freight — and carry S. Shattock to Boston. In six weeks the vessel anchored in that harbor.
It was on the First-day of the week, nevertheless many citizens who
were expecting letters, or anxious to hear the news, went on board;
but it had been agreed that no letters should be delivered, and no
information given of the business on which they had come, until the
messenger had gone on shore and delivered the mandamus; so all
were told that no letters would be delivered until the next day.
The visitors returning into the town, reported having seen S. Shattock, the banished Quaker, on board, which produced no little excitement among the citizens, and especially among the members of
the Quaker-hanging court.

"The next morning Samuel Shattock, the King's deputy, and
Ralph Goldsmith, the commander of the vessel, went on shore; and
sending the men that landed them back to the ship, they two went
through the town to the Governor, John Endicott's door, and
knocked. He sending a man to know their business, they sent
him word their business was from the King of England, and that
they would deliver their message to none but the Governor himself. Thereupon they were admitted to go in, and the Governor

came to them, and commanded Shattock's hat to be taken off, and having received the deputation and mandamus, he laid off his own hat ; and ordering Shattock's hat to be given him again, he looked upon the papers, and then going out, went to the Deputy Governor, and bid the King's deputy and the master of the ship to follow him. Being come to the Deputy Governor, and having consulted with him about the matter, he returned to the two aforesaid persons and said, ' We shall obey his majesty's command.' After this, the master of the ship gave liberty to the passengers to come ashore, which they did, and met together with their friends of the town, to offer up praises to God for this wonderful deliverance."

The Council having met. issued an order to the keeper of the prison to set at liberty all the Quakers then in confinement.

Fearing lest advantage might be taken of their having gone beyond the authority granted in the charter of the Colony, and the opprobrium their course had excited in England, so as to deprive them of the government, the Council resolved to send the chief "minister," John Norton, and Simon Broadstreet, a principal Magistrate, over to England, to make such explanations and present such reasons for their action, as might remove the unfavorable opinions prevailing there, and ward off any unpleasant consequence therefrom. On arriving there, they found the high church party, then in power, looked on them very coldly, and some Royalists in favor at Court, wished to have them tried, so that they were glad to escape being called officially to account, and to return home so soon as they could get away.

George Fox gives in his journal the following account of his interview with them : "Some time after this, several New England Magistrates came over, with one of their priests. We had several discourses with them concerning their murdering our friends, the servants of the Lord ; but they were ashamed to stand to their bloody actions. At one of those meetings I asked Simon Broadstreet, one of the New England Magistrates, Whether he had not an hand in putting to death those four servants of God, whom they hanged for being Quakers only, as they had nicknamed them ? He confessed he had. I then asked him, and the rest of his associates then present, Whether they would acknowledge themselves to be subjects to the laws of England ? And if they did, by what law they had put our friends to death ? They said, they were subjects to the laws of England, and they had put our friends to death by the same law as the Jesuits were put to death here in England. I asked them then, Whether they did believe those Friends of ours, whom they had put to death, were Jesuits or jesuitically affected? They said, Nay. Then, said I, ye have murdered them, if ye have put them to death by the law that Jesuits are put to death here in England, and yet confess they were no Jesuits. By this it plainly appears ye have put them to death in your own wills, without any law. Then Simon Broadstreet, finding himself and his company ensnared by their own words, said, Did we come to catch them? I told them, they had catched themselves, and they might justly be questioned for their lives; and if the father of William Robinson, who was one of those that were put to death, was in town, it was probable he would question them, and bring their lives into jeopardy. Hereupon they began to excuse themselves, saying, 'There was no persecution now amongst them;' but next morning we had letters from New England, giving us account that our friends were persecuted there afresh. Thereupon we went to them again, and showed them our letters, which put them both to silence and to shame. In great fear they seemed to be, lest some should call them to account and prosecute them for their lives, especially Simon Broadstreet; for he had at first before so many witnesses confessed, 'He had a hand in putting our friends to death,' that he could not get from it; though he afterwards through fear shuffled, and would have unsaid it again. After this he and the rest soon left the city, and got back to New England again. I went also to Governor Winthrop, and discoursed with him about these matters; but he assured me, 'He had no hand in putting our friends to death, or in any way persecuting of them, but was one of them that protested against it.'"

But though the command of the King disappointed whatever expectation the rulers may have entertained of taking the lives of other members of the "cursed sect" by hanging, yet, as has been seen, it by no means mitigated their intolerant bigotry, or moved their determination to prevent the hated Quakers taking root in the soil of Massachusetts, if it could be prevented by the persevering infliction of the severest physical suffering. How steadily and unmercifully they pursued the inhuman course they had marked out, the few instances already given, and the records of the different courts fully attest. As it is undesirable to recur to this painful subject again, it may be here stated, that as death removed the members of the Court that had first passed and executed the iniquitous punitive laws against Friends—and the circumstances attending the deaths of many of them were remarkable--persecution in New England subsided. But as Friends increased in numbers, so as to render it necessary to build more meeting-houses to accommodate the many converts that flocked to their meetings, the "ministers," who could not bear to see people resorting to other places than their own steeple-houses for divine worship, repeatedly stirred up the Magistrates to acts of persecution, in order to stop it; and occasionally the law for scourging was carried into execution. The last instance of this kind was at Boston, in 1677, when a woman Friend from Barbadoes, named Margaret Brewster, who had come to New England to warn the inhabitants of the approach of a pestilence that would sweep many away, believing it to be required of her, entered one of the public places of worship in Boston, clothed in sack-cloth, with her face blackened, and ashes on her head, as a sign. Being taken before the Court, with four other Friends, who accompanied her, she told them that she had felt this service required of her by her Divine Master, and had not been willing to give up to perform it until brought so low by sickness that her life was despaired of, when she yielded; and now, if it was the will of the Almighty that she should lay down her life for having performed her duty, she was content. She was ordered to be stripped to the waist and have twenty lashes. This was done, and two days after, twenty-two Friends were subjected to the same punishment, simply because they were attending their place of worship. But this act of barbarism produced such an excitement among the people, that on the next First-day the meeting-house of Friends was so greatly crowded, and so much disapprobation of the course pursued by the Court was expressed, that the members of it became alarmed, and hearing some time after that the home government was dissatisfied with their proceedings, the law fell into disuse, and whipping Quakers came to an end.

It is worthy of note that not long after the warning given by Margaret Brewster, a fatal epidemic, then called the "Black Pox," spread throughout New England, carrying many of the inhabitants to the grave.

Repeated complaints having been made to the home government that the Massachusetts Colonies were executing laws contrary to those of England, a Commission was sent over in 1664, to examine and rectify them; but the rulers refused to comply with their direction. But in 1682, the General Court in Boston, finding that the complaints had assumed a much more grave form, and there was danger of losing their charter, authorized its agent near the royal Court, to offer the King a bribe of two thousand guineas if he would interfere, and stop the proceedings. They, however, were not successful, and in 1683, a *quo warranto* was issued, for them to show cause why, in consequence of the violation of the terms of their charter, by many of the laws being opposed to those of England, it should not be forfeited. Conscious that they could make no valid defence, they allowed· judgment to go by default, and the charter was taken away.* A new charter was afterwards granted by William and Mary.†

CHAPTER XV.

Friends' Marriages declared Legal — John Perrot and his Party — Sufferings under the "Convential Act"— Neal's account — Duty of Publicly Assembling for Divine Worship — Beginning of Persecution in London — Cases before Brown, the Lord Mayor — Trial of J. Crook — Necessity for Friends being cautious about Pleading to Indictments — Letters from Prisoners.

IN 1661, Judge Archer, in one of the Courts in England, gave judgment that the marriages of Friends were legal. A person had brought suit to obtain possession of some property belonging to a child whose father was deceased, and mother married a second time; basing his claim on the assumption, that the marriage of the father and mother was not according to the laws of England, and therefore the child was illegitimate, and could not inherit. The Judge charged the jury, that the fully expressed consent and declaration of the par-

---

* Fowler's Local Laws of Massachusetts, pages 29, 30.

† Governor Endicott was stricken with a disease of so loathsome a character, and the offensiveness of the smell was so great, that his attendants could hardly bear to be with him, and so he died.

Major-General Adderton, who upbraided Wenlock Christison with pronouncing judgments that never,were fulfilled, was soon after thrown from his horse and instantly killed.

John Norton, the priest who attempted to justify the barbarous cruelty inflicted on William Brend, and urged the execution of William Robinson and M. Stevenson, was struck with death soon after returning home from his place of worship on First-day, and was heard to say, the hand, or the judgment of the Lord, is upon me, and sunk down and died.

Richard Bellingham, who became Governor after Endicott, became deranged, and so continued until his death.

ties, const tute marriage, as Adam took Eve for his wife in Paradise. The jury brought in a verdict for the child, thus substantiating the marriage; after which the marriage of Friends was never called in question.

As Friends believed marriage was an ordinance of God, they held that He alone could rightly join any therein, and that the intervention of a priest or minister, was not only uncalled for, but added nothing to the sacredness of the marriage covenant. The opinion that the solemnization of the rite, was a function belonging to a minister of the gospel, Friends knew was altogether unscriptural, but it was cherished by the clergy, as it augmented their .importance, and added to their revenue.

Conscious, that to secure happiness in married life, it was of the greatest importance there should be union between the parties in spiritual views as well as in temporal concerns; and that where this is not the case, the natural consequences are uneasiness and disagreement on the most serious of subjects; and that the offspring of such connection, are liable to grow up with no fixed religious opinions, or with opposing sentiments and feelings, sometimes leading to the interruption of that love and harmony which should reign in the family, Friends required their members to choose their companions for life, from among those of their own Society. This practice has proved a great blessing to the members and the Society, and its abandonment must lead to laxity of family discipline, uncertainty as to religious profession, and weakness in the Body.

After the return of John Perrot—who has been mentioned already —to London, elated by the attention paid him by several Friends, on account of his supposed sufferings in Rome, and his apparent sanctity, as evinced by his appearance and manner, he soon began to manifest a spirit of self-exaltation, and to claim a deeper sight and sense in spiritual things than other Friends had attained. [1661.] As an evidence of this he gave out, he had seen that the custom among Friends of taking off the hat at the time of public prayer, was a mere formality and in conformity with the spirit of the world; and that it was wrong to shave off the beard. Both these notions he carried into practice, and a considerable number of Friends, deceived by the plea of greater spirituality, joined with him, and thereby created a party opposed to George Fox, and the great body of sound, substantial Friends. This caused much grief and exercise to George Fox, who felt deeply the injury, disunity arising from unsound notions, would do to the Society, and the occasion it would give to its enemies to misrepresent and traduce it. He accordingly gave forth a declaration to all his fellow professors, warning them, that "Whosoever became tainted with the spirit of John Perrot, it will perish;" and concluding, he warns the disaffected, "O! consider! the light and power of God goes over you all, and leaves you in the fretting nature, out of the unity which is in the everlasting light, life and power of God. Consider this before the day be gone from you, and take heed that your memorial be not rooted out from among the righteous."

Great labor and care were bestowed by Friends, not only to prevent the spread of this defection, but to bring those back who were carried away by it; but it continued to give trouble for several years. Perrot himself continued to decline more and more from the principles of truth, of which he had once made so high a profession; so that after going to reside in America, he professed to feel that it was not right to assemble for the purpose of Divine worship, unless moved specially thereto by the internal monitor; and finally, he threw off all appearance and profession of a Friend, and having obtained an office under the government, became an exacter of oaths, and an enemy to those he had formerly professed to be united with in the bonds of Christian fellowship.

It has been mentioned already, that an Act of Parliament had been passed [1661-2], requiring every one holding office, as Judge, Magistrate, Clerk, town officer, &c., to deny the legality of the "Solemn League and Covenant," or that it was binding; and also to take the "sacrament" according to the rites of the "Episcopal Church," at least once within a year of the time of entering office. This was to exclude all "Dissenters" from those offices; so that their places might be filled by persons disposed to carry out the designs of the "Church" and Court party. The Commissioners appointed to see that this law was executed, had been so busily engaged in the work, that by the beginning of 1662, the time when the law especially aimed at Friends went into effect, those who were likely to be called on to execute it, were in no wise disposed to relax its severity. Although the title of the Act against Friends alludes only to their refusal to take oaths, yet provision is made in the law itself, to prevent more than five of them, over sixteen years of age, assembling for Divine worship, and if they persisted in doing so, to punish them in the severest manner. Other Dissenters from the "established Church," were liable to suffer for non-conformity, and holding their own religious meetings. How firmly they stood for their rights and religion, cannot here be set forth ; doubtless some of them suffered for obeying the dictates of conscience.

Neal, in his history, says, "Before the Conventicle Act took place, the laity were courageous, and exhorted their ministers to preach till they went to prison ; but when it came home to themselves and they had been once in jail, they began to be more cautious, and consulted among themselves how to avoid the edge of the law, in the best manner they could. For this purpose their assemblies were frequently held at midnight, and in the most private places ; and yet, notwithstanding all their caution, they were frequently disturbed ; but it is remarkable that under all their hardships, they never made the least resistance, but went quietly along with the soldiers or officers, when they could not fly from them." "So great was the severity of these times, that many were afraid to pray in their families, if above four of their acquaintance, who came only to visit, were present. Some families scrupled asking a blessing on their meat, if five strangers were at the table. In London, where the houses join, it was thought the law might be evaded, if the people met in several houses, and heard the minister through a window, or hole in the wall ; but it seems this was overruled, the determination being in the breast of a single mercenary justice of the peace."

Friends had long been inured to suffering, and it was now evident their sincerity and fortitude would be put to the severest test, while braving the malice and cruelty of their enemies, and patiently resigning their property, their liberty and their lives, rather than forego their testimony to public worship, or flinch from the performance of the duty required of them when assembled for that purpose. Governed by the convictions of Divine Grace on their minds, and the principles taught in the holy Scriptures, they could not compromise the testimonies of the gospel committed to them to illustrate before the world, nor shrink from confessing Christ openly before men, by refusing to meet boldly in his name at their accustomed places for worship, and there striving to worship Him, who is a Spirit, in spirit and in truth. As witnesses for the truth, and to the inalienable right of liberty of conscience in all matters of religion, they were bound to bear a faithful testimony against the unrighteous assumption of the "Church" and clergy, against the arbitrary and tyrannical course of the government, as well as against the profanity, debauchery and practical infidelity that had overrun the country. While they thus made themselves hated by many of the high professors, and scorned by the multitudinous libertines and worldlings, who longed to see them swept out of their way, they showed themselves to be a peaceable and unresisting people, who, however much injured and trampled on, would seek no revenge, but if smitten on one cheek, would rather turn the other for a blow, than strike back.

In the speech of George Whitehead before the House of Commons, when the Bill against Friends was under consideration, he said, that if the Bill should become a law, it would give encouragement to wicked, rude and lawless persons to abuse Friends, even beyond the intention of the framers of the law; and almost as soon as it came into operation this was made manifest. It appears that the first who made an attack on Friends in London, on account of their assembling for divine worship, was one Philip Miller, who, without being in any office, or having warrant or authority, went into Friends' meeting, in Johns street, followed by a rabble from the street, and flourishing a cane, seized upon whom he pleased, and then, procuring a constable, had them brought before a Magistrate, who committed them to prison. A few days after he came to the same meeting, bringing a constable with him. He ordered all assembled to depart, and finding they did not obey, he began beating those about him with his cane, and charged the constable to bring such as he chose to select—among whom was John Crook, a valued minister—before a Magistrate. This Magistrate required them to promise to appear before the Court of Justices at Hick's Hall the next morning, and dismissed them. The next morning, on their appearing before the Court, nine of them were committed to Newgate. This was but one instance of very many similar; for often common soldiers and others of low character, broke in violently where Friends were engaged in solemn worship, beat and dragged both men and women, sometimes tearing the clothes off their backs, and when asked for their authority, held up their clubs or swords, and said those were their authority. It appeared as though those in "church" and State, who aimed at destroying the Society, supposed that by carrying out their iniquitous laws at once, and making a clean sweep of all the more influential Friends, ministers and others, and committing them to prison, others would be intimidated and discouraged, and thus the meetings be broken up and discontinued.

Sewel speaking of the persecution at this time says: "There was published in print a short relation of the persecution throughout all England, signed by twelve persons, showing that more than four thousand and two hundred of those called Quakers, both men and women, were in prison in England; and denoting the number of them that were imprisoned in each county, either for frequenting meetings, or for denying to swear, &c. Many of these had been grievously beaten, or their clothes torn or taken away from them; and some were put into such stinking dungeons, that some great men said, they would not have put their hunting-dogs there. Some prisons were crowded full of both men and women, so that there was not sufficient room for all to sit down at once; and in Cheshire, sixty-eight persons were in this manner locked up in a small room; an evident sign that they were a harmless people, that would not make any resistance, or use force. By such ill-treatment many grew sick, and not a few died in such jails; for no age or sex was regarded, but even ancient people of sixty, seventy, and more years of age, were not spared: and the most of these being tradesmen, shop-keepers and husbandmen, were thus reduced to poverty; for their goods were also seized for not going to church, (so called,) or for not paying tithes. Many times they were fain to lie in prison, on cold nasty ground, without being suffered to have any straw; and often they have been kept several days without victuals: no wonder therefore that many died by such hard imprisonments as these.

"At London, and in the suburbs, were about this time no less than five hundred of those called Quakers, imprisoned, and some in such narrow holes, that every person scarcely had conveniency to lie down; and the felons were suffered to rob them of their clothes and money. Many that were not imprisoned, nevertheless suffered hardships in their religious meetings, especially that in London, known by the name of Bull-and-Mouth. Here the trained bands came frequently, armed generally with muskets, pikes and halberds, and conducted by a military officer, by order of the city magistracy; and rushing in, in a very furious manner, fell to beating them; whereby many were grievously wounded, some fell down in a swoon, and some were beaten so violently, that they lived not long after it. Among these was one John Trowel, who was so bruised and crushed, that a few days after he died. His friends therefore thought it expedient to carry the corpse into the aforesaid meeting-place, that it might lie there exposed for some hours, to be seen of every one. This being done, raised commiseration and pity among many of the inhabitants; for the corpse, beaten like a jelly, looked black, and was swelled in a direful manner."

The jury which was called by the Coroner in the above case,

though satisfied from the evidence that a murder had been committed, refused to return any verdict, for fear of its bringing a heavy fine on the city.

But however indefatigable and merciless the persecution, and however grievous the suffering, if it sifted out some who were either unfaithful to their convictions, or had never been fully convinced of the precious truths, for maintaining which Friends were now constantly in jeopardy of their liberty and lives, it failed entirely to effect the object had in view by their enemies. When beaten and dragged out of their meeting-houses, so soon as the opportunity presented they went into them again. When the houses were taken possession of and Friends locked out, they met in the streets before them, and thus the audience was often largely increased; and often when one minister, while speaking, was pulled down and taken to prison, another was prepared to take his or her place, declaring the truths of the gospel, and encouraging the brethren and sisters to unyielding obedience to manifested duty. Even children, under the influence of that love for Christ and his cause, which is begotten by walking in accordance with the manifestations of Divine Grace, were made willing to take part in suffering for the good cause, and, hand in hand with their elders, to persevere in meeting for divine worship.

Robinson, the Lieutenant of the Tower, sent two boys to Bridewell for being at meeting; the one thirteen and the other sixteen years of age. Besse, in his "Collection of the sufferings" of Friends, says, "The constancy of these young lads was remarkable; who having their arms put into the stocks, and there so pinched for the space of two hours, that their wrists were very much swollen, yet continued undaunted; nor could the keepers force them to work, they asserting their innocence, and refusing to eat except at their own charge. They wrote also, during their imprisonment, an epistle to Friends' children, exhorting them to stand faithful to their testimony against all unrighteousness." It would be impossible, within the prescribed limits, to give a detailed account of the many grievous cases that were continually occurring. The cruelty practised on Friends, not only when beaten and otherwise maltreated when their meetings were assailed and broken up, but when brought before the Magistrates, was great and almost universal. Brown, the Lord Mayor, distinguished himself by the ferocity of his treatment and his implacable hatred of Friends. Two or three instances illustrative of the course he pursued may be given: they are taken from Sewel.

Daniel Baker, mentioned in the first, was a minister, and has been already mentioned in the account of the imprisonment of Catharine Evans and Sarah Chevers.

"About midsummer [1662], Daniel Baker, with four others, were taken by a band of soldiers from the Bull-and-Mouth meeting, and carried to Paul's yard, where, having been kept for some hours, they were brought to Newgate; but in the evening they were brought before Alderman Brown, to whom Baker with meekness said, 'Let the fear of God and his peace be set up in thy heart.' But Brown fell a laughing, and said, 'I would rather hear a dog bark;' and using more such scoffing expressions, he charged Baker, &c., with the breach of the King's law in meeting together. To which Baker said, 'The servants of God in the apostles' days, were commanded to speak no more in the name of Jesus; and they answered, and so do I too, whether it be better to obey God than men, judge ye.' He also instanced the case of the three children at Babylon, and Daniel who obeyed not the King's decrees. But Brown grew so angry, that he commanded his men to smite Daniel on the face. This they did, and pulling him four or five times to the ground, they smote him with their fists, and wrung his neck so, as if they would have murdered him. This these fellows did to please Brown, showing themselves to be ready for any service, how abominable soever."

There being no charge made against these Friends, Brown as usual, tendered them the oath of allegiance, and committed them to prison, there to remain until they would take it.

"One John Brain, being taken in the street, and not in any meeting, was brought by some soldiers before Brown; who, seeing him with his hat on, ordered him to be pulled down to the ground six or seven times, and when he was down, they beat his head against the ground, and stamped upon him; and Brown, like a mad-man, bade them pull off his nose; whereupon they very violently pulled him by the nose. And when he got up, they pulled him to the ground by the hair of his head, and then by the hair pulled him up again. And when he would have spoken in his own behalf against this cruelty, Brown bade them stop his mouth. Whereupon they not only struck him on the mouth, but stopped his mouth and nose also so close, that he could not draw breath, and was liked to be choked: at which actions Brown fell a laughing, and at length sent him to jail.

"Thomas Spire, being brought before Brown, he commanded his

hat to be taken off; and because it was not done with such violence
as he intended, he caused it to be put upon his head again, saying,
'It should not be pulled off so easily.'   Then he was pulled down to
the ground by his hat, and pulled up again by his hair.   William
Hill being brought before him, he commanded his hat to be pulled
off, so that his head might be bowed down: whereupon he being
pulled to the ground, was plucked up again by the hair of his head.
George Ableson was thus pulled five times one after another to
the ground, and plucked up by his hair, and so beaten on his face,
or the sides of his head, that he staggered, and bled, and for some
days was under much pain.

"Nicholas Blithold being brought before Brown, he took his hat
with both his hands, endeavoring to pull him down to the ground;
and because he fell not quite to the ground forward, he pushed him,
to throw him backwards; and then he gave him a kick on the leg,
and thrust him out of doors.   Thomas Lacy being brought before
him, he himself gave him a blow on the face; and Isaac Merrit,
John Cook, Arthur Baker, and others, were not treated much better;
so that he seemed more fit to have been a hangman, than an alderman, or justice."

In order that our readers may form some truthful conception of
the course generally pursued by the Courts before which they were
arraigned, the following extracts are taken from an account of the
trial of John Crook, published shortly after it occurred.   As already
stated, he had been taken from a meeting in London, by a person,
not an officer, and without warrant or authority. [1662.]

"C. Judge.— Call John Crook to the bar; which the crier did
accordingly, he being amongst the felons as aforesaid.

J. C. being brought to the bar:

C. Judge.— When did you take the oath of allegiance?

J. C.— I desire to be heard.

C. Judge.— Answer to the question, and you shall be heard.

J. C.—I have been about six weeks in prison, and am I now called
to accuse myself?   For the answering to this question in the nega-
tive, is to accuse myself, which you ought not to put me upon; for,
Nemo debet seipsum prodere.   I am an Englishman, and by the law
of England I ought not to be taken, nor imprisoned, nor dis-seised
of my freehold, nor called in question, nor put to answer, but according to the law of the land; which I challenge as my birthright, on
my own behalf, and all that hear me this day; (or words to this
purpose.)   I stand here at this bar as a delinquent, and do desire

that my accuser may be brought forth to accuse me for my delinquency, and then I shall answer to my charge, if any I be guilty of.

C. Judge.—You are here demanded to take the oath of allegiance, and when you have done that, then you shall be heard about the other; for we have power to tender it to any man.

J. C.— Not to me upon this occasion, in this place; for I am brought hither as an offender already, and not to be made an offender here, or to accuse myself; for I am an Englishman, as I have said to you, and challenge the benefit of the laws of England.

. . . .

Ch. Judge.— We sit here to do justice, and are upon our oaths; and we are to tell you what is law, and not you us: therefore, sirrah, you are too bold.

J. C.— Sirrah is not a word becoming a judge : for I am no felon : neither ought you to menace the prisoner at the bar: for I stand here arraigned as for my life and liberty, and the preservation of my wife and children, and outward estate, (they being now at the stake;) therefore you ought to hear me to· the full, what I can say in my own defence, according to law, and that in its season, as it is given me to speak: therefore I hope the Court will bear with me, if I am bold to assert my liberty, as an Englishman, and as a Christian; and if I speak loud, it is my zeal for the truth, and for the name of the Lord; and mine innocency makes me bold —

Judge.— (Interrupting John Crook.) It is an evil zeal.

J. C.— No : I am bold in the name of the Lord Almighty, the everlasting Jehovah, to assert the truth, and stand as a witness for it. Let my accuser be brought forth, and I am ready to answer any Court of justice.

Judge.— Sirrah, you are to take the oath, and here we tender it to you; bidding the Clerk read it.

J. C.— Let me see mine accuser, that I may know for what cause I have been six weeks imprisoned, and do not put me to accuse myself by asking me questions; but either let my accuser come forth, or otherwise let me be discharged by proclamation, as you ought to do.

Judge Twisden.— We take no notice of your being here otherwise than of a straggler, or as any other person, or of the people that are here this day; for we may tender the oath to any man. And another judge spake to the like purpose.

J. C.— I am here at your bar as a prisoner restrained of my liberty, and do question whether you ought in justice to tender me the oath on the account I am now brought before you, because I am supposed to be an offender; or else why have I been six weeks in prison already? Let me be cleared of my imprisonment, and then I shall answer to what is charged against me, and to the question now propounded; for I am a lover of justice with all my soul, and am well known by my neighbors, where I have lived, to keep a conscience void of offence, both towards God and towards man.

Judge.— Sirrah, leave your canting.

J. C.— Is this canting, to speak the words of Scripture?

Judge.— It is canting in your mouth, though they are Paul's words.

.   .   .   .

J. C.— By what law have you power to tender it [the oath]?

Judge.— By the third of King James.

The prisoner desired the statute to be read, which the Court refused.

Judge.— Hear me.

J. C.— I am as willing to hear as to speak.

Judge.— Then hear me: you are here required to take the oath by the Court, and I will inform you what the penalty will be, in case you refuse; for your first denial shall be recorded, and then it' shall be tendered to you again at the end of the sessions; and upon the second refusal you run into a premunire, which is the forfeiture of all your estate, (if you have any,) and imprisonment.

J. C.— It is justice I stand for; let me have justice, in bringing my accuser face to face, as by law you ought to do, I standing at your bar as a delinquent; and when that is done, I will answer to what can be charged against me, as also to the question; until then, I shall give no other answer than I have already done—at least at present."

He was then ordered to be taken out of the Court.

"On the Sixth-day of the week, in the forenoon following, the Court being seated, John Crook was called to the bar.

C. Judge.— Friend Crook we have given you time to consider of what was said yesterday to you by the Court, hoping you may have better considered of it by this time; therefore, without any more words, will you take the oath? And called to the Clerk, and bid him read it."

Very much the same ground was again gone over as had been traversed when J. C. was previously before the Court; the Judges striving to induce him to plead to the indictment of not being willing to take the oath, and he refusing to plead until he knew his accusers, and for what he had been a prisoner for more than six weeks. J. C. had occupied the position of a Magistrate, was somewhat acquainted with the law, and saw the object the Judges had in view, who, knowing that he could not take an oath, were so strenuously urging him to plead guilty or not guilty.

Judge. — Mr. Crook, hear me: you must say, guilty, or not guilty; if you plead not guilty, you shall be heard, and know how far the law favors you. And the next thing is, there is no circumstance whatsoever that is the cause of your' imprisonment, that you question, but you have as a subject, your remedies, if you will go this way, and waive other things, and answer guilty, or not guilty; and what the law affords you, you shall have, if you do what the law requires you; or else you will lose the benefit of the law, and be out of the King's protection.

J. C. — Observe how the Judge would draw me into a snare, viz.: By first pleading (guilty, or not guilty,) and when I have done so, he and his brethren intend suddenly to put me, (as an outlawed person,) out of the King's protection; and how then can I have remedy for my false imprisonment? &c.

. Judge. — You must plead guilty, or not guilty.

J. C. — I do desire in humility and meekness to say, I shall not; I dare not betray the honesty of my cause, and the honest ones of this nation, whose liberty I stand for, as well as my own; as I have cause to think I shall, if I plead to the present indictment, before I see the faces of my accusers.

Judge. — The most arrant thief may say he is not satisfied in his conscience.

J. C. — My case is not theirs, yet they have their accusers: and may not I call for mine? And therefore call for them, for you ought to do so: as Christ said to the woman, Woman, where are thine accusers? So you ought to say to me, Man, where are thine accusers? — (Interruption.)

The Judges still insisted it was no matter how it happened that he was before them, they found him there, and had the power to tender him the oath, and to punish him if he refused to answer to the indictment drawn against him; and J. Crook, with equal inflexibility claiming, that as the law declared " No man is to be taken or imprisoned, or be put to answer, without presentment before justices, or matter of record, or by due process, or writ original, according to the old law of the land; and if anything from henceforth, be done to the contrary, it shall be void in law, and holden for error," he therefore had a right to know, how and why it was that he had been first put in prison, and then brought there, without knowing who was his accuser, without presentment, or due process; and that until he was righted of these illegalities, or proclaimed by the Court not to have been found guilty of any act that made him a prisoner, it had no right by law to consider him in a situation to have the oath of allegiance administered.

"Ch. Judge.— When you have (once) sworn, you may not be put upon it again, except you minister occasion on your part.

J. C.— Is this the judgment of the Court, that the oath (once) taken by me is sufficient, and ought not to be tendered a second time, without new matter ministered on my part?

Judge.— Yes; you making it appear you have (once) taken it.

J. C.— Is this the judgment of the whole Court? For I would not do anything rashly.

Judges.— Yes, it is the judgment of the Court. (To which they all standing up, said, Yes.)

J. C.— Then it seems there must be some new occasion ministered by me after I have (once) taken it, or it ought not to be tendered to me the second time.

Judges.— Yes.

J. C.— Then by the judgment of this Court, if I may make it appear that I have taken the oath (once) and I have ministered no new matter on my part, whereby I can be justly charged with the breach of it, then it ought not to be tendered to me the second time: but I am the man that have taken it (once), being a freeman of the city of London, when I was made free; witness the records in Guildhall, which I may produce, and no new matter appearing to you on my part; if there do, let me know it; if not, you ought not, by your own judgment, to tender me it the second time; for *de non apparentibus et non existentibus eadem ratio est.**

Judge.— Mr. Crook, you are mistaken, you must not think to surprise the Court with criticisms, nor draw false conclusions from our judgments.

J. C.— If this be not a natural conclusion from the judgment of the Court, let right reason judge; and if you recede from your own judgments in the same breath, (as it were,) given even now, what justice can I expect from you? For, if you will not be just to yourselves, and your own judgments, how can I expect you should be just to me?

* That which doth not appear, is to be judged of as that which doth not exist.

Judge.— Mr. Crook, if you have taken it, if there be a new emergency, you are to take it again ; as for instance, the King hath been out of England, and now is come in again.   . . .   We have no more to do, but to know of you, whether you will answer (guilty, or not guilty,) or take the oath, and then you shall be freed from the indictment: if you will not. plead, clerk, record it: What say you ?   Are you guilty, or not guilty ?

J. C.— Will you not stand to your own judgments ?   Did you not say, even now, that if I had (once) taken the oath, it ought not to be tendered to me the second time, except I administered new matter on my part that I have not kept it, &c.   But no such matter appearing, you ought not to tender it to me the second time, by your own confession, much less to indict me for refusal.

Judge.— If you will not plead, we will record it, and judgment shall be given against you : therefore say, guilty, or not guilty, or else we will record it.   (The clerk beginning to record it.)

J. C.— Before I answer, I demand a copy of my indictment ; for I have heard it affirmed by counsel learned in the law, that if I plead before I have a copy, or have made my exceptions, my exceptions afterwards against the indictment will be made void : therefore I desire a copy of the indictment.

Judge.— He that said so, deserves not the name of a counsel ; for the law is, you must first answer, and then you shall have a copy. Will you plead guilty or not guilty ?

J. C.— If my pleading guilty or not guilty, will not deprive me of the benefit of quashing the indictment, for insufficiency, or other exceptions that I may make against it, I shall speak to it.

Judge.— No, it will not.   Will you answer, guilty or not guilty. If you plead not, the indictment will be found against you : will you answer ?   We will stay no longer.

J. C.— As to the indictment it is very large, and seems to be confused, and made up of some things true, and some things false ; my answer therefore is, what is true in the indictment I will not deny, because I make conscience of what I say, and therefore, of what is true, I confess myself guilty, but what is false, I am not guilty of.

Judge.— That is not sufficient, either answer guilty, or not guilty, or judgment will be given against you.

J. C.— I will speak the truth, as before the Lord, as all along I have endeavored to do ; I am not guilty of that which is false, contained in the indictment, which is the substance thereof.

Judge.— No more ado ; the form is nothing, guilty or not ?

J. C.— I must not wrong my conscience. I am not guilty of what is false, as I said before.

Recorder.— It is enough, and shall serve turn. Enter that, clerk."

"The seventh day of the week, called Saturday.

Silence being made, John Crook was called to the bar. The clerk of the sessions read something concerning the jury, which was impanelled on purpose, (as we said,) the jury being discharged who were eye-witnesses of what passed between us and the Court: and this jury, were divers of them soldiers, some of whom did by violence and force pull and haul Friends out of their meetings, and some of us out of our houses; and these were of the jury by whom we were to be tried. The clerk reading the indictment, (as I remember.)

J. C.— I desire to be heard a few words, which are these, that we may have liberty till the next quarter sessions to traverse the indictment, it being long and in Latin, and like to be a precedent; and I hope I need not press it; because I understood that you promised, and (especially the Recorder, who answered, when it was desired, you shall,) that we should have counsel also, the which we cannot be expected to have had the benefit of as yet, the time being so short, and we kept prisoners.

Judge.— We have given you time enough, and you shall have no more; for we will try you at this time, therefore swear the jury."

As the indictment, which was long and in Latin, including many technicalities in reference to their refusing to take the oath, J. Crook and his fellow-prisoners, claimed that by law they were entitled to traverse it and take legal counsel respecting their cause. This, however, was denied them.

There was much noise and confusion in the Court, and one of the Friends addressing the Court:

"Judge.— Stop his mouth, executioner. (Which was accordingly done.)

Prisoners.— Then we cried out, will you not give us leave to speak for ourselves? We except against some of the jury, as being our enemies, and some of them who by force commanded us to be pulled out of our meetings, contrary to law, and carried us to prison without warrant, or other due process of law; and shall these be our judges! We except against them.

Judge.— It is too late now, you should have done it before they had been sworn jurymen. Jury, go together; that which you have to find, is whether they have refused to take the oath, or not, which hath been sworn before you that they did refuse; you need not go from the bar."

" Then we cried for justice, and that we might be heard to make our defence, before the jury gave their verdict; but the Judge and Recorder said, we should not be heard, crying again, stop their mouths, executioner; which was done accordingly with a dirty cloth, and also endeavored to have gagged me, striving to get hold of my tongue, having a gag ready in his hand for that purpose : and so we were served several times. Then I called out with a loud voice, Will you condemn us without hearing? This is to deal worse with us than Pilate did with Christ, who, though he condemned him without a cause, yet not without hearing him speak for himself; but you deny us both."

The question being put by Isaac Gray, whether, as in criminal cases, if bail was given the case could not be tried at the next Court, the Chief Justice replied that, though they had the power to postpone, they would not do so. Whenever any of the prisoners attempted to speak, the Court ordered the executioner to stop their mouths; which he did.

" J. C.—You might as well have caused us to be murdered before we came hither, as to bring us here under pretence of trial, and not give us leave to make our defence; you had as good take away our lives at the bar, as to command us thus to be abused, and to have our mouths stopped : was ever the like known. Let the righteous God judge between us. Will you hear me? You have often promised that you would."

The confusion in the Court continued : some saying one thing and some another.

" Judge.— Jury, give in your verdict.

J. C.—Let me have liberty first to speak, it is but a few words, and I hope I shall do it with what brevity and pertinency my understanding will give me leave, and the occasion requires; . . . . (Interrupted. The Court calling again to the executioner to stop my mouth; which he did accordingly with his dirty cloth, as aforesaid, and his gag in his hand.)

Judge.— Hear the jury :

Who said something to him, which was supposed to give in the verdict, according to his order; for they were fit for his purpose, as it seems, they beginning to lay their heads together, before we had spoken anything to them, only upon his words.

Judge.— Crier, make silence in the Court.

Then the Recorder, taking a paper into his hand, read to this purport, viz.: The jury for the King do find that John Crook, John Bolton, and Isaac Gray, are guilty of refusing to take the oath of allegiance; for which you do incur a premunire, which is the forfeiture of all your real estates during life, and your personal estates forever; and you to be out of the King's protection, and to be imprisoned during his pleasure: and this is your sentence.

J. C.—But we are still under God's protection."

Then the prisoners were remanded to Newgate, where J. Crook found opportunity to make a narrative of the whole trial, which was printed as aforesaid, together with the Latin indictment, in which he showed several errors, either by wrong expressions or by omissions.

To oblige Friends to incur the penalty of premunire, by which they lost all their personal estate, and forfeited their real estate during life, while they were placed without the protection of the law, became the primary object of the Judges and Magistrates before whom they were brought for trial. It was confidently believed they could not long stand against this despoiling law, as it would strip them of everything, and place them in a condition wherein any and every one might abuse them at their will, and the law could give them neither protection nor redress. But it was forgotten there was a power above that of man, and that "He that dwelleth in the secret place of the Most High, shall abide under the shadow of the Almighty." Thus it proved with those valiant but patient sufferers for the testimony of Jesus, whom the wrath of man had devoted to destruction, but whom the Lord upheld; frustrating the design of their enemies, and often shielding and supporting them in a remarkable manner.

The hesitancy of Friends, when on trial before a Court or a Magistrate, to give a direct answer to the charge preferred against them, arose from no unwillingness to confess having acted in accordance with their religious principles, nor from a desire to shrink from an open avowal of the testimonies of the gospel, which they believed themselves acquired to maintain. But such were the wording of some of the laws they might be charged with violating, and the construction given to them by the Judges, and such the manifest desire of most of those before whom they were arraigned, to extort from them some admission that might be taken advantage of by the Court or Magistrate, to declare them guilty by confession, and so pronounce sentence on them at once, without allowing the case to go before a jury, that they were at all times in danger of being ensnared, and deprived of any hope of the justice that might possibly be obtained if a trial was allowed; and hence their frequent refusal to plead at once to the charge, or the indictment, if one was prepared.

They had no wish to be made martyrs, and objects as they were of the implacable enmity of the "Church" and State, they knew that several of the laws put in force against them, had been made, long before, under special circumstances, and to repress people altogether different from themselves, and had become almost obsolete. They were, therefore, desirous to avail themselves of the few rights yet left them as Englishmen, and to trust that among a jury of twelve men, some one might be found that would be willing to stand up against the extortion and cruelty he saw practised on his fellow countrymen.

Space cannot be allowed, to enter into many details of the grievous sufferings Friends were now enduring, because they could not conscientiously either abstain from meeting for the public worship of Almighty God, or, in obedience to the command of Christ and his apostle, they dare not swear; or, believing that the ministry of the gospel must be freely exercised, by those who are gifted by Christ for the service, they could not pay tithes. The jails throughout England were almost filled with them, both men and women; and such was the noisomeness of the holes and dungeons into which multitudes of them were crowded, that many laid down their lives therein, or contracted disease, from the painful or enfeebling effects of which they never recovered. The following will illustrate how those taken at the meetings were treated, after they got out of the hands of such men as the Lord Mayor of London, and others employed in consigning them to these dismal abodes. Also the deep feeling of brotherly love and Christian sympathy that prevailed among this despised and persecuted flock, who counted not their lives dear unto themselves, so that they might finish their course with joy, and the ministry which they had received of the Lord Jesus, to testify the gospel of the grace of God.

The first was written by one of the prisoners in Newgate, London, and published at the time that most of the prisons in that city and its suburbs were similarly crammed with Friends [1662]:

"We are now, about seven scores of us, prisoners in this place, remaining upon the accounts before mentioned; and divers of our Friends, when first brought into Newgate, were put into a very nasty, stinking place, called the Hole, where they always put condemned persons between their sentence and execution; and some Friends have been kept there for twenty-four hours, and then put into the Chapel, so many together, that they could not all lie upon the floor, but were crowded and thronged in a pitiable manner; some lying in hammocks, and some having no lodging at all; but divers have been necessitated to lie upon the leads all night, out of doors; and so thronged have we been within, that we were near stifled with the extraordinary heat; insomuch that it hath been dangerous in causing sickness and diseases. But the mercy of the Lord hath preserved us generally in health, except some few, who had been visited with sickness for a time, and only two have departed this life; one of which was a fresh lively young man, who being put in the dark, noisome Hole before mentioned, where [condemned] prisoners are put, took his sickness there, and on his death-bed, he would often cry out of the noisome, stinking prison, as the cause of his distemper. And also it was the judgment of both the juries that passed on each of the dead bodies — for any of the prisoners dying, a jury must pass on them, to find out the cause of their death — that though they died of a natural sickness, yet the occasion of their sickness might possibly be their strait imprisonment in such noisome prisons, and so many put together. Yet are not all these things regarded, but we are still thronged up and detained in cruel bonds; there being a great many poor men among us, whose poor families are exposed to ruin thereby; their poor wives and children crying out daily for want of husbands and fathers; their trades ruined, and their customers complaining; and thus the ruin of many is threatened, by reason of this hard imprisonment. Yet, little notice at all can be taken of this by any in authority, but all hearts are shut up, and compassion fled away, and the innocent suffer under the oppression of men, and no man regards it."

The next, which was presented to the Mayor and Sheriffs of London, referring to the above account, after reciting the suffering inflicted on these poor prisoners, "some of them being poor housekeepers and others among them poor servants," whose families "are exposed to utter ruin by reason of their imprisonment," continues, "Therefore we, their friends and brethren, who are one with them in their sufferings, and afflicted with them, and do own the cause for which they suffer, do desire that you would take into consideration their sad estate, and find some way how they may be relieved, that so their families may not be utterly ruined, nor their persons exposed to death. If no other way can be found for their relief, if they may not have the liberty to follow their occasions [occupations] for some weeks, or until such time as you shall call for them — which we desire on their behalf— we are ready to give our words that they shall again become prisoners, as you shall appoint them. And if no other way can be found, ther we, a certain number of us, *do present our bodies to you, offering them freely to relieve our afflicted and oppressed brethren, and are ready to go into their places, and to suffer as prisoners in their room* for your security, that so many of the poorest of them, as we are here, may have their liberty to go about their needful occasions, whether it be for some weeks, or until you shall call for them, as you see meet in your wisdom. All which we do in humility of heart and sincerity of our minds, and in the fear of God and love to our brethren, that they may not perish in prison, and in love to you, that innocent blood and oppression may not come upon you, but be prevented from ever being charged against you."

This moving appeal was signed by about thirty Friends; but though showing the fervent love existing among the members, so that they were willing to hazard their lives for each other, it fell upon ears closed to every cry for mercy or justice, from those who were not willing to sacrifice their sense of religious duty, and conform to the form of worship marked out by the hierarchy of the "established church," and the dictates of the demoralized Parliament.

CHAPTER XVI.

Account of T. Ellwood — Prison Life — Deaths in Prison — Death of R. Hubberthorn and E. Burrough—Wm. Ames—Persecution at Colchester—Meetings kept up — Divine Support — Testimonies to Friends' steadfastness — Account of Stephen Crisp.

THOMAS ELLWOOD gives in his Journal a graphic description of life in prison as Friends had to endure it, parts of which will be introduced; first, however, giving some notice of the writer. He was the son of Walter Ellwood, a member of a highly respectable family, and was born in Crowell, Oxfordshire, in 1639. The family, while residing in London, were on intimate terms with Lady Springett, who afterwards became the wife of Isaac Penington. T. Ellwood's early education was good, but his father removing to his estate at Crowell, near the close of the revolutionary war, he was not sent to college, and being greatly addicted to field sports, his further literary improvement was neglected. From the account he gives of himself, it appears that though he took delight in fashionable dress, manners and associations, he was preserved from running into gross evils.

In 1659, when Thomas Ellwood was about twenty years of age, he accompanied his father on a visit to Isaac Penington, who having, as already related, married the widow Springett, and with his wife joined themselves to Friends, was living at Chalfont, about fifteen miles from Crowell. Being invited to attend a meeting of Friends near by, where were both Edward Burrough and James Naylor, they went. The former preached, and his words went home to the heart of T. Ellwood, and affected him in a manner as " he had not till then felt from the ministry of any man." On coming back to the house of I. Penington, in the evening, the servants were called in, and a religious opportunity had in the family. E. Burrough having spoken on " The universal free grace of God to all mankind," the elder Ellwood undertook to argue against the doctrine, but the son soon saw that his father could nôt maintain his ground. The impression made at the meeting on T. Ellwood's mind continuing, he went to another meeting of Friends which he heard was to be held at High Wycomb. In this meeting he was thoroughly convinced of the truth as held by Friends, and there is much instruction to be gained from the narrative he gives of the work of regeneration as experienced by him. Although it was to be expected, that as they minded the manifestation of the same Divine Grace, it would bring them under similar baptisms, and lead them into the adoption of the same testimonies as witnesses for the truth, yet it is striking, confirming and encouraging, to mark how similarly the work of sanctification, justification and perfect redemption was carried on in those devoted and eminent Christians, who were early brought into communion with Friends by convincement.

The experience of those of them who have left records of their religious birth, growth and establishment in the Truth, though differing widely as regards the circumstances under which they were placed, yet in relation to the necessity of taking up the daily cross, and witnessing to the world the requirements of the spiritual religion of Jesus, by supporting all those testimonies which have made Friends a peculiar people from their rise to the present time, answered to each other as face to face in a glass.

"Now was all my former life ripped up, and my sins by degrees were set in order before me. And though they looked not with so black a hue and so deep a dye as those of the lewdest sort of people did, yet I found that all sin, even that which had the fairest or finest show, as well as that which was more coarse and foul, brought guilt, and with and for guilt, condemnation on the soul that sinned. This I felt, and was greatly bowed down under the sense thereof. Now also did I receive a new law, (an inward law superadded to the outward,) the law of the Spirit of life in Christ Jesus, which wrought in me against all evil, not only in deed and in word, but even in thought also; so that everything was brought to judgment, and judgment passed upon all. So that I could not any longer go on in my former ways, and course of life, for when I did, judgment took hold upon me for it. Thus the Lord was graciously pleased to deal with me in somewhat like manner as He had dealt with his people Israel of old, when they had transgressed his righteous law; whom by his prophet He called back, and required to put away the evil of their doings, bidding them first cease to do evil, then learn to do well, before he would admit them to reason with him, and before He would impart to them the effects of his free mercy. Isaiah i. 16, 17.

"I was now required by this inward and spiritual law (the law of the Spirit of life in Christ Jesus), to put away the evil of my doings, and to cease to do evil. And what in particular was the evil which I was required to put away and cease from, that measure of the divine Light, which was now manifested in me, discovered to me; and what the light made manifest to be evil, judgment passed upon.

"So that here began to be a way cast up before me for me to walk in; a direct and plain way, so plain that a wayfaring man, how weak and simple soever, though a fool to the wisdom and in the judgment of the world, could not err while he continued to walk in it; the error coming in by his going out of it. And this way with respect to me I saw was that measure of divine Light which was manifested in me, by which the evil of my doings, which I was to put away and to cease from, was discovered to me. By this divine Light then I saw, that though I had not the evil of the common uncleanness, debauchery, profaneness, and pollutions of the world to put away, because I had, through the goodness of God, and a civil education, been preserved out of those grosser evils, yet I had many other evils to put away and to cease from; some of which were not by the world, which lies in wickedness, accounted evils; but by the Light of Christ were made manifest to me to be evils, and as such condemned in me. As particularly, those fruits and effects of pride, that discover themselves in the vanity and superfluity of apparel, which I, as far as my ability would extend to, took, alas! too much delight in. This evil of my doings I was required to put away and cease from, and judgment lay upon me till I did so. Wherefore, in obedience to the inward law, which agreed with the outward, I took off from my apparel those unnecessary trimmings of lace, ribands, and useless buttons, which had no real service, but were set on only for that which was by mistake called ornament; and I ceased to wear rings.

"Again: the giving of flattering titles to men, between whom and me there was not any relation to which such titles could be pretended to belong. This was an evil I had been much addicted to, and was accounted a ready artist in: therefore this evil also was I required to put away and cease from. So that thenceforward I durst not say, Sir, Master, My Lord, Madam, (or My Dame,) or say Your Servant, to any one to whom I did not stand in the real relation of a servant, which I have never done to any.

"Again: respect of persons, in uncovering the head, and bowing the knee or body in salutations, was a practice I had been much in the use of. And this being one of the vain customs of the world, introduced by the spirit of the world instead of the true honor, which this is a false representation of, and used in deceit, as a token of respect, by persons one to another, who bear no real respect one to another; and besides, this being a type and proper emblem of that divine honor which all ought to pay to Almighty God, and which all, of all sorts, who take upon them the Christian name, appear in when they offer their prayers to Him, and therefore should not be given to men. I found this to be one of those evils, which I had been too long doing; therefore I was now required to put it away, and cease from it.

"Again: the corrupt and unsound form of speaking in the plural number to a single person, You to one, instead of Thou, contrary to the pure, plain, and single language of truth, Thou to one and You to more than one, which had always been used by God to men, and men to God, as well as one to another, from the oldest record of time, till corrupt men, for corrupt ends, in later and corrupt times, to flatter, fawn, and work upon the corrupt nature in men, brought in that false and senseless way of speaking, You to one; which hath since corrupted the modern languages, and hath greatly debased the spirits and depraved the manners of men.   This evil custom I had been as forward in as others, and this I was now called out of, and required to cease from.

"These, and many more evil customs, which had sprung up in the night of darkness and general apostasy from the truth and true religion, were now by the inshining of this pure ray of divine Light in my conscience, gradually discovered to me to be what I ought to cease from, shun, and stand a witness against.

"But so subtilly, and withal so powerfully did the Enemy work upon the weak part in me, as to persuade me that in these things I ought to make a difference between my father and all other men; and that therefore, though I did disuse these tokens of respect to others, yet I ought still to use them towards him, as he was my father.   And so far did this wile of his prevail upon me, through a fear lest I should do amiss, in withdrawing any sort of respect or honor from my father, which was due unto him, that being thereby beguiled, I continued for a while to demean myself in the same manner towards him, with respect both to language and gesture, as I had always done before.   And so long as I did so, standing bare before him, and giving him the accustomed language, he did not express, whatever he thought, any dislike of me.

"But as to myself, and the work begun in me, I found it was not enough for me to cease to do evil, though that was a good and great step.   I had another lesson before me, which was to learn to do well; which I could by no means do, till I had given up, with full purpose of mind, to cease from doing evil.   And when I had done that, the Enemy took advantage of my weakness to mislead me again.   For whereas I ought to have waited in the Light, for direction and guidance into and in the way of well doing, and not to have moved till the divine Spirit, (a manifestation of which the Lord had been pleased to give unto me, for me to profit with or by) the Enemy, transforming himself into the appearance of an angel of light, offered himself in that appearance to be my guide and leader into the performance of religious exercises.   And I, not then knowing the wiles of Satan, and being eager to be doing some acceptable service to God, too readily yielded myself to the conduct of my enemy, instead of my friend.

"He thereupon, humoring the warmth and zeal of my spirit, put me upon religious performances in my own will, in my own time, and in my own strength; which in themselves were good, and would have been profitable unto me, and acceptable unto the Lord, if they had been performed in his will, in his time, and in the ability which He gives. But being wrought in the will of man, and at the prompting of the Evil One, no wonder that it did me hurt instead of good.

"I read abundantly in the Bible, and would set myself tasks in reading; enjoining myself to read so many chapters, sometimes a whole book, or long epistle, at a time. And I thought that time well spent, though I was not much wiser for what I had read, reading it too cursorily, and without the true guide, the Holy Spirit, which alone could open the understanding, and give the true sense of what was read. I prayed often and drew out my prayers to a great length; and appointed unto myself certain set times to pray at, and a certain number of prayers to say in a day; knowing not, meanwhile, what true prayer was. This stands not in words, though the words which are uttered in the movings of the Holy Spirit, are very available; but in the breathing of the soul to the Heavenly Father, through the operation of the Holy Spirit, who maketh intercession sometimes in words, and sometimes with sighs and groans only, which the Lord vouchsafes to hear and answer.

"This will-worship, which all is that is performed in the will of man, and not in the movings of the Holy Spirit, was a great hurt to me, and hindrance of my spiritual growth in the way of truth. But my Heavenly Father who knew the sincerity of my soul to Him, and the hearty desire I had to serve Him, had compassion on me; and in due time was graciously pleased to illuminate my understanding further, and to open in me an eye to discern the false spirit, and its way of working, from the true; and to reject the former, and cleave to the latter.

"But though the Enemy had by his subtlety gained such advantages over me, yet I went on notwithstanding, and firmly persisted in my godly resolution of ceasing from and denying those things which I was now convinced in my conscience were evil."

As the Light of Christ shone more clearly on his soul, T. Ellwood came to see that he had been deceived, in supposing he might omit witnessing to all its requirements when before his father, and he felt that he must be willing to use the plain language of thou and thee to him, and decline uncovering his head when with him, as a mark of respect.* By faithfully acting in accordance with what he saw to be his religious duty in this respect, he soon incurred his

* It was then the custom to wear the hat in the house, and for children to uncover the head in token of respect.

father's displeasure, who repeatedly beat him with both fists and cane, took away all his hats, and thus confined him to the house, and most of the time to his room, for several months. At length I. Penington and his wife coming to pay a visit to the family, persuaded the father, when they were leaving, to allow his son to accompany them home ; where he resided for many weeks, and on his return to his father's house, finding him still offended with his hat and language, he was content to eat with the servants, so long as he and his father lived together. He became firmly established in the Truth, and after his death, the Friends of the meeting to which he belonged, bore testimony that he was " A man to whom the Lord had given a large capacity beyond many, and furnished with an excellent gift, whereby he was qualified for those services in the church, in performance of which he did shine as a star, which received its lustre and brightness from the glorious Sun of righteousness." He was not a minister.

He narrates, that being in London not very long after his convincement [1662], he attended the meeting of Friends held in the house of Humphrey Bache; around which a crowd collected "ready to receive the Friends as they came forth, not only with evil words, but with blows ; which I saw they bestowed freely on some of them that were gone out before me, and expected I should have my share of when I came amongst them. But quite contrary to my expectation, when I came out, they said one to another, ' Let him alone; don't meddle with him ; he is no Quaker, I 'll warrant you.' This struck me, and was worse to me than if they had laid their fists on me, as they did on others. I was troubled to think what the matter was or what these rude people saw in me, that made them not take me for a Quaker. And upon a close examination of myself with respect to my habit and deportment, I could not find anything to place it on, but that I had then on my head a large mountier-cap of black velvet, the skirt of which being turned up in folds looked, it seems, somewhat above the then common garb of a Quaker; and this put me out of conceit with my cap."

But in 1662, he was taken from the Bull-and-Mouth meeting, and, with many others, committed to Old Bridewell. He thus describes the accommodations there, and the manner in which the prisoners passed their time.

" This room in length, for I lived long enough in it to have time to measure it, was three-score feet, and had breadth proportionable to it. In it, on the front side, were very large bay-windows, in which stood a large table. It had other very large tables in it, with benches round; and at that time the floor was covered with rushes, against some solemn festival, which I heard it was bespoken for. Here was my *nil ultra*, and here I found I might set up my pillar.

"But I was quickly put out of these thoughts by the flocking in of the other Friends, my fellow-prisoners; amongst whom yet, when all were come together, there was but one whom I knew so much as by face; and with him I had no acquaintance. For I having been but a little while in the city, and in that time kept close to my studies, I was by that means known to very few.

"Soon after we were all gotten together, came up the master of the house after us, and demanded our names; which we might reasonably have refused to give, till we had been legally convened before some civil Magistrate, who had power to examine us, and demand our names; but we, who were neither guileful nor wilful, simply gave him our names, which he took down in writing.

"It was, as I hinted before, a general storm which fell that day, but it lighted most, and most heavy upon our meetings; so that most of our men Friends were made prisoners, and the prisons generally filled. And great work had the women, to run about from prison to prison, to find their husbands, their fathers, their brothers, or their servants; for accordingly as they had disposed themselves to several meetings, so were they dispersed to several prisons. And no less care and pains had they, when they had found them, to furnish them with provisions, and other necessary accommodations. But an excellent order, even in those early days, was practised among the Friends of that city, by which there were certain Friends of either sex appointed to have the oversight of the prisons in every quarter; and to take care of all Friends, the poor especially, that should be committed there.

"This prison of Bridewell, was under the care of two honest, grave, discreet, and motherly women, whose names were Anna Merrick, (afterwards Vivers,) and Anne Travers, both widows. They, so soon as they understood that there were Friends brought into that prison, provided some hot victuals, meat and broth, for the weather was cold; and ordering their servants to bring it, with bread, cheese, and beer, came themselves also with it, and having placed it on a table, gave notice to us, that it was provided for all those that had not others to provide for them, or were not able to provide for themselves. And there wanted not among us a competent number of such guests.

"As for my part, though I had lived as frugally as I possibly could, that I might draw out the thread of my little stock to the utmost length, yet had I by this time reduced it to tenpence, which was all the money I had about me, or any where else at my command. This was, but a small estate to enter upon an imprisonment with, yet was I not at all discouraged at it, nor had I a murmuring thought. I had known what it was moderately to abound, and if I should now come to suffer want, I knew I ought to be content; and through the grace of God I was so. I had lived by Providence before, when for a long time I had no money at all, and I had always found the Lord a good provider. I made no doubt, therefore, that he who sent the ravens to feed Elijah, and who clothes the lilies, would find some means to sustain me with needful food and raiment; and I had learned by experience the truth of that saying, 'Nature is content with few things.'

"Although the sight and smell of hot food was sufficiently enticing to my empty stomach, for I had eaten little that morning, and was hungry, yet considering the terms of the invitation, I questioned whether I was included in it; and after some reasonings, at length concluded, that while I had tenpence in my pocket, I should be an injurious intruder to that mess, which was provided for such as perhaps had not twopence in theirs. Being come to this resolution, I withdrew as far from the table as I could, and sat down in a quiet retirement of mind, till the repast was over; which was not long, for there were hands enough at it to make light work of it.

"When evening came, the porter came up the back stairs, and opening the door, told us, if we desired to have anything that was to be had in the house, he would bring it us; for there was in the house a chandler's shop, at which beer, bread, butter, cheese, eggs, and bacon, might be had for money. Upon which many went to him, and spake for what of these things they had a mind to, giving him money to pay for them. Among the rest went I, and intending to spin out my tenpence as far as I could, desired him to bring me a penny loaf only. When he returned, we all resorted to him to receive our several provisions, which he delivered; and when he came to me he told me he could not get a penny loaf, but he had brought me two halfpenny loaves. This suited me better; wherefore returning to my place again, I sat down and eat up one of my loaves, reserving the other for the next day. This was to me both dinner and supper; and so well satisfied I was with it, that I could willingly then have gone to bed, if I had had one to go to; but that was not to be expected there, nor had any one any bedding brought in that night.

"Some of the company had been so considerate as to send for a pound of candles, that we might not sit all night in the dark; and having lighted divers of them, and placed them in several parts of 'that large room, we kept walking to keep us warm.

" After I had warmed myself pretty thoroughly, and the evening was pretty far spent, I bethought myself of a lodging, and cast mine eye on the table which stood in the bay window, the frame whereof looked I thought somewhat like a bedstead. Wherefore, willing to make sure of that, I gathered up a good armful of the rushes wherewith the floor was covered, and spreading them under that table, crept in upon them in my clothes, and keeping on my hat, laid my head upon one end of the table's frame instead of a bolster. My example was followed by the rest, who gathering up rushes as I had done, made themselves beds in other parts of the room; and so to rest we went.

" I having a quiet, easy mind was soon asleep, and slept till about the middle of the night; and then waking, finding my feet and legs very cold, I crept out of my cabin, and began to walk about apace. This waked and raised all the rest, who finding themselves cold as well as I, got up and walked about with me, till we had pretty well warmed ourselves; and then we all lay down again, and rested till morning.

"Next day, all they who had families, or belonged to families, had bedding brought in, of one sort or other, which they disposed at the ends and sides of the room, leaving the middle void to walk in. But I, who had nobody to look after me, kept to my rushy pallet under the table for four nights together, in which time I did not put off my clothes; yet, through the merciful goodness of God unto me, I rested and slept well, and enjoyed health, without taking cold.

" In this time divers of our company, through the solicitations of some of their relations or acquaintance to Sir Richard Brown, (who was at that time a great master of misrule in the city, and over Bridewell more especially,) were released; and among these one William Mucklow, who lay in a hammock. He, having observed that I only was unprovided with lodging, came very courteously to me, and kindly offered me the use of his hammock while I should continue a prisoner. This was a providential accommodation to me, which I received thankfully, both from the Lord and from him; and from henceforth I thought I lay as well as ever I had done in my life.

"Amongst those that remained, there were several young men who cast themselves into a club, and laying down every one an equal proportion of money, put it into the hand of our friend Anne Travers, desiring her to lay it out for them in provisions, and send them in every day a mess of hot meat; and they kindly invited me to come into their club with them. These saw my person, and judged of me by that, but they saw not my purse, nor understood the lightness of my pocket. But I, who alone understood my own condition, knew I must sit down with lower commons. Wherefore, not giving them the true reason, I, as fairly as I could, excused myself from entering at present into their mess, and went on as before to eat by myself, and that very sparingly, as my stock would bear. And before my tenpence was quite spent, Providence, on whom I relied, sent me in a fresh supply."

Having received money from William and Isaac Penington, and from his father, he says:—"Now was my pocket from the lowest ebb risen to a full tide. I was at the brink of want, next door to nothing, yet my confidence did not fail, nor my faith stagger; and now on a sudden I had plentiful supplies, shower upon shower, so that I abounded, yet was not lifted up; but in humility could say, 'This is the Lord's doing.' And, without defrauding any of the instruments of the acknowledgments due unto them, mine eye looked over and beyond them to the Lord, who I saw was the author thereof, and prime agent therein; and with a thankful heart I returned thanksgivings and praises to Him. And this great goodness of the Lord to me I thus record, to the end, that all into whose hands this may come may be encouraged to trust in the Lord, whose mercy is over all his works, and who is indeed a God near at hand, to help in the needful time. Now I durst venture into the club, to which I had been invited; and accordingly, having by this time gained an acquaintance with them, I took an opportunity to cast myself among them: and thenceforward, so long as we continued prisoners there together, I was one of their mess.

"And now the chief thing I wanted was employment, which scarce any wanted but myself; for the rest of my company were generally tradesmen, of such trades as could set themselves on work. Of these divers were tailors, some masters, some journeymen, and with these I mostly inclined to settle. But because I was too much a novice in their art to be trusted with their work, lest I should spoil the garment, I got work from an hosier in Cheapside, which was to make night-waistcoats, of red and yellow flannel, for women and children. And with this I entered myself among the tailors, sitting cross-legged as they did, and so spent those leisure hours with innocency and pleasure, which want of business would have made tedious. And indeed that was in a manner the only advantage I had by it; for my master, though a very wealthy man, and one who professed not only friendship but particular kindness to me, dealt I thought but hardly with me. For, though he knew not what I had to subsist by, he never offered me a penny for my work till I had done working for him, and went after I was released, to give him a visit; and then he would not reckon with me neither, because, as he smilingly said, he would not let me so far into his trade, as to acquaint me with the prices of the work, but would be sure to give me enough. And thereupon he gave me one crown piece, and no more; though I had wrought long for him, and made him many dozens of waistcoats, and bought the thread myself; which I thought was very poor pay. But, as Providence had ordered it, I wanted the work more than the wages, and therefore took what he gave me, without complaining."

Having been taken before the Court, which refused to hear their plea of false imprisonment, without trial or sentence; but tendered the oath of allegiance and sent them to Newgate, he thus speaks of their further imprisonment;

" And as soon as the rest of our company were called, and had refused to swear, we were all committed to Newgate, and thrust into the common side.

" When we came there, we found that side of the prison very full of Friends, who were prisoners there before, as indeed were, at that time, all the other parts of that prison, and most of the other prisons about the town; and our addition caused a great throng on that side. Notwithstanding which, we were kindly welcomed by our friends whom we found there, and entertained by them, as well as their condition would admit, until we could get in our own accommodations and provide for ourselves.

" We had the liberty of the hall, which is on the first story over the gate, and which, in the day-time, is common to all the prisoners on that side, felons as well as others, to walk in, and to beg out of; we had also the liberty of some other rooms over that hall, to walk or work in during the day. But at night we all lodged in one room, which was large and round, having in the middle of it a great pillar of oaken timber, which bore up the chapel that is over it. To this pillar we fastened our hammocks at the one end, and to the opposite wall on the other end, quite round the room, and in three degrees, or three stories high, one over the other; so that they who lay in the upper and middle row of hammocks, were obliged to go to bed first, because they were to climb up to the higher by getting into the lower. And under the lower rank of hammocks, by the wall sides, were laid beds upon the floor, in which the sick, and such weak persons as could not get into the hammocks, lay. And, indeed, though the room was large and pretty airy, yet the breath and steam that came from so many bodies, of different ages, conditions, and constitutions, packed up so close together, was enough to cause sickness amongst us, and I believe did so; for some were not long there, yet in that time one of our fellow prisoners, who lay on one of those pallet beds, died."

During the year 1662, there died in the prisons of London, twenty Friends; and seven contracted diseases therein, which proved fatal not long after their discharge. Among those who thus became martyrs for the religion they professed, were two, Richard Hubberthorn and Edward Burrough, who were eminent as ministers of the gospel, and for the boldness with which they faced opposition, and the meekness but firmness they manifested under insult and cruel abuse. A conversation between the former and King Charles, in which Richard explained many of the principles held by Friends, and the King gave him the assurance " upon the word of a king," that Friends should not suffer for their opinions on religion, so long as they lived peaceably, has already been narrated. Nevertheless, under the authority of an Act specially designed to root Friends out, to which the King had given his sanction and signature, this servant of Christ, R. Hubberthorn, was forcibly haled out of a meeting for divine worship held at the Bull and-Mouth meeting-house, brought before R. Brown, who seizing the brim of his hat, dragged his head down nearly to the ground, and after otherwise abusing him, committed him to Newgate, then closely packed with Friends. Being of but feeble constitution, he soon sickened, and in about two months laid down his life. A day or two before his death he said to some who were trying to minister, the best they could, to his wants, that "He knew the ground of his salvation and was satisfied forever in his peace with the Lord:" and a few hours before his release, to a woman Friend, " Do not seek to hold me, for it is too strait for me, and out of this straitness I must go; for I am to be lifted up on high, far above all."

E. Burrough, while preaching at the Bull-and-Mouth meeting-house had been pulled down, and carried before Brown; who committed him to Newgate, where he laid several weeks before he was brought to trial. The Court, under what law was not known, sentenced him to pay a fine of twenty marks, and to be kept in jail until that sum was paid, which under the circumstances was equivalent to imprisonment for life. He was then in the twenty-eighth year of his age, and during the ten years since he had received a gift in the ministry, his gospel labors had been incessant with his. pen, as well as by word of mouth; he was indefatigable, as he was anointed for the service, to promote the cause of truth and righteousness in the earth, to build up the church of which he was so honored a member, and to encourage and strengthen his brethren and sisters to bear with fortitude and patience the close trials permitted, in divine wisdom, to come upon them. In his interviews with those in authority, which were many, both in the time of Cromwell and after the restoration, this undaunted soldier of the cross never shrank from declaring to them the truth, when called to testify against the iniquity of their proceedings, or to warn them of the judgments that would be visited upon them if they persisted in wrong doing.

Ever since his first coming to London, in 1654, E. Burrough appears to have been deeply interested in the planting, watering and growth of the church there; and though often called away by a sense of duty to labor in other fields, he generally hastened back to that city, to engage in the arduous service of promulgating the gospel among its mixed multitudes; who often listened to his well-known voice, dividing the word aright to professor and profane, and proving that the weapons of his warfare were not carnal, but mighty through God to the pulling down of strongholds, casting down imaginations, and every high thing that exalted itself against the knowledge of God. Previous to his coming to London the last time, he appears to have had a sense, that though young in years, his day's work was nearly accomplished; having at several meetings. which he attended when on his way there, taken an affectionate farewell of Friends, as not expecting to see them again: and as has been mentioned already, at Bristol he spoke of going up to London to lay down his life for the gospel.

After he was taken sick from the infected atmosphere the prisoners were obliged constantly to breathe, by some means the King was informed of it, and of the manner in which the prisoners were crowded into small apartments, and he sent a special order to the Sheriffs to release him and a few others named. It shows how well the Sheriffs understood the King's character, that, at the instigation of Brown the Lord Mayor and some other Magistrates, equally inimical to Friends, this order was never executed, and there appears to have been no further notice taken of the matter at Court.

During the time of his sickness, his fervent concern for the preservation and prosperity of Friends was unabated. He was often engaged in supplication for them, and sometimes for their persecutors. In reference to his own state, he said, " I have had the testimony of the Lord's love unto me from my youth ; and my heart, O Lord ! has been given up to do thy will." "There is no iniquity lies at my door, but the presence of the Lord is with me, and his life, I feel, justifies me." Being sensible that his end was fast approaching, he observed, " Though this body of clay must turn to dust, yet I have a testimony that I have served God in my generation ; and that Spirit, which hath lived and acted and ruled in me, shall yet break forth in thousands." The morning of the day on which he died, he said, " Now my soul and spirit is centred in its own being with God, and this form of person must return whence it was taken." Soon after he quietly departed this life ; having been in the prison about eight months. He died on the 14th of the Second month, 1662, in the twenty-eighth year of his age.

William Ames, who had been arrested, without warrant, with S. Fisher,and three other Friends at a private house,was also imprisoned in Bridewell, where he was soon taken sick. As he had been for some years residing in Holland, had come over to England on a visit, and was well known at his adopted home, it was thought this influenced the Magistrates to discharge him ; fearing lest he would die on their hands. He returned to Amsterdam, but soon after died there.

The notice of the cruelty practised upon, and the suffering endured by, Friends in London and its environs, is a fair representation of the kind of treatment they received throughout the different counties of England, wherever and whenever the priests and the Magistrates were prepared to gratify their new-born and fanatical zeal for the " Episcopal Church," or to indulge their bigoted hatred of dissenters, especially of the unresisting Quakers. In some places where those arrested could have their cause brought before juries not packed by the Court, they were declared not guilty as in form indicted ; but in such cases, the Court almost universally tendered them the oath of allegiance, and committed them to prison.

At Colchester, in Essex, the person who was Mayor of the city, in that year, 1662, appeared willing to resort to any barbarity in order to prevent the Friends there holding their meetings for divine worship.   Having arrested and committed to the dismal jail of the place, a number of those who met, among whom was Stephen Crisp, — and finding that course did not deter others from assembling as usual, he employed a portion of the county soldiers, who went to the meeting-house, first beat a number of those assembled, then broke out the windows, destroyed the forms and benches, and carried several Friends to prison.   The house was then fastened up so that Friends were obliged to meet in the street.   This they continued to do twice in the week, however wet and cold the weather might be, feeling it to be their duty, whatever suffering it might cost them.   This had continued not many weeks, when a troop of horse, armed with swords and carbines, rode furiously among them, and began at once to beat whoever came in their way, with their sabres and guns, bruising and maiming men and women, young and old, and breaking into the houses wherever they might take shelter. Nearly a dozen were dragged or driven to the prison, where they were shut up.   The next First-day, the troopers having supplied themselves with large clubs, in addition to their other weapons, again rushed in among those who were holding their meeting in the street, knocked down several, who lay insensible on the stones, and bruised and beat others in so dreadful a manner that it was days before they could take off their clothing, or feed themselves.   One of the unresisting sufferers, on the blade of the sword flying out of the hilt from the violence with which the soldier laid on his blows, picked it up and returned it to him, saying, " I will give it thee again.   I desire the Lord may not lay this day's work to thy charge." After having thus broken up the meeting, four of the soldiers met a poor invalid at a considerable distance from the place of meeting, and riding up to him, asked whether he was a Quaker?   He not denying it, they began to beat him, and continued it until some who witnessed their brutality, believing they would kill him, rescued him out of their hands, and took him into a neighboring house : he was long entirely disabled, and rendered incapable to do anything towards providing for his family.

The constant imprisonment of some, and maiming of others, lessened the number of these faithful testimony-bearers to the obligation to meet for the public worship of God, but those who were left, relaxed not in going twice a week to the place of meeting, in the street.   The same merciless persecution was continued, and the soldiers had iron barbs driven into their clubs, which being sharpened, penetrated the flesh when a blow was given. One man about seventy years of age being struck with a heavy club, survived the blow but a few days. A merchant of repute in the town, was being beaten so fearfully, after having been knocked down, that his wife, fearing he would be killed, threw herself on his body, and received on her own person the blows still laid on. Giles Barnardiston, who had been educated at the University, and had been a Colonel in the army, and a man of note in every respect, now an humble self-denying Quaker, was indefatigable in his labors and exhortations for the encouragement of his persecuted fellow-members, and willingly took his part in the suffering, constantly attending the meetings, and freely hazarding his life in support of his religious testimony.

But here, as in other places, the patience, Christian fortitude and endurance, of those who acted from a sense of religious duty, and of the reverent worship they owed to their Father in heaven, finally wearied out the malice and intolerant cruelty of their persecutors ; and though this fearful storm, with an occasional lull, was kept up for years, it never succeeded in forcing Friends to give up their meetings, or inducing them to relax in the testimony they had borne from the beginning, against priestcraft and its works of darkness, and to the inalienable right to enjoy, liberty of conscience. The fiercer the storm raged the deeper the roots of the Society struck into the hearts of those who loved its principles, and the more firmly were its faithful members established on that foundation, against which the gates of hell cannot prevail. It was the testimony of not a few of those who assembled for divine worship, in different places, where they were constantly expecting to be attacked and their lives put in jeopardy, that such was the sense given them of the immediate presence of Him who had promised to be in the midst of the two or the three gathered in His name, and so sweetly were their hearts filled with his peace and love, that no thought of danger or suffering pressed upon them ; and in the midst of clamor and blows, their souls overflowed with gratitude and praise to his eternally worthy Name : thus confirming what was written by William Leddra, the day before his martyrdom, " Alas! alas! what can the wrath and spirit of man, that lusteth to envy, aggravated by the heat and strength of the King of the locusts, which came out of the pit, do unto one that is hid in the secret places of the Almighty, or unto them that are gathered under the healing wings of the Prince of Peace? under whose armor of light they shall be able to stand in the day of trial, having on the breast-plate of righteousness, and the sword of the Spirit, which is their weapon of warfare against spiritual wickedness, principalities, and powers, and the rulers of the darkness of this world, both within and without."

The open, undisguised manner, and unflinching constancy, with which Friends kept up their religious meetings, so fixed the attention of the party in power on them, that other dissenters, who, with some exception of the Baptists, generally shrunk from publicly assembling for worship, escaped with but little suffering. Neal's observation respecting the course of the Presbyterians, has already been given, and though he never manifests much esteem for Friends, he bears this testimony to their firmness under this trial: "Indeed the Quakers gloried in their sufferings, and were so resolute as to assemble openly at the Bull-and-Mouth, near Aldergate; from whence the soldiers and other officers dragged them to prison, till Newgate was filled, and multitudes died by close confinement in the several jails. The account published about this time says, there were six hundred of them in prison, merely for religion's sake, of whom several were banished to the plantations. Sometimes the Quakers met and continued silent, upon which it was questioned whether such an assembly was a conventicle for religious exercise; and when they were tried for it in order for banishment, they were acquitted of the banishment, and came off with a fine, which they seldom paid, and therefore continued in prison."

Baxter is another witness, who cannot be accused of any undue partiality for Friends: he says, "Here the Quakers did greatly relieve the sober people for a time, for they were so resolute, and so gloried in their constancy and sufferings, that they assembled openly at the Bull-and-Mouth, near Aldergate, and were dragged away daily to the common jail, and yet desisted not, but the rest came the next day. Abundance of them died in prison, and yet they continued their assemblies still."

Orme, who wrote the life of Baxter, remarks on this passage, "Had there been more of the same determined spirit among others, which the Friends displayed, the sufferings of all parties would sooner have come to an end. The Government must have given way, as the spirit of the country would have been effectually roused. The conduct of the Quakers was infinitely to their honor." In another place the same author observes, "The heroic and persevering conduct of the Quakers, in withstanding the interference of Government with the rights of conscience, by which they finally secured those privileges they so richly deserve to enjoy, entitles them to the veneration of all the friends of civil and religious freedom."

Stephen Crisp, of whom mention has been made, as having been made a prisoner at Colchester, was a native of that town, having been born there about the year 1628. In his journal he says, "So soon as I can remember, and so soon as I was capable of understanding, He [the Lord] made me to understand that which consented not to evil, but stood in my soul as a witness against all evil; and manifested that I should not lie, nor steal, nor be stubborn, nor be disobedient; but should behave myself in meekness and quietness, and set truth before me as that which was better than falsehood. This same witness, even in the days of my childhood, ministered peace and boldness to me, when I hearkened to the counsel of it. But there was a contrary nature and seed in me, that was of this world, and not of God; which inclined unto evil, and unto the way and manner of this evil world, as most suiting the carnal mind, and an eye began to open in me that saw, rather what was acceptable with man, than what was well pleasing to God." As he grew to manhood, though he ran into many of the vanities pleasing to the young, yet his religious thoughtfulness, and sensitiveness to the monitions of the internal Monitor, did not forsake him, and having heard much about election and reprobation, he tried to persuade himself that he was one of the elect, by comparing his spiritual condition with what he was told were the " signs of a true believer." But alas! he says, "here was yet but the blind leading my poor blind soul. This was not the balance of the Sanctuary, and when I had got a little peace and quietness, and thought to hold it, alas! it would soon be shattered and broken. When God's pure witness arose in me, that I might be weighed in the true balance, oh! then I found I was much too light." Like very many others who were concerned about their soul's salvation, in that day he went from one set of religious professors to another, seeking certainty and rest, but finding neither. He joined in membership with the Baptists, and was strict in the performance of outward ordinances, but still found he did not obtain dominion over his evil propensities, nor enter into that peace which he supposed the Lord's children should enjoy.

Speaking of having opened his condition to some whom he thought might help him, he remarks, "But well might I say, miserable comforters I found them all to be; for they would bid me apply the promises by faith, and suck comfort out of the Scriptures; and tell

of the Apostle's state, mentioned in Romans vii., and assure me it
was so with him, yet he was a servant of Jesus Christ; and such
like deceitful daubings, as they had daubed themselves with, in like
manner dealt they with me, not considering the Apostle called that
a wretched and undelivered state, as I might well do mine." "As
for the priests and professors of those times, most of them would
boast of experiences and of zeal, and of assurances of the love of God,
and what comfort they enjoyed by thinking or meditating on the
sufferings of Christ for their sins, &c. But alas! thought I, I can
think of these things as well as you, but my wound still remains
fresh, and I see that I am as one of the crucifiers, while I live in
sin, for which He died."

His first information respecting Friends, came through the many
reports disparaging and misrepresenting them; and yet he took
notice they were always said to be undergoing "cruel mockings and
grievous sufferings patiently." In 1655, James Parnel came to
Colchester. Stephen Crisp says, that when he first saw him, thinking he was but a youth, and not knowing the Spirit and power that
were in him, he thought to withstand him, and so began to question
him. But, he continues, "I quickly came to feel that the Spirit of
sound judgment was in him, and the witness of God arose in me,
and testified to his judgment, and signified I must own it; it being
just and true." He attended a meeting appointed by James, where
he "Heard him declare the everlasting gospel in the name and
authority of the Lord, which I could not, with all my wisdom and
knowledge, withstand, but was constrained to own and confess to
the truth." Although he owned the truth of the doctrine preached,
yet he confessed to it only in his understanding, his spirit not being
willing to bow to the cross inseparable from its practical application; and so, he says, "I held it in the same part with which I
[had] withstood it, and defended it with the same wisdom by which
I [had] resisted it; and so was yet a stranger to the cross that was to
crucify me, and was at liberty, in the discoursative spirit, to lay out
my wits and parts for the truth."

This state of things continued for a few weeks; but knowing now
that that within him, which was reproving him for evil, and making
known the way he was called to walk in, was no other than the
Grace of God, which alone could bring him salvation, he yielded to
its discoveries, and permitted it to make manifest his true condition.
"O! then, I cried out, in the bitterness of my soul, what hath all
my profession profited me? I am poor and blind and naked, who

thought I had been rich and well adorned." After describing
the many fears and sore conflicts through which he passed when his
sins were being called to judgment beforehand, and while that Word
which is sharper than a two-edged sword was dividing, as between
the joints and the marrow, and showing unto him the thoughts and
intents of his heart, he observes, "After long travail, strong cries,
and many bitter tears and groans, I found a little hope springing
in me, that the Lord in his own time would bring forth his seed,
even his elect seed, the seed of his covenant, to rule in me. This
was given me at a time when the sense of my own unworthiness had
so overwhelmed me in sorrow and anguish, that I thought myself
unworthy of any of the creatures. Then did the hope of the resurrection of the just spring in me, and I was taught to wait on God,
and to eat and drink in fear and watchfulness, showing forth the
Lord's death till He should come to be raised to live and reign in
me."

He appears to have been attending the meetings of Friends
during this time, for he narrates, "Upon a time, being weary of my
thoughts in the meeting of God's people, I thought none was like
me, and it was but in vain to sit there with such a wandering mind as
mine, which though I labored to stay it, yet could not, as I would.
At length I thought to go forth, and as I was going, the Lord
thundered through me, saying, That which is weary must die. So
I turned to my seat and waited, in the belief of God, for the death
of that part which was weary of the work of God, and grew more
diligent in seeking death, that I might be baptized for the dead;
and that I might know how to put off the old man with his deeds,
and words and imaginations, his fashions and customs, his friendship and wisdom, and all that appertained to him; and the cross of
Christ was laid upon me and I bore it." Though he had so much
to suffer, yet he says, "Oh! the secret joy that was in me in the midst
of all my conflicts and combats, [for] I had this confidence, that if
I did but take up the cross, I shall obtain victory, for that is the
power of God through faith to salvation, and as I have found it so in
some things, so I shall do in all, in due time."

Referring to the effect produced by this transforming power of
Divine Grace, operating in the secret of the heart, he remarks,
"The more I came to feel and perceive the love of God, and his
goodness to flow forth upon me, the more was I humbled and bowed
in my mind to serve Him, and to serve the least of his people among
whom I walked. As the word of wisdom began to spring in me, and

the knowledge of God grew, so I became as a counsellor to them that were tempted in like manner as I had been; yet was I kept so low, that I waited to receive counsel daily from God, and from those that were over me in the Lord, and were in Christ before me; against whom I never rebelled nor was stubborn."

In 1659, S. Crisp, a gift in the ministry of the gospel having been conferred upon him by the Head of the Church, gave up to travel into Scotland, where he labored to turn the people from darkness to light, and from the power of Satan unto God. Returning, he continued his gospel labors in various parts of England, sharing with his brethren and sisters in the Truth, in the many afflictions meted out to them, being repeatedly imprisoned, and suffering much abuse in the faithful performance of religious duties. He went on religious visits into Holland, Friesland, and other parts of Europe, thirteen times; being earnestly engaged to strengthen the hands of those who were convinced of the principles of the gospel, as held by Friends, and concerned to live in accordance with them. He was also often instrumental in mitigating or removing the persecution to which they were, in many places, subjected. His various epistles and other writings show him to have been a man of good understanding and considerable literary culture, but above all, of large religious experience, and deeply instructed in the mystery of divine things.

CHAPTER XVII.

ANOTHER Friend who became an eminent minister, and was indefatigable, both by preaching and by his writings, in endeavoring to promote the cause of truth and righteousness in the earth, was Isaac Penington, who was also undergoing imprisonment at that time in Aylesbury jail. [1661.] He was the son of Isaac Penington, of London, one of the Magistrates of that city, who at one time during the Commonwealth, had been made its Lord Mayor. The son appears to have been from his youth unusually serious and thoughtful about religion, earnest in seeking for the pearl of great price, and deeply sorrowing that with all the efforts he made he did not find it. He says, "My heart from my childhood was pointed towards the Lord, whom I feared and longed after from my tender years. I felt that I could not be satisfied with, nor indeed *seek* after the things of this perishing world; but I desired a true sense of and unity with that which abideth forever. There was something still within me which leavened and balanced my spirit almost continually; but I knew it not so distinctly as to turn to it, and give up to it entirely and understandingly. In this temper of mind I earnestly sought after the Lord, applying myself to hear sermons, and read the best books I could meet with, but especially the Scriptures, which were very sweet and savory to me. Yea, I very earnestly desired and pressed after the knowledge of the Scriptures, but was much afraid of receiving men's interpretations of them, or of fastening any interpretation upon them myself; but waited much and prayed much, that from the Spirit of the Lord I might receive the true understanding of them, and that He would endue me with that knowledge which I might feel to be sanctifying and saving."

Isaac Penington's father was a rigid Presbyterian, and it is probable that from his instructions and the religious associations into which he was thrown, the son imbibed the notion of unconditional election and reprobation. Be that as it may, this perversion of gospel truth, acted upon his sensitive nature, so as to produce deep depression, not only because of feeling there was no certainty of his being among the elect, but also, if true, on account of the dark shadow it cast on the justice and mercy of the Creator, and the hopeless condemnation of myriads of his fellow creatures, created for everlasting destruction. In after-life he came to see that he had been betrayed into this grievous error, by undertaking to interpret the Scriptures by his own intellectual powers. In reference to this he says, "I have known it indeed to be a bitter thing to follow this wisdom, as that which could make me truly understand the Scriptures." From the position occupied by his family, and having received a university education, the way was open for him to aspire to a conspicuous standing in the society of the gay and courtly, and to reap largely of the wealth and honors of this world; but from the tenor of some of the works he wrote some time before he joined with Friends, it would seem he had a true sense of the vanity of earthly pleasures and possessions, and preferred the reproaches of Christ, to enjoying the pleasures of sin for a season.

He was married to Mary Springett, widow of Sir William Springett, who died in 1643, aged twenty-three years. She was one who, like others in that day of religious unsettlement and inquiry, had gone the round of professing religionists, seeking the living among the dead, and, when wearied with the unsatisfying search, had turned to the world, and striven to draw from its gayeties and pleasures, at least forgetfulness of the longing after good and its reward, that had once filled her heart. Disgusted and sick at heart, at the hollowness and insincerity she witnessed in those with whom she associated, she again and again reverted to the religious convictions and aspirations of former days, and in anguish of spirit, after some years, she resolved once more to seek for help from on high, to find out the way of peace and salvation. She again set herself earnestly to work to obtain that without which could be found only within her, and to give herself to circumspect walking and serious meditation. " Sometimes," she says, " I would be melted into tears, and feel an inexpressible tenderness; but not knowing what it was from, and being ready to misjudge all religion, I thought it was some influence from the planets which governed my body. But I durst not regard any thing in me being of, or from God, or that I felt any influence of his spirit on my heart. . . . In the condition I have mentioned of weary seeking and not finding, I married my dear husband, Isaac Penington. 'My love was drawn to him because I found he saw the deceit of all mere notions about religion: he lay as one that refused to be comforted, until He came to his temple 'who is truth and no lie.' All things that had only the *appearance* of religion were very manifest to him, so that he was sick and weary of *show*, and in this my heart united with him, and a desire was in me to be serviceable to him, in this his desolate condition, for he was as one alone, and felt miserable in the world."

Of their first intercourse with Friends she gives the following account: " One day as my husband and I were walking in a park, a man that for a little time had frequented the Quakers' meetings, saw us as he rode by, in our gay and vain apparel. He spoke to us about our pride, at which I scoffed, saying, ' He a public preacher, indeed! preaching on the highway.' He turned back again, saying, he had a love for my husband, seeing grace in his looks. He drew nigh to the pales, and spoke of the Light and Grace of God that had appeared to all men. My husband and he having engaged in discourse, the man of the house coming up invited the stranger in. He was but young, and perceiving my husband was too able for him in the fleshly wisdom, said he would bring a man next day, who would better answer all his questions and objections, who, as I afterwards understood, was George Fox. He came again the next day, and left word that the Friend he intended to bring could not well come; but some others, he believed, would be with us about the second hour; at which time came Thomas Curtis and William Simpson. My mind had been somewhat affected by the discourse of the night before; and though I thought the man weak in the management of the arguments he brought forward to support his principles, yet many Scriptures which he mentioned stuck with me, and felt very weighty. They were such as showed me the vanity of many of my practices; which made me very serious, and soberly inclined to hear and consider what these other men had to say. Their solid and weighty carriage struck a dread over me, for they came in the authority and power of the Lord to visit us. The Lord was with them, and all we who were in the room, were made sensible at that time of the Divine power manifestly accompanying what they said. Thomas Curtis repeated a Scripture that struck out all my inquiries and objections, 'The doctrine is not mine, but His who sent me. If any man will *do his will*, he shall know of the doctrine, whether it be of God, or whether I speak of myself.' "

But though the truths declared had reached the witness for God in the secret of their souls, neither Isaac Penington nor his wife were disposed to look favorably on the despised Quakers, and the religion they inculcated. The gate was too strait and the way too narrow for them to enter and walk in, while the strong man armed was keeping the spiritual house. They had long been *seeking* to enter, but not knowing the Stronger than he to bind the strong man, they had not been able. She observes, " I never had peace or quiet from sore exercise of mind for months, till I was, by the Lord's judgment, brought off from all those things which I found his Light made manifest to be deceit, bondage, vanity and the spirit of the world. The giving up these things cost me many tears. I felt that by the world I would be regarded as a fool, and that my honorable position must be sacrificed if I took up the cross, and acted contrary to the fashions and customs that prevailed in the world and among my acquaintances. My relations made this cross a very heavy one; but at length I gave up all." After thus passing through many sore baptisms and "giving up all," she adds, " I then received strength to attend the meetings of this despised people, which I had intended never to meddle with. I found they were truly of the Lord, and my heart owned them and honored them." [1656.]

Isaac Penington writes as follows, " At first acquaintance with this people, that which was of God in me opened, and I did immediately in my spirit own them as children of my Father, truly begotten of his Light by his own Spirit. But the wise, reasoning part presently rose up, contending against their uncouth way ; for which I did disown them, and continued a stranger to them, and a reasoner against them for about twelve months. By weighing and considering things in that way, I was still further and further off from discerning their leadings by the Spirit of God into those things. But at length it pleased the Lord to draw out his sword against that part in me, turning the wisdom and strength thereof backward ; and again to open that eye in me wherewith He had given me to see the things of his kingdom, in some measure, from a child. And then I saw and felt them grown in that life and spirit, which I, through the treachery of the fleshly-wise part, had been estranged from. And now, what bitter days of mourning I had over this, the Lord alone fully knows. Oh! I have known it indeed to be a bitter thing, to follow this wisdom as that which could make me truly to understand the Scriptures. The Lord hath judged me for it, and I have borne a burden and condemnation for *that* which many at this day wear as a crown." Speaking of the peace and certainty to which he had attained, after that he had fully given up to believe in and act in accordance with the principles of the gospel as held by Friends, he says, "Blessed be the Lord! there are many at this day who can truly and faithfully witness, that they have been brought by the Lord to this state. We have thus learned of Him, not by the high, striving, aspiring mind, but by lying low and being contented with a little ; if but a crumb of bread, yet bread ; if but a drop of water, yet water. And we have been contented with it, and thankful to the Lord for it. Nor was it by thoughtfulness and wise searching, or deep considering with our own wisdom and reason that we obtained this, but in the still, meek and humble waiting have we found it."

It appears from letters addressed by I. Penington to his father, that the latter was much incensed at his son joining with Friends ;

a people whom he contemned and despised. In these letters the son refutes the charges brought by his father against Friends and their principles, and in the fervor of honest conviction, and the solicitude of filial love, labors not only to justify his own course, but to convince his parent of the errors in his belief, and the indispensable necessity of knowing the work of regeneration to be carried on and perfected under the transforming power of the Holy Spirit, which leads to taking up the cross. How far this difference in religious views may have produced estrangement between the families does not appear. The last letter from Isaac to his father which has been published, is dated near the close of 1658, and the events that followed, soon after the restoration of King Charles, in the early part of 1660, closed all intercourse between them. The Alderman, as has been already stated, had been a member of the Commission appointed by Parliament to try Charles I., and which had condemned him to death. Of that Commission, or Court, nearly fifty were still living, when it was resolved to restore the banished King, Charles II., to the throne. Alderman Penington, with several others of those judges, relying on the declaration made from Breda by the returning King, "That no crime whatsoever committed against us or our royal father, before the publication of this, shall ever rise in judgment, or be brought in question against any of them," &c., came forward, accepted the pardon, and took the oath of allegiance.

But in about three months after Charles was seated on the throne, all of those who had sat in judgment on his father, who could be found and secured, were brought to a trial and condemned to death as regicides. Among these — twenty-nine in number — were eighteen, who, with Alderman Penington, had given themselves up, relying on "the word of a king" they should not be held responsible for their former acts. Of these eighteen, the punishment of fourteen was changed from death, to imprisonment for life, and confiscation of all their personal and real estates. Under this sentence, Alderman Penington was committed to the Tower under the custody of Sir John Robinson, the Lieutenant. Whether he was prompted to it by others, or it was the legitimate fruit of his own innately cruel disposition, certain it is these prisoners were subjected to inhuman treatment, and in a little while Isaac Penington's father sunk under it and died. His estate was bestowed by the King on the Bishop of Worcester and the Duke of Grafton, leaving Isaac and his family dependent on the estate of his wife.

During this time of sore persecution and trial, when it seemed as though the enemies of Friends would be permitted, by filling the jails, wherein many died, and constantly breaking up their meetings for divine worship, to keep them from spreading a knowledge of their religion among the people, many of those who by the extraordinary gifts conferred upon them and their faithful labors in the service of the Lord, were looked up to as judges and counsellors in the church, sent forth epistles to their fellow-professors; exhorting them to patience and faithfulness under suffering, and encouraging them to look beyond present afflictions, to the blessed recompense of reward; under the ·assurance that the omnipotent and omniscient One, who was cognizant of all their sorrows and evil treatment, would recompense them by the abounding of his love, and in his own time, open a way for their escape from the wrath of man.

George Fox, knowing the grief that had spread among Friends on account of the death of Edward Burrough, sent forth a few lines as follows: "Friends, Be still and quiet in your own conditions, and settle in the Seed of God, that doth not change; that in that ye may feel dear Edward Burrough among you in the Seed, in which and by which he begat you to God, with whom he is; and that in the Seed ye may all see and feel him, in which is the unity with him in the life; and so enjoy him in the life that doth not change, which is invisible.   G. F."

He also wrote and published the following, as showing the rise and ground of persecution.

1662. "All the sufferings of the people of God in all ages, were because they could not join in the national religions and worships which men have made and set up, and because they would not forsake God's religion and his worship which He had set up. You may see through all chronicles and histories, that the priests joined with the powers of the nations; the magistrates, soothsayers, and fortune-tellers, all joined against the people of God, and did imagine vain things against them in their councils. When the Jews did wickedly, they turned against Moses; when the Jewish kings transgressed the law of God, they persecuted the prophets; as may be seen in the prophets' writings. When Christ, the substance came, the Jews persecuted Christ, his apostles, and disciples. And when the Jews had not power enough of themselves to persecute answerable to their wills, then they got the heathen Gentiles to help them against Christ, and against his apostles and disciples, who were in the Spirit and power of Christ.   G. F."

Francis Howgil likewise addressed his suffering friends, informing them what he had seen in the vision of Light, respecting the Lord's will, concerning the people He had raised up, and who were now suffering so much from those who hated or despised them. That they were dear in his sight, and He would take care of and deliver them. One passage of this extraordinary address may be quoted, to give an idea of its character, "I have brought them to the birth, yea, I have brought them forth; I have swaddled them and they are mine. I will nourish them and carry them as on eagles' wings; and though clouds gather against them, I will make my way through them; though darkness gather together on a heap and tempests gender, I will scatter them as with an east wind, and nations shall know they are my inheritance, and they shall know I am the living God, who will plead their cause with all that rise up in opposition against them."

Very many were the exhortations and letters of encouragement sent forth, often from those who were themselves in dismal jails or dungeons, but whose righteous zeal for the good cause, and love for their brethren could not be bound, nor quenched by the malice or cruelty of their persecutors.

It has been mentioned that King Charles, on hearing of the sickness of E. Burrough, for whom, though he had dealt so plainly with him, he evidently had an esteem, had ordered his release; which, however, was not obeyed. It is probable the information communicated to him of the dreadful condition of the Friends confined in the jails of London and its environs, reminded him of his repeated promises to some of them, that they should not suffer for their principles, and touched whatever feeling he may have had for their sufferings, and his own honor. For near the close of the year 1662, with the consent of his privy council, he issued a proclamation, in which, after alluding to his declaration from Breda, that liberty of conscience should be enjoyed by all his *peaceable* subjects, he says, he is glad to renew that assurance, and also that he would bring the subject before Parliament, in order to induce that body to concur, by an act for the purpose, with his exercise of the power of dispensing with enforcing the penalties provided for non-conformity in worship. Accordingly at the opening of the next session of Parliament, in his speech, he brought the subject before it, and proposed the enactment of a law recognizing what he believed to be a right within his prerogative, to grant indulgence to peaceable dissenters, under such circumstances as he thought called for it; so that they might not be forced to leave the country, or to conspire against its peace.

Parliament, however, was not disposed to relax in any manner
the severity of the laws it had enacted against those who did not
comply with the form of religion it had established. It declared
the King's proclamation from Breda contained no promise, but a
mere expression of what was then his intentions, upon the terms of
the Parliament agreeing to it; and that they, as the representatives
of the nation, were unwilling that he should carry those intentions
into effect.

The King's pecuniary embarrassments, to relieve which he was
dependent on Parliament, were quite sufficient to paralyze his feeble
effort to moderate the bigoted zeal of that intolerant body, and to
induce him to withhold any further interference on behalf of his
suffering subjects, and nothing more was done. But the public
expressions of the King's views, had the effect of restraining, in
some measure, the violence of the Magistrates and others, in and
about London; so that there was less cruelty practised by them on
Friends during 1663, than before and after.

It appeared evident, that it was the design of the party in power
and their subalterns, to shut up as many of the ministers among
Friends as they could lay their hands on, with the hope that by thus
arresting their gospel labors, the other members of the Society would
be brought more easily to succumb to the power, kept actively employed against them. But in this they were disappointed. Especially were they desirous to get hold of George Fox; who nevertheless, was moving about from place to place attending the regular
meetings of Friends, and often addressing large concourses of people
in places where Friends had no regularly established meeting-houses.
He went down from London to Bristol, accompanied by Alexander
Parker and John Stubbs; and though persecution of Friends was
rife there, and some Friends, fearing lest he would be arrested, tried
to dissuade him from going to their usual place of worship, yet he
was at their meeting two First-days in succession, and preached to
large congregations, and escaped being taken by the soldiers who
came to break up the assembly, by their coming either too early or
too late. As the Mayor of Bristol was exceedingly desirous to arrest
him, and the soldiers were on the alert to find where he was and
take him, it was remarkable they should have failed as they did;
and George says, " It was indeed the immediate power of the Lord,
that preserved me out of their hands at Bristol, and over the heads
of all our persecutors; and the Lord alone is worthy of all the
glory, who did uphold and preserve for his name and truth's sake."

Being at a place called the Barnet-hills, where lived a Captain Brown, a Baptist, whose wife was a Friend, he says, "This Captain Brown, after the Act for ' Breaking up Meetings ' came forth, being afraid his wife should go to meetings, and be cast into prison, left his house at Barrow, and took a place on these hills, saying, ' His wife should not go to prison.' And this being a free place, many priests and others fled thither as well as he. But he, who would neither stand to truth himself nor suffer his wife, was in this place, where he thought himself safe, found out by the Lord, whose hand fell heavily upon him for his unfaithfulness ; so that he was sorely plagued, and grievously judged in himself for flying and drawing his wife into that private place. We went to see his wife, and being in the house, I asked him, how he did ? ' How do I ! ' said he, ' The plagues and vengeance of God are upon me, a runagate, a Cain as I am. God may look for a witness for me, and such as me ; for if all were not faithfuller than I, God would have no witness left in the earth.' In this condition he lived on bread and water, and thought it was too good for him. At length he got home again with his wife to his own house at Barrow, where afterwards he was convinced of God's eternal truth, and died in it. A little before his death he said, ' Though he had not borne a testimony for truth in his life, he would bear a testimony in his death, and would be buried in his orchard ; ' and was so."

At Swanington, in Leicestershire, George Fox was arrested while sitting in a private house, by a Lord Beaumont, who came with a company of soldiers. Having also arrested the other Friends who were in the house, Beaumont had them guarded through the night, and the next morning brought before him, when he committed them to Leicester jail ; the mittimus stating they were " to have had a meeting." When the assize came on, the usual course of tendering the oath of allegiance was pursued by the Court, inasmuch as their commitment by Lord Beaumont had been illegal. They were sent back to the prison, and as the streets were filled with people gazing at them, George " declared the truth to them " as he walked along ; and for some cause, which was supposed to have been a letter written by Lord Hastings, from London, and which George Fox had in his possession, but had not shown — in a little while they were all set at liberty. This was in 1662.

The old device of getting up reports of an intended insurrection of the republicans, and the separatists or dissenters, was again resorted to, and it was said this was to take place somewhere in the north of

England.   Contrary as it was to their known peaceable principles
and conduct, it was nevertheless pretended that Friends were implicated in this attempt at uprising, and it thus afforded a plea for persisting in outrages inflicted on them because of their refusing to
take the oath of allegiance, and assembling for the purpose of Divine
worship.   George Fox had gone north, and was at York when he
heard this report of a plot.   Knowing that if not devised for the
purpose, it would be made use of to strengthen the hands of the
persecutors of Friends, he wrote, and had printed, an address to
Friends; in which, after declaring that Friends had nothing to do
with plots, he advised them to be very circumspect in their conduct,
so as to give no ground for their enemies to take advantage of them.
Having sent copies of this to the King and several officers in the
government, he continued his gospel labors; going through Westmoreland, and continuing on southward into Wales; thence returning north, went as far as Carlisle, and turning back, came again
into Westmoreland.   Wherever he went he heard of the excitement stirred up by the rumored plot, and the efforts made to arrest
Friends.   Yet he had large meetings, and many continued to be convinced by his ministry; and though one Justice Fleming had in open
session, at Kendal, offered five pounds to any one who would take
him, and a man who had just left the Court, saw him, and said to his
companion, " There is George Fox," he arrived at Swarthmoor un-
touched.   Speaking of his labors and his preservations while in Cumberland, he says, " So eager were the Magistrates about this time to
stir up persecution in those parts, that some offered five shillings,
some a noble a day, to any that could apprehend the speakers among
the Quakers; but it being now the time of the Quarter Sessions in
that county, the men who were so hired were gone to the Sessions
to get their wages, so all our meetings were at that time quiet."

1663.   At Swarthmoor he learned that Colonel Kirby had sent
his Lieutenant there for him; who had not been satisfied until he
had searched chests and trunks, to see if he was concealed therein.
That night George felt that it would be right for him to go to
Colonel Kirby, and inquire what he wanted with him.   The next
morning he rode over to Kirby-hall, where he found not only the
Colonel, but several of the gentry, and the two justices, Fleming,
one of whom, had offered five pounds for his apprehension.   On
George Fox telling the Colonel why he came, and asking him if
he had anything against him? the Colonel assured him, " as he was
a gentleman," that he had nothing against him; but that Mrs. Fell

must not keep great meetings at her house, for it was against the law. When taking leave, the Colonel shook him by the hand, and repeated that he had nothing against him, and others present said " he was a deserving man."

This seemed very fair, but it was all outside show. In a few days there was a meeting of justices and deputy lieutenants, and a warrant was issued for the apprehension of George Fox. He heard of it the day it was done, and he could readily have gone out of the neighborhood ; but he says, " I considered there being a noise of a plot in the north, if I should go away, they might fall upon Friends, but if I gave myself up to be taken, it might prevent them, and Friends would escape the better ; so I gave myself up to be taken, and prepared against they came." The officer who came to Swarthmoor for him would not show any order or warrant, but laid his hand on his sword, and said that was order enough.

Margaret Fell accompanied her guest to Houlker Hall, where they found a considerable company of Magistrates and officers assembled. These at once entered on an examination of George Fox. There were many frivolous questions asked him, and then they examined him in relation to his knowledge of the plot. But his answers were so clear and explicit, and several of the Magistrates having to own they had received George's paper against the plot, that they found there was no ground for accusation against him, on that account. He told them that not very long before, he had been sent up from the north by Col. Hacker to O. Cromwell, charged with being engaged in a plot to bring in King Charles, and asked where were they, or what were they doing in those days? Finding they had no sufficient plea for holding him, George Middleton, who was known to be a Papist, ordered a Bible to be brought and the oath of allegiance tendered him. Some who were ashamed of taking advantage of him in that way, objected, and desired he might be discharged ; but the voice of the majority prevailed, and he was asked to take the oath, which he refused. When about to make out the mittimus to send him to Lancaster jail, some of them relented, and said they would be content to take his word to appear at the next session, which receiving, he was dismissed and returned to Swarthmoor.

At the sessions, George Fox appeared according to his promise, and after undergoing some questioning in regard to wearing his hat before the Judge — it being taken off by an officer — and what he knew of the plot, the oath was tendered him, to which he replied he could not take any oath, because Christ and his apostle James had forbidden it. Justice Rawlinson tried to entrap him, by asking him, if he thought it *unlawful* to swear? but he was aware of the law which imposed banishment or a heavy fine on those who inculcated the opinion that it was *unlawful* to swear, and he therefore kept to the simple ground that swearing was forbidden in the New Testament. Finding they could not obtain, any advantage over him, they committed him to prison in Lancaster castle, for refusing to swear. Several other Friends were sent to the prison at the same time; some for not swearing and some for meeting to worship; so that the prison was crowded. As many of these prisoners were in low circumstances, the wives and children of such suffered great privation; and Friends who had the opportunity, were so urgent and incessant in their application to the Magistrates for relief, that at last an order was issued for the release of some of the Friends from prison."

George Fox mentions there were four Friends in the prison [1663], sent there by the Countess of Derby, for tithes; who had been lying there for two years and a half. One of them, Oliver Atherton, being of feeble constitution. the long confinement in the damp, unventilated apartment had entirely prostrated him, and it became apparent, that unless removed, death would soon close his suffering. The four Friends drew up a statement of his condition, also giving the reasons why they could not conscientiously pay tithes, and sent it, by the hands of the sick man's son, to the Countess; also praying her to have compassion on the dying man, and not bring the guilt of his death upon her. One of her servants greatly abused the son when he took the statement, and drove him from the house; nevertheless the letter addressed to the Countess was put in her hands. But she heeded it not, and continued the imprisonment. When the son informed his father there was no mercy for him, he remarked, "She has been the cause of shedding much blood, but this will be the heaviest blood that ever she spilt," and soon after died. When Friends were taking the remains to the parish where he had lived, they had notices stuck up in divers places, "This is Oliver Atherton of Ormskirk parish, persecuted to death by the Countess of Derby, for good conscience-sake towards God and Christ, because he could not give her tithes:" and setting forth why he could not pay tithes, his long imprisonment, her hard-heartedness towards him, and the manner of his death, &c. The rage of the Countess at this exposure was great, but her efforts to punish those in the places where the notices had been allowed to be put up, only served to draw more general attention to the case; and in three weeks from the death of her victim she also died.

Towards the latter end of the year 1663, George Fox, who had been kept in prison for many weeks, was brought before the Court held by Judge Twisden. The proceedings in his case are thus narrated by him: "When I was set to the bar, I said, 'Peace be amongst you all.' The Judge looked upon me and said, 'What! do you come into the Court with your hat on?' Upon which words, the gaoler taking it off, I said, 'The hat is not the honor that comes from God.' Then said the Judge to me, 'Will you take the oath of allegiance, George Fox?' I said, 'I never took any oath in my life, nor any covenant or engagement.' 'Well,' said he, 'will you swear or not?' I answered, 'I am a Christian, and Christ commands me "not to swear;" so does the apostle James; and whether I should obey God or man, do thou judge?' 'I ask you again,' said he, 'Whether you will swear or no?' I answered again, 'I am neither Turk, Jew, nor Heathen, but a Christian, and should show forth Christianity.' I asked him, If he did not know that Christians in the primitive times, under the ten persecutions, and some also of the martyrs in Queen Mary's days, refused swearing, because Christ and the apostle had forbidden it? I told him also, they had experience enough, how many had first sworn for the King and then against him. But as for me I had never taken an oath in my life. My allegiance did not lie in swearing, but in truth and faithfulness; for I honor all men, much more the King. But Christ, who is the Great Prophet, the King of kings, the Saviour and Judge of the whole world, saith, I must 'not swear.' Now, whether must I obey, Christ or thee? For it is tenderness of conscience, and in obedience to the command of Christ, that I do not swear; and we have the word of a king for tender consciences. Then I asked the Judge, If he did own the King? 'Yes,' said he, 'I do own the King.' Why then, said I, dost thou not observe his declaration from Breda, and his promises made since he came into England, 'That no man should be called in question for matters of religion, so long as they live peaceably?' If thou ownest the King, said I, why dost thou call me in question, and put me upon taking an oath, which is a matter of religion; seeing thou nor none else can charge me with unpeaceable living?' Upon this he was moved, and looking angrily at me, said, 'Sirrah, will you swear?' I told him 'I was none of his Sirrahs, I was a Christian; and for him, an old man and a Judge, to sit there and give nick-names to prisoners, it did not become either

his gray hairs or his office.'   'Well,' said he, 'I am a Christian too.'
'Then do Christian works,' said I. 'Sirrah!' said he, 'Thou thinkest
to frighten me with thy words.'   Then catching himself, and looking aside, he said, 'Hark! I am using the word (Sirrah) again;' so
checked himself. I said, 'I spoke to thee in love; for that language
did not become thee, a judge. Thou oughtest to instruct a prisoner
in the law, if he were ignorant and out of the way.'   'And I speak
in love to thee too,' said he. 'But,' said I, 'Love gives no nick-
names.'   Then he roused himself up, and said, 'I will not be afraid
of thee, George Fox. Thou speakest so loud, thy voice drowns mine
and the Court's; I must call for three or four criers to drown thy
voice: thou hast good lungs.' 'I am a prisoner here,' said I, 'for
the Lord Jesus Christ's sake; for his sake do I suffer, for Him do I
stand this day, and if my voice were five times louder I should lift
it up, and sound it out for Christ's sake, for whose cause I stand
this day before your judgment-seat, in obedience to Him who commands 'not to swear;' before whose judgment-seat you must all be
brought, and must give an account.'   'Well,' said the Judge,
'George Fox, say, Whether thou wilt take the oath, Yea or Nay?'
I replied, 'I say as I said before, Whether ought I to obey God or
man, judge thou! If I could take any oath at all, I should take this;
for I do not deny some oaths only or on some occasions, but all
oaths, according to Christ's doctrine, who hath commanded his
'Not to swear at all.'   Now if thou or any of you, or any of your
ministers or priests here, will prove that ever Christ or his apostle,
after they had forbid all swearing, commanded Christians to swear,
then I will swear.'   I saw several priests there; but not one of them
offered to speak.   Then said the Judge, 'I am a servant to the King,
and the King sent me not to dispute with you, but to put the laws
in execution; therefore tender him the oath of allegiance.' 'If thou
love the King,' said I, 'why dost thou break his word, and not keep
his declarations and speeches, wherein he promised liberty to tender
consciences? I am a man of a tender conscience, and in obedience to Christ's command I cannot swear.'   'Then you will not
swear,' said the Judge; 'Take him away, gaoler.'   I said, 'It is for
Christ's sake that I cannot swear, and for obedience to his command
I suffer; and so the Lord forgive you all.'   So the gaoler took me
away; but I felt the mighty power of the Lord was over them all.

  "The sixteenth of the same month I was brought before Judge
Twisden again, who was somewhat offended at my hat; but it being
the last morning of the assize, before he was to go out of town, and

not many people there, he made the less of it. He asked me, 'Whether I would traverse, stand mute, or submit.' But he spoke so fast, it was hard to know what he said. However I told him, 'I desired I might have liberty to traverse the indictment, and try it.' Then said he, 'Take him away, I will have nothing to do with him, take him away.' I said, 'Well, live in the fear of God, and do justice.' 'Why,' said he, 'have not I done you justice?' I replied, 'That which thou hast done hath been against the command of Christ.' So I was taken to the jail again, and kept prisoner till the next assizes.

"Some time before this assize, Margaret Fell was sent prisoner to Lancaster jail by Fleming, Kirby, and Preston, Justices; and at the assize the oath was tendered to her also, and she was again committed to prison to lie till the next assize."

1664. Three months after, George Fox was again brought before the Court, now presided over by Judge Turner. "The jury being impanelled, the Judge asked the justices, 'Whether they had tendered me the oath at the sessions?' They said, 'They had.' Then he bid, 'Give them the book, that they might swear they had tendered me the oath at the sessions.' They said 'They had.' Then he bid, 'Give them the book, that they might swear they had tendered me the oath according to the indictment.' Some of the justices refused to be sworn; but the judge said, he would have it done, to take away all occasion of exception. When the jury were sworn, and the justices had sworn 'they had tendered the oath according to the indictment,' the Judge asked me, 'Whether I had not refused the oath at the last assizes?' I said, 'I never took an oath in my life, and Christ, the Saviour and Judge of the world, said, "Swear not at all."' The Judge seemed not to take notice of my answer; but asked me, 'Whether or no I had not refused to take the oath at the last assize?' I said, 'The words that I then spoke to them were, that if they could prove, either judge, justices, priest, or teacher, that after Christ and the apostle had forbidden swearing, they commanded that Christians should swear, I would swear.'"

The jury being sworn and the indictment read, G. Fox said to the jury they could not find him guilty on that indictment, for it had many gross errors in it. The Judge forbid him to speak to the jury, but *he* would do that; and he then told them he had the authority to tender the oath to any man, and premunire him if he would not take it; and therefore they must bring in the prisoner guilty, seeing he had refused to take the oath. George asked him what was the use then of having the form of a trial, and he demanded of the jury to do him justice; but they obeying the Judge, found him guilty. Then George told them and the Court they had forsworn themselves, for the indictment was untrue.

In the afternoon, both George Fox and Margaret Fell were brought before the Court to receive sentence, and the latter, who had also plead her own cause in the morning, desired that sentence should be deferred in her case, until next day, as she had employed counsel to examine the charge for her. G. Fox told the Court he asked for justice and not for mercy, as that was for those who had committed evil; but he desired them to send some suitable person to see the prison, or room, in which he was kept; for it was so bad, no one of them would put their creatures into it; and that Colonel Kirby — who was then on the bench — had said, "I should be locked up and no flesh alive should come to me." The Judge replied, that "when sentence was passed, he would leave me to the favor of the jailer." The Court concluded to defer passing sentence until the next day, and some of the justices, accompanied by Colonel Kirby — who, notwithstanding he had told George Fox "he had nothing against him," had urged on this prosecution — went to look at his prison. When they got to the room, they feared to go into it, the floor was so bad and dangerous, and the whole so open to the wind and rain. Kirby then said, the prisoner should be removed to a more convenient place before long.

The next morning, being again brought before Court, the Judge asked George Fox what he had to say why sentence should not be passed upon him. George then took up the indictment, clause by clause, and by questioning the Judge as to what the law required, he showed him that according to his answers, it was full of serious errors, and that even the Magistrates on the bench, who had sworn they had tendered him the oath in Court on the day mentioned in the indictment, had perjured themselves; for there was no Court held on that day. The Judge could not deny the fatal errors pointed out, but acknowledged them, and as George was going on to point out others, he said, "Nay, I have enough, you need say no more." George then asked "Am I at liberty, and free from all that has been done against me in this matter?" "Yes, said the Judge, you are free from all that has been done against you;" and then starting up in a rage, he said, "I can put the oath to any man here, and I will tender it to you again." George demanded his liberty. "You are at liberty, said the Judge, but I will put the oath to you again. Give him the book."

After George had called on the people assembled, to observe how he was treated, and that the Judge was trying to ensnare him, the jury was called and the oath read; whereupon he took the Bible in his hand, and opening it, after he was asked whether he would swear, said, "Ye have given me a book to kiss, and to swear on, and this book which ye have given me to kiss, says, 'Kiss the Son,' and the Son says in this book 'Swear not at all,' and so says also the apostle James. I say as the book says, yet ye imprison me. How chance ye do not imprison the book for saying so? How comes it that the book is at liberty among you, which bids me not to swear, and yet ye imprison me for doing as the book bids me?" While saying this he held up the Bible, open to where Christ forbids to swear. The book was then jerked out of his hand, and the Judge again asked him if he would swear? He then addressed the Court, gave the reasons why he did not swear, and declaring that throughout his life his yea had always been yea, and his nay, nay, more reliable than many men's oaths, as they had seen in yesterday's proceedings; but that if the Court, or any of their priests, would show him, where or how the command of Christ had been repealed, he would then take the oath.

Being again brought before the Court in the afternoon, the new indictment against him was read; the Judge charging the officers to see there was no error in it this time. Being asked what he had to say to it, he replied that as it was long, and he had heard it imperfectly, he was not prepared to traverse it, and he asked until the next session to examine it. He then told the Judge that he (G. F.) and all his friends were against all plots or disturbances of the government, and they were quite willing that any violation of their yea or nay should be punished the same as perjury. The Judge replied, he wished the laws were otherwise than they were. They, however, recommitted him to the same wretched prison, there to lie until the next session; Colonel Kirby again ordering the jailer "to keep him close, and suffer no flesh alive to come to him; for he was not fit to be discoursed with by men."

George Fox says in his journal, "I was put into a tower, where the smoke of the other prisoners came up so thick, it stood as dew upon the walls, and sometimes it was so thick that I could hardly see the candle when it burned; and I being locked under three locks, the under-jailer, when the smoke was great, would hardly be persuaded to come up to unlock one of the uppermost doors, for fear of the smoke, so that I was almost smothered. Besides, it rained in upon my bed, and many times, when I went to stop out the rain in the cold winter-season, my shirt was as wet as muck with the rain that came in upon me while I was laboring to stop it out. And the place being high and open to the wind, sometimes as fast as I stopped it the wind blew it out again. In this manner did I lay all that long cold winter, till the next assize, in which time I was so starved with cold and rain, that my body was greatly swelled, and my limbs much benumbed."

1664. At the Spring session of the Court, George Fox was again brought before it. He had carefully examined the indictment found against him, and though Judge Turner had charged the officers to examine it well, and the Judge himself had read it over, yet George found several of the same grievous legal errors in it that had quashed the former one. G. Fox in allusion to this, remarks, "Surely the hand of the Lord was in it, to confound their mischievous work against me, and to blind them therein." Some of the officers of the Court, having sworn that the oath was tendered to him according to the indictment, Judge Twisden—who now presided—asked him what he had to say? for he would not dispute with him about anything but in point of law.

George then asked the Judge, "Whether the oath was to be tendered to the King's subjects only, or to the subjects of foreign princes? He replied, 'To the subjects of this realm; for I will speak nothing to you,' said he, 'but in point of law.' Then, said I, look in the indictment, and thou mayest see the word subject is left out of this indictment also. Therefore, seeing the oath is not to be tendered to any but the subjects of this realm, and ye have not put me in as a subject, the Court is to take no notice of this indictment. I had no sooner spoke thus, but the Judge cried, 'Take him away, jailer, take him away.' So I was presently hurried away. The jailer and people looked when I should be called for again; but I was never brought to the Court any more, though I had many other great errors to assign in the indictment."

To complete the injustice and illegality of the proceedings, after George was sent away, the Judge asked the jury if they were agreed, and they said they found for the King. But he was not brought before the Court again, neither could he hear there was ever any sentence publicly passed upon him; though it was reported that he was premunired; and he was kept in prison on this charge, altogether over three years. During the whole of this time, though those who came out of curiosity, or some evil motive, were admitted to his dismal abode, Friends were jealously excluded, so that he says he was as one dead to the Society at large.

George Fox had now been a prisoner in Lancaster Castle over eighteen months, with no accommodations fit for a human being, and exposed to the inroads of the weather, let it be as inclement as it might. By reason of his long and close confinement, he became greatly weakened; but, he says, "The Lord's power was over all, supported me through all, and enabled me to do service for Him, and for his truth and people; as the place would admit." This service was in writing and having published answers to several books that had come out against the principles held by Friends; in showing the unlawfulness of tithes; and in pointing out that which is of the world, and that which is of God; to encourage his fellow professors to stand firm in the day of trial, relying on the Lord alone.

Col. Kirby, and others of the Magistrates, who had been instrumental in having him thus immured, who felt keenly the exposure that had been made of their hypocrisy and malice, and the comments of the people upon them, became very uneasy at having their victim kept so immediately in their own neighborhood; where the parties and the circumstances were generally known. Kirby wished much to have G. Fox sent beyond sea, so as to be entirely out of the way, but at all events to get him out of Lancashire.

Application being made to the King and Council, an order was procured for his removal. So he was brought out of his wretched room in the Tower, and though they offered him wine, which he refused, they would not allow him any time to refresh himself, and change his clothes, which, from being kept constantly in dense smoke, had become offensive; but they put him on a horse, though through weakness he could hardly keep in the saddle, and carried him fourteen miles that night. They would not tell him where they were going with him; but guarded by a Marshal and a company of troopers, he was hurried along, while the people crowded the streets of the towns through which he passed, to gaze upon him. Many Friends who heard of his being on the road, hastened to meet and speak with him which was a mutual comfort to them. At York he was put into a large chamber, and the greater part of two troops of horse came to look at him, some of whom put impertinent questions to him; but he took no notice of these, and soon felt himself called to preach the gospel to them; which he did, and they became quiet and respectful. He was kept two days at York, and Lord Frecheville, the commander of the soldiers, visited him, obtained from him an account of the manner in which he had been treated, and was not only civil but loving towards him. The day after this visit, he was sent under an escort of four or five soldiers to Scarborough Castle. [1665.]

On his first introduction to this Castle, as he was so weak that he frequently fainted, they allowed him a tolerably comfortable room, and would occasionally permit him to go into the open air, accompanied by a sentry ; but this indulgence lasted not long. Soon they put him into a room, much like the one he had occupied at Lancaster Castle ; that is, open to the wind and rain, and filled with dense smoke whenever a fire was made. Sir Jordan Crosland, the Governor of the castle, who was a Papist, after some time came to see his prisoner, and could hardly find his way out of the room in consequence of the smoke, and George told him, he thought it must be his purgatory he had put him into. They consented to his expending between two and three pounds, to repair the room so as to keep out the rain and improve the draft of the chimney ; and when it was done, they took him out of it, and put him in another that had neither hearth nor chimney, and which being close to the sea, the wind would blow the rain and spray into it, " so that," he says, " the water came so over my bed, and ran about the room, that I was fain to skim it up with a platter." Here, his friends shut out from him — for though many travelled far to see him, almost every one was denied admittance — he was obliged to make what arrangement he could with others, to supply him with the necessaries of life, and sometimes the soldiers would take for themselves the food and drink that was purchased with his money. His food was generally bread, and water with wormwood steeped in it. When his clothes were wet with the rain, he had no fire to dry them, and in consequence, his body and limbs became greatly swollen.

But neither the inhumanity of his oppressors nor the sufferings of his body, could overcome his Christian patience and fortitude, nor induce him to forego the principles and practices he had learned in the school of Christ. Many persons of note in the world came to see him, some to tantalize him, and some to find fault with his religious views ; but they always found him prepared to give a reason for the hope that was in him, and often to declare unto them the truth as it is in Jesus. Threats of violence were often made, and on one occasion the Deputy Governor told him, the King, knowing the influence he had among the people, had sent down an order, that if there should be any stir in the nation, to hang him over the wall of the castle. But none of these things moved him, and on another occasion, when they were talking much about hanging him, he told them, "If that was what they desired, and it was permitted them, I was ready, for I never feared death nor sufferings in my life, but I was known to be an innocent, peaceable man; free from all stirrings and plottings, and one that sought the good of all men."

Thus with Christian love and constancy he returned good for evil, and finally so wrought upon the Governor and officers, that their conduct towards him was entirely changed, and they came to treat him with respect, and even kindness. The officers in speaking of him to others would say, "He was as stiff as a tree and as pure as a bell, for we could never bow him."

After being immured in Scarborough more than a year, George Fox addressed a letter to the King, giving an account of the cause of his imprisonment, and the cruel usage he had received from the hands of those who had charge of him, and that he had been informed no one but the King could release him. He had previously, on the occasion of the Governor of the Castle going to London, requested him to speak to Esquire Marsh and some others of influence, respecting his case, the severity, and length in time, of his sufferings, &c.; which, on his return, the Governor assured him he had done, and that Marsh had said, he would "go a hundred miles barefoot" for his liberty. Two Friends in London called on Esquire Marsh, who willingly undertook, if a correct account of George Fox's case was drawn up, to have it delivered to the Master of Requests, and thus brought before the King. This was accordingly done, and the King signed an order for his release. So soon as the order was obtained, one of the Friends, John Whitehead, carried it down to Scarborough, and delivered it to the Governor of the Castle. Upon its receipt, the Governor interposing no obstructions and requiring no sureties, released his prisoner; furnishing him with a passport as follows:

"Permit the bearer hereof, George Fox, late a prisoner here, and now·discharged by his Majesty's order, quietly to pass about his lawful occasions, without molestation. Given under my hand at Scarborough Castle, this first day of September, 1666.

JORDAN CROSLAND, Governor of the Castle."

. So happy was the effect of G. Fox's Christian conduct on the Governor, that ever after he treated Friends kindly, and did what he could to shield them. G. Fox observes, it was remarkable that very many of those who were instrumental in bringing himself and other Friends under the action of the Court, by which he was premunired, and in subjecting him to the cruelty inflicted on him in prison, soon after either died, or fell into practices that obliged them to flee out of the country. Four of the Magistrates active in the Court, died in a comparatively short time after, as did the constable and the deputy constable, the jailer at Lancaster, and the Sheriff; so that when G. Fox was again in that country, nearly all his old persecutors were gone. Colonel Kirby, though not cut off by death, never prospered after.

It has been mentioned that Margaret Fell, after pleading her own cause, informed the Court she had employed counsel to examine the indictment, and show cause why she should not have sentence passed upon her. The next morning her counsel pointed out many errors in the indictment, and pleaded for arrest of judgment. But the Judge refused to recognize these errors, and proceeded to pass sentence on her, which was, that " She be put out of the King's protection, and forfeit all her estate, real and personal to the King, and suffer imprisonment during life." In the account of this persecution which was published, she says, in reference to the close of her trial : " But the great God of heaven and earth, supported my spirit under this severe sentence, so that I was not terrified ; but gave this answer to Judge Turner, who passed the sentence, ' Although I am out of the King's protection, yet I am not out of the protection of Almighty God." She complained to the Court that the room in which she was imprisoned, admitted the rain freely, and was not fit for any human being to remain in. The Judge said this ought not to be ; but it does not appear that any change was made ; and this well educated, noble woman, who, her life long, had been accustomed to all the domestic comforts and refinements of good society, was incarcerated in that dismal cell ; where she remained twenty months before she could persuade her jailer to allow her to go home for a short time to see her family ; and after her return she was kept prisoner four more years. [1664.]

CHAPTER XVIII.

Arrest and Trial of F. Howgil — Imprisonment and Death of F. Howgil — John Audland — Suffering on account of Tithes — Value of the Testimonies suffered for — Conventicle Act — Short imprisonments of Friends, in order to transport them on the third offence — Trials at Hertford — Cruel conduct at London — Trials at London — Judge's charge — Dead bodies of two Friends seized and secretly buried — Grand Jury threatened for not finding a Bill against Friends — Hannah Trigg — False witnesses — Sentence of Banishment — Refusal of Captains to carry Friends away — Banished Friends put on Shore — Embargo laid on all vessels that would not carry Quakers — Mortality in Prisons — Persecution in the Isle of Man.

TOWARDS the latter part of the year 1663, Francis Howgil being engaged in his lawful business at the market-place in Kendall, was taken by the high constable before some Magistrates who were sitting at a tavern; who tendered him the oath of allegiance, and committed him to prison, there to be kept until the next session of the Court to be held at Appleby. When brought before the Court, which was held by Judge Twisden, the usual course was pursued of tendering the oath, and an indictment was found by a jury.

The Judge seemed inclined to moderation, offering Francis until the next assizes to prepare for his trial; but requiring that he should give surety for his appearance at the Court, and for his good behavior, and that he would not go to meeting, in the mean time. To this, however, Francis objected, offering to give his word that, unless something should occur that would prevent, he would be present when called for, but declining to give surety for good behavior, or not to attend meeting. Two of the Justices — Flemming and Musgrave — were very bitter against him, the former, representing that as Francis "was a great speaker among the Quakers, if they got rid of him, probably they [the Quakers] could not get along without him. The latter thought the Courts were not sufficiently severe on the Quakers; for notwithstanding all that was done, they continued to hold their meetings and to increase. Francis was remanded to jail until the next assizes.

When brought before the Court at its next session, Judge Turner presided, and F. Howgil presented a paper in which he declared he was bound to observe the substance of all that was contained in the oath, and was ready so to declare before the Court; and he desired that it might be taken, instead of his being required to swear, as he

declined that, solely on the ground of conscientious scruple. There
was much passed in relation to the principles of Friends, as regards
swearing, declining to own the "Church" established by law, and the
obligation to obey all laws which did not contravene the commands
of Christ. But the Judge not being prepared to controvert what
Francis advanced, finally required him to speak to the indictment
and nothing else. It then appeared, that although Judge Twisden
had given him until this assize to traverse the indictment, Francis
had never been allowed to have a copy of it nor to hear it read.
The Judge paid no regard to this, but ordered the jury to find a
verdict, which they did, of guilty. In the course of the interlocu-
tion that occurred after the prisoner was asked what he had to
say, why sentence should not be passed upon him, F. Howgil
cited several authors, who showed that for the first three hundred years of the Christian era, the disciples of Christ refused to
swear, and that at different times since, very many Christians declared it to be contrary to Christ's command. The Judge expressed his surprise at this, but would not allow it to have any
weight.

"Judge.— Well, I see you will not swear, nor conform, nor be
subject, and you think we deal severely with you, but if you would
be subject, we should not need.

F. Howgil.— Yes, I do so think indeed, that you deal severely
with us for obedience to the command of Christ. I pray thee,
canst thou show me that any of those people for whom this act was
made, have been proceeded against by the statute? though I envy
no man's liberty.

Judge.—O, yes! I can instance you many up and down the country
that are premunired. I have pronounced sentence myself against
divers.

F. Howgil.— What! against Papists?

Judge.— No.

F. Howgil.— What then! against Quakers? So I have heard.
It seems then, that Statute which was made against the Papists,
thou lettest them alone, and executest it against the Quakers.

Judge.— Well, you will meet in great numbers, and do increase;
but *there is a new Statute which will make you fewer.*

F. Howgil.— Well, if we must suffer, it is for Christ's sake, and
for well doing.

Judge.— In a faint low voice.— You are put out of the King's
protection, and the benefits of the laws. Your lands are confiscated

to the King during your life, and your goods and chattels forever and you are to be prisoner during your life.

F. Howgil.— Hard sentence for obeying the command of Christ; but I am content, and in perfect peace with the Lord; and the Lord forgive you all.

Judge.— Well, if you will yet be subject to the laws, the King will show you mercy.

F. Howgil.— The Lord hath showed mercy to me, and I have done nothing against the King, nor the government, nor any man, blessed be the Lord, and therein stands my peace. It is for Christ's sake I suffer, and not for evil doing."

He was then sent back to prison, where he was kept until his death, which occurred near the close of the year 1668. His wife and some Friends were allowed to be with him during the time of his last sickness, to whom he spoke repeatedly of his peaceful feelings, and his full confidence that the Lord would support all those who were faithful in maintaining his cause. Among other expressions are the following: " I say again, God will own his people, even all those that are faithful; and as for me, I am well, and am content to die. I am not at all afraid of death; and truly one thing was of late in my heart, which I intended to have written to George Fox and others, even that which I have observed; which is, That this generation passeth fast away. We see many good and precious Friends, within these few years, have been taken from us, and therefore Friends have need to watch, and be very faithful, so that we may leave a good, and not a bad savor, to the next succeeding generation; for you see that it is but a little time that any of us have to stay here." " He was content to die, and was ready; and he praised God for the many sweet enjoyments and refreshments he had received on that, his prison-house bed, whereon he lay, freely forgiving all who had a hand in his restraint." A little while before his departure, he said, " I have sought the way of the Lord from a child, and have lived innocently as among men, and if any inquire concerning my latter end, let them know that I die in the faith in which I lived, and suffered for." He had been in that prison over four years.

Amid the severe suffering meted out to those who stood unflinchingly for the doctrines and testimonies held by Friends, in the year 1663, died John Audland; who as has been before mentioned, was one of those ministers, that with many more people were convinced of the truth, at the memorable meeting at Firbank Chapel in 1652.

He was one of the first ministers who engaged in that service before the Society was fully formed, and was eminently instrumental in spreading a knowledge of the doctrine of the Light of Christ, bestowed on every man to bring him salvation, and the gospel testimonies springing from it. Though at the time of his convincement occupying a priest's office, and having a congregation among the Independents, when he heard the gospel preached with convincing power, by one who had comparatively little of the learning of the schools, he confessed that all his great profession availed nothing, for "The day of the Lord was upon it, and the fire of his Word consumed it as dry stubble." He submitted to take up the daily cross, and to bear what the Lord was pleased to lay upon him, in order to obtain that peace which Christ bestows upon his humble, cross-bearing disciples. He became a zealous minister, spending his time, strength and substance freely, for the promotion of the cause he had espoused ; and when he came to lay down his life, though his frame was greatly wasted by Consumption, and his physical strength prostrated, yet he was enabled to praise his Redeemer for all his tender mercies to his soul, and to pour it out in fervent prayer, that Friends "might be preserved in the Truth, out of the evil of the world," and that "the gospel might be spread and published, to the gathering of all that pertain to Israel." He was thirty-four years of age at the time of his death.

The brief accounts given of the trials at different courts of the Friends mentioned, are representative of large numbers that took place at almost, if not quite every session, in different parts of the kingdom ; representative, as to the arbitrary and unjust character of the proceedings, and the vindictive punishment inflicted, for no other offence than obeying the dictates of an enlightened and sensitive conscience. The jails were kept crowded not only with those who were arrested and punished for being found convened for the purpose of Divine worship, and those who scrupled to take an oath ; but also with hundreds of Friends who were prosecuted for tithes.

The suffering from the latter cause, was very severe ; for not only was the head of and provider for the family, often shut up in jail, where he was not allowed to do anything for the support of his family, but seizures of cattle, goods and furniture, were frequently so remorselessly made, that little or nothing was left for the use or support of the wife and dependent children. Great havoc was also made of the property — often small in amount — of Friends, on whom fines were imposed for some religious act, construed into a crime. Thus thousands of pounds were forcibly distrained, from those who dare not do otherwise than act in accordance with the religion of Christ, as they understood it, and stand as witnesses to the self-denying requirements of his gospel, as He had sealed them by his Spirit on their understandings. As the great body of the Society was composed of those who were in the middle and the humbler walks of life, dependent on their own exertions for the means of subsistence, it may be readily conceived into how great straits, and often positive suffering, those dependent on the labor of the hands of the head of a family, were often brought, when the little substance possessed was swept away, or the caretaker shut up in prison by some unjust judge, bent on forcing him into conformity, or some avaricious priest, determined to exact the last penny of tithes which the law, and it alone, awarded him.

To meet, and as far as possible relieve the distress thus caused; accounts of suffering were sent up regularly to Friends in London, and subscriptions raised from the brethren throughout the whole land; so that pecuniary help could be extended where needed, by suitable committees, and no Friend or his family be allowed to become dependent on public charity.

It is no easy thing, unless brought under the same government of the Spirit of Christ, that required Friends of that day to maintain these testimonies, in the midst of that crooked and perverse generation, to realize their unalterable importance, or rightly to estimate the painful cost, at which those valiant soldiers of the cross, finally purchased the enjoyment of the right of liberty of conscience, and transmitted to succeeding generations the privilege of possessing in peace and quietness, the full exercise of the duties belonging to the religion of Christ; a privilege which very many of them laid down their lives, in their efforts to secure.

Disappointed in the result of the persecuting laws made in former reigns, and again brought into operation, and dissatisfied with the failure of the Act directed specifically against Quakers, to prevent them from holding their meetings for Divine worship, or to lessen their number, it was decided by the Council and Parliament, to resort to other measures for ridding the country of non-conformists, and especially the irrepressible Society of Friends.

In the trial of Francis Howgil, Judge Twisden told him, "There is a new statute which will make you fewer." This statute was entitled "An Act to Prevent and Suppress Seditious Conventicles." The avowed object of this Act, was to "provide further and more speedy remedies, against the growing and dangerous practices of seditious sectaries and other disloyal persons, who, under pretence of tender consciences, do at their meetings contrive insurrections, as late experience hath showed." It was apparently aimed at all non-conformists, and as it was well known that the principles held by Friends, restrained them from taking part in any insurrection, or movement hostile to the government, and as their whole deportment and published declarations had shown, they were strictly and practically governed by those principles; patiently and passively submitting to the laws that inflicted such severe punishment on them, it might have been supposed this law was not intended to apply to them, and would not be enforced upon them. But it is worthy of note, that the penalties of fine and imprisonment which it prescribes, were but rarely imposed on members of other dissenting Societies, and it is doubtful, whether sentence of banishment was executed under it in England, upon any but Friends. It was not so much to impose new punishments, as to make the convictions more speedy, and the penalties to be inflicted more immediate and certain. It provided, [1664] "That if any person of the age of sixteen years or upwards, being a subject of this realm, at any time after the first day of July, which shall be in the year of our Lord, one thousand six hundred sixty and four, shall be present at any assembly, conventicle or meeting, under color or pretence of any exercise of religion, in other manner than is allowed by the liturgy or practice of the Church of England, in any place within the kingdom of England, dominion of Wales, and town of Berwick-upon-Tweed; at which conventicle, meeting, or assembly, there shall be five persons or more assembled together, over and above those of the same household; then it shall and may be lawful to and for any two justices of the peace of the county, limit, division, or liberty wherein the offence aforesaid shall be committed, or for the chief magistrate of the place where such offence aforesaid shall be committed, (if it be within a corporation where there are not two justices of the peace,) (2) and they are hereby required and enjoined upon proof to them or him respectively made of such offence, either by confession of the party, or oath of witness, or notorious evidence of the fact, (which oath the said justices of the peace, and chief magistrate respectively, are hereby empowered and required to administer,) to make a record of every such offence and offences under their hands and seals respectively; (3) *which record so made, as aforesaid, shall to all intents and purposes, be in law taken and adjudged to be a full and perfect conviction* of such offender for such offence; and thereupon the said justices and chief magistrate *respectively*, shall commit every such offender, so convicted as aforesaid, to the jail or house of correction, there to remain without bail or mainprise, for any time not exceeding the space of three months; unless such offender shall pay down to the said justices or chief magistrate, such sum of money not exceeding five pounds, as the said justices or chief magistrate (who are hereby thereunto authorized and required) shall fine the said offender at, for his or her said offence." The money to go for the relief of the poor of the parish.

For the second offence, convicted in the same manner, the fine or imprisonment was to be doubled.

For the third offence, convicted in the same manner, the "offender" is to be committed to jail or house of correction until the next session of Court, where he is to be indicted, and tried, and if found guilty, he "shall be transported beyond the seas, to any of his Majesty's foreign plantations (Virginia and New England excepted), for seven years, or to pay one hundred pounds," &c. In case such banished persons escape or return before the end of the time specified, they shall be adjudged to be felons, and suffer death, " *without benefit of clergy.*" Justices, Sheriffs, or any person they may deputize, are authorized to break up all such conventicles or unlawful assemblies, and to take into custody as many of the company assembled as they may think proper.

Persons who allowed their dwellings, barns or other houses to be used for holding these conventicles, were liable to the same pains and penalties as those who attended them.

If any one sentenced to transportation had not property sufficient to defray all the expense, he was to be made over to the master of the ship, or his assigns, to serve as a laborer for five years.

Fearing perhaps that some of the subordinate officers might have too much humanity to carry the law into complete execution, it was provided, that should any constable or other officer neglect or refuse to execute the warrants and distraints granted and ordered under this law, such officer shall forfeit five pounds for every such neglect or refusal; one half of that sum to be given to whoever may bring suit therefor; and if any jailer permit a person who has been committed to his custody for any offence under this Act, to go at large; or shall permit any person at large, to join with such prisoner in any act of worship " differing from the rites of the church of England," he shall forfeit the sum of ten pounds for every such offence.

By the last provision it was determined to put a stop to a prisoner (a Friend) visiting his family for a short time, so as to see after their means of maintenance; and also to prevent any who were not prisoners, but were visiting those who were, uniting with them in meetings for worship.

The iniquitous character and cruel provisions of this Act, drew forth expositions and comments, not only from Friends, but from persons of other religious Societies. Its interference with what might occur in the privacy of domestic life; its encouragement of eaves-droppers and informers; its contemplated effect of sending out of the country numerous citizens of good moral repute, industrious, and contributing to the public welfare and wealth; whereby husbands and wives would be separated, and families of helpless children might be left destitute and with none to care for them, were set forth; and those in power were warned, that such wickedness would sooner or later bring the judgments of an offended God upon the people. George Whitehead published a pamphlet, in which, after showing the irrational and unchristian course pursued by the government, and the injustice and inhumanity that must accompany the execution of the law, he declared that Friends could no more adopt the suggestion made by some who professed to desire they should not suffer by it, of meeting in their own houses privately to the number of five, for worship, than Daniel could have made his prayers secretly, and not with open windows, three times a day, after the King had issued his decree forbidding it. "Since then," he says, " our meetings are kept in obedience to the Lord God, and according to the freedom he hath given us, we may not leave off *our testimony for God* in that case; but we must be faithful to Him, *whatever we suffer on that account*. For neither the threatenings of men, nor their severity nor cruelty acted against us, how far soever it may be extended, can make us *to forsake the Lord in not keeping our assemblies*, or to be ashamed of Christ before men, lest hereafter He be ashamed of us before his Father which is in heaven."

Such was the unscrupulous haste with which the enemies of Friends sought to carry out what they fondly hoped would prove the means of their extermination, that although the law did not go into effect until the first of the Seventh month, in the year 1664, yet on the 12th and 13th of the next month, eight Friends were arraigned before Orlando Bridgeman, presiding over the Court held in Hertford; being indicted for the third offence under this Conventicle Act.

Fully aware that Friends acted in this matter from a sense of religious duty ; and let the consequences be what they might, they dare not decline the due attendance at their places for public worship, their persecutors resolved to avail themselves of this faithfulness to the requiring of their Divine Master, in order to hasten their banishment from their native land. Accordingly, after violently assaulting and breaking up a meeting, the Magistrates would send large numbers to jail, to be kept there for a few days. This constituted the first offence. When set at liberty ; for many of them were not detained for the small fine imposed—the same individuals would soon be found at their meetings again, and being arrested and once more committed for a short time, the same course was pursued ; until, on the third arrest and committal, they were indicted therefor, and held liable to banishment. Thus, from the middle of the Seventh month, to the end of the first week in the Ninth month, in 1664, there were nine hundred and seventy Friends taken from the different meetings in London, at different times, and committed to Bridewell or Newgate.

At the trial at Hertford, before Judge Bridgeman, though the witnesses swore the prisoners had met together over the number of five, and were taken at the times and places specified, yet they could not say they heard any of them speak, or do anything when in the meeting ; they were merely sitting still. After hearing the evidence, the grand jury thought it insufficient to prove the indictment, and they returned it *ignoramus*. As this was a legal return, and given in due form, the prisoners should have been discharged thereon, but the Judge was not willing to be so quickly deprived of his prey; and addressing the jury, he said, angrily, " My masters, what do ye mean to do ? will ye make a nose of wax of the law, and suffer the law to be baffled ? Those that think to deceive the law, the law will deceive them. Why do ye not find the bill ? " One of the jury replying, it became them to be wary, for they were upon men's lives, for aught they knew. No, said the Judge, I desire not their lives, but their reformation. He then sent them out again, with such instructions, that when they returned they had found the bill.

When arraigned, the usual question of guilty or not guilty being put to the four, who were to be tried together, they replied not guilty, and further, that they had transgressed no *just* law. But, said the Judge, " ye have transgressed *this* law," having the " Conventicle Act " in his hand. He then told them, that having been twice convicted before, of the same offence, as the record proved, if they were now found guilty the sentence would be transportation for seven years; and to show them that he had no wish to push the law to its highest severity, but, if possible, to induce them to conform, he would be willing to pass by their two former offences, if they would promise not to go any more to their meetings : but this must be done before their cases went to the jury. He then put the query, " Will ye promise to meet no more?" They answered, they could make no such promise.

In his charge to the jury the Judge instructed them, " Ye are not to expect a plain, punctual evidence against them for anything they said or did at their meeting; for dumb men may speak to one another, so as they may understand each other by signs; and they . themselves say, that the worship of God is inward in the Spirit, and that they can discern spirits, and know one another in spirit. So that if ye find, *or believe in your hearts,* that they were in the meeting under color of religion in their way, though they sat still only, it was an unlawful meeting; and their use and practice not according to the liturgy of the church of England; for it allows and commands when people meet together in the church, that divine service shall be read," &c. He also told them that the law *had nothing whatever to do with conscience,* it was merely to prevent the government being undermined, and that they must find for the King, &c. Under these instructions the jury in the course of an hour brought in a verdict of guilty.

"Judge.—Addressing the four prisoners. What can ye say for yourselves that judgment of transportation should not pass against you?

Prisoners.—We are innocent, and have transgressed no just law. If we must have that sentence, we give up our bodies freely into the hands of the Lord; the will of the Lord be done.

Judge.— Have ye nothing more to say?

Prisoners.— Nothing, but that we are innocent.

Judge.—Then hearken to your sentence. Ye shall be transported beyond the seas, to the Island of Barbadoes, there to remain seven years."

To the two prisoners brought next before the Court, the Judge said, he had heard so good an account of one of them, that he was willing to show them so much favor, as to grant them until the next term of the Court, to consider the matter better for themselves. They replied, We have transgressed no law of God, nor wronged any man; we desire it not, we leave it to the Court. The Judge then said he would not grant it. The other three prisoners were then brought to the bar, that all might be tried together. The testimony respecting one of the latter was that he was not in the meeting, but was taken a short distance from the door of the meeting-house, with his face turned from it. The Judge tried to impress the jury, that in the latter case, the circumstantial evidence was sufficient to convict; but they returned a verdict of guilty for four, but not guilty for the other. To the usual inquiry what they had to say why judgment of transportation should not be given against them? they replied, " We are innocent, and have not offended any just law of God or man, to deserve that sentence. We leave it to the witness for God in thy and your consciences." The Judge then said, " Ye have offended against this law — having the act before him — which is made by the King and Parliament, and executed by us, their subordinate ministers; if it be not righteous and just, we must answer for that." He then condemned them to transportation to Jamaica, there to remain seven years. Before the Court rose up, the Judge informed the prisoners that if each of them would pay down one hundred pounds, before the Court broke up, they would be acquitted of all that had passed, and he would adjourn until the afternoon to give them time to think well of it. In the afternoon, being asked if they would pay the £100, they all answered, No, and the Court closed.

Before noticing the occurrences attending the attempted execution of the sentences passed upon these Friends, it will be well to speak of some two or three of the trials that took place in London. Such, however, was the ferocious spirit with which this extreme of persecution was carried on, that the number of Friends prosecuted at different Courts was so great, it would carry this narrative far beyond the limits assigned, to enter into a detailed account of one-fourth of them. The same spirit inspired the actors in these scenes that prompted the Puritans in New England to torture with the stocks, the scourge, and the branding-iron, and, in the bitterness of their vindictive passion, finally to resort to the gallows, in order to rid themselves of those who would bear witness to the truth, and expose spiritual wickedness in high places. Sharp and severe as were the means resorted to for this purpose, in America, comparatively few Friends lost their lives there, by the hands of those who hated them; while in England, hundreds were sacrificed by the slow torture inflicted in its horrible prison-houses and dungeons; and in some cases, punishments harder to bear than death itself, were inflicted on citizens, against whom nothing was charged but non-

conformity to the religious profession established by law. The
spirit of this world is always at enmity with God, and when it as
God, sitteth in the temple of God, showing itself that it has usurped
the place of God, it matters not what may be the outward profession
of the worshippers, if possessed of sufficient power, they will betray
having imbibed more or less the spirit of him who was a murderer
from the beginning.

It has been already mentioned how large a number were crowded
into the jails in London, in the course of a few weeks after the Conventicle Act took effect.   The same cruel treatment, when breaking
up a meeting as before described, was continued towards those who
were found assembled, and those who were picked out for the prisons.
One quotation from Besse may be given as an illustration.

"On 21st of the Seventh month [1664], were committed to Newgate, from Miles-end Green meeting-house, eleven persons for two
days, and from the Peel, twenty-nine persons for four days.   On the
same day, about nine in the morning, the City Marshal and other
officers, with constables and their assistants, came to the Bull-and-
Mouth meeting, and haled out by force all or most present, and then
withdrew into the street, where the assembly continued ; and soon
after, the doors being opened, returned into the house, where one
began to preach, but was instantly haled out, and sent to Guild-Hall.
The meeting still continuing, the Lord Mayor, with the Sheriffs, and
Alderman Brown, came in.   Brown with his wonted fury, kicked
some, pulled others by the hair and pinched the women's arms until
they were black ; and thus with his own hands, shamefully abused
others.   The Mayor causing the doors to be shut, sent about one
hundred and fifty-nine of them to Newgate for four days; where
they had not room enough to sit down, nor scarcely to stand, being
close shut up, without respect to age or sex, among felons and murderers.   The rest of them — about twenty-seven — were sent to
Bridewell."

Having by the course adopted, obtained a number of prisoners
who stood committed for the third infraction of the law, it was resolved to bring some of them to trial.   Accordingly at the Sessions
in the Old Bailey held Ninth month, 1664, Judge Keating addressed
the grand jury in relation to Friends and their principles; the ani-
mus of which charge may be understood from a few extracts: " Because this day was appointed for the trial of these people, and inasmuch as many are come hither, expecting what will be done, I will
say something concerning them and their principles, that they may

not be thought worthy of pity, as suffering more than they deserve; for they are a stubborn sect, and the King has been very merciful to them. It was hoped that the purity of the Church of England, would, ere this, have convinced them; but they will not be reclaimed. They teach dangerous principles: this for one; That it is not lawful to take an oath. You must not think their leaders believe this doctrine, only they persuade these poor ignorant souls so; but they have an interest to carry on against the government, and therefore will not swear subjection to it, and their end is rebellion and blood. You may easily know they do not believe themselves what they say, when they say *it is not lawful to take an oath,* if you look into the Scriptures. That text (Matthew v.) where our Saviour saith, 'Swear not at all,' will clear itself from such a meaning as forbids swearing, if you look but into the next words; where it is said, ' *Let your communication be yea, yea, nay, nay;*' and it is said, '*An oath is an end of all strife.*' This for the New Testament; and the old is positive for swearing, and they that deny swearing, deny God a special part of his worship." He then enters into a declamation respecting the importance of swearing: that no government can stand, and no laws be executed without it, &c., &c.

He is not much more happy in his exposition of the object in view, in thus prosecuting Friends for attending their meetings. He says, "Whereas, they pretend in their scribbles, that this Act against Conventicles, doth not concern them, but such as, under pretence of worshipping God, do, at their meetings, conspire against the government. This is a mistake, *for if they should conspire,* they would then be guilty of treason, *and we should try them by other laws.* But this Act is against meetings; to prevent them of such conspiracy; for they meet to consult to know their numbers, and to hold correspondence, *that they may in a short time be up in arms.*"

He then went on to inform the jury, that in serving his Majesty at York, he had found that plots were carried on at these meetings, and four or five of the speakers, chief leaders in rebellion, had been hung; inducing the jury to believe they were Quakers. That the law was a merciful law, merely banishing for seven years on the third offence, and it had nothing to do with worshipping God according to their conscience, for the Quakers could do that in their own families, if not more than five were present.

After thus endeavoring to prejudice the jury by falsehood and invective, the Judge wished to proceed at once to the trial of several of the prisoners, but it appeared none but a boy from Newgate was present. Upon the query being put to him; whether he was not at the Bull-and-Mouth meeting on such a day? he replied, " I was not." Whereupon. the Judge observed, that with all their pretensions to truth, the Quakers could lie, to promote their interest, or escape suffering. The lad persisting in his declaration, the Judge said, We shall prove you were there; will you stand to your profession? Yes, said he, and seal it with my blood. It was then ordered that the witnesses of the fact be called. But no one could be found to give evidence against him. The Judge manifested his angry maliciousness by observing, " Here is a disappointment," and threatening that some should suffer for it, dismissed the jury.

Two Friends who had been kept in prison for some time, dying soon after their release, their bodies were put in coffins, and taken to the Bull-and-Mouth meeting-house, in order that the burial should take place thence. The Mayor and several of the Magistrates hearing of this, and fearing that the spectacle of the funeral might awaken commiseration in the minds of those who witnessed it, issued an order to the churchwardens of the parish, to go that night, seize the bodies, and bury them at once in the church-yard. With this warrant, the Marshal, and several other men with halberds, went at midnight to the meeting-house, and roused up the family that lived in one part of it. Upon the latter asking what was the matter, and what they had come for? the officer replied, they had come " *to search for a meeting.*" The door was at once opened, that they might see there was no meeting being held ; whereupon they went in, took possession of the coffins and their contents, and carried them away to the place designated, to be buried, without their families or friends knowing anything about the matter.

Sixteen Friends were tried at the sessions in the Tenth month, 1664. The grand jury, dissatisfied with the evidence, refused to find a bill. The Judges threatened them, and finding that while they were together, they were unwilling to return the indictment, they took them apart, and by threats of heavy fines, and persuasion that they need not regard anything more than that more than five of the prisoners were together at a given time, they brought over a majority to agree to find a bill. One of the majority afterwards published a pamphlet entitled, " The wounded heart, or the Juryman's Offences," in which he confessed how wrong he had acted, under the influence of fear.

The Friends being found guilty, when brought up for sentence the next day, and the usual question asked, why sentence should not be pronounced against them, one of them, a young girl named Hannah Trigg, replied, that she was not sixteen years of age. The Judge told her "*She lied.*" A certificate signed by two women, testifying that they were present at the birth of Hannah Trigg, and that it occurred on the 20th of the month called August, 1649, showing she was but fifteen years of age, was then handed to the Court; but they refused to take any notice of it; sentencing the girl with the others, and sending her back to prison. The Judge was so confused or confounded when passing the sentence, that he declared the prisoners had transgressed the laws of the *Commonwealth*, and ordered some of them to be transported to *Hispaniola*, an island belonging to Spain. Four married women were condemned to imprisonment for eleven months.

Hannah Trigg, who was but a delicate girl, soon sunk under the close confinement and poisonous atmosphere of her prison-house, and died. The inhuman officers refused to allow her mother and other relatives, to have the sad consolation of paying the last kind offices to her remains; but had them carried to the ground appropriated for the interment of felons who died in prison; and upon arriving there, finding no grave was prepared, they left the corpse on the ground, saying they would make a grave in the morning. The poor sorrowing mother, who had followed the dead body of her child to its last resting-place, could do no more than watch by it during the livelong night.

Trials of similar character as those already noticed, were now going on at every session of the Court in London, and occasionally in other parts of England. The persecuting Judges and Magistrates did not always succeed according to their wishes. In one case, where sixteen were tried before Judge Hide, at the Old Bailey, such was the contradiction, and false swearing of some of the officers who were used as witnesses, that one of the jury, addressing the Judge, said, " My lord, I beseech you let us be troubled with no more such evidence; for we shall not cast men on such evidence as this." But the Judge, palliating the want of truthfulness, rebuked the juryman for being too scrupulous. The jury brought in a verdict that four were " not guilty," and the others " guilty of meeting, but not of fact." The Judge being displeased, demanded of them, what they meant by " not guilty of fact." They replied, that though there was evidence of their meeting at the Bull-and-Mouth, there was no evidence of their meeting contrary to the liturgy of the Church of England. The Judge tried all in his power to change them; but neither persuasion nor menaces could induce them to alter their verdict, and the Court, exasperated at the failure, bound six of them in £100 each, to appear at the King's Bench Bar, at the next session. By a publication issued towards the close of the year (1664,) it was shown there were at that time between six and seven hundred Friends in prison, and the records prove that in the two years, 1664 and 1665, upwards of two hundred were sentenced, in different parts of the nation, to banishment. It is a noticeable fact, although the principal ministers in the Society continued their labors incessantly, going from place to place, when not confined in prisons, strengthening and encouraging their fellow-members to stand firmly in the midst of the terrible storm that was beating upon them, yet no one of them was brought to trial for a third violation of the Act, and no one of them sentenced to banishment.

Of those who were under sentence of transportation, some died in prison before passage to the places they were to go, could be obtained; some were released by their relatives, who were not Friends, paying the £100 fine, and there were a very few instances of apostacy from the faith, and drawing back in the last hours of the bitter trial. Seven of the Friends sentenced by Judge O. Bridgeman, at Hertford, as already narrated, were brought to London by the jailer; who agreed with the Captain of the ship Anne, of London, to take them; some to Barbadoes, and some to Jamaica; the understanding being, they were undertaking the voyage of free will. But when the Captain found they were to be banished as convicts under the Conventicle Act, he refused to receive them on board his ship. The jailer applied to Albemarle, Secretary of State, and swore that the Captain knew the condition of the prisoners when he contracted to take them; and although the Captain took two witnesses with him to the Secretary, who were willing to swear that the jailer had represented to the Captain that the men for whose passage he contracted were free men, and would take some goods with them, Albemarle refused to hear them, and told the Captain he must take them.

The prisoners, in the meantime, were unfeelingly treated, being kept pent up in a small dark room, at an inn. On the night of the 14th of the 10th month, they were forced into a boat and rowed to the ship, which laid in the stream. The Master being on shore, they were received on board, but on his return, taking their word, that they would come back when he sent for them, he put them on shore, with a certificate they were there by his permission. From that time until the first of the Eleventh month, — six weeks, — the Captain and crew, made every effort to get the vessel down the river, and out to sea; but were continually frustrated, either by storm, head wind or something that prevented the vessel getting under sail. Six times the prisoners were put on shore, and six times, in obedience to the Captain's order, they returned on board again. On the evening of the thirty-first day of the Tenth month, the prisoners were sent on shore for the last time, the Captain directing them to meet him at Deal. He met them there some days after, and in the presence of several witnesses, informed them, he was resolved not to carry them; and to clear them of any blame in the matter, he gave them a certificate as follows:

"Whereas there were seven men, called Quakers, brought on board my ship, called the Anne of London, by Wm. Edmonds, jailer of Hertford, viz.— giving their names — all which have continued waiting upon my ship from London to Deal, from the 14th of September last till this day. And I seeing that Providence hath much crossed me hitherto; whereby I perceive that the hand of the Lord is against me, that I dare not proceed on my voyage to carry them? they being innocent persons, and no crime signified against them worthy of banishment; and that there is a law in force, that no Englishman shall be carried out of his native country contrary to his will; and also my men refuse to go the voyage if I carry them; which will be much to my hindrance — men being very scarce, by reason of the long press. For these reasons, therefore, and many more, *I will not carry them.* These are therefore to certify any person or persons who shall question them, that they did not make an escape; but I put them on shore again to go whither they please. All this is certified under my own hand, this 10th day of November, 1664." This certificate was signed by the Captain and four witnesses.

The next morning the ship got under sail, and the principal officer at Deal, to whom complaints had been made that the Friends had escaped; and who had had an interview with the Captain, told them that "he could witness that the ship went away from them, and not they from it." They then said to the officer that if he, as a Magistrate, had any thing to say to or do with them, he might do it. He replied, nothing, but to wish them well. After returning to their families in London, they wrote to the King and Council a recital of all the facts of the case; telling where they then were, and furnishing them with a copy of the Captain's certificate.

The statement and certificate were read in a full Council, and under pretence of there having been collusion between the Captain and prisoners, an order was issued by it, for the recommitment of the Friends to prison; where they laid between seven and eight years.

Near the close of the year 1664, Edward Brush, Robert Hays and James Harding were placed on board a vessel and sailed for the West Indies. R. Hays, who was sick when carried on board, died soon after, but the others arrived at Jamaica, and lived through the term of years assigned them. E. Brush afterwards returned to England. These were the only Friends on whom the sentence of banishment was fully executed. The Master of the vessel that took out the above named three Friends, carried with him an order of the King and Council, directed to the Governor, requiring him to receive the prisoners, and if they did not pay the expense of transportation, &c., to cause them to be employed as servants during the time specified in their sentence.

The Captains of the shipping generally, becoming apprehensive that their voyages would prove disastrous if they were accessory to the forcible expatriation of their countrymen, refused to receive any Friends aboard their vessels, and it became impossible to carry the sentences of the Courts into effect. To meet this difficulty, an embargo was laid on all vessels in port; none being allowed to sail without a " pass " from the Admiral. This " pass " was withheld from every vessel intending for the West Indies, unless the Captain agreed to carry with him a certain number of condemned Friends. In the meantime the jails were so crowded that the mortality was great. In Newgate alone, during 1664, twenty-five Friends died, either while prisoners, or soon after being discharged, from disease contracted within its walls. The bodies of several of those who died in prison were withheld from their relations, and buried in the felons' graveyard.

Friends who were wellknown for their extensive labors, and their devotion to the cause of Christ, and who, by the Lord's providence, were free from sentence of transportation and from long imprisonments, were untiring in their efforts to relieve their suffering brothers and sisters; to strengthen them in the faith, and encourage them in faithfulness to their divine Master. William Crouch, himself one of the sufferers, alluding to this period, says, " In the time of this great persecution and exercise, which attended Friends and their families, by separating husbands from their wives, fathers from their children, masters from their families, children from their parents; for no other cause but meeting together to worship God, as they were persuaded in their consciences; no crime being laid to their charge, nor doing evil to any man; the Lord was at this time, very near to support them, and by fresh visitations of his Spirit to quicken them, and to encourage each other to a steadfast and constant perseverance in their testimony for God, and the cause in which they were engaged."

The firmness and Christian endurance with which some, in very humble life, adhered to their religious convictions, amid persecution and long continued suffering, were strikingly exemplified by the few who embraced the principles of the gospel as held by Friends, in the Isle of Man. The Island was in the possession and under the government of the Earl of Derby, who exercised almost absolute power, and it was within the ecclesiastical jurisdiction of the Bishop of Sodar and Man. The "clergy" on the Island appear to have been early prejudiced against and inimical to Friends, so that when James Lancaster and Catharine Evans had come there and engaged in declaring the truths of the gospel to the people, they were quickly arrested,— the latter being taken out of her bed,— and sent out of the Island. Whether it was through the instrumentality of those Friends, or by the immediate enlightening and instruction of the Holy Spirit, is not known, but there were a few of the inhabitants brought into fellowship with Friends, embracing the doctrines and testimonies they were called on to uphold.

The persecution began in the time of the Commonwealth, and various means were tried to force the little company to give up meeting together for Divine worship, and conform to the rites and ceremonies of the "Church." Fines and imprisonment were the lot of most of them, and some were banished from the Island.

In 1657, William Callow was kept in prison for eight weeks, for having spoken reprovingly to one of the "ministers," whom he heard abusing the Quakers. From him and J. Christen ten bushels of oats were distrained, and carried to the barn of the Magistrate who ordered the levy; and the next First-day the priest gave public notice, that any of the poor of the parish might go and take whatever corn they wanted. Many went, but none would take what was offered them. The next week one poor man took a portion, and expressed his determination to come and get more; but it so happened that before he had consumed what he then took, he died, and the people interpreted this sad event to be a Divine judgment; no one would have anything to do with what was left, so that it was spoiled. This was in 1657.

These poor men, Callow and Christen, were fishermen, procuring the means of sustenance for themselves and families from the sea. In 1659, coming on shore, after having been out all night in the wet and cold, they were suddenly seized and hurried to prison; where they were kept for several days, charged with not paying 2d. for the bread and wine, and for tithes. The same treatment was meted out to them by the priest, in 1660. In 1662, this priest having brought suit before another priest, who acted as judge, had them thrust into a vault or dungeon, dug out under the graveyard; and there kept without beds, fire, light, or any other conveniences, for a demand of 18d. for bread and wine, of which, of course, they had never partaken. At the end of sixteen days, some of their neighbors, fearing lest they would die before the priest would release them, paid the amount demanded, and thus rescued them. In the beginning of the winter of that year, these two Friends, with four others, were confined in an old tower, for fifteen weeks, without fire or candle, though the weather was cold. The charge was neglecting to go to "church," and attending the meeting of Friends.

An order being issued from the Bishops' Court in 1664, to imprison all Quakers who, after being admonished, refused to attend "church," the men were committed, and W. Callow's wife being ill, apparently nigh unto death, he was allowed to go to her for two days; but before she was so far recovered as to be able to walk, she, and all the other women Friends, being told they had been excommunicated, were, with their children, by an order from the Bishop, conveyed to the noisome dungeon or vault under the graveyard, where the men were shut up; the officer before he left them, pronouncing what he called, "The Bishop's curse" upon them. In this wretched abode they were kept several months. But supported by an unseen Hand, they endured all the hardships imposed upon them, and remained patiently firm in maintaining their religious principles and testimonies.

Finding it impracticable to force these poor but good soldiers of Jesus Christ to deny their Master or his religion, it was resolved by their implacable prosecutors to banish them from the Island. They were carried on board a ship, lying at Douglass; but as soon as the sailors learned the circumstances of the case, they all left the ship; declaring to the Captain they would not " be hired to carry people out of their native country, contrary to their will; neither would they sail with him, if he consented to carry them." He was obliged to return the Friends to the shore, and immediately on his sailors coming on board again he left. The Captains and crews of other vessels likewise refused to carry the Friends.

1665. Some days after, about midnight, Wm. and Mary Callow were taken out of bed, and without being allowed to provide themselves with a change of clothes, or any other necessaries, were conveyed by soldiers on board a vessel that had come into the harbor; while Evan and Jane Christen were, in like manner, hurried on board another vessel, the sails of which had been seized and were detained, until the Captain submitted to receive them—and the Friends were thus sent away to Ireland. On arriving at Dublin, the authorities, after examining the Captains, forbid their being landed, and ordered them to be carried, in one of the ships, whence they came. The Captain of the ship, instead of returning with them to the Isle of Man, carried the Friends to Whitehaven, in Cumberland, England, and put them on shore, with a certificate of the circumstances under which they and he had been placed.

A Justice of the Peace in Whitehaven, being informed by the four Friends — who were without any means for their support — how they had been treated, he issued an order to have them at once replaced on board the ship that had brought them, and commanded the Captain to take them back to their home. The Captain had no alternative but to receive them; but when he sailed, instead of obeying the command to return them to the Isle of Man, he took them again to Dublin. Arrived there, he was not allowed to land them, until he gave security that he would take them away with him, and land them on the Isle. They were then allowed to come on shore, where they remained until the vessel was ready to sail; when, relying on the word of the Captain, and the obligation he had assumed to return them to the place of their nativity, they again went on board. But contrary to his engagement, and in entire disregard of their feelings, the Captain carried them back to Whitehaven, and put them on shore.

1666. Hopeless of being allowed to return to their home, without permission being obtained from the Earl of Derby or the Bishop of Man, the two men Friends resolved, though it was in the midst of winter, to seek one or both of these arbiters of their place of abode, and solicit a retraction of the order that had banished them from the home where they were known, and where they had passed honest and honorable lives, and who had thus exposed them to be driven from place to place, as though unworthy of a dwelling on earth. While their husbands were engaged in this attempt, the two women were sent on board the ship and taken by the Captain to the Isle of Man, where, immediately on their arrival, they were shut up in prison.

Having found the residence of the Earl, the two men Friends made repeated efforts to obtain an interview with him but failed, and after a long time, he sent them a message to apply to the Bishop, stating where he could be found. Accordingly, they repaired to the place designated, and after waiting long, finally obtained an audience with the Bishop, and the Dean of the island. Besse gives the substance of the conversation that passed between these dignitaries and the two persecuted exiles, and it is remarkable as well as affecting, how these poor unlearned Christians were enabled to plead their cause, and set forth in clear language, the religious principles by which they were actuated. But it was in vain. Both Bishop and Dean refused to permit them to return to their families, unless they would conform to the Church; and contended that it was not persecution to punish them for non-conformity.

After some months, the two Friends resolved to face all difficulties, and make an effort to see their wives and children once more, who were suffering greatly from the absence of their loving caretakers. They therefore embarked for the Island, but on their arrival, and it becoming known, the Master of the vessel was ordered not to allow them to land. After keeping them some time, the Master petitioned the Bishop to allow him to put them on shore, to be at their homes until he was ready to sail again, when he would transport them to England. This was reluctantly granted, on condition that security was given by the Captain not to sail without them. When the ship was ready to depart, soldiers were sent to their houses, who took them on board, amid the cries and tears of their distressed families; the Captain weeping with them, at the affliction they were under. Before they got off, an attorney came to them, with an order from the Bishop and four others, to seize upon and sequestrate whatever goods, or property, whether real or personal, they, or any other Quaker or Quakers on the Island, might be found possessed of; all of which was to "accrue and belong" to the Lord Bishop.

On landing at Newhaven, William Callow concluded to apply once more to the Earl of Derby; which he did; but he rejected his application, refusing to take any further notice of him. Anxious to obtain the interest of some one high in authority, W. Callow had a statement of their cases laid before the Duke of York and Prince Rupert: and the latter showed so much interest in his suffering condition, as to address a letter to the Earl of Derby; in which he urges, that, insomuch as nothing but being a Quaker was alleged against Callow, he might be allowed to join his family, without any injury being sustained by the inhabitants of the Isle of Man. Derby, however, would not accede to the request, and so replied to the Prince.

While prosecuting his unsuccessful suit with the Earl, W. Callow received a letter from his wife, dated in the 11th month, 1666, stating she was sick and in prison; and that as both she and Jane Christen were *enceinte*, they had written to the Bishop, imploring him to allow them to return to their former homes until Spring, that they might endeavor to procure things necessary for themselves and children, and they would engage to come back to the prison, when the cold weather was passed away. But the haughty prelate replied, that unless they would conform, and receive absolution, they should stay where they were; and if death was the consequence, they would be self-murderers.

In his distress on account of the helpless situation of his wife and children, and his separation from them in their sufferings, William believed it would be right for him, to make another effort to rejoin them; but before he did so, he drew up a statement of the manner in which he, with others, had been driven from one place to another, the sport of merciless men, for more than three years, and the suffering he and his family were still enduring. He once more appealed to the Earl and the Bishop to show some mercy, and allow him to be with his family, and support them by the labor of his hands; seeing the Bishop had taken possession of all the little property he had once owned. This statement was put into the Earl's hands; but he turned a deaf ear to the touching appeal, and sent William word, that unless he would conform, he should not go to his Island to poison its inhabitants.

[1667.] The Bishop having determined to banish from the Island the four women Friends, had had them seized at the different places where they were staying, and conveyed to prison; whence, as has been seen, W. Callow's wife had written him the letter mentioned. Great cruelty was practised on them, by the soldiers while executing the Bishop's orders: one of the women being between seventy and eighty years of age, and very feeble, and W. Callow's wife very sick at the time. Having obtained a vessel for the purpose, the women

with the young children, were brought down to the beach for embarkation. Here a most pitiable scene was witnessed. When the
boat was about to push off, Wm. Callow's wife was about to take
her children with her; but the soldiers said they had orders not to
allow them to go, and also to seize any extra clothing the women
might have, if they did not pay the fees demanded. Entreaty was
disregarded, and the women were dragged into the boat; one leaving four, and another five weeping children on the beach, without
father or mother to care for, provide for, or protect them, while the
mothers with their agonized maternal feelings, were forced on board
the ship, unfurnished with sufficient clothing, or other necessaries.
The Bishop now had public notice given, that whoever would compound for William Callow's estate, should have a full title made to
him therefor.

Arrived in Cumberland, the women were there joined by the
banished men Friends; but the Magistrates of Whitehaven, where
they had been landed, after making inquiry into the circumstances
of their case, and finding there had been no legal proceedings, trial
or sentence, but merely the arbitrary commands of the Bishop and
his officers to banish them, ordered all of them to be sent back to
Man. Again they were put on board a vessel, and in the Fifth
month of 1669, they were landed at Douglass, the principal port of
the Isle of Man; two of the women having young children. The
night of that day they were again dragged out of their beds, by
soldiers, the women not being allowed to dress themselves, or their
young children properly, and were forced on board the vessel that
had brought them over, where they were kept under guard until
she sailed — no one from the shore, but their persecutors, being
allowed to communicate with them — and were carried over to Dublin. They had been on shore there but a few days, when the Mayor
and some of the Aldermen of that city, issued an order, in which
they stated, that it appearing these natives of Man had been convicted of no crime, nor afforded any legal trial, but were banished
without their consent, they therefore required they should be put
on board a vessel and returned to their native place.

Launched once more upon the deep, they encountered a storm,
and the Captain, when he neared the shore of the Isle of Man, sent
the women off in a boat. Information of the landing of these poor
women having reached the Bishop, he, with the Governor, ordered
the vessel having the men on board to be watched, to prevent them
from being put on shore. The Bishop then sent soldiers to seize the

women and convey them on board again. The soldiers finding Jane Christen with her husband — who was not a Friend — took her away at night from him and their children, and put her on board the ship; but William Callow's wife was so ill, they did not attempt then to remove her. The Captain of the vessel being taken before the Governor, represented to him how greatly the females had suffered while at sea, and his fears that if they were forced to leave in their present weak condition, it would prove too much for them. The Bishop, however, was inexorable : he ordered a messenger to be sent to "raise the parish people," and have William's wife carried to the place where the ship was lying, and she put on board. The messenger returned, saying, he found the woman so near the time of confinement, he was afraid to attempt to move her. The Bishop repeated his order; to be executed forthwith; and the soldiers going to her bedside, insisted on her getting up: they took her forcibly away, not allowing her to provide herself with any extra clothing, &c., and carried her on board the vessel. Three of the neighbors who had been ordered to assist in removing her, were so affected with her deplorable condition, and the savage cruelty perpetrated, in dragging her out of the house, and away from her children, that they wept, and refused to be accessory to the crime : for this the Bishop afterwards had them imprisoned. The poor Friends, who it may be truly said could find no certain dwelling-place or rest for their feet, were carried over and landed at Peel, in Lancashire; whereupon two Justices of that place ordered them to be, as soon as possible, sent back to the Isle of Man. In compliance with this order, on the 6th of the Eighth month, 1669, William Callow and Jane Christen, were put on board one vessel, and Evan Christen and Alice Coward on board another; William's wife, having an infant but a few days old, being obliged to be left behind. When the vessels arrived with them at the island, a guard was sent on board, who kept the Friends close prisoners. On the 1st of the Ninth month, the Governor sent for W. Callow, and when brought before him, he asked him if he would not like to go to Virginia? William told him he had no business there. The Governor then informed him they had resolved to send him there. A long conversation ensued, in which William declared he had committed no wrong, had never been put upon trial, and demanded that he should have a trial under the laws of England. But the Governor told him he had written an order to have him transported to Virginia, and he would take the responsibility : answering for it to his Lordship. Two soldiers were then commanded to take him on board a vessel, then lying in the harbor, bound to America.

The Master of the ship appeared disposed to be kind to the suffering Manksman; but when the sailors came to understand how it was, that William was about to be sent away from his home, his wife, and his children, they told the Captain they would not make the voyage if he consented to carry him; for, said they, "They had never heard of a ship that carried Quakers, against their will, that prospered." Finding his men determined, the Captain solemnly promised them, that after getting away from the island, he would land the Quaker in Ireland; which he did; putting William on shore about forty miles north of Dublin. William went direct to that city, and at once sailed for Whitehaven to join his wife. In the mean time, the other Friends were once more expelled from their native place, and carried into Scotland, whence they travelled into England, where, it would appear, they were at last all allowed to remain.

Thus were these innocent and harmless Christians for years made the sport of the malice of an implacable Bishop, and the tyranny of a proud, hard-hearted noble. It was remarked of the two vessels whose owners or Captains had *volunteered* to carry these Friends away from their homes, that one was shortly after wrecked, and all on board perished; the other was greatly disabled while lying in the port of the Isle of Man, and the Captain lost his lading and all his money.

CHAPTER XIX.

WHILE the Magistrates were so industrious in breaking up the meetings of Friends, and inflicting wanton and cruel punishment on those who continued to meet together to offer that worship which is in spirit and in truth, little or nothing appears to have been done by them to stay or lessen the contagion of debauchery, profanity and other vices, that had spread through all ranks of society. The " clergy," absorbed generally in securing and enjoying the revenues of their benefices, exacted tithes and other sources of income with unmerciful rigor, were not unfrequently intemperate in their habits, and far more bent upon enforcing uniformity, than promulgating or practising the requirements of the moral law. Luxury and pride marked the manners and habits of those considered the higher classes ; while extravagance in dress, in eating and drinking, and indulgence in low sports were carried to great length, among most who could obtain means for the indulgence. The history of the time, as given by those best acquainted with it, justifies the assertion, that the great majority of the people, from the Court down to the rabble, came within the description denounced by the prophet, as those who " draw iniquity with cords of vanity, and sin as it were with a cart-rope."

From the time of their rise, Friends had been conspicuous from the unwavering controversy they maintained, not only against the vices commonly denounced as such by all religious professors, but against all those habits and customs of society that fostered the pride of the human heart, or were likely to betray into things inconsistent with the character and duties of a self-denying disciple of Christ ; who, while enjoying the blessings of heaven with cheerfulness, ought to pass the time of his sojourning here in fear of offending his Lord and Master. Hence, while their assertion of the scriptural doctrine of the headship of Christ in his church, and the equal standing of its members, according to the gifts which He conferred upon them, struck at the unauthorized assumptions of the clergy, and called forth their enmity and opposition ; so the simplicity of their manners, and style of living, the plainness of their dress and address, and the uniformity of carriage observed towards high and low, were a palpable rebuke, not only to the rich and great, but to all who conformed to the fashions and follies of the age.

Springing up as they did in the time of Puritan rule, and very many of the early converts coming from the more scrupulous of the high professing sects of that day, they had adopted the plain, unornamented apparel worn by their consistent members ; and as the religious principles they embraced, forbade compliance with the changing fashions, unless for real use and service — the lawful ends of clothing — they soon became known by their peculiar apparel as well as their mode of speech. Thus as witnesses to the spirituality of the Gospel, to the necessity of taking up the daily cross in things which the world professed to esteem of little or no account, but the non-observance of which it would not tolerate, drew upon them the scorn and hatred of the worshippers of the god of this world; who, like Demetrius of old, feared that if they continued to turn away much people, their idols would be despised, and their magnificence destroyed.

In the language of one of the early members, " These things [their plainness of speech, behavior and apparel] to be sure gave them a rough and disagreeable appearance with the generality, who thought them turners of the world upside down, as indeed in some sense they were; but in no other than that wherein Paul was so charged; viz., to bring things back into their primitive and right order again. For these and such like practices of theirs were not the results of humor, or for civil distinction, as some have fancied ; but a fruit of an inward sense, which God through his holy fear had begotten in them."
. . " But God having given them a sight of themselves, they saw the whole world in the same glass of truth, and sensibly discerned the affections and passions of men, and the *rise* and *tendency* of things; what it was that gratified the ' lust of the flesh, the lust of the eye, and the pride of life,' which are not of the Father, but of the world."

With a Court composed mostly of libertines and their mistresses, an " established church," which, though like that of Sardis, had a few who had " not defiled their garments," was under the control of men who used all the arts of priestcraft to obtain the honors and power of this world; who showed that the principal care about their flocks was to strip them of the fleece, and who while professing to be representatives of the Prince of Peace, made unrelenting war on all who would not bow down to the image they had set up; with wickedness stalking abroad with brazen front, unshamed and unrestrained, while those who strove to serve the Most High, and bring all the tithes He required into his storehouse, were persecuted, often unto death, because they could not conform, and yet obey the dictates of an enlightened conscience; it is no marvel, that many began to fear that the Almighty would visit the nation with his judgments, and in some way avenge his own elect, who cried unto him day and night. Neal and Baxter both speak of the licentiousness, as well as cruelty, that prevailed; of the foreboding of calamity, and of the afflictions that visited the nation, as judgments incurred.

Several Friends had been concerned to warn the Court and Parliament more particularly, and the people generally, that judgments were impending over the land, and that unless there was a change for the better, dire calamity would ensue. George Fox the younger, in 1661, had put forth a fervent address and expostulation; in which he declared he had seen in the Light of the Lord that many of the people would be taken away, and "that an overflowing scourge, yea, even a great and terrible judgment was to come upon the land, and that many in it would fall and be taken away." When the Courts began to sentence Friends to transportation, [1664] George Bishop addressed the King and Parliament in these words, " Thus saith the Lord, meddle not with my people because of their conscience to me, and banish them not out of the nation, because of their conscience; for if you do, I will send my plagues upon you, and you shall know that I am the Lord."

Through the intrigues of the French Monarch, war broke out between the English and Dutch nations, and it soon began to be seen, that with all their high pretensions and arrogant scorn of those who were not of the church of England, the sycophants of the Court were unable to contend with the statesmen and naval force of the Republic. Peculation and incapacity were the prominent features of the administration of the affairs of the nation. The Dutch swept the ocean of English shipping, blockaded their seaports, put an end for the time to all trade, and sailed up the Thames, so near to London that their guns were heard in that city, and they burned the fleet that lay in the river. During the two and a half years the war continued, England was drained of much of both blood and treasure, and when it ended, discontent and murmuring pervaded the people.

In the autumn of 1664, a few cases of the Plague occurred in London, outside the walls. It excited some apprehension, but as it did not then assume the character of an epidemic, there was no general alarm at its presence. In the early months of 1665 it reappeared, and began gradually to creep from one locality to another, until the whole city and its environs became affected, and a carnival of death set in, such as had very rarely if ever been experienced in Great Britain before. Notwithstanding that as the pestilence increased, thousands left the city, hoping to escape the contagion, the mortality continued to progress; until in the Ninth and Tenth months of 1665, the numbers that died in a week varied between six and eight thousand. Large pits were dug in different parishes, into which hundreds of bodies were thrown indiscriminately, and covered over with earth, when filled to within three or four feet of the surface.

The face of London was now altogether changed. All trade was stopped; horror or despair was depicted on the countenances of most of those who were seen in the streets; the stillness that reigned was broken by the groans and shrieks of the suffering and the dying; while the rumbling of the dead-cart by day and at night was mingled with the cry of the attendants, "*Bring out your dead.*" Grass grew in the streets once crowded with the busy multitude; almost all the public buildings were shut up, and hundreds of houses were deserted by their former tenants. The Plague having spread into many parts of the country, especially in villages, carried, as was supposed, by those fleeing from the city, the inhabitants were greatly alarmed, and often refused to allow those travelling to pass along the roads, or find a resting-place in their respective neighborhoods; so that, although London was the chief seat of the desolating scourge, its appalling calamities were felt throughout the kingdom.

Notwithstanding the message to the people by this awful visitation, was so loud and solemn, to break off their sins by righteousness, and their iniquities by showing mercy to the poor, yet it did not overcome the hardness of heart to which continuation in sin always gives rise. It is said that robbery and murders were never so numerous as during the height of the pestilence; and this can be easily understood: for where people arrive at that pitch of wickedness that they neither fear God nor regard man, their crimes will multiply with the temptations presented, and the facility with which they may be perpetrated. But it is an astonishing fact, that even when this confessed judgment of the Almighty was making itself felt, by the removal by death of thousands in a week, the persecutors of Friends did not cease the unrelenting cruelty they had been practising so long. In the latter end of the Fifth month, 1665, there were one hundred and twenty men and women lying in the jails in London, under sentence of banishment. Besides these, Newgate and Bridewell were crowded with other Friends, sent there for the first or second offence against the Act. The meetings for worship, which Friends felt bound to keep up notwithstanding the pestilence, were assailed in the usual manner, and even after the Plague had entered the jails, and was proving fatal among the prisoners, the Magistrates continued to send innocent men and women into their pestilential atmosphere, knowing it was most probable they would never leave them alive. These deadly cells of Newgate and Bridewell were thus kept thronged, and in the former above fifty-two Friends laid down their lives as witnesses to the truth as it is in Jesus. Of this number, twenty-two had been condemned to banishment. Of the number of deaths among Friends in the other prisons, no account is given.

George Whitehead, who, under a sense of duty, came into London in the time of the Plague, and continued there, visiting the sick, looking after the welfare of those in prison, and in other ways assisting to help and comfort his suffering brethren and sisters, in an epistle which he afterwards addressed " To the remnant of Friends and chosen of God, whom He hath yet preserved to bear their testimony, in and about the city of London," thus testifies respecting the closing scenes of many whose death he witnessed :

" And the life, peace, satisfaction and comfort that many innocent Friends felt, and that some expressed and signified on their death-beds, I am a living witness of, for them ; having some times, as the Lord hath drawn me in his love, been present with many of them when they were very low in the outward man, and with divers when upon their death-beds in that destructive prison of Newgate, and some other places. Yea, when sorrow and sadness have seized upon my spirit, and my heart and soul have been pierced and wounded, when I have seen the sad sufferings of so many harmless lambs, on their sick beds in these noisome holes and prisons ; yet at the same time having a deep sense and knowledge of the Lord's love and care to them in that condition, and truly felt his life and power stirring amongst them ; this on the other hand has refreshed and revived my spirit ; knowing that Christ, their salvation and redemption was manifest to and in them, though in that suffering state, as they have followed and obeyed Him through sufferings and tribulation. With such, to live was Christ in that state, and to die was gain ; it being through death that the Lord had appointed the final deliverance of many from the cruelties and rod of their oppressors, and from the evil to come. The faithfulness, uprightness and innocency of divers of those that were taken away, their constancy of spirit to the Lord and his living truth, their unfeigned love for the brethren — by which it was evident they had passed from death unto life — and that living and faithful testimony they bore for the Lord in their lifetime, being well known and manifest amongst us ; their memorial is truly precious to us, and never to be forgotten ; and we are satisfied that they are counted worthy for the Lord, and the world was not worthy of them."

Although the embargo on the vessels in port, unless furnished with a " pass," subjected the captains trading to the West Indies to great inconvenience and loss, yet so fully were they convinced of the iniquity of banishing innocent men and women from their families and country, that they refused to receive them on board their ships; and thus it was that so many were kept in jail, waiting the execution of their sentences. At length a man named Fudge offered to take such as might be put on board his vessel; and fifty-five were brought out of Newgate, embarked in a barge, and rowed to where the vessel was lying. [1665.] The Captain was on shore when they came alongside, and the sailors all refused to do anything towards getting them on board. The jailers and other officers told the seamen these men and women were the King's goods, and tried what they could to persuade them to assist, but they would not raise a finger in the work; so that after with great labor placing four on the deck, the officers gave out and took the others back to Newgate. In about three weeks they were again taken down to the ship, and soldiers were sent to assist in removing them into her. Efforts were again made to induce the sailors to assist in transferring the prisoners from one vessel to another, but they steadily refused, and the soldiers were obliged to do the work themselves, which they did with great brutality.

There were now fifty-nine on board, of whom eighteen were women. The men were all crowded between decks, where there was not height sufficient to stand upright. But this vessel, like the one which the seven banished Friends had been put on board,—who were afterwards sent on shore by the Captain, because he believed the hand of the Lord frustrated all his attempts to leave the shores of England,—was continually hindered by some unforeseen circumstance, from getting down the river. Fudge, the Captain, was arrested for debt, and could not continue in command, and it was seven months from the time the Friends were forced to embark in her, before she reached *Land's End*. During this long delay the Plague broke out among the prisoners and crew, and twenty-seven of the former died of it. The day after the ship got out to sea, she was captured by a Dutch privateer, and carried into Horn, in North Holland; whence, when it was found they would not be exchanged as prisoners of war, the Friends were sent home, being furnished with a certificate of the facts, and a passport.

It was to be expected that a pestilence of so contagious a character and so fatal in its effects, as to sweep off one hundred thousand of the inhabitants of London, in the comparatively short time of its visitation, would include among its victims some of the Friends residing there, besides those who being placed by the Magistrates where the poison was in its most virulent form, could hardly hope to escape its fatal effects. A number died, and as the deplorable condition of the city paralyzed almost all trade, the bereaved families were often left helpless and suffering. To meet the exigency, and make the needful provision for the widows and orphans, some Friends, both men and women, devoted themselves to the work of administering relief; holding regular meetings once in the week for receiving information, and devising the best modes for meeting the needs of the cases presented. As Friends in the country became aware of the suffering and wants of their brethren and sisters in the stricken city, they manifested that brotherly love and sympathy one for another, which was a marked feature in their religious character, by not only contributing of their substance, but by several of the more substantial members going up to London as with their lives in their hands, in order to lend their aid in the arduous work required; to suffer with them, and by both example and precept, to encourage and strengthen them in the performance of their social and religious duties. Among those who were drawn thus to visit Friends in London, were Alexander Parker, George Whitehead and Josiah Cole, all eminent ministers.

In this year, [1665,] Samuel Fisher, of whom some account has been given, died in prison, in London, having been kept there closely for over eighteen months.

As the testimony of one entirely unconnected with Friends, to the worth of this learned man, but meek and exemplary Friend, the following from the pen of the editor of Neal's Puritans, is of interest: "There died in prison this year, Mr. Samuel Fisher, a man of great parts and literature, of eminent piety and virtue, who reflected honor on each denomination of Christians with which, through the change of his sentiments, he became successively connected. . . . In 1623, at the age of eighteen, he became a student in Trinity College, Oxford, where he took the degree of Master of Arts, and then removed to New Inn. At the University he distinguished himself by his application and proficiency, gained an accurate knowledge of Greek and Roman Antiquities, and was particularly given to the study of rhetoric and poetry. . . . In 1632, he was presented to the vicarage of Lidd, in Kent, a living of £500 per annum. Here he had the character of a very powerful preacher, united with humility and affability of carriage. While in this situation, in consequence of frequent conversation with a Baptist minister, he was led into an examination of the questions concerning baptism, which ended in his embracing the opinions of the Baptists, being baptized by immersion . . . having freely resigned his living, and returned his diploma to the bishop. . . . He rented a farm and commenced a grazier.· . . . . During his connection with the Baptists he baptized some hundreds, and was frequently engaged in public disputes in vindication of their sentiments. . . . . He was deemed an ornament to the sect, and one of the chief defenders of its doctrine. In 1654, he embraced the principles of the Quakers, and became an active and laborious minister among them. He preached at Dunkirk against the idolatry of the priests and friars, and in company with another Friend, travelled on foot over the Alps to Rome, where they testified against the superstitions of the place, and distributed some books among the ecclesiastics, and left it without molestation. After his return he suffered among Protestants the persecution he escaped among the Romanists. The greater part of the last four years of his life was spent in prison, and after two years' confinement in the White Lion prison, in Southwark, he died, ' in perfect peace with God, in good esteem both with his friends and many others, on account of the eminence of his natural parts, and acquired abilities as a scholar, and of his exemplary humility, social virtues, and circumspect conversation as a Christian ; in meekness instructing those who opposed, and laboring incessantly by his discourses and by his writings, to propagate and promote true Christian practice and piety.' "

William Caton also died in this year, in Amsterdam, where he had been married to a Dutch woman of high repute among Friends of that place, and continued to reside.

In 1662, after the re-establishment of Episcopacy in England, it was introduced again into Scotland as the national religion—after an interruption of twenty-four years—notwithstanding a very large portion of the people was opposed to it. Sharp was made Archbishop, and several bishops were assigned benefices in different parts of the country. Burnet's account of the character of these men, represents most of them to have been very unfit for holding any office in a professed Christian church; especially the Metropolitan, whom the writers of the time describe as a man whose conduct was regulated by no good principle. The Scotch Parliament, like that of the sister

Kingdom, was compliant to the wishes of the royalists and the high church party. It annulled the laws passed since 1633, which were in favor of Puritanism, declared the "solemn League and Covenant" unlawful, and commenced a series of oppressive acts, which inflicted sufferings that wore out the patience of, and finally drove the persecuted Covenanters — who did not hold to the peaceable principles of the Gospel as Friends did—into insurrection and rebellion. A Court of Ecclesiastical Commission was instituted, which acted as though governed by the same principles as the Spanish Inquisition ; passing sentence without allowing it to be known who was the accuser, what was the evidence of guilt, or what defence could be made by the accused. Having risen in arms, attended at first with some success, the Covenanters were totally defeated at Pentland ; and the pretext being thus obtained, there followed a succession of judicial murders, imprisonment, fines, and proscription, that stamped the administration and executive with indelible disgrace.

The whole course of these events illustrates how much better it is to obey the precepts of Him who knows what is in man, and sees the end from the beginning, than to give place to the dictates of passion or corrupt human reason ; remembering that He can and will support and preserve all who adhere to the principles of his gospel, and in the midst of danger and persecution seek not to avenge themselves or to resist evil by violence, but resign themselves and their cause into the hand of their almighty Father. One of their historians, speaking of the Scotch Presbyterians under this severe persecution, says, " Many were exorbitantly fined, unjustly imprisoned, oppressed by soldiers, plundered by dragoons, and a lawless Highland host. Multitudes were forced to wander about in dens and caves of the earth. Not a few were tortured by boots, thumb-kins, fire-matches, &c. Some were beheaded, others were hanged and quartered ; women as well as men suffered death : some of them were hanged and others drowned : prisons were crowded, and ships were loaded with prisoners, who were banished from their native country ; of whom many perished."

With the feeling that prevailed, it was not to be expected that Friends would escape with any less suffering than had accompanied the rise and slow increase of the Society in that part of Great Britain. George Keith joined himself to Friends, after having been educated in the Presbyterian faith, and taken the degree of Master of Arts in the University of Aberdeen, of which city he was a native. Going to the " church " in Aberdeen, in 1665, and attempting to declare the principles which he had adopted, he was knocked down and beaten by the bell-hanger, and then committed to the jail. Four other Friends were taken from their meeting in the same city and shut up in what was called the Iron House, among thieves and murderers. The same course towards Friends was pursued in other parts of Scotland, but the persecution was never so general nor so barbarous as in England. It did not produce the effect desired, for several, members of the different congregations, continued to leave them, and join themselves to the persecuted Quakers.

Among those who united themselves to Friends in 1666, was David Barclay of Ury, " descended from an ancient and honorable family;" and near the close of the same year his son Robert Barclay, who afterward wrote the famous "Apology for the True Christian Divinity," became convinced of the truth of the doctrines held by Friends and willingly cast in his lot among them.

Until past middle life David Barclay had spent most of his time in the army, having entered into service under Gustavus Adolphus, King of Sweden, and risen to the rank of Colonel. During the civil wars in Great Britain he was in active service as commander of cavalry, and appears to have been engaged in many conflicts, and important services. He was appointed Governor of Strathboggie, a strong military position. His wife was a Gordown,* whose family was connected with that of James I., of England. He was repeatedly elected to Parliament. After the restoration he was committed a close prisoner to Edinburg Castle. Here he was kept for a considerable time, but finally was liberated without any specific charge having been brought against him. Prior to his imprisonment, however, disgusted with the injustice and hypocrisy he saw in the world, and anxious to devote the remainder of life to obtaining a knowledge and the practice of religion, he retired from the occupation and associations that had heretofore engrossed his attention, and gave his time to reading the New Testament, as the means, as he thought, of acquiring the knowledge of the religion of Christ in its original purity. Hearing there was a people called in derision Quakers, who though everywhere spoken against as great sticklers for an uncompromising testimony against the corrupt ways of the world, were nevertheless admitted to be truthful, honest and unflinching in upholding what they believed to be right, he concluded there must be something in their religion different from that of ordinary professors. Having occasion to go up to London he there

* Afterwards spelled Gordon.

met with some Friends, and by conversation with them, and yielding to the enlightening influence of the Holy Spirit, he became convinced that this evilly entreated people held the truths of the gospel
in their purity. He did not, however, at that time, conclude to
join the Society. During his imprisonment in Edinburg Castle
he met with John Swinton, likewise a prisoner; who though he had
been one of the Judges of the Court of Sessions, and a member of
the Council of State for the Government of Scotland, had become a
Friend. The intercourse between them served to remove any doubts
or fears D. Barclay — who was a cautious man — might have had,
respecting the scriptural soundness of the religion professed by
Friends, and that they held themselves ready to give up all for its
sake. He therefore joined himself to the Society, and ever after
adorned it by his exemplary life and conversation; meekly enduring the scorn and suffering which his conscientious course brought
upon him.

Walter Scott, who was a descendant of John Swinton, gives the
following account of his ancestor: "The celebrated John Swinton,
of Swinton, nineteenth baron in descent of that ancient and once
powerful family, was, with Sir William Lockhard, of Lee, the person
whom Cromwell chiefly trusted in the management of Scottish
affairs during his usurpation. After the restoration, Swinton was
devoted as a victim to the new order of things, and was brought
down in the same vessel which conveyed the Marquis of Argyle to
Edinburgh, where that nobleman was tried and executed. Swinton
was destined to the same fate. He had assumed the habit and entered into the Society of the Quakers, and appeared as one of their
number before the Parliament of Scotland. He renounced all legal
defence, though several pleas were open to him, and answered in
conformity with the principles of his sect; that at the time these
crimes were imputed to him, he was in the gall of bitterness and
bond of iniquity; but that God Almighty having since called him
to the Light, he saw and acknowledged these errors, and did not
refuse to pay the forfeit of them, even though, in the judgment of
the Parliament, it should extend to life itself. Respect to fallen
greatness, and to the patient and calm resignation with which a
man once in high power expressed himself under such a change of
fortune, found Swinton friends; family connections, and some interested considerations of Middleton the Commissioner, joined to
procure his safety; and he was dismissèd, but after a long imprisonment and much dilapidation of his estates."

At what time John Swinton joined the Society of Friends'is not mentioned, nor whether his convincement was by instrumental means or through the immediate illuminating, convincing power of Divine Grace; but as he is mentioned by Alexander Jaffray as one with whom he took counsel on religious matters, when he (Jaffray) felt himself required to give up the ordinances and ceremonials of the Presbyterian Society, it is probable he had long been a seeker after the knowledge of vital religion, and was ready to embrace the doctrines and testimonies of the gospel as held by Friends, when he first heard them preached.   Indifferent as he seemed to the result of his trial before the Scotch Parliament, whether he should be condemned to death or not, such was the love that filled his heart towards his fellow-men, and his sense of duty to do what he could for the salvation of their souls, that while shut up in the castle of Edinburgh, he labored so assiduously to communicate a knowledge of the truth among his fellow prisoners, that the Governor, fearing the spread of his religious views, shut him up in solitary confinement for many weeks, permitting no intercourse to be held with him.

Robert Barclay was born at Gordonstown, the seat of his mother's family, in 1648, and received some part of his education at the best schools in his native country.   At an early age, his father sent him to Paris, and entered him as a student in the Scottish College in that city, of which his uncle was Rector.   Here he made so great progress in his studies, as to attract the notice of the different masters and to secure the approbation of his uncle; who offered to make him his heir, if he would agree to remain with him.   Although his early training had been in the principles of the strictest sect of Presbyterians, yet, being now thrown into the society of Roman Catholics, he became somewhat tinctured with several of their superstitious notions, and though he had become a proficient in the Latin and French languages, had acquired a considerable knowledge of Greek, and bid fair to become eminent as a scholar, his father, fearing lest he might be induced to embrace the Popish religion, brought him home when in his seventeenth year.   His return to Scotland was in 1664, two years before his father joined with Friends.   Although so young his mental powers were far more developed than is ordinary at that age, and he continued to improve them, both by study, by reading and by association with men of intellectual culture.

Anxious to make himself more fully acquainted with the differences in religious opinion that were separating his countrymen into sects, bitterly opposed to each other, he visited extensively among his relatives and friends, who made different profession ; especially among his Catholic relatives, in different parts of the country. He observed the change that had taken or was taking place in his father's views and habits, and was deeply impressed by the circumspect conduct, and religious feeling that marked his every-day life; but when David Barclay was imprisoned in Edinburgh Castle, the Governor denied him any intercourse with his son. D. Barclay, however, was very anxious his son should not adopt any form. of religion from imitation, or any other motive than heartfelt conviction, and therefore thought it right, seeing, that though young, he was more than ordinarily capable to examine and judge for himself, to leave him to be guided in this matter by his own convictions. Removed from the influence of his Roman Catholic associates in Paris, and at liberty to compare the tenets of that apostate "Church," with the plain teachings of the New Testament, he soon became extricated from the notions with which it had in some measure ensnared him, and was left free to turn his mind seriously to seek for the pearl of great price.

It does not appear that R. Barclay became a convert to Friends' principles, through the medium of preaching ; though there has been a tradition handed down, that he was deeply impressed by these few words, uttered by a minister in the first meeting of Friends which he attended : " In stillness there is fullness, in fullness there is nothingness, in nothingness there are all things." In the " Ury Record," it is stated, " He came by the power of God to be reached, and made to bow before the truth." He, speaking of himself, says, " Who not by strength of argument, or by particular disquisition of each doctrine, and convincement of my understanding thereby, came to receive and bear witness to the Truth ; but by being secretly reached by this Life. For when I came into the silent assemblies of God's people, I felt a secret power amongst them which touched my heart ; and as I gave way unto it, I found the evil weakening in me, and the good raised up ; and so I became thus knit and united unto them, hungering more and more after the increase of this power and life, whereby I might find myself perfectly redeemed." [1667.]

Having given himself up to walk in obedience to the Divine will, as manifested through the inward appearance of the Spirit of Christ Jesus, Robert Barclay, though but in the twentieth year of his age, found himself called to a life of great watchfulness and dedication ; by which he became an able witness of the regenerating power of

Divine Grace, established upon the everlasting Rock and foundation of prophets and apostles, and prepared to receive a gift in the ministry. Through the remainder of his comparatively short life, he labored abundantly to bring others to a knowledge of the truth as it is in Jesus, and to defend the true Christian divinity as set forth in the Holy Scriptures, from the assaults and cavils of the ignorant or unbelieving; and his labor was, and continues to be, greatly blessed in the Lord. His father placed him upon his estate at Ury, accompanied by a Friend named Falconer, who had at different times suffered imprisonment on account of faithfulness to his religious principles; and a meeting of Friends was soon held in the house there. Robert was at that time but nineteen years of age.

The number of Friends in Scotland continued slowly to increase. There never being those large convincements, which often followed the promulgation of the doctrines they held, in England; nor was their persecution, though often very severe, of that barbarous character which disgraced the party in power in the sister kingdom. This result was not owing to any less bitterness and hate on the part of the clergy and bishops, but because the civil power was in the hands of men not always disposed to allow it to be made use of to gratify the ungoverned passions of the "ministers" of the so-called Church. Several of the Magistrates not only refused to impose the fines and imprisonment which the ecclesiastics sought to inflict, but sometimes made use of their authority, to set free some whom they were convinced were illegally or cruelly punished.

Early after the Plague had begun to spread in London, the Court removed to Oxford, and while it was ravaging the city, the Parliament was convened in the same town. [1664–5.] Whatever sobering effect it may have produced on others, the pestilential scourge does not appear to have so impressed either King or Parliament, as to induce the former to attempt to reform himself and his immoral court, or the latter to cease their vain and unchristian attempts to enforce uniformity in religion. It was said that the King having inquired whether any Quakers died with the disease, and learning that such was the case, remarked that then the pestilence could not be regarded as an evidence of Divine displeasure at the treatment they received; forgetting that the righteous are often taken from the evil to come; and that though one event, so far as regards death, happens to the evil and the good, yet the chastisements of the Almighty are inflicted to arouse the bad to a sense of their wickedness, to induce them to repent and to amend their ways. Even Defoe, speaking of the members of the Court having escaped the Plague, says, " For which I cannot say that they ever showed any great token of thankfulness, and hardly anything of reformation ; though they did not want being told that their crying vices might, without breach of charity, be said to have gone far in bringing that terrible judgment upon the whole nation."

1665. The Parliament, untaught by the failure of its previous efforts to change, by force, men's religious convictions, or by the trouble, loss and misery spread over the nation, by its vain attempt to oblige all the people to support what it chose to call the " Church," proceeded to enact another penal law against Dissenters, which was styled, " An act to restrain non-conformists from inhabiting corporations." This Act prescribed an oath to be taken, that it was not lawful to take up arms against the King, or against his person by his authority, or against those commissioned by him, or to attempt to change the government. It also set forth, that whereas, " many vicars, curates, lecturers and other persons in holy orders" had not subscribed to the Act of Uniformity, and yet undertook to preach in unlawful assemblies, instilling their poisonous principles of schism, &c., therefore, all such persons shall not, after "the 24th of March " ensuing, come or be within five miles of any city, town-corporate, or borough represented in Parliament, wherein they may have, since the Act of Oblivion, been parson, vicar, &c., or preached in any conventicle — before they have subscribed to the afore-mentioned oath before a Magistrate, &c., under a penalty of £40 ; one-third to be paid to the person sueing for it. And if they do not take the oath, they shall also be incapable of teaching in any school, or to take boarders, or tablers, for instruction, under a like penalty. The offenders in either case may be committed, by two justices, to prison for six months. Though this law was ostensibly aimed at the clergy of the Presbyterians, Baptists and Independents, and it wrought them much suffering, it was, nevertheless, principally made use of as a means for distressing Friends.

It might seem from the contemplated suffering likely to result from the operation of this Act, that the Court and Parliament, so far from regarding the depopulating of London by the Plague as a retribution for the profligacy of the people, or for their cruelty towards Dissenters, must rather have construed it as a judgment for not taking more severe measures for their extermination. Certainly they manifested no disposition to relent in their persecution,

but went on with the same arrogant intolerance, to allow no man to
judge for himself in what manner or form he should worship and
serve his Creator. The cry of oppression and suffering, though finding entrance at the ear of the Lord of Sabaoth, appeared to make
no other impression on their feelings, than to embitter them still
more, if possible, against the non-conformists, and to seek, by whatever means they could command, to punish and destroy them. It
is not surprising, therefore, to find the great fire in London, that
followed not long after the disappearance of the Plague, spoken of
by several writers of that day, as another just judgment of the
Almighty for the persevering wickedness of the Court and people.
Its origin was never clearly ascertained, though the Committee
appointed by Parliament to investigate the matter, reported having
received evidence of fire-balls having been thrown into houses by
certain Papists, who had fled from the country. A Frenchman, who
afterwards was shown to have been insane, was convicted and executed on his own confession, which probably was a mere delusion.

The fire commenced on the 2d of September, 1666, near where
the Monument now stands, and continued to burn between three
and four days, laying in ashes nearly the whole of the city within
the walls. Thirteen thousand two hundred dwelling-houses and
shops, eighty-nine "churches," many public buildings, school-houses,
libraries, &c., were consumed, including the great "Cathedral of St.
Paul." Merchandise, furniture, and goods of various kind, and of
enormous value were destroyed, and very many were reduced, as by
a stroke, from comparative wealth to poverty, by its terrible ravages.
The inhabitants, driven unexpectedly from their homes, could carry
but little away with them, and were often glad to escape with their
lives, leaving their household goods behind them. Cabins and tents
were hastily erected on the fields around ; where many of those who
had been rich were glad to find lodging and shelter ; while hundreds
were forced to wander away to seek for food and temporary protection. It was an awful calamity, and for a while stayed the hand of
persecution.

John Evelyn, in his Diary, containing much of historical interest,
thus records his observation of the fire : "September 3d [1666], the
fire continued all this night — if I may call that night which was
light as day for ten miles round about—after a dreadful manner,
when conspiring with a fierce east wind in a very dry season. I went
on foot to Bankside in Southwark, and saw the whole south part of
the city burning, from Cheapside to the Thames, and all along Corn

hill, Tower Street, Fenchurch Street, Gracious Street, and so along to Bainard's Castle, and was taking hold of St. Paul's church. The conflagration was so universal, and the people so astonished, that from the beginning—I knew not by what despondency of fate—they hardly stirred to quench it. So that there was nothing heard or seen but crying and lamentation; and running about like distracted creatures. . . . All the sky was of a fiery aspect like the top of a burning oven, the light being seen above forty miles round about for many nights. The poor inhabitants were dispersed about St. George's Fields and Moorfields, as far as Highgate; several miles in circle; some under tents, some under miserable huts and hovels; many without a rag or necessary utensil, bed or board; who from delicateness, riches and easy accommodations in stately and well-furnished houses, were now reduced to extremest misery and poverty."

Many Friends suffered great loss of goods, &c., by the fire.

Two or three days before the fire began, a Friend from Huntingdon, named Thomas Ibbit came to London, and went through the streets, with his clothing loose and disarranged, proclaiming that a judgment by fire would lay waste the city. In an interview which some Friends obtained with him in the evening of one of those days, on being asked what was the origin of his concern, and the authority of his message? he informed them that he had a vision of the fire, and a sense of the impending judgment for some time; but that he had put off coming and declaring it, as he was commanded, until, as he said, he felt the fire in his own bosom. Before he left the city he saw his prediction fulfilled, and London in flames. This quick confirmation of what he believed to be the word of the Lord through him, proved too much for his Christian steadfastness. Whether he became inflated with spiritual pride, or, what is more probable, the exciting circumstances around him unsettled his brain and deprived him of the use of his reason, he gave himself up to the extravagant notion that the same omniscient Being who had enabled him to foresee the coming event, would give him power to stop the devouring element. He therefore placed himself in front of the advancing flames with outstretched arms, and had not some of his friends dragged him away, it seemed probable he would have paid the penalty of his infatuation with his life. He afterwards recovered from his frenzy, and confessed the error into which he had been betrayed.

The liberation of George Fox from Scarborough Castle after having been a close prisoner there and at Lancaster, very nearly three years, as already stated, took place the day before the great fire in London broke out. His physical system had suffered greatly from the cruel usage he had endured, so that his stiffened, swollen limbs, were hardly able to bear the weight of his body, and his strength was so reduced he could with difficulty ride on horseback. Nevertheless, his mind, ever active and mainly bent on promoting the cause of truth and righteousness, with which he felt that the interests of the Society he had been so instrumental in gathering was inseparably connected, would not permit him to seek recovery by indulgence in ease and retirement. He engaged at once in his usual religious labors, and as he was able to bear it, travelled through several counties, holding meetings, many of which were large, visiting his friends in many places, proclaiming the truths of the gospel, and holding out the word of admonition and encouragement, suited to the day of severe suffering. After thus laboring in the north he turned south, and slowly made his way once more to London. [1666.] He makes but little comment in his Journal upon the condition in which he found things there; merely saying, " Being come to London I walked a little among the ruins and took good notice of them. I saw the city lying, according as the word of the Lord came to me concerning it several years before." Varied, as may be supposed, must have been his emotions, as he reflected on the past scenes in which he had been a deeply interested actor in the great city now in ruins. The earnest gospel labors of himself and his friends and fellow ministers, who but a few years before had come up from the north to " declare the word of the Lord ; " the numbers that had been gathered into communion with them out of the multitude that thronged its streets ; the dreadful suffering through which they had passed, and were still enduring ; the difficulties and occasional disorder attending the influx of members into the Society, not yet uniformly concrete and reduced to systematic government ; and the removal from works to rewards, of many of those devoted, highly gifted men, who, as sons of thunder or consolation, had proved themselves eminently qualified to share with him in the great work, to which, in the ordering of the glorified Head of the church, he had been called would all press upon him. But he knew the good cause was in the hands of One who was all-sufficient for the work.

The violence of persecution was stayed for a time, and George Fox, after attending the remaining meetings in London — the Bull-and-Mouth meeting-house having been burnt—travelled into some of the southern counties, attending the regular meetings of Friends, and often holding public meetings, which were large. On his return to London, he was engaged with other Friends, in holding a series of meetings with those, who, having imbibed the notion first started by J. Perrot, of not taking off the hat in time of public prayer, and some other inconsistencies in relation to the good order of the Church, had given Friends no little trouble in some places; creating party spirit and strife. But as several who had been caught with this delusion, seeing the evil consequences arising from it, had become uneasy with their course, and desirous to have the breach healed, it was concluded to appoint a meeting, to which all of them who were willing, were invited to come. Referring to this meeting, G. Fox says, "Several meetings we had with them, the Lord's everlasting power was over all, and set judgment on the head of that which had run out. In these meetings, which lasted whole days, several who had gone out with John Perrot and others, came in again, and condemned that spirit which led them to 'keep on their hats when Friends prayed, and when themselves prayed.' Some of them said, 'Friends were more righteous than they;' and that 'If Friends had not stood, they had been gone and had fallen into perdition.' Thus the Lord's power was wonderfully manifested, and came over all."

Thomas Ellwood, who in the infancy of his religious life, had been caught with this innovating spirit, but was soon favored to see its evil origin and escape from its withering influence, observes in his Journal, "But when that solemn meeting was appointed at London, for a travail in spirit on behalf of those who had thus gone out, that they might rightly return, and be sensibly received into the unity of the body again, my spirit rejoiced, and with gladness of heart I went to it, as did many more of both city and country; and with great simplicity and humility of mind, did honestly and openly acknowledge our outgoings, and take condemnation and shame to ourselves. And some that lived at too remote a distance in this nation, as well as beyond the seas, upon notice given of that meeting and the intended service of it, did the like by writing, in letters directed to and openly read in the meeting; which for that purpose was continued many days. Thus in the motion of Life were the healing waters stirred; and many, through the virtuous power thereof, were restored to soundness; and indeed not many were lost."

CHAPTER XX.

WHILE still in London, George Fox gives the first notice of the concern which was upon him, to establish a uniform system of Church government, for the now numerous and widespread Society of Friends. He says: "Then I was moved of the Lord to recommend the setting up of five Monthly Meetings of men and women in the city of London, besides the women's meetings and the Quarterly Meetings, to take care of God's glory, and to admonish and exhort such as walked disorderly or carelessly, and not according to truth. For whereas Friends had only Quarterly Meetings, now truth was spread and Friends grown more numerous, I was moved to recommend the setting of Monthly Meetings throughout the nation. And the Lord opened to me what I must do, and how the men's and women's Monthly and Quarterly Meetings should be ordered and established in this and other nations; and that I should write to those where I came not, to do the same."

Twenty years had elapsed since, in obedience to the command of Christ his Saviour, George Fox had first gone forth to proclaim among the people the truths of the gospel, as they had been made clear to his understanding by the same Holy Spirit that had inspired holy men of old to record them in the sacred Scriptures. Early in his mission he had been given to see "The harvest white, and the seed of God lying thick in the ground, and none to gather it," and for this he had "mourned with tears." He had witnessed the general agitation and unsatisfied seeking of the people on the subject of religion, while through years of strife and bloodshed, the doctrines of Christianity, and the form of government for the professed Church of Christ, were looked upon as questions that could and must be decided at the point of the sword. Going forth without scrip or purse, but with his feet shod with a preparation of the gospel of peace, he had witnessed the convincing power attending the preaching of that gospel, with a measure of the Holy Ghost sent down from heaven: and how, by the Light of Christ in the soul, people were brought to see, to comprehend, and to embrace the simple spiritual religion of which He [Christ] was the Author. His soul had been bowed under sympathy with and grief for them, while he saw them enduring suffering, and even death itself, rather than forego the peace that passeth understanding; obtained by obedience to that Light, in the denial of self, in renouncing the manners and fashions of a vain world, and its forms of religion, corrupted by the contrivances of men. He had seen a noble band of valiant soldiers of the cross quickly raised up, and equipped by the Captain of Salvation, with weapons, " not carnal, but mighty through God to the pulling down of strongholds, casting down imaginations, and every high thing that exalteth itself against the knowledge of God." Notwithstanding the bigoted, and passionate opposition of other religious professors to the distinguishing doctrine they preached—Christ within, or a measure of his Spirit given to every man for his salvation—some falsely declaring that it depreciated the necessity for, or the value of the one great propitiatory offering made on Calvary, for the sins of the whole world ; some equally untruly asserting, that it was a blasphemous assumption of a divinity in man, as a created being; while others derided it as a misconception of natural conscience, arising from ignorance and superstition—yet, he knew it met the Witness for Truth in the minds of the hearers, who had long been seeking the way of salvation, and who received it joyfully. Thus tens of thousands had been brought to experience for themselves, the efficacy of obedience to " that inward Light, Spirit and Grace," which he had been commanded to turn people to, when first commissioned to go forth on his errand of love and mercy, and had found, as he had declared they would find, that by it, " all might know their salvation and their way to God." From almost every denomination of professing Christians, they had been gathered; and those who were faithful, under the teaching of the Divine gift or Grace, had learned to speak the same language, to believe in and maintain the same doctrines and testimonies, and patiently to submit, not only to the reproaches and revilings of men, but to the cunningly devised tortures of their implacable enemies.

But as the Scripture doctrine of reconciliation to God by the death of his Son, and of justification by faith in Christ risen and glorified, had been corrupted by Protestants generally ; by supposing that men obtain remission of sins, and are justified in the sight of God, by a self-wrought belief in, and application to themselves, of the atoning death and sufferings of Christ on Calvary, without the transforming operation of his Holy Spirit on the soul ; so this doctrine of the Universal Saving Light, or Grace of God which bringeth Salvation, and which hath appeared unto all men, was liable to be perverted and abused; by supposing that it brought man into an equality with Christ, or rendered his propitiatory sacrifice for the sins of mankind unnecessary, or without effect for salvation. It might also be invoked as authority to sanction or cover up individual aberration from the strait and narrow way of self-denial, or to justify insubordination to the restrictions and injunctions of church government.

Friends had become a numerous body; those who professed to hold the principles inculcated by them, and who attended their meetings, were considered its members, without any rules for their formal admission having been adopted, and the Society was held responsible for their conduct; its enemies narrowly watching for any occasion whereby, through them, they could bring odium upon it. Though persecution and suffering kept it generally clear of those who were not sincere in their profession, and consistent therewith in their lives and conversation, yet experience had already been had, in the cases of J. Naylor and his followers, and of J. Perrot and his abettors, of the perversion of Christian doctrine, and the disorder and disunity into which it led. Besides this, such is human frailty, and the powerful influence of self, that, as our Saviour told his disciples, "it must needs be that offences come;" and the means were required by which the offender might be reclaimed, or the Church and cause of Truth exonerated from the reproach his or her conduct might otherwise bring upon it. George Fox, therefore, saw that the time had come when the Society should be organized in distinct meetings for taking charge of the affairs of the church, and a system of church government instituted, based upon the principles laid down by Christ for the treatment of an offending brother.

It has been seen that the unity of faith and practice, which had drawn Friends together into one body, springing as it did from the love of God shed abroad in their hearts, created and fostered a deep interest in each other's welfare; and when the fellowship of suffering for their Christian faith was added thereto, by the general persecution they underwent, it led to the exercise of a spirit of kindness and unselfish benevolence, that sought for opportunities to relieve distress, to administer help and encouragement, and to communicate, in every way, as they had ability, to each other's welfare.

It was for promoting and carrying out this good work, as well as for promulgating the Gospel, that "General Meetings" had been held in different parts of England, of which mention is made in several Friends' Journals. One such was held at Swannington, in 1654; one at Edge Hill in 1656; one at Balby in 1658, and one at the house of John Crook, in the same year. At these meetings the wants and sufferings of Friends in different places were made known; and besides relief being afforded, admonition and directions were issued, as to the course to be pursued in the discharge of domestic, social and religious duties; and also for a cheerful compliance with the requirements of civil government, where such compliance did not conflict with the maintenance of the testimonies of the Gospel which Friends were called to uphold.

George Fox thus speaks of one of these " General Meetings" held at Skipton, in 1660; giving an insight of their character, and of some of the business that occupied the time and attention: " To this meeting came many Friends out of most parts of the nation; for it was about business relating to the church, both in this nation and beyond the seas. Several years before, when I was in the north, I was moved to recommend to Friends the setting up of this meeting for that service; for many Friends suffered in divers parts of the nation, their goods were taken from them contrary to law, and they understood not how to help themselves, or where to seek redress. But after this meeting was set up, several Friends who had been Magistrates, and others who understood something of the law, came thither, and were able to inform Friends, and to assist them in gathering up the sufferings, that they might be laid before the Justices, Judges, or Parliament. This meeting had stood several years, and divers Justices and Captains had come to break it up; but when they understood the business Friends met about, and saw Friends' books, and accounts of collections for relief of the poor, how we took care one county to help another, and to help our Friends beyond sea, and provide for our poor that none of them should be chargeable to their parishes, &c., the Justices and officers confessed that we did their work, and would pass away peaceably and lovingly, ' commending Friends' practice.' Sometimes there would come two hundred of the poor of other people, and wait till the meeting was done, for all the country knew we met about the poor, and after the meeting, Friends would send to the bakers for bread, and give every one of those poor people a loaf, how many soever there were of them; for we were taught ' to do good unto all, though especially to the household of faith.' "

While these " General Meetings," which appear to have been held at irregular intervals, and to have been composed of Friends appointed to that service, in different counties, served not only for transacting such business as is mentioned in the extract, but to bind the members more closely together as one body, and produce more unity of action, and more general understanding of the condition of the Society, and the progress making in the great work assigned it, there were other things that required more prompt and continued attention than these General Meetings could render; such as ministering to the necessities of those who were deprived of the care and labor of the head of the family by imprisonment; or stripped of their means of subsistence by heavy fines, or exorbitant levies for tithes; supplying food and raiment for those languishing in jails, where otherwise they would have been without these necessaries; the registration of deaths, and births — for from the rise of the Society, the children of Friends appear to have been considered its members—to take care in regard to proceeding in marriage; to collect and transmit to the Friends in London appointed to receive them, accounts of sufferings; and to exercise a spiritual care over the flock. For attention to these varied duties Quarterly Meetings were first instituted, composed of a few suitable Friends deputized thereto by the several meetings in one or two counties. These Quarterly Meetings appear to have exercised very similar functions to those since confided to Monthly Meetings.

In 1666, however, the great increase of members in the Society; the exigencies of the time from the implacable persecution by their enemies; the manifested necessity to take more efficient measures for reclaiming or disowning those who fell away from the religious principles of Friends, or otherwise walked disorderly, as well as to watch over one another in love, and encourage each other in spiritual as well as temporal matters, all contributed to render it needful, that a more perfect arrangement should be made, for the preservation of good order in the church, and the building up of the members on the most holy faith; and accordingly, as has been stated, George Fox was moved to establish Monthly Meetings throughout the Society.

No doubt other substantial Friends were instrumental in this work of organization and systematizing the church government of the Society; but, it is evident that upon George Fox the burden of the work was principally laid by the Head of the Church, and he labored in it assiduously, notwithstanding his physical weakness and suffering; so that in 1668, he says, "The men's Monthly Meetings were settled throughout the nation. The Quarterly Meetings were generally settled before. I wrote also into Ireland, Scotland,

Holland, Barbadoes, and several parts of America, advising Friends to settle their men's Monthly Meetings in those countries; for they had their Quarterly Meetings before." These Monthly Meetings attended to much of the business that had previously engaged the care of the Quarterly Meetings; the latter receiving reports from those Monthly Meetings subordinate to them, and extending advice and assistance to them, as circumstances required.

· The rapid increase of Friends in London, following the first preaching of the gospel within its walls by Edward Burrough, Francis Howgil, and others called there to labor in the work of the ministry, and the peculiar circumstances surrounding Friends in that large city, had early made it necessary to institute a supervisory meeting, to take charge of the affairs of the infant Society in the city and the places immediately surrounding it. William Crouch mentions in his memoirs, that soon after taking the Bull-and-Mouth for a meeting place (1655), "The ancient Friends about the city did sometimes meet together, to the number of eight or ten, sometimes a few more were added, . . . to consult about and consider the affairs of Truth, and to communicate to each other what the Lord opened to them for the promotion thereof; and also to make such provision to supply all necessary occasions, which the service of the church might require." This was called "The two weeks' Meeting," and it appears to have exercised authority as to matters of arrangement and disciplinary oversight, over the various meetings and members embraced in the London district.

When suffering from persecution increased, and the jails were filled with Friends, a similar meeting composed of women Friends was established; to which was especially confided visiting the sick and feeble, and ministering to their necessities, as also to look after the widows and orphans.

These meetings continued steadily to perform their functions until 1666, when, as has been before mentioned, George Fox advised the setting up of five Monthly Meetings in and about London; which was done. The two weeks' Meeting, though the extent of its jurisdiction was thus greatly lessened, still continued to have under its care, for several years, those Friends residing within the old walls of London, and was particularly charged with the necessary arrangements for and the oversight of marriages.

As yet there was no regular Yearly Meeting; though there appears to have been a General Meeting of Ministers from all parts of the nation, assembled in London in 1668, which issued an epistle.

of advice and instruction to the different meetings and members. Again, in 1672, another General Meeting of similar character convened in London, in which it was agreed " That for the better ordering, managing and regulating the public affairs of Friends, relating to the truth and service thereof, there be a general meeting of Friends held at London once a year, in the week called Whitsun-week ; to consist of six Friends for the city of London, three for the city of Bristol, two of the town of Colchester, and one or two from each of the counties of England and Wales." The proposed meeting assembled according to appointment the next year, and it was then concluded to discontinue this annual representative meeting until " Friends in God's wisdom shall see a further occasion : " but the general meeting of Ministers to be kept up.

Of the duties of these General Meetings of Ministers, besides issuing advice and directions to Friends generally, information is given by the following extract from an exhortation by George Fox in 1674. " Let your General Assemblies of the Ministers, examine as it was at the first, whether all the ministers that go forth into the counties, do walk as becomes the gospel ; for that you know was one end of that meeting, to prevent and take away scandal, and to examine if all who preach Christ Jesus, do keep to his government, and in the order of the gospel, and to exhort them that do not."

In 1677, the Yearly Meeting of Ministers in London again extended an invitation to the Quarterly Meetings to send representatives to the meeting to be held at the same time in the next year in London, " For the more general service of Truth and the body of Friends, in all those things wherein we may be capable to serve one another in love." This representative meeting was held accordingly, and after transacting its business, renewed the invitation to the different Quarterly Meetings to send their representatives next year ; which was done ; and from that time to the present, a similar representative body has met annually not only in London, but in every other Yearly Meeting of Friends, and exercised supreme supervisory and legislative power over its subordinate branches.

Referring to its own establishment, the Yearly Meeting says, in one of its epistles issued some years after it was first regularly held, " The intent and design of our annual assemblies, in their first constitution, was for a great and weighty oversight and Christian care of the affairs of the churches, pertaining to our holy profession and Christian communion ; that good order, true love, unity and concord may be faithfully followed and maintained among us."

The Yearly Meeting continued to be composed exclusively of the representatives regularly appointed from time to time, to attend and take part in its deliberation and action, from the year 1677, when it was instituted, until more than a quarter of the next century had passed by. Then it was concluded that the Yearly Meeting of London should consist of the members of the General and the Quarterly Meetings in Great Britian, and that representatives should be sent to it from the Half Year's Meeting in Ireland. The appointment of representatives from all the Quarterly Meetings was continued; who were expected to give account of and to answer for the respective meetings which sent them, and to them was confided the duty of nominating a clerk for the meeting, and his assistants. Members had the right to appeal from the judgment of the Monthly and Quarterly Meetings to which they belonged to the Yearly Meeting: its decision in all cases is final.

As has been seen, Friends were undergoing great persecution and much suffering during the time when the Yearly Meeting was first established, and cases of distress were frequently occurring, requiring the speedy care and intervention of Friends who could have prompt access to those in authority, and labor for their relief; who also might embrace any opportunity that presented, to restrain the hands of those who were active in spoiling Friends of their goods, and to mitigate, as far as possible, the application of oppressive laws. For these purposes a corresponding committee had been kept in London [1666], to receive accounts of cases of suffering, and extend help and counsel as they were enabled. It was therefore now concluded, that this corresponding committee, together with other Friends appointed by the Quarterly Meetings, should meet regularly, in London, so often as might be agreed upon, in the interval between the conclusion of one Yearly Meeting and the beginning of another; to represent the Yearly Meeting during its recess, and take the charge of these and other matters brought to its notice; and from the character of its principal business at that time, it took the name of The Meeting for Sufferings. [1677.]

Thus was a system of church government organized throughout the Society, which while it avoided laying any undue restriction on individual spiritual liberty, yet provided for that subjection of the members to the authority of the church, which insured order, preservation and edification, so long as it was allowed to have free action; and which by fully recognizing the Headship of Christ in the church, left free the exercise of every gift which He bestowed, and aimed at promoting a consistent and circumspect conversation among the members, and the mutual edification of each other in love.   Universal in its application and simple in its working, this system of church government, when exercised in the Spirit of the Saviour of men, while it holds every member accountable to the meeting in which his right of membership rests, for his conduct and the religious principles he inculcates, gives him the right to receive the extension of every care and encouragement which a religious Society can properly bestow, to meet his wants, and prompt the devotion of his heart to the service of his Creator.

No code of Christian discipline had yet been authoritatively agreed upon; but at different times some of the Friends, who had given full proof of their large experience in things pertaining to the welfare and extension of the kingdom of Christ, had written epistles to the members and meetings; pointing out the duties that were to be performed and the line of action to be observed in order to keep the camp clean, and to bring the members forward in the performance of their services in religious, social and civil life.   Besides these highly valued advices, similar epistles emanating from the General Meetings, were received and observed, as clothed with an authority which was not to be disobeyed or gainsaid.   But in 1668, George Fox drew up and had sent to the respective meetings, a document containing his sense of what should claim the attention and care of meetings for discipline, and the manner in which they should manifest that care over their members.   It was entered upon the minute-books of many meetings, and as it shows the various subjects which the Society, in its early days, was concerned to take in charge, and also the religious concern and comprehensive grasp of that pre-eminent Elder and pillar in the Church, extracts from it are here given:

"Friends' Fellowship must be in the Spirit, and all Friends must know one another in the Spirit and Power of God.

" First. — In all the meetings of the country, two or three being gathered from them to go to the General Meetings, for to give notice one to another, if there be any that walk not in the truth, and have been convinced and gone from truth, and so dishonor God, that some may be ordered from the meeting to go and exhort such, and bring to the next General Meeting what they say.

" 2ndly. — If any that profess the truth, follow pleasures, drunkenness, gamings or are not faithful in their callings and dealings, nor honest nor just, but run into debt, and so bring a scandal upon the truth, Friends may give notice to the General Meeting (if there be any such) and some may be ordered to go and exhort them, and bring in their answer next General Meeting.

"3rdly.—And if any go disorderly together in marriage, contrary to practice of the holy men of God, and assemblies of the righteous in all ages; who declared it in the assemblies of the righteous, when they took one another; (all things being clear,) and they both being free from any other, and when they do go together, and take one another, let there not be less than a dozen Friends and relations present (according to your usual order) having first acquainted the Men's Meeting, and they have clearness and unity with them; and that it may be recorded in a book according to the word and commandment of the Lord; and if any walk contrary to the truth herein, let some be ordered to speak to them and give notice thereof to the next General Meeting.

. . . .

"6thly.— And all such as marry by the Priests of Baal, who are the rough hands of Esau, and fists of wickedness and bloody hands, and who have had their hands in the blood of our brethren, and are the cause of all the banishment of our brethren, and have spoiled so many of their goods, casting into prison, and keep many hundreds at this day — such as go to them for wives or husbands, must come to judgment, and condemnation of that spirit that led them to Baal, and of Baal's priests also; or else Friends that keep their habitations must write against them and Baal both; for from Genesis to the Revelations you never read of any priest that married people; but it is God's ordinance, and whom God joins together let no man put asunder; and they took one another in the assemblies of the righteous when all things were clear. Therefore, let all these things be inquired into and brought to the General Meeting, and from thence some ordered to go to them and to return what they say at your next meeting. And all these, before they or any of them be left as heathens or written against, let them be three or four times gone to; that they may have Gospel order, so that if it be possible they may come to that which did convince them, to condemn their unrighteous doings that so you may not leave a hoof in Egypt.

. . . .

"8thly.— And in all your meetings let notice be given to the General Meetings of all the poor; and when you have heard that there are many more poor belong to one meeting than to another and that meeting thereby burdened and oppressed, let the rest of the meetings assist and help them ; so that you may ease one another, and help to bear one another's burdens, and so fulfil the law of Christ, and so see that nothing be lacking, according to the apostle's words. Mark, nothing lacking, then all is well. . . . So there is not to be a beggar now amongst the Christians, according to the law of Jesus, as there was not to be any amongst the Jews, according to the law of God.

  .   .   .   .

    " 10thly.— And that notice be taken of all evil speakers, backbiters, slanderers and foolish talkers and idle jesters; for all these things corrupt good manners, and are not according to the saints and holy ones; whose words are seasoned with salt, ministering grace to the hearers.

    " 11thly.— And all such who are tale carriers and railers, whose work is to sow dissension, are to be reproved and admonished : for such do not bring people into the unity of the Spirit, but by such doings come to lose their own conditions.

    " 12thly.—And all such as go up and down to cheat by borrowing and getting money of Friends in by-places (and have cheated several).

    " 13thly.—And if there happen any differences between Friend and Friend of any matters, and if it cannot be ended before the General Meeting, let half a dozen Friends from the General Meeting be ordered to put a steady end thereto ; that justice may be speedily done, that no difference may rest or remain amongst any : (and let your General Meeting be once in every quarter of a year, and to be appointed at such places as may be most convenient for the most of Friends to meet in). So that the house may be cleansed of all that is contrary to purity, virtue, light, life, and Spirit and power of God. So that Friends may not be one another's sorrow and trouble, but one another's joy and crown in the Lord.

    "14thly.— And all Friends see that your children be trained up in the fear of the Lord ; in soberness and holiness, and righteousness, temperance and meekness, and gentleness, lowliness and modesty in their apparel and carriage ; and so to exhort your children and families in the truth ; that the Lord may be glorified in all your families; and teach your children when they are young, then will they remember it when they are old, according to Solomon. So that your children may be a blessing to you and not a curse.

  .   .   .   .

    " 16thly.—And also that Friends do buy necessary books for the

registering of births, marriages, and burials, as the holy men of God
did of old ; as you may read through the Scriptures; that every one
may be ready to give a testimony and certificate thereof, if need require, or any be called thereunto.

"17thly.—And also that the sufferings of Friends (of all kinds of
sufferings) in all the counties be gathered up and put together, and
sent to the General Meeting, and so sent to London, to Ellis Hookes;
that nothing of the memorial of the blood and cruel sufferings of
your brethren be lost, which shall stand as a testimony against the
murdering spirit of this world, and be to the praise of the everlasting power of the Lord in the ages to come; who supported and upheld them in such hardships and cruelties; who is God over all,
blessed for ever. Amen.

"18thly.— And let inquiry be made concerning all such as do
pay tithes, which makes void the testimony and sufferings of our
brethren who have suffered, many of them to death ; by which many
widows and fatherless have been made, and which is contrary to the
doctrine of the apostles and the doctrine of the martyrs, and contrary to the doctrine of the righteous in this present age; all such
are to be inquired into, and to be exhorted.

. . . .

"Dear Friends be faithful in the service of God, and mind the
Lord's business, and be diligent, and bring the power of the Lord
over all those that have gainsaid it; and all you that be faithful go
to visit them all that have been convinced, from house to house,
that if it be possible you may not leave a hoof in Egypt; and so
every one go seek the lost sheep and bring him home on your backs
to the fold, and there will be more joy of that one sheep than the
ninety-nine in the fold.

"And my dear friends live in the wisdom of God, that which is
gentle and pure, from above, and easy to be entreated, and bear one
another's infirmities and weaknesses, and so fulfil the law of Christ;
and if any weakness should appear in any of your meetings, not for
any to lay it open and tell it abroad ; that is not wisdom that doth
so, for love covers a multitude of sins, and love preserves and edifies
the body, and they that dwell in love dwell in God, for He is love,
and love is not provoked. And, therefore, keep the law of love,
which keeps down that which is provoked, for that which is provoked hath words which are for condemnation, therefore let the law
of love be amongst you, it will keep down that which is provoked
and its words, and so the body edifies itself in love.

"Copies of this to be sent all abroad amongst Friends in their men's meetings. [1668.]   G. F."

This may be considered the basis upon which, under the leading and authority of the Head of the Church, the code of discipline was shaped and extended, according as the varying circumstances of the Society rendered needful. Many years elapsed before Queries were regularly sent to the subordinate meetings, to be answered.

CHAPTER XXI.

Friends in Ireland—Persecution there—Cruelty of Geo. Clapham—Efforts of Wm. Edmundson to rescue Friends from his oppression — Interview of W. E. with the Lord Lieutenant — W. E.'s service at Londonderry — Meetings for Discipline set up in Ireland — G. Fox visits Ireland — Admiral Penn — Account of Wm. Penn — Death of R. Farnsworth — Continued Persecution — Lord Clarendon — Death of Thomas Loe — Josiah Cole and F. Howgil

IRELAND had had several ministers of the gospel raised up from among those who were convinced of the truth as held by Friends, and through the instrumentality of these, many others had been brought to a knowledge of the way of life and salvation, and to conform in all things to the doctrines and testimonies of the gospel which distinguished Friends. Like their fellow professors in England and other places, they gave evidence of the sincerity of their religious convictions, and the sure foundation on which their faith was built, by the patience, meekness and devotedness with which they bore the multiplied wrongs and cruelties heaped upon them, as well as by the love and sympathetic fellowship that subsisted among them.

1660. Several ministers from England, were concerned to travel throughout the principal parts of the Island, preaching the everlasting gospel, strengthening the hands of those of the same household of faith, and bringing many off from the lifeless forms of the religion they professed, to join with those who were not ashamed to confess Christ before men, by taking up the daily cross, and living in conformity with the restraining, self-denying precepts of his gospel. Among these ministers were John Burnyeat and Robert Lodge, who, landing in the North of Ireland, travelled pretty generally through the settled parts of the different provinces, declaring "the true faith in Jesus," undergoing great hardships, and suffering much abuse from the ignorant people. They were repeatedly imprisoned; but He in whose service they were engaged, made way for their liberation, and supported them under all their trials. Rutty, in his "Rise and Progress," speaking of these two Friends, says, "They were imprisoned several times, besides other abuses that they received, because of the testimony they had to bear in towns and steeple-houses, against hireling priests: and thus having labored in the gospel together for the space of twelve months, and been instrumental in the convincing and gathering of many to the truth, being clear of their service here, in the Seventh month 1660 they took shipping for England."

Thomas Loe, another eminent minister from England, spent considerable time in Ireland, travelling often on foot. In Rutty's account it is stated, that in 1657 he came into Dublin, "Where he declared the day of the Lord through the streets thereof, preaching the word of life and salvation, from James' gate until he came to Lazar's hill." . . . . "He had blessed service, and many were convinced by him."

1660. A few of the Magistrates were very inimical to Friends, and made use of their power to persecute them. Thus a Judge named Alexander, caused five Friends who had been sent to jail at Carlow, for being found at a meeting for worship, but were declared *not guilty* by the jury, to be again indicted, and obtaining a verdict against them, he fined them £320. At Cork he fined three other Friends for the same offence £1190, and at Waterford he imposed a fine of £580 on nine Friends for a similar *offence*. At Limerick he fined the Friends who had assembled to hold a meeting, £40 a piece and kept them in prison four months, when they were released by an order from the Lords Justices.

William Edmundson, who, with most of the men Friends of the meeting to which he belonged, had been excommunicated by the Bishop's Court, because of their not attending at the so-called church, and refusing to pay tithes, church dues, &c., continued indefatigable in his labors to serve his Divine Master and the cause of his suffering people. He gives the following account, which may be taken as illustrating the character of the persecution Friends throughout the nation had to endure, more especially from the priests, in consequence of their faithful adherence to their Christian principles.

"1665. Having my liberty, I found a concern on my mind to solicit the Government against the priest's fierceness and cruelty; for George Clapham, priest of Mountmelick, endeavored to prevent the miller grinding corn for our families, or any speaking or trading with us or any of our families. He watched the market and Friends' shops, and those whom he saw or knew to deal with us, he sent the Apparitor to summon to the Bishop's Court, and so forced them to pay him and the Apparitor money to get free from trouble; they being afraid of the Bishop's Court, it bore such a great name. This priest told his hearers, that if they met any of us in the highway, they should shun us as they would shun the plague; and if they owed us anything, they need not pay it, or if they knocked us on the head, the law would bear them out. At which the people were much troubled, and in general, their love declined from the priest, and drew towards Friends; and they would offer their servants to carry our corn to the mill, that we might get bread for our families, or any other kindness they could do for us."

" I drew up a statement of several of his gross proceedings, and got many of his own people to sign it, who had been abused; then I went to Dublin and petitioned the Government; who with the Primate took notice of it, and the Privy Council resented it, being contrary to all law and rule. They sent an order for the priest and Apparitor to appear before the Council; where they were sharply reproved, and would have been punished, for the Primate said, he would make them examples. But I told him we desired nothing but to be quiet, and to live peaceably in our callings, and that they should desist from their cruelty. The Primate, who was also Chancellor, said, if they did not desist we should write to him, and he would make them examples to the nation. So I forgave them, and let all proceedings fall. This gained much on the minds of many chief men in authority."

1665. " Priest.Clapham was very angry against me, although I had forgiven him, being very greedy and covetous. One time he took my neighbor's horse and car, came to my house, and loaded up and carried away a great deal of cheese: also at that time he took away much goods, corn and wearing-clothes from Friends of our meeting; for some church dues, as he said. While I was at a meeting in Mountmelick, where I used to attend when at home, he — being a Justice of the Peace — sent a constable to apprehend me, and made a mittimus to send me to Maryborough jail; but the Earl of Mountrath, superseded his warrant, and set me at liberty, until the assizes. When the assizes came on, he [the Earl] stood by me against the said priest, who had drawn up two indictments against me; and when they came into Court, four lawyers, one after the other, pleaded for me; though I knew nothing of them nor gave them any fee. But the Lord gave us place in the minds of the people, and their hearts yearned towards us; so that as I passed through them in the Court-house, they would say, 'The Lord bless you, William! the Lord help you, William!' The indictment was quashed, and the priest hissed at by the Court, to his shame."

"Another time, this priest Clapham indicted several Friends of our meeting, at the assizes at Maryborough, and one, for being at a meeting on such a day, which he called an unlawful assembly, and for not being at church, as he called it, on the same day. [1665.] He also indicted me for not paying a levy or assessment towards the repairs of his worship-house; though the wardens and constables had before taken from me for the same, a mare worth three pounds ten shillings. Several Friends were thus proceeded against, and we were fined, and an order given to distrain our goods; on which account I rode to Dublin, and petitioned the Lord-lieutenant and Council. I and one other Friend were admitted into the Council chamber to state our grievance, and had a very fair hearing, the Judge being present who gave judgment against us at the assizes. The Council gave their judgment that the proceedings were illegal. The Lord-lieutenant wished to know why we did not pay tithes to the ministers? I showed him out of the Scriptures that the law was ended which gave tithes, and the priesthood changed which received them, by the coming and suffering of Christ; who had settled a ministry on better terms, and ordered them a maintenance. He would know what maintenance the ministry would have? I told him, Christ's allowance; and I showed him from the Scriptures what that was, as the Lord opened them to me by his Spirit and power, which gave me wisdom and utterance, and set home what I said to their understandings. There were three Bishops present, and not one of them replied in all this discourse, though so nearly concerned in it. In conclusion, the Lord-lieutenant bid God bless us, adding, we should not suffer for not going to their public worship, neither for going to our meetings. This quieted the priests, and it soon went abroad that the Quakers had the liberty of their religion, which was a great ease to Friends, for we had been often imprisoned, and had much goods taken from us on that account."

But though persecution was thus somewhat restrained in Ireland, it was by no means stopped. Shortly after the relief obtained, William Edmundson, with several other Friends, was taken from a meeting and put into prison. [1667.] "There (he says) we had liv-

ing, powerful meetings; many Friends and friendly people came out
of the country to them, and though under suffering, we had a sweet,
heavenly, refreshing time, for the glory of the Lord shone amongst
us.   The priest of the town .kept his worship in the session-house,
and it being under one roof with the jail, we could hear him at his
worship; likewise he and his people could hear us at ours.   The
Lord's power, so confounded him that he could not get on in his
devotion, but left the place and came no more to worship there
while we were prisoners.   The Lord's power, truth and testimony
were over them all, everlasting praises to His great name."

William Edmundson, who was eminently gifted by his divine
Master, and made use of as a nursing-father in the infant Society
in Ireland, was often called into services requiring great faith and
Christian boldness.   He mentions that on one occasion [1668], " I
was moved of the Lord to go from my own house to Londonderry,
to warn them to repent, or the Lord would bring a scourge over
them.   So, in obedience to the Lord, I went; and when I came there
it happened to be a day of humiliation, as they called it; being at
the time the Plague was in London.   They were gone to their worship
at the Cathedral, and I was moved of the Lord to go there.   When
I came to the door, the man who used to ring the bells, met me, and
took me by the hand and led me near the pulpit, where the Bishop
was preaching.   He thought he had got a Presbyterian convert, and
did not take off my hat until he saw the people gazing at me, when
he took it off and laid it by.   I stood there until the Bishop had
done preaching; the people's eyes were on me, and I spoke what the
Lord gave me to say, warning them to repent, or the Lord would
bring a scourge over them, *and scale their walls without a ladder.*
The Bishop called to the Mayor and officers to take me away, but
the dread of the Lord's power was over them ; they all sat still and
did not molest me.   When I had delivered the Lord's message I
went towards the door, where the man who led me in met me, and
took me by the hand, having my hat in his other hand; he led me
to the door, put my hat on my head, and bid God speed me well."

" I went to my lodgings, which was a public house kept by John
Gibson, who, with his wife, was convinced of the truth.   There I
was moved to write a paper to the Bishop and Magistrates, and the
next day I went to the Bishop's house with it, he living in the city.
I knocked at the door, and the man who led me in and out of the
worship-house the day before, opened the door, and made his
apology, that he did me no harm at the church.   I told him

he did well, and asked him for the Bishop. He said he was gone to dinner and a great many gentlemen with him, and he told me it would be better for me to come when they had dined.

"I went back to my lodgings, and in a little time came again, and they having then dined, I sent my paper to them; and they sent a priest to call me up. As I was going up the stairs the word of the Lord said unto me, 'I will make thee a wall of brass.' There were the Bishop, the Governor, the Mayor, several justices of the peace, priests and others, in a great dining-room; the Bishop sat with his hat on and the rest all stood bare-headed. When I came into the room the Bishop rose up from his seat, put off his hat, and met me with several low bows; but I was as a wall of brass, and stood in the power of the Lord that was with me, which smote him. Then he sat down and told me what I had said at their worship the day before was true, and he preached the same, and pointed to the priests, saying they preached the same, and therefore there was no need of me. I told him the more preachers of truth the better, and there was need enough; and he being a Bishop ought to encourage me. He said he must know what I came to the city for, and who sent me, and he bade the Mayor examine me. So the Mayor came from among the rest, and asked me where I dwelt? I told him in the Queen's county. He asked what trade I was? I told him, a plough-man. He asked my business there, and who sent me? I told him the Lord Jesus Christ sent me, to warn them to repent, or He would lash them with his judgments. As I declared this, the Lord's power reached him, and he could not refrain from tears, being a tender spirited man; so he went back behind the rest."

"The Bishop seeing this, was amazed, and bid two of his waiting-men take me into the buttery and make me eat and drink. They took me by the arms down the stairs, and bid me go into the buttery to eat and drink. I told them I could not eat or drink there; but they urged me, saying, I heard their lord command them to make me eat and drink. I asked them if they were Christians at that house? They said, Yes; then said I, let your yea be yea, and your nay be nay, for that is Christ's command. I said I will not eat nor drink here, and you take no notice of it, being accustomed to break your yea and nay. They stood silent and let me go, for the Lord's power astonished them, and was over them all."

"I went to my lodgings and was moved of the Lord to write a paper and put it on the gates of the city, and to declare the Lord's message through the streets. Accordingly, I wrote a paper that evening, and in the morning went first to the Mayor, and told him the message I had to the city. He said the Bishop had chided him the day before, because he did not send me to prison; but he did not intend to do it so long as the law would bear him harmless, and wished he had me living by him, and then I should soon have another to help to suppress wickedness. I went from the Mayor, and beginning near Water-gate, sounded the Lord's message through the streets: it was dreadful to the people, and several ran as if before naked swords. As I came near the main guard, a soldier being at the door mocked, but in the dread of the Lord's power I looked in at the guard-house door, and cried, Soldiers! all repent. The soldiers on the guard were smitten as men affrighted, for the power of the Lord was mighty, in which I performed this service; and when I had done, I put a paper on the gates, as the Lord moved me. Being clear, I left the city and visited Friends' meetings in the North, and they admired the Lord's goodness that carried me through that service without a prison."

"The day I left Londonderry, the Bishop took his journey towards Dublin, and as I was informed by those who said they heard him, he preached a sermon before the Lord-lieutenant and government, against the Quakers; comparing us to Corah, Dathan and Abiram, and urging them with many arguments to suppress us; but he was taken sick in the worship house, carried to his lodging, and died; having preached his last sermon against the Lord's people and servants, who truly fear him."

William Edmundson subsequently remarks, that the people of Londonderry had reason to remember, and did remember and speak of the prophetic warning delivered to them; when in the siege, by the army of King William, "Thousands died for want of bread, and through other miseries, the Lord having scaled their walls without a ladder, yet suffered not their enemies to get the city by force of arms, or scaling ladders."

As has been already stated, George Fox had written to Friends in Ireland, advising the setting up of meetings for discipline, and William Edmundson,—whom Rutty in his history speaks of " as the chief instrument in this land [Ireland] for the spreading of truth, and preserving of Friends faithful therein,"—had labored untiringly in the work. "Provincial Meetings" had been set up, which met every six weeks, performing the same duties as Quarterly Meetings in England. In 1669 George Fox crossed over ·to Ireland on a religious visit, and assisted in establishing a·more general and efficient system of church government; setting up men's and women's meetings throughout the nation; many of which were held every two weeks; and instituting a general Half Year's meeting, to meet in Dublin, which sent representatives to London. W. Edmundson, speaking of the settlement of these meetings, says, " I was much eased by them, as I told George Fox at that time; for I had a great concern in those things, which had lain heavy upon my spirit for several years before, and this gave every faithful Friend a share of the burden. I travelled with George Fox from place to place in the several provinces."

George Fox, after narrating the many efforts made in different places during this visit to arrest and imprison him, says, " Yet the Lord disappointed all their counsels, defeated all their designs against me, and by his good hand of Providence preserved me out of all their snares, and gave me many sweet and blessed opportunities to visit Friends, and spread truth through that nation. For meetings were very large, Friends coming to them far and near, and other people flocking in. The powerful presence of the Lord was preciously felt with and amongst us, whereby many of the world were reached, convinced, gathered to the truth, and the Lord's flock was increased, and Friends were greatly refreshed and comforted in feeling the love of God."

Again, " A good, weighty and true people there is in that nation, sensible of the power of the Lord God, tender of his truth; and very good order they have in their meetings; for they stand up for righteousness and holiness, which dams up the way of wickedness. A precious visitation they had, and there is an excellent spirit in them, worthy to be visited." [1669.]

It was in Ireland that William Penn, who joined the Society of Friends in 1666, first formed acquaintance with some of its members. He was the son of William Penn, who, trained to nautical life, had by his genius and courage, risen rapidly in the navy, until at the age of twenty-nine he became " Vice-Admiral of the Straits." From the account of his life and public career, given by Granville Penn a descendant, he appears to have been a man who made self-interest a leading principle of conduct, but who while eagerly coveting wealth and honor, was never accused of being corrupt as a public servant. His son William was born in 1644, and resided with his mother at Wanstead, in Essex, while his father was absent with the fleet over which he had command.

Owing to information received by Cromwell through some of

the spies kept by him in attendance upon the exiled Charles and his Court, that, notwithstanding he had sanctioned the promotion of Admiral Penn and largely rewarded him by an estate in Ireland, for some losses he had sustained there, he was secretly making overtures to bring the squadron he commanded into the service of the Royalists, he lost favor with the Protector.   On his return from an unsuccessful expedition against the Spanish West India Islands, he was deprived of his command and thrown into prison, whence Cromwell generously liberated him at his own humble petition.   He then took his family over to Ireland, where he continued to reside for some years, on the estate which Cromwell had had bestowed upon him, and which was near Cork.

In a manuscript written by Thomas Harvey, reciting an account given to him by William Penn, of some of the circumstances of his early life, and which was first published in " The Penns and Peningtons," by M. Webb, it is stated, " That while he was but a child living at Cork with his father, Thomas Loe came thither.   When it was rumored a Quaker was come from England, his father proposed to some others to be like the noble Bereans, and hear him before they judged him.   He accordingly sent to T. Loe to come to his house ; where he had a meeting in the family.   Though William was very young, he observed what effect T. Loe's preaching had on the hearers.   A black servant of his father's could not restrain himself from weeping aloud ; and little William looking on his father, saw the tears running down his cheeks also.   He then thought within himself, ' What if they would all be Quakers ! '   This opportunity he never quite forgot ; the remembrance of it still recurring at times."   William Penn was then about eleven years of age, and was being educated by a private tutor.

On the retirement of Richard Cromwell from the position for which he had been appointed by his father, Admiral Penn declared for Charles Stuart, and lost no time for going over to the continent to pay court to him whom he had no doubt would soon be recalled to the throne.   Charles employed him in secret service, and rewarded him by the honors of knighthood, and by becoming his debtor for one hundred pounds.

When a little over fifteen years of age, William Penn entered as " a gentleman commoner," at Oxford, where he remained three years ; distinguishing himself as a hard and successful student.   After the Restoration, the Court set to work to remodel the University, by displacing those who held Puritanical opinions, or who had found favor during the Commonwealth, and installing others, friendly to the re-established church, and the lax moral principles then prevailing. Dr. Owen, conspicuous as a scholar and a strict religionist, was ejected to make room for a royalist partisan, and the students became divided into parties, applauding or denouncing the changes made.

There is reason to believe, from observations made by W. Penn himself, that throughout his youth he was repeatedly visited by the Day-Spring from on high, convicting him of that which was evil in his ways, and bringing him into serious thoughtfulness. While at college his associates appear to have been those of a religious cast of character like himself, and who with him were greatly influenced by the teaching and advice of Dr. Owen. It so happened that while much controversy was going on among the scholars relative to religious opinions and practices, Thomas Loe came to Oxford, and held several meetings. To these meetings W. Penn and his associates went, and a deep impression was made upon their minds by the powerful preaching of this devoted servant of Christ. They declined being present at what were now the regular "services" of the college, and did not refrain from speaking depreciatingly of what they designated as the "popish doctrines and usages" reintroduced among them. For this they were lectured and fined. With the ardor and indiscretion of youth, this supposed indignity was highly resented by them. They not only held private meetings for worship and religious exhortation and prayer, but some of them refused to wear the student's gown and cap, and in some instances tore them off of those they met. How far William Penn was implicated in the latter wrong-doing is not known; but his positive refusal to wear the usual garb, his bold denunciation of the doctrine and practices he believed to be wrong, and his courageous defence of the gospel truths he had heard from Thomas Loe, brought upon him the enmity of the Masters in power, and he was expelled the University.

Admiral Penn, who had set his heart upon preparing his son for realizing to the full, the ambitious hopes and aims entertained by himself for his family, appears to have been little qualified to understand his son's character, or to rightly estimate the principles that actuated him. His pride was mortified, and, as he thought, his promising schemes were blasted. He received William with anger, and for a time would hardly deign to speak to him. Accustomed to command, and to be obeyed without question, he ordered him to give up his newly formed views of religious duty, and to hold no further intercourse with those who had shared in his rebellious opinions and course. Enraged on finding that his authority, though seconded by the filial affection of his child, was powerless for removing his religious convictions, he resorted to the use of his cane; followed by solitary confinement in his room, and then banishment from the family.

It was not long, however, before his good sense convinced him that the object he had in view was not to be obtained by severity. He resolved to change his mode of attack, and try if what could not be gained by force, might not be brought about by the seductions of a life of gaiety and pleasure. Learning that a number of young men, sons of persons considered to be of high families, were about to go on to the continent and spend some time in study and travelling, he decided to send William with them. Accordingly, furnished with letters that would introduce him into what the world considered the best society, he went to Paris; and fascinated by the courtly and gay scenes of the company into which he found himself welcomed, as an admired guest, he soon caught the worldly spirit that presided over their festivities, and his serious, Quaker-like impressions appeared to pass away, like the morning dew before the burning rays of the sun. He did not, however, allow pleasure to wean him from study. He went to Saumur, and placing himself under the tuition of the learned Moses Amyrault, applied himself to the study of the language and literature of the country, embracing the philosophic basis of divinity. Travelling into Italy he made himself acquainted with its language, and gratified his taste for the works of the Masters in art.

On the breaking out of the war with the Dutch, the Admiral called his son William home, where he arrived after an absence of two years. All trace of the religious seriousness and conscientious restraint that had marked his conduct and manner when he left, was gone, and his father was delighted to find his son wearing the carriage, and displaying the accomplishments of a self-possessed man of the world. He was at once introduced at Court, and had the opportunity to become acquainted with many who stood high in the brilliant but profligate society that filled the saloons of Whitehall.

William Penn now entered Lincoln's Inn as a student of law, and in 1665, when twenty-one years of age, there seemed every probability of his making an accomplished courtier, and a successful competitor for the honors of this world. Few could enter life with more flattering, and apparently better grounded prospects of attaining to all that would gratify a mind with strong intellectual powers, and naturally ambitious of preferment. His manly form, blooming with health, betokened physical strength and endurance. His disposition, though lively and active, was marked by docility and sweetness. He possessed ready wit, and his good mental abilities had been well developed and trained by careful culture, and strengthened by extensive and profound literary attainments. Men high in power and place smiled upon him; his father enjoyed close intimacy with the Duke of York, heir presumptive to the crown, and eagerly sought to secure for his son the glory and riches of the world which courted his acceptance.

The Admiral having been appointed by the Duke of York, to accompany him in command of the fleet, took William as one of his staff; but after a short absence the latter was sent home with a dispatch to the King. The Plague was now spreading in London, and soon the whole aspect of the city was sadly changed. The awful scenes of death that were daily occurring and struck the stoutest hearts with dismay, brought to the sensitive mind of the gay young man, conviction of the uncertainty of life, and warning of the necessity to prepare for its sudden termination. The Holy Spirit again broke up his false rest, showed him the emptiness of all worldly grandeur, and wooed him to follow Christ Jesus in the regeneration.

After a cruise of about two months his father returned, flushed with success in the sanguinary contest in which he had been engaged. He found William again serious, and indisposed to continue the course upon which, but a short time before, he had exultantly entered. The increased honors and emoluments heaped on the victorious sailor by the royal brothers, made him still more fearful lest the foolish whimsies — as he thought them — of his son, would yet disappoint his hopes of the hereditary honors that might be settled upon him. Large accession to his Irish estate, derived from royal bounty as a reward for the service rendered, made it necessary that some one should look after his interest there; and having experienced the good effect—as he considered it—of placing his son within the dazzling circle of gay and fashionable life, he hurried him across the channel, with letters of introduction to the Duke of Ormund, then Lord Deputy of Ireland.

William found the viceregal Court comparatively free from the dissipation and loose morals of that which surrounded Charles II., and he soon seemed to enter heartily into the enjoyment it afforded. He joined an expedition, sent under the command of Lord Arran, to quell an insurrection that broke out among the garrison at Carrickfergus, and for a while was so excited by the spirit and enterprise attending active military life, that he became anxious to adopt. it as a profession. But his father, when consulted on the subject, decidedly objected, and it was given up.

But He who watches over the workmanship of his hand, and seeks to save that which is lost, was not leaving William Penn to wander in the paths of folly, without the reproofs of instruction, and in mercy, by his witness in the heart, inclining him to accept those reproofs as the way to life; and it was not long before he was brought to a stand, and made to feel that he must then make his election between the life of a votary of this world, and that of a self-denying disciple of a crucified Saviour.

Shangarry Castle, the newly acquired estate of the Admiral, was near to Cork, and when not employed in bringing the place and the affairs connected with it into order, William was often in the town, where he had been well acquainted when a boy. Having one day, while there, gone into the shop of a woman Friend whom he had formerly known, to make a purchase, and finding she did not recognize him, he introduced himself, and entered into conversation with her; recalling to her recollection the meeting held by Thomas Loe at his father's house. Upon her expressing surprise at his memory of the events, he replied, he thought he would never forget them, and that if he knew where that Friend was, he would go to hear him again, though it was an hundred miles off. She told him he need not go so far, for that Friend was now in Cork, and was to have a meeting the next day. Curious again to hear one who had arrested his attention when a boy, and seriously impressed him by his ministry, when at Oxford, he went to the meeting; and after a time Thomas Loe stood up with the expression, " There is a faith that overcomes the world, and there is a faith that is overcome by the world." It struck deep into the heart of William Penn, who was then made to feel keenly that he had been long striving against or slighting his known duty to his Maker, and allowing the world to overcome the drawing of his heavenly Father's love, to bring him out from the thraldrom of sin; and as the preacher, with fervid eloquence, dwelt on the fruits of such faith, he was thoroughly broken down, and wept much. After the meeting he went with T. Loe to a Friend's house, where they had a free conversation, and from that time he became a regular attender of the meetings of Friends. As the Light of Christ shone with more and more clearness upon his soul, he saw how grievously he had departed from the right way of the Lord, and was brought under deep repentance therefor. Convinced of the truth of the doctrines held by Friends, he heartily embraced them, and firmly resolved to live and die by them, whatever sacrifices it might cost him.

Being at a meeting in Cork in 1667, he, with others, was arrested by officers who came to break the meeting up, and was sent to prison; though the Magistrate, who recognized him as the son of the lord of Shangarry Castle, offered to set him at liberty if he would give his word "to keep the peace," which he refused. From the prison he addressed a letter to the Earl of Ossory, giving an account of the arrest and imprisonment of himself and friends, showing their innocence, and pleading the liberty of conscience demanded by the precepts of the gospel. An order was immediately despatched by the Earl for his release; and as it was soon noised abroad that Admiral Penn's son had turned Quaker, the Earl wrote to his father, communicating the information. Startled and annoyed by the intelligence, the Admiral ordered William to come home immediately, which he did. Josiah Cole, of whom mention has been made before, met him at Bristol, accompanied him to London, and being deeply interested for his stability and preservation, went with him to his father's house. Fully as William had adopted the principles of Friends, and many as were the baptisms he had already passed through, he had not yet adopted the plain dress that distinguished them from others; and his father observing this, and that his rapier still hung by his side, hoped that his friend the Earl had been wrongly informed; and he treated him and his friend during the evening with ordinary courtesy, without alluding to the report that had reached him.

Observing, on the next day, that William did not uncover his head when he came into his presence — in those days men generally wore their hats in the house — and that he used thee and thou when addressing him, he demanded an explanation. William frankly told him, that having been convinced of the truth of the religion of the Quakers, he was conscientiously scrupulous against taking off his hat as a token of respect, using the plural language, or compliments. An angry altercation on the part of the father, and deeply distressing on the part of the son succeeded, and was more than once repeated. Finally, the former, finding that neither argument nor threats could shake the latter's firm conviction that to comply with his father's wishes, would be to violate his duty to his Lord and Master, told him he might thee and thou whom he pleased, and keep on his hat, except in the presence of the King, the Duke of York, and himself; but to or before these he should not thee nor thou, nor stand covered; and the son, moved by his father's distress and his own filial affection, asked time for consideration before giving a decisive reply. This was reluctantly granted, though he was forbidden to see any Friend, and William retired, to pour out his soul in prayer for right direction and strength to follow it. At their next interview William told his father that he could not comply with his wishes without violating his duty to his God, and must therefore decline. Irritated at what he considered his son's obstinacy, and foolish determination to sacrifice the worldly honors soliciting his acceptance, for a mere whim, the Admiral upbraided him in no measured terms, and when convinced that he would not be changed, turned him out of doors, with the threat that he would disinherit him. Before leaving his home and family, William assured his father how deeply he was grieved; not so much because of his being driven from his paternal roof and brought to poverty, as because he incurred his displeasure, and was thought by him to be an undutiful child : he then left the house, resigned to make the sacrifice required, and "Choosing rather to suffer affliction with the people of God, than to enjoy the pleasures of sin for a season; esteeming the reproach of Christ greater riches than the treasures of Egypt; for he had respect unto the recompense of reward." Friends who knew the circumstances under which Wm. Penn was placed, received him gladly; and his mother, who yearned over the son of her love, and greatly mourned the course pursued towards him, took means to have him supplied with money sufficient to obtain food and raiment, and so managed as to have an occasional interview with him. It was not long after, that laying aside his rapier and all ornamentation of dress, he appeared in the plain garb of a Quaker.

Some years after, when writing respecting the trials that befell him about this time, he speaks of " The bitter mockings and scornings that fell upon me, the displeasure of my parents, the cruelty and invective of the priests, the strangeness of all my companions and what a sign and wonder they made of me; but above all, that great cross of resisting and watching against my own vain affections and thoughts."

As he was given up to endure the baptisms necessary for his

purification and refinement, his Divine Master brought him up out of the horrible pit, set his feet upon Himself, the Rock of ages, and made him a partaker of the powers of the world to come; and having thus prepared him for the work, bestowed on him a gift in the ministry of the gospel of life and salvation   He first came forth in this service in 1668, about two years after his convincement under the ministry of T. Loe, and in the twenty-fourth year of his age. His uniformly consistent conduct, and careful maintenance of affectionate filial respect toward his exasperated parent, finally won upon him so far that he permitted him to take up his abode in his house; though it was long after he had been so living, before he would have much intercourse with him.   But when, sharing in the persecution which Friends were then suffering, his son was cast into prison, it was said he secretly used his influence to obtain his liberty.

In 1667, Richard Farnsworth, who has been mentioned as one of the band of ministers which, shortly after the great convincement that attended the early preaching of George Fox, was sent forth, and earnestly engaged in promulgating the truth, first throughout the Northern Shires of England, and then in various parts of Great Britain, deceased in London, whither he had come in gospel love. He was a faithful laborer in the Lord's cause, and willingly took his share of the suffering so generally inflicted on Friends on account of their adherence to what they believed to be the faith once delivered to the saints.   Daniel Roberts in his account of his father, John Roberts, relates, that two women Friends who were at the house of the latter, having recommended him to go to R. Farnsworth — who was then in Banbury jail for the testimony of Truth — to obtain more information respecting the principles of Friends, he went; and finding the two women Friends there, whom the jailer would not admit, he requested they might be allowed to accompany him to the prisoner, and it was granted.   They were " conducted through several rooms to a dungeon, where Richard Farnsworth was preaching through the grating to the people in the street.   Soon after they came in he desisted; and after a little time of silence, turning to them, spoke to this purpose.   That Zaccheus being a man of low stature, and having a mind to see Christ, ran before and climbed up into a sycamore tree; and our Saviour knowing his good desires, called to him, ' Zaccheus, come down, for this day is salvation come to thy house.'   Thus, Zaccheus was like some in our day who are climbing up into the tree of knowledge, thinking to find Christ there.   But the word now is, Zaccheus come! come down! for that which is known of God is manifested within. This, with more to the same purpose, was spoken with such authority, that when my father came home, he told my mother he had seen Richard Farnsworth, who had spoken to his condition as if he had known him from his youth. From that time he patiently bore the cross."

A short time before his death, being sensible that his end was near at hand, Richard addressed those about him in the following words: "Friends, God hath been mightily with me, and supported me at this time, and his presence and power have encompassed me all along : God hath appeared for the owning of my testimony. I am filled with his love more than I am able to express. God hath really appeared for us. Therefore I beseech you, Friends, here of the City of London, be you faithful to the testimony which God hath committed to you."

Severe persecution was going on in many parts of England, and one William Armorer, in Berkshire, so distinguished himself by his persevering oppression of Friends in that Shire, and his implacable cruelty towards those he brought within his power, that an account of his acts and the suffering Friends had to endure from him, was published, giving the particular cases, time and places. They were much the same as many of those which have been already narrated, though some evinced peculiar malignity of feeling on the part of this persecutor, who was bent upon robbing and imprisoning all who openly professed the principles of Friends, and were within the reach of his authority. There were, however, political causes at work, which, by unsettling the depository of power, and causing commotion among those who were desirous to control the government, took attention, in part off from enforcing conformity to the " established Church," by constant persecution of Dissenters. The vices of the Court kept the King constantly poor, and having to go again and again to the House of Commons for the means to continue his follies, the latter began again to encroach on the prerogatives and functions of the executive branch of the government, and to augment its own power, by a crafty use of its command over the purse. They became dissatisfied with Clarendon, Chancellor of England, and the head of the administration, and boldly called him to account. He was hated by one party of royalists, anxious to be made rich by confiscating the property of the Puritans, because he inflexibly insisted on the strict observance of the " Indemnity Act," and was equally disliked by another party at Court, on account of his circumspect morals, and his felt rebuke of their own licentiousness; while, as the author of the penal laws, and the principal promoter of other severe measures resorted to, to crush the Dissenters, he was looked upon by them as a bigot, and devoid of the common feelings of humanity. His proud and arrogant manner, especially towards those whom he thought were aiming to acquire power, disgusted many in the Parliament; while the common people, who blindly attributed to him most of the great evils that had befallen the nation, failed not to give him ample proof of how unpopular he was with them. The King having taken the great Seal from him, and the Commons impeached him for high crimes and misdemeanors, he became so alarmed at the probable result, that he fled the country, and Parliament passed an act sentencing him to perpetual exile; thus meting to him in full measure, for his crimes, that punishment which he had been the cause of meting to so many much better men than himself, for adhering to their religious principles.

Those who succeeded Clarendon in place and power, probably impressed by his fate with the fickleness of popular favor, and the distracted condition of the country, appeared desirous to remove the great discontent of the Dissenters, by letting the execution of the laws against them sleep, and conniving at their meeting together for public worship. Consequently, for a short time, Friends were not so universally and persistently harassed and imprisoned.

In 1668 Josiah Cole was gathered from works to rewards. He joined the Society in 1654, and became a faithful laborer in the Lord's vineyard, as has been noticed in the account of his services and sufferings when in America. William Penn, in his testimony concerning him, says, "His declarations to the ungodly world were like an axe or a sword, sharp and piercing, being mostly attended with an eminent appearance of the dreadful power of the Lord; but to the faithful and diligent, O! the soft and pleasant streams of life immortal that have run through him, to the refreshing of the Lord's heritage."

As he felt the chill of death creeping over him — George Fox and Stephen Crisp being with him — he uttered many weighty expressions; among the last of which were, "For my part I have walked in faithfulness to the Lord, and I have thus far finished my testimony, and have peace with the Lord. His majesty is with me, and his crown of life is upon me. So mind my love to all Friends." Then addressing S. Crisp, he said, "Dear heart! keep low in the holy Seed of God, and that will be thy crown forever. A minister of Christ must walk as He walked." He died in the arms of the two Friends above named.

It was also in this year (1668,) that Francis Howgil died in jail, as has been mentioned in the account of his trial and imprisonment. Thomas Loe, another eminent servant and minister of Christ, who, in the course of his service in the Church, had been instrumental in turning many to righteousness, was called away from the church militant to enter upon his reward in the church triumphant. When on his death-bed, he said to William Penn, who, with other Friends, was waiting on him, "Bear thy cross and stand faithful to God; then He will give thee an everlasting crown of glory, that shall not be taken from thee. There is no other way which shall prosper than that which the holy men of old walked in. God hath brought immortality to light, and life immortal is felt. Glory! glory! to Him, for He is worthy of it. His love overcomes my heart; nay, my cup runs over, glory be to his Name forever." To George Whitehead he remarked, "The Lord is good to me; this day He hath covered me with glory," and as life was leaving his body he sang, " glory, glory to Thee forever!" and so sank to sleep in Jesus.

CHAPTER XXII.

Dispute of G. Whitehead and W. Penn with Thos. Vincent—"Sandy Foundation Shaken"— Imprisonment of Wm. Penn—No Cross, no Crown—" Innocency with her Open Face " — Unjust Suspicion of W. Penn's Soundness in Christian Faith—W. P. released from the Tower — Address of Marg. Fell to King Charles II.—Her Release from Prison — Marriage of G. Fox and M. Fell — Epistle of G. F.—Visit of J. Burnyeat to America — Defection of T. Thurston — Perrot's Principles in America— Numerous Friends engaged in Religious visits to W. Indies and America — G. Fox in America — W. Edmundson in America — Friends in N. and S. Carolina — Friends obtain control of New Jersey — Emigration to N. J.—Settlement of Meetings in N. J.

THE Baptists and Presbyterians were now holding their meetings for worship publicly, and as it was no uncommon thing for some among their congregations to leave them and join with Friends, many of their ministers, chagrined at the loss of members of their flock, resorted to the common usage of misrepresenting the doctrines held by the "Quakers." Among others, one Thomas Vincent, a Presbyterian clergyman, having lost some of his congregation, who were convinced of Friends' principles, indulged in such gross denunciation of, and calumnies respecting the Society, that George Whitehead and William Penn deemed it their duty to call him to account, and demand of him a public examination of the charges he so boldly made, that Friends held damnable doctrines.

1668. Accordingly, a meeting was assembled in the Presbyterian place of worship, composed principally of Vincent's congregation; and he, with several of his clerical brethren to assist him in the dispute, accused Friends of holding the damnable heresy of denying there being three distinct and separate persons in the Godhead. The disputation was altogether unsatisfactory. Vincent and his abettors failed to prove their charge, which they attempted to do by syllogisms, because they could not show the truth of the second or minor proposition; and the two Friends failed to obtain opportunity to explain what Friends' doctrine really was. When Vincent had got through with what he desired to say, he fell upon his knees and began to repeat over a prayer, after finishing which, he and his assistants left the house, desiring the people to do so likewise. But as Friends desired them to remain and listen to their declaration of what they did believe, and many of them were disposed to do so, the lights were put out, and to prevent an uproar, Friends left and the assembly dispersed. Vincent promised to give another opportunity for continuing the debate, but could never be brought to comply with his promise; though George Whitehead and William Penn went to his meeting-house and, waiting until he had got through with his "service," requested him to give them the opportunity to examine and refute the charges he had made against Friends, but he pleaded not having time, and went directly away.

As this attempt at a public debate on controverted points of belief had excited great interest, and was a subject of much conversation throughout the city, William Penn wrote and had published a tract, which he entitled " The Sandy Foundation Shaken ;" in which he controverted the three positions taken, or propositions advocated by Thomas Vincent, viz.: One God subsisting in three distinct and separate-*persons*. The *impossibility* of God pardoning sinners, without a plenary satisfaction. The justification of *impure* persons by an imputative righteousness. [1668.]

Zealous to refute the error of there being three *persons* in the Godhead; and to prove the unscriptural character of the assertions that God *could not* pardon sin " upon repentance, without Christ paying his justice, by suffering *infinite vengeance and eternal death* for sins past, present and to come," and that the righteousness of Christ was imputed to impure persons and they thereby justified, William Penn was not so guarded in the language he used in treating on these mysteries, but that he was misunderstood by many, and supposed to be unsound on the fundamental doctrines of the proper divinity, and meritorious death and atonement of Christ.

The tract attracted general attention, and gave deep offence to some of the Prelates; who, either thought it beneath their dignity to enter into argument with a polemic so young, and as they might think, so unskilled in divinity; or, as being more in accordance with their practice and the spirit of the times, and more likely to silence their opponent, they applied to the Secretary of State and induced him to issue a warrant for his arrest; which Wm. Penn hearing of, went and voluntarily gave himself up, and was committed to the Tower. It was evident that Wm. Penn had some bitter enemies, for a letter was picked up near where he had been standing when he surrendered himself, which contained matter of so treasonable a character, that Lord Arlington, the Secretary of State, on receiving and reading it, went immediately to the Tower and had an interview with him, in which he soon satisfied himself that Wm. Penn knew nothing of the note, and was innocent of any conspiracy.

There had been no indictment, no trial, conviction, nor sentence passed upon the prisoner, and yet he was kept in solitary confinement for about eight months; during which time most of his family and friends were forbidden access to him, and the "Bishop of London" sent him word he should either make a public recantation or die in prison. But though thus closely immured as to his body, his spirit was free, and the word of the Lord was not bound. He prepared himself to weary out the malice of his enemies by patience and meekness, and to be resigned to lay down his life within the walls of the Tower, if the sacrifice was called for, rather than violate his conscience.

To occupy his time profitably, and, so far as he had ability, promote the cause of truth and righteousness, he employed his pen; and his thoughts, probably taking their direction and coloring from the afflictive circumstances under which he, and many other members of the Society to which he was joined, were then placed, he wrote the work, since become so celebrated, "No Cross, No Crown." This treatise is admitted to be of extraordinary merit; not only in a literary point of view, considering the short time, and the circumstances under which it was produced, but in the clear and cogent manner in which it presents the sinful indulgences of the great body of the professors of christianity, and enforces the self-denying requisitions of the religion of Christ.

Finding that some parts of his " Sandy Foundation Shaken," had been misunderstood or misrepresented, so as to give currency to the charge of his being unsound in relation to the divinity and atonement of Christ, William Penn at once wrote an explanation of what had been misrepresented, and in exposition of his views on these cardinal points of Christian faith. [1668.] This was entitled, " Innocency with her Open Face." In this work he says, " Let all know, that I pretend to know no other name by which remission, atonement, and salvation can be obtained, but Jesus Christ the Saviour, who is the power and wisdom of God." Asserting his full belief in the divinity of Christ, he observes, " He that is the everlasting Wisdom, the divine Power, the true Light, the only Saviour, the creating Word of all things, whether visible or invisible, and their Upholder by his own power, is without contradiction, God; but all these qualifications and divine properties are, by the concurrent testimony of Scripture, ascribed to the Lord Jesus Christ, therefore, without scruple, I call and believe him really to be the mighty God."

In replying to Dr. John Collenges, some years after the publication of " The Sandy Foundation Shaken," who had at that time brought forward exceptions to its doctrines, William Penn again explicitly asserts his full belief in the proper divinity of, and atonement made by, Christ; and in the doctrine of Justification as held by Friends at that time and ever since. " I do *heartily believe* that Jesus Christ is the only true and everlasting God, by whom all things were made that are made, in the heavens above or the earth beneath, or the waters under the earth: that He is as omnipotent, so, omniscient and, omnipresent, therefore God." And in regard to the atonement and justification, he thus writes, "He that would not have me mistaken, on purpose to render his charge against me just, whether it be so or no, may see in *my apology* for ' The Sandy Foundation Shaken,' that I otherwise meant than I am charactered. In short, I say, both as to this and the other point of justification, that Jesus Christ was a *sacrifice for sin*, that He was set forth to be *a propitiation for the sins of the whole world;* to declare God's righteousness, *for the remission of sins that are passed,* &c.; to all that repented and had faith in his Son. Therein the love of God appeared, that He declared his good-will *thereby* to be reconciled; Christ bearing away the sins

that are passed, as the scape-goat did of old ; not excluding inward
work; for till that is begun, none can be benefited ; though it is not
the work, but God's free love that remits and blots out; of which
the death of Christ, and his sacrificing himself was a most certain
declaration and confirmation. In short, *that* declared remission to
all who believe and obey, for the sins that are past; which is the
first part of Christ's work (as it is a King's to pardon a traitor before
he advanceth him,) and hitherto the acquittance imputes a righteousness—inasmuch as men, *on true repentance* are imputed as clean
of guilt as if they had never sinned—and thus far are justified—but
the *completion* of this by the working out of sin inherent, must be
by the Power and Spirit of Christ in the heart, destroying the old
man and his deeds, and bringing in the new, and everlasting righteousness. So that which I wrote against, is such doctrine as extended Christ's death and obedience, *not to the first,* but to this second
part of justification ; not the pacifying of conscience as to past sin ;
but to complete salvation without cleansing and purging from all
filthiness of flesh and spirit, by the internal operation of his holy
power and Spirit."

Notwithstanding William Penn is thus clear and explicit in cor-
recting the misunderstanding of his Christian faith, to which some
of his expressions in "The Sandy Foundation Shaken " had given
rise, and in his full avowal of his belief in the Deity of Christ, and
the atonement made by Him for the sins of mankind; as also in the
doctrine of justification by faith in Him ; yet those who are anxious
to represent Friends as Socinians, or as denying the atonement of
Christ, are still so unjust to his unequivocal and widely published
opinions on these points, and so ungenerous to his character and
memory, as well as untruthful in their representation of Friends,
as to claim him as authority for their disbelief in these fundamental
doctrines.

Though he had addressed a communication to Lord Arlington,
Secretary of State ; on whose warrant he was committed to the
Tower—in which he denied the charges brought against him, so far
as he had been able to ascertain them ; declaring they were the result of ignorance and malice, and requesting that he might have an
audience with the King, in order to hear the accusation of his enemies,
and have an opportunity to defend himself; or if he could not have
access to the King, then to be brought, with his accusers face to
face, before him, the Secretary of State; it was disregarded, nor was
the rigor of his confinement abated. "Innocency with her Open

Face," had, however, produced a change of public feeling towards him; and his father, who could not but respect the consistent firmness and Christian endurance of his son, and who had himself been passing through a severe ordeal from the machinations of his enemies in the House of Commons, visited him in his dungeon, and began to use the influence he continued to hold with the Duke of York and the King, on his behalf. Whether at his instance or not is not known, but Arlington, though declining to give audience to William Penn himself, sent the King's Chaplain, Stillingfleet, to have an interview with him, and ascertain what concessions he would be willing to make to the offended hierarchy. Their conversation appears to have been conducted in a friendly spirit and manner; the Chaplain holding up the brilliant future that would be realized by Penn, if he would recant some of his opinions; and dwelling on the favorable disposition of the Duke of York and the King, towards him. William told him, "The Tower is the worst argument in the world," and that nothing could induce him to violate his conscientious convictions; so there seemed nothing gained. But suddenly and unexpectedly an order came from the King for his release, and he left the gloomy confines of his prison-house without making any concession, or accepting a pardon. The discharge was believed to have been the work of the Duke of York, and William ever cherished a grateful feeling towards him for this generous act. [1669.]

Although the trials of Margaret Fell and of George Fox had taken place at the same time, in the same court, and both had been premunired and sent to prison, yet George was liberated more than a year before Margaret was suffered to return to her home and children. She was set free by the King's order in 1668, having been incarcerated four years and six months. During her confinement, she wrote several dissertations, which were published, and kept up correspondence with most of the Friends of eminence in the Society. In 1666, she had addressed the King from her prison — Lancaster Castle — in mild but plain and pointed language. She reminded him of the course that had been pursued by the government for six years; bringing hundreds of the servants of Christ to untimely graves, and the oppression and bondage it had inflicted, and was still inflicting, on an innocent, harmless and peaceable people, and recited a promise the King had made to her, in one of her interviews with him, that "If they [Friends] were peaceable, they shall be protected." She pointed out how the Bishops had refused to give Friends an opportunity to declare and explain to them their doctrines, principles and practices; and that she had warned him 'to beware of their counsel, or it would prove his ruin; touching on several other points. "And now," she says, "I ask thee, for which of these things hast thou kept me in prison three long winters, in a place not fit for human beings to live? A place where storm, wind and rain enter, and which is sometimes filled with smoke; so that it is much 'wonder I am alive; and this only because the power and goodness of God have been with me." Then after referring to the warnings which had been given by Friends, to those who were in power before him, to which they would not give heed, she continues, "Now after all my sufferings, in the same feeling of love that I visited thee in the beginning, I once more beseech thee to fear the Lord God, by whom Kings rule, and princes decree justice; who sets up one and pulls down another at his pleasure. And let not the guilt of the breach of that word that passed from thee at Breda, lie any longer on thy conscience; but perform as thou promised in thy distress." But Charles II. was too deeply immersed in the folly and licentiousness of his Court, to care about the weal or woe of a virtuous, Christian woman, shut up in prison a hundred miles off; and so no notice was taken of the letter. Friends, however, did not cease to use all the influence they could command, to obtain the liberty of their suffering brethren and sisters; but as Margaret Fell was a person whose character and presence commanded respect, some about the Court feared her, and it was not until 1668, as before stated, that an order was granted by the King and Council for her discharge.

After the marriage of her daughter Mary to Thomas Lower, which took place about two months after her return to Swarthmoor, and placing her youngest daughter Rachel at the school established for Friends' children at Shacklewell, M. Fell felt herself called to visit the different prisons throughout the country, where any Friend or Friends were confined. She appears to have been engaged in this service about a year, during which time she was doubtless instrumental in administering help and consolation to many, suffering similar affliction for the Truth, as that of which she had been so large a partaker.

At the conclusion of this service, she tarried for some time at her daughter Isabel Yeomans, then residing in Bristol, where she was joined by George Fox, not long after his return from Ireland. He gives the following account of their marriage:

1669. "After this meeting in Gloucestershire, we travelled till we came to Bristol; where I met with Margaret Fell, who was come to visit her daughter Yeomans. I had seen from the Lord a considerable time before, that I should take Margaret Fell to be my wife; and when I first mentioned it to her, she felt the answer of Life from God thereunto. But though the Lord had opened this thing to me, yet I had not received a command from Him for the accomplishing of it then. Wherefore I let the thing rest, and went on in the work and service of the Lord, according as He led me; travelling in this nation, and through Ireland. But now being at Bristol, and finding Margaret Fell there, it opened in me from the Lord that the thing should be accomplished. After we had discoursed the matter together, I told her, 'If she also was satisfied with the accomplishing of it now, she should first send for her children:' which she did. When the rest of her daughters were come, I asked both them and her sons-in-law, 'If they had anything against it, or for it?' and they all severally expressed their satisfaction therewith. Then I asked Margaret, 'If she had fulfilled her husband's will to her children?' She replied, 'The children knew she had.' Whereupon I asked them, 'Whether, if their mother married, they should not lose by it?' I asked Margaret, 'Whether she had done anything in lieu of it, which might answer it to the children?' The children 'said, 'She had answered it to them, and desired me to speak no more of it.' I told them, 'I was plain, and would have all things done plainly: for I sought not any outward advantage to myself.' So our intention of marriage was laid before Friends both privately and publicly, to their full satisfaction, many of whom gave testimony that it was of God. Afterwards, a meeting being appointed on purpose for the accomplishing thereof, in the public meeting-house at Broad Mead in Bristol, we took each other in marriage; the Lord joining us together in the honorable marriage, in the everlasting covenant and immortal Seed of life. In the sense whereof, living and weighty testimonies were borne thereunto, by Friends in the movings of the heavenly power, which united us together. Then was a certificate, relating both to the proceedings and the marriage, openly read, and signed by the relations, and by most of the ancient Friends of that city; besides many others from divers parts of the nation." The Certificate is dated the 18th of Eighth month, 1669; he was in his forty-sixth year, and she ten years older.

After spending a week in Bristol they travelled North, but the Lord's work was not allowed to be neglected, and in a little while they took leave of each other; Margaret going towards her old home at Swarthmoor, now become the property of her daughters by the terms of their father's will, and George Fox travelling through different Shires to London.

The following epistle, addressed by George Fox to the several Quarterly Meetings, is given to show the benevolent care which rested on his mind for the welfare of all classes in the Society, and as indicating the watchful oversight and assistance given by the different branches of the church, in order to preserve all the members within its immediate influence and control, and to promote their present and future well-being.

" My dear Friends : —Let every Quarterly Meeting make inquiry through all the Monthly and other Meetings, to know all Friends that are widows, or others that have children to put out to apprenticeships, so that once a quarter you may set forth an apprentice from your Quarterly Meetings ; so that you may set four in a year in each county, or more if there be occasion. This apprentice, when out of his time, may help his father or mother, and support the family that is decayed ; and in so doing, all may come to live comfortably. This being done in your Quarterly Meetings, ye will have knowledge through the county, in the Monthly and Particular Meetings, of masters fit for them, and of such trades as their parents or you desire, or the children are most inclined to. Thus being placed out to Friends, they may be trained up in the Truth, and by this means, in the wisdom of God, you may preserve Friends' children in the Truth, and enable them to be a strength and help to their families, and nursers and preservers of their relations in their ancient days. Thus also, things being ordered in the wisdom of God, you will take off a continual maintenance, and free yourselves from much cumber. For in the country, ye know, ye may set forth an apprentice for a little to several trades, as bricklayers, masons, carpenters, wheelwrights, ploughwrights, tailors, tanners, curriers, blacksmiths, shoemakers, nailers, butchers, weavers of linen and woollen, stuffs and serges, &c. And you may do well to have a stock in your Quarterly Meetings for that purpose. All that is given by any Friends at their decease, except it be given to some particular use, person, or meeting, may be brought to the public stock for that purpose. This will be a way for preserving of many that are poor among you ; and it will be a way of making up poor families. In several counties it is practised already. Some Quarterly Meetings set forth two apprentices ; and sometimes the children of others that are laid on the parish. You may bind them for fewer or more years, according to their capacities. In all things the wisdom of God will teach you ; by which ye may help the children of poor Friends, that they may come to support their families, and preserve them in the fear of God. So no more, but my love in the everlasting Seed, by which ye will have wisdom to order all things to the glory of God. G. F."

"LONDON, the first of the 11th month, 1669."

George Fox was likewise much concerned that schools should be established, where the children of Friends could obtain liberal education ; and Friends, under his advice, had instituted two boarding-schools, the one at Shacklewell being for girls only, and that for boys at Waltham. The subject of education engaged the attention of Friends almost so soon as meetings were settled, and efforts were early made to secure the means for conferring upon the children of both rich and poor, such learning as would fit them for conducting business, and engaging in the duties of social and civil life. Meetings, both smaller and larger, had this important matter frequently before them ; and the members were often reminded of the duty resting upon them, to see that their offspring had opportunity afforded to acquire learning " in whatsoever things were civil and useful in the creation ; " and above all things that they should be kept under religious restraint and training, so as to grow up in the nurture and admonition of the Lord. Before the end of the century there were from fifteen to twenty seminaries opened.

Friends by no means ignored the use of human reason in the knowledge and work of religion. But they rejected the idea that reason, however developed by culture, and aided by the study of the sacred truths recorded in the Scriptures, is a light or a power sufficient of itself to guide or to enable man to walk in the way of salvation. Christ is the alone Author and Finisher of the saints' faith, and his Light communicated to the soul by the measure of the Holy Spirit, purchased for every human being, must make manifest the things that belong to the soul's peace ; guide, guard and strengthen man in the exercise of his intellectual faculties, as he enters and takes step after step in the strait and narrow way that leads to life eternal. "The natural man receiveth not the things of the Spirit of God, for they are foolishness unto him ; neither can he know them, because they are spiritually discerned."

In 1664, John Burnyeat, whom George Fox calls " a pillar in the house of God," after visiting Ireland, set sail for the plantations in America, stopping on the way at Barbadoes, and visiting the Friends

in that Island. Quite a considerable number of professors with
Friends were settled in that place, and several meetings regularly
held. There were several valuable Friends residing on the Island,
and J. Burnyeat was constantly engaged in religious service among
them for more than three months.

Besse, in his Collection of the Sufferings of Friends, states that
the gospel testimonies, in the faithful support of which Friends in
Barbadoes suffered most, were, to the peaceable principles of the
religion of Christ, and their consequent refusal to bear arms; to the
obligation imposed by the injunction of Christ, Swear not at all,
and their declining to take an oath; and to the headship of Christ
in the church, and his command to those whom He ordains for the
ministry, Freely ye have received, freely give, their unwillingness
therefore to pay tithes or church rates. Beside these, they were
exposed to imprisonment for assembling for the purpose of Divine
worship. There were thirty-six in the common jail at one time for
this; how long they were detained is not stated. The equivalent
of the value of any article in the island was in pounds of sugar, and
fines were levied and rated by that standard. Besse gives a large
number of cases of suffering reported to the Governor and Council,
in an Address presented to them by Friends; showing that between
1664 and 1669 there had been taken property equal in value to
111,124¼ pounds of sugar.

The same course was pursued by the Governor and Council for
several years; increasing the fines, however, so that the next report
of the amount of goods of different kinds, taken between 1669 and
1673, was valued at about 350,000 pounds of sugar. A law was
also enacted to prevent the Quakers having slaves attending their
meetings for worship, and heavy fines were levied on them therefor;
also where it was shown that Friends had had them collected for
the purpose of instructing them in the contents of the Holy Scriptures.

The same persecuting course was pursued towards Friends in the
Islands of Jamaica, Nevis, Antigua and the Bermudas; where many
Friends suffered severely at different times.

John Perrot, when he found he had lost credit and standing in
England; had gone over to the West Indies and America, and in
both places promulgated his peculiar views. Here he took a step
further than in England, and beside objecting to taking off the hat in
time of prayer, as being a mere form, he declared it wrong to have
regular times appointed for offering public worship to the Almighty,

and that it was not right for a Friend to attend at meetings for worship, unless feeling a special call thereto.

John Burnyeat, speaking of his labors in Barbadoes [1664–5], says, "There I also met with many who had been hurt by John Perrot, and carried away with his imaginations." He then speaks of the "high notions and vain conceits of this apostate," and observes, "Such as were taken with his notions, were led out of true order into looseness and such a liberty, that the cross in most things was laid down by them, and their own wills followed, and Truth's testimony let fall. But he run out of the Truth so far at last, that many began to see him and what his spirit led to; and so came to see their own loss, and returned back to their first love; and the power of the Lord went over that dark Spirit, with all the vain imaginations they had been led into thereby, and so Friends were gathered into their former unity."

Leaving the Island, J. Burnyeat sailed for Maryland, where he landed in the Second month of 1665. Friends must have increased largely in that Province, for he says, "I travelled and labored in the work of the gospel in that Province that summer, and we had large meetings; and the Lord's power was with us, and Friends were greatly comforted, and several were convinced." But he states that Thomas Thurston—who has been spoken of as a fellow laborer with Josiah Cole in the work of the ministry in several of the Colonies, and who had been imprisoned in Maryland for a year — had fallen into the errors of J. Perrot, and drawn a party after him, opposed to Friends and their good order. " Great was the exercise and the travail — says this devoted servant of Christ — which was upon my spirit day and night, both upon the truth's account, which suffered by him, and also for the people, who were betrayed by him to their hurt, and were under a great mistake." Another instance of the fallibility of all, even those who " Have tasted the good word of God and the powers of the world to come," and their liability to fall from grace unless obeying the injunction of the Saviour, " What I say unto you I say unto all, watch! watch and pray, lest ye enter into temptation."

1665–6. The "labor and travail in the Lord's wisdom and power," of J. Burnyeat and other faithful Friends, were effectual in searching out the wrong spirit; the delusion and evil doings of T. Thurston were exposed, and "Most of the people came to see through him, and, in the love of God, to be restored into the unity of the Truth again." But such was not the case with him who had been the means of perverting and misguiding them. He, says J. B., " was lost to truth, and became a vagabond and fugitive, as to his spiritual condition, and little otherwise as to the outward."

The unsound notions of J. Perrot had been industriously disseminated by him among Friends in Virginia, while he was visiting there; and many of them having been but recently convinced of the truth as held by Friends, and with but little experience, they too were caught with their apparent greater spirituality, and many of them imbibed them. Once brought under the controlling influence of a spirit which prompted to self-exaltation, and to set at naught the judgment of the church, as come to under the guidance of heavenly wisdom, one step out of right order opened the way for another, and it was not very long before they who had formerly stood so firm, and suffered so much for the cause of Truth, were carried captive by the spirit of the world, and gave up the attendance of the meetings for Divine worship. "Thus — J. Burnyeat writes — by which he [J. Perrot] judged Friends' practices and testimony in and for the Truth, to be but forms; and so pretending to live above such things, he drew Friends from their zeal for the Truth, and their testimony therein so far that they avoided every thing that might occasion suffering. Thus they being seduced or bewitched, as the Galatians were, into a fleshly liberty, the offence of the cross ceased, and the power was lost; and when I came there it was hard to get a meeting among them." Through much effort he at length succeeded in having a meeting held, to which many of them came, and "The Lord's power was with us and among us, and several were revived and refreshed, and through the Lord's goodness and his renewed visitations, [were] raised up into a service of life, and in time came to see over the wiles of the enemy."

As to John Perrot himself, after having wrought so much mischief in the Society, he finally settled in Jamaica; where he threw off the plain appearance of a Friend, and became not only irreligious, but indulged in habits of gross licentiousness, and at last died greatly in debt.

1670. On a second visit to America by J. Burnyeat, he found things much improved among Friends in Virginia and Maryland. "I found a freshness among them — he observes — and many of them were restored and grown up to a degree of their former zeal and tenderness; and I found a great openness in the country, and had several blessed meetings." This was in 1672; during which year a large number of eminent ministers among Friends were travelling through the provinces in America; among whom were George Fox, William Edmundson, Thomas Briggs, John Rouse, Robert Wid, ders, &c.

All these Friends, with Elizabeth Hooten, had embarked in 1671, in the same ship at London, for religious service in the West Indies and America; and after spending some time on the Islands, where, according to the accounts contained in the Journals of G. F. and W. E., their labors were much blessed, most of them crossed over to Maryland. Elizabeth Hooten, however, died at an advanced age, in great peace and joy, while they were in Jamaica.

In consequence of the many slanders circulated respecting the .doctrines held by Friends, their enemies endeavoring thereby to persuade the people that they were unsound in the fundamental doctrines of the Christian religion, George Fox, while in Barbadoes, as he says in his Journal, " With some other Friends, drew up a paper to go forth in the name of the people called Quakers, for the clearing truth and Friends from those false reports," and had it presented to the Governor, Council and other principal men in authority. From that clear and emphatic declaration of doctrine, the following is taken:

" Whereas many scandalous lies and slanders have been cast upon us, to render us odious; as that ' We deny God, Christ Jesus, and the Scriptures of truth,' &c. This is to inform you, That all our books and declarations, which for these many years have been published to the world, clearly testify the contrary. Yet, for your satisfaction, we now *plainly and sincerely* declare, That we own and believe in the only Wise, Omnipotent, and Everlasting God, the Creator of all things in heaven and earth, and the Preserver of all that He hath made; who is God over all, blessed for ever; to whom be all honor, glory, dominion, praise and thanksgiving, both now and for evermore! And we own and believe in Jesus Christ, his beloved and only begotten Son, in whom He is well pleased; who was conceived by the Holy Ghost and born of the Virgin Mary; in whom we have redemption through his blood, even the forgiveness of sins; who is the express image of the Invisible God, the firstborn of every creature, by whom were all things created that are in heaven and in earth, visible and invisible, whether they be thrones, dominions, principalities, or powers; all things were created by Him. And we own and believe that He was made a sacrifice for sin, who knew no sin, neither was guile found in his mouth; that He was crucified for us in the flesh, without the gates of Jerusalem;

and that He was buried, and rose again the third day by the power
of his Father, for our justification; and that He ascended up into
heaven, and now sitteth at the right hand of God. This Jesus, who
was the foundation of the holy prophets and apostles, is our foundation; and we believe there is no other foundation to be laid but that
which is laid, even Christ Jesus: who tasted death for every man,
shed his blood for all men, is the propitiation for our sins, and not
for ours only, but also for the sins of the whole world: according as
John the Baptist testified of Him, when he said, 'Behold the Lamb
of God, that taketh away the sins of the world.' John i. 29. We
believe that He alone is our Redeemer and Saviour, the Captain of
our salvation, who saves us from sin, as well as from hell and the
wrath to come, and destroys the devil and his works; He is the Seed
of the woman that bruises the serpent's head, to wit, Christ Jesus, the
Alpha and Omega, the First and the Last. He is (as the Scriptures of truth say of him) our wisdom, righteousness, justification,
and redemption; neither is there salvation in any other, for there is
no other name under heaven given among men, whereby we may
be saved. He alone is the Shepherd and Bishop of our souls: He
is our Prophet, whom Moses long since testified of, saying, 'A prophet shall the Lord your God raise up unto you of your brethren
like unto me; him shall ye hear in all things, whatsoever he shall
say unto you: and it shall come to pass, that every soul that will
not hear that prophet shall be destroyed from among the people.'
Acts ii. 22, 23. He is now come in Spirit, 'and hath given us an
understanding, that we know Him that is true.' He rules in our
hearts by his law of love and life, and makes us free from the law
of sin and death. We have no life, but by him; for He is the
quickening Spirit, the second Adam, the Lord from heaven, by
whose blood we are cleansed, and our consciences sprinkled from
dead works, to serve the living God. He is our Mediator, who makes
peace and reconciliation between God offended and us offending;
He being the Oath of God, the new covenant of light, life, grace,
and peace, the author and finisher of our faith. This Lord Jesus
Christ, the heavenly man, the Emanuel, God with us, we all own
and believe in; *He whom the high-priest raged against, and said, he
had spoken blasphemy; whom the priests and elders of the Jews took
counsel together against, and put to death; the same whom Judas betrayed for thirty pieces of silver, which the priest gave him as a reward for his treason;* who also gave large money to the soldiers to
broach an horrible lie, namely, 'That his disciples came and stole

him away by night whilst they slept.' After He was risen from the dead, the history of the Acts of the apostles sets forth how the chief priest and elders persecuted the disciples of this Jesus, for preaching Christ and his resurrection. *This, we say, is that Lord Jesus Christ, whom we own to be our life and salvation.*

"Concerning the Holy Scriptures, we believe they were given forth by the holy Spirit of God, through the holy men of God, who (as the Scripture itself. declares, 2 Pet. i. 21,) 'spoke as they were moved by the Holy Ghost.' We believe they are to be read, believed, and fulfilled (He that fulfils them is Christ); and they are 'profitable for doctrine, for reproof, for correction, for instruction in righteousness, that the man of God may be perfect, thoroughly furnished unto all good works,' 2 Tim. iii. 17, and are able to 'make wise unto salvation, through faith which is in Christ Jesus.' We believe the Holy Scriptures are the words of God; for it is said in Exodus xx. 1, 'God spake all these *words*, saying,' &c., meaning the ten commandments given forth upon Mount Sinai. And in Rev. xxii. 18, saith John, 'I testify to every man that heareth the *words* of the prophecy of this book, if any man addeth unto these, and if any man shall take away from the *words* of the book of this prophecy', (not the Word), &c. So in Luke i. 20, 'Because. thou believest not my *words*.' And in John v. 47, xv. 7, xiv. 23, xii. 47. So that we call the Holy Scriptures, as Christ, the apostles, and holy men of God called them, viz., the words of God."

After a tempestuous voyage of over six weeks, they arrived in Chesapeake Bay, in the Second month of 1672; and landing near the mouth of Patuxent River, they learned that John Burnyeat had appointed a meeting at West River, for all the Friends in the Province of Maryland. To that meeting these Friends at once went, and George Fox says of it, "A very large meeting this was, and held four days; to which, besides Friends, came many other people, divers of whom were of considerable quality in the world's account, . . . who seemed well satisfied with the meeting." In the meeting for business, "for establishing the blessed order of the gospel of Christ Jesus," J. Burnyeat observes, "George Fox did wonderfully open the service thereof to Friends, and they with gladness of heart received advice in such necessary things as were then opened to them, and all were comforted and edified."

There was great eagerness among the inhabitants of Maryland and Virginia to hear George Fox, when it became known that he was in the country. There were very few professed ministers of the

gospel, connected with other religious Societies, to be found in those
Provinces; though much care had been taken to make known the want
of the people in this respect, and to hold out such pecuniary inducements as their circumstances would allow them to offer. Consequently, as the presence and services of a minister were deemed necessary
by them for holding a meeting for worship, comparatively few were
held, and it was a rarity to hear a sermon delivered. When therefore it was noised abroad that the "great founder of the Quakers,"
was come among them to preach the gospel, the people crowded to
his meetings. Officers of the highest rank, both civil and military,
followed him from place to place, and several were convinced.

1672. Referring to a General Meeting, held at Treadhaven, G.
Fox says, "This meeting held five days. The first three we had meetings for public worship, to which people of all sorts came; the other
two were spent in the men's and women's meetings. To those public meetings came many Protestants of divers sorts, and some Papists;
amongst whom were several Magistrates and their wives, with other
persons of chief account in the country. Of the common people, it
was thought there were sometimes a thousand at one of those meetings;
so that though they had enlarged their meeting-place, and made it as
big again as it was before, it could not contain the people. I went
by boat every day four or five miles to the meeting, and there were
so many boats at that time passing upon the river, that it was almost
like the Thames. The people said, 'There were never so many boats
seen there together before;' and one of the Justices said, 'He never
saw so many people together in that country.' It was a very heavenly meeting, wherein the presence of the Lord was gloriously
manifested, Friends were sweetly refreshed, the people generally
satisfied and many convinced; for the blessed power of the Lord
was over all: everlasting praises to his holy name forever! After
the public meetings were over, the men's and women's began, and
were held the other two days: for I had something to impart to
them, which concerned the glory of God, the order of the gospel, and
the government of Christ Jesus. When these meetings were over,
we took our leave of Friends in those parts, whom we left well
established in the truth."

Though Friends increased largely in Maryland and Virginia,
they continued to suffer much in support of their testimony against
oaths, and bearing arms. They were despoiled not only by heavy
fines levied upon them, but by being debarred from collecting debts
due from persons disposed to cheat; from being prevented serving

as executors, and from occupying other offices which would have enabled them to protect themselves, and render essential service to the community.

1671. William Edmundson appears to have been the first ministering Friend who travelled into Carolina, and he encountered great hardships in his journey. Two Friends from Virginia agreed to accompany him, and they set out on horseback, having nothing to guide them through the wilderness but an occasional marked tree. Becoming entangled in swamps and rivers, and he who was to be guide, becoming uncertain what course to take, Wm. Edmundson says, "I, perceiving he was at a loss, turned my mind to the Lord, and as He led me, I led the way. So we travelled in many difficulties until about sunset; then they told me they could travel no further, for they both fainted, being weak-spirited men. I bid them stay there and kindle a fire, and I would ride a little farther; for I saw a bright horizon appear through the woods, which travellers take for a mark of some plantation. I rode on to it and found it was only tall timber trees without under-wood. But I perceived a small path which I followed until it was dark, and rained violently: then I alighted and set my back to a tree, until it abated. It being dark and the wood thick I walked all night between two trees, and though very weary I durst not lie down on the ground, for my clothes were wet to my skin. I had eaten little or nothing that day, neither had I anything to refresh me, but the Lord. In the morning I returned to seek my two companions, and found them lying by a great fire of wood." William continuing to lead the way, they arrived at the place they wished to reach; which was the house of a Friend named Henry Phillips, who had joined the Society in New England, and moved into North Carolina. The family had not seen a Friend for seven years, and wept for joy, on meeting their visitors. The people, sparsely scattered through the country, rejoiced to hear the sound of the gospel. William had meetings in several places, and though he says they "seemed to have little or no religion, and sat down in the meetings smoking their pipes," yet, he adds, "The Lord's testimony arose in the authority of his power, and their hearts being reached by it, several of them were tendered, and received the testimony."

1672. Not long after William Edmundson had returned out of North Carolina, it was visited by George Fox, Robert Widders, and two other Friends. The Friends were courteously received and entertained by the Governor, and George Fox represents, "The people were tender, and much desired after meetings." While at the Governor's house, a doctor present denied the doctrine of Universal Saving Light, which Friends preached ; saying it was not in the Indians. George Fox states, " Whereupon I called an Indian to us, and asked him, ' Whether or no, when he did lie, or do wrong to any one, there was not something in him that did reprove him for it ? He said there was such a thing in him that did so reprove him ; and he was ashamed when he had done wrong, or spoken wrong.' So we shamed the doctor before the Governor and people ; insomuch that the poor man ran out so far, that at length he would not own the Scriptures." There was a rapid increase in the Society in North Carolina, and it was not long before meetings for discipline were established among them.

It should be stated to the credit of those who held and exercised authority in the governments of North and South Carolina, that no attempt was ever made by them to abridge or trespass upon the rights of conscience. Friends enjoyed unlimited freedom in the promulgation and practice of their religious principles, and repeatedly occupied the more responsible posts in the government.

While in North Carolina as in Virginia, George Fox was drawn in Christian feeling towards the aborigines of the country, and he repeatedly obtained opportunities to proclaim the truths of the gospel to them, and to invite them to partake of the unsearchable riches of Christ. After a meeting in North Carolina, at which the Governor and his Secretary were present, he says : " I went from this place among the Indians, and spoke to them by an interpreter, showing them, ' That God made all things in six days, and made but one woman for one man ; and that God did drown the old world because of their wickedness. Afterwards I spoke to them concerning Christ, showing them that He died for all men, for *their* sins, as well as for others ; and had enlightened them as well as others ; and that if they did that which was evil He would burn them ; but if they did well they should not be burned.' There was among them their young king and others of their chief men, who seemed to receive kindly what I said to them."

The account given by George Fox of his perilous journey in returning out of Virginia into Maryland, and to the place of embarkation for England, gives a vivid picture of the wilderness condition of the country, and the difficulties and dangers the travellers had to encounter. He and his companions appear to have crossed Chesapeake Bay in an open boat, and pursued their course in the same kind of conveyance on different rivers; occasionally landing, holding meetings, and crossing sections of the country on horseback. Day and night they were exposed to the severe cold of an inclement winter, amid heavy snows, and often without the means to obtain warmth or other refreshment. But he seemed never to grow weary in the service of his Lord and Master; having learned in whatsoever condition that service brought him, therein to be content. He says, " Having travelled through most parts of that cuontry [the different colonies], and visited most of the plantations, having alarmed people of all sorts where we came, and proclaimed the day of God's salvation amongst them, our spirits began to be clear of those parts of the world, and draw towards old England again." He embarked for home on the 21st day of the Third month, 1673.

Attracted by the mildness of the climate, the good condition of the soil, and above all, the accorded right to partake of all the benefits of citizenship, without their religious faith and testimonies being interfered with, some Friends had settled in different parts of South Carolina,—probably prior to G. Fox's visit in North Carolina, —and though there is no account of any of the ministers who came over from England in the early establishment of the Society in other colonies, visiting them, they must have soon increased in number and exercised much influence. In an epistle from G. Fox to Friends in Charleston, dated Twelfth month, 1683, after expressing his satis- faction at having received a letter from them, giving an account of their meeting in that town, he says, " My desire is that you may prize your liberty, both natural and spiritual, and the favor that the Lord hath given you; that your yea is taken instead of an oath; as that you do serve both in assemblies, juries and other offices without swearing, according to the doctrine of Christ; which is a great thing, worth prizing. And take heed of abusing that liberty, or losing the savor of the heavenly salt, which seasons your lives and conversation with truth, holiness and righteousness: for you know when the salt hath lost its savor, it is good for nothing but to be trodden under foot of men."

Some time about the year 1684, John Archdale, a member among Friends, was chosen to be Governor of South Carolina, and while in the office, corresponded with George Fox; giving him some account of the state of the country, of the condition of Friends, and some circumstances connected with the conduct of the Indians.

During the time of severe suffering through which Friends were passing in Great Britain after the Restoration [1661] as was natural, on finding that redress or abatement of their grievances were almost beyond hope, they seriously entertained a project for finding homes somewhere beyond the reach of their fellow-men, who seemed bent on extirpating them by the slow process of the cruel punishments inflicted for their religious faith. George Fox, in common with several other prominent members, seriously contemplated the purchase of a tract of land from the Indians in North America; where not the whole body of Friends in Great Britain, but such as felt themselves free to leave their native land, might emigrate and enjoy the right of worshipping the Almighty according to the dictates of their consciences.

Josiah Cole while engaged in religious service in America [1661] was commissioned to look out, and enter into treaty for such a resting place; and at one time he had several interviews with the chiefs of the Susquehanna Indians, in order to treat with them for a part of their territory. Owing to a war coming on between that tribe and another, the proposed purchase fell through. But when New Jersey was finally brought under the government of Charles II. by the treaty between the English and Dutch in 1674, and Berkeley — who with Carteret was Proprietary of the Colony — was disposed to sell his share in it, it was bought by Edward Billinge and John Fenwick, two Friends, for £1,000 [1675]; it being understood that the purchase was made for the benefit of such members of the Society as chose to avail themselves of it.

Friends from New York and New England had occasionally settled on the eastern side of New Jersey, and as early as 1670 there was a meeting for worship regularly held at Shrewsbury, and another at Amboy. A Monthly Meeting was shortly after established at Shrewsbury. George Fox, when on his way from New England to Maryland and Virginia [1672], passed through Shrewsbury, and says, "On First-day we had a precious meeting there, to which Friends and other people came from far, and the blessed presence of the Lord was with us." . . . "They are building a meeting-house in the midst of them, and there is a Monthly and a General Meeting set up, which will be of great service in those parts, for keeping up the gospel order and government of Christ Jesus."

A disagreement arising between the two Friends who were purchasers from Berkley, it was a considerable time before it was adjusted; William Penn as Arbitrator finally bringing it to a settlement. Billinge having become embarrassed in his circumstances, made over all his right and title to four Friends—of whom William Penn was one — for the benefit of his creditors. [1676.] Fenwick being desirous to go over to New Jersey, borrowed a sum of money, for which he gave a mortgage on such part of the territory as pertained to him, with liberty to the mortgagees to sell the land, until their claim was satisfied. He, however, on arriving in the Delaware, settled at a spot on the side of a creek that emptied into the river, gave his intended village the name of Salem, and began at once to make grants of land to settlers.

The four Friends acting for the creditors of Billinge [of whom William Penn was the most active], took steps to have a line run between that part of New Jersey still remaining in possession of Carteret, one of the original proprietors, and that which had now come into their possession. It extended from Little Eggharbor to where the 41° of North latitude crosses the Delaware river, and the two portions afterwards were called East and West Jersey. A form of government was agreed on for West Jersey, and a declaration of fundamental principles to be incorporated in it, consented to; among which was the stipulation, "No person to be called in question or molested for his conscience, or for worshipping according to his conscience."

These fundamental laws were adopted in 1676, and a description of the Province was published in England. At once so many began to make preparation to become settlers therein, that the four Friends, fearful that some of their brethren might be hurried into so important a step unadvisedly, issued an address, in which they extend a caution, " Lest any of them, as is feared by some, should go out of a curious and unsettled mind, and others to shun the blessed cross of Jesus; of which several weighty Friends have a godly jealousy upon their spirits; lest any unwarrantable forwardness should act or hurry any beside or beyond the wisdom and counsel of the Lord, or the freedom of his Light and Spirit in their own hearts, and not upon good and weighty grounds."

Many Friends of good estates, and highly esteemed for their religious standing and experience, crossed the Atlantic to this land of liberty, and between 1676 and 1681 about fourteen hundred had arrived and settled, principally in the country bordering the eastern shore of the Delaware. These immigrants suffered the privations and hardships incident to beginning civilized life in an unbroken wilderness, surrounded by savages, who were dependent in great measure upon the uncertain supplies of the chase for their own sus-

tenance, and who rarely laid up much in store for future wants.
But by uniform uprightness in all their dealings with these children
of the forest, and their Christian kindness towards them, they soon
gained their good will, and in times of scarcity, excited their sympathy; so that often they were relieved by voluntary offerings of
corn and meat from these untutored red men, when it seemed as
though otherwise they must have suffered for food.

Proud, in the preface to his History of Pennsylvania, gives in a
note an account of these trials, drawn up by one of the Friends who
settled in New Jersey, containing the following passages:

"A providential hand was very visible and remarkable in many
instances that might be mentioned, and the Indians were even rendered our benefactors and protectors. Without any carnal weapon,
we entered the land and inhabited therein, as safe as if there had
been thousands of garrisons; for the Most High preserved us from
harm both of man and beast." "The aforesaid people [Friends]
were zealous in performing their religious services; for having at
first no meeting-house to keep a public meeting in, they made a
tent or covert of sail-cloth to meet under; and after they got some
little houses to dwell in, then they kept their meetings in one of
them till they could build a meeting-house."

Being thus impressed with a just sense of religious duty, meetings
were soon established in different places, and in the early part of
1678, a Monthly Meeting was regularly constituted at Burlington;
which being embarrassed by persons coming within its limits and
professing to be Friends, but bringing no certificates, addressed an
epistle to London Yearly Meeting in 1680, in reference thereto,
which is believed to be the first communication of the kind received
by that meeting from a meeting of Friends in America.

The settlements of Friends on the part of New Jersey bordering
on the Delaware River increasing, meetings were settled at Wood-
bury Creek, Cooper's Creek, Rancocas, and other places, as the land
was taken up. Salem was the first meeting of Friends held in West
Jersey, and in the course of comparatively short time, a Quarterly
Meeting was held there, composed of the members of Salem and
Newtown Monthly Meeting. A Quarterly Meeting appears to have
been established at Burlington about the year 1680, which extended
its jurisdiction over the Monthly Meeting at Shrewsbury.

General notice having been spread among Friends throughout
the Colony, a General Meeting was held at Burlington in the Sixth
month of 1681. It held four days, and the times and places for

holding meetings for worship and discipline were decided on. It was also agreed to hold a Yearly Meeting for worship at Salem, in the Second month of each year, and that the Yearly Meeting for discipline should assemble at Burlington in the Seventh month of every year.

In 1679, George Carteret, the proprietor of East Jersey, died, and by his will directed the whole of his portion of the Province to be sold to pay his debts. It was bought by twelve persons, nearly all of whom were Friends, William Penn and Ambrose Rigge being among them. These associated twelve more with them as proprietors, and in 1683, they chose Robert Barclay, of Ury, to be Governor of the Province for life, who exercised the functions of his office by deputy for two years. A large number of Presbyterians, driven from their homes in Scotland by the inhuman treatment of the government incited by the prelates and clergy, during the attempt of the latter to fasten the Episcopal Church polity upon the people of that portion of Great Britain, came over and settled in East Jersey, where they increased and became a leading portion of the Christian Church. Friends multiplied about Shrewsbury, Amboy, Rahway, and a few other settlements, but they were never so numerous in East as in West Jersey.

CHAPTER XXIII.

Purchase of Pennsylvania by W. Penn—Form of Government established by W. Penn — Rapid Settlement by Friends—Meetings set up—Indian Treaty — Yearly Meeting—Friends in New York and New England—Visits of J. Burnyeat, G. Fox and W. Edmundson — Dispute with Roger Williams — Further Check to Persecution in N. England — Spirit of Persecution still alive — Wm. Edmundson again in America — At Hartford.

IN the course of the business which necessarily claimed his attention as a trustee or a proprietor of the province of New Jersey, William Penn naturally had his thoughts frequently directed towards the settlements of his countrymen on the far distant shores of America; and having been disappointed in the part he took in English politics, in an unsuccessful effort to procure the election of his friend Algernon Sidney to Parliament, his interest in that section of the world increased, and his mind became occupied with the idea of settling a free Colony in the.pathless wilderness on the other side of the Atlantic; where men should live under an elective government, enact the laws by which they were to be controlled, admit of no master, but all share in equal rights, and rest in the enjoyment of civil and religious liberty. Witnessing the success that attended the removal of Friends to New Jersey, where they were freed from the cruel persecution they had endured while in Great Britain, under which their brethren at home were still suffering grievously, he became desirous to obtain the control of such portion of the yet unappropriated territory over which the King of England claimed the sovereignty, as would enable him to found a Colony, and " make a holy experiment "— as he called it — of opening an asylum for the oppressed of every land; where there should be secured equality of political and civil rights, universal liberty of conscience, personal freedom, and a just regard for the rights of property.

Admiral Penn at different times had loaned money to the British government, and to the Duke of York; which the costly profligacy of the Court had prevented being repaid, and with the interest accruing, it amounted at that time to between sixteen and seventeen thousand pounds sterling. In 1680, William Penn petitioned the King, that in order to cancel the debt, he should grant him the tract of country bounded on the east by the Delaware River, and on the south by Lord Baltimore's Province of Maryland; while the western and northern limits were undefined; though the latter was not to interfere with the Province of New York. But William Penn was by no means popular at the Court. The courtiers despised him for his strict conscientiousness: the clerical party hated him for his Quakerism, and open opposition to their assumed place and power; while the active interest he had taken in promoting the return of Sidney — a known Republican — to Parliament, had given offence to the King and Duke. Private interests and jealousies were also enlisted against him, and the agents of Lord Baltimore and Sir John Werden, deputy for the Duke of York, were assiduous in their efforts to thwart him, and defeat his application.

But he was a man not easily turned aside from pursuing that which he thought right to attain. The Earl of Sutherland was his firm friend in the Privy Council, and there were several other persons of note who took warm interest in the success of his colonial project. Penn sought and obtained an interview with the Duke of York, and succeeded in changing his feelings towards himself, and his views relative to the policy of the grant. But, perhaps, the most cogent argument with the King and Council was, the persistent presentation by one of the latter, that if the grant was withheld, the money due must be forthcoming. There were many vexatious delays and disappointments; but finally the boundaries of the Province being adjusted, as was then thought clearly and definitely, and such clauses introduced into the terms of the patent or charter, as were deemed necessary to secure the paramount authority of the King, Charles affixed his signature to it on the 4th of the Third month, 1681. Wm. Penn proposed to call his Province, New Wales; but the Secretary, who was a Welshman, would not consent to it. He then suggested Sylvania, to which the King prefixed Penn, out of respect to the late Admiral; and though William objected to it, as savoring of vanity in him, it was determined to adhere to that name.

This is not the place to enter into an account of the provisions of the Charter, but it may be stated, that William Penn was made sole and absolute proprietary of the Province; with power, with the assent of the freemen residing therein, to make all necessary laws, provided they were not inconsistent with the laws of England; to grant pardons or reprieves, except in cases of wilful murder or treason, and to enjoy all such duties on imports or exports, as the representatives of the people might assess. There was a clause in the Charter — inserted at the solicitation of the Bishop of London — that whenever twenty of the inhabitants should petition the said Bishop for a preacher, he should be permitted to reside in the Province.

Being now feudal sovereign of so extensive a territory, so far as the act of the King and Council could make him, Wm. Penn published a description of the natural features and resources of the country, and invited those who were disposed to change their place of abode, and prepared to emigrate, to resort to Pennsylvania, and under its Christian government and special privileges, secure the blessings of freedom and political equality. He did not disappoint his friends in their expectation of the benign form of government he afterwards instituted. It was democratic in its spirit, and its provisions were liberal, and fitted to meet the demands of the broad principles of popular rights, as they were from time to time developed. The article in relation to liberty of conscience deserves to be noticed, as the public declaration of the principles of Friends on that point, where they had the power of government in their own hands.

"Almighty God being only Lord of Conscience, Father of lights and spirits, and the author as well as object of all Divine knowledge, faith and worship; who only can enlighten the mind, and persuade and convince the understanding of people, in due reverence to his authority over the souls of mankind: It is enacted by the authority aforesaid, [General Assembly met at Chester, 12th month, 4th, 1682,] that no person now, or at any time hereafter living in this Province, who shall confess and acknowledge one Almighty God, to be the Creator, upholder and ruler of the world, and that professeth him or herself obliged in conscience to live peaceably and justly under the civil government, shall in any wise be molested or prejudiced for his or her conscientious persuasion or practice; nor shall he or she at any time be compelled to frequent or maintain any religious worship, place or ministry whatever, contrary to his or her mind; but shall freely and fully enjoy his or her Christian liberty in that respect, without any interruption or reflection. And if any person shall abuse or deride any other, for his or her different persuasion and practice in matter of religion, such shall be looked upon as a disturber of the peace, and be punished accordingly."

There were no oaths exacted, and no provision made for military defence. He exempted from the penalty of death two hundred crimes for which that punishment was inflicted in England, though life was to be forfeited for wilful murder. With a view of connecting reformation with punishment by imprisonment, prisoners were to be kept at work, and subjected to moral discipline. And it was enacted "That as a careless and corrupt administration of justice draws the wrath of God upon Magistrates, so the wildness and looseness of the people provoke the indignation of God against a country; therefore, that all such offences against God, as swearing, cursing, lying, profane talking, drunkenness, drinking of healths, obscene words, and several other scandalous acts particularly named, treasons, misprisions, duels, murders, felony, sedition, maims, forcible entries, and other violences to the persons and estates of the inhabitants of the Province; all prizes, stage-plays, cards, dice, may-games, gamesters, masques, revels, bull-baiting, cock-fightings, bear-baitings, and the like, which excite the people to rudeness, cruelty and irreligion, shall be respectively discouraged and severely punished, according to the appointment of the Governor and freemen in provincial council and general assembly."

George Fox had repeatedly expressed his Christian solicitude for the colored people held as slaves, at that time, by Friends. He had strongly urged upon all who held them, to see to their instruction, especially in the truths of the gospel as recorded in the Scriptures; that after serving for a certain time they should be freed, and that provision should be made for their comfortable enjoyment of old age. William Penn, in the charter he granted to "The Free Society of Traders," inserted the following article, showing how fully he sympathized in this feeling of G. Fox's, and his desire to promote manumission after a term of service. "Black servants to be free, at fourteen years, and, on giving to the Society two-thirds of what they can produce on land allotted to them by the Society, with stock and tools. If they agree not to this, to be servants until they do."

There were about two thousand inhabitants—exclusive of Indians —mostly English, Swedes and Dutch, when William Penn took possession of his Province. The well known character of the Proprietor, the strong inducements offered by the system of government proposed, and the natural advantages from soil and climate of the newly opened domain, all acted as powerful incentives to emigrate; not only to men who were struggling hardly and uncertainly at their native home for the means of subsistence, but to others, who, though with sufficient to live comfortably where they were, were anxious to escape from the intolerant oppression of a Court and hierarchy bent on-enforcing the alternatives of conformity to certain prescribed dogmas of their own construction, or suffering, if not ruin, by imprisonment or deprivation of estate.

William Penn arrived in Pennsylvania in 1682, and in that year and the two following, fifty vessels came into the Delaware river, bringing several thousand emigrants; the most of them from Great Britain, and some from Germany. Nearly all of them were professors with Friends, and many, substantial consistent members, who came under a sense of religious duty, and made the practice of the religion they had embraced, the primary object of life. Some had the benefit of a liberal education, while the great body, farmers, mechanics or tradesmen, had acquired but the rudiments of English school learning. Many possessed considerable property, paying cash for the land they took up; and, generally, the others soon found means to make themselves independent.

Those who came first, as was to be expected, had to encounter the difficulties and privations usually attending pioneers in an uncultivated forest. Some who brought the frames of small houses with them, were not long in obtaining a comfortable shelter; but very many were obliged to content themselves with hastily constructed shanties, under the over-arching branches of trees; while some dug caves in the bank of the river, and made out to obtain in them some of the comforts of a home. This was before William Penn came out, but Richard Townsend, who came in the same ship with him, thus speaks of his experience. "At our arrival we found it a wilderness; the chief inhabitants were Indians: there were some Swedes, who received us in a friendly manner; and although there was a great number of us, the good hand of Providence was seen in a particular manner, in that provisions were found for us by the Swedes and Indians, at very reasonable rates; as well as brought from divers other parts, that were inhabited before. Our first concern was to keep up and maintain our religious worship, and in order thereto, we had several meetings in the houses of the inhabitants; and one boarded meeting-house was set up, where the city was to be, (near the Delaware;) and as we had nothing but love and good will in our hearts one to another, we had very comfortable meetings from time to time, and after our meeting was over, we assisted each other in building little houses for our shelter."

The high motives that prompted them to exile themselves from their native land, and the fervent religious concern to be engaged in promoting the spread of the Redeemer's Kingdom, which warmed their hearts, enabled them to bear all they had to endure with cheerfulness. One of them thus expresses himself: "Our business in this new land, is not so much to build houses, and establish factories, and promote trade and manufactures, that may enrich ourselves (though all these things, in their due place, are not to be neglected), as to erect temples of holiness and righteousness, which God may delight in; to lay such lasting frames and foundations of temperance and virtue, as may support the future superstructures of our happiness, both in this and the other world."

Prior to the purchase of Pennsylvania by William Penn, some Friends had crossed out of Jersey, and settled on and near the west bank of the Delaware. [1677.] As usual, they had begun holding meetings for Divine worship as soon as they were fixed in homes, and these meetings were kept up; being attached to the Monthly Meeting held in Burlington. With the increase of colonists was a corresponding increase of meetings; so that in the First month of 1683, Friends informed their brethren in England, "In Pennsylvania there is one [a meeting] at Falls, one at the Governor's house [Pennsbury], one at Colchester river, all in the county of Bucks; one at Tacony, one at Philadelphia, both in that county; one at Darby, at J. Blunston's, one at Chester, one at Ridley, and one at Wm. Ruse's at Chichester. There be three Monthly Meetings of men and women, for Truth's service; — in the county of Chester one; in the county of Philadelphia one, and in the county of Bucks, another. And [we] intend a Yearly Meeting in the Third month next. Here our care is, as it was in our native land, that we may serve the Lord's truth and people.

. . . . Dear Friends and brethren, we have no cause to murmur; our lot is fallen every way in a goodly place, and the love of God is, and is growing among us, and we are a family of peace within ourselves, and truly great is our joy therefor."

The following is the Introductory Minute entered on the Minute Book of the Monthly Meeting of Friends established in Philadelphia.

" The first meeting of Friends to treat of business occurring among themselves, was at Philadelphia yᵉ ninth day of yᵘ 11th month, being yᵉ third day of yᵉ week in yᵉ year 1682; the proceedings whereof were as followeth, viz. :

" The friends of God belonging to the meeting in Philadelphia, in yᵉ Province of Pennsylvania, being met in yᵉ fear and power of yᵉ Lord, at yᵉ present meeting-place, in yᵉ said city, yᵉ ninth day of yᵉ 11th month, being yᵉ third of yᵘ week, in yᵉ year 1682. They did take into consideration yᵉ settlement of meetings therein, for yᵉ affairs and service of Truth; according to that Godly and comely practice and example which they had received and enjoyed with true satisfaction amongst their friends and brethren in yᵉ land of their nativity; and did then and there agree, that yᵉ first third-day of yᵉ week in every month shall hereafter be yᵉ Monthly Meeting day for yᵉ men's and women's meetings, for yᵉ affairs and service of Truth, in this city and county, and every third meeting shall be the Quarterly Meeting of yᵉ same."

In taking possession, and in the settlement of Pennsylvania, it had been a subject of much solicitude and care with William Penn, that the whole conduct of the settlers in their intercourse with the aborigines, should be so marked with kindness, and with consideration for their rights and national customs, as to secure their good will and influence them to live in peace and harmony with the new comers upon their soil. Before coming over himself he had appointed three Commissioners to see to the necessary arrangements for the reception and settlement of the colonists, to lay out the site for a town, and to treat with the Indians. By these he sent an address to the latter, in which he tells them it is his desire to enjoy the country over which he had been made Governor, "With their love and consent, that we may always live together as neighbors and friends;" and as he had heard that in some places impositions had been practised upon them which had produced animosity and revenge, it was his sincere desire, and should be his practice, and the practice of those he should send, to treat with them justly for their lands, and to make and preserve a firm treaty of peace. [1681.]

When, after his arrival on the shores of the Delaware, he had met the Colonial Assembly elected by the inhabitants, and the necessary laws were enacted, and had transacted some other business immediately pressing upon him, he gave the necessary attention to select the location of the future city, to which he gave the name of Philadelphia. Afterwards he went on to New York, and visited Friends there and on Long Island and in New Jersey. On his return from this journey, he took the necessary measures to have the chiefs of the tribes of Indians occupying that portion of the Province which was likely to be soon required by the settlers, to meet him in council. The place of meeting was in Shackamaxon, a little north of the city, and on the Delaware river. There, under the wide-spread branches of a noble elm tree, was held the treaty of friendship and perpetual peace between the natives, the Governor, and the immigrant Friends, which has become world renowned as the *Great Indian Treaty*. Made in good faith and honesty, by both parties, this treaty was defaced by no oaths, and remained unbroken so long as Friends held the reins of power in the government. Under its provisions, there sprung up a confiding intimacy between the red men and the white; and so long as the Christian policy inaugurated by William Penn and his brethren in religious profession, was adhered to, there was no case of wrong or misunderstanding occurred, which was not speedily settled and removed by resort to the peaceable and just means provided for in its stipulations.

Thus the benign and peaceable principles of the gospel, as laid down by Christ and his Apostles and adopted by Friends, were closely adhered to and fully tested in the settlement of Pennsylvania; and the experience of seventy years of uninterrupted peace and prosperity, while the Province was under the control of Friends, conclusively proves how far they exceed all other rules and motives of conduct, however devised by the wisdom of man or enforced by military power. The enlightened and liberal policy of the settlers, together with the simplicity of manners and refinement, evinced in their domestic and social economy and general intercourse, contributed to the powerful attraction exerted by the Colony on all who were disposed to escape from the tyrannous exactions and almost continuous commotions agitating and embittering civil society in Europe.

The just and loving manner in which William Penn treated the Indians from the beginning of his intercourse with them, and the peaceable principles, not only professed, but continually acted on by the settlers, beside gaining the confidence of the tribe immediately surrounding them, spread their fame to others more distant; so that during the stay of the Proprietor, when on his first visit to his Province, he made treaties of friendship and amity with nearly twenty different tribes. Nor were the expenditures for the land purchased, a mere nominal sum, palmed upon the ignorant natives, easily caught with showy goods, and unaccustomed to estimate things at their real value. From the accounts preserved of these bargains and sales, it appears, that during his lifetime, the Proprietor expended over twenty thousand pounds in the purchase of that portion of the soil which was ceded to him by the aborigines; and yet they were not required to abstain from hunting or fishing within its boundaries, and the laws were so framed as to give them the protection of citizens.

The influx of settlers was unprecedented; the forest began to be cleared, and dwellings were put up rapidly. The soil yielded abundantly, and no calamity occurred for years to check the rapid increase of inhabitants, or create doubts and dissatisfaction as to the course they had taken, in removing from their native country. New meetings for worship were established, as the new-comers took up lands in the counties contiguous to the city; so that in 1684, Wm. Penn wrote, there were eighteen in all, and all were brought within the order of church government, as laid down in the discipline then adopted.

The Friends from this Province attended the Yearly Meeting held in Burlington, New Jersey, in the Seventh month of 1683. The holding a General Meeting of Friends in the middle and southern Provinces having claimed the consideration of that meeting, the following minute was made thereto:

" Whereas this meeting judged it requisite for the benefit and advantage of Truth, and mutual comfort of Friends, that a General Yearly Meeting might be established for the Provinces in these parts, northward as far as New England, and southward as far as

Carolina, that by the coming of Friends together from the several parts where the Truth is professed, the affairs thereof may be better known and understood; and to the end the same may be assented to by Friends in those parts and places, as above mentioned, it is agreed that William Penn, Christopher Taylor, Samuel Jennings, James Harrison, Thomas Olive and Mahlon Stacy do take sure methods, by writing to Friends or speaking, as may best fall out for their conveniency, in order to have the same established."

In 1683, a few weeks after the adjournment of the Yearly Meeting held at Burlington, a General Meeting was held in Philadelphia, but if minutes of its proceedings were made they were not preserved. Yearly Meetings were again held in 1684, in both Burlington and Philadelphia. By the latter an epistle was sent to Friends in London, in which is the following: "At the two aforementioned General Meetings, we had such a blessed harmony together, that we may say we know not that there was a jarring string among us. Glorious was God in his power amongst us. A great multitude came of many hundreds, and the gospel bell made a most blessed sound. There was the men's and women's meetings at both places, in their precious services, to inspect into Truth's matters, in what related to them; and God gave them wisdom to do it, and all was unanimous."

It appears from this, that at that early day, women Friends held a Yearly Meeting in those two Provinces, and there is evidence that one or both of them also addressed an epistle to their sisters in England.

In 1685 there were present at the General Yearly Meeting held in Philadelphia, Friends who had been appointed to attend from Rhode Island, and from the Quarterly Meetings of Choptank and Herring Creek, in Maryland; and after solid deliberation it was concluded to establish one General Yearly Meeting for Friends of Pennsylvania and west New Jersey and adjacent Provinces; to be held alternately at Burlington and Philadelphia, beginning at Burlington in 1686. A General Meeting continued to be held at Salem, New Jersey, and from accounts given in Journals of Friends who attended it at different times, it would appear that it exercised some control over the meetings in its neighborhood.

Having brought the account of the settlement of New Jersey and Pennsylvania by Friends up to the above date, it is now time to return to the condition of the Society in other Colonies, where Friends had long had meetings established.

The persecution of Friends in the Colony of New Amsterdam

[New York], had been stopped by the Dutch Government, as has been already stated; but while the Province remained under the control of the Dutch, and for some time after it came into possession of the English, there were no Friends settled in the town. On Long Island, there had been many convinced of the truths of the gospel as held by Friends; and the Society continued to increase there; several meetings being settled in different neighborhoods.

While on his religious visit to America in 1666, John Burnyeat visited the meetings in New York and Long Island, and again when on a similar errand in 1671–2, he had much religious service among Friends in those places. Being at the Half-Year's Meeting, which was held at Oyster Bay, on Long Island, he found that the defection started by J. Perrot, had spread among some making profession with Friends in those parts. He states, that in this meeting for transacting the affairs of the Church, "Several rose up in a wrong spirit, against the blessed order of the Truth." They had written a book, principally against G. Fox and some epistles of advice written by him, in reference to the right ordering of the Meetings for Discipline. This book, which was in manuscript — some of the ringleaders insisted upon reading before the meeting, and Friends sat still until they had gone through it. J. Burnyeat then took it up, part by part, and "Cleared George Fox and Friends in our godly care and intent, and opened the service and benefit of such things as they cavilled at." He also "Reprehended them for their falsehoods and slanders, with which they had hurt the minds of several young and newly convinced Friends." This service was blessed, and many were thus rescued from the snare into which they had fallen. "The Lord's power broke in upon the meeting, and Friends' hearts were broken, and great meltings in the power were among us, and in the same we blessed the Lord and praised Him, and prayed unto Him, and they were bowed and went away."

[1672.] At the next Half-Year's Meeting, George Fox was in attendance. It was a large assemblage, Friends coming to it from all the settlements on the Island. George Fox mentions in his Journal, "On Third-day were the men's and women's meetings, wherein the affairs of the Church were taken care of. Here we met with some bad spirits, who were run out from truth into prejudice, contention and opposition to the order of truth, and to Friends therein. These had been very troublesome to Friends in their meetings there and thereabouts, formerly, and it is like would have been so now; but I would not suffer the service of our men's and women's meetings to be interrupted and hindered by their cavils. I let them know, 'If they had anything to object against the order of truth which we were in, we would give them a meeting another day on purpose.' And indeed I labored the more, and travelled the harder to get to this meeting, where it was expected many of these contentious people would be; because I understood they had reflected much upon me when I was far from them. The men's and women's meetings being over, on the Fourth-day we had a meeting with those discontented people; to which as many of them as would did come, and as many Friends as had a desire were present also; and the Lord's power broke forth gloriously, to the confounding of the gainsayers. Then some, that had been chief in the mischievous work of contention and opposition against the truth, began to fawn upon me, and cast the blame upon others; but the deceitful spirit was judged down and condemned, and the glorious truth of God was exalted and set over all; and they were all brought down and bowed under. Which was of great service to truth, and great satisfaction and comfort to Friends; glory to the Lord for ever!"

William Edmundson also visited New York in 1672, and held a meeting in the town, at the Inn where he lodged. He remarks, "It was a good meeting, some of the chief officers, Magistrates and leading men of the town being at it, who were very attentive, the Lord's power being over them all." He then went to Long Island and attended the meetings of Friends there; after which he went to Shelter Island where he met G. Fox, James Lancaster, Christopher Holder and others; and at the hospitable home of Nathaniel Silvester, they embraced the opportunity of recounting their several travels and exercises during their sojourn in America, and to encourage each other to faithfulness in the work assigned them.

Shelter Island received that name, it is probable, from its having been a place of shelter for many who had been driven from the main land by those in authority: who persecuted Friends wherever they had them in their power. It was near the eastern point of Long Island, and was under the exclusive control of N. Silvester, the sole proprietor; who purchased it either when he first became a Friend, or he was convinced of the principles of Friends, soon after he obtained possession of it. Here the weary exiles, on account of religion, always found a home and a heart to receive, to succor and refresh them; so that the kindness and liberality of N. Silvester were widely known and highly appreciated by Friends in America and Great Britain.

Among other religious services on the Island, George Fox says, "The day after, being First-day, we had a meeting there. In the same week, I had a meeting among the Indians, at which were their king, with his council, and about an hundred Indians more. They sat down like Friends, and heard very attentively, while I spoke to them by an interpreter, an Indian that could speak English well. After the meetings they appeared very loving, and confessed what was said to them was truth."

George Fox appears to have visited the meetings on Long Island very generally, and to have labored to get Friends into the right order of the discipline as established and carried out in other parts of the Society. After accomplishing this, accompanied by other ministers from England, he went on to Rhode Island to be at the Yearly Meeting for New England, which was held at Newport, in the Fourth month of 1672. This Colony had maintained its enlightened policy of toleration of all Christian professors, and consequently it afforded a safe and inviting home for Friends. G. Bishop, in his "New England Judged," states that a Yearly Meeting of Friends was held there, as early as 1661,— several years before the London Yearly Meeting was established,— from which time it had been regularly held; extending its jurisdiction over all the meetings in New England, New York, and it is probable further South.

George Fox thus alludes to his attendance of the meeting: " As soon as the wind served we set sail, and arrived in Rhode Island, the thirtieth of the Third month; [1672] where we were gladly received by Friends. We went to Nicholas Easton's, who was Governor of the Island; where we lay, being weary with travelling. On First-day following, we had a large meeting; to which the Deputy Governor and several Justices came, and were mightily affected with the truth. The week following, the Yearly Meeting for Friends of New England, and other Colonies adjacent, was held in this Island; to which, besides many Friends who lived in those parts, came John Stubbs from Barbadoes, and James Lancaster and John Cartwright from another way. This meeting lasted six days. The first four were spent in general public meetings for worship; to which abundance of other people came. For having no priests in the Island, and no restriction to any particular way of worship, and the Governor and Deputy Governor, with several Justices of the Peace, daily frequenting meetings, it so encouraged the people, that they flocked in from all parts of the Island. These public meetings over, the men's meeting began, which was large, precious, and weighty.

The day following was the women's meeting, which was also large and very solemn. These two meetings being for ordering the affairs of the church, many weighty things were opened, and communicated to them by way of advice, information, and instruction in the services relating thereunto; that all might be kept clean, sweet, and savory amongst them. In these, several men's and women's meetings for other parts were agreed and settled, to take care of the poor, and other affairs of the church, and to see that all who profess truth, walk according to the glorious gospel of God."

From the number of places where there were meetings of Friends, mentioned by William Edmundson, John Burnyeat and George Fox, it is evident that the Society had largely increased in Rhode Island, and that its members exercised much influence in the management of the affairs of the Colony. On more than one occasion, a Friend was elected Governor of the Province. Although Roger Williams had uniformly maintained the right to liberty of conscience in religion, within the Colony of Rhode Island, yet he was strongly prejudiced against Friends, and strenuously opposed the spread of their doctrines. There were other causes besides differences of religious opinions, which had embittered his feelings against them. Many years before the period now spoken of, there had been a sharp rivalry between him and William Coddington for the governorship of the Colony,—the latter having embraced the principles of Friends,— and William had been appointed to the station of Governor by the home Government. Roger went over to England on that account, and after much labor, succeeded in having his rival displaced. Two years after his return he was chosen Governor; but some time prior to the visit of William Edmundson to the Colony, the people had elected Friends to fill the offices of Governor, Deputy Governor, and Magistrates. In addition to these supposed grievances, many of his own flock — Baptists — had joined in membership with Friends.

1672. While William Edmundson was in that part of the country, R. Williams put forth fourteen propositions, designed to invalidate the scriptural soundness of the doctrines Friends promulgated, and challenged them to a public dispute upon the points of faith designated; appointing Newport as the place for discussing seven of them, and Providence the other seven. William Edmundson joined with other Friends in answering this challenge, and he says, that "a great concourse of people of all sorts gathered" in Friends' meeting-house at Newport. Wm. Edmundson remarks, "When those propositions, as he called them, came to be discoursed of, they were all mere slanders and accusations against the Quakers; the bitter old man could make nothing out; but on the contrary, they were turned back upon himself." "The testimony of Truth in the power of God, was set over all his false charges, to the great satisfaction of the people." This dispute lasted three days.

At Providence, where there was a great gathering of Presbyterians, Baptists, and Ranters, William Edmundson told R. Williams, that as they had spent so much time at the meeting at Newport, and that he [R. W.] had made nothing out, and he [W. E.] had other religious service to perform, he could not now give more than one day to answering his "false accusations." "We answered all his charges against Friends, and disproved them." "We had a seasonable opportunity to open many things to the people, appertaining to the kingdom of God, and way of eternal life and salvation. The meeting concluded with prayer to Almighty God, and the people went away satisfied and loving."

1666. The unchristian intolerance of the Presbyterians in Massachusetts and Connecticut, had received a further check from the Court in England, by its injunction, that as they were "indulged with the liberty of being of what profession of religion they pleased," they should permit "all persons of civil lives, to enjoy the same liberty of conscience, and to worship in the way they thought best," —an expression of Christian principle which the Government issuing it, was itself far from practising. But though this, in measure, restrained the rigid professors in New England from exercising the cruelty they had practised when they had their own way, yet some, especially those who held the offices of Magistrates and ministers, showed that the persecuting spirit still ruled in their hearts, by occasionally, where the people manifested a strong disposition to desert their common places of worship, and attend the meetings of Friends, resorting to the cat-o'-nine-tails, as the most powerful argument they could command, for convincing Friends of what they denounced the unsound doctrines they preached.

In the year 1666, John Burnyeat travelled through a large part of Massachusetts, and speaks of no obstructions being thrown in his way. He says, "About the latter end of the Sixth month I took my journey towards Sandwich; and when I was clear there, I took my journey by Plymouth to Tewkesbury, and so to Marshfield and Scituate, and to Boston, and I visited Friends and had meetings. From Boston I went to Salem, and so on to Piscataqua. When I was clear there, I returned back through the meetings, and came to Hampton, Salem, Boston, Scituate, Marshfield, and so by Tewkesbury and Plymouth to Sandwich; and from thence, through the woods to Ponyganset; and from thence over unto Rhode Island."

When, during his second visit to the Colonies in 1672, the same minister was at Scituate, he encountered some "Elders of their church," who charged him with being a heretic. In the dispute which took place, upon their declaring that the Scriptures were their rule, he replied, then they must abide by the rule laid down by Christ, " By their fruits ye shall know them ;" and so, he says, " I went on to reckon up the fruits of their Church ; which were, to fine and take away goods for not coming to their worship ; to imprison ; to whip with cruelty ; to cut off ears ; to burn in the hand ; to banish upon pain of death ; to hang ; for they had hanged four of our Friends. If they could prove by Scripture that those were the fruits of a Christian church, I would yield." The elders could not deny nor get over this kind of reasoning, and J. B. remarks, " They were confounded, some of themselves having been actors in persecution." When at Boston, John Stubbs and James Lancaster, who just before had been travelling with J. Burnyeat, were arrested, together with three other Friends, put in prison, and then banished out of the Colony. This was in 1672.

As has been before stated, the last. instances recorded of cruel whipping of Friends in New England was in 1677.

George Fox appears from his Journal not to have gone further North or East than Rhode Island. Being anxious, if possible, to reclaim some of the Ranters, who occasionally came to the meetings of Friends, and behaved in a rude and indecorous manner, he appointed a meeting especially for them ; but to which, he says, came many Friends and others ; and the Lord "gave him power over them, to his praise and glory." Accompanied by the Governor he went to Providence, where "The Lord whom we waited upon, was with us, and his power went over all, and his blessed Seed was exalted and set above all." With the Governor still as his companion, he visited Narraganset, where he had several meetings, attended by the principal inhabitants of the place. There was great openness to hear the doctrines he preached, and several received them, and joined the Society. He says, that at one place, " I heard that some of the Magistrates said among themselves, " If they had money enough they would hire me to be their minister." This was where they did not well understand us and our principles ; but when I heard of it, I said it was time for me to be gone ; for if their eye was so much to me, or and of us, they would not come to their own teacher." This was prior to his visit to Shelter Island.

After getting through with what was required of him in this part of the country, George Fox returned again into Maryland, and so into Virginia and Carolina, as has been already narrated. On the 23d of the Third month, 1673, he embarked for his native country, where he arrived after a voyage of about five weeks : he landed at Bristol.

In the year 1675, William Edmundson, under the constraining influence of gospel love, again visited the Colonies in America. After spending five months engaged in the service of the gospel in Barbadoes, where several were convinced under his ministry, he sailed for Rhode Island ; where he landed in about three weeks. At that time New England, with the exception of Rhode Island, was engaged in the war with King Philip ; but the Governor of that Province, being a Friend, was unwilling to take any part in the bloody contest, and refused to issue any commission for raising or officering troops. The Indians committed great carnage and destruction of property ; killing the inhabitants, not only in open combat, but in the fields, on the roads and by their firesides ; so that people of all other religious professions but Friends, carried arms with them on all occasions, even when they assembled for the purpose of Divine worship. It was a remarkable circumstance, that though property was destroyed by the savages in other parts of the colony, yet they made no incursion on the Island itself, and no Friend was killed.

Wm. Edmundson travelled northeastward towards Piscataway, though it was thought very dangerous ; but, he says, " I committed my life to God who gave it ; " and " I travelled in many places, as with my life in my hand, leaving all to the Lord who rules in heaven and earth." At different places on the road going and returning, he speaks of meeting with many Friends who were glad of his coming among them, especially in that time of trial, and they had " precious and comfortable meetings." He had two meetings at Marblehead. " Many resorted to them, and several were convinced and received the truth."

1676. In Boston and its vicinity, he was brought under " great exercise," on account of some who, he says, professed with Friends, but lived not in the truth, " who did much hurt, and hindered the Lord's work." He went from Boston to Rhode Island, in a vessel owned by Edward Wharton, who had been so great a sufferer during the hot persecution under Endicott and his coadjutors, and who was still living in Salem.   Friends in Rhode Island were yet under much trial, on account of the people who did not profess with them, being bent on participating in the Indian war, and endeavoring to implicate the government, in giving sanction and assistance to carrying it on.   It was a great strength to the Governor and other officers, to have the company of this resolute and devoted servant of the Prince of Peace, at this juncture ; and he observes, " Friends were glad of my coming, and it pleased God that it was to good purpose in several respects ; the faithful and honest-hearted among them were much helped and strengthened by my being there.   I stayed some time among them, and had many blessed and heavenly meetings to worship God ; also men's meetings for church affairs."

While laboring there he was seized with a malignant disease, then carrying off many of the inhabitants.   He observes, " Then some spirits whom I had dealt with for their looseness, were glad, and thought their curb and rein were taken off ; but the Lord healed and raised me up, so that in about ten days, I was able to appear in public meetings . . .   and the Lord carried me over all."

Finding it laid upon him to go to New Hartford, in Connecticut, and knowing that the men in authority in that Colony were greatly opposed to Friends, and at that time much excited against them, it brought him under severe exercise of mind, before he was made willing to give up to expose himself among them.   Arriving at New London he essayed to have a meeting, but the Presbyterians would not permit it.   He, however, appointed a meeting a short distance out of the town ; but before it was over, he says, " The constables and other officers came with armed men, and forcibly broke up our meeting, haling and abusing us very much ; but the sober people were offended at them."

James Fletcher offering to accompany him to New Hartford, they set off on horseback, through the wilderness, without a guide, and after a hard day's ride, arrived at an inn within a few miles of the town.   Leaving James here the next morning, William walked into New Hartford, and it being the First day of the week, he went to the " Church," and remained until the " service " was concluded. Having then spoken " what the Lord gave me," the minister and Magistrates soon went away ; but most of the people remaining, he had full opportunity to relieve himself of his apprehended duty.   In the afternoon he went to another place for worship ; where, while the minister and people were assembled, they had an armed guard set, to keep off the Indians. Here, he says, "I declared the way of salvation to them a pretty while; but, by the persuasion of the priest, the officers haled me out of the worship-house, and hurt my arm so that it bled." It was a very cold day, and Wm. Edmundson had had nothing to eat all day. He appealed to the officer having him in charge — who was complaining of the severity of the cold — if it was Christian usage they were subjecting him to. He was troubled, tried to excuse the priest and Magistrates, and then took him to an inn. The people thronged to see and hear him, so that he had an opportunity of freely discoursing with them, and he observes, "Truth's testimony was over all." The next morning the officer sent him word he might go where he would, and he went back to meet his companion.

William Edmundson again went through the perils and hardships of a journey through the wilderness, from New York to Maryland, and from there on into Carolina. He speaks of having many "blessed meetings," with Friends and others, after his arrival in Maryland, and also in Virginia. But he suffered greatly from the exposure in an open boat to the snow, sleet, and severe cold, when crossing the inlets and bays, as also on the rivers. He was, however, mercifully carried through all, and enabled to labor faithfully in word and doctrine, and in the affairs relating to Gospel order. He says, referring to the state of the Society in Virginia, "There was indeed need enough for help, for things were much out of order, and many unruly spirits to deal with. I had good service and success, for the Lord blessed his work in my hand." This was in 1677.

As the whole distance between the Settlements in Virginia and those in North Carolina was at that time considered too dangerous to be traversed by any but armed bands; not only on account of the hostility of the Indians, who were murdering the whites, almost wherever found in that section of the country, but also on account of the sanguinary war then being waged between the Governor, Sir William Berkeley and his partisans, and Colonel Bacon and his partisans, Friends were very unwilling Wm. Edmundson should attempt the journey, and for some time he hesitated to start. But having appointed a meeting where none had been held before, and walked in the evening preceding, some distance with a young man, the son of the widowed Friend at whose house William had been staying, he was called up in the night, to be told that the young man was dead. "Then," he says, "the word of the Lord came to me, saying, all lives are in my hand, and if thou goest not to Carolina, thy life is as this young man's; but if thou goest, I will give thee thy life for a prey." So, accompanied by an "ancient man Friend," he went, and had "meetings in several places" in that colony; and having "settled things among Friends," he found himself at liberty to return home; and there being a vessel from Bristol in Elizabeth river, he took passage in her, and arrived in Ireland after a tempestuous voyage.

CHAPTER XXIV.

Lull of Persecution in Great Britain—George Fox reported to have turned Presbyterian — Third "Conventicle Act"— T. Ellwood's Criticism Thereon— Character of Informers and Magistrates — G. Fox and an Informer — Terrible Persecution — Church of England "Service" performed at Friends' Meeting-House—Horsleydown Meeting-House Torn Down—Ratcliff Meeting-House Wrecked — Trial of Wm. Penn and Wm. Mead — Jury Fined— Defendants Kept in Prison—Death of Admiral Penn—Trial and Suffering of other Prisoners before the same Court — Lieutenant of the Tower— Wheeler Street Meeting-House and Gilbert Latey — Constancy and Faithfulness of Friends — Illness of G. Fox — Domestic Trials of his Wife.

IN recurring to the condition of the Society in Great Britain, it may be remembered there had been a lull in the storm of persecution, for a little time after the great fire in London; [1666] the loss and distress incurred by this calamity, and by the disastrous events of the war with the Dutch, had so occupied the government and people as, in some measure, to divert their attention from the persecution of Dissenters.

The King in his address at the opening of parliament in 1668, had expressed his willingness to sanction a more moderate policy towards those who dissented from the "Established Church," and his privy Council favored the trial. But the "Lords Spiritual," and the House, quickly intervened to prevent any mitigation of the rigor of the laws against Dissenters; and Charles, a Roman Catholic at heart, was too indifferent to religion in any form, to persevere in carrying out whatever good intention he might have had; and fearing to cross their bigoted zeal, he complied with their demands, and issued his Proclamation for again enforcing the laws against conventicles, &c.

The fire of persecution, nevertheless, burnt more fitfully and with less heat, and it again became a subject of serious consideration with several of those who were more deeply interested in the interests of the country, whether something more ought not to be attempted, in order to remove the objections of some classes among the Dissenters, to amalgamating with the Established Church, and to extend a modified toleration to others, who could not be induced to give up their own organizations and modes of worship. Accordingly, some of those holding high offices, together with two of the more moderate Bishops, prepared proposals of concessions to be made, and communicated them to some Dissenting ministers, who advised with the principal members of their congregations. A bill was prepared by the Lord Chief Justice, intended to carry these views into operation ; but the knowledge of it coming to some of the prelates who had not been consulted, at the time when the Parliament was again convening, they—more especially Archbishop Sheldon—set themselves to work, and succeeded in preventing the proposed bill being presented to the House.

The amended " Conventicle Act " expired by limitation in 1670, and the usual prelude to the enactment of some other legal device for harassing, preying upon, and if possible eradicating, those who would not support episcopacy, in its unchristian demands and pretensions, was again put in practice. Reports were spread abroad through the country, of intended insurrections of Presbyterians and Catholics, and that their design was to overturn the government. When George Fox returned from his visit to Ireland in 1669, he landed at Liverpool, and after holding several religious meetings in Lancashire and Cheshire, he passed into Gloucestershire ; where he heard a report, in several places, that he had turned Presbyterian, and that he was to be at a large meeting in a yard, where a pulpit was already set up for him to preach ; and he says, he saw the yard and the pulpit set in it.

He observes, " The occasion of this strange report, as I was informed, was this. There was one John Fox, a Presbyterian priest, who used to go about preaching ; and some, changing his name from John to George, gave out that George Fox was turned from a Quaker to be a Presbyterian, and would preach at such a place on such a day. This begat such curiosity in the people, that they went thither to hear this Quaker turned Presbyterian, who would not have gone to have heard John Fox himself. By this means it was reported they had got together above a thousand people. But when they came there, and perceived they had a trick put upon them, that he was but a counterfeit George Fox, and understood that the real George Fox was hard by, several hundreds came to our meeting, and were sober and attentive."

Some time after, this John Fox got into a quarrel with the parish priest who had succeeded him in the living he formerly enjoyed; and in a contest that took place in the "steeple-house," between them and their respective partisans, a common Prayer Book was destroyed, and the supporters of J. Fox gave utterance to expressions construed to be treasonable. This was quickly published, but in such language as gave the impression, that the treasonable expressions were from "George Fox the Quaker." The report of a large and tumultuous meeting being held by George Fox turned Presbyterian, and of the treasonable words expressed, was spoken of in Parliament as a cause of complaint and suspicion; so that George thought it needful to obtain certificates from some of the members of the House, who were acquainted with John Fox, testifying that he was the person implicated, and not George Fox the Quaker. Nevertheless this report was made use of among others to unsettle the minds of the people, and induce them to think there was need for severe measures to keep down the Dissenters; all of whom were considered to be political malcontents. The law against Dissenters that had just expired, while inflicting indescribable suffering on those who were brought under the operation of its provisions, had failed in its object; partly because of its severity in imposing enormous fines, long imprisonments and banishments; the last being so repugnant to the feelings of the people as to prevent its being executed. It was therefore determined to try another method; which by enlisting the cupidity of the depraved class, willing to prey upon the property of others for obtaining the means to gratify their own sensual indulgences; and using the almost unrestrained judicial functions of officials clothed with absolute power, it was hoped would so impoverish and harass those who met together for Divine worship in a way differing from the "Church of England," as to render them unable to live in their native country. Accordingly a third "Act to prevent and suppress seditious Conventicles," was passed by Parliament, and received the royal assent in the Fourth month of 1670.

By this Act it was declared unlawful for more than five persons beside a family to assemble for performing Divine worship "in any other manner than according to the Liturgy and practice of the Church of England." Where this was violated, the "offender" or "offenders" were to be fined five shillings for the first "offence," and ten for the second. The preacher or teacher to be fined twenty pounds for the first offence, and forty for the second. Those permitting such meetings to be held in their house, or on their premises, were to be fined twenty pounds. The oaths of two witnesses to be sufficient proof, and the record of a Magistrate under his hand and seal to be a perfect conviction, and to be certified to the next Court of Quarter Sessions. The fines were to be levied on the goods and chattels of the offender, and if he was too poor to satisfy the demand, then to be levied on the goods and chattels of any other person or persons, thus convicted of having been present. The fines of preachers or teachers, were to be in like manner levied upon them, or if they are without goods or chattels, which could be distrained, then upon any other person convicted of being present; and in like manner upon the house where the meeting was held; provided in either of these latter cases not more than £10 or half the fine, was to be taken. The money thus obtained, was to be divided, one-third to the King, one-third to the poor, and the remaining third to the informers. Justices, Constables, &c., were authorized to break into the place where the meeting was held, or said to be holding. Justices were to be fined £100 if refusing to act, and Constables, &c., £5. All clauses of the Act "Shall be construed most largely and beneficially for the suppressing of conventicles, *and for the justification and encouragement of all persons to be employed in the execution thereof.*" No warrant or mittimus was to become void on account of defects in form; the goods and chattels of a convicted offender were to be seized wherever found, and a husband was liable for the fines imposed on his wife, whether he was present or not.

Thomas Ellwood, who was a sufferer from this iniquitous law, and active in defeating its profligate and abandoned executioners, in their attempts upon others, says of it —

"Firstly. It broke down and overrun the bounds and banks, anciently set for the defence and security of Englishmen's lives, liberties, and properties, viz.: Trial by juries. Instead thereof, directing and authorizing justices of the peace, and that too privately, out of sessions, to convict, fine, and by their warrants, distrain upon offenders against it; directly contrary to the Great Charter.

"Secondly. By that Act the informers, who swear for their own advantage, as being thereby entitled to a third part of the fines, were many times concealed, driving on an underhand private trade; so that men might be and often were convicted and fined, without having any notice or knowledge of it, till the officers came and took away their goods; nor even then could they tell by whose evidence they were convicted. Than which, what could be more opposite to common justice, which requires that every man should be openly charged, and have his accuser face to face, that he might both answer for himself before he be convicted, and object to the validity of the evidence given against him.

"Thirdly. By that Act, the innocent were punished for the offences of the guilty. If the wife or child was convicted of having been at one of those assemblies, which by that act was adjudged unlawful, the fine was levied on the goods of the husband or father of such wife or child, though he was neither present at such assembly, nor was of the same religious persuasion that they were of, but perhaps an enemy to it.

"Fourthly. It was left in the arbitrary pleasure of the Justices, to lay half the fine for the house or ground where such assembly was holden, and half the fine for a pretended unknown preacher; and the whole fines of such and so many of the meeters as they should account poor, upon any other or others of the people, who were present at the same meeting, not exceeding a certain limited sum; without any regard to equity or reason.".

Efforts have been made to exonerate the Bishops and clergy from the odium of being the active instruments in procuring the passage of this abominable law, and we will not undertake to examine whether it owed its paternity more to the ecclesiastical than to the civil power. It is undeniable, however, that after it came into force, several of the Bishops and most of the clergy, were eager and active to have it executed. Archbishop Sheldon exerted himself to enlist all his suffragans in the service, urging them to use their influence to the utmost, for carrying out the provisions of the law. In a letter to one of his Bishops, which Calamy recites, we find this language. "And now, my Lord, what the success may be we must leave to God Almighty; yet, my Lord, I have this confidence under God, that if we do our parts, now at first seriously, by God's help, and the assistance of the civil power, considering the abundant care and provision the Act contains for our advantage, we shall, in a few months, see so great an alteration in the distraction of these times, as that the seduced people, returning from their seditions and self-seeking teachers to the unity of the Church, and uniformity of God's worship, it will be to the glory of God, the welfare of the Church, the praise of his Majesty's government, and the happiness of the whole Kingdom." The substance of this letter was directed to be communicated to all the clergy of each diocese.

Thomas Ellwood says in his journal, " That some of the clergy of most ranks, and others who were excessively bigoted to that party, used their utmost efforts to find out and encourage the most profligate wretches to turn informers; and get such persons into parochial offices as would be most obsequious to their directions, and prompt at their beck to put this law into most rigorous execution." Persons of plausible manners, and capable of assuming different characters, were employed to insinuate themselves into the company of different Dissenters, pretending to unite with them, and thus obtain knowledge of the preachers, and principal persons connected with them; and on the first fitting occasion to inform against them. One thus commissioned by the Vice Chancellor of Oxford, came into Buck's county, and first tried to pass himself off on Friends; but being rebuffed by them, and when drunk, having betrayed his employment, he went among the Baptists in another part of the country, and having induced one of them to converse freely with him about the times and the laws, accused him before a Magistrate of speaking treasonable words; which would have cost him his estate and liberty, but that his accuser's former character being found out, he became alarmed and fled the country. But associating a man with him as an accomplice, who had been in jail for stealing a cow, they entered upon the business of regular informers. There were a number of instances of Justices resigning their positions and leaving the bench, because they could not conscientiously be the instruments for executing a law they felt to be infamously unjust, and which left them no option whether to act or to decline, unless they were willing, in the latter case, to incur the heavy penalty of £100.

This law was intended to act with the same merciless severity on all Dissenters, and wherever the opportunity offered, it was generally executed on all. But Presbyterians, Baptists, and Independents, thought themselves justified in bending to the storm. Neal says, " The Non-conformist ministers did what they could to keep themselves within the compass of the law; they preached frequently twice a day in large families, with only four strangers, and as many under the age of sixteen as would come; and at other times, in places where people might hear in several adjoining houses; but after all, infinite mischiefs ensued; families were impoverished and divided," &c., &c.

This Act went into operation the 10th of the Third month 1670; but in some parts of the country, it took time for the machinery to be provided to carry it into effect. In the cities and towns it began its work at once. In London the meeting-houses of Friends were shut up by the civil authority. On the First-day, directly after the Act went into operation, George Fox went to Grace-church Street meeting. "I found," he says, "the street full of people, and a guard set to keep Friends out of their meeting-house. I went to the other passage out of Lombard street, where also I found a guard, but the court was full of people, and a Friend was speaking among them. When he had done I stood up." He had not spoken long, when an informer and some soldiers came, and pulling him down, took him and others to go before the Mayor. As they went along, the informer said to one of the company, "It would never be a good world, till all the people came to the good old religion that was two hundred years ago." George said, "Art thou a Papist? what! a Papist an informer?" This got to be known among the people, who were at that time greatly excited against the Papists. When at the Mayor's house, some present asked G. Fox for what he was taken up? He desired them to ask the informer, and also what was his name? The man refused to tell his name, and on one of the officers saying he would have to tell it; and asking why he was intruding himself among the soldiers, he became frightened, and attempted to escape. One of the officers asked, "Have you brought people here to inform against, and now will you go away before my Lord Mayor comes?" He, however, slipped out through the door; but no sooner did he get into the street than the crowd shouted "A Papist informer! a Papist informer!" and G. Fox, fearing lest the mob would do him bodily injury, desired the soldiers to rescue him; which they did, and brought him into the house again. He attempted to escape the second time, but the soldiers had again to bring him back, lest the people would maim him. They took him into an adjoining house, where he so altered his appearance, that he was able to sneak off, without being recognized. There were some Presbyterian and Baptist teachers examined at the same time, who were convicted; but when George's turn came, there was no one to inform against him and the other Friends; after some discourse as to their coming within the purview of the law, the Mayor discharged them; first taking their names and residences.

As giving some idea of the course pursued by Friends under these trying circumstances, it may be mentioned, that upon G. Fox being thus liberated, he went immediately back to Grace-church Street meeting; but found the meeting held in the street was over, and most of the Friends gone to their homes. At the other meeting-houses Friends were kept out, and in some instances several were taken away, but were not long detained; and George says, "A glorious time it was, for the Lord's power came over all, and his everlasting truth got renown. For as fast as some that were speaking were taken down, others were moved of the Lord to stand up and speak, to the admiration of the people; and the more because many Baptists and other sectaries left their public meetings, and came to see how the Quakers would stand."

Persecution now ran riot; and the power being by design placed in the hands of the most profligate and debased, glad to avail themselves of the opportunity granted them to rob, under sanction of law, the goods of the religious and industrious, rapine, havoc and impoverishment were spread over the nation by the graceless informers, abetted by a venal magistracy, eager to share in the plunder. As was to be expected, where the money or goods seized, came into the hands of the unscrupulous officials, very little of it was parted with, for either the King or the poor. As the people, especially in the country, very generally refused to buy the goods thus taken, the few who were willing to be accessories after the fact, bought them for a fourth or third of their value; thus affording the myrmidons of the law opportunity to repeat their seizures, until, in many instances, the victims were stripped of everything they possessed. The records contain accounts of many instances where Friends in humble circumstances had everything, — beds, bedding, clothing, and the implements used in their business taken away. The sick were dragged out of bed, their beds and clothing seized, and they obliged to lie upon straw. Cradles, and the vessel in which food for infants was preparing, were sometimes carried off. In one case a Constable having reported to the Magistrate, that he had stripped the house of every thing but some loaves of bread, he was ordered to return and bring them, and if he could not sell them, to feed them to the Magistrate's horses.

But the storm, biting and incessant as it was, was no more effective in deterring Friends from assembling for the purpose of worshipping their Almighty Father in heaven, than that which had been raised under the former "Conventicle Acts." Grievously spoiled and cruelly abused as they were, they knew their enemies could truthfully allege nothing against them but that which concerned the law of their God; and in the sincerity of their hearts, they made their appeal unto Him, with full confidence that He would extend his fatherly, protecting care over them, would cause the wrath of man to bring Him praise, and, when He saw it was enough, would restrain the remainder of wrath, and limit the rage and cruelty of their merciless tormentors.   Deprived of the use of their meeting-houses, they assembled as, near to them as they could get; and beaten, bruised, imprisoned and fined, as many of each company were almost sure to be, the next meeting-day found others at the same place, engaged in the performance of the same indispensable duty; ready to encounter, with meekness and patience, the wrath of their persecutors, and to suffer for the maintenance of their rights as men, and their obligation as Christians.

1670. In London, after some weeks' trial of violent exclusion of Friends from their meeting-houses, beating of drums to drown the voice of the speakers, and barbarous abuse of those who met in the streets, without any prospect of being successful in their extermi- nating intentions, it was resolved by the church party to try other measures.   A clergyman was appointed to attend at Grace-church Street meeting-house, and conduct service there in accordance with the manner of the "Established Church." Accordingly, accompanied by a guard of soldiers, he repaired to the place, drawing a crowd of idle rabble after him; whose curiosity prompted them to witness "the Episcopal service" conducted by a priest in a Quaker meet- ing-house.   His first sermon was on Love and Charity, and when he got through, George Whitehead stood up, and preached on the same virtues; showing how inconsistent persecution for religion, which Friends were then enduring, was with those virtues.   He was pulled down, carried before the Lord Mayor, and though he pleaded that even according to the late Act it was a lawful as- sembly, and that no one denied he had preached the gospel, yet the Mayor said, that as soon as the priest had done, it became a con- venticle, and though he believed he (G. W.) had done good, yet he fined him forty pounds.

When the priest came to the meeting-house on the next First- day, he found Friends already assembled, and holding their meet- ing in the court.   His heart failed him, and he held back, until a double guard of soldiers were brought; who made way for him to the door of the house; but some of the mob assembled to see the "sport," deriding him, he slunk away.   The next meeting-day, the soldiers went by the time it was light in the morning, and prevented Friends from entering their house, or assembling in the court; and so the priest had the "service" all his own way, with the few auxili- aries who were willing to hear him.   Thus by picketing the street and court with soldiers, and arresting the Friends who came into it, the priest managed to go through his performance in the gallery of the meeting-house, for three or four weeks; but as he could get no respectable audience, it was obliged to be given up.

Exasperated at finding the ill success attending the infliction of fines, imprisonments, beatings, and other inhumanities, for keeping Friends from assembling for the purpose of Divine worship, an order was adopted by the King and Council, on the 29th of the Seventh month, 1670, Sandcroft, the Archbishop of Canterbury, being present, to demolish the meeting-house at Horsleydown, in Southwark; and Christopher Wren, "Surveyor-General of his Majesty's Works," was directed to execute it. The congregation worshipping there had been continually subjected to the brutality and vile indecencies of the soldiery let loose upon them; but with an undeviating constancy and humble trust, had persevered in obeying God rather than man; submitting patiently to be despoiled of their goods, and to undergo whatever else the wrath of man was permitted to impose upon them. The destruction of their meeting-house was an act of mere arbitrary power, and the military were employed in carrying it out. On the 20th of the Eighth month, a company of soldiers, with carpenters and others, went to the place and pulled down the whole house; carting away the windows, doors, lumber, &c.; which were sold, and the money kept. The next meeting-day, the Friends met on the rubbish of their demolished house, and held their meeting, until they were assaulted by the soldiery, beaten, and dragged away.

The precedent thus set, John Robinson, Lieutenant of the Tower, so far as appears, of his own will and authority, first broke up, or carried away all the forms from Friends' meeting-house at Ratcliff; and finding that Friends continued to meet there, though without benches to sit on, he sent his soldiers, who made a wreck of the whole house; carrying away in carts such portions as could be made further use of, or might be sold. But here, as at Horsleydown, Friends did not neglect to meet on the ruins, or as near as the infuriated soldiers would allow them to come, and so kept up their meetings; where the Lord was pleased to be with them, and to give them to partake of his blessed love and peace in the presence of their enemies. [1670.]

It would swell this work far beyond its prescribed limits, to narrate a tithe of the grievous sufferings endured by Friends, during this season of bitter persecution. Their treatment in London, bad as it was, was thought to be less severe than in many other parts of the kingdom. Yet in that city, it was a common occurrence for those who attended their meetings for worship, to be beaten with the muskets of the foot-soldiers, and the sabres of the dragoons, until the blood ran down upon the ground; women, sometimes young maidens, were maltreated in the most shameful manner; sometimes, fastened by a rope to the saddlebow of the horseman, and made to run, or be thus dragged through the streets; sometimes, after beating the unresisting sufferers, the soldiers would shovel up mud and filth out of the kennels and dash it over their persons; and in cases where the citizens, alarmed, or ashamed at the inhuman treatment by the savage soldiers, opened their doors to bring their inoffensive victims under shelter, or in other ways attempted to befriend them, they only brought upon themselves abuse and loss, by the resentment they incurred. Friends represented to the Magistrates the illegality of the course usurped by the military, and some of them attempted to put a stop to it; but their authority — if it was exerted in good faith — was disregarded, and the violence and outrage went on.

In order to find excuse for legally imposing longer imprisonment upon Friends, the Magistrates of London resolved to have those taken at their meetings, indicted for riot. On the 14th of the Eighth month, 1670, William Penn and William Mead were taken from the meeting held in the street, as near to Grace-church meeting-house as they could get; the former being engaged in ministry at the time. They were brought to trial on the 1st of the Ninth month, before the Mayor — Samuel Starling, — the Recorder — John Howell, — several Aldermen and the Sheriffs. Wm. Mead had formerly been a Captain in the Commonwealth's army, but having embraced the truths of the Gospel as held by Friends, he of course gave up all connection with military life, and is mentioned in the indictment, as a linen-draper, in London; though it is probable he resided most of his time in Essex, where he had a considerable landed estate. He afterwards married a daughter of Margaret Fell.

The indictment charged that they, with other persons, to the number of three hundred, with force and arms, unlawfully and tumultuously assembled together on the 15th day of August, 1670, and the said William Penn, by agreement made beforehand with William Mead, preached and spoke to the assembly; by reason whereof, a great concourse and tumult of people continued a long time in the street, in contempt of the King and his law, to the great disturbance of his peace, and to the terror of many of his liege people and subjects.

The character of the trial might be judged by the first incident that occurred. Being brought before the Court on the 3d of the Ninth month, an officer took off their hats on their entrance; whereupon the Mayor angrily ordered him to put them on again; which being done, the Recorder fined them forty marks apiece, for alleged contempt of Court, by appearing before it with their hats on. This trial has become celebrated, not only on account of the ability with which William Penn — then in his twenty-sixth year — defended his cause, and sustained the inalienable rights of Englishmen, but for the inflexible firmness of the jury in maintaining their own rights, and adhering to their conscientious convictions; notwithstanding the iniquitous determination of the Court, to enforce its own will, to convict and punish the prisoners at the bar, and to oblige the jury to become their tools for that purpose.

The indictment was incorrect, even in the statement of the time when the offence was said to have taken place; as it was on the 14th of the month, and not on the 15th, and therefore it ought to have been quashed by the Court, and the prisoners discharged. The evidence of the three witnesses examined, was altogether inconclusive, but William Penn boldly said to the Court, " We confess ourselves to be so far from recanting or declining to vindicate the assembling of ourselves, to preach, pray or worship the eternal, holy, just God, that we declare to all the world, that we do believe it to be our indispensable duty to meet incessantly on so good an account; nor shall all the powers upon earth be able to divert us from reverencing and adoring the God who made us." He then asked the Court, to tell him upon what law the indictment and proceedings were founded. The Recorder answering, the common law, Penn requested him to tell him, what law that was; for if it was common, it must be easy to define it. But the Recorder refused to tell him, saying it was *lex non scripta,* and it was not to be expected that he could say at once what it was, for some had been thirty or forty years studying it. Penn observed, that Lord Coke had declared that common law was common right, and common right the great chartered privileges confirmed by former Kings. The Recorder, greatly excited, told him he was a troublesome fellow, and it was not to the honor of the Court to suffer him to go on; but Penn calmly insisted that the Court was bound to explain to the prisoners at their bar, the law they had violated, and upon which they were being tried ; and he told them plainly that unless they did so, they were violating the chartered rights of Englishmen, and acting upon an arbitrary determination to sacrifice those rights, to their own illegal designs. Whereupon the Mayor and Recorder ordered him to be turned into the bail-dock. W. Penn —"These are but so many vain exclamations ; is this justice or true judgment ? Must I, therefore, be taken away because I plead for the fundamental laws of England ? Then addressing himself to the jury, he said, 'However, this I leave upon your consciences who are of the jury, and my sole judges, that if these ancient fundamental laws which relate to liberty and property, and are not limited to particular persuasions in matters of religion, must not be indispensably maintained and observed, who can say he hath right to the coat upon his back. Certainly our liberties are openly to be invaded, our children enslaved, our families ruined, and our estates led away in triumph, by every sturdy beggar and malicious informer, as their trophies, but our pretended forfeits for conscience-sake. The Lord of heaven and earth will be judge between us in this matter.' The hearing of this emphatic speech was so troublesome to the Recorder, that he cried, 'Be silent there.' At which W. Penn returned, 'I am not to be silent in a cause wherein I am so much concerned, and not only myself, but many ten thousand families besides.' "

Penn being thrust into the bail-dock, Wm. Mead was called up, and was asked if he was present at the meeting ? Which question he refused to answer, on the ground that he could not be required to accuse himself. He then told the jury that the indictment was false in many particulars, and that Wm. Penn was right in demanding the law upon which it was based. It charged him with assembling by force and arms, tumultuously and illegally, which was untrue ; and he informed them of Lord Coke's definition of a rout or riot, or unlawful assembly. Here the Recorder interrupted him, and endeavored to cast ridicule on what he had said, by taking off his hat and saying, "I thank you for telling us what the law is." On Mead replying sharply to a taunting speech of Richard Brown, the old and inveterate enemy of Friends, the Mayor told him "He deserved to have his tongue cut out." He, too, was put into the bail-dock, and the Court proceeded to charge the jury. Whereupon, Wm. Penn cried out with a loud voice to the jury, to take notice, that it was illegal to charge the jury in the prisoners' absence, and without giving them opportunity to plead their cause. The Recorder ordered him to be put down. Wm. Mead then remonstrating against such "barbarous and unjust proceedings," the Court ordered them both to be put into a filthy, stinking place, called "the hole." After an absence of an hour and a half, eight of the jury came down agreed, but four stayed up and would not assent. The Court sent for the four, and menaced them for dissenting. When the jury was all together, the prisoners were brought to the bar, and the verdict demanded. The Foreman said, Wm. Penn was guilty of speaking in Grace-church Street. The Court endeavored to extort something more, but the Foreman declared he was not authorized to say anything but what he had given in. The Recorder, highly displeased, told them they might as well say nothing. and they were sent back. They soon returned with a written verdict, signed by all of them, that they found Wm. Penn guilty of speaking or preaching in Grace-church Street, and Wm. Mead not guilty. This so incensed the Court, that they told them they *would* have a verdict they would accept, and that "they should be locked up without meat, drink, fire or tobacco; you shall not think thus to abuse the Court. We will have a verdict, by the help of God, or you shall starve for it." Against this outrageous infraction of justice and right, Wm. Penn remonstrated, saying, "My jury, who are my judges, ought not to be thus menaced; their verdict should be free, and not compelled; the Bench ought to wait upon them, but not forestall them. I do desire that justice may be done me, and that the arbitrary resolves of the Bench may not be made the measure of my jury's verdict." The Recorder cried out, "Stop that prating fellow's mouth or put him out of Court." Penn insisted that the agreement of the twelve men was a verdict, and that the Clerk of the Court should record it; and, addressing the jury, he said, "You are Englishmen; mind your privileges; give not away your right!" To which some of them replied, "Nor will we ever do it."

The jury were sent to their room, and the prisoners to jail, the former being deprived of food, drink, and every accommodation. The same verdict was returned the next morning; calling from the Bench upbraiding and threats, similar to those so lavishly bestowed on the jury before; the Recorder, in his passion, going so far as to say, "Till now, I never understood the reason of the policy and prudence of the Spaniards in suffering the Inquisition among them; and certainly, it will never be well with us till something like the Spanish Inquisition be in England." Again the jury was sent back to their room, and the prisoners returned to Newgate; both being so kept for another twenty-four hours; the jury without victuals, drink, or other accommodations. The next morning they were again brought into Court, and the u ual question respecting their verdict being put, the Foreman first replied, " You have our written verdict already." The Recorder refusing to allow it to be read, the Clerk repeated the query : How say you, is Wm. Penn guilty or not guilty? the Foreman answered : Not guilty. The same verdict was given in the case of Wm. Mead. The jury being separately questioned, they all made the same reply. The Recorder, exasperated at their decision and firmness, after pouring out his invectives upon them, said, The Court fines you forty marks a man, and imprisonment till paid.

Wm. Penn now demanded his liberty; but the Mayor said, No, you are in for your fines. " Fines! for what?" replied Penn. For contempt of Court, was the answer. Penn then declared, that according to the laws, no man could be fined without trial by jury; but the Mayor ordered him and Mead first to the bail-dock, and then to the jail; where the jury was likewise consigned.

But this noble stand of the jury for law and right was not allowed to terminate in the punishment of these upright men, and the continued gratification of the revenge of the unjust Judges. After ineffectually demanding of the Court their release two or three times, a writ of *habeas corpus* was granted by Judge Vaughan; who upon hearing the case, decided their fine and imprisonment illegal, and set them free.

William Penn, anxious to have the cases of himself and his friend reviewed by a Superior Court, wrote to his father; affectionately desiring him not to interfere to have him released. But the old man, who was fast declining, and anxious to have the company and attentions of his son, to whom he was not only reconciled, but on whose filial affection and care he had learned to lean for comfort and support, was not willing to wait the tardy process of law; and therefore paid the fines of both the Friends, and had them set free. The Admiral survived but a few days the liberation of his son; in which time he sent one of his friends to the King and Duke of York, to make his dying request, that, so far as they could, they would hereafter befriend his loved son; which both promised to do. Addressing his son, shortly before his death, he said, "Son William, if you and your friends keep to your plain way of preaching, and your plain way of living, you will make an end of the priests to the end of the world." Again — sensible it is probable of the wrong he had before committed in his course towards his son — he said emphatically, "Let nothing in the world tempt you to wrong your conscience. I charge you, do nothing against your conscience; so you will keep peace at home, which will be a feast to you in the day of trouble."

Near the close of this year [1670], William Penn was again arrested, at Wheeler Street meeting, by some of the officers of Robinson, Lieutenant of the Tower, who had sent them there for the purpose, and he was taken before him. His examination, as published, shows his Christian courage and firmness, as he exposed the duplicity of Robinson, in his profession of friendship for him; and asserted his innocence of the charges made against him. He was sent to Newgate for six months; during which time he drew up an account of the memorable trial at the Old Bailey; also several dissertations which were afterwards published as tracts: one of these was, "The great Case of Liberty of Conscience, once more briefly Debated, and Defended by authority of Scripture, Reason, and Antiquity."

At the same session of the Court, which had acted, as has been narrated, in the cases of Penn and Mead, there were thirteen other Friends tried; among whom was Thomas Rudyard; who being well instructed in the law, and versed in the application of it, had rendered himself very obnoxious to the Magistrates, by repeatedly and successfully extricating Friends from their grasp, whom they were endeavoring illegally to punish. Twice they had had him arrested and imprisoned, with the hope he could thus be kept out of their way; but both times he was set free by due process of law. Now he was taken at meeting, and with other Friends, was to be tried on indictments similar to those of Penn and Mead. The Court having sent the first jury to jail, proceeded to have another empanelled; taking care to have men on it who they knew would not be likely to thwart their designs. The prisoners claimed, that as the former jury had been sworn to try their cases, no other could legally have their cases brought before them. To this the Court would give no other reply than that it *overruled* the objection; and when several of the jurors were challenged, as being incompetent and unfit to try the case, the same reply was made. One of the prisoners saying, that such an answer was arbitrary, unless it was shown to be founded on law, the Recorder told him he should be gagged, and deserved to have his tongue bored through with a red-hot iron. The same kind of treatment as had marked their former proceeding, was indulged towards these Friends; their hats were taken off by an officer, then by order of the Court put on, and they fined for contempt, and at the conclusion of the evidence, on attempting to plead in their own defence, they were thrust into the bail-dock ; the jury was charged while they were thus absent from the Court, the Recorder instructing it, they must bring them in guilty ; which it was quite ready to do.

When, at the close of the session, the prisoners were brought into Court to receive sentence, they were prepared with exceptions to arrest judgment ; but they found the sentences had already been given ; and without their knowing what the sentences, thus passed in secret, were, they were hurried back to jail.   They afterwards discovered that fines of different amounts had been imposed, and imprisonment until paid.   To gratify the special hatred towards Thomas Rudyard, his fine was one hundred pounds.

But Newgate was so crowded with prisoners, there was no room to receive these just condemned, and regardless as the Magistrates were of the suffering resulting from over-crammed apartments, they found it absolutely necessary to procure another place for the safe-keeping of these innocent convicts.   Learning that the keeper of a place called " The Dog," near Newgate, and a person who had been confined there, had just died of Spotted Fever, that place was selected to confine these Friends in ; and strict orders were given not to allow any one of them to go out on any occasion.   The previous course of the Magistrates gave rise to the suspicion that this place was chosen with a hope that the contagious disease of which the two had died, might be still lurking about the premises, and thus assist the authorities in getting rid of some of the Quakers, whom they found it impossible otherwise to destroy.   Be that as it may, their victims were preserved in health, it may have been, to their chagrin and disappointment ; certainly beyond the expectation of the prisoners' friends.

Thus, iniquity and violence exalted themselves in what ought to have been courts of justice ; and so far were the actors from shame or condemnation — knowing that the last Conventicle Act was designed to entrap and oppress honest people, who dared to dissent from the " Episcopal Church," and to encourage the protection of all who were base enough to violate justice and truth in order to effect the end designed — that a short time after these memorable trials, the Court of Magistrates voted one hundred pounds, as a gift to Alderman Brown, for his valuable services at that session of the Old Bailey.

Robinson, Lieutenant of the Tower, having, as stated, destroyed Friends' meeting-house at Ratcliff, decided to pursue the same course with that in Wheeler street. The members becoming aware of this determination, some of them waited on him, requesting sufficient delay to allow of their communicating his intention to the owner: who was then in the North of England. This was granted; but he assured them that if the owner did not come before him in three weeks, at the end of that time he would not leave one stone of the house upon another. The owner was Gilbert Latey, who was sent for as fast as was then possible. Upon learning the danger in which the house stood, he at once had it formally leased to a Friend, who took possession of it as his tenant. All the necessary arrangements having been legally made, Gilbert appeared before Robinson prior to the expiration of the appointed time; when the following conversation is reported to have taken place:

"Robinson. — So you are the owner of this place?

Gilbert. — I am; and of several others too.

Robinson. — How dare you own any meeting-house, contrary to the King's law?

Gilbert. — I owned that meeting-house before the King had any such law.

Robinson. — I find you are a pretty fellow; and pray who lives in the meeting-house?

Gilbert. — My tenant.

Robinson. — Your tenant! What is your tenant?

Gilbert. — One that I thought good to grant a lease to.

Robinson.—Then you have a tenant that has taken a lease from you.

Gilbert.—Yes."

Robinson now saw that he was completely foiled, and turning to the other Friends who were present, said, " I think you have now fitted me. You have brought a fellow to your purpose. Had your friends been all as wise as this fellow, you might have had your other meeting-houses as well as this."

Taking the hint from this circumstance, Friends took the same course with other meeting-houses, and thus preserved them from destruction by the governmental authorities.

It is certainly a remarkable circumstance, that notwithstanding all the elaborate pains taken by the vindictive churchmen and venal Parliament, seconded by a faithless King and a profligate Court, to force Dissenters into a hypocritical conformity with the " church" established by law; and the degraded character of the men they enlisted as instruments to carry their cunningly devised scheme into effect; the havoc that was made of the means of subsistence, and the suffering inflicted by every means of punishment at the command of their enemies, yet Friends boldly and unflinchingly endured it all, rather than abate one jot in the maintenance of their right to worship the Almighty according to the dictates of their consciences. Through the conflict, far more galling to the spirit of a man than physical warfare, that, with brief intervals, lasted for years, they kept the banner, given them to display because of the Truth, constantly aloft, and finally secured the triumph of religious liberty, by wearing out the wrath and cruelty of their oppressors with meekness, patience, and long-suffering endurance.

The testimony of Neal, given in his history of the Puritans, may be again cited as coming from one who was far from being prejudiced in favor of Friends: it is partly quoted from Burnet. He says, referring to the time of which we have been treating, " The behavior of the Quakers was very extraordinary, and had something in it that looked like the spirit of martyrdom. They met at the same places and hour as in times of liberty, and when the officers came to seize them, none of them would stir: they went altogether to prison; they stayed there till they were dismissed; for they would not petition to be set at liberty,* nor pay the fines set upon them, nor so much as the prison fees. When they were discharged, they went to their meeting-houses again ·as before, and when the doors were shut up by order, they assembled in great numbers in the street before the doors; saying they would not be ashamed nor afraid to own their meeting together, in a peaceable manner, to worship God: but in imitation of the Prophet Daniel, they would do it more publicly, because they were forbid. Some called this obstinacy, others firmness; but by it they carried their point, the government being weary of contending against so much perverseness." The last word shows this was written in no laudatory spirit; but it cannot depreciate the inflexible Christian conduct that extorted such a testimony.

There being a little abatement in the heat of persecution in London, George Fox, towards the latter part of 1670, travelled through different parts of the country, inciting and encouraging Friends to faithfulness in the maintenance of their meetings, and patient en-

---

* This is a mistake, as they repeatedly presented their suffering case to the King.

durance of the suffering brought upon them therefor.   Before returning to London, he was taken sick, and his nervous system became so affected, that he lost both sight and hearing.   He believed this sickness was partly in consequence of the baptism of his spirit into a sense of the condition of those who were oppressing the truth and Friends; whom he designates as " man-eaters."   He says, " I was sensible I had a travail to go through, and therefore desired that none but solid, weighty Friends, might be about me. Under great sufferings and travails, sorrows and oppressions, I lay for several weeks; whereby I was brought so low and weak in body, that few thought I could live.   Some that were with me, went away, saying, ' They would not see me die;' and it was reported both in London and in the country, that I was deceased; but I felt the Lord's power inwardly supporting me."   When so far recovered that he began to have perception of light, he requested to be taken in a carriage, slowly from place to place; staying two or three weeks at the house of one Friend after another.   In the course of this slow moving from one part of the country to another, convalescence went on; but his weakness continued long so great he could hardly stand. A few days before the death of Amor Stoddard, who had been a faithful minister of and sufferer for the Truth, George Fox was taken to see him, and says, "I was moved to tell him, ' He had been faithful as a man, and faithful to God; and that the immortal Seed of Life was his crown.'"   He also wrote the following epistle to Friends:

" My dear Friends:—The Seed is above all.   In it walk; in which ye all have life.   Be not amazed at the weather; for always the just suffered by the unjust, but the just had the dominion.   All along ye may see, by faith the mountains were subdued, and the rage of the wicked, with his fiery darts, were quenched.   Though the waves and storms be high, yet your faith will keep you, so as to swim above them; for they are but for a time, and the truth is without time. Therefore keep on the mountain of holiness, ye who are led to it by the light, where nothing shall hurt.   Do not think that anything will outlast the truth, which standeth sure; and is over that which is out of the truth.   For the good will overcome the evil, the light darkness, the life death, virtue vice, and righteousness unrighteousness.   The false prophet cannot overcome the true; but the true prophet, Christ, will overcome all the false.   So be faithful, and live in that which doth not think the time long.   G. F."

During all this time Margaret Fox was again in jail at Lancaster, having been committed there by order of the King and Council, on the old sentence of premunire; with the consent, if not at the instigation, as was believed, of her son George, who was greatly exasperated at his mother marrying George Fox. George Fell was a barrister, a free liver, indulging in the manners and habits of a man of the world, and not unfrequently straitened for means to meet his expenses. Whether advised or not of his mother's intended marriage with George Fox, does not appear; but he became greatly incensed when he found it had taken place, and at once set to work to dispossess her and her daughters of Swarthmoor Hall. By the will of Judge Fell, his widow was to forfeit her right in the Hall should she again marry, and the daughters to come into possession of it. But the son, who was greatly prejudiced against them all, because of their having become Friends, was determined, if he could accomplish it, to drive them away from their home, and obtain it for himself.

CHAPTER XXV.

Imprisonment of I. Penington and T. Ellwood—I. P. and Earl of Bridgwater —Cruel treatment by the latter of the former — I. P. liberated by the Court in London—Testimony of a fellow prisoner—Wm. Dewsbury—His concern for J. Perrot—Great Imprisonment of Friends in York—Long Imprisonment of W. Dewsbury — Epistle by W. D.—Political Affairs—Royal Proclamation to suspend the Penal Laws against Dissenters — Friends liberated from Prison—Effects of their patient Suffering—Controversy with the Baptists — Dissatisfaction of the People — Proclamation Revoked — Arrest and Imprisonment of G. Fox — G. F.'s persecution by Parker — Interviews with G. F. in prison—Friends in Scotland—Alexander Skene—Queries addressed by A. Skene—Efforts of the Clergy to suppress Friends—Judges in Scotland admit an Affirmation instead of an Oath.

IT was not only in support of their religious obligation to keep up their meetings for Divine Worship, against the claim of tithes, and the unlawfulness of oaths, that Friends were called to suffer grievously; but for their obedience to their divine Lord and Master, in refusing those common and corrupt tokens of false honor to their fellow mortals, which marked the habits and manners of men of the world, and were intended to gratify pride, or promote self-interest.

In 1665 Thomas Ellwood and Isaac Penington were arrested and committed to the common jail, while attending the burial of a Friend; a Magistrate of the county choosing to construe the company of relatives and friends convened to pay the last office of respect to the departed, into a conventicle. Coming up to the procession, he knocked the coffined corpse off the shoulders of the Friends who were carrying it, into the street of the little town through which they were passing to the graveyard; and it laid for hours thus exposed before it was interred; when it was taken from the widow, and buried in what was called the unconsecrated portion of the "Church" ground. The Friends named, with eight others, who had been in attendance at the funeral, were kept in jail until the assize, when the Judge refused to hear their case, and the Magistrates who had committed them, discharged them at the end of a month from the time of holding the Court, without any trial having been granted them.

But I. Penington, having had occasion to address the Earl of Bridgwater, the latter took great offence because Isaac, in writing to him, had not used the term "My Lord," nor signed his letter "Your humble servant;" and he determined to punish him therefor. Accordingly, about four weeks after his recent discharge from the jail, I. Penington was again arrested and committed to Aylesbury prison, on a mittimus granted by the deputy-lieutenant of the county; which directed the jailer to keep him in safe custody, *during the pleasure* of the Earl of Bridgwater; and the Earl declared he should "lie in prison till he would rot," unless he publicly apologized for having addressed him as he did, and again address him as his rank demanded.

I. Penington's wife had not been able to leave her chamber since the birth of their last child, when her husband was thus taken from her, at the behest of the proud Earl; and doubtless the separation was a severe trial to her. The following letter shows the state of mind to which that meek and pure-hearted husband had attained. It was written from the jail.

1665. "My dear true Love.—I have hardly freedom to take notice of what hath passed, so much as in my own thoughts; but I am satisfied in my very heart, that the Lord, who is good, hath ordered things thus, and will bring about what He pleaseth thereby. Why should the fleshly-wise, reasoning part murmur, or find fault. Oh! be silent before the Lord, all flesh within me! and disturb not my soul in waiting on my God, to perceive what He is working in me and for me, and which He maketh these uncouth occurrences con-

duce unto. One thing have I desired of the Lord, even that I
may be his, perfectly disposed of by Him, know nothing but Him,
enjoy nothing but in his life and leadings. Thus must I give up
and part with even thee, my most dear and worthy love, or I cannot be happy in my own soul, nor enjoy thee as I desire.

"I find my heart deeply desiring and breathing after the pure
power of the Lord to reign in me; yet dare I not choose, but beg
to be taught to wait; and to be made willing to drink the residue
of the cup of suffering, both inward and outward, until the Lord
see fit to take it from my lips. Oh, my dear! say little concerning
me; plead not my cause; but be still in thy own spirit, and await
what the Lord will do for me; that all the prayers which, in the
tenderness of my soul, I have often put up for thee, may have their
full effect upon thee. My dear, be my true yoke-fellow, helpful to
draw my heart toward the Lord, and from everything but what is
sanctified by the presence and leadings of his life. I feel, and
thou knowest that I am, very dearly thine.   I. P."

The Earl, knowing that as his victim had broken no law, he
must be liberated if brought before Court, and that his friends were
fully expecting Isaac's discharge at the next assizes, exerted his influence with the Judges and other officers, and prevented his case
being called for trial. This flagrant prevention of justice took
place at every session of the Court for at least a year, and probably
more; for I. Penington was committed in the Sixth month of
1665, and an appeal to the Magistrates on behalf of his persecuted
Friends and himself, is dated from the jail, near the close of the
Fourth month of 1666. In this appeal, he says: "I have been and
still am a patient sufferer for well-doing, blessing the Lord who re-
deemeth and preserveth the souls of his children out of evil-doing,
and who bringeth his indignation and wrath, with great perplexity
and misery, upon nations and upon persons, who set themselves in
opposition to Him."

It has been mentioned, that when Isaac Penington's father was
sentenced for his participation in the trial of Charles I., all his
estate was confiscated to the King; and the greater part of it had
been bestowed by the King on the Duke of Grafton. But the
Grange at Chalfont had not been taken from his son Isaac, and he
had continued to reside there. While, however, he was thus kept
a prisoner, at the instigation of some one — and it was believed to
have been the Earl of Bridgwater—he was dispossessed of this home,

and his family turned out and obliged to seek a dwelling place; wherever the different members could find one. Some unprincipled persons, who knew that I. Penington could not take the needful oath to bring suit for money, due and withheld by the debtor, taking advantage of his conscientiousness, refused to pay him money they owed him, and thus completely impoverished him. In addition to this, one of his wife's relatives, knowing that she was bound by the same scruples against swearing as her husband, brought a suit to dispossess her of great part of the estate she inherited from her former husband; had the cause thrown into Chancery, where there was no redress except upon an oath, and thus succeeded in robbing her of it, because she could not verify her just title, by complying with the law. "Thus," she says, "we were stripped of my husband's estate, and wronged of great part of mine. After this, we were tossed up and down from place to place, to our great weariness and charge; seeing no place to abide in in this country, near to meetings; which had formerly been held at our house at Chalfont."

Some time after the publication of an address to the Magistrates, put forth by I. Penington, the Earl of Ancram, whether moved by it, or by the notorious injustice committed on the innocent sufferer, interfered, and succeeded in having him discharged from jail. He had, however, been liberated little more than three weeks, when the Earl of Bridgwater again persuaded the Deputy Lord-lieutenant to have him arrested, and sent to Aylesbury prison. Apparently anxious to rid themselves of this pious, unresisting Christian gentleman, they now had him shut up in a damp, cramped, unhealthy apartment; where he was soon taken sick, and in the course of a short time brought so low, that his life was despaired of; and it appeared as though his implacable enemies would succeed in their efforts to move him out of the way. But it pleased his heavenly Father, whom it was his greatest delight to serve, to raise him up from his bed of languishing, and restore him to comparative health and strength. The unprincipled Earl was unrelenting; he persisted in saying he should apologize for not addressing him as My Lord, and publicly give him that title, and subscribe himself his obedient servant; and none of the Judges were willing to incur his displeasure, for the sake of a poor despised Quaker; so that little hope was entertained of his again escaping. But a relative of Mary Penington, becoming acquainted with the circumstances of her husband's unrighteous persecution, took out a writ of *habeas corpus*, and had the case brought before the Court in London ; where, upon examination, there was found to be no charge recorded against him ; there was no cause to try, and he was at once set free. This was in 1668.

In 1672, I. Penington having gone to visit some Friends who were prisoners in Reading jail, a Magistrate of that place hearing he was there, sent for him, and on his appearing before him, tendered him the oath of allegiance; which he informing the Magistrate he could not conscientiously take, he was committed to the prison. He was kept there closely for twenty-one months ; when he was liberated by the King, at the time he issued his order to discharge all Friends who were incarcerated on suits of the crown.

One of the Friends who was a fellow-sufferer with I. Penington, bears this testimony concerning him while he was a prisoner : " Being made willing by the power of God, to suffer with patience, cheerfulness, contentedness and true nobility of spirit, he was a good example to me and others. I do not remember that ever I saw him cast down or dejected during the time of his close confinement, or ever heard him speak hardly of those that persecuted him ; for he was of that temper to love enemies, and to do good to them that hated him ; having received a measure of that virtue from Christ his Master, that taught him so to do. Indeed I may truly say, in the prison he was a help to the weak, being made instrumental in the hand of the Lord for that end. Oh ! the remembrance of the glory that did often overshadow us in the place of our confinement ; so that indeed the prison was made by the Lord, who was powerfully with us, a pleasant palace. I was often, with many more, by those streams of [spiritual] life, that did many times flow through him, as a vessel, greatly overcome with a sense of the pure presence and love of God, that was plentifully spread abroad in our hearts."

Although William Dewsbury, when engaged in the service of his Lord, as a minister of the gospel, appears to have been greatly favored, and to have had many seals to the convincing power and efficacy of his ministry, yet it was permitted, in divine wisdom, that he should prove himself to be a faithful witness to his full conviction of the divine origin and obligation of the doctrines he preached, and the self-denying testimonies he exemplified in his daily life, by the meekness and Christian cheerfulness with which he bore imprisonment during nearly the whole of the last twenty-five years of his life. He had been greatly distressed with the course pursued by J. Perrot, and in an epistle addressed by him

" To all the faithful in Christ," in the year 1663, the following passages occur, " Oh! how did my bowels yearn for the preservation of John Perrot, in doing what I could to draw and separate him from that spirit which gave forth the paper that propagated the keeping on of the hat in prayer, and reflected upon those that called upon the name of the Lord with their heads uncovered. But after much counselling of him in tender love, to stop that paper from going abroad, and he would not be separated from that spirit which gave it forth, I cleared my conscience, in the word of the Lord. And now, in my freedom in God, I declare to the children of Zion, what the judgment is that did arise in my heart; to this purpose :— John, if thou propagate what thou hast written in this paper, thou wilt wound more hearts and cause more trouble of spirit among the tender-hearted people of the Lord, than when the temptation entered James Naylor; who deeply suffered; but the Lord restored him again by true repentance. And as to my particular, it is not my nature to be found striving with thee, or with any upon the earth; but having declared the truth to thee, I will return to my rest in the Lord; and let every birth live out the length of its day, and let time manifest what is born of God," &c.

In 1660, William Dewsbury was confined, first in Ouse-bridge prison in the city of York, then in York Tower; whence in 1661 he was removed to York Castle. The cause for imprisonment was refusal to take the oath of allegiance. At one time in the year 1661, there were five hundred and thirty-six Friends shut up in the prisons of Yorkshire; five hundred and five of whom were crowded into the Castle; where five of them died from diseases brought on by the unhealthiness of their quarters. From this imprisonment he was liberated by the proclamation of King Charles II., issued just after he came to the throne. Several of the extraordinary epistles which he sent abroad to his brethren and sisters, while they were suffering so grievously for the testimony of Jesus, in which he strives to build them up on the most holy faith, and to bring home to them a renewed sense of the consolations of the gospel, were dated from York Castle or dungeon.

He had been at liberty but a few months, when he was again sent to Warwick prison, with several other Friends. [1661.] He had given thanks after supper at an inn; which was construed by the informer and Magistrate into preaching at a conventicle. Again the oath of allegiance was tendered, and as the Friends could not take it they were sent to the jail; where some of them were kept for ten years. How W. Dewsbury was extricated from this imprisonment is not recorded; but in a short time after his commitment, he was in London; where he wrote an address to his suffering brethren, dated in the Twelfth month of 1661, from Newgate prison. Discharged from there in 1662, he returned to his family and home; earnestly engaged however at different places in the work of the ministry, by which many were convinced, and, under the operation of the Holy Spirit in their hearts, converted. In the Fifth month of that year, he was taken from his home, and again committed to York Castle, on the charge of being "a ringleader among the Quakers." Here he was closely kept until the fore part of 1663, when he obtained a release. But towards the latter part of that year, he was again sent prisoner to Warwick common jail; where he remained in close confinement until some time early in 1672, over eight years. While thus enduring bonds for the testimony of Jesus, he continued to enjoy that life which is hid with Christ in God, and his pen was not idle; but employed again and again to address his fellow-professors and sufferers.

One of these epistles, written when the Courts were sentencing Friends to transportation, was addressed to "My dear, honorable brethren, who are or may be sentenced to be transported to the isles beyond the sea, for the testimony of the name of the Lord Jesus." Another was to "Those from whom the Lord hath suffered or shall suffer their dear and tender husbands to be separated beyond the seas or elsewhere, for the testimony of the Lord Jesus Christ." The latter breathes such a sweet, loving, but steadfast spirit, that it may well have a place here.

"Dear handmaids, whom the Lord hath counted worthy to part with your dear and tender husbands for his name — assuredly many put their shoulders to help to bear the burdens of your trials in this day. O, the tears and breakings of heart, that are poured forth before the Lord, for your dear husbands, for you and your dear children! Ye are families of many prayers, and assuredly shall be known to be families of many mercies. Be content with your cup handed forth to you, and bless the name of the Lord, that you are accounted worthy to be the first fruits. What could the Lord do more for you, than count you worthy to suffer in this nature, and give you such husbands, who are set as lights in the face of all people; let it be seen that you love the Lord Jesus more than your dear husbands. Stand over the affectionate part, and solace your souls in the love and life of the Lord Jesus, your eternal husband, and the comforter of your earthly husbands. He will make us all rejoice in whatever He calls us unto; we diligently watching and judging ourselves, and resting in the Light, and in the will of God. In which, the Lord establish you; for whom your brother breathes daily to the Lord, to strengthen you and your dear husbands, and all who love the Lord Jesus Christ, in whom fare you well.

W. D."

In 1672 there was a temporary suspension of persecution of Dissenters; more relieving to Friends than others, because of their being the chief sufferers. King Charles, constantly in need of money to meet the expenses of himself and his Court, and strongly inclined to openly embrace the Romish religion, which his brother, the Duke of York, had for some time avowed and practised, had entered into a secret treaty with Louis the XIV. of France; by which, for a stipulated sum, to be paid him annually, he had bound himself, and as far as he had the power, the government of England, to make public profession of the Catholic faith; to employ the strength of England in assisting the French monarch to conquer the United Provinces, and in support of the claim of the House of Bourbon to the throne of Spain, in case of the death of the young and sickly reigning Sovereign of that Kingdom. Parliament had been induced by representation of the cabinet — then called the Cabal — that it was necessary for the support and enlargement of the fleet, to vote a large sum of money — nearly a million of pounds — which being the chief service the King and his Council cared for it to perform, it was at once prorogued. The suspicion of the nation had long been aroused, by the marriage of the King to a Catholic princess, the proclivity of several of the members of the Court towards that religion, and the openly acknowledged preference of the Duke of York for it, that a design was covertly entertained to bring the Catholics again into power. It was therefore necessary that the initiatory steps for carrying out the secret treaty with France, should be taken slowly and stealthily.

Professing to be moved by the sufferings of a large portion of his subjects, and his strong desire to promote domestic union and peace, the King issued, in 1672, a Proclamation; in which, claiming the right inherent in his royal person, and in virtue of his supreme authority in ecclesiastical matters, as head of the church, he suspended the execution of all penal laws against those who did not conform to the doctrine, discipline and government of the " church established by law."

False as were the avowed motives, and arbitrary the power assumed for this ostensibly laudable act, the act itself was one of indescribable relief to those who were paying the penalty of the infraction of those laws, in supporting the truths of the gospel, and the right of liberty of conscience.

Friends, ever on the alert to relieve their suffering brethren, at once took steps for availing themselves of the provisions of the proclamation. George Whitehead, Thomas Moor and Thomas Green, waited on the King and Council. In the interview, these Friends again took occasion to assure the King, that the refusal of Friends to take the oath of allegiance, was solely because they felt themselves restrained by the command of Christ, and his Apostle James, not to swear; and that it was not from any disloyalty to him or disrespect to his government. The King told them he would pardon their friends. It being said, that as they were innocent they needed no pardon, and that the order from the King would be all-sufficient for their release, the Council informed the Friends that such a release would not free the prisoners from the penalties they had incurred; and unless they were cleared by the King's pardon, they would be liable to be re-imprisoned, and their fines, and the sentence of premunire, would still hang over them. The necessary letters-patent were then made out; the Lord Keeper (Orlando Bridgeman) voluntarily remitted his fees; and as the number of Friends in the different jails throughout the country was so large, that the fees for procuring their separate discharge would have amounted to a great sum, the King ordered that the pardon, though comprehending so many, should be charged but as one. There were upwards of four hundred names of Friends included in it, and it required eleven skins of parchment for a fair copy.

The Solicitors employed by other Dissenters, now applied to Friends to assist them in obtaining a similar discharge of those professing with them, who were in prison; and Friends, as George Whitehead remarks, "were glad of it, and that they partook of the benefit through our industry." Friends advised them to apply to the King for liberty to have the names of their friends included in the letters-patent, already procured by Friends; which they did, and obtained his consent, and among these names was that of John Bunyan. The act of pardon completed, it required great contrivance and labor to carry it as quickly as possible to the different jails,

where Friends,were shut up, and have it obeyed by the liberation
of the prisoners. But Friends in London were too heartily interested in the welfare of their brethren and sisters, to halt because of
the trouble or expense; they pursued the good work they had in
hand, unremittingly, overcame all obstacles, and in a little while
had the gladdening assurance that all those who came within the
scope of the letters-patent, were now at liberty; not a few of whom
had been suffering the hardships of prison life for many years; Wm.
Dewsbury, as before stated, was one thus liberated.

The conduct of Friends during the season of conflict and persecution through which they had been passing, had made a strong impression upon many members of other Dissenting Societies, and
these had not hesitated to acknowledge that it was their unconquera-
ble firmness, and unresisting suffering, that had baffled the unrighteous schemes of the dominant hierarchy and subservient civil authorities, to enforce uniformity of profession and modes of worship;
and had in great measure screened other sects from the severity of the
punishment, which, had they been faithful to their profession, would
have reached them. This led many to examine into the religious
principles of Friends, and to compare the course pursued by them
with that of many of their own pastors and fellow professors. The
consequence was, that considerable numbers were convinced of the
scriptural soundness of those principles, and joined in fellowship
with the Society. This was especially the case from among the
Baptists; insomuch that when under the protection of the King's .
proclamation, they were not afraid to appear openly before the
public, some of their preachers, who had lost many of their former
hearers, brought railing accusations against Friends, both in their
pulpits and by publishing pamphlets. One of their ministers named
Hicks, had printed and spread abroad, "A Dialogue between a
Christian and a Quaker." In this he represented the "Quaker" as
uttering many unscriptural and absurd opinions; which the "Christian," of course, easily refuted and proved to be unsound. The
whole was so worded as to impress the reader with the belief that
it was a correctly reported conversation, that had actually taken
place.

William Penn soon published a reply, entitled, "The Christian
Quaker, and his Divine Testimony Vindicated," in which he not
only exposed the disingenuousness of attributing to Friends sentiments they never held or promulgated, and the folly of thus setting .
up a mere man of straw to be overturned; but he explained and

enforced the doctrine of the Light of Christ, or the Spirit of Truth being furnished to all men. That it emanates from Christ, who the Scriptures declare, is the true Light that lighteth every man that cometh into the world: that it convinces of sin, and leadeth all who co-operate with it out of sin and into all truth; consequently it bears testimony to the Divinity of the Lord Jesus Christ, and to all his offices; to his atonement, as the propitiatory sacrifice for the sins of the whole world; to his Mediatorship, and to his being the Advocate with the Father; and that this doctrine of the Light of Christ in the soul of man, is a distinguishing characteristic of the Society of Friends.

There was another pamphlet, entitled, " The Dialogue Continued," and a third; to all which replies were made, and the scriptural soundness of the doctrines held by Friends fully established.

The Baptist ministers having made a personal attack upon the character of Wm. Penn and George Whitehead, the latter entered a complaint thereof, to some of the leading men in their Society, and asked that an opportunity be given them to clear themselves and their religious belief of the charges made. A meeting was appointed by the Baptists at a time when the Friends implicated were away from London; and on some Friends in that city being informed of it, they gave notice that Wm. Penn and G. Whitehead were too far away to receive word of the meeting, and to get to the city in time to attend it; and therefore they desired it might be postponed for a few days. This, however, was not granted, but the meeting assembled, and as there were none to controvert what was said, of course the charges were declared to be proved.

Upon Wm. Penn being informed of what had occurred, he at once came to London, and demanded another meeting, where the complaint made against Friends might be investigated. At first this was opposed; but was finally acceded to; and at the meeting appointed, Thomas Hicks and Jeremy Ives spoke on behalf of the Baptists, and Wm. Penn, George Whitehead and George Keith, on behalf of Friends. The dispute, which appears to have been principally about the distinction between the manhood and the deity of Christ — the Baptists refusing to enter into an examination of the charges brought against Friends, but attacking William Penn's " Christian Quaker,"— was inconclusive and unsatisfactory, as to settling the points of difference. Again Friends endeavored to obtain another conference, but the Baptists refused; whereupon Friends appointed a meeting to be held at their own house in

Wheeler Street, and invited Hicks and the others of their opponents who were willing, to come to it. Hicks, who was the author of a charge that Friends were not Christians, refused to attend; but Ives, and some others, were sent, who altogether objected to any examination of the charges made, and of course Friends could obtain no acknowledgment of the injustice done them. One good consequence however resulted, in that many of the Baptist congregation left them and joined Friends.

Several Friends were now much engaged in preparing controversial writings, in defence of the doctrines they held and preached, and in exposing and refuting the charges brought against them, as being unsound in the Christian faith. Disagreeable as this mode of warfare was, it was found that the more closely the religious faith of the Society was sifted and tested, the more it was proved to be consonant with Scripture, and the greater the number that embraced it.

Taking into consideration how frequently Friends who were called to the work, were engaged abroad in ministerial labors; and how often and long many of those not engaged as ministers, as well as the latter, were shut up in prisons, it is surprising the promptness with which they replied to every printed attack made upon them or the doctrines they preached; how freely they resorted to the press to give a general knowledge of the principles they held; to refute error; to expose the evil spirit and fruits of persecution, and to promote holiness of life and conversation. Printing in that day was expensive; but, robbed and spoiled as they were of their outward substance, by unjust fines and the levies of merciless priests, and often maimed or enfeebled by the punishments inflicted by their persecutors, it is remarkable that they yet found means for defraying the expense of publishing and circulating the great number of works they wrote. This is one of the striking evidences of their considering everything they had — talents, time, and property — as belonging to the gracious Giver of all things we enjoy; and that it was their duty to serve Him and his cause first, and themselves afterwards.

Productive of relief to Dissenters as was the proclamation of the King, releasing them from the further action of the penal laws for enforcing conformity, it came from too doubtful and polluted a source, to allow expectation of its long continuance. The object had in view was rather relief to Popish recusants, than favor to the great body of the people that refused to be included in the Established Church. That portion of the large sum voted by Parliament for

the increase of the navy, which the King and Court had been enabled to appropriate for their own use, was soon squanderéd. A
flagrant breach of public faith, in refusing to refund money that
had been temporarily loaned to the government, by the goldsmiths
of London, and obliging the lenders to be satisfied with the interest
allowed upon the principal, gave rise to great monetary distress
and disorder.   There was increasing dissatisfaction with the influence Roman Catholics were obtaining in different ways, and even
very many of the Non-conformists, who had managed to conceal or
screen themselves while the storm of persecution raged, joined in
publicly denouncing the assumption of arbitrary power, by which
the King had proclaimed toleration, and claimed the prerogative
to set the laws of the realm at naught.   Louis the XIV. found the
expenditure required to carry on the war with three powers on the
Continent so great, that he could not pay the sum by which he had
subsidized Charles, and the latter could do without anything else,
better than money to pay for his debaucheries. The murmured
discontent of the people, was not to be disregarded, the want of
money pressed, and there was no alternative but to reassemble Parliament, which had been repeatedly prorogued, and trust to the
policy and chicanery of the "Cabal," to manipulate it into compliance with the royal will and exigencies.

1673. When assembled, the first step taken by the Commons was
to give the King to understand, that his proclamation of toleration
was contrary to the spirit of the Constitution, and inconsistent with
the limited power with which the sovereign of Great Britian was
invested.   A demand was made for its withdrawal, and the King
and Council were given clearly to understand, that until that was
done, they need look for no supply of pecuniary means to carry
on the war, or to meet the other necessities of the government.
Charles, at first, appeared inclined to insist upon what he claimed
as his prerogative; but some of his ministers cowered before the
determined tone of the House, and withdrew their support from the
unpopular measure; and as money was a *sine qua non* with the
King, he yielded to the demand, revoked the declaration he had
made, and promised not to pursue such a course again.

Doubtless this action of the Parliament in restriction of despotic
power, sprung from a noble motive in some, to secure the acknowledged liberties of the people, and so far it deserves praise; but
there can be as little doubt, that with many others, it had its origin
in their hatred of Dissenters, and their unwillingness to see them in

the enjoyment of the exercise of their religion, freed from the severe punishments they had inflicted on them therefor.

The priests, Magistrates and informers were once more let loose, to reap their harvest of unrighteous gains; and Friends, as before, came under the cruel scourge of the infamous law of 1670.

George Fox, who with his wife had been travelling among Friends and holding meetings, being in Worcestershire, was with his son-in-law, Thomas Lower, apprehended, while at a Friend's house, and committed by Henry Parker, a justice of the peace, to the county jail; the charge against them being, that they were holding large meetings to the prejudice of the established church. The mittimus was dated December 17th, 1673. After their incarceration, some Friends accompanied Margaret Fox and her daughters, more than one of whom appear to have been with her, to their home in the North.

At the session of the Court there was nothing found against the prisoners, as they had been taken out of a private house, where there was no conventicle held, and Thomas Lower was discharged; but the Court tendered the oath of allegiance to George Fox, and upon his telling the Magistrates that he could not break Christ's command by taking an oath, he was recommitted to the prison; and his son-in-law, refusing to be liberated while his father was kept prisoner, went with him. After some time the case was removed to the Court of the King's Bench, in London, by a writ of *habeas corpus;* and from the manner in which the proceedings were conducted, and the conduct of the Judges towards George Fox, there was reason to believe his liberation would soon take place. The Sheriff of Worcester was discharged from the care of him, and he was placed in the custody of the "keeper" of the King's Bench Court. But Justice Parker, who was his present persecutor, having come to London and obtained an interview with the Judges, they had George again brought before them, and gave an order to have him remitted to the Worcester sessions. He was, however, upon his promise to appear, permitted to take his own time and way for going there. He stayed in London some time, attended the Yearly Meeting, and then travelled leisurely to Worcester, for he was still infirm and weak, and appeared at the session. Parker again succeeded in having the oath tendered to him, and he was recommitted for refusing to take it. At the instance of some of the Magistrates who were friendly to him, he was permitted to have the liberty of the town until the next session.

While thus a prisoner at large, George Fox embraced the opportunities that presented, to spread a knowledge of the truth ; as will be seen by the following extracts from his Journal :

" At one time came three non-conformist priests and two lawyers to discourse with me ; and one of the priests undertook to prove, ' That the Scriptures are the only rule of life.' After I had defeated his proof, I had a fit opportunity to open to them, ' The right and proper use, service, and excellency of the Scriptures ; and also to show, that the Spirit of God which was given to every one to profit withal, the grace of God which bringeth salvation, and which hath appeared to all men, and teacheth them that obey it to deny ungodliness and worldly lusts, and to live soberly, righteously, and godly in this present world ; that this, I say, is the most fit, proper, and universal rule which God hath given to all mankind to rule, direct, govern, and order their lives by.'

" Another time came a common-prayer priest, and some people with him. He asked me, ' If I was grown up to perfection ? ' I told him, ' What I was, I was by the grace of God.' He replied, ' It was a modest and civil answer.' Then he urged the words of John, ' If we say that we have no sin, we deceive ourselves, and the truth is not in us.' He asked, ' What did I say to that ? ' ' I said with the same apostle, " If we say that we have not sinned, we make him a liar, and his word is not in us ; " who came to destroy sin, and to take away sin. So there is a time for people to see that they have sinned, and there is a time for them to see that they have sin ; and there is a time for them to confess their sin, and to forsake it, and to know the blood of Christ to cleanse from all sin.' Then the priest was asked, ' Whether Adam was not perfect before he fell ? and whether all God's works were not perfect ? ' The priest said, ' There might be a perfection as Adam had, and a falling from it.' But I told him, ' There is a perfection in Christ above Adam, and beyond falling ; and that it was the work of the ministers of Christ to present every man perfect in Christ ; for the perfecting of whom they had their gifts from Christ ; therefore they that denied perfection, denied the work of the ministry, and the gifts which Christ gave for the perfecting of the saints.' The priest said, ' We must always be striving.' I answered, ' It was a sad and comfortless sort of striving, to strive with a belief that we should never overcome.' I told him also, that ' Paul, who cried out of the body of death, did also thank God who gave him the victory through our Lord Jesus Christ.' So there was a time of crying out for want of victory, and a time of praising God for the victory. And Paul said, ' There is no condemnation to them that are in Christ Jesus.' The priest said, 'Job was not perfect.' I told him, God said Job was a perfect man, and that he did shun evil; and the devil was forced to confess, that 'God had set an hedge about him; which was not an outward hedge, but the invisible, heavenly power.' The priest said, 'Job said, He chargeth his angels with folly, and the heavens are not clean in his sight.' I told him, 'That was his mistake, it was not Job said so, but Eliphaz, who contended against Job.' 'Well, but,' said the priest, 'what say you to that Scripture, 'The justest man that is, sinneth seven times a day?' 'Why truly,' said I, 'I say there is no such Scripture;' and with that the priest's mouth was stopped. Many other services I had with several sorts of people between the assizes and the sessions." Here he must be left for the present.

Such was the strength and bitterness of the feeling prevailing among the Presbyterians in Scotland, against the Episcopal system of religion, which had been established by law and force in that section of the United Kingdom, that the attention of the ruling power there was kept so much occupied with efforts to introduce their own forms of worship, and to suppress the determined opposition of the great body of the people;—who, in their hearts, preferred the Puritan Synod and the outlawed "Conventicle"—that for a considerable time, Friends, as a body comparatively small in number escaped general persecution; except such as consisted in the denunciations and misrepresentations of the "ministers," and the abuse of the lower classes. But it was a noted circumstance, that among the early converts to the religious principles of Friends, in Scotland, especially at Aberdeen and its vicinity, were men and women who had long been conspicuous as strict religious professors; and who, by the exemplary purity of their lives, and devotedness to their duties, in both civil and religious society, had acquired very considerable notoriety and influence in the community. Among such as these, were Alexander Skene, one of the Magistrates of Aberdeen, and Tho n Mercer, "Dean of Guild;" both of whom withdrew from the "church," and joined Friends.

The former had been a violent opponent of "Quakers;" insomuch, that on one occasion he had declared, "It were well to take that villain, George Keith, and hang him up at the cross of Aberdeen." Having been, soon after this speech, seized with spasms in the muscles of the mouth and cheeks, producing what is termed *risus sardonicus,* he believed it was inflicted on him for his passion and furious speech against an innocent man; and being thereby brought seriously to examine into his own spiritual condition, and to give obedient heed to the "reproofs of instruction," he became convinced not only that he had been in the gall of bitterness, but that he must adopt the religion of the "Quakers" he had so much despised; and he was favored with ability to take up the daily cross and join with Friends in their work and suffering.

The loss of several of their highly esteemed members greatly excited the "ministers;" who feared the effect it would have on others in their congregations; and these fears were increased by the spread of some queries on the subject of worship, addressed to the ministers, by A. Skene. As these show the uniformity of views respecting the spiritual nature of the religion of Christ, and the necessity of waiting for ability from Him to perform any religious act, into which the early members of the Society were led, wherever and however brought to a knowledge of the truth, they may claim a place in these pages.

First. "Should any act of God's worship be gone about without the motions, leadings and actings of the Holy Spirit?"

Second. "If the motions of the Spirit be necessary to every particular duty, whether should He be waited upon, that all our acts and words may be according as He gives utterance and assistance?"

Third. "Whether every one that bears the name of a Christian, or professes to be a Protestant, hath such an uninterrupted measure thereof [the sensible prompting of the Holy Spirit] that he may, without waiting, go immediately about the duty?"

Fourth. "If there be an indisposition and unfitness at some times for such exercises, at least as to the spiritual and lively performance of them, ought they to be performed in *that* case and at *that* time?"

Fifth. "If any such duty be gone about under pretence that *it is in obedience to the external command*, without the spiritual life and motion necessary, whether such a duty thus performed can *in faith be expected to be accepted of God;* and not rather reckoned as a bringing of 'strange fire' before the Lord? seeing it is performed, at best, by the strength of natural and acquired parts, and not by the strength and assistance of the Holy Ghost: which was typified by the fire that came down from heaven; which alone behoved to consume the sacrifice, and no other."

Sixth. "Whether such duties gone about in the mere strength of natural and acquired parts, either in public or in private, be not as *really*, upon the gross matter, *an image of men's invention, as the Popish worship?* though not so gross in the outward appearance? and, therefore, whether it be not as real superstition to *countenance* any worship of that nature, as it is to *countenance* Popish worship, though there be a difference *in the degree?*"

Seventh. "Whether it be a ground of offence or just scandal, to countenance the worship of those, whose professed principle it is neither to speak for edification, nor to pray, but as the Holy Ghost shall be pleased to assist them in some measure, more or less; without which they rather choose to be silent, than to speak without this influence."

The Bishop of Aberdeen summoned a convention of ministers, who sent a messenger to the King's Council at Edinburgh, with a petition, that it would "Take some effectual course to curb and rid the land of the Quakers, who were increasing among them." The Council, however, declined to pass any new ordinance, but referred the petitioners to an Act that had been passed some time before; that all who withdrew "from the parish church, be admonished by the preachers before two sufficient witnesses," and then after a continued absence of three more weeks, "they be fined one-eighth of their valued rents."

This was considered too mild a punishment, by the ministers; but they set about giving the legal notice to Friends, and in order to mulct them in the fines, they prevailed upon the Magistrates of Aberdeen, to pass an ordinance: "That no Quaker should be made a burgess or freeman of that City; that whosoever received a Quaker into his house, without leave of the Magistrate, should be fined five shillings; and that if any person should let a house for Quakers, either to meet or dwell in, he should be fined £28 2s. 6d. sterling." But to the great chagrin of the persecutors, just as they were about to inflict the suffering prepared, the King's Proclamation of Indulgence came forth, and stopped the hands stretched out to seize upon the property of their honest neighbors and town's people. Friends in Scotland as in England, looked upon this as a providential interference, and with many other Non-conformists, accepted it with gratitude.

Friends also obtained relief in another case of conscience, in which many of them had suffered greatly. The law required, that unless there was a witness to the contraction of a debt, it could not be legally collected, unless the debtor refused to take an oath that he did not owe the money claimed. As Friends could neither take an

oath themselves, nor call upon others to take one, some of them had
been made a prey repeatedly, by dishonest persons bringing claims
against them altogether false and unjust; but from which Friends
could not clear themselves by oath ; and again, by such persons refusing to pay debts they justly owed to Friends; relying on the
want of evidence, and their known conscientiousness in relation to
swearing.

The Supreme Judges, witnessing the great injustice thus perpetrated upon men whom they believed to be honest and sincerely
conscientious, adopted a resolution, that in such cases the simple
declaration of a Friend to the truth of the statement he made,
should be accepted. This was long before the affirmation of a
Friend was made legal in England.

CHAPTER XXVI.

Robert Barclay—Death of A. Jaffray—Severe persecution begun at Aberdeen
—Dispute of R. Barclay and G. Keith with Students—Barclay's Apology
—Friends imprisoned in Aberdeen—Sympathized with by other Friends—
Letter of Princess Elizabeth—G. Fox sentenced to Premunire—Carried to
London on *Habeas Corpus*—Discharged—Account of Richard Davies—G.
Fox, while too feeble to travel much, writes Epistles, &c.—Friends visit
Holland—Great Spoliation of Friends—Unjust constructions of the " Con-
venticle Act"—The King and Church Party inexorable—Interview of G.
Whitehead and W. Crouch with the Bishop of Canterbury.

IN 1669, Robert Barclay was married to Christian — daughter
of Gilbert and Margaret Molleson. Gilbert had been one of
the Magistrates of Aberdeen, and now, with his wife, was a highly
esteemed member amongst Friends. So incensed were the "ministers," that a marriage should take place without any of them being
allowed to officiate in it — it being the first one so solemnized in that
city — that they applied to the Bishop, and through him procured
a summons of R. Barclay, to appear before the Privy Council at
Edinburgh, to answer for an unlawful marriage. But the account
states, " This matter was so overruled of the Lord, that they never
had power to put their summons into execution, so as to do any
prejudice."

At Ury, where David Barclay and his son Robert were settled,
a Monthly Meeting was established in 1669 ; also " a more public or

general meeting" was held there half-yearly; the first of which is mentioned as remarkable for the convincement "of several people of good account." Meetings "for transacting the affairs of the Church," were set up in different localities in Scotland, as circumstances called for them.

Young as Robert Barclay was, when, under the transforming power of the Grace of God, he forsook the alluring pleasures and honors of the world, to bear the cross of Christ, and espouse the cause of truth and righteousness in the midst of a crooked and perverse generation, he soon gave unmistakable evidence, that with all his intellectual acuteness, and his acquired store of learning, he had come to realize that "The fear of the Lord is the beginning of wisdom, and the knowledge of the holy is understanding." It is recorded of him that he passed through many humbling and heart-searching baptisms; by submitting to which, and keeping his spiritual eye single and fixed on Christ, the Author and Finisher of the saints' faith, he was favored with a clear view and understanding of many of the mysteries of the Kingdom of heaven, the purity and spirituality of the gospel of Christ, and the mixed and corrupt professions of religions prevailing in the world. As a minister, he is said to have borne a faithful testimony to the truth; clearly setting forth the doctrines contained in the Holy Scriptures; fearlessly rebuking spiritual wickedness in high places, and urging the indispensable necessity for the natural man to be brought under the quick and powerful operation of the Word of God, sharper than any two-edged sword, piercing even to the dividing asunder of the soul and spirit, and of the joints and marrow; and is a discerner of the thoughts and intents of the heart. Some of the services required of him were of a very humiliating character; as that which he performed in the early part of 1673 — then in his twenty-sixth year — when he went through the principal streets of Aberdeen, clothed in sackcloth, as "a spectacle unto men;" that he might awaken them to a true sense of their condition, and the necessity for abasement and repentance, for having despised the day of the Lord's visitation, and made merry over His witness in their hearts. He afterwards wrote an address to the inhabitants of that city, which breathes the loving, truthful spirit of an ambassador of Him who came to seek and to save that which was lost.

Shortly before this, when travelling with John Swintoune — or Swinton — they visited the few Friends, who held a meeting at Kinnaber; where they with others were arrested and committed to prison, and were there kept a considerable time; but exactly how long, or how their liberation was effected, is not mentioned.

While Friends were enduring much suffering in Scotland, they received an epistle from their fellow-believer and sufferer, William Dewsbury, dated Warwick, Eighth month, 1672; which conveys the Christian sympathy and evangelical spirit which marked that devoted servant of the Lord. The following short extract is from it. "The Almighty God keep all your garments clean in his holy power, and in it exercise you to the building up of one another on your most holy faith; that in the pure, chaste love, you may grow up in the unity of the Spirit, and bond of peace, to shine forth as the morning stars, to enlighten the people in that nation. . . . . And seeing God hath called you to be the first fruits, and to make you a blessing; as you wait to be ordered of the Lord, then will my expectation be answered in behalf of the holy Seed, whom my soul loves in that land."

In the early part of 1673, Alexander Jaffray, who has been mentioned as one of the earliest convinced in Scotland, of the doctrines of Friends, and who had been a faithful witness through much suffering to the virtue and power of the principles he professed, died, after an illness of twelve days. In the course of his last sickness, he remarked, "That it was a great joy and comfort in that trying hour, that ever he had been counted worthy to bear testimony to, and suffer for, that invaluable principle, of Christ's inward appearance in the hearts of the children of men; visiting all by his Light, Grace, or Good Spirit, which convinceth of sin; and that the great judgment and condemnation of many in the nation, especially the religious professors, was, and would be, their having so slighted and despised, yea, hated this Divine Light, and the witnesses of it."

The King having withdrawn his proclamation in favor of Dissenters, the Council at Edinburgh issued an order against "house or field conventicles," and requiring every head of a family to sign a bond obliging themselves and those under their control, not to keep or be present at any such assemblies. The ministers and Magistrates of Aberdeen were prompt to avail themselves of this device, for persecuting Friends. They went to their meeting-house, while assembled for worship, ordered them away, and on their refusing to leave, had them forcibly expelled. But on their ejectors departing, Friends quietly reassembled in the house, and R. Barclay and G. Keith were engaged in the ministry.

Friends were then fined, and a ministering Friend from England, was put in the Tolbooth, where he was kept over three months. They were afterwards denounced by name at the market-cross, as rebels against the State, and their personal property declared forfeited to the King's use.

Besides his engagements as a minister, Robert Barclay employed his pen in defence of, and in promulgating, the truth. In 1673, he published his "Catechism or Confession of Faith;" and forasmuch as the enemies of Friends charged them with denying or undervaluing the Scriptures, he used in it Scripture text altogether, for replies to the interrogatories upon points of Christian doctrine.

Having prepared and published some "Propositions," embracing the "Chief principles and doctrines of Truth," as held by Friends; and for rescuing his fellow believers from the unjust charges of unbelief in the great fundamental truths of the Christian religion, and the odium cast upon them; Robert Barclay offered to defend them where those charges had been made, and against those who had thus traduced Friends. But the "ministers" of Aberdeen declined to meet him, and on the 14th of Second month, 1675, he and George Keith, met several students of "divinity," in the presence of many hundred people. Although the Friends were desirous to enter upon the controversy, with the ministers and teachers themselves, yet, finding they would not come forward, they disputed with the students for about three hours; when the latter began treating the serious subjects under consideration with great levity, then resorted to personal abuse, and finally employed "clods and stones," ending the dispute in tumult and disorder. The students claimed that they had gained a victory; but the evidence of the superior argumentation of the Friends was, that four students, who took no personal part in the controversy, were convinced of the soundness of the doctrines advocated by Friends, joined the Society, and had published a statement of the grounds upon which they had changed their religious views.

The "Propositions," thus put forth by R. Barclay, were the basis on which he afterwards, under a sense of religious duty, constructed his celebrated "Apology for the true Christian Divinity; being an Explanation and Vindication of the Principles and Doctrines of the People called Quakers;" which was published in 1675, and which has been acknowledged, put forth, and recommended by the Society ever since, as a correct, fair and unimpeachable exposition of its true principles and doctrines. Henry Tuke, a Friend of high standing in England, writing for the "Christian Observer," in 1804, says of this standard work, "The first publication of the work, was under the sanction of the Society. . . . It was first printed in Latin; has since passed through eight editions in English, under the sanction of the Society, besides one printed in Dublin, and another at Birmingham, by Baskerville. It has likewise undergone three editions in German, two in Dutch, two in French, one in Spanish, and one in Danish; also a second edition in Latin. All, or most of these in foreign languages, have likewise been at the direction and expense of the Society, and a year never elapses without a public recognition of the work by the Society at large, by reading over a list of books in their Annual Meetings, in order to consider the republishing of such as are nearly out of print. Nor is this all; it is a book, so far as my knowledge extends the *only* book, which has been given by the Society to many of the public libraries in Europe, as well as to some Sovereigns and Ambassadors, for conveying a correct information of their principles, and for counteracting those misrepresentations with which adversaries. . . have endeavored to impress the public mind." Prior to the publication of the above notice of "Barclay's Apology," it had been endorsed and published by the Yearly Meeting of Friends in New England, and since by Philadelphia Yearly Meeting, through its representative body; again by London Yearly Meeting, and also by private individuals, as a standard work; exhibiting in full the doctrines and Christian faith which the Society of Friends believe to be in strict accordance with the Scriptures of Truth.

The Society of Friends has always believed that the Holy Scriptures were written by holy men under Divine inspiration; that they contain a revelation of the mind and will of the Almighty, and a declaration of the fundamental doctrines and principles relating to the work of the salvation of the soul; that they are *a* rule of faith and practice, obligatory on all who have a knowledge of them; and that whatever is contrary to them, is to be considered a delusion of Satan. They, being the *words* of God, and a Divine record of Christian faith, are therefore the only outward standard or test, by which controversies respecting that faith or belief, should be tried. Therefore, in thus fully endorsing the principles and practices inculcated and defended in "Barclay's Apology," and at various times and by succeeding generations, presenting it to the world as a true, clear and unequivocal declaration of the faith held and taught by it, the Society of Friends has never intended to convey the idea or opinion, that it claimed for that work the same estimation or authority as for the Hóly Scriptures; but that the author of the Apology, under the enlightening influence of a measure of the same Spirit that dictated the Scriptures, had been enabled to demonstrate in it, what are the Christian doctrines set forth in the sacred records, as they are understood, embraced, lived up to, and promulgated by true Friends.

The doctrines and testimonies so ably set forth by Barclay, are in exact unison with those preached, practised, and otherwise inculcated, by George Fox, and all those faithful men and women who labored with him in the work of the gospel in their day; many of whom bore testimony to his growth and establishment in the immutable truth, and their unity with his labors for the promotion of truth and righteousness. To this day, the work has remained unrefuted, and it continues to be fully acknowledged by all those who can rightly claim to be Friends.

In 1676, the Council at Edinburgh issued a declaration of the continued force of former Acts against Conventicles, and enjoining Sheriffs and Magistrates to have them executed. This incited the civil and ecclesiastical rulers in Aberdeen to renewed persecution of Friends, and in a few weeks thirty-four of them were lodged in prison; where they were kept some time before being brought to trial. When the trial came on, although it was shown that the indictments were incorrect, and the witnesses called were illegal on account of their connection with the prosecution, yet, because they would not bind themselves not to go to their meetings again, seven of them were fined, each one-fourth of their respective annual rents, for going to their own meeting, and one-eighth of the same, for not attending at the established public worship; three of them another eighth, for their wives' similar transgression; and two of them— John Skene and George Keith—were ordered to give bonds not to preach again, under penalty of five thousand marks, or to be banished the kingdom.

The Friends were again shut up in a filthy prison, until the fines levied could be distrained; which was intrusted to one George Melville; who, as he obtained opportunity, carried off goods, horses, cattle, &c., belonging to the Friends, far exceeding the amount claimed. As some were liberated upon their fines being collected, other Friends were committed; and as those discharged were soon found at their meetings again, they were also recommitted. By the malignant cruelty of some of those in power, the prisoners were subjected to great suffering; being sometimes crowded in rooms so small they could not all lie down at the same time ; and sometimes, by the boarding up of the windows, to prevent Friends preaching to the people in the streets, the circulation of air was so impeded, that there was imminent risk of suffocation. Some physicians of the town having expressed the opinion, that the close confinement in the contaminated atmosphere, and the other severe usage to which they were daily subjected, were endangering the lives of the prisoners, some of their relatives and friends applied to the Mayor and Bailie, to allow some of them to be removed to another place of confinement : but he refused ; saying, " He would pack them like salmon in a barrel, and though they stood as close as the fingers on his hands, they should have no more room ; and if they had not room in the chambers they might lie on the stairs ;" which was a narrow passage, admitting of but one to pass at a time.

Three of the Friends who had been longest kept in prison and were most cruelly treated by the persecuting Magistrates, were Patrick Livingston, George Gray and Andrew Jaffray. They were ministers, and under a sense of duty, found themselves engaged to preach the gospel to the people from the windows of the Tolbooth of Aberdeen ; often having a large audience in the street, especially on market days. To prevent this, which was attended with several convincements that greatly enraged the Magistrates, those three Friends were separated from their fellow prisoners, and thrust into a close vaulted cell at the top of the jail, where murderers were usually confined. The only aperture for the admission of light and air, was a hole through the thick wall, with an iron grating at each end. The place was infested with vermin, and in summer was excessively hot, and those kept in this horrid cell seemed literally buried alive. But the three Friends, through the preserving power of Him, whom they were striving to serve in simplicity and sincerity, were kept cheerful and well, and it is said, " Their very natural voices strengthened, and [were] raised up as trumpets, mightily to sound forth God's glorious truth and power, through the said hole in the wall, and though four or five stories high, and [the hole] double grated, as aforesaid, so that their faces could not win near to see the street below, yet they were distinctly heard all over the street by the people, who the more frequently got together." Finding that their own cruelty, and the patient endurance of suffering by the Quaker preachers, were working the effect they most dreaded or hated, the Magistrates, after seven weeks' trial of the " iron house," as it was called, returned the three Friends to the same quarters as were occupied by their fellow professors.

While these Friends were thus enduring suffering for their testimony to the truth, and to keep a conscience void of offence towards God and towards man, they were visited by epistles from several of their brethren in religious profession; who themselves knew what it was to undergo bonds and afflictions in the same good and noble cause. Isaac Penington, William Penn, Gavine Lawrie, Hector Allane and others, thus manifested their love and sympathy; and gave proof how the faithful members of the Society were united in the fellowship of the gospel, and concerned to watch over each other for good, and to encourage and serve one another as members of the same household of faith.

David Barclay was one of the prisoners, and of the sufferers in his estate by the seizures of the rapacious Melville; but during all the forepart of this severe persecution, Robert Barclay was absent from Scotland; having gone on a religious visit into England, and after performing that service, going on a similar errand into Holland and parts of Germany.

It was during this visit on the continent that R. Barclay first became acquainted with Elizabeth, Princess Palatine, and a mutual friendship was formed which continued through life, a correspondence being kept up between them. On his return from this journey, while at London, he heard of the imprisonment of his father and other Friends at Aberdeen. He at once drew up a statement of the case of the suffering Friends in Scotland, and had it presented to the King, through the Duke of Lauderdale. The King and Council, however, decided to refer the matter to the Privy Council, at Edinburgh, and that body, knowing well that neither the King nor Lauderdale would give further attention to the matter, took no effectual measures for liberating Friends at Aberdeen; but David Barclay was discharged from prison.

R. Barclay had not been long at home before he was arrested while attending a meeting for worship in Aberdeen, and with three other Friends, was shut up in its noisome jail. While thus a prisoner, the fact having become known to his friend, the Princess Elizabeth, she at once addressed a letter to her brother, Prince Rupert, who stood high at the Court of Charles II.; and as it may be considered characteristic of the feelings and sentiments of that personage, who will be again mentioned, it may well claim a place here.

" Herford, December 19th, 1673. Dear Brother. I have written to you some months ago by Robert Barclay, who passed this way, and hearing I was your sister, desired to speak with me. I knew him to be a Quaker by his hat, and took occasion to inform myself of all their opinions; and finding they were so submiss to the Magistrates in real, omitting the ceremonial, I wished in my heart the King might have many such subjects. And since, I have heard that notwithstanding his Majesty's gracious letter, on his behalf, to the Council of Scotland, he has been clapped up in prison with the rest of his friends; and they threaten to hang them; at least those they call preachers among them, unless they subscribe their own banishment; and this upon a law made against other sects, that appeared armed for the maintenance of their heresy — which goes directly against the principles of those, who are ready to suffer all that can be inflicted, and still love and pray for their enemies. Therefore, dear brother, if you can do anything to prevent their destruction, I doubt not but you would do an action acceptable to God Almighty, and conducive to the service of your royal Master: for the Presbyterians are their main enemies; to whom they are an eyesore, as bearing witness against all their violent ways.

"I care not though his Majesty see my letter: it is written no less out of humble affection for him, than in a sensible compassion of the innocent sufferers. You will act herein according to your own discretion; and I beseech you still consider me as, yours

ELIZABETH."

As has been already stated, George Fox was, in 1674, a prisoner at large in Worcester, waiting for trial at the next Quarter Session of the Court, to be held in the Second month. At that session, when he pleaded the errors in the indictment, he was overruled by the Court, and the oath being tendered to him again, which he refused to take, the jury was instructed to bring him in guilty; which they did. At the Sessions in the Fifth month, he was again arraigned. He pointed out many errors in the indictment, which the Judge acknowledged were errors; but nevertheless he ordered the jury to bring in a verdict, and as they hesitated, the Court instructed them that it having been testified that George Fox had refused to take the oath when tendered to him at the last sessions, that was enough: whereupon they brought him in guilty. The Judge then told him he warned him of the sad sentence he had incurred. George asked him if he was going to pass sentence upon him now; for he had many reasons to give why he should not be sentenced on that indictment, it being so defective. The Judge replied, he was about to show him the danger he was in of a premunire, but he did not deliver it as a sentence, but as an admonition. The Court then ordered him taken away. After George was gone, the Judge ordered that what he had told him, as an admonition, should be recorded as his sentence; and thus he was made a prisoner for life under the premunire.

George Fox being thus incarcerated, with no prospect of release, his wife came to Worcester, to be with and take care of him. A full statement of his case, and of the legal errors in his trials, was drawn up by her and their son-in-law, Thomas Lower, and presented to the Judge who held the next assizes; but he would give no opinion, except that they might bring suit upon the alleged invalidity of the trial. G. Fox was soon after taken sick, and became so ill that his life was despaired of. He, however, was sensible that the time for his dismissal from service was not yet come, and he says, the word of the Lord came to him, that He " had a great deal more work for me to do for Him, before He took me to himself." When he was convalescent, his wife went to London, sought and obtained an interview with the King, and ' laid her husband's hard case fully before him. He referred her to the Lord Keeper ; who told her the only way to obtain a release, was by the King's pardon. This George refused to accept; for, he declared, " I would rather have lain in prison all my days, than have come out in any way dishonorable to Truth."

Richard Davies, a Friend, of Wales, having come to visit his honorable and beloved friend in prison, G. Fox gave him an account of the circumstances of his case, and Richard being impressed with the manifest illegality of some of the proceedings, suggested that application should again be made for a writ of *habeas corpus*, and another trial be had before the Judges of the King's Bench. He also proposed that a Welsh Counsellor, named Corbet, then in London, should be employed to conduct the case. George Fox felt free to proceed at once on this course; so the necessary writ was obtained, and they went up to London; George in a coach, being yet too weak to ride on horseback.

He says in his Journal: " We came to London the eighth of the Twelfth month, and the eleventh I was brought before the four Judges at the King's Bench, where Counsellor Corbet started a new plea. He told the Judges, ' They could not imprison any man upon a premunire.' Whereupon the Chief Justice, Hale, said, ' Mr. Corbet, you should have come sooner, at the beginning of the term, with this plea.' He answered, 'We could not get a copy of the re-turn and the indictment.' The Judge replied, 'You should have told us, and we would have forced them to have made a return sooner.' Then, said Judge Wild, 'Mr. Corbet, you go upon general terms; and if it be so as you say, we have committed many errors at the Old Bailey, and in other Courts.' Corbet was positive, that by law they could not imprison upon a premunire. The Judge said, 'There is summons in the statute.' 'Yes,' said Corbet, 'but summons is not imprisonment, for summons is in order to a trial.' 'Well,' said the Judge, 'we must have time to look in our books, and consult the statutes.' So the hearing was put off till next day.

"The next day, they chose rather to let this plea fall, and begin with the errors of the indictment; and when they came to be opened, they were so many and gross, that the Judges were all of opinion the 'indictment was quashed and void, and that I ought to have my liberty.' There were that day several great men, lords and others, who had the oaths of allegiance and supremacy ten-dered to them in open Court, just before my trial came on; and some of my adversaries moved the Judges, that the oaths might be tendered again to me, telling them, 'I was a dangerous man to be at liberty.' But Judge Hale said, 'He had indeed heard some such reports, but he had also heard many more good reports of me;' so he, with the rest of the Judges, ordered me to be freed by Proclamation. Thus after I had suffered imprisonment a year and almost two months for nothing, I was fairly set at liberty upon a trial of the errors of my indictment, without receiving any pardon, or coming under any obligation or engagement at all; and the Lord's everlasting power went over all, to his glory and praise. Coun-sellor Corbet got great fame by it; many of the lawyers told him, 'He had brought that to light which had not been known before, as to the not imprisoning upon a premunire;' and after the trial, a Judge said to him, 'You have obtained a great deal of honor, by pleading George Fox's cause so in Court.'"

As Richard Davies, who had been so helpful in obtaining a new trial for George Fox, whereby he was honorably discharged, was a Friend of great integrity; of whom George Whitehead testifies, "He was a preacher of Christ and his righteousness, in his conversation, as well as in doctrine and ministry; wherein he was exemplary to the believers;" and as he was one of, if not the first in North Wales, convinced of the doctrines and testimonies of the Gospel as held by Friends, it may be well to give a short sketch of his convincement.

From the account given by him, it is evident, that from youth he was a sincere seeker after truth, and conscientiously concerned to embrace every means and opportunity that presented for obtaining a knowledge of it; being much given to studying the Scriptures, and frequenting the meetings of the Independents. Believing himself called to engage in many religious exercises, he was often occupied in exhortation, and in making long prayers; but he remarks of himself and his companions, though "The Lord did then beget true hungerings and thirstings in our souls after Him," yet "We knew not the Lord, as we ought to have done; namely, by his Light, Grace and Spirit shining in our hearts, to give us the light of the knowledge of the Son of God ; which knowledge keeps a man meek and humble."

About the year 1656, he says, "Our ministers told us there was a sort of people come up in the North, called Quakers, that were a people of strange posture and principles : saying that it was the last days and times which Christ spoke of in the twenty-fourth of Matthew, 'Many shall come in my name and deceive many,'" verse v.: 'For there shall arise false Christs and false prophets, and shall show great signs and wonders; insomuch that if it were possible, they shall deceive the very elect,' verse xxiv. This sort of people, called Quakers, were much preached against: they told us they were the false prophets; that they denied the Scriptures and all ordinances, and also denied the very Christ that bought them," &c.

He thus states his first personal knowledge of Friends: "About the year 1657, there came a poor man, in a mean habit, to my master's house, named Morgan Evan, of South Wales: he had met with the people called Quakers in his travels, and was convinced of the truth. This poor man discoursed my master about the principles of Truth, and I being in the shop about my calling, my mistress came and said, 'Why do you not go to help your master? for there is a Quaker at the door, that hath put him to silence.' I, hearing this, made haste and took my Bible under my arm, and put on what courage I could, to dispute with that poor man ; but he proved too hard for us all. When I went to them, they were upon [the use of] the words *Thee* and *Thou*, and I peremptorily asked him, what command he had to speak *Thee* and *Thou?* for I did acknowledge to him that it was the language of God to Adam, and the language of the Scriptures ; but, said I, that is not enough for us in this day ; we must have a command for it. To which he answered, 'Hold fast the form of sound words which thou hast heard of me.' I asked him whether that was Scripture? He asked me whether I would deny it? and I told him he was to prove it. Then he took the Bible out of my hand, and turned to 2d Timothy, i. 13, which he read, and told me that *Hold fast* there, was a command; which I knew very well, both the Scripture and the command. But to prove him further, I desired him to read a little more of that chapter, both backward and forward, which he freely did, and then asked me, Why I did require that of him? I told him we heard that the Quakers denied the Scriptures, and that they would not read them. He said there were many false reports about them. And truly when he read the Scriptures so readily, I concluded in myself that what was reported of them was not true, and he saw that he had reached to the Witness for God in me. Then he exhorted me to take heed to that Light that shined in my heart, and showed me my vain thoughts, and reproved me in secret for every idle word and action; saying, 'That was the true Light which lighteth every man that cometh into the world,' and that in that Light I should see more light, and that it would open the Scriptures to me, and that I should receive a measure of the same Spirit that gave them forth. Further he told me, It was ' The more sure word of prophecy,' unto which I did well, if I took heed, ' as unto a light that shineth in a dark place, until the day-dawn, and the day-star arise in your hearts;' 2 Peter, i. 19. And he spoke much of the inward work, and the operation of God's Holy Spirit upon the soul; recommending me to the 'Grace of God that bringeth salvation,— teaching us that denying ungodliness and worldly lusts, we should live soberly, righteously and godly in this present world:' Titus, ii. 11, 12. And so he departed from our house, and I set him a little along on his way."

Awakened by this humble instrument in the Lord's hand, to a far deeper insight of the spirituality of the Christian religion, and its transforming work upon the soul, than he had ever had before, Richard Davies found that the place of beginning and carrying on the change from a state of nature to a state of grace, was in the vineyard of his heart. He says, " The more I waited in that Light to which he [M. Evan] recommended me, the more my former peace, and that in which I formerly took comfort, were broken; and herein I came to see that our former building could not stand; for we built with that which the apostle called wood, hay and stubble. Here I came to a loss of all my former knowledge, and my former performances proved but a sandy foundation." Earnestly and sincerely desirous to come to a knowledge of the truth as it is in Jesus, he was sorely afraid lest he might be deceived by the Quakers; for he "had read and heard that Satan himself is 'transformed into an angel of Light.'" As he came under the teaching of the Spirit of Truth inwardly revealed, he found himself obliged to "Take leave of all my former teachers, and many times went to the woods and other by-places, where none might see me, to wait upon the Lord ; where I was much broken and tendered by the power of God." There being no one in that part of the country who could counsel or sympathize with him in his inward conflicts and outward trials, he fervently petitioned that, if it were right, he " Might see that poor man once again ; for I knew not where to see the face of any called a Friend ; and it pleased God that he came again that way, and I desired my master and mistress to give him lodging, and that he might be with me, to which they consented."

In the course of their conversation, R. Davies learned the views of Friends in relation to the nature of Christian baptism, and the use of bread and wine; " which," he observes, "gave me some satisfaction ; " and after they parted, " I saw him no more for several years." Under the enlightening influence of Divine Grace, he came to see that it was a mistake to call the Scriptures the *Word* of God, inasmuch as that title belongs to Christ; who was in the beginning, before the Scriptures were written; and that it was also wrong to suppose that *eternal life* was to be obtained in those sacred records ; but all must come to Christ, as He is inwardly revealed to the soul, as the Way, the Truth, and the Life. In this way, as obedience accompanied the knowledge received, he became more and more fully instructed in the mysteries of the Kingdom of heaven, and willingness was wrought to take up the daily cross and follow his spiritual Leader. He came to see clearly the true nature of the baptism of Christ, and of feeding on His flesh and blood ; that both were inward and spiritual ; the one being the washing of regeneration, through the renewing of the Holy Ghost, and the other the communion with Christ as He comes into the soul, and gives it to partake of the food which He supplies.

" God showed me," he observes, " the customs of the nation were vain, and our language not according to the language of God's people, recorded in the Scriptures of truth." It cost him much to give up the use of the language, fashions, and compliments in which he had been educated, and which were practised by all around him; but when convinced by the Holy Spirit in his heart, that it was

right and needful, he gave up, in childlike obedience, thus to become as a fool for Christ's sake. He says, "Thus I was conscientiously concerned to speak the pure language of thou and thee
to every one, without respect of persons; which was a great cross to
me."

His master — who was convinced of many of the doctrines and
testimonies held by Friends, but was unfaithful thereto — found no
fault with Richard for using the plain language to him; "But when
I gave it to my mistress, she took a stick and gave me such a blow
upon my bare head, that made it swell and sore for a considerable
time. She was so disturbed at it, that 'she swore she would kill
me, though she would be hanged for me;' the enemy had so possessed her, that she was quite out of order; though before she had
seldom, if ever, given me an angry word." Notwithstanding the
hard usage he met with, he continued faithful, and to perform his
"work and service" honestly and justly; "not with eye-service as
man-pleasers: but in singleness of heart, as the servant of Christ,
doing the will of God from the heart;" and in course of time, though
the rage and evil-intention of his mistress continued long, yet being
taken ill after he had gone to live at another place, she was favored
to see the sinful condition she had fallen into, and told her husband,
"She could not die until she had asked his [Richard's] forgiveness,
and desired he might be sent for." Richard sent word, that he had
long before freely forgiven her; and some time after, he states, "It
pleased God to order it so, that she had a visit from me before she
went out of this world; and very comfortable and acceptable it was
to her, and in a little time she ended her days in peace, and was
buried in Friends' burying-place."

It soon became the talk of the place, that Richard Davies had
become a Quaker. and the minister of the parish where his parents
lived, went to them and told them, "That I had gone distracted, and
that they should see for some learned man to come to me, and restore me to my senses." His parents were greatly grieved and displeased with him, and when he first went to visit them after his
change, both father and mother turned their backs upon him; his
father saying, "They had thought to have comfort in him, but now
they expected he would go up and down the country crying, Repent,
Repent." This treatment plunged him into great distress; but he
had brought to his remembrance the language, "When my father
and my mother forsake me, then the Lord will take me up: teach
me thy way, O Lord! and lead me in a plain path, because of mine

enemies." " At. length," he says, " my mother came tenderly to me, and took a view of me, looking on my face, and she saw that I was her child, and that I was not, as they said, bewitched or trans-formed into some other likeness — which was reported of Quakers then, and that they bewitched people to their religion, &c. . . . And when I discoursed with her out of the Scriptures, her heart was much tendered and affected with the goodness of God towards me; she went to see my father, and when she found him, said to him, ' Be of good comfort, our son is not as was reported of him, we hope to have comfort of him yet.' " Finding it laid upon him to go to the place of worship where the minister officiated, who had told his parents he was distracted, R. Davies, when there, waited until the "service" was ended, and then called upon the priest to defend the false doctrine he had just promulgated; and if he [R. Davies] was distracted, as he had said, to labor for his restoration. But Richard, and a young man who had been convinced previously by his conversation, and had followed him to the " steeple-house," were laid hold of, and put in prison, where they were kept that night; the Magistrate, on examination the next mording, discharging them, as they had broken no law.

Under a sense of religious duty, R. Davies visited many of his former associates, setting before them the errors of their ways, and expounding to them the doctrines of the gospel and the require-ments of the way of righteousness; and two or three of them were convinced and embraced the truth. He states, " When we had come to the number of four, it was with me that we ought to meet together in the name of the Lord; for I remembered the promise of Christ, who said, ' Where two or three are gathered together in my name, there am I in the midst of them.' So we all agreed to meet together, but none of us had a house of his own to meet in. We determined therefore to meet upon a hill, in a common, as near as we could for the convenience of each other; we living some miles distant one from another. There we met in silence, to the wonder of the country. When the rain and weather beat upon us on one side of the hill, we went to the other side. We were not free to go into any of the neighbors' inclosures, for they were so blind, dark and ignorant, that they looked upon us as witches, and would go away from us, some crossing themselves with their hands about their foreheads and faces."

Two of these young converts having been sent out of that part of the country by their relatives, and another proving unfaithful,

Richard was left to hold the meeting alone, which he appears to have done until the end of his apprenticeship, when he went up to London, and there followed his business. But in the course of a short time, he found it required of him to return to his former place of residence in Wales ; in order to stand there as a witness for the Truth ; but he was rebellious, greatly preferring to remain where he was, where he had the company and encouraging countenance of other Friends. He resisted the conviction of this duty until he was visited with severe and painful illness, when he was made willing to resign himself to the Lord's disposal ; who provided him with a suitable wife ; one who, under a sense of religious duty, was willing to leave all, and rest content in the field and service of the Lord appointed for them. They removed to Welch Pool in Wales, where R. Davies, who had received and now exercised a gift in the ministry of the gospel, labored abundantly ; suffering frequent imprisonments, and often very cruel treatment, from those who strove to prevent the spread of truth and righteousness, by persecuting Friends who labored to promote the cause of Christ. Many were convinced of the principles and testimonies held by Friends, and large meetings came to be settled in that part of Wales, where Richard Davies, singly and alone, had been led, through the inshining of the Light of Christ, to understand and adopt those principles and testimonies ; and by faithfulness to the same divine Guide, had been made instrumental to open the way for their spread, and to gather the converts thereto, into a visible church. His was another striking instance, added to the many that occurred in that day, of the uniformity of the operation of the Spirit of Truth, in leading its obedient subjects out of the errors which they had adopted by education and association, and into a knowledge of and practical conformity to the doctrines and testimonies of the gospel, as Friends were called to uphold them ; even when far separated one from another, and surrounded by circumstances wholly opposed to the reception and advancement of those self-denying principles. It is written " In the mouth of two or three witnesses every word may be established," and the multiplicity of such instances may well establish the verity of the religion Friends have ever professed.

After the clearance of George Fox from all the charges that had been brought against him, and his freedom proclaimed in open Court, he attended the Yearly Meeting in London in 1675, and then proceeded North on his way to Swarthmoor ; travelling slowly, and visiting meetings regularly held or appointed, as he journeyed. Incessant labor in the promotion of the cause of Truth, and frequent imprisonments in cold, damp and noisome prisons, with several severe sicknesses brought on thereby, had so shattered his constitutional vigor and impaired his strength, that he was now a confirmed invalid, and he spent nearly two years at Swarthmoor, the home of his wife and her daughters; unable to travel far, and endeavoring to regain physical ability to renew his arduous labors in the service of his beloved Lord and Master. During this period of enforced retirement from active participation in the work carried on by the Society, he was by no means idle; but employed his pen, either in dissertations on specific points of Christian doctrine and practice, in counselling and encouraging his fellow professors, in defending the civil and religious rights of his persecuted brethren, or in warning those who made use of the power they held, to inflict punishments upon others who were conscientiously striving to live in accordance with the Divine law written in their hearts. Within these two years he had published more than a dozen different works of this character. Besides these, he made a collection of the several epistles he had at different times addressed to Friends, and also of many of the communications sent by him to those in power, &c., &c.

In 1676 he sent a general epistle to the Yearly Meeting, sitting in London; in which he alludes to the ranting spirit that had sprung up among Friends in some places, opposing the idea of need for, and the execution of, the discipline; as well as the men's and women's meetings set up for carrying it into effect. In the first month of 1677, having in some measure regained strength for the journey, he left his home and proceeded southward; stopping frequently and laboring fervently among Friends and others, for the promotion of that blessed cause, which was dearer to him than his natural life; that so his fellow professors might be built up on their most holy faith, and others might come to know and embrace the truth as it is in Jesus. He arrived in London towards the close of the Third month, and he says: " In my journey I observed a slackness and shortness in some that professed the truth, in keeping up the ancient testimony against tithes." He therefore was " moved of the Lord " to issue an epistle to Friends on that subject; which, after alluding to the abrogation of all tithes under the gospel, and the inconsistency of preaching against a man-made and hireling minis- try, while contributing to its support; he thus concludes : " Consider how many faithful servants and valiants of the Lord have laid down their lives against them, in this day of the Lord; and in the days of the martyrs they did witness against them. Consider also what judgments have come upon those that spoiled Friends' goods, and cast them into prison for tithes and maintenance. Therefore in the power of the Lord maintain the war against the beast, and do not put into his mouth lest he cry peace to you; *which peace you must not receive*, but it must be broken and thrown out by the Spirit of God. Then in the same spirit ye will receive the peace from the Son of peace, which the beast and the world, with all their earthly teachers for the earth, made by man, cannot receive nor bereave you of. Therefore keep your authority and dominion in the power, Spirit, and name of Jesus, in whom is my love to you.   G. F.

   "Third month, 1677."

   In the Fifth month of this year [1677] in company with Robert Barclay, William Penn, George Keith, John Furly, and some other Friends, he crossed over to Holland; where, and in Germany, they were engaged in religious service for several months.

   In the mean time, the unrelenting persecution of Friends went on unremittingly in many parts of England; as has been seen, it did in Scotland. Not only did they suffer inhuman treatment, under color of the "Conventicle Act," for meeting to worship the Author of their lives, and of all their sure mercies; but they were stripped of their substance, and kept for indefinite periods, in prison-houses and dungeons, by rapacious priests; suing them, for their unceasing tithes, in ecclesiastical courts, and upon writs *de excommunicato capiendo*, obtaining power to incarcerate them at their will. It is not necessary to enter into further particulars of individual suffering; but the following, taken from Sewel, will suffice to show, that the cruel treatment continued, which began with the determined effort to break down the faithfulness of Friends to their religious convictions, and oblige them to bow to the arrogant claims and behests of a proud and irreligious priesthood. Since the short-lived experiment of the King to suspend the action of the penal laws against Dissenters, in order to screen the Catholics from their operation, neither Court nor Church relaxed in the determination to gratify, to the full, their relentless opposition to the Quakers.

   "The Act against seditious Conventicles gave opportunity to the malicious to disturb the religious meetings of the Quakers, who never met in a clandestine manner, but always publicly: and on this account fines were extorted from them; to which may be added, that oftentimes they were still very ill-treated, and most grievously abused, as among the rest at Long Claxton, in Leicestershire, where some women were dragged by the neck along the street; and among these a widow, the skin of whose neck was rubbed off by this rudeness; and an ancient woman, above seventy, was violently cast down to the ground. Some of the men were dragged by the hair; and others by their legs, besides the many blows given them : and some were trodden upon till the blood gushed out of their mouths and noses. Yet all this they bore patiently, without making any resistance; whereby it happened sometimes that some who had not the gift of preaching, reached others by their patient suffering; showing by their meek behavior, that their works did agree with their Christian profession: and though many were robbed of all they had, even clothes and beds not excepted, yet they continued steadfast without fainting; though often it was called a meeting when some were come together, not properly to perform religious worship, as hath been related already."

The law having put it into the power of the most covetous and the most depraved, to lodge complaints against Dissenters; and obliged Magistrates to take the oath of such, as sufficient evidence of the charge sworn to; and enjoined Justices to construe every provision of the laws, in favor of the party prosecuting; Friends could rarely meet together in number over five, for any purpose whatever, without some one being found, who, coveting what little property they might possess, was willing to perjure himself by swearing they were holding a Conventicle; and to insist eagerly upon receiving a writ to take away whatever property could be found. Thus where Friends met together to bury their dead, where a few words of comfort to the bereaved were expressed; or of exhortation to those at the side of the open grave were uttered; or where they met to confer about relieving the necessities of the poor ; such occasions were again and again construed into unlawful assemblies, and made a pretext for stripping many a housekeeper of almost, if not quite, everything that could be found and taken away. In some instances the dead were not suffered to rest in their graves ; but the latter were re-opened, and the bodies taken up, the coffins broken, and the remains thus left exposed to public gaze; in order, by thus harrowing up the feelings of relatives and friends, they might be induced to pay the priest his charge for reading the burial service over the corpse of their beloved and lost companion.

Moved by the pressure of these grievous sufferings, Friends made an appeal to the Judges, when about to enter on the duties of their several Circuits, [1674] as follows: " Many of our friends called Quakers, being continued prisoners, many prosecuted to great spoil by informers, and on *qui tam* writs, and by presentments and indictments, for £20 *per mensem,* in divers counties through England, only on account of religion and tender conscience towards Almighty God, we esteem it our duty to remind you of their suffering condition, as we have done from time to time ; humbly entreating you, in the Circuits, to inquire into the several causes of their commitments, and other sufferings which they lie under; and to extend what favor you can for their ease and relief : praying the Almighty to preserve and direct you."

But all the efforts of Friends to stay the hand of violence from inflicting its merciless blows upon their unresisting fellow-members, as well as the attempts of other Non-conformists to procure some alleviation of the unjust and tyrannical impositions, under which many of their number were suffering, were vain. The King, indifferent to the true interest of religion in any form, and anxious to comply with the requisitions of the French monarch, who again paid him his liberal stipend ; and with the wishes of the profligate women and men who disgraced his Court, and intrigued for the gratification of their own selfish and corrupt propensities — most of whom were either secretly or openly Papists — turned a deaf ear to the remonstrance that reached him. Conscious that the enormity of the deceitful and unpatriotiq course he was pursuing, had roused the passions of a large portion of the people, and called up a powerful party, watching for an opportunity to crush the Popish conspirators and their schemes, he gave countenance to the oppression and punishment of all those whom the high church party, on whom he mainly relied, denounced and sought to exterminate.

Neal says : " The mouths of the high-church pulpiteers, were encouraged to open as loud as possible. One in his sermon before the House of Commons, told them that the Non-conformists ought not to be tolerated, but to be cured by vengeance. He urged them to *set fire to the fagot,* and to teach them by scourges or scorpions, and open their eyes with gall."

The law against Conventicles allowed of an appeal from the judgment of a Magistrate to the next Court of Quarter Sessions ; but Friends soon found that little relief, but often great additional cost, resulted from an attempt to avail themselves of this provision of the Act. The fines imposed by the Magistrates had to be first paid into the hands of the Judges who were to hear the appeal; and though in many cases the most flagrant perjury was shown to have been committed by the informers, there was hardly an instance, where the first judgment was set aside; but almost universally where an appeal was prosecuted, some plea was found by which the money deposited was kept, and the appellant mulct in heavy expenses, under the character of Court charges.

William Crouch having been heavily fined, on the oath of an informer, who swore to his being at a meeting on a certain day, when no such meeting was held, appealed, and narrates the result as follows; which may serve as a representative case. " The informer having sworn to a wrong day, upon which I was convicted for ten pounds; which I deposited, and entered my appeal, which came in course to a trial, where I had retained counsel to plead. A jury being sworn, my cause was called among others, and witnesses were examined: after which, the jury going forth to agree upon their verdict, Thomas Jenner [who was the Judge] goes from the bench, and in some little time returns. The jury coming in with their verdicts, and having dropped my cause, *it was called again for a new trial;* T. Jenner saying, 'a *slip* in the record should not serve [my] turn.' Whereupon I made application to my counsel; who advised me to withdraw my appeal, to prevent a worse consequence; for, says he, they are resolved to carry it. So I suffered the loss of my money, and all the charges."

1670. Although so often repulsed in their applications to obtain the little justice which the laws allowed, the impositions and spoliations inflicted by the abandoned creatures who, as informers, preyed upon Friends, became so grievous and enormous, that George Whitehead and William Crouch thought it their duty to represent their case to the Bishop of Canterbury; in the hope, that as he had much interest at Court, and much authority with the Episcopal clergy, he might be induced to use them for putting a stop to the iniquitous trade of the informers. " We went to the Bishop of Canterbury "—Doctor Sandcroft — says William Crouch, " at his home at Lambeth, to complain of the irregular proceedings against us, the Quakers, upon the Conventicle Act, by informers who swore falsely; by which many were convicted, and distresses made accordingly; which we informed him of, and that it was a dishonor to their Church." To which he replied, with great unconcernedness of mind, and without much regard, " *That a ship could not be built*

without some crooked timber."   On which reply, Wm. Crouch justly
remarks, " It was to the church we referred the dishonor by false
evidences, and it was to that reference the Bishop made answer;
where *crooked timber*, it seems, is so useful; crooked because contrary to straight, not upright; not to be squared by an equal rule;
but bending and warping from it, false to truth, liars, and forswear-
ing themselves; yet useful, in the Bishop's sense for the Church,
the ship."   Of course no relief was to be obtained from that quarter.

CHAPTER XXVII.

Forerunners of a Change—Miserable End of many Informers—Confession of
   One — Notice of Wm. Baily — Meetings in Holland—Wm. Penn's Address
   to the King of Poland—Sufferings of Friends on the Continent — Embden
   — Visits to Elizabeth Princess Palatine — Letter of the Princess to G. Fox
   — R. Barclay's efforts for Relief of Friends in Scotland — Restiveness of
   some under the Discipline — Insubordination of Wilkinson and Story —
   Their Defection from the Principles of Friends—Efforts to Reclaim them—
   Separation — Some Reclaimed — Publications called forth by the Ranting
   Spirit — Jeffrey Bullock.

THOUGH Friends continued to be harassed and impoverished by
   the disgraceful means, through which the policy of the Court
and Church was prosecuted, that policy was gradually working a
decided change in the views and feelings of the people, and preparing the way for a more radical revolution in the government, than
many at the time anticipated.   In the Established Church itself, party
lines were drawn between " High Church," and " Low Church ; " the
former insisting upon the absurd dogma of " apostolic succession ; "
on all the arrogant claims of prelacy, and the right of enforcing
conformity to their ritual; while the latter took a more common-
sense and Christian view of their commission and functions, and
were prepared to concede to Dissenters the right to worship according to the dictates of conscience.   Alarmed at the evident subserviency of the King to Louis XIV., and at the stealthy, but persistent
encroachment of the Romanists upon governmental power, a strong
party, called the " Country Party," began to see, that in order to
thwart the designs of the Court, and obtain power to crush out the
hopes and expectations of the Papists, who, under the tuition of
Jesuits, were aiming to bring the kingdom under the ecclesiastical

domination of the Pope, it was necessary to obtain the help of Dissenters in the elections for Parliament; and that this was not likely to be accomplished, while they were so cruelly persecuted. Beside this, the natural disposition of Englishmen, where their passions or prejudices are not deeply enlisted, to demand "fair play," and to sympathize with those struggling for the enjoyment of natural rights, began to excite disgust at the continued exhibition of a heartless tyranny, on the part of the party in power; and called forth the expression of disapprobation of the penalties to which they saw their fellow-countrymen subjected, for no other offence than striving to obey God rather than man, in the matter of religious worship. So that notwithstanding the increasing boldness with which Charles and the parasites of his Court, claimed the inalienable authority of his prerogatives, and the "Established Church," vaunted its unquestionable right to condemn and eradicate whatever it deemed contrary to its creed or its interests, beneath the surface, a political and ecclesiastical revolution was incubating; which, in the course of a few years, changed the character of the government, and, in good measure, restored many of the rights now withheld from the subjects.

The business of an informer, and of those who colleagued with them, though it seemed an easy way of living upon other people's property, did not prove a profitable occupation. Sewel and Gough narrate many instances, strikingly exhibiting the miserable end to which members of both these classes came, and the almost uniform poverty and wretchedness attending the latter days of those who had devoted themselves to serving the Church by preying upon the goods and persons of Friends. The former says: "But none of the persecutors seemed to take notice, or to regard such instances; for they let their rage loose against the Quakers, who, for all that, continued in patience, though they did not think it unlawful to give notice of the grievous oppression their friends suffered, to those that were in authority, lest they might have excused themselves as ignorant of these violent proceedings. Therefore it was not omitted to publish, in public print, many of those crying instances that have been related here, and to present them to the King and Parliament, with humble addresses to that purpose. But all this found but small entrance."

One instance narrated by Sewel is worthy of notice here; inasmuch as it demonstrates that even those who have given themselves up to work wickedness, and set themselves in opposition to others conscientiously striving to walk in obedience to the Lord's commands, may be brought to conviction and repentance of their guilt, and, through mercy, experience forgiveness. Mathew Hyde, who was of respectable family, and not an open informer, but who, Sewel says, " made it his business, during the space of about twenty years, publicly to contradict the Quakers in their meetings, and to disturb them in their worship of God, when brought to his death-bed, was brought under great condemnation and distress; as William Penn once, in the presence of many, had told him would be the case, ' and that the time would come when he would be forced to confess to the sufficiency of that Light he then opposed, and to acknowledge that God was with those called Quakers.' With the prospect of death before him [1676] he sent for G. Whitehead; and when he came, said to him: ' What I have to say, I speak in the presence of God. As Paul was a persecutor of the people of the Lord, so have I been a persecutor of you, his people, as the world is who persecute the children of God.' More he spoke, but being very weak, his words could not well be understood. Then G. Whitehead resumed, ' Thy understanding being darkened, when darkness was over thee, thou hast gainsaid the truth and people of the Lord; and I knew that that Light which thou opposedst would rise up in judgment against thee. I have often, with others, labored with thee, to bring thee to a right understanding.' To which Hyde said: ' This I declare, in the presence of God and of you here, I have done evil in persecuting you, who are the children of God, and I am sorry for it. The Lord Jesus Christ show mercy unto me, and the Lord increase your number, and be with you." . . . . . . " G. Whitehead resumed: ' I desire thou mayest find mercy and forgiveness at the hand of the Lord. How is it with thy soul? Dost not thou find some ease?' ' I hope I do,' answered Hyde; ' and if the Lord should lengthen my days, I should be willing to bear a testimony for you; as publicly as I have appeared against you.' His wife then said, ' It is enough; what can be desired more?' ' If,' queried Whitehead, ' the Lord should not lengthen out thy days, dost thou desire what thou sayest should be signified to others?' ' Yes,' answered Hyde, ' I do; you may; I have said as much as I can say.' " In about two hours after this interview, he quietly breathed his last. It was of him that William Penn published a brief account, in his tract entitled " Saul Smitten to the Ground."

In 1675 died William Baily, who had long been a minister in

the Society of Friends, and often a great but patient sufferer for the testimony of Jesus. He was a Baptist minister at the time of his convincement of the truth as held by Friends; which took place in 1656, under the ministry of George Fox. Having come under the transforming power of Divine Grace, as manifested to his soul, he willingly took up the cross, and denied himself of all that he saw was contrary thereto; and, walking in the Light, he came to experience the blood of Christ to cleanse him from sin, and to give him dominion over the temptations of Satan. Having, in the course of time, received a gift in the ministry of the gospel, he became a zealous preacher of the truth, which his spiritual eyes had seen and his hands handled; accepting, with much resignation, the fines, imprisonments, beatings, and other modes of persecuting, which were the common lot of his fellow-professors. On one of the occasions when an Episcopal priest came to officiate at Grace-church Street meeting — and, though attended by a guard of soldiers, failed, from shame, or some similar cause, to enter on the "service"— William Baily, who was preaching to the multitude gathered there, was arrested and sent to Newgate, on a charge of abusing the priest, though he had not spoken a word to him, nor had the priest made any attempt to officiate. He was afterwards fined between thirty and forty pounds for alleged trespass and contempt. He followed the sea for a living, and, when in port, always took the opportunity presented for spreading a knowledge of the gospel as held by Friends. He died when on a voyage home from Barbadoes. Being sensible that his end was near, he took those about him by the hand, exhorting them "to fear the Lord, and then they need not fear death. Death," said he, "is nothing in itself; for the sting of death is sin. Tell the Friends in London, who would have been glad to see my face, I go to my Father and their Father, to my God and their God. Remember my love to my dear wife. She will be a sorrowful widow; but let her not mourn too much, for it is well with me." His wife was the Mary Fisher who was so cruelly used at Boston, and who afterwards travelled to Adrianople, and had an interesting interview with the Turkish Sultan.

It has been mentioned that George Fox, William Penn, Robert Barclay and other Friends went over, on religious service, to Holland, and travelled into Germany in 1677. From the accounts given by G. Fox and William Penn — the latter of whom published a Journal of his travels and labors on that occasion — the number of members in Holland appears to have been quite considerable. The Friends from England all attended a General Meeting of men and women, held in Amsterdam; of which William Penn says, "The Lord, who is setting up his own Kingdom, by his own power, owned us with his blessed presence, and opened us in that wisdom and love, that all things ended with peace, great concord and comfort; many things being spoken, especially by our dear friend George Fox, that were of good service, and I hope will dwell with them forever."

At that meeting it was agreed, "That henceforth a Yearly Meeting be held at Amsterdam; unto which Friends in the Palatinate, Hamburg, Lubeck and Frederickstadt, &c., be invited; of which meeting there shall be given notice to the Friends of the Yearly Meeting at London; to be kept always on the Fifth day of that week, which is fully the third week following after the Yearly Meeting in London." Through the instrumentality of these Friends, co-operating with others assembled, a code of Discipline was adopted, and Monthly and Quarterly Meetings set up in different parts where Friends were settled: thus bringing the Society in that country into a similar organization and government to those which had been established in Great Britain and America.

Letters being received from the few Friends living at Dantzic, in Poland, setting forth the cruel treatment they were suffering from the civil authorities, Wm. Penn prepared an address to the King of Poland on their behalf; explaining to him the Christian faith held by Friends, and earnestly entreating him to give the subject his serious consideration and action; "That we may no longer lie under these, not only unchristian, but unnatural severities; but receive that speedy and effectual relief, which becometh Christian Magistrates to give to their sober and Christian people." 1677.

This remonstrance does not appear to have obtained relief for the sufferers. The Magistrates of Dantzic, finding that imprisonment did not induce the three of their fellow-citizens who had embraced the principles of Friends to give them up, or make them willing to promise they would not again meet together for the purpose of Divine worship, ordered that they should be banished beyond sea; and that if they should return, they should be kept in the House of Correction, "or punished with some other hard punishment." Pursuant to this decree, the three Friends were put on board a ship and sent to England.

But this severity, exercised without knowing or endeavoring to ascertain what the principles were, which those innocent men had embraced ; or what other effect those principles would exercise on their conduct and conversation, than inducing them to withdraw from attendance on the priests, and endeavor to worship in accordance with the dictates of their own consciences, could not shut out the light of Truth, in that dark community ; and several more of the inhabitants came to be convinced, and met together to hold their religious meetings. The rabble, incited by the absurd reports spread concerning Quakers, broke into the house while Friends were holding their meeting; abused those found there, took away their hats and other things they could carry off, and became so riotous that the Magistrates arrested all the Friends present — six in number — and committed them to prison.

This persecution was kept up for years, for in 1678, Stephen Crisp, writing from Amsterdam, states " At Dantzic the Rulers have sentenced Friends to depart in eight days, or to be led out [of the city] by the hangman ; and have brought out two ; who, when the man had left them, went to a Friend's house in the suburbs, and after some time to their own houses; whence they were brought to prison ; and we expect daily to hear of their being all banished, that will not give security not to come to meetings." The sufferings of those who were confined in the " House of Correction " must have been great, as they represent their being kept chained by the wrist, two and two together, fed upon bread and water, and allowed no bedding but straw.

In 1685, seven years later than the letter of S. Crisp, the epistle of London Yearly Meeting contains the following : " The Lord has been pleased to influence the King of Poland and the Magistrates of Dantzic, moderately to resent the applications made to them in behalf of the said suffering Friends and brethren ; although most of them, by means of their former great sufferings, were reduced to so low a condition in the world, that they are not yet able to support themselves and families."

So early as 1662 a few persons in East Friesland, were convinced of the doctrines and testimonies held by Friends ; which so alarmed the priests, that a synod was convened, which presented a petition to the Court, at Lewarden, in which they say, " Whereas the wicked sect of the Quakers are found in these United Provinces, and also sprung up here in East Friesland, you are desired to watch against it in time, that that *devilish error* might not creep in farther." This called forth a proclamation forbidding a Quaker to come into the country, under penalty of imprisonment for five years in the Rasp-house. The priests were authorized to examine any suspected person, and a reward of twenty-five gilders was offered to any one who would discover a Quaker. This law led to many inconveniences, affecting the people generally; it became unpopular, and after a short trial was repealed. It does not appear that other oppressive measures were resorted to for several years; but about 1672, there being a small number of Friends in the city of Embden, the civil authorities there began to treat them with much severity. Some were cruelly beaten, some kept shut up in a dungeon and allowed nothing but bread and water; some fined beyond all they possessed, and some were banished.

Stephen Crisp, who labored much in the work of the gospel on the continent of Europe, states that the first person who embraced the principles of Friends in Embden, was a physician, named John William Hasbert; and he gives the following account of the sufferings of the little company which found themselves constrained to stand as witnesses for the truths of the gospel as revealed to their spiritual understanding. "At first they sat down, about ten persons, in Dr. Hasbert's house, to wait upon the Lord; and when this was noised about the city, the wicked One stirred up the priests and rulers against them; and they stirred up the rude and ignorant people to assault them; to mock, reproach and revile them, and the rulers fell quickly to fining, imprisoning, threatening and banishing those weak and tender plants, in an almost unheard of manner. They banished some, sixteen or twenty times, spoiling them of all they had, save their clothes, and at last fell upon them also; taking away their coats, boots, gloves, aprons, &c., and driving them through the street, almost naked, aboard the ships that were to carry them away: all which and much more, by the mighty power of the Lord, did these innocent, harmless lambs bear with great patience and quietness, and were not dismayed at all at these cruelties. For the Lord had regard to his name, and to their innocent cry, and supported them, and doth support them; and they have found it true, that those who wait upon the Lord renew their strength. Blessed be the Lord forever."

William Penn, moved by the accounts received in England at that time, of the grievous hardships, these, his fellow professors, were enduring, addressed the Council and Senate of Embden; endeavoring to inculcate Christian principles of charity and good-will, and to influence them to toleration of religious freedom, and a course of treatment of those who differed from them in religious faith, more in consonance with the commands and example of Christ and his apostles. [1675.] It was written in Latin; and when in that city two years after, W. Penn visited the President of the Council of State, told him that he was the author of that address, and reasoned and pleaded with him on behalf of the Friends there. He says, "The President was astonished to see what manner of men we were; but after a little time he comported himself with more kindness than we expected at his hands." He expressed much opposition to Friends, but before they parted, he told W. P., that if he would again write a remonstrance to the Senate, and tell them what he desired them to do, he would himself present it, and show he was not so much an enemy to Friends as they thought.

Persecution, however, though occasionally mitigated, did not cease at Embden for some years; and it is probable that it would not have ceased, even when it did, in 1686, had it not been found that the imprisonment, banishment and other punishments inflicted for religion's sake, on a class of citizens, many of whom were master mechanics, and others engaged in important manufacturing concerns, had materially lessened the trade and standing of the city; and that it was probable, if continued as heretofore, would destroy its former prosperity altogether. Convinced of this, the Magistrates resolved not only to revoke their intolerant laws, but to issue a declaration of their determination to grant Friends freedom, and all the rights and privileges of other citizens, and to enjoy the religion they believed to be required of them to maintain. They sent a communication to that effect to Friends at Amsterdam, and another of similar import to Friends in England; manifesting no little anxiety to induce those in membership with them, to settle in Embden. Friends of Amsterdam addressed the Rulers at Embden, acknowledging this act of Christian liberality, and returning thanks therefor.

The same course of persecuting those who professed with Friends was pursued at the free city of Hamburg, and in other towns in Germany; where William Caton, William Ames, George Rolfe and some other ministers of the gospel, had labored with more or less success, to promulgate the pure, spiritual views of the religion of Christ, which they had themselves found to answer to the dictates of his Spirit to their souls.

In that age of bigotry and intolerance, Holland was distinguished for abstaining from enacting laws designed to interfere with the right of liberty of conscience; nevertheless, as has been already related, the Magistrates sometimes sanctioned, or at least connived at the infliction of illegal abuse of innocent persons; who, through misrepresentation, had incurred the prejudice and hatred of the lower classes in the towns. Thus, at different times, some of those who professed with Friends were cruelly treated, either by persons in authority, who abused their power to gratify their wounded pride or unsanctified zeal; or by the rabble, who, in blind excitement, sought to destroy what they did not comprehend, but supposed to be inimical to the interest of their religious leaders.

George Fox, with two or three Friends who accompanied him, appears to have travelled pretty extensively in Holland, Friesland and some parts of Germany; holding meetings with those who professed with Friends, and others, being obliged however to depend on an interpreter to communicate with his hearers.

In the course of the travels of William Penn, Robert Barclay and George Keith, in Germany, they visited Elizabeth, Princess Palatine of the Rhine, at her Court at Herwerden. She was the oldest daughter of Frederick V., Elector Palatine, and at one time King of Bohemia; her mother being the sister of Charles I. of England. She is represented to have been a woman of good natural capacity, well educated, and of amiable disposition and manners; and to have governed her small territory with good judgment and much consideration for the welfare of her subjects. Having been brought under the power of religion, she manifested strong interest in others who were sincere in their religious convictions, and was opposed to interference with liberty of conscience. Having become acquainted with the religious tenets of Friends, by conversation with R. Barclay and Benjamin Furly, who visited her in 1676, and with women Friends from Amsterdam, she found them to answer to the convictions of Truth on her own mind; and she not only gladly received Friends when they came to see her, but in her letters to several of the more prominent members among them, and to others at the English Court, she unhesitatingly expressed her high estimation of them, and her disapproval of the persecution to which those that held them were subjected.

The Friends named, having requested permission to have a religious opportunity with her, it was readily granted; she having in her family at that time the Countess of Hornes, her intimate friend, and a French lady. Of this interview, William Penn thus writes in his Journal: "I can truly say it, and that in God's fear, I was very deeply and reverently affected with the sense that was upon my spirit of the great and notable day of the Lord, and the breaking in of his eternal power upon all nations; and of the raising of the slain Witness to judge the world; who is the Treasury of life and peace, of wisdom and glory, to all that receive Him in the hour of his judgments, and abide with Him. The sense of this deep and sure foundation, which God is laying as the hope of eternal life and glory for all to build upon, filled my soul, with an holy testimony to them, which in a living sense was followed by my brethren; and so the meeting ended about the eleventh hour."

In the afternoon they held another meeting with them, which was also so remarkably favored, that Wm. Penn says: "Well, let my right hand forget its cunning, and my tongue cleave to the roof of my mouth, when I shall forget the loving-kindness of the Lord, and the sure mercies of our God to us, his travailing servants, that day."

Subsequently, on their return towards Holland, these Friends again stopped at Herwerden, and upon informing the Princess of their arrival, they were again gladly received by her and her friends. A meeting being held with them and some others whom they had invited, the next morning, Wm. Penn states in his Journal: "About eight the meeting began, and held till eleven, several persons of the city, as well as those of her own family, being present. The Lord's power very much affected them, and the Countess was twice much broken while we spoke. After the people were gone out of the chamber, it lay upon me from the Lord, to speak to them two, — the Princess and the Countess — with respect to their particular conditions; occasioned by these words from the Princess, 'I am fully convinced: but Oh! my sins are great.' While I was speaking, the glorious power of the Lord wonderfully rose, yea, after an awful manner, and had a deep entrance upon their spirits; especially the Countess, so that she was broken to pieces: God hath raised, and I hope fixed, his own testimony in them."

The next day they had a parting interview in the chamber of the Princess, which was equally favored. "Magnified be the name of the Lord, He overshadowed us with his glory. His heavenly, breaking, dissolving power richly flowed amongst us, and his ministering angel of life was in the midst of us."

George Fox having written a letter to the Princess from Amsterdam, she returned him a reply, as follows:

HERTFORD, 30th of August, 1677.

"Dear friend: — I cannot but have a tender love to those that love the Lord Jesus Christ, and to whom it is given, not only to believe in Him, but also to suffer for Him; therefore, your letter and your friends' visits have been both very welcome to me. I shall follow their and your counsel, as far as God will afford me light and unction; remaining still your loving friend,   ELIZABETH."

The Friends mentioned, who had been diligently laboring on the continent, returned to England in the Autumn of 1677. Robert Barclay had preceded the others a short time, and, when again in London, he concluded to apply once more, to some of those who had the authority to interfere, on behalf of Friends in Scotland. Accordingly, he sought and obtained an interview with the Duke of York, and having ascertained that the Duke of Lauderdale was then in Scotland, he requested the Duke of York, to write to him in such terms that he would have to act at once in favor of those who were kept prisoners. It was characteristic of Barclay's honest boldness and straight-forwardness, that he told the Duke, unless he would write " in that style wherein Lauderdale might understand that he was serious in the business, and did really intend the thing he did write concerning, should take effect," he desired, " he would excuse himself the trouble" of writing at all. The Duke took his plain dealing in good part, and told him he would write as he desired, for himself (R. Barclay) and his father; but would not meddle with the other Friends who were prisoners. He accordingly gave Robert the desired letter; which no doubt was duly delivered to Lauderdale.

At what time after this Robert Barclay was again imprisoned is not clearly narrated; but the family records state, that some time subsequent to his return home, David Barclay and his son were released from prison, " By an order from the Court, with a reprimand for meddling with either of them." The same record also mentions, that Robert Barclay afterwards procured the liberation of the other Friends, who were detained after them.

It has been stated, that in the year 1666, George Fox, under a sense of Divine requiring and direction, had been engaged in setting up Meetings for discipline of different grades and authority, throughout the Society; and that through the enlightening influence of the same Divine wisdom, certain rules and regulations had been adopted and brought into action, for the establishment of right order in the church, and the preservation of the members in conduct and conversation consistent with the doctrines and testimonies of the Gospel as held by Friends. In this work of church organization and government, the leading members in different parts of the Society, men eminent for their devotion to the cause of Truth, and their deep insight of the mysteries pertaining to the Kingdom of Christ, had been more or less, personally engaged, or had accorded to it their full sanction and support. The principles of church government adopted, recognized unequivocally and as indispensable for their proper application, the Headship of Christ; and a distinguishing feature was the uniform inculcation of the necessity for those who were engaged in carrying them into practice, to wait for, and act under a measure of his holy Spirit; in accordance with the Apostolic injunction, to bear one another's burdens and so fulfil the law of Christ; and that if a man be overtaken with a fault, they who are spiritual, should restore such an one in the spirit of meekness. From the testimony handed down to succeeding generations, this ecclesiastical polity and administration appear to have tended greatly to the preservation and edification of the Society, from their first introduction.

But although the Society was largely kept free, by continued and severe persecution, from nominal professors, who were unconvinced of its religious tenets, or unwilling to suffer for them; yet there were numbered among its members those who, unchanged by the power of the religion, to the truth of which they assented, were indisposed to be restrained by the discipline it had adopted; and who desired to be left free to speak and to act in accordance with what they claimed to be the sense of right and wrong, revealed in their own breasts; without reference to the judgment of their fellow-members, either individually, or collectively, as a church. This had early shown itself in the case of John Perrot and his followers; and now, undeterred by the sad course and destructive consequences that had followed their indulgence in this ranting spirit, by that misguided party, it again manifested itself in the north of England, under the leading of two ministers, named John Story and John Wilkinson, who were members of Westmoreland Quarterly Meeting.

From the accounts preserved, and the character of the publications of Wilkinson and Story, or their abettors, there is reason to believe, that not keeping in that humility and watchfulness which would have preserved them from aspiring after great things, or courting popularity, these two men took offence at the extension of counsel by some of their more experienced brethren, who were anxious for their preservation and deepening in the Truth; and allowed secret envy and spiritual pride to prompt them to reject and denounce the care of the church, and to seek to build themselves up, by forming a party from among those like-minded with themselves. They soon began to preach doctrines more conformable to the inclinations of the unregenerate man, than Friends believed the gospel of Christ could sanction, and which consequently were more agreeable to those who were unwilling to bear the daily cross in the practice of self-denial. Having thus drawn a number to unite with them, they boldly claimed that each one should be left to regulate his course by the Light of Christ in himself, without being amenable to others. They therefore denounced the discipline and the meetings for discipline, as encroachments on the right of private judgment, similar to that practised by the church of Rome; and as George Fox had been mainly instrumental in their institution, their crimination of and invectives against him were loud and unsparing.

The first steps in error were not long in opening the way for others; and as they became more and more alienated from Friends, and lost the life of Truth, these dissatisfied members contended that they must be left to their own sense, as to whether it was required of them to assemble for the purpose of worship, under the certainty of incurring the penalty of abuse, imprisonments or fines; and that a like personal conviction must authorize a refusal to pay tithes, &c. They clothed their opposition to the authority and restraints of the church, under the specious pretext of contending for the sufficiency of the Light of Christ in the soul, to guide and keep it from all error, as well as to lead into all truth; and referred to the earlier days of the Society, as showing there was no need for church organization, or prescribed rules, to regulate the conduct of those who made profession of the same principles. Hence they declared that George Fox and other members who stood high in the Society, and had originated or promoted the institution of the discipline, were thereby usurping authority over the consciences of their fellow members, and seeking to lord it over the heritage of God.

Friends of Westmoreland Quarterly Meeting labored abundantly and affectionately with Wilkinson and Story, to convince them of the error into which they had fallen, and to induce them to be reconciled to those who were really their best friends, by giving up their opposition to the order established in the Society, and returning to take their right places in the body. But they treated these Christian efforts with contempt, and persisted in their revolutionary course. Seeing that this state of feeling, unless removed, must lead into an open breach, Friends of that Quarterly Meeting drew up a statement of the case, and the points involved in controversy; and requested several of the most experienced Friends in the adjoining counties, who were altogether unimplicated in what had already occurred, to sit in judgment on the points involved. Accordingly, those Friends appointed a meeting and invited all the parties to be present, and make their own statements and explanations. The meeting was held; but Wilkinson and Story, with their adherents, refused to be present; and the Friends called in from other counties, adjourned the meeting to the next day, and went personally around to the several malcontents, urging them to meet with them and their fellow members of the Quarterly Meeting; in order that all complaints might be fully investigated, truth cleared of all reproach, and harmony restored.

The next day the second meeting was held; but the disaffected again refused to meet with them. John Burnyeat, who was one of the Friends called in as referees, in his account of the matter, says, "So we gave a hearing a second time to the Friends; and then we of Yorkshire and Cumberland withdrew, and among ourselves viewed the whole matter,— for it was in writing,— and opened our hearts one unto another. And waiting upon the Lord, there fell a weighty concern upon us for the Truth's sake, and the blessed order thereof, with our holy testimony we had been raised up into, which by them, had been slighted, scorned and reproached, so that we could not pass it by; but in the power of the Lord God, which was dreadful among us, we gave judgment against that spirit, which was grown so high, loose and fleshly, as thus to undervalue the testimony of God, and the bringing forth of his holy power in the churches of Christ; by which all may be kept sweet, clean and in good order. And when we had cleared ourselves in the rising and springing up of the Word of Life, and drawn up our testimony in writing, we gave it unto Friends there, and so departed." These two meetings were held in 1675.

Uninfluenced by the Christian labor and concern of their fellow members, unless it was to make them more litigious and determined to have their own way, this dissatisfied party went on in opposition to and railing against Friends who stood firm and upright in the Truth. The latter, sincerely desirous to rescue them from the spirit of contention and confusion into which they were so obviously betrayed, and finding that the disaffection was spreading into other parts of the Society, in 1676, made another effort to remove the cause of difficulty, by appointing another meeting in Yorkshire; to which they were invited. At it, four days were spent in endeavoring to convince them, that as each member was enlightened by a measure of the same Holy Spirit, it will lead all who are faithful to its openings and requirings, into the same path of self-denial; the maintenance of the same gospel truths, and the unity and fellowship of Christ's disciples; and they that walk in the Light as He is in the Light, will have fellowship one with another. It was urged that God was a God of order in all the churches, and his Spirit required nothing inconsistent with itself; therefore the church acting collectively under the influence of the same Spirit that governed the members individually, would require nothing of the members contrary to the will of its holy Head. The church has power to establish such rules and regulations as will not only prevent disorder and scandal among its members, but also guard them from violating those principles and testimonies, for the support and promulgation of which they were voluntarily associated together. It is the exclusive prerogative of the Almighty to enlighten and regulate the conscience, and man is accountable to Him alone for his convictions of what is right and what is wrong; but in his outward conduct and conversation, he is amenable not merely to civil government, but to the religious society or church in which he holds membership, and whose character and standing are implicated by his deportment. If not satisfied with the doctrines it holds or the discipline it adopts, he is not obliged to remain a member; and if he voluntarily sanctions doctrines inconsistent with the faith of the church, or violates its testimonies or the rules it has enacted, it has the authority to declare him no longer a member.

There being a large number of eminent ministers and others at this meeting [1676], many testimonies were borne against the spirit that was leading into separation; and earnest entreaty was made that those who had been caught with it, might be willing to submit to the judgment of the Church, and be restored to unity and oneness with their brethren; the former judgment given against them being confirmed. But though both Wilkinson and Story seemed touched by the Christian love and uprightness of Friends, and expressed some sorrow for having " given cause of offence to the Church of God," the change in their views and feelings was not deep enough to humble them, so as to induce them to retrace the steps they had taken, and give up their separate meetings. The Yearly Meeting in that year, therefore, being brought under deep religious concern on their account, addressed an epistle to those two members, specially, as leaders in the separation, and another to their followers; in both which, expostulation and entreaty were again employed to bring them out of their error, and back into the bosom of the Church. Some honest-hearted members, who had been deluded by the profession of Wilkinson and Story, that all they wanted was to return to the principles and practices of Friends in the beginning, and secure liberty for each one to act in accordance with his own conviction of duty, came to see wherein they were deceived, humbly confessed their error, and gladly returned among Friends. This separation, nevertheless, continued to give trouble to Friends for several years; but the spirit of division and self-dependence rife among these discontented persons, in the course of time worked its legitimate result, and those who came not back to Friends, fell to pieces, and dwindled away. In the course of the controversy, [1676-7] William Penn wrote " A Brief Examination of Liberty Spiritual," and Robert Barclay, "The Anarchy of the Ranters." George Fox wrote an epistle against separations, and Thomas Ellwood, George Whitehead, and other Friends, in like manner exposed the errors of the seceders, and defended the truth and the Society.

Among the deep trials which Friends were thus introduced into by false brethren, about this time, was one arising from the apostasy of Jeffery Bullock; who, having fallen away from faith in the gospel as held by the Society, promulgated the anti-Christian notion, that the Grace of God which bringeth salvation, having appeared unto all men, it rendered inoperative, and destroyed any benefits resulting from the coming and sufferings of our Lord and Saviour Jesus Christ.

As usual with those who bring in false doctrine, and attempt to have it substituted for that held by Friends, he claimed the right to sow his anti-Christian sentiments within the pale of the Society; took offence at being opposed and rebuked by some of those who stood firmly for the faith held by it, and persisted in his disbelieving and disorganizing course; drawing a few followers after him. Labor proving unavailing for his recovery, he was disowned by the Quarterly Meeting to which he belonged. The testimony of disownment is long, setting forth the error of J. Bullock, and the Christian doctrine of Friends. The following extracts will show its character:

" For the clearing of the precious truth of God, professed by us, his people called Quakers, from the occasion of stumbling and reproach, given by Jeffery Bullock's pernicious doctrine, in affirm-

ing that he neither expects justification nor condemnation by that
Christ that died at Jerusalem : These are to certify all Friends, and
friendly people whom it may concern, that we testify against this
doctrine as stated by him, as both pernicious and anti-Christian,
and contrary to plain Scriptures, *and the constant testimony faithfully borne amongst us from the beginning,*" &c., &c. . . . . .
" And further, we cannot own any such doctrine or words (by
whomsoever spoken) as tend to undervalue the sufferings, death,
and blood of Christ. For not only a reconciliation was made and
declared through his death, but all his sufferings, and his being
the one universal Offering and Sacrifice, did contribute to man's
redemption, and the salvation of all that *truly* believe in his Name ;
though without the washing of regeneration, and being born again
of the living Word and Spirit of Life, none do really partake of
eternal salvation, or that redemption which is obtained through the
blood of Christ, who gave Himself for us, that He might redeem us
from all iniquity."

Some years after [1686] J. Bullock came to see the delusion into
which he had fallen, and published " Several Testimonies against
that evil spirit by which he had been led to oppose the truth and
people of God."

CHAPTER XXVIII.

Increase and Suffering of Friends in Ireland — J. Banks' Service in Ireland
— Disorders among some Members — Catharine Norton — Wm. Edmund-
son and other Friends shut up in a Dungeon — W. E. before the Bishop's
Court — Account of J. Banks — Account of Benj. Bangs — " Popish Plot "
— Friends persecuted as " Popish Recusants " — G. Fox addresses Parlia-
ment — Friends petition the King and Parliament — Efforts to relieve
Friends frustrated — Fires of Persecution rekindled — Wm. Dewsbury in
Jail — Sufferings of Friends at Bristol — Prisons filled — Wishes of the
Mayor and Citizens disregarded by the Persecutors — Faithfulness of the
Women and Children — Case of Isaac Dennis, a persecuting Jailer — Gen-
eral Persecution and Faithfulness — Epistles of Encouragement — Epistle
of G. Fox.

FRIENDS continued to increase in number in Ireland, although,
like their brethren in other places, they were exposed to much
suffering ; chiefly on account of tithes, though they were not unfrequently persecuted on account of faithfully supporting other testi-

monies. Their unwillingness to take an oath sometimes subjected them to much loss. On this account they addressed the Lord-Lieutenant and Council, in 1673, stating "That whereas they durst not, on any account, take an oath, as being forbidden by Christ, wicked men laid hold on this, their conscientious scruple, to ensnare and defraud them, by causing them to be subpœnaed into Chancery, where their answers, without an oath, would not be admitted. For instance, in the county of Wexford, Thomas Holme, having about £200 due to him from one Captain Thornhill, for which judgment was obtained against him in common law, was subpœnaed into Chancery by Thornhill, where he well knew Thomas could not answer on oath; and so this Friend lost his debt." Several instances of similar iniquitous action are given; in one of which the Friend not only lost a considerable sum due him, but was subjected to an additional loss of £70, before he could get rid of the exactions of his debtor. This cause of suffering continued in Ireland for many years.

William Penn paid a visit to Friends in Ireland, and by his influence obtained the release of many of his brethren who were at that time imprisoned. In 1671 John Banks made a general religious visit to Friends throughout that nation, and was instrumental in convincing many, of the doctrines he preached, and in establishing some meetings. When in Dublin, he felt it laid upon him to go to Wicklow, and have a meeting with the inhabitants there: no Friend having yet held a meeting in that place. On his arrival, notice was spread that an English Friend would hold a meeting there the next day; which, coming to the ears of the priest of the place, he applied to the Governor of the Castle to prevent the meeting being held. When John and the Friends with him were about leaving the house where they had lodged, to go to the meeting, their landlady entreated them not to attempt to go along the street, for there was a guard of musketeers waiting to take him; at the same time kindly offering to show them a back way. But John Banks told her, though "I accept of thy love, I must not go any private way; for I have a testimony to bear for the Lord, in love to the people." They got to the place of meeting unmolested; but so soon as the meeting was settled, the soldiers came in, and their commander required John to go before the Governor. Upon J. B. asking to see his warrant for arresting him, he held up his halberd, saying, "This is my warrant."

The Governor had with him his wife, the priest, and some others,

and when John Banks entered, the priest said to the Governor,
"Sir, this is the deceiver, this is the deluder that is come from England to delude the people; I hope you will do justice and execute
the law." The Governor made no reply, and J. Banks stood still
until the priest had fully unburdened himself of his invectives.
He then said, addressing the priest, "Thou sayest I am a deceiver
and a deluder." The priest cried out with violence, "So thou art,
so thou art." "Have patience, continued John, and let thy moderation appear, and hear what I have to say in my own vindication;
.for I will not admit thy assertion as proof. I have had patience to
hear thee: art thou a minister of Christ?" "Yes," said the priest,
"I am." John replied, "But if I prove thee a liar, as by the witness of these people thou art, in charging me with what thou canst
bring no proof for, thou art out of the doctrine of Christ, and of
consequence no minister of his: therefore *thou art* a deceiver and
a deluder of the people." The priest made no reply; and many
people having by this time crowded into the room where they were,
John took the opportunity to explain to them and the Governor,
what were the religious principles held by Friends, and concluded
by exhorting them to sobriety and watchfulness. Nevertheless,
the Governor committed him, and two of the Friends with him, to
the prison.

The jailer was very friendly, and allowed the Friends the use of
a room, and all who wished it, to come into them. So they held a
meeting, and John Banks preacded so convincingly, that several
embraced the doctrines of Friends, and in time, joined with them
in membership. The three were kept in prison but three days.
After being liberated, John went into the north of Ireland, and on
his return to Dublin, he received a letter from Wicklow, stating
the people there were desirous he would hold another meeting among
them. . He felt free to comply with their request, and a meeting
was held without interruption, and so many joined with Friends,
that a regular meeting was established in the town.

1674. Friends in Ireland did not escape the troubles occasioned
by persons arising among them who run into excesses, and others
who were unwilling to live under the daily cross and know it to keep
them in the strait and narrow way, in which the disciple of Christ
must walk. Persecution had for a while been very fierce at Cork,
and many Friends had suffered there severely for the cause and
testimony of Truth; nevertheless, both there and in Dublin, several
nominal members adopted the notions of Muggleton, and ran into

looseness of conduct, bringing discredit and much trouble on the Society. William Edmundson, who had been absent for some time in America, on religious service, returned in 1674; and he says, "When I landed I went to Cork, to the Province Meeting, which was at hand, and presently found there was cause for my spirit to be pressed to hasten over for the preservation of the church's peace; some being gone into the loose, foolish imaginations of Muggleton, and others, both of England and of this nation, into the liberty of their wills and carnal affections, from the cross of Christ and self-denial; which caused great trouble and difference among Friends, both in Cork and Dublin, and in several other places. We had much exercise before we got things brought into order and settled; but the Lord's power was with us, and went over all. He still gave an understanding to place judgment in the right line; praises to his name forever."

In 1678, a woman Friend named Catharine Norton, visited the northern parts of Ireland, in the work of the ministry. She was a native of Ireland, of a good family named McLaughlin, and had received her education at Londonderry. When sixteen years of age, she had emigrated to Barbadoes, and there married. When George Fox and the Friends who accompanied him were in that Island, she was convinced at one of the meetings held by them, embraced the truth, as held by Friends, in all sincerity and perseverance; and becoming firmly established in the truths of the gospel and a life consistent therewith, she received a gift in the ministry, and was made an able minister of the new covenant. When on this religious visit to her native country, she preached in some places, as at Lurgan, on a market-day, in the Irish language. She held some public disputes, with those who sought to prevent the spread of the principles held by Friends, and her services are represented to have been "to the satisfaction and edification of Friends." Rutty, in his "Rise and Progress," speaks of her as "Well qualified for the service, being of sound judgment, large in testimony, of good utterance, had of her own to distribute, and did not make the gospel chargeable."

In 1682, Benjamin Bangs, a minister from England, in good esteem for his religious life and services, spent nearly a year in travelling among Friends in Ireland; and we learn from him that at that time he attended one hundred and eighty meetings of Friends on the Island.

William Edmundson in the year 1682, with his friend Robert Jackson, under the prosecution in the Bishops' Court, by a priest named Lloyd, who had become curate for George Clapham, the notorious persecutor of Friends — now a lunatic — had been excommunicated, and confined in a dungeon; where none but the worst malefactors were usually shut up. Here the two Friends were kept twenty weeks. During this time their friends did not fail to visit them frequently in their dismal abode, and William says, " We had many precious good meetings." These two Friends being tenants of the Lord of Ely, he heard of the suffering they were enduring, and applied to the Bishop to have them released, and the latter ordered that they should appear at his Court at Kildare. Of the conference at this Court, William gives a full account, from which the following is taken. " Accordingly we came, and there were the Bishop and about ten or twelve priests, the Lord of Ely and his steward, with several other persons of account in the world, and a great concourse of people. One Dean Sing, was Chancellor of the Court: John Burnyeat and Anthony Sharp accompanied me, yet went not in, but stood at the door where they could both see and hear us. The Bishop began to discourse with me concerning tithes which I was unwilling to enter upon, being sensible of my own weakness; but he urged: then the Lord, by his Divine Spirit, gave me wisdom and understanding, and brought Scripture into my memory fluently; so that I proved tithes to be ended, and that it was anti-Christian either to pay or receive them in these gospel times; which was opened so clear to the understandings of the people, that there seemed to be great satisfaction in the Court. Then Dean Sing stood up before them all and said, if he had known me as well before as he did now, I should not have suffered; with several other expressions of kindness." The Court questioned the prisoner respecting ministry, faith and Divine worship, on all which points he says, " My understanding was clear, ripe and ready, through the assistance of the Lord's blessed Spirit, to answer;" and so fully and clearly did he show forth the Christian ground upon which Friends rested their testimony against tithes and formal worship, and their dissent from the " Church of England," that the Bishop enjoined him to give him what he had then said, in writing; dismissed the two Friends until the next Court, and ordered the Sheriff to let them have their liberty in the meanwhile. At the next Court the Bishop offered to *absolve* them; but William let him know they would not come under any of their ceremonies, and so spoke, that the Bishop at last " Bid God make us good Christians, and wrote to the Sheriff to discharge them; " which was done.

Among the Friends who were frequently and extensively engaged in visiting the meetings and members in Ireland was John Banks, who has been already mentioned. He was born in Cumberland, England, and received so good an education that at fourteen years of age he kept a school, and read the Scriptures and " a homily " to the people who came to hear him, on the First-day of the week. He also practised singing psalms and praying; for which, however, he says, he " had no liking." On one occasion a man who was considered a great scholar, but intemperate, told this youthful officiator, that he read very well, but he did· not pray in the right form, and that he would write to him and teach him how to pray ; which he did. But when John had read over the prepared supplication, he says, " I was convinced of the evil thereof, by the Light of the Lord Jesus, which immediately opened to me the words of the apostle Paul concerning the gospel he had to preach ; that he had it not from man, neither was he taught, but by the revelation of Jesus Christ. In answer to which it arose in me, ' But thou hast this prayer from man, and art taught it by man ; and he one of the worst of many.' So the thread of the Lord fell upon me, with which I was struck to my very heart, and I said in myself, ' I shall never pray in this wise.' " Receiving an inward intimation to go to a meeting of those called Quakers, he went ; and such was the effect produced, that he refused to receive any of the compensation provided for him, on account of his clerical services. Previous to his going to this meeting, however, he remarks, " It pleased the Lord to reach my heart and conscience by his pure, living Spirit, in the blessed appearance thereof, in and through Jesus Christ ; whereby I received the knowledge of God, and the way of his blessed truth, by myself alone in the fields, before I ever heard any one called a Quaker preach, and before I was at any of their meetings. But the First-day that I went to one, the Lord's power so seized upon me in the meeting, that I was made to cry out, in the bitterness of my soul, in a true sight and sense of my sins; which appeared exceeding sinful. On the same day, as I was going to an evening meeting of God's people, scornfully called Quakers, by the way I was smitten to the ground, with the weight of God's judgment for sin and iniquity, which fell heavy upon me, and I was taken up by two Friends.' " Being now given up to allow the Light of Christ Jesus to shine into his dark heart, his sins were set in order before him, and brought to judgment. He observes, " As I travelled under the ministration of condemnation and judgment for sin and transgression, great was the warfare I had with the enemy of my soul ; who, through his subtlety, sought to betray me from the simplicity of the truth, and to persuade me to despair, as though there was no mercy for me. Yet in some small measure, I knew the Lord had shown mercy to me, which he mixed with judgments for my sins past. But the experience I had gained in the travail of my soul, and the faith begotten of God in my heart, strengthened me to withstand the enemy, and his subtle reasonings. I overcame the wicked One, through a diligent waiting in the Light, and keeping close to the power of·' God ; waiting upon Him, in silence, among his people ; in which exercise my soul delighted." Again, he says, "My prosperity in the Truth, I always found, was being faithful to the Lord in what He manifested, though in but small things ; unfaithfulness in which, is the cause of loss and hurt to many in their growth in the Truth." And further, "Thus I came clearly to see that it was not safe for me to sit down satisfied with what I had passed through, or the victory I had already obtained ; but to travel on in faith and patience, and watch diligently in the Light of Jesus Christ, where the true power is still received. For notwithstanding the many deliverances, and strength and victory I had experienced, the Lord, according to the greatness of his wisdom, was pleased to make me sensible of my own weakness, and that there was no strength to stand, nor place of safety for me to abide in, but in His power ; and under a sense thereof I was humbled, bowed and laid low."

Thus keeping in the school of Christ, and submitting to his discipline, John Banks became deeply versed in the things that belonged to salvation, and in the mysteries of the kingdom of heaven ; and in course of time was entrusted with a gift in the ministry ; in the exercise of which he became eminent. One more extract from his Journal is worthy of close consideration to all in the present day. "Oh ! the comfort and divine consolation we were made partakers of in those days ; and in the inward sense and feeling of the Lord's power and presence with us, we enjoyed one another, and were near and dear one to another. But it was through various trials and deep exercises, with fear and trembling, that thus we were made partakers. Blessed and happy are they who know what the truth has cost them, and hold it in righteousness."

As John Banks was not only a deeply experienced servant of Christ, but one who was well versed and extensively engaged in promulgating the religious faith of Friends, the following short extracts from his "Testimony concerning his faith in Christ," and that of Friends, may properly have a place here: "I believe in the same Lord Jesus Christ, the Son of God, for remission of sins and the salvation of the soul; even He which was conceived of the Holy Ghost, born of the Virgin Mary, who made a good confession before Pontius Pilate, and was crucified without the gates of Jerusalem; dead and buried and rose again the third day, and ascended into glory, far above all heavens, that He might fill all things," &c. . .• . . "But blessed, praised and magnified be the worthy name of the Lord our God forever, who hath opened and cleared our understandings by his power; whereby we know Him in whom we do believe; which is not to believe in the Light within, distinct from Christ; as if people could believe in the Light and not in Christ. But we believe in both as one; knowing and being clear in our understanding, that no separation can be made betwixt Christ and the Light that comes from Him; which shines in the hearts of all true believers, and shines in the darkness of unbelievers, and therefore the darkness cannot comprehend it. So we as truly believe in the same Christ, who laid down his body and took it up again, as well as in his Light within; and we have benefit to salvation by the one as well as by the other, and of both, they being one; and we are willing to lay hold of every help and means, God, in and through Jesus Christ, has ordained for our salvation."

1671. Another Friend mentioned as having labored extensively in Ireland is Benjamin Bangs; who, born in Norfolk, England, came up to London with the man to whom he had been bound as an apprentice, and continued residing there for some years. He was one of the "wardsmen" summoned by Sir John Robinson, Lieutenant of the Tower, to unite with the soldiers, when he ordered the destruction of Friends' meeting-house at Ratcliff. Speaking of the transactions of that day, B. Bangs remarks, "Those who appeared in arms, had orders to let all the Quakers come in that would, but to suffer none to go out until the Justices came; who when they approached, treated the Quakers with very rough language; calling them rogues and rebels for meeting there contrary to law, and began to take their names. After this was done, they were permitted to go out; and they not pulling off their hats to the Justices, the rude people in the yard plucked them off and threw them over the wall; but they who were friends to them [the Quakers] saved what they could, and restored them to the owners; others, who had a mind to make a prey, got a good hat and left a bad one." Being one of the guard sent with three Friends committed to the New prison, one of them addressing him, said, "Thou hast an innocent countenance, and dost not look like a persecutor." "No," Benjamin replied, "it was much contrary to my inclination:" the Friend added, "We believe thee and freely forgive thee." This, he says, produced tenderness of heart towards Friends. But he had no thought of taking part with this suffering people; and his mother, who had joined Friends, having written to him, desiring him to frequent the meetings of Friends, it so offended him, that at first he would not read the whole letter through. But, he says, on the First-day following, "I went to take a walk under the arches in Covent Garden, and after a little time, a solid concern came over my mind, and this arose in my thoughts, 'What is the matter that thou canst not read thy mother's letter?' with that I went and sat down on a large stone, and read the letter with pleasure, and it arose in my mind to go to a meeting. The enemy of all righteousness suggested, 'Thou knowest not where a meeting is;' but it very intelligibly opened to my understanding, Go down to Charing-cross, and there thou shalt see some of that people; follow them." He went, saw five or six persons whom he recognized to be Friends; he followed them, and, he says, "Their habit, with their solid behavior, affected me."

In the meeting, though he remarks he could not keep his thoughts fixed on the preaching, yet he came in measure to see his own lost condition, and was "made sensible that there was a spiritual warfare to be passed through, and that no staidness of mind could be attained to, till the inward enemies of the soul came to be destroyed," and that it was required of him to get into inward retirement. So great was the effect produced upon him by the impressions made on his mind in that meeting, that one of his near friends, observing his great seriousness, inquired what had taken place; and on Benjamin narrating the circumstances, he remarked "He had never heard anything like it; it must be something supernatural, or it could never have had such an effect upon you. And he was so far reached and convinced, that he soon after forsook his former profession, and joined himself to the Quakers." It is further stated by Benjamin Bangs, "Several young men, who heard of the manner of my convincement — I think through the young man who was my companion — were so reached and affected therewith, and seeing my grave and solid behavior, who they heard had before been very wild, that they came also to embrace the Truth; so that I was made, very early, an instrument for the convincement of several."

But some time after, letting in the temptation to believe that he was so firmly established "he would never do anything disagreeable to the Truth," the arm of preservation and defence was withdrawn; and he so far lost his good estate as to grow careless, and to satisfy himself with the belief, that as he now knew how to attain to the knowledge he had so longed for, he might take more liberty, and be more in earnest at a future time. He indulged in this, until he "became ashamed to meet his friends in the street;" but he states that at a certain time, "As I sat at work, the word of the Lord came to me, 'This is thy day; harden not thy heart;' which so struck me, that I trembled." He was now brought to see how he had fallen away; and he goes on: "My exercise was very great; my tongue is too short to express it, and my pen to describe it; and the way to get back to what I once enjoyed, I found by experience to be very narrow. For if I took a wrong step, either by word or a vain thought, my inward Instructor made it manifest that it did not belong to me; I had something else to do."

By close watchfulness and implicit obedience to the manifestations of the Light of Christ, he was favored to bear the baptisms necessary for his purification; and came to know what it was to be truly grafted into Christ, the living Vine; and he makes the acknowledgment, "It is good for me that I have been thus afflicted; for now I know something of what it is to buy the truth; for it had cost me but little before."

Notice has been taken of the condition of political parties in England, and of the spread and embittering of dissatisfied feeling among the people at large; produced, in part, by the prevalent sense that by the foreign policy pursued by the King and his counsellors, the country was occupying a low and humiliating position among the nations; in part by forebodings of some scheme being designed, to undermine the constitutional rights of the citizens, and destroy all civil liberty; and perhaps more than anything else, by the hatred and fear in the great body of the people, of the Romish religion, and the suspected secret machinations of the Papist recusants, to obtain the free exercise of their religion, and once more seize the reins of government. In this state of discontent and uncertainty, the whole nation was startled and thrown into violent ferment, by the revelations of one Titus Oates, a degraded clergyman in the "Church of England." He is said to have once professed the Romish faith, and to have passed some portion of his life in a college of the Jesuits on the continent. In 1678, he boldly declared that he had become acquainted with a carefully concocted plan, devised by the hierarchy at Rome, and having its ramifications throughout the country; to bring into action the means, by which the whole power and all the places of honor and profit in the government, were to be secured by, and kept in the possession of, the Papists. He asserted that the profuse shedding of blood was to be no obstruction to carrying out the designs of the plotters; and that they stood ready at the first opportunity to rise, and by massacre or any other means, wholly to overturn the present condition of the nation.

Some circumstances occurring at the time, supposed to corroborate this tale of a "Popish Plot," the nation became distracted with an insane terror and credulity. Nothing seemed too bad or too incredible not to be eagerly accepted by the excited populace, as part and parcel of the Jesuitical conspiracy prepared for their destruction; and Parliament, participating in the general hallucination, insisted upon the Duke of York being excluded from the Privy Council; gave expression to their jealousy of the influence of the Queen, and impeached the High Treasurer; who had received money from the French monarch. A new *test* Act was passed, and a proposition made to exclude the Duke of York from the throne. The King, fearing lest an investigation would be gone into that would lead to a knowledge of transactions, which he was particularly desirous to keep concealed, in the First month of 1679, dissolved the Parliament; which had been in existence almost ever since his restoration, nearly eighteen years; leaving the whole nation in an unreasoning, passionate ferment, and the officers appointed to administer the laws, subject to the contagious excitement that was hurrying the populace into the wildest excesses.

Friends, of course, had nothing to do with these political turmoils, nor with the supposed Popish plot, that was so deeply agitating the nation; but it was made a means for increasing the power of their enemies, and multiplying their sufferings. However violently parties opposed each other, and however implacable their hatred of each other, they seemed to unite, as on common ground, in the persecution of the Quakers. In addition to former pretended causes for punishment, many of the ribald informers and corrupt Magistrates, now boldly accused them of being Popish recusants; and maliciously enlisted the prejudices and passions of the people on that subject, to inflict on defenceless Friends the havoc of goods and personal suffering, they were, in measure, restrained from meting out on the dreaded Catholics. Nor was it this class only that took advantage of the excited state of the people to add to the sufferings of Friends; for some who were of account in the "established church," took much pains to spread the impression, that though the Quakers might not be Papists, yet they were plotters against the government. To meet and, if possible, prevent the effect intended to be produced by this calumny, George Fox put forth a declaration as follows; addressed more particularly to the new Parliament.

"It is our principle and testimony, to deny and renounce all plots and plotters against the King, or any of his subjects; for we have the Spirit of Christ, by which we have the mind of Christ, who came to save men's lives, and not to destroy them: and we would have the King and all his subjects to be safe. Wherefore we do declare, that we will endeavor, to our power, to save and defend him and them, by discovering all plots and plotters, which shall come to our knowledge, that would destroy the King or his subjects: this we do sincerely offer unto you. But as to swearing and fighting, which in tenderness of conscience we cannot do, ye know that we have suffered these many years for our conscientious refusal thereof. And now that the Lord hath brought you together, we desire you to relieve us, and free us from those sufferings: and that ye will not put upon us to do those things, which we have suffered so much and so long already for not doing; for if you do, ye will make our sufferings and bonds stronger, instead of relieving us."

In 1680, Friends presented to the King and Parliament a brief relation of the sufferings they had undergone, since the restoration of the King; showing, that beside all the grievous imprisonments which had been inflicted on over ten thousand of them, the havoc made of their property, &c., two hundred and forty-three of their members had died in prison; several of whom came to their death from the inhuman beatings they had received, when meeting to worship their Almighty Father in heaven. They also set forth the iniquitous prosecutions they were subjected to, in the Exchequer, as Popish recusants; whereby two-thirds of the estate of the Friends thus prosecuted, were seized in the King's name, though it was well known they were Protestant Dissenters. The exorbitant fines, &c., imposed by the Bishops' Courts, were likewise shown, as also other unjust proceedings. William Penn, George Whitehead and William Mead, went before a committee of the House, and clearly demonstrated the truth of the statements made, and the inhumanity of the course pursued towards their harmless brethren; so that Sir Christopher Musgrave, himself a zealous Churchman, expressed his disgust at the treatment Friends received; saying, "The prisons were filled with them, many of them had been excommunicated for small matters, and that it was a shame and scandal for their Church, to use the Quakers so hardly on every trivial occasion."

As Friends did not partake in the popular feeling of hostility towards the Roman Catholics, and were, on principle, opposed to the harsh measures pursued towards them on account of their religion, they were careful, while thus exhibiting the injustice of punishing them [Friends] as "Popish recusants," to make known likewise their disapproval of the persecution of the Catholics. Thus in his speech before the Committee of the House, William Penn makes use of the following language:

"I would not be mistaken. I am far from thinking it fit, that Papists should be whipped for their consciences, because I exclaim against the injustice of whipping Quakers for Papists. No; for though the hand pretended to be lifted up against them, hath, I know not by what direction, lit heavily upon us, and we complain, yet we do not mean that any should take a fresh aim at them, or that they must come in our room. We must give the liberty we ask, and cannot be false to our principles, though it were to relieve ourselves; for we have good-will to all men, and would have none suffer for a truly sober and conscientious dissent on any hand. And I humbly take leave to add, that those methods against persons so qualified, do not seem to me to be convincing, or indeed adequate to the reason of mankind, but this I submit to your consideration."

A Bill was reported to the House, releasing Protestants from the penalties of certain laws relating to Non-conformists, and exempting others from similar penal statutes; on condition of their subscribing a declaration of allegiance, and assembling with open doors. But the Presbyterians, claiming to be included within the Established Church, so that they might participate in its emoluments, proposed such amendments to or alterations in the Bill, that though it was committed, it was not perfected or passed. Both Houses, however, passed an Act exempting Protestant Dissenters from the penalties imposed by the Acts of Elizabeth, against Popish recusants; though it was strongly opposed by the Bishops, in the House of Lords. When it was to have been presented to the King for his signature, it was suddenly missing; having been secreted by the "Clerk to the Crown," it was said, by Charles' direction.

The King, who had come to the determination to rule by his own absolute power, informed Parliament that he was about to prorogue them; and both Houses at once passed resolutions, that the Acts against Popish recusants ought not to be used against Protestant Dissenters; and that the prosecution of the latter was weakening the Protestant interest, and giving encouragement to Papists. The laws, however, were not changed. This Parliament was soon after dissolved, and another elected, which assembled at Oxford; but it manifesting the same kind of feeling, and the same determination to exclude the Duke of York from succession to the throne, the King, in a passion, dissolved it; and siding entirely with the party which had received the title of Tory, in opposition to the other now called Whig, the measures taken were more the product of party hate and animosity, than for the ease of the people, or bettering the condition of the country. The Bishops and high-churchmen generally sided with the tories, and unblushingly supported the arrogant assumptions of the King and Court; while the latter, turned out of office every one suspected of not favoring the tyrannical measures now pursued, in order to retain and extend the power usurped.

Friends in London, owing to the moderate sentiments and kindly feelings of the then Mayor and Sheriff, had for the last year been permitted to escape the keen edge of persecution; but the Court, by its unjustifiable interference, had those officers, contrary to the wishes of the citizens as expresed by a vote, turned out of place, and succeeded by others prepared to do its bidding. In a little time after, the King took away the charter of the city, and would not restore it, without a stipulation, that thereafter he should have a veto in the appointment of its chief officers. Soon the fire of persecution was again kindled against Friends there, and many were made to suffer deeply from it. The informers, who in most places had become so detestable to the people that they were either ashamed or afraid to pursue their nefarious trade, now returned to their prey; and were gladly welcomed by the party desirous to profit by their insolence and depravity. Several of the clergy enlisted in the infamous service themselves; first disturbing or breaking up meetings, and then giving information of the presence of persons, whom and whose families they assisted to ruin, by fines and imprisonments.

George Whitehead, who was charged with being a Jesuit, appeared to be an object of their implacable hate. Again and again he was fined as a preacher among the Quakers; so that in a comparatively short time, he had goods taken from him valued at nearly £73; but by an appeal against two of the seizures, which were so illegally made, that the decision had to be in his favor, he recovered a little over £11, out of about £50 worth of goods that had been seized and sold; the balance remaining in the hands of the informer and Magistrates.

William Dewsbury, who had been for a short time out of prison and living at his own home, was once more taken up, upon the charge of being a Jesuit and connected with the Popish plot, and sent to his old quarters in Warwick jail; and although the notorious Oates gave a certificate that neither he nor any other Friend, was in any way connected with the plot, and that William was entirely innocent of the charges brought against him, his enemies found means to gratify their ill-will towards him. He was kept shut up in prison, until liberated by the proclamation of King James II.; about six years after his committal. It was during the time of this last imprisonment in Warwick jail — which made up about nineteen years that he was confined in that wretched abode — that he lost by death a little grandchild, named Mary Samm; who had continued with him in his bonds; waiting upon him, and contributing not a little to his enjoyment. She was but little over twelve years of age, and the account given by her grandfather, of her religious exercises and expressions, during her last illness, shows her to have been remarkably mature in religious understanding.

The necessity to observe brevity will not admit of entering into many particulars of the sore persecution, now unrelentingly enforced against Dissenters, by corrupt officials, throughout England, Scotland, and Ireland; of which, as usual, Friends bore the severest part. It is probable that Friends were made to feel it the more keenly, because of it becoming known, that in the elections which had necessarily occurred on the dissolution of Parliament, they had pretty generally cast their votes in favor of candidates opposed to the Court and high-church party; and William Penn had taken an active part, both by pen and personal influence, to have his friend Algernon Sidney returned; who was specially disliked by the party in power; in which, however, he was disappointed.

As on former occasions, Friends' meetings were now generally broken up by armed bands; the meeting-houses taken from them, obliging them to meet together in the streets, or in other places, as near to them as they were allowed to come; personal violence was continually resorted to, while fines and imprisonments were the lot of the more conspicuous among them. Still, they were borne above it all, and kept faithful to their testimony, being supported by Divine power; and, as George Whitehead says, comforted by the inward assurance that the Lamb and his followers should finally have the victory. At Bristol their persecution was particularly persistent, barbarous, and regardless of all form of law.

The three principals, most conspicuous in the inhuman treatment meted out to Friends in that city at that time [1682] were the Sheriff, named Knight, an Alderman, named Olyffe, and an Attorney named Helliar. These, with their subordinates, appear to have reached an extraordinary depth of wickedness, and to have given unrestrained license to their evil passions. They first laid a fine of £5 on one of Friends' meeting-houses, under pretence that it was required to defray the expense of the "trained bands;" and as it was not paid, they took the seats, forms, chairs, &c., out of the house, and encouraged the rabble to break the windows, &c. Finding Friends continued their meeting there, they attacked them while assembled; beat some of them and sent some to Newgate. They broke down the galleries, and carried off the partitions; then took possession of the house, and boarded up the doors. Having thus disposed of one of the meeting-houses, they proceeded to enact the same destruction at the other; raising such a riot by the mob they enlisted in the service, that the whole neighborhood was in an uproar; to the terror of the peaceable inhabitants; for which they endeavored to make Friends responsible. Whenever Friends assembled for Divine worship, they were assailed in the most brutal manner, both men and women suffering alike from the violence and insolence of the low men and boys, who served the higher officers, generally led on by Helliar; while the most abusive and often obscene language, was poured out upon them. Fines were levied upon them without stint, and the jails crowded almost to suffocation. A widow, named Elizabeth Batho, had her house seized, the windows broken, her goods thrown out, and she obliged to give place to another tenant, whom the self-authorized trio put in. The goods seized for the fines levied, were generally of two or three times more value than the sum demanded; and the Sheriff sold them in obscure places, where those who coveted them could get them at a mere nominal price. From seven Friends they took goods worth over £100 in five days' time; and there was no possibility of obtaining redress. Fifty of the members were prosecuted

as " Popish recusants," for the purpose of bringing them under the
sentence of premunire. The Sheriff and Alderman Olyffe sent
men and women to jail, at their own option, without regard to trial
or law ; until the rooms into which they were crowded, became so
full, they had not sufficient space to hold the necessary beds ; and
the atmosphere, from want of proper ventilation, became poisonous.
The prisoners represented their suffering condition to the Mayor ;
stating there were nine beds in one room of thirteen feet square.

The Mayor and Aldermen generally disapproved of the barbarous
course pursued towards Friends, and were desirous to afford them
relief ; but their good intentions were frustrated by the Sheriff,
Knight ; who, knowing that he would be approved and supported
by those in power at Court, refused to comply with the direction of
the Mayor ; not only in regard to affording relief to the prisoners,
but also as to stopping the disposing of goods seized, in alehouses ;
and the private convictions, and commitments privately made,
according to the will of one Sheriff and one Alderman.

The commitments to prison still going on, some of the citizens
accompanied the other Sheriff of the city, to inspect the condition
of the prisoners ; who published a certificate, in which they say that
eighty-five of those in jail " were of the people called Quakers,
who were unreasonably thronged to four, five, six, seven and nine
beds in a room ; many necessitated to lie on the ground, in a filthy
place, which had been a dog-kennel, to the hazard of their lives,"
&c. This statement producing no change, two Friends went up
to London, and with George Whitehead were admitted before the
King and Council ; where, though some members of the Council
endeavored to prevent any notice being taken of their statement, its
exhibition of the illegality as well as cruelty of the proceedings at
Bristol, was so clear, that an order was issued to the Magistrates of
that city, to allow the prisoners better accommodations ; whereupon
some of them were taken out of Newgate, and shut up in another
place. But the three confederate persecutors cared little for this
intervention ; they soon filled up the places that had been vacated
in Newgate, and gave ground for the same complaints of the noisomeness of the quarters, as were heard before. Four physicians
of the city now visited the prison ; and afterwards certified that it
was so full and noisome, and the prisoners so straitened for room to
rest, as had a tendency to suffocate and destroy them.

Like the former testimony, this had no effect on the men who
were equally regardless of justice and humanity ; they kept up their

outrages on the Friends who were left to assemble at their religious meetings; and finding that those who were crammed within the prison walls, continued to devote part of their time to performing the duty of Divine worship, Knight, Helliar, and the jailer, named Isaac Dennis, broke violently upon them while thus engaged; drove them out of the room, put irons upon one of them, and thrust him into the place usually reserved for condemned felons. On one such occasion, while Friends were holding their meeting in the common hall, Knight seized a Friend who had spoken a few words, and threw him headlong down the stairs; and he, narrowly escaping with his life, was thrust into the felons' apartment.

When the Quarter Sessions was held at Bristol, the Magistrates who were favorable to Friends, discharged the greater part of them, on their promise to appear at the next sessions; but in the course of a short time, Knight and Helliar had sent the most of them back to their old quarters. Finding that when the men were nearly all incarcerated, the women continued to hold their meetings, they resolved to sweep them off also; and quickly, the women Friends were shut up in prison with their husbands, brothers, and sons; so that it was not long before one hundred and sixty Friends were locked up. Among the women were Barbara Blaugdone and Catharine Evans, of both of whom notice has been taken before.

The parents being thus prevented from maintaining a public testimony to the indispensable duty of assembling for Divine worship, the children, undismayed by the persecution inflicted on their nearest and dearest caretakers, came together regularly at the place appointed, and held the meeting with decorum and solidity; bearing with becoming patience, the ribald jests and derision lavished on them. Being under the age that would have exposed them to the lash of the law, they were, nevertheless, not exempted from the illegal and cowardly efforts of the vindictive persecutors, when they found that taunts and jeers had no effect to deter them from keeping up the meeting. Some were put in the stocks and kept there for hours; and some were severely whipped with whalebone whips. Helliar sent eleven boys and four girls to Bridewell; and when they were brought before the Deputy Mayor the next morning, flattery and threats were freely used, in order to induce them to give up their meeting; but not being moved by either, they were sent back to jail; Helliar charging the jailer to procure a new cat-o'-nine-tails for use on the morrow. But the Magistrates interfered to prevent the whipping; though Helliar, to gratify his cruel disposition, strongly urged it. The jails soon became so crowded that no more could be got into them; the spotted fever broke out among the prisoners, of which three Friends died, and no redress or abatement of suffering could be obtained; unless at the price of sacrificing religious principles. That this almost incredible bigotry and malignity were approved at Court, is proved by the fact, that the King rewarded Knight, the Sheriff, who was the leading spirit in the implacable persecution, with such dignity as the order of Knighthood could confer on such a man.

The jailer at Newgate, in Bristol, Isaac Dennis, has been mentioned, and it seemed as though an evil spirit might have taken possession of him and his wife; so continued and outrageous was the cruel treatment they inflicted on the Friends placed under their custody. Their ingenuity was taxed to add injury to their bonds, and to throw every obstacle they could, in the way of the relief they sought, and such as was occasionally proffered. He refused to allow the nursing and comforts which the relatives or friends of the sick were solicitous to bestow; positively denied there was any fever in the jail, and assured the Magistrates, when inquiry was made of him, there was abundance of room for the accommodation of those in the prison; afterwards declaring, that all he wanted was to have no fewer packed in a room than would allow of his closing the door. But the measure of his iniquity was filled up, and on being taken sick, his anguish of mind was indescribable. He proclaimed aloud, that " he had sinned out the day of Grace; there was no help, and no hope for him." Yet he requested some of the Friends to pray for him; and they tried to impress upon him, that as he was brought to a sense of his manifold sins, he might hope it was evidence that he was not entirely cast off; but in his despair, he replied, " I thank you for your good hope, but I have no faith to believe;" and he sank into death in this awful condition.

Though the persecution of Friends at Bristol was carried on by men of more brutal and obdurate hearts than some others, yet it may be received as a type of that which prevailed throughout the kingdom, during the years 1681, 1682, 1683 and part of 1684. Notwithstanding its severity, Friends continued almost universally faithful in support of the testimonies of the gospel for which they were called to make a good confession before many witnesses; though there were some few among them who made shipwreck of faith and a good conscience; and it is probable that others may have been induced, by the bonds and afflictions abiding them at home, to emigrate to New Jersey or to Pennsylvania. Many epistles of counsel, comfort and encouragement were written by George Fox, William Dewsbury, George Whitehead and other eminent members in the Society, to their suffering brethren; and it was a remarkable circumstance, obtaining notice at the time, that so many of these dedicated servants and ministers, escaped imprisonment, and were actively engaged in going from place to place, visiting those in bonds; administering to their necessities, and laboring to build them up on the most holy faith, and to confirm them in accepting with all joy the privilege of not only believing in Christ, but of being counted worthy to suffer for him.

In the epistle written by George Fox, he exhorts his brethren, "Take care that all your offerings be free, and of your own, that has cost you something; so that ye may not offer of that which is another man's, or that ye are entrusted withal and not your own." And he reminds them that in former times of great suffering, how great a care was on the minds of Friends on that account. That where any had goods which they had bought on credit, and had not yet paid for them, they felt constrained to go to their creditors, and inform them that as they [the debtors] were liable to have at any time all that they had taken from them, they desired to return such goods as had not been paid for; for they would not have any man to suffer for them; neither would they by suffering, offer up anything but what was really their own, or what they were able to pay for. And thus many received their goods again, which "wrought a very good savor in the hearts of many people; seeing such a righteous, just and honest principle in Friends." He enjoins that this course may continue to be observed, and then suffering for the testimony of Jesus will bring a blessing.

Other Non-conformists were very generally suppressed; their ministers when caught officiating in their private meetings, being subjected to heavy fines and imprisonment, from which some of them suffered severely. Sewel, who may be considered a contemporary historian, says, "All other Protestant Dissenters were now suppressed; for they were restrained from exercising any public worship; and some there were, who, in their nocturnal meetings, would pray God, that it might please Him to keep the Quakers steadfast, that so they might be as a wall about them, in order that other Dissenters might not be rooted out. And yet these, to render the Quakers odious, formerly had been very active in setting them forth in very ill colors. But the said people continued now so valiant, and without fainting, that some of their persecutors have been heard to say, that the Quakers could not be overcome, and that the devil himself could not extirpate them."

In 1683, George Fox paid a second visit in Holland. He had been spending some time in London and its vicinity, "Laboring in the work of the Lord, being frequent at meetings, and visiting Friends that were prisoners, or that were sick; and in writing books for the spreading of truth, and opening the understandings of the people to receive it." After attending the Yearly Meeting in that city, which he says was "A blessed, weighty one, wherein Friends were sweetly refreshed together; for the Lord was with us and opened his heavenly treasures amongst us," he embarked, with several other ministering Friends, and was at the Yearly Meeting in Amsterdam. Upon getting through with his service in that country, which occupied but a few weeks, he returned; and going to London, his health being feeble, and there being much to be attended to for the service of the Society that required being near the Court, he and his wife spent many months in that city; during which time he was, as usual, assiduously employed in promoting the welfare of others and of the good cause.

CHAPTER XXIX.

Triumph of the King and Church Party—Death of Charles II.—Accession of James II.—Petition and Statement of Friends—Attempt of the Duke of Monmouth—Release of Friends from Imprisonment—Examination into the Conduct of Informers—Their Iniquity Exposed—Epistle of G. Fox—Death of D. Barclay and of Anne Whitehead—Liberty of Conscience Granted—Acknowledgment of Gratitude by Friends—R. Barclay's efforts to relieve Friends in Scotland—End of Persecution in Scotland—R. Barclay in Public Affairs—Attacked by a Highwayman—Death of R. Barclay—Testimonials—Defection towards King James—Imprisonment of Bishops—William, Prince of Orange, invited to take the Throne—William and Mary declared King and Queen—Wm. Penn at the Court of King James—Wm. Penn arrested—Death of W. Dewsbury.

THE Court and High Church party had now triumphed over all opposition. The rabid excitement following the discovery of the Popish plot had passed away, and advantage had been taken of the reaction that succeeded, to brand zeal against Popery as the spirit of faction. The constitution of England had become a dead letter. The liberties and rights of the people were delivered up to the Crown. The Rye-house plot — as it was called — had given the tories an opportunity to gratify their hatred and revenge on some of those they deemed their most dangerous enemies; and some of the noblest blood in the nation had been poured out on the block. The Bishops, and nearly all their clergy, sided with the Court, and employed the pulpit to inculcate the doctrine of the divine right of Kings, and the obligation of unresisting obedience to whatever he [the King] required. This, with the advocacy of conformity to "the church," and the right and expediency of rooting out all Dissenters, was the main burden of their weekly teaching. Many of the clergy were commissioned as Magistrates, in order to facilitate the collection of their tithes, and more speedily and surely to punish those who did not pay, or who absented themselves from "the church." The small party of clergy denominated "low churchmen," who were known to be averse to the arrogant assumptions and slavish opinions of their more courtly brethren, and opposed to the furious persecution of the Non-conformists, were denounced as betrayers of the church; and everything in church and State seemed prepared for passive obedience, when Charles should be succeeded by his Romanist brother.

This event came sooner than was expected. In the Second month of 1685, Charles, in the midst of his corrupt Court, was seized with a disease, that in the course of two or three days terminated his profligate life. In his last hours he showed his want of faith in the prelates that approached his bed—one of whom summoned courage to say, "It is time to speak out, for, Sir, you are about to appear before a Judge who is no respecter of persons,"—by giving little or no heed to what they had to say, and refusing to partake of the bread and wine which they urged upon him as the Lord's supper. He, however, when asked, said he was sorry for what he had done amiss, and allowed the absolution they professed to give, to be pronounced over him. But soon after they were sent out of his room by the Duke of York, and he gladly received the services of a Popish priest; confessed to him, and obtained his absolution; swallowed with great difficulty the bread he gave him, and fixed his dying gaze on the crucifix he presented; thus, though a practical skeptic while living, dying a member of the Romish church.

Before noticing the progress of events among Friends during the brief reign of James II., it may be well to notice the death of Isaac Penington and his wife. After his release from the prison at

Reading, Isaac had been permitted to remain quietly at his home at Woodside, where he employed his time in helping Friends in their meeting, in the neighborhood, and in promoting the cause of Truth by the use of his pen. In 1679, with his wife, he went on a visit into Kent, where, after spending some time, he was seized with his last sickness, which in a few days terminated his life. His sorrowing widow survived him about three years; dying at Worminghust, the residence of her daughter, Gulielma Penn, the wife of William Penn.

1685. It is one of the remarkable instances illustrating the fickleness of popular opinion, and the inconsistency with which mere worldlings act, that the Duke of York, against whom, as a Catholic, there had been, but a short time before, such determined hostility shown by Parliament and the people, that he had been obliged to withdraw himself from notice, and retire into Scotland, succeeded his brother on the throne, as James II., amid the acclamations of nearly all classes, without riot or the exhibit of any rebellious feeling. He at once threw aside the privacy with which he had heretofore attended on the religious rites of the Romish Church; had a new pulpit erected at the Court, for a Popish priest; and on the advent of what is called "Passion Week," he had mass publicly celebrated at Westminster. Nevertheless, he declared that he was determined to protect the "Church of England"—of which he was the official head — and maintain the liberties of the people. Congratulatory addresses were sent to him from most parts of the Kingdom; those from Oxford and Cambridge being no less servile than others that indulged in greater adulation. Some historians have recorded one, which is represented as coming from the Quakers; couched in curt and uncouth expressions; such as they supposed corresponded with Friends' plainness of speech. It was fictitious, and probably designed to cast odium on the Society.

The first address made by Friends to King James, was presented more than a month after he ascended the throne. It was called forth by a sense of duty to seek relief from the grievous suffering they had been subjected to, almost ever since their rise as a distinct body of Christian professors, and which they continued to endure. This Address was accompanied by a petition to the Sovereign and Parliament, for the extension of clemency and help; and the following passages from the latter give some insight of the unmerciful treatment that Friends had been long, and were then, undergoing. It shows, "That of late, above one thousand five hundred of the said people, both men and women, having been detained prisoners in England, and part of them in Wales, (some of which, being since discharged by the Judges, and others freed by death, through their long and tedious imprisonment,) there are now remaining, according to late accounts, about one thousand three hundred eighty and three; above two hundred of them women. Many under sentence of premunire, both men and women, and more than three hundred near it; not for denying the duty, or refusing the substance of allegiance itself, but only because they dare not swear; many on writs of excommunication and fines for the King, and upon the act for banishment: besides, above three hundred and twenty have died in prison, and prisoners, since the year 1660; near one hundred whereof, by means of this long imprisonment, as it is judged, since the account delivered to the late King and Parliament, in 1680; thereby making widows and fatherless, and leaving them in distress and sorrow: the two last hard winters' restraint, and the close confinement of great numbers in divers jails, unavoidably tending towards their destruction, their healths being evidently impaired thereby."

. . . .

"Besides these long-continued and destructive hardships upon the persons of men and women, as aforesaid, great violences, outrageous distresses, and woful havoc and spoil, have been and still are, frequently made upon our goods and estates, both in and about this city of London, and other parts of this nation, by a company of idle, extravagant, and merciless informers, and their prosecutions upon the Conventicle Act; many being convicted and fined, unsummoned and unheard in their own defence. As also on *qui tam* writs, at the suit of informers, who prosecute for one-third part for themselves, and on other processes, for twenty pounds a month, and two-thirds of estates seized for the King; all tending to the ruin of trade, husbandry, and farmers, and the impoverishing of many industrious families; without compassion shown to widows, fatherless, or desolate: to some, not a bed left to rest upon; to others, no cattle to till their ground, nor corn for bread or seed, nor tools to work withal: the said informers and Sheriff's bailiffs in some places being outrageous and excessive in their distresses and seizures, breaking into houses, and making great waste and spoil. And all these and other severities done against us by them, under pretence of serving the King and the Church, thereby to force us to a conformity, without inward conviction or satisfaction of our tender consciences, wherein our peace with God is concerned, which we are very tender of." Ap-

pended to this petition was a list of the number of Friends, prisoners
at that time, in forty of the counties of England; amounting to one
thousand four hundred and sixty.

Action on this just and affecting representation, of the barbarous
manner in whic an innocent and peaceable people, under a professedly Christian government, were persecuted on account of adherence to their scriptural faith, as well as petitions from other Non-conformists for relief, was prevented by the attempt of the Duke of
Monmouth, to obtain possession of the throne; in consequence of
which, the Parliament was prorogued, and the whole attention of
the King and Court directed to the suppression of the insurrection.
When that was accomplished, much time was occupied in wreaking
vengeance on those implicated in the unsuccessful invasion and outbreak; so that the "bloody assize" under the presidency of the
brutal and sanguinary Jeffreys, is one of the very dark stains on
English history. As the Duke of Argyle, who had taken an active
part in this effort to drive James from the throne, was a Presbyterian; and it was supposed that the representatives of the Puritans
were generally inimical to the house of Stuart, the laws against them,
in common with other Dissenters, were now much more rigorously
enforced; and not only in Scotland, where they were hunted and
shot down by the notorious Claverhouse and his savage dragoons;
but in England, they were made to feel, much more severely than
before, the hatred and malice of their enemies.

But the Parliament had given great offence to James, who had
appointed several Papists in different offices, by calling in question
his authority to absolve any from the action of penal laws; and also
by calling on him to put in execution the laws against all who were
not members of the "Established Church." Himself a Roman
Catholic, it was not to be expected that he would be instrumental
in punishing others for making profession of the religion he publicly acknowledged as the only true one; and whatever his motives
may have been, he had always avowed himself averse to persecution
for religious belief. There was, therefore, some ground for the
expectation entertained by many, that liberty of conscience, in
regard to forms of religion, would be granted.

Friends, ever on the alert to extricate themselves from the grasp
of the merciless men who were making them their prey, appointed
some of their number to wait upon the King, and renew their solicitations for the release of their brethren and sisters, from the
noisome prisons and dungeons where they were shut up, and where

they had been kept closely immured, some for five, some for ten and some for fifteen years or more. Their persevering efforts were crowned with success. On the 15th day of the Third month, 1686, a warrant was issued by the King to the Attorney-General, commanding that those Quakers who had been convicted, or were in process of conviction of premunire, for not swearing, for not coming to church; or who had been returned into the Exchequer and in charge for twenty pounds *per mensem;* or were lying in prison upon writs *de excommunicato capiendo,* should be forthwith discharged from jail; and that all fines, forfeitures, or sums of money charged upon any of those commonly called Quakers, be stopped and discharged; and a *nolle prosequi* be entered in all cases where it may be necessary to carry the intention of this warrant into execution. Friends took immediate steps to have this warrant duly executed; and in a little time, nearly fifteen hundred of their members came forth from their prison-houses, once more to enter on the enjoyment and the duties of life and liberty.

Encouraged by the disposition manifested by the King and his Council, Friends persevered in their efforts to have other of their remaining grievances redressed; for though the royal mandate had relieved so many from imprisonment, the laws against " Non-conformists " and " Popish recusants," were still in force, and informers had not slackened their nefarious employment. Accordingly a statement of numerous instances of the perjuries, illegal robberies, and embezzlements committed by informers, and Magistrates in league with them, was drawn up, and signed by a number of Friends; who stated they were prepared to prove the charges they made. They petitioned for the appointment of a Commission to examine into their allegations, in the presence of those so charged. The statement was favorably received, [1686] and the petition granted; Commissioners being appointed, who notified the Friends of the time for meeting, and summoned the informers named. At the first meeting, the complainants with their witnesses numbered over fifty, and the informers in the outset sought to discourage and harass them by their vulgar abuse and ribald invectives; especially directed against George Whitehead; who had long been a special object of their malice, and a victim of their plundering, and who now conducted the proceedings for Friends. But the Friends went on undeterred, quietly reporting the circumstances attending the respective cases, and producing the proof of the correctness of their charges.

Thirty-four cases were investigated, and the most flagrant perjury, illegal violence, and exorbitant seizures and carting away of goods, chattels, &c., which were never fully accounted for, were irrefragably proved ; so that the informers could make no defence. In numerous cases warrants had been granted by Magistrates, to levy on the personal effects of individuals, for each offence said to have been committed at a specified time ; the Magistrate charging ten pounds for every such warrant : thus making his fees in some cases amount to fifty pounds.

The Commissioners adjourned for ten days. The informers hoping to prevent some of the Friends most actively engaged in the examination, from proceeding farther in it, went to Grace-church Street meeting, and had four of them arrested and taken before the Lord Mayor ; where they were detained until late at night, waiting to hear the charges against them. Their accusers not appearing, the Mayor directed they should be bound by recognizance to appear at the sessions, and to be of *good behavior* in the meantime. This they refused to do, as it implied they had done some wrong, which they denied. He then drew a mittimus to send them to prison ; but on reflection — probably sensible there was a different feeling towards the Quakers at Court, than had reigned for so long a time — he discharged them, upon their promise to appear at the assizes. When they appeared at the sessions, there was no evidence against them, and they were discharged.

At the next sitting of the Commissioners, a lawyer attempted to defend the informers ; but the further cases produced were so outrageously illegal, and the evidence so overwhelming, that he was soon silenced ; and the Commissioners told Friends they need go no further, as they were fully convinced of the truth of their allegations, and would report accordingly. Nevertheless, when George Whitehead got to see the report they had drawn up, he found it very defective ; in not stating the perjuries, the robberies, and the illegal extortions committed by the informers ; and he remonstrated against the evident intention to palliate their course. They consented to make some alteration ; but one of them told him they found they had a critical business on hand, for they had received a message, from " one who stood high in the Church," to beware not to lessen the power of the informers, for they were of great service to the Church. The report being presented, it was referred to the Lord Chancellor, with direction to have such illegal proceedings corrected, and to see that testimony should be taken from none but those of reputable character. Beside this, the King let it be known, that it was his wish to have a stop put to the work of the informers, and that they should be discountenanced by Judges and Magistrates. On a succeeding application to the King, it was further ordered, that a *nolle prosequi* be entered in the Courts, to stay proceedings against Friends under indictments as "Popish recusants," and to forbear pursuing any process against those whose names were given, or others under similar suits. As the character of the Acts and the penalties attached, applicable to such cases, were excessively severe; the latter, under some circumstances, involving the loss of life as well as of all estate; although it was an entire perversion to apply them to Friends; yet this order of the King was a great relief; rescuing many who had been unjustly prosecuted, as "Popish recusants," from imprisonment and the confiscation of their estates. [1686.] One Friend, Richard Vicris, had been condemned to death, under those laws; but upon the removal of his case, by a writ of *habeas corpus*, to the Court of the King's Bench, he was liberated by proclamation.

When the Yearly Meeting assembled in London, in this year (1686), there was great rejoicing; there being many Friends in attendance — some of them eminent ministers — who had, for years, been prevented from assembling with their brethren, by being imprisoned; and who, now, by the good providence of the Divine Master they were endeavoring to serve, in simplicity and sincerity, were once more permitted to unite with their fellow-professors, in harmonious labor for the honor of Truth, and in returning thanksgiving and praise to Him for his merciful interference for their deliverance.

George Fox, ever watchful to promote the cause of Truth, and to incite Friends to a close adherence to the pure and spiritual doctrines they professed, and a life and conversation consistent therewith, fearful lest the freedom from suffering, might betray some into lukewarmness and carelessness, respecting the religious duties incumbent upon them, addressed them in the following words of caution and counsel:

"FRIENDS: — The Lord, by his eternal power, hath opened the heart of the King to open the prison-doors, by which about fifteen or sixteen hundred are set at liberty; and hath given a check to the informers; so that in many places our meetings are pretty quiet. So my desires are, that both liberty and sufferings, all may be sanctified to his people; and Friends may prize the mercies of the Lord in all things, and to Him be thankful, who stilleth the raging waves of the sea, and allayeth the storms and tempests, and maketh a calm. And therefore it is good to trust in the Lord, and cast your care upon Him, who careth for you. For when ye were in your jails and prisons, then the Lord did, by his eternal arm and power, uphold you, and sanctified them to you; and unto some he had made them as a sanctuary; and tried his people, as in a furnace of affliction, both in prisons and spoiling of goods. And in all this the Lord was with his people, and taught them to know that the earth is the Lord's, and the fulness thereof; and that He is in all places; who crowneth the year with his goodness.— Psalm lxv. Therefore let all God's people be diligent and careful to keep the camp of God holy, pure and clean; and to serve God, and Christ, and one another, in the glorious, peaceable gospel of life and salvation; which glory shines over God's camp; and his great Prophet, and Bishop, and Shepherd is among or in the midst of them, exercising his heavenly offices in them; so that you his people may rejoice in Christ Jesus, through whom you have peace with God. For He that destroyeth the devil and his work, and bruises the serpent's head, is all God's people's heavenly foundation and rock to build upon; which was the holy prophets' and apostles' rock in days past, and is now a rock of our age; which rock and foundation of God standeth sure. And upon this the Lord God establish all his people. Amen. GEORGE FOX.

"London, the 25th of the Seventh month, 1686."

In this year died David Barclay of Ury, who, as has been before mentioned, from a noted warrior, became a peaceable and spiritually-minded Friend, suffering cheerfully the malice and abuse of those who hated him for his religion's sake. In the course of his last illness he uttered many expressions, giving evidence of the heavenly state of his mind, and his preparation for entering into those joys prepared for the righteous. "I shall now go to the Lord, and be gathered to many of my brethren who are gone before me." "The Lord is nigh." "The perfect discovery of the Day-Spring from on high, how great a blessing it hath been to me and my family." "The Truth is over all." At the last he poured out his soul in praise and prayer: "Praises to the Lord! Let now thy servant depart in peace. Into thy hands, O Father, I commit my soul, spirit and body. Thy will, O Lord, be done on earth, as it is done in heaven;" and thus breathed his last, in the seventy-sixth year of his age.

Anne Whitehead also deceased in this year. Her maiden name was Anne Downer, and she was one of the first of those, who were convinced in the city of London, of the principles of Truth as held by Friends. She never swerved from a practical exemplification of the religion she professed, and was ever·laborious and watchful to serve the cause of Christ, and those who, like herself, had espoused it; going at one time two hundred miles on foot to minister to the necessities of G. Fox and other Friends, then in prison in Launceston. She was a widow when she was married to George Whitehead. Her ministry was sound and edifying, being the means of convincing many. Near her close she said to those about her dying bed, "There is no cause for you to be troubled or concerned, for I am well and in peace." "God knoweth my integrity, and how I have been, and walked before him." "I have done with all things in this life, and have nothing that troubles me, but am in true peace and ease every way."

In 1687, the King issued a general declaration of liberty of conscience to all his subjects, ordering the penal laws concerning ecclesiastical affairs, not to be executed. This was taking the same step his brother had been obliged to retrace; claiming the right from the prerogative of the Crown, irrespective of the action of Parliament. Probably having in view the exaltation into power of members of the Romish church, the King had broken with the high-church party; strongly and loudly censuring the cruel and unchristian policy so long pursued by the "Church of England" towards Non-conformists. Convinced that the hierarchy, who ever had their eye on the emoluments of the "church," would exert the great influence they wielded, to retain their position, and persecuting power they had long possessed, and strained to its utmost limit, James resolved on, and by some means, did effect, such a change in the Judges, that a sufficient number of those who continued to hold the office, gave a judgment in favor of the absolute dispensing power of the Crown, especially in ecclesiastical affairs. The "Test Act," was therefore virtually abrogated, and the way opened to advance Papists to offices of honor, profit and influence. Both Court and Church — now placed in antagonism to each other — became desirous to conciliate the Dissenters; and hence interference with them in their religious exercises came to a stop.

Although Friends in London had previously expressed to the King their acknowledgment of gratitude for the exemption from persecution he had secured for them, the Yearly Meeting, in 1687, prepared an address to him; expressing "The humble and grateful acknowledgment of his peaceable subjects called Quakers, in this kingdom, for release from the spoil and suffering they had so long endured." A committee was appointed to present it; which was done, and it was properly received; its reading to the King and Council being preceded by a speech from William Penn. This distinguished Friend had much influence in the Court, and there is no doubt the regard for him, felt by the King, was favorably exerted to induce his Sovereign to assist those to whom he was closely united in religious fellowship.

It has been mentioned, that some time after the return of Robert Barclay from London, in 1677, where he had applied to the Duke of York in order to obtain the release of the Friends then suffering greatly in prisons in Scotland, he himself had been imprisoned, with his father; and that they were liberated by an order from Court, which also forbade further meddling with them. There can be no doubt that King James, then Duke of York, used his influence and authority to allay or arrest the persecution of Friends in Scotland; which Archbishop Sharpe had done, and continued to do, all in his power to promote and increase in its violence and severity, with the hope of extirpating the "Quakers." R. Barclay did not cease in keeping the Duke informed of the grievous sufferings of his friends and fellow-countrymen; and it is probable that through this means he had been induced to interfere secretly on their behalf. The last disturbance of Friends' meeting in Aberdeen, and imprisonment of the principal Friends in attendance, was in the Ninth month of 1679. The latter were detained but a few hours; and active persecution for holding their meetings, ceased at that time in Scotland. The testimony is left upon record, that throughout the whole time the effort was kept up in that country to drive Friends, by the force of bodily suffering, by ruinous fines, and accumulated impositions, from attending their meetings for divine worship, or to sacrifice their religious principles in other respects, their meetings were constantly held at the appointed times, and the number of members increased. When the greater part of the men were in prison, the women with the children held the meetings with unflinching constancy, and no settled meeting on any occasion ceased to be regularly held.

It was remarkable, that the three "ministers" in Aberdeen, who had exerted themselves against Friends more furiously and implacably than any others, all lost their positions about the same time; one dying, and the others being deposed and ordered to give up preaching. Meldrum, who, of the three, was perhaps the most bitter, and utterly regardless of the suffering he inflicted, could never after obtain permission to officiate as a minister. In view of the tragic death of Archbishop Sharpe—whom Burnet, Cruickshank, and other historians characterize as one of the most unprincipled and hypocritical men of that age — the closing paragraphs in the address of Robert Barclay to him, which, as stated before, was delivered when Friends were patiently bearing the affliction he was heaping upon them, are worthy of notice: "So the God of truth, whom we serve with our spirits in the gospel of his Son, and to whom vengeance belongs (so we leave it), would certainly, in his own time and way, avenge our quarrel, in case thou should prove inexorable towards us; whose dreadful judgments should be more terrible unto thee, and much more justly to be feared, than the *violent assaults* or *secret assassinations* of thy other antagonists. That thou mayst prevent both *the one and the other*, by a Christian moderation, suitable to the office thou layest claim to, is the desire of thy soul's well-wisher, R. B." In the third month of 1679, as the Archbishop was passing over a moor, in his coach and six, he was waylaid by six " covenanters," who dragged him from his carriage, and brutally murdered him, reminding him as they dealt the fatal blows, that he was *an apostate, a betrayer*, and *a persecutor*.

Although it is anticipating the regular course of events, this may be a suitable place to notice some of the few circumstances in the closing years of the life of Robert Barclay, which have been left on record. In 1682, the Earls of Perth and of Melfort, together with the other proprietaries of New Jersey, in North America, elected him Governor of East Jersey; gifting him, at the same time, with a large tract of the land, and appropriating five thousand acres more, to be bestowed as he might see proper. King Charles II.'s letter, confirming the appointment, states that "such is his known fidelity and capacity," he was to hold the government for life; though no successor should have the office for more than three years.

As his influence with James, while he was Duke of York, was considerable, it appears not to have diminished when the latter was made King; and that influence, so far as it went, was ever improved for the benefit of Friends, and others who applied to him when in difficulty. Thus "Sir Ewen Cameron," or Cameron of Lochiel, as he was called, "who had married R. Barclay's sister, having become entangled in a serious difference with the Duke of Gordon, when other means had failed to remove it, R. Barclay went to London, obtained an interview with the King, and had the whole matter fully laid open before three of the Scottish Lords, who consented to act as arbitrators; by which he succeeded in obtaining a satisfactory settlement of the whole dispute. It may have been on his return home from London on this occasion, in 1683, that, while riding through Stonegatehole in Huntingdonshire, the party, consisting of his brother-in-law, G. Molleson, a merchant of Holland, himself and wife, were attacked by highwaymen. The merchant was shot through the thigh, and died a few days after; G. Molleson was robbed; but when the highwayman presented his pistol at R. Barclay, Robert took him calmly by the arm, saying, "How comes thou to be so rude?" The robber trembled so, that his pistol dropped to the ground, and he made no further attempt to take anything from him.

In 1685, he went up to London; while there, participating and sympathizing with his friends, in their trials, and the efforts they were then making to obtain relief. He again went to that city in 1687, being urgently requested so to do by George Fox; who was solicitous to obtain whatever influence R. Barclay had with the King, to arrange and forward measures for the relief of Friends, and of Dissenters generally. It is probable that at that time he attended the Yearly Meeting. His last visit to London, was in 1688, when he took his son Robert with him, then in the seventeenth year of his age. This youth had already become so firmly established in the principles and practice of vital religion, that his father hesitated not to introduce him at Court, where he was much noticed. During the time he was in that city, which was several months, R. B. had frequent interviews with the King, who was then in much trouble on account of the state of affairs in the nation.

After his return from this visit to the metropolis, he appears to have remained near his home, laboring in the work of the ministry in his own and neighboring meetings. In 1690, he accompanied James Dickenson, an eminent minister, residing in Cumberland, England, to the meetings of Friends in the north of Scotland. Shortly after his return to Ury, he was seized with severe illness attended by high fever, which prostrated him at once, and terminated his life in eight or nine days. James Dickenson was with him during his last sickness, and bore testimony that the Lord's love and power were sweetly manifested to and in him. He was fully sensible of his approaching end, desired a message of his love to be given to all his friends, particularly to *dear* George Fox; saying, " God is good still; and though I am under a great weight of sickness and weakness as to my body, yet my peace flows." " This I know, that whatever exercises may be permitted to come upon me, they shall tend to God's glory and my salvation; and in that I rest." He died on the third of the Eighth month, 1690, in the forty-second year of his age.

The death of this accomplished scholar, and deeply experienced Christian, was felt to be a great loss to the Society. Having in early life received the inshining of the Day-spring from on high, he closed in with obedience to its manifestations, and became willing to sell all that he had, in order to become possessed of " the pearl of great price;" and under the leading of the Spirit of Truth, he turned his back on the allurements of the world, and, from full conviction of the scriptural soundness of their religion, joined himself to the persecuted Quakers. By doing his heavenly Father's will, he came to know experimentally of the doctrine that is of God, and he devoted time, talents, and all his many acquirements, to its exposition and defence.

George Fox gave forth " A testimony concerning our dear brother in the Lord, Robert Barclay, who was a wise and faithful minister in Christ, and wrote many precious books in the defence of the truth, in English and Latin, and after translated into French and Dutch. He was a scholar and a man of parts, and underwent many calumnies, slanders and reproaches, and sufferings for the name of Christ; but the Lord gave him power over them all."

William Penn, after speaking of him as a minister, a learned man, and of his domestic and social relations, says, " These eminent qualities, in one who employed them so serviceably, and who had not lived much above half the life of man, aggravated the loss of him, especially in that nation where he lived." And in reference to his " Apology for the true Christian Divinity," he remarks, " The book *shows so much for us* and *itself too*, that I need say the less; but recommend it to thy serious perusal, Reader, as that which may be instrumental, with God's blessing, to inform thy understanding, confirm thy belief, and comfort thy mind about the excellent things of God's Kingdom."

Similar testimonials from other eminent members of the Society were given, showing how highly Robert Barclay was esteemed as a faithful servant of Christ, and a writer who fairly and clearly set forth and defended the doctrines and testimonies of the Gospel as held by Friends.

It has been stated that King James had granted liberty of un-molested worship to all Non-conformists; previously, however, to so doing, aware that he was giving great offence to the high church party, by thus rescuing their prey out of their hands, and also to the great majority of the people, by the favor he was showing to the Roman Catholics; and that they were looking with anxious expectation towards the Prince of Orange and his wife, regarding the latter as the rightful successor to the throne; he took the necessary means to obtain an expression of the sentiments of those high personages on the subject. William Penn, who was about to visit the Conti-nent, was deputed by him to see the Prince and his wife, in order to ascertain their feeling and wishes in reference thereto. Other agents were afterwards employed. But when James found, that while they freely approved of toleration to all Protestant Dissenters, and the repeal of the penal laws against them, they were altogether opposed to abrogating or suspending the laws against Papists, he took offence at it, and resolved to carry out his own views, regardless of the wishes or opposition of the high church party, or others. The declaration, unmodified, was therefore published, and steps were taken to in-duce those who shared in the elective franchise, to give their votes for such candidates for Parliament as would sanction this measure.

The Bishops having been directed by an Order in Council, to have the declaration read in all their Churches, most of them declined to comply; and seven of their number waited on the King, with an humble representation of the reasons why they refused to obey; the principal being, that the dispensing power of the King had been declared void by Parliament. Exasperated at their recusancy, James sent them to the Tower; where they were kept prisoners for some time; their incarceration greatly increasing the public excite-ment and discontent. 1688.

The doctrine of unlimited obedience, and absolute non-resistance to the King, so long preached by the Bishops and clergy, was now disavowed, and they professed a willingness that the liberty con-ferred by the King, should be granted to *Protestant* Non-conform-ists. Their previous severities having been publicly called to mind by some one, they attributed the statement to Friends, and declared, "That the Quakers belied them, and reported that they (the Bishops) had been the cause of the death of some of them." It was not true that Friends had had anything to do with the allegation publicly made against the Bishops; nevertheless, Robert Barclay, who was then in London, visited the seven in the Tower, and while assuring them that Friends were not the authors of what had been published, yet gave them such undeniable proofs, of cases where Friends had been kept in ·jail by their orders, until they died; although certificates from physicians who were not Friends, that longer detention must prove fatal, had been presented them, together with applications for the sick prisoners to be discharged, that they could not gainsay it.

The imprisoned Bishops being tried, were acquitted; and the rejoicing of the populace on the occasion, was heartily responded to by the troops; to the chagrin of the King and Court. Infatuated with the idea of the sacredness of his royal prerogatives, and blindly bigotted in the superstitious faith he had embraced, James, with undeniable good intentions towards those whom he knew had been borne down by both the Puritan and the high church party, pursued a course, so favorable to Popery and adverse to Protestantism, that he alienated the affections of those attached to the "Established Church," or to the Dissenters; and so filled the minds of his subjects with a fear that their liberty and their religion were to be sacrificed, in order to erect an absolute monarchy, and again establish Papal supremacy, that many of the more influential in the kingdom resolved to drive him from the throne, and put it in possession of the Princess of Orange and her husband.

William Henry, Prince of Orange, was a grandson of Charles I.; his mother being Mary, daughter of that Sovereign of England. His wife was the daughter of James II.; their marriage having been brought about by Charles II., in the hope that by promoting this connection of the daughter of the then Duke of York, with the head of the house of Nassau, who was the acknowledged leader of the Protestant alliance on the Continent, he would so greatly gratify his subjects, as to appease their discontent with his own disgraceful policy. Notwithstanding their father's predilection for Popery, his daughters, by King Charles' express command, had been educated in the Protestant faith, and two of them were married to Protestant Princes. Mary was the eldest, and at that time apparent heiress of the Crown of England; her marriage with William of Orange, took place on the fourth of November, 1677.

It is not necessary to enter far into the political events of the time; but it may be stated, that the Prince of Orange, being invited by the leaders of the malcontents — including most of the Bishops, and the Universities—came over to England with an army of twelve thousand men; and being joined by a large number of those who were set against James, by his rash and impolitic conduct, the latter became alarmed for his personal safety, and fled to France. [1688.]

When it is borne in mind, that the High Church party had been engaged for years, in preaching the "Divine right" of hereditary Kings, and — while boasting of their own unlimited loyalty — declared that any resistance to this sacred right, or to acts emanating from it, was contrary to the Christian religion, and damnable; it can be considered no other than indubitable evidence of a deplorable lack of religious principle, and indeed of common morality, that this same party, through its chief dignitaries and leaders, when apprehensive that its wealth and place were in danger of being wrested from it, was among the first to enter into a combination to overturn their King's power. To bring another Prince, who could not then claim their allegiance, into the country; and thus give rise or strength to a revolution, which, it must have been seen, would almost inevitably drive their legitimate Sovereign from the throne. The after conduct of many of its chief members, when they were disappointed by not regaining all they had been forced to relinquish, further confirms the conclusion, that self-interest and self-exaltation were the primary objects kept in view by them.

A Convention having been assembled, it was resolved into a Parliament; which declared the throne vacant by the King's abdication — though he had left a statement, that he went only to seek assistance — and the crown was offered to William and Mary. The offer being accepted, they were declared King and Queen of Great Britain; their coronation taking place in the Fourth month of 1689.

During the time of contention and commotion preceding the flight of James, Friends, in common with other Non-conformists, enjoyed immunity from suffering, except that arising from their testimony against a hireling ministry; which brought them under the exactions of the priests, for tithes; and the losses often sustained in consequence of their refusing to take an oath. One of their number, however, conspicuous for his zeal as a Friend, and his intimacy with the King, was exposed to much suspicion and calumny; and finally brought into no little trouble by the part he was supposed to have taken, in the affairs transacted, and the influence he was credited with having exerted, to promote some of the measures of Court.

Allusion is made to William Penn, who, as has been mentioned, was commended by his father, on his death-bed, to the good offices of the then Duke of York, and who had received no small favor at his hands. The respect and kind feeling of the Duke for William Penn appear to have continued after he became King; and a sense of gratitude and Christian interest, in measure, bound the man he had befriended, to his royal benefactor. He was almost daily at Court, and as often, his interest there was employed on behalf of those with whom he was united in religious fellowship, or of others who solicited his aid; which his kindness of heart prompted him not to refuse. His house in Kensington was daily thronged with persons who sought his mediation to promote their interests, or desired to engage him to present their petitions or addresses to the King. He received all with courtesy, and aided those he could, with cheerfulness.; and no one ever charged him with making gain of his position or influence. Nevertheless, in this way, it is probable, he appeared in cases where greater prudence would have restrained him from interfering. Certainly he made many and bitter enemies, who hesitated not to proclaim him to be a Jesuit, a hypocrite, and an enemy to the Protestant interest. Accustomed to calumny as a Friend, and conscious of his innocence, William Penn allowed these slanders to possess the public ear, until they came to be credited by many who, without any particular prejudice against him, supposed that, like other emissaries of Rome, he was in league with the King in trying to subvert the religion and constitutional liberties of the nation. At length the Secretary for the Plantations, who knew Penn well, and was greatly grieved with the manner in which he was traduced, and fearful of the ultimate result of his persistently declining publicly to defend himself, addressed him by letter; reciting the charges industriously circulated against him, and earnestly requesting he would notice and refute them. To this letter William Penn replied, taking up each accusation separately, and showing the untruth and the absurdity of all. He did not hesitate to acknowledge the gratitude and kind feeling he entertained towards King James, and that on some occasions, when his opinion had been sought on matters affecting the nation, he had given it; but he declared, that on all such occasions, he had advocated liberty of conscience, and the best interest of Protestant England; and he challenged any one to come forward and show to the contrary. Notwithstanding this explanation of his intimacy at Court, and his positive denial and refutation of the many false stories raised about him, the feeling produced by them was not entirely removed; and in the last month of 1688, as he was walking in Whitehall, he was suddenly summoned to appear before the Lords of the Council. Some of the Council, who were inimical to him, required him to give sureties for his appearance on the first day of the next term of Court. On his appearance there, his case was postponed until the next session; when there appeared to be no accuser or accusation against him, and he was declared clear, in open court.

In this year [1688] died that devoted and eminent servant of Christ, and patient sufferer for his cause, William Dewsbury. He was among those who were released from long confinement, by the intervention of King James, when he issued his warrant for the discharge of Friends, and the suspension of the penal laws against them, on their first application to him. He had been arrested as a Jesuit, at the time of the great excitement respecting the "Popish plot;" and though it was shown there was no ground for the accusation made against him, the vindictive malice of his persecutors, and the unjust and illegal action of the Magistrates, induced and enabled them to keep him a prisoner during all the time that elapsed from the outbreak of the terrible popular excitement mentioned, to the first year of the short reign of King James. Though greatly debilitated, and his health permanently impaired, by his long confinement in noisome jails, and other cruelties inflicted on him; so that it was difficult and painful for him to walk, he, nevertheless, after his release, visited Friends at some of their meetings. But finding himself too feeble to travel much, he addressed an epistle to Friends generally, which, he says, was " Given forth in the moving of the peaceable spirit and word of reconciliation in the Lord Jesus Christ: to whom are my prayers, that all who are convinced, may wait to be made of the number of the slain of the Lord, and conformable to Christ in his death. That they may witness his quickening power to raise them up in the resurrection of life, to enter into the gates of Zion, and dwell in the city of New Jerusalem: peace is within her gates, and quietness among all that have their habitation therein, having salvation for walls and bulwarks; and [they] are blessed of the Lord, and preserved by Him, to the honor of his name forever. Amen." He went up to London, to attend the Yearly Meeting, in 1688. While there, he preached a remarkable sermon, which has been.handed down in print. It is said the congregation he addressed
· was over two thousand. Being taken ill, he was unable to attend

the Yearly Meeting, but sent a short letter to it, informing of the reason of his absence. He was favored to reach his home by short journeys, and lived but about two weeks after. A few days before his death, several Friends being present in his chamber, though very weak, he addressed them very fervently, testifying to the power of the religion Friends professed, and the goodness of God as manifested to them. "Therefore," said he, "Friends, be faithful, and trust in the Lord your God: for this I can say, I never, since [his convincement,] played the coward; but joyfully entered prisons as palaces; telling my enemies to hold me there as long as they could. And in the prison-houses I sang praises to my God, and esteemed the bolts and locks put upon me as jewels; and in the name of the eternal God, I always got the victory. For they could keep me no longer than the determined time of my God. . . . . My departure draws nigh. Blessed be my God, I am prepared; I have nothing to do but to die, and put off this corrupt, mortal tabernacle, this flesh that has so many infirmities. But the life that dwells in it ascends above all, out of the reach of death, hell and the grave; and immortality and eternal life are my crown for ever and ever." Thus triumphantly departed this aged, deeply experienced, and suffering follower of the Lord Jesus, to enter on the unceasing enjoyment of those heavenly felicities which are laid up for all those who love Him and his appearing in their hearts.

CHAPTER XXX.

Act of Toleration — Friends obtain a Modification of the Language — Confession of Faith — S. Crisp's Address to Friends — Death of Alex. Parker — Little persecution in Ireland — Warning by W. Edmundson — War — Raparees — Services of Wm. Edmundson for his Neighbors — Cruel Treatment of W. E. — Efforts to take the Life of W. E. — Testimony relative to the Faithfulness of Friends in Ireland during the War — Increasing Weakness of G. Fox — Epistles by G. Fox — Last Sickness and Death of G. Fox — Death of J. Burnyeat — Death of Thomas Salthouse.

THE government being now in the hands of a King and Parliament, united in the policy of maintaining the Protestant religion, one of the first subjects that occupied the attention of the latter, was so to modify the laws in relation to professors of different forms of that religion, as would strengthen the coalition among them, that had effected the recent revolution. King William was a Calvinist, but had always advocated liberty of conscience. This brought on him the dislike and opposition of the "high church" party; which, though ready to unite with other professors in opposition to the late King, when they felt their own interest likely to succumb to the power of a Catholic Sovereign, were now desirous to return to their former supremacy and arbitrary oppression. The House of Lords, where the Bishops exerted their influence most effectually, rejected a bill that had passed the Commons, 3d month, 1689, to remove the "Sacramental test," as it was called; so as to admit all Protestants to hold office under the government. But as the Bishops, when feeling the weight of King James' resentment, had declared to him they "Were willing to come to such a temper towards Dissenters as shall be thought fit, when the matter came to be considered and settled in Parliament," their hands were so far tied, as to cripple them from much opposition to the enactment of "The Act of Toleration;" which exempted Protestant subjects, dissenting from the "Church of England," from the penalties of certain laws designed to force them to conformity.

As it was of importance to Friends, that the terms and phraseology of this Act should be such as to allow them to participate in its benefits, George Whitehead and three others of them, attended at Parliament; and on finding that the Bill had a confession of faith attached to it, which included a declaration that the Scriptures were the *word* of God; an appellation which Friends, believing to be peculiarly applicable to Christ, the eternal Word that was from the beginning, therefore declined giving to those sacred writings — exerted themselves to have it expunged. They soon found that this confession had been so framed, with the expectation and intention, on the part of some, who imagined that Friends were not Christians, of excluding them from its provisions. A confession of the faith of Friends was therefore drawn up, and laid before the House, by a member friendly to them; whereupon the four Friends in attendance were examined in relation thereto; and gave such full statements of their Christian belief, and the reasons therefor, that the confession of faith presented, was accepted. It is as follows: "I profess faith in God the Father, and in Jesus Christ his eternal Son, the true God, and in the Holy Spirit, one God blessed forever; and do acknowledge the Holy Scriptures of the Old and New Testament, to be given by Divine inspiration."

As certain questions had been propounded, Friends likewise presented to Parliament, a Declaration of the faith held by the Society, from which the following is taken:

" Question.— Do you believe the divinity and humanity of Jesus Christ, the eternal Son of God? or that Jesus Christ is truly God and man?

Answer.— Yes, we verily believe that Jesus Christ is truly God and man, according as Holy Scriptures testify of him; God over all, blessed forever; the true God, and eternal life; the one Mediator between God and man; even the man Christ Jesus.

Question.— Do you believe and expect salvation and justification by the righteousness and merits of Jesus Christ, or by your own righteousness or works?

Answer.— By Jesus Christ, his righteousness, merits and works, and not by our own. God is not indebted to us for our deservings, but we to Him for his free Grace in Christ Jesus; whereby we are saved through faith in Him, not of ourselves; and by his grace are enabled truly and acceptably to serve and follow Him as He requires. He is our all in all, who worketh all in us that is well-pleasing to God.

Question.— Do you believe remission of sins and redemption, through the sufferings, death and blood of Christ?

Answer.— Yes, through faith in Him as He suffered and died for all men, gave himself a ransom for all, and his blood being shed for the remission of sins; so all they who sincerely believe in and obey Him, receive the benefits and blessed effects of his suffering and dying for them. They, by faith, in his name, receive and partake of that eternal redemption which He hath obtained for us, who gave himself for us, that He might redeem us from all iniquity. He died for our sins, and rose again for our justification; and if we walk in the Light as He is in the Light, we have fellowship one with another, and the blood of Jesus Christ, his Son, cleanseth us from all sin."

The Act provided that Dissenters should hold their meetings for worship, &c., without molestation, the doors of their meeting-houses being unfastened; but it imposed the taking of an oath of allegiance; which, as Friends could not take an oath, would yet have excluded them from toleration. But the manner in which Friends, from their rise, had illustrated their conscientious adherence to the peaceable principles they professed; and the religious character of their scruples against swearing, satisfied many of those who did not unite with them in their belief, that no danger to the State was to be apprehended from their declining to take this oath. It was therefore finally decided to accept in lieu thereof, the following declaration:

"I, A. B., do sincerely promise and solemnly declare, before God and the world, that I will be true and faithful to King William and Queen Mary; and I do solemnly profess and declare, that I do from my heart abhor, detest and renounce, as impious and heretical, that damnable doctrine and position, that Princess excommunicated or deprived by the Pope, or any authority of the see of Rome, may be deposed or murdered by their subjects, or any other whatsoever. And I declare that no foreign prince, person, prelate, state, or potentate, hath or ought to have, any power, jurisdiction, superiority, pre-eminence, or authority, ecclesiastical or spiritual, within this realm."

Thus Friends — in common with other Dissenters — were legally tolerated, and two of the principles and practices connected with their religious convictions — the duty of publicly assembling for the worship of the Almighty, and the obligation to obey the command of Christ not to swear — which unreasonable and wicked men had long taken advantage of, to wrong and oppress them, were no longer causes of legal offence and persecution; though the latter still exposed them to wrong, and deprived them of some rights which others enjoyed. The oppressive and anti-Christian yoke of tithes, however, still rested heavily upon them; one clause of the Act of Toleration specially providing, that no part of it should be so construed, as to exempt any Dissenters from paying tithes, or other parochial dues, to the church or minister; nor from prosecution in an ecclesiastical Court or elsewhere, therefor. [1689.]

Friends, however, from their disuse of the "ordinances," as they are called, escaped some exactions to which other Non-conformists were still liable. The provisions of the Toleration Act were such, that it did not altogether relieve other Dissenters from the pressure of the several penal laws against them; all of which remained unrepealed. They were held liable to be called on to give assent to the canon of the "Church of England," in reference to the "Eucharist," and also to admit the truth of by far the greater part of the "thirty-nine articles." The enjoyment of the right of liberty of conscience in relation to the profession and practice of religion, was therefore far from being established; and the "State Church" continued to hold the power in its hands to oblige all to contribute, in some way, to its support.

That Friends looked upon this release from suffering, which they had long and patiently borne, as a result of Divine interposition in promotion of the Lord's own sacred cause of truth and righteousness, there can be no doubt; and they were fully aware, that to

Him were to be ascribed the praise and gratitude that were due. Thus in an epistle addressed to Friends, by Stephen Crisp, about that time, is the following: " And, Friends, consider of the great works that this mighty arm of the Lord hath brought to pass in the general, as well as in the particular; how many contrivances have been framed, and laws and decrees made to lay you waste, and to make you cease to be a people, and how have the wicked rejoiced thereat, for a season, crying, 'Aha! thus would we have it; they are all now given up to banishments, to imprisonments, to spoils and ruins; now let us see if that invisible Arm they trust in can deliver them.' ، O Friends! how hath your God been your support in the midst of all these exercises! and when He hath pleased, how hath He quieted the sharpest storms, and turned back the greatest floods and torrents of persecution that ever you met! and how hath He confounded his and your enemies, and brought confusion upon the heads of them that sought your hurt! Were not these things wrought by the power of God? Did your number, your policy, your interest, or any thing that might be called your own, contribute anything to these your great preservations and deliverances? If not, then let God have the glory, and acknowledge, to his praise, these have been the Lord's doings, and are marvellous in our eyes."

Another clause in this epistle indicates the trials Friends had to endure even in that day, from "false brethren;" who thought the path which had been marked out for them by the Head of the Church, was too strait and narrow; and were desirous to do away the offence of the cross. It also shows that faithful Friends adhered to the principles which they had seen, in that Light which could not deceive, were inseparable from the gospel in its purity, and to the practices resulting from them. He says, "Again, dear Friends, consider how the wicked one hath wrought in a mystery among yourselves, to scatter you, and to lay you waste from being a people as at this day; how many several ways hath he tried; raising up men of perverse minds, to subvert and to turn you from the faith, and from the simplicity that is in Christ Jesus our Lord; and to separate you from that invisible Power that hath been your strength, and to separate you one from another, and by subtle wiles to lead you into a false liberty above the cross of Christ; and sometimes by sowing seeds of heresy and seditions, endeavoring to corrupt the minds of whom they could, with pernicious principles; but oh, how have their designs been frustrated, and the authors thereof confounded and brought to naught: and how have you been preserved as a flock under the hand of a careful Shepherd, even unto this day; which ministers great cause of thanksgiving unto all the faithful, who have witnessed the working of this preserving power in their own particulars."

In 1689, died Alexander Parker, who had long been looked up to as a judge and a valiant in Israel. He was a man of noble presence, strong intellectual endowments and good education. He was born in Lancashire, was convinced of the truth as held by Friends, early after George Fox began his labors as a minister of Jesus Christ, and was himself soon called into the same service. By close adherence to the dictates of the Spirit of Christ to his soul, he became eminent in the exercise of the gift he had received. He travelled much with George Fox, sharing with him the hardships and cruel treatment to which he was exposed. He came up with him to London, when Colonel Hacker sent him to the then Protector, and was with him in different parts of Great Britain; and also in Holland in 1684. After his marriage, his home was in London, when not engaged in religious service in other places; and while at home, his time and attention were much devoted to serving the Society; which led him frequently into interviews with members of the Privy Council and of Parliament. Like others of his fellow-professors, he suffered frequent imprisonments and much cruel abuse, but he was sustained by the invisible Arm of Divine power; and when he had filled up his measure of service and of suffering, he quietly and peacefully exchanged the toils and vicissitudes of time for the full fruition of those joys which are eternal.

Friends in Ireland, though exposed to suffering on account of their refusal to pay tithes, which often brought them under the oppression of rapacious priests, who prosecuted them in ecclesiastical Courts, and by exorbitant costs and fees, made great havoc of their substance, were nevertheless almost free from the enormous spoil and merciless persecution, inflicted on their brethren in England and Scotland; through the instrumentality of unprincipled informers and Magistrates. While other Dissenters, almost universally throughout that Island, deserted their meeting-houses, and either met privately, or declined altogether to hold public worship, on account of the Conventicle Act, Friends continued their religious meetings for worship and discipline as heretofore; and though occasionally disturbed, the former were largely attended by others than members, and thus a knowledge of the truths of the Gospel continued to spread, and there were many convinced thereby. In 1684, having received information, that many Friends in England had been reduced to great straits by the ravenous informers, the National Meeting, actuated by that sympathetic love one for another, and mutual interest in each other's well being, which characterized the members of the Society everywhere, directed voluntary subscriptions to be raised for the relief of their suffering fellow-professors; and several hundred pounds were sent over to England, to be distributed among those in need.

But though now comparatively exempt from persecution, William Edmundson had a sense given him of great calamities near at hand, and says, that after attending the National Meeting, in 1685, he visited Friends in the North, and other places; and "A weighty sense came upon my spirit, of great exercises and trials approaching, which would try us all, and that the Lord would spread the carcasses of men on the earth, as dung. So in the Spirit and power of the Lord, I faithfully and plainly warned Friends and others of it, in many public meetings; and often, in the Lord's movings, advised Friends to lessen their concerns in the world, and be ready to receive the Lord in his judgments, which were at hand; and to flee unto Him for succor, that they might have a place of safety in Him."

As has been already seen, King James, in his scheme for gradually introducing Catholics into the government, manifested a willingness to favor all Dissenters from the Church of England; and in accordance with this policy, those in authority in Ireland, appointed some Friends in different places, to serve as Corporators, or as Magistrates. This brought forth from a General Meeting of Friends there, an epistle of advice to those who had consented to serve in those stations; and George Fox, being informed of the circumstance, addressed a letter to William Edmundson, in which he says, "As for those Friends of Dublin, Cork, Limerick and other places, that have taken those offices of Aldermen and Burgesses upon them, they must consider and be wise; for if they keep to Truth, they can neither take an oath, nor put an oath to any one; neither can they put on their gowns, and strange kind of habits; as Friends have considered it here, when they talk of putting them in such places." He also reminds them, that they cannot attend at their feasts, nor join in any formalities, &c.

The King having removed his brother-in-law, the Earl of Clarendon, from the office of Lord-lieutenant of Ireland, bestowed it upon the Earl of Tyrconnel, a bigoted Papist; who soon manifested a determination, by his displacements and appointments, to transfer the various offices and the power, from the Protestants into the hands of Roman Catholics. Not only those in command of the military, but Judges, Magistrates, and other civil officers, were Catholics; and as the greater part of the inhabitants belonged to that church, and had been much oppressed by the former government, they rejoiced to take part with King James, in his contention for the crown, and to embrace the opportunity to gratify their thirst for revenge and plunder. When war between the two adverse parties fairly broke out, nearly the whole Island was overrun with the hostile armies. Large numbers of the Irish banded together, and under the name of· Raparees, became the terror of the country. Unrestrained by military law, these armed guerillas murdered, often indiscriminately, all whom they wished to rob, and often burned whatever they could not carry off.

During this season of awful wickedness and calamity, which lasted over two years [1688, 1690], it was a remarkable circumstance, that Friends were generally favored by those in authority; and William Edmundson continued to exert no little influence with the higher officers in the government. In many parts of the country, they nevertheless suffered grievously; so that it was estimated that in the time mentioned, their loss in property amounted to £100,000.

William Edmundson having been instrumental in stopping the plundering by some of the Irish, and having a few of those who had been engaged in it, arrested and punished; although he afterwards interceded for the offenders, and obtained their release, with the restoration of the horses that had been taken from them, yet the animosity of many of the common soldiers, and the subordinate officers, was greatly excited towards him. On one occasion, in 1690, a company from the army of King William, came into his neighborhood, drove off about five hundred cattle and horses, and took one of his neighbors, named Dunn, who had been a soldier, with his father and brothers, intending to hang him. William being requested to interfere on behalf of this poor man, and also of those who were robbed, went after the soldiers, and overtaking them about four miles off, interceded with the officers, to give up their prey. He says, "So with much discourse and arguments to this purpose, the two captains seemed willing to release all, if the soldiers could be prevailed on. I rode with them to the head of the party; but they were very angry, and would need have killed the Irish, who had followed for their cattle. Whereupon I quitted my horse and ventured my life among the rude soldiers, to save the Irish ; and with much ado, and the captains' assistance, got them moderated, on condition to give them a small part of the cattle, to release the rest. Then I mounted my horse, and sought out the man they had stripped for hanging. When I found him, I threw him my riding coat to put on, and desired one of the captains to assist me in finding him that had taken his clothes." When discovered, William spoke to ·the soldier in such a manner, that he undressed himself and returned the clothes to their rightful owner ; and finally, William succeeded in obtaining the release of the father and the sons, with most of the cattle.

Speaking of the National Meeting held in Dublin in 1690, to which Friends went at the risk of their lives, William says, " We had a heavenly, blessed, powerful meeting, and Friends were more than ordinarily glad one of another in the Lord Jesus, who had preserved us alive, through so many dangers, to see one another's faces again."

But though so devoted in support of the cause of Truth, and so serviceable in helping others, William Edmundson had to undergo great suffering himself. His house was surrounded on the 23d of the 9th month, 1690, by a large band of Raparees, who set fire to it. He narrates, " When we could stay no longer for the fire, I made conditions with them, and opened the doors, and went out ; but they soon broke their conditions, though they bound themselves with many oaths. They took what plunder they could get from the fire ; which being very fierce, destroyed the greater part. . ·. One of them at my request, lent me an old blanket of my own to wrap about me, and they took away all my cattle. They took me and my two sons that night through rough places, bushes, mire and water to the knees in cold weather ; where our bare feet and legs were sorely hurt, and bruised." Having held a council in the morning, it was resolved to shoot William and hang his two sons. " Then I told them, if I died they were my witnesses I was innocent, and God would revenge my blood. . . . Then they hoodwinked my two sons to hang them, and having prepared two fire-locks to shoot me, they came to hoodwink me also ; but I told them they need not, for I could look them in the face, and was not afraid to die." At this juncture a lieutenant Dunn came up — he was one of the brothers whom W. E. had rescued from a company of soldiers, as related — who interposed, and took the father and sons to Athlone, about twenty miles off. This journey they were forced to perform without other clothing or much food. At Athlone they were near being murdered in the street; but were again saved from death by a man, who said he knew William, and that he was a righteous man; and who had sufficient influence with the savage rabble to prevent their deadly purpose. When brought before the Governor of the Castle, and William had made himself known to him, the former wept to see him in such a case, said he knew him well, and had often been entertained at his house. He put the father and sons under the care of an officer, and had them supplied with bread, meat and drink. William continues, " We lay upon the bare floor which was very cold and hard; we wanting clothes, and my strength being much spent, I was not likely to continue long, if the Lord had not provided succor for me."

Succor came through a Friend named John Clibborn; who, hearing of William being a prisoner at Athlone, went there at the risk of his own life, and so far as was in his power, contributed towards relieving his necessities. After some time, this Friend prevailed on the Governor — who was desirous to release William, but was afraid of the Raparees who were in the town — to allow him to take him home with him. William found that the Dunns, whom he had so greatly befriended at the risk of his own life, having joined the Raparees, were become his bitter enemies, and had incited the armed band to make this attack on him. One of the sons, who was a lieutenant, having, when in command of a band of his outlaws, met William's wife, who with the help of some neighbors was removing the leather, &c., from her son's tanyard, they seized everything they could carry away. The neighbors escaped, but the Raparees caught William's wife, and though the weather was cold, and she far advanced in years, they stripped her entirely naked; in which condition she was obliged to walk two miles before she could find shelter. From this barbarous treatment she never recovered, but died about seven months after. The perfidious and ungrateful Dunns met a quick retribution, being killed the next day in a fight.

William Edmundson continuing a considerable time at the home of J. Clibborn, a Colonel Bourk, who was in command of a company of Irish, stopping there, showed great kindness towards him, and assured him he would procure his liberty when he went to Athlone, for he believed he was an honest man. Accordingly, when the opportunity presented, he interceded so effectually with the Governor of Athlone, that William and his sons were set at liberty. William returned to Mount Melick; his dwelling-house, on his farm at Rosenallis, having, as before stated, been burned.

Part of the English army having come into the neighborhood of Mount Melick, the General commanding it, hearing how greatly William had suffered, sent for him; and after conversing with him, ordered him to accompany him to Rosenallis; and on arriving there, a garrison was quartered in the town. The Catholics of the neighborhood, imagining that William had been the means of having the soldiers stationed there, in order to restrain their depredations, and prevent them from harboring their friends, became greatly incensed at him. They resolved to be revenged, and in order to gratify their vindictive passions, employed several Raparees to lie in wait on the road between Mount Melick and Rosenallis, and shoot him as he passed along. These miscreants having concealed themselves, two of the neighbors called on William, pretending great friendship for him, and earnestly requesting him to go to Rosenallis, in order to use his influence with the officers there, on their behalf; as they stood much in need of it. Willing to oblige them, he would have gone, but was hindered by something that occurred. Two days after, they came again, repeating their request, adding, that his own outhouses were being destroyed. But, William says, " I was restrained by a secret Hand that knew their evil design, and would not suffer me to fall into their snare." The next morning three respectable men travelling on the road, were murdered by these ruffians, who then fled the country, and most of their employers or abettors followed them.

Rutty, after giving several instances of severe suffering endured by Friends in Ireland, and the manner in which relief was often afforded, states, " These particulars may show the eminent, providential hand of the Lord over Friends, and his care and kindness to preserve them in the midst of such great perils, and many more might be instanced; and though in those times, many of the English neighbors fell by the hands of those bloody murderers, yet we know of but four, that we could own to be of our Society, in all the nation, that fell by the hands of cruelty; and two of them too forwardly ventured their lives, when they were lost." Speaking of the effect those severe trials had upon Friends, he remarks, " Friends generally were low in their minds, and their hearts open one to another; so that those who had something left were willing to communicate to those who were in want, and Friends that were driven from their dwellings, did generally return to their places; and the National Men's Meeting took care that in every Quarter, Friends should be supplied for the present, with such necessaries as time and their ability did afford; and great care was taken in Friends settling, that they might settle near together for the benefit of meetings, to serve the Lord." Again, in referring to the danger to life, through which Friends were obliged to go to their religious meetings, and their faithfulness in keeping them up, he adds, "And the Lord was pleased to accompany them in their meetings, with his glorious, heavenly presence, and the truth gained ground, and Friends came more into esteem than formerly, in the minds of many, both rulers and people, through their innocent, wise deportment in the fear of God." [1690.]

George Fox, having become so enfeebled that he could no longer bear to make long journeys, spent the greater part of the last three years of his life in and around London; where he found the most opportunity and convenience for serving the Society, and promoting the spread and establishment of those doctrines and testimonies, into the belief, promulgation and support of which, he and his fellow-laborers had been led, by the unerring Spirit of Truth. During this time, when not otherwise engaged, he continued to employ his pen; writing many epistles and exhortations for the preservation of the members in the practical illustration of the principles they professed, and for the edification of the Church. He was particularly concerned, that Friends should not be caught with the teaching of those who had not experienced in themselves, the transforming working of Divine Grace, the Power of God unto Salvation. In one of his addresses, he says, "Doth not all that which is called Christendom, live in *talking* of Christ's and of his Apostles' words, and the letter of the Scriptures? and do not their priests minister the letter, with their own conception thereon, for money? though the Holy Scriptures were freely given forth from God and Christ, and his prophets and apostles. Yet the Apostle says, 2d Cor. iii. 6: 'The letter killeth; but the Spirit giveth life.' The ministers of the New Testament are not ministers of the letter, but of the Spirit, and they sow to the Spirit, and of the Spirit reap life eternal. But people spending time about old authors, and talking of them and of the outward letter, this doth not feed their souls. For talking of victuals and clothes doth not clothe the body, nor feed it. No more are their souls and spirits fed and clothed, except they have the bread and water of life from heaven to feed them, and the righteousness of Christ to clothe them. Talking of outward things and spiritual things, and not having them, may starve both their bodies and souls: therefore quench not the·Spirit of God, which will lead to be diligent in all things."

He was interested in the effort made by Friends, to have the Act of Toleration so framed as to give them relief, as well as other Dissenters; and as his strength would allow, he took part in the different affairs of the Society, as brought to view in the central position he occupied. The Yearly Meeting in London of 1689, he speaks of as "A very solemn, weighty meeting; the Lord, as formerly, visiting his people, and honoring the assembly with his glorious presence, to the great satisfaction and comfort of Friends." When in London he generally attended all the meetings in regular course; but the atmosphere of the city so affected him, that after a short tarriance, he was obliged to go to one or other of his step-sons-in-law to recruit. In 1690, observing that some of the younger members were indulging in some of the fashions of the world, and some among those advanced in years devoting their time and talents to accumulating wealth, he says, " I was moved to give forth the following paper, as a reproof to such, and an exhortation and warning to all Friends, to beware of, and keep out of those snares."

" To all that profess the truth of God. My desires are that you walk humbly in it; for when the Lord first called me forth, He let me see that young people grew up together in vanity and the fashions of the world, and old people went downwards into the earth, raking it together; and to both these I was to be a stranger. And now, Friends, I do see too many young people that profess the truth, grow up into the fashions of the world, and too many parents indulge them; and amongst the elder some are declining downwards and raking after the earth. Therefore, take heed that you are not making your graves while you are alive outwardly, and loading yourselves with thick clay, Hab. ii. 6. For if you have not power over the earthly spirit, and that which leadeth into a vain mind, and the fashions of the world, and into the earth; though you have often had the rain fall upon your fields, you will but bring forth thistles, briers, and thorns, which are for the fire. Such will become brittle, peevish, fretful spirits, that will not abide the heavenly doctrine, the admonitions, exhortations, and reproofs of the Holy Ghost, or heavenly Spirit of God; which would bring you to be conformable to the death of Christ, and to his image, that ye might have fellowship with Him in his resurrection. Therefore it is good for all to bow to the name of Jesus, their Saviour, that all may confess Him to the glory of God the Father. For I have had a concern upon me in a sense of the danger of young people's going into the fashions of the world, and old people's going into the earth, and many going into a loose and false liberty, till at last they go quite out into the spirit of the world, as some have done. The house of such hath been built upon the sand on the sea-shore, not upon Christ the Rock; that are so soon in the world again, under a pretence of liberty of conscience. But it is not a pure conscience, nor in the Spirit of God, nor in Christ Jesus; for in the liberty in the Spirit there is the unity, which is the bond of peace; and all are one in Christ Jesus, in whom is the true liberty: and this is not of the world, for He is not of the world. Therefore all are to stand fast in Him, as they have received Him; for in Him there is peace, who is the Prince of Peace, but in the world there is trouble. For the spirit of the world is a troublesome spirit, but the Spirit of Christ is a peaceable Spirit: in which God Almighty preserve all the faithful, Amen.   G. F.

"Gooses, the 1st of the Second month, 1690."

Having again attended the Yearly Meeting held in the Fourth month of 1690, he remarks of it, "The Lord's wonted goodness was witnessed, his blessed presence enjoyed, and his heavenly power livingly felt, opening the hearts of his people unto Him, and his divine treasures of life and wisdom in and unto them; whereby many useful and necessary things relating to the safety of Friends, and the honor and prosperity of truth, were weightily treated of, and unanimously concluded."

Cheering and consoling must it have been to this valiant and un-wearied soldier of the cross, now rapidly descending to the grave, to be able to use the following language in the closing paragraph of the last epistle he wrote; which was addressed to his "Dear Friends and Brethren in the Lord Jesus Christ," in Ireland; who were then suffering grievously, as has been related. "As for the affairs of Truth in this land and abroad, I hear that in Holland and Germany and thereaway, Friends are in love, unity and peace; and in Jamaica, Barbadoes, Nevis, Antigua, Maryland and New England, I hear nothing, but that Friends are in unity and peace. The Lord preserve them all out of the world, (in which there is trouble) in Christ Jesus, in whom there is peace, life, love and unity, Amen."

The following account of the closing hours, death, and burial of George Fox is given at the conclusion of his Journal, and probably was drawn up by Thomas Ellwood, who prepared the Journal for the press:

"The next day, after he had written the foregoing epistle to Friends in Ireland, he went to the meeting at Grace-church Street, which was large (it being on the First-day of the week:) and the Lord enabled him to preach the truth fully and effectually, opening many deep and weighty things with great power and clearness. After which having prayed, and the meeting being ended, he went to Henry Gouldney's (a Friend's house in White-hart Court, near the meeting-house): and some Friends going with him, he told them, 'He thought he felt the cold strike to his heart, as he came out of the meeting;' yet added, 'I am glad I was here; now I am clear, I am fully clear.' As soon as those Friends were withdrawn, he laid down upon a bed, as he sometimes used to do, through weariness after a meeting, but soon rose again; and in a little time laid down again, complaining still of cold. And his strength sensibly decaying, he was fain soon after to go into the bed; where he lay in much contentment and peace, and very sensible to the last. And as, in the whole course of his life, his spirit, in the universal love of God, was set and bent for the exalting of truth and righteousness, and the making known the way thereof to the nations and people afar off; so now, in the time of his outward weakness, his mind was intent upon, and wholly taken up with that: and he sent for some particular Friends, to whom he expressed his mind, and desire for the spreading Friends' books, and truth thereby in the world. Divers Friends came to visit him in his illness, unto some of whom he said, 'All is well: the Seed of God reigns over all, and over death itself. And though,' said he, 'I am weak in body; yet the power of God is over all, and the Seed reigns over all disorderly spirits.' Thus lying in a heavenly frame of mind, his spirit wholly exercised towards the Lord, he grew weaker and weaker in his natural strength; and on the third day of that week, between the hours of nine and ten in the evening, he quietly departed this life in peace, and sweetly fell asleep in the Lord; whose blessed truth he had livingly and powerfully preached in the meeting but two days before. Thus ended he his day in his faithful testimony, in perfect love and unity with his brethren, and in peace and good-will to all men, on the 13th of the Eleventh month, 1690, being then in the 67th year of his age.

"Upon the 16th of the same month (being the sixth of the week, and the day appointed for his funeral), a very great concourse of Friends, and other people of divers sorts, assembled together at the meeting-house in White-hart Court, near Grace-church Street, about

the middle-time of the day, in order to attend his body to the grave.
The meeting was held about two hours, with great and heavenly
solemnity, manifestly attended with the Lord's blessed presence and
glorious power; in which divers living testimonies were delivered,
from a lively remembrance and sense of the blessed ministry of this
dear and ancient servant of the Lord, his early entering into the
Lord's work at the breaking forth of this gospel day, his innocent
life, long and great travels, and unwearied labors of love in the
everlasting gospel, for the turning and gathering many thousands
from darkness to the light of Christ Jesus, the foundation of true
faith; the manifold sufferings, afflictions, and oppositions, which he
met withal for his faithful testimony, both from his open adversaries
and from false brethren; and his preservations, deliverances, and
dominion in, out of, and over them all, by the power of God; to
whom the glory and honor always was by him, and is and always
ought to be by all, ascribed.

"After the meeting was ended, his body was borne by Friends,
and accompanied by very great numbers, to Friends' burying-ground
near Bunhill fields; where, after a solemn waiting upon the Lord,
and several living testimonies borne, recommending the company
to the guidance and protection of that Divine Spirit and Power, by
which this holy man of God had been raised up, furnished, supported, and preserved to the end of his day, his body was decently
committed to the earth; but his memorial shall remain, and be
everlastingly blessed among the righteous."

George Fox left a package, with the superscription, "Not to be
opened before the time;" which, being examined after his death,
was found to be an epistle, addressed, "For all the children of God,
everywhere, who are led by his Spirit, and walk in his Light; in
which they have life, unity, and fellowship with the Father, and
the Son, and one with another." It is as follows:

"Keep all your meetings in the name of the Lord Jesus, that be
gathered in his name, by his light, grace, truth, power and Spirit;
by which you will feel his blessed and refreshing presence among
you and in you, to your comfort, and God's glory.

"And now, Friends, all your meetings, both men's and women's
Monthly, Quarterly, and Yearly, &c., were set up by the power,
Spirit, and wisdom of God; and in them you know that you have
felt his power, and Spirit, and wisdom, and blessed refreshing presence among you, and in you, to his praise and glory, and your comfort: so that you have been a 'city set on a hill, that cannot be hid.'

"And although many loose and unruly spirits have risen betimes to oppose you and them, in print and other ways, you have seen how they have come to nought. The Lord hath blasted them, brought their deeds to light, and made them manifest to be trees without fruit, wells without water, wandering stars from the firmament of God's power, and raging waves of the sea, casting up their mire and dirt; and many of them are like the dog turned to his old vomit, and the sow that was washed, turned again to the mire. This hath been the condition of many, God knoweth, and his people.

"Therefore all stand steadfast in Christ Jesus, your Head, in whom you are all one, male and female, and know his government; of the increase of whose government and peace there shall be no end; but there will be an end of the devil's, and of all that are out of Christ, who oppose it and him, whose judgment doth not linger, and their damnation doth not slumber. Therefore in God and Christ's light, life, Spirit, and power, live and walk, that is over all (and the Seed of it) in love, in innocency, and simplicity. In righteousness and holiness dwell, and in his power and Holy Ghost, in which God's kingdom doth stand. All children of new and heavenly Jerusalem, that is from above, and is free, with all her holy, spiritual children, to her keep your eyes.

"As for this spirit of rebellion and opposition, that hath risen formerly and lately, it is out of the kingdom of God and heavenly Jerusalem; and is for judgment and condemnation, with all its books, words, and works. Therefore Friends are to live and walk in the power and Spirit of God that is over it, and in the Seed that will bruise and break it to pieces. In which Seed you have joy and peace with God, and power and authority to judge it; and your unity is in the power and Spirit of God, that doth judge it; all God's witnesses in his tabernacle go out against it, and always have and will.

"Let no man live to self, but to the Lord, as they will die in Him; and seek the peace of the Church of Christ, and the peace of all men in Him: for 'blessed are the peacemakers.' Dwell in the pure, peaceable, heavenly wisdom of God, that is gentle, and easy to be entreated, that is full of mercy; all striving to be of one mind, heart, soul, and judgment in Christ, having his mind and Spirit dwelling in you, building up one another in the love of God, which doth edify the body of Christ, his Church, who is the holy Head thereof. Glory to God through Christ, in this age and all other ages, who is the Rock and Foundation, the Emanuel, God with us, Amen, over all, the beginning and the ending. In Him live and walk, in whom you have life eternal; in Him you will feel me, and I you.

"All children of New Jerusalem, that descends from above, the holy city, which the Lord and the Lamb is the light of, and is the temple; in it they are born again of the Spirit: so Jerusalem that is above, is the mother of them that are born of the Spirit. These that come and are come to heavenly Jerusalem, receive Christ; and He giveth them power to become the sons of God; and they are born again of the Spirit: so Jerusalem that is above, is their mother. Such come to heavenly Mount Sion, and the innumerable company of angels, to the spirits of just men made perfect, and to the Church of the Living God written in heaven, and have the name of God written upon them. So here is a new mother, that bringeth forth a heavenly and spiritual generation.

"There is no schism, no division, no contention, nor strife in heavenly Jerusalem, nor in the body of Christ, which is made up of living stones, a spiritual house. Christ is not divided, for in Him there is peace. Christ sayeth, 'In me you have peace.' And He is from above, and not of this world; but in the world below, in the spirit of it, there is trouble; therefore keep in Christ, and walk in Him. Amen.   G. F.

"Jerusalem was the mother of all true Christians before the apostasy; and since the outward Christians are broken into many sects, they have got many mothers; but all those that are come out of the apostasy by the power and spirit of Christ, Jerusalem that is above is their mother (and none below her); who doth nourish all her spiritual children.   G. F."

"Read at the Yearly Meeting, in London, 1691."

In this year (1690), the Society met with another great loss by the death of John Burnyeat; who, as has been seen, was a faithful and laborious servant in the Church of Christ: of whom his friends testify, that "Being called by Grace to the knowledge of the Lord, his truth and power, and receiving the same in faith, love and obedience, came to witness the effectual working thereof, to his sanctification; and so became a vessel of honor, fitted for his Master's use, even Christ, and learned to rule his own house well; in washing first the inside, and the outside appearing clean also." "He was a man of an excellent spirit, and of deep experience in the things of God and mysteries of his kingdom; which were richly made manifest unto him, and it was his delight to be meditating therein; whereby his experience was daily increased unto the conclusion of his days." " He did greatly delight to read the Holy Scriptures, and would often, and with great earnestness, advise Friends frequently to read the same, and the young and tender in years more especially; as also Friends' books, wherein the principles of truth were treated of; that so none might be ignorant of the principles of the true Christian religion, now again preached and clearly held forth."

He had for some years resided in Ireland, and being out on a religious visit, after attending the Monthly Meeting at New Garden, he came to the house of John Watson, where he was taken ill; his last sickness continuing twelve days. He was entirely sensible throughout the whole time; saying, " He was finely at ease; and quiet in his spirit." To his friend J. Watson, he observed, " That he ever loved the Lord, and the Lord loved him from his youth, and he felt his love." He deceased in the Seventh month, in the sixtieth year of his age, " And is gone to his rest with the Lord, and his works follow him."

Thomas Salthouse also departed this life in 1690. He was an inmate of the family of Judge Fell, when George Fox made his first visit there, in 1652, and with William Caton, was convinced by his powerful ministry; and having embraced the truth as it is in Jesus, and allowed the transforming power of Divine Grace to crucify the " old man and his deeds," and to bring forth the new man created unto holiness, he remained faithful throughout the many sufferings he had to endure, for the cause of truth and righteousness; finishing his course with joy, prepared to enter into the rest and peace of heaven.

CHAPTER XXXI.

Troubles of William Penn—Seclusion of W. P.—W. P. acquitted — Death of S. Crisp — Account of John Richardson — Account of Thomas Story — Account of Thomas Chalkley — Relief to Friends in Barbadoes — Increase of Friends in Pennsylvania—Trials of Friends in Pennsylvania on account of Military demands — Remonstrance against Slavery by Friends at Germantown — Friends and Slavery — Yearly Meeting of Pennsylvania and New Jersey — Harmony among Friends.

NOTWITHSTANDING the alienation of the kindly feelings of the people, by the impolitic course pursued by James, and their apparent determination to maintain William and Mary on the throne, the self-exiled monarch resolved to continue whatever effort he could make, with the assistance of his friend Louis XIV., to regain the crown of Great Britain.   There were many who had stood high in State and Church, who refused to take the oath of allegiance to the reigning royal pair.   These were termed Nonjurors and Jacobites, and intrigues and covert conspiracies were, for a long time, rife among them.   Naturally, this gave rise to suspicion and distrust on the part of the party in power.   From this cause William Penn was subjected to no little trouble; his intimacy with the former King affording ground to prejudice the minds of many against him. He had already been arrested and discharged, there being no specific charge brought against him.   But some letters from James having been intercepted, among them was found one addressed to him.   He was again brought before the Privy Council, and some of those present, saying the circumstances required sureties from him, he urgently requested to be allowed to appear before King William himself.   This was granted, and after a conference of two hours, the King was prepared to acquit him of being implicated in any treasonable correspondence with James.   Some of the Council, however, were not satisfied without bail being given to appear at Court.   On coming before the Court, he was again discharged.   While King William was conducting the campaign in Ireland, where James was at the head of an army, fighting for possession of that Island, a conspiracy in favor of the latter was discovered, originating in Scotland. Queen Mary ordered the seizure of many supposed to be hostile to the government, and among them William Penn was again included. How long he was detained does not appear, but at the Michaelmas term of the Court (1690), he was once more cleared of any complicity with ·the opponents of the government.   For many months he had been making preparation to revisit Pennsylvania, and on his discharge, he hastened to have every thing ready to embark; but before he could complete his arrangements, he was again brought into difficulty, more serious than at any time before, on account of his connection with the Court of King James.   King William had crossed over to Holland, to be present at a Congress held at the Hague, and his absence emboldened the disaffected to enter into another plot, for restoring James, who was then at the Court of Louis XIV.   Two of their number started to cross the channel, and have an interview with their absent Sovereign; but the plot was discovered, and these emissaries, with their papers, seized.   One of them was hung, the other, in order to save his life, gave testimony against several of the nobility, and implicated William Penn in the conspiracy. A warrant for his arrest was issued, and on his return from the funeral of George Fox, he narrowly escaped once more being made a prisoner.

In what manner he was said to be connected with the conspiracy, or what was the specific charge brought against him, is nowhere clearly stated; but as Lord Preston — one of the captured messengers — declared he was one of the plotters, and a man of the name of William Fuller, swore to the correctness of Preston's statement, the matter assumed a serious aspect. As the origin of the plot was believed to have been among the Catholics, the same misrepresentations of Penn being a Jesuit in disguise, were again brought forward, and the passions of the people being much inflamed against the intriguing Papists, it was thought a fair trial could not be obtained for him. Under these circumstances, some accounts represent that William Penn voluntarily secluded himself where he could not be easily seen; waiting until a time should arrive when he might have a fair opportunity to clear himself; while others state, that having been examined before the Privy Council, he was ordered to remain a prisoner in his own house, under surveillance. The latter is the more probable, as he could hardly have supposed he could escape the search the government would make for him; especially as he kept up intercourse with his friends. Thus, in the Third month of 1691, he addressed an epistle to the Yearly Meeting in London, in order to remove any unfavorable impression that might have been made in the minds of his brethren by his forced seclusion. In this he says, "My privacy is not because men have sworn truly, but falsely against me: for wicked men have laid in wait for me, and false witnesses have laid to my charge things that I knew not; who have never sought myself, but the good of all, through great exercises; and have done some good, and would have done more, and hurt to no man; but always desired that truth and righteousness, mercy and peace, might take place amongst us."

During his retirement he employed his pen diligently, producing several works of much value. The refusal of Friends in Pennsylvania to contribute money for the erection of forts or for other military purposes, had given great offence to the home government, and the enemies of Penn took advantage of this, and of the position he was now in, with charges of treason hanging over him, to obtain an order from the King and Council, in the early part of 1692, to annex the government of Pennsylvania to that of New York, then presided over by Colonel Fletcher. Penn remained shut out from the world, and deprived of opportunity to serve the cause of truth and righteousness, and his brethren of the same faith, except by his pen, for more than two years; his character stained in the estimation of some, and his valuable services forgotten by many others, who, perhaps, thought he had indeed fallen to rise no more. But there were men of eminence, who had never believed William Penn guilty of the crime laid to his charge, and were awaiting the right opportunity to have justice done to his position and character. Among these was the celebrated John Locke, who esteemed him, not only as a man of exalted virtue and great literary attainment, but as a personal friend. He applied to King William for a pardon; but William Penn was too conscious of innocence, and too fully persuaded that in due time his innocence would be made manifest to the world, to be willing to accept of any release that would imply he had been guilty. In the meantime, Lord Preston, who had made the charge against him, had fled the country, and Fuller, his witness, having been detected in perjury, was, by order of Parliament, tried as an impostor, in the Court of the King's Bench, found guilty, and sentenced to stand in the pillory. Lords Ranelagh, Rochester, and Sydney, now waited on the King, and stating that the name of William Penn had never been found in any of the letters or papers connected with the conspiracy, and that the charge against him rested solely on the accusation of two men who were known to be unworthy of belief, urged upon him the injustice and hardship of his case. The King appears to have heard them patiently, and replied that William Penn was an old acquaintance of his; that he had nothing to allege against him, and that he might follow his business as freely as ever. Afterwards, the King gave an order to the principal Secretary of State for his freedom; which was communicated to him in the presence of the Marquis of Winchester. He, however, sought and obtained a hearing before the Privy Council; and after a full examination of the charges, he was honorably acquitted. The cloud that had long obscured his standing and services was now dispelled, and he returned to his family and friends, to resume the position he had before attained in the church, and in civil society. His wife survived his release but little more than two months.

In 1692, the Church lost one of its most valuable and deeply experienced members, by the death of Stephen Crisp. He had been an indefatigable and efficient laborer in his Master's work and service, ever since his convincement by the youthful J. Parnel, in 1655; continuing until near the close of his life, to promulgate the truths of the Gospel as held by Friends, and to enclose all whom he could gather, within the Gospel net. He was a copious writer; many of his epistles and addresses evincing the depth of his knowledge in the mysteries of Christ's kingdom, and retaining a savor that makes them still refreshing as well as instructive to the true believer. He attended the Yearly Meeting in London, and was shortly after taken ill. Removing to Wandsworth, he continued suffering from the inroads of disease, until the 28th of the Sixth month, when he departed this life, in the sixty-fifth year of his age; laying down his head in peace with the Lord. His friends testify of him, "He was zealously and conscientiously affected for the peace and prosperity of Friends in every place; and for that cause diligently labored among them; and when he was not able to ride or travel much, by reason of his distemper, as in former days, he continued chiefly in the town of Colchester, and in the city of London, in the Lord's work and service, as long as strength and ability of body lasted." . . . . "He would often call to the people, to come and try the sufficiency of the Grace of God, a measure of which was committed to them; and whether it was not able to save from sin; yea, to the utmost, all such as received and obeyed it. He divided the word aright, and turned many from darkness to light: many mourners have been comforted by him; and many tender-hearted helped through their inward exercises and conflicts of spirit; and he hath been a strength to them in their spiritual warfare."

While most of those who had been called and had given themselves up to the work, in the first breaking forth of the Lord's light and power for the gathering of the Society, were being taken from works to rewards, others were being brought into the service, and entrusted with gifts for the spread of the truth and the edification of the Church. It is instructive to observe, that the experiences of these, in the way and work of religion, the transformation from a state of nature to a state of grace, and of acceptance as true disciples of Christ, as left on record by several of them, correspond in all respects with those of the eminent servants to whom reference has already been made; showing that the ways of the Most High are equal, and that they who enter the kingdom of righteousness and peace, must go in by Christ the door, wearing his yoke and bearing the daily cross. As they thus come to do the will of their Father in heaven, they obtain a practical knowledge of the doctrine that is of Him; and thus these new converts came to understand and adopt the doctrines and testimonies which Friends had promulgated from the beginning.

John Richardson was born of parents who had joined Friends from convincement—his father being a minister—and was educated, while young, with care. He was early sensible of the strivings of the Holy Spirit, to keep him from evil, and lead him in the way of life and salvation. His father dying when he was but thirteen years of age, and his mother marrying a second husband, who was a Presbyterian, he was left very much to pursue his own way. Favored with the reproofs of instruction, he was restrained from running into gross evils, and finally made willing to yield to manifested duty, and enter upon the straight and narrow way. He thus records some of his experiences in the work of regeneration, before he had yet attained to man's estate. " I now came to witness that Scripture to be fulfilled which sayeth, ' When the Lord's judgments are in the earth '—or earthly hearts of men—' the inhabitants learn righteousness ; ' and notwithstanding there was an aversion, in my wild nature, to the people in scorn called Quakers, as also to the name itself, yet, when the afflicting hand of the Lord was upon me, for my disobedience, and when, like Ephraim and Judah, I saw, in the Light, my hurt and my wound, I bemoaned myself, and mourned over that just principle of Light and Grace in me, which I had pierced with my sins and disobedience. Although that ministration of condemnation was glorious in its time, yet great were my troubles, which humbled my mind, and made me willing to deny myself of everything which the Light made known in me to be evil ; I being in great distress, and wanting peace and assurance of the love of God to my soul ; the weight of which so humbled my mind, that I knew not of any calling, people, practice, or principle, that was lawful and right, which I could not embrace or fall in with. This was surely like the day of Jacob's troubles and David's fears. I saw that the filth of Zion was to be purged away by the Spirit of judgment and of burning ; that this is the way of the deliverance and recovery of poor man out of the fall, and the time of the restoration of the kingdom to God's true Israel." Yielding to the secret manifestations of the Light of Christ, and bearing the baptisms of the Holy Ghost and fire, he became a vessel clean and fitted for the Master's use, patiently enduring many deep mortifications and sufferings, to keep a conscience void of offence towards God, and towards man ; and was made a deep and powerful minister of the new covenant, and an instrument to turn many to righteousness.

Thomas Story, who joined Friends somewhere about 1690, had been educated, in profession with the " National Church ; " and having received a good education, and acquired the accomplish- ments, as they were called, of a gentleman, had a fair prospect of rising to note in society. He studied law, and commenced practice in Carlisle. From early life he appears to have been sensible of the operation of Divine Grace upon his mind, though at first not clearly recognizing what it was that rebuked him for evil, and invited him to choose the good. "Though I did not know or con- sider," he says, " what this reprover was, yet it had so much influence and power with me, that I was much reformed thereby from those habits which, in time, might have been foundations for greater evils ; or as stocks whereon to have engrafted a worse nature, to the bringing forth of a more plentiful crop of grosser vices." . . . "In process of time, as the motions of corruption and sin became stronger and stronger in me, so the Lord, in great goodness and mercy, made manifest to my understanding, the nature and end of them ; and having a view of them in the true Light, and the dan- ger attending them, they became exceedingly heavy and oppressive to my mind. And then the necessity of that great work of regener- ation was deeply impressed upon me ; but I had no experience nor evidence of it wrought in me hitherto. This apprehension greatly surprised me with fear, considering the great uncertainty of the continuance of the natural life ; and it began to put a secret stain upon the world and all its glory, and all that I had to glory in ; though I kept these thoughts within my own breast, not knowing of any soul to whom I could seriously and safely divulge them." Continuing to give heed to the Light of Christ shining into his dark heart, he came step by step to cease to do evil and to learn to do well. He observes : " Hitherto I had known the Grace of God in me only as a manifester of evil and of sin ; a word of reproof, and a law condemning and judging those thoughts, desires, words, pas- sions, affections, acts, and omissions, which are seated in the first nature and rooted in the carnal mind." . . . " By this Divine Grace I was, in good degree, enlightened, reformed, and enabled to shun and forbear all words and acts known to be evil, and moral right- eousness was restored in my mind, and thereby brought forth in me."

Abiding in this exercised state, he persevered in seeking a clearer knowledge of God and the attainment of greater " moral righteousness;" but he says, "Yet I did not know the Divine Grace in its own nature, as it is in Christ; not as a word of faith, sanctification, justification, consolation and redemption; being yet alive in my own nature. The Son of God was not yet revealed *in me,* nor I, by the power of his holy cross, mortified and slain; being without the knowledge of the essential truth, and in a state contrary to Him, and unreconciled." While in this condition, he states, that " Being alone in my chamber, the Lord broke in upon me unexpectedly; quick as lightning from the heavens, and as a righteous, all-powerful, all-knowing, and sin-condemning Judge; before whom my soul, as in the deepest agony, trembled, was confounded and amazed, and filled with such awful dread, as no words can reach or declare. My mind seemed plunged into utter darkness, and eternal condemnation appeared to inclose me on every side, as in the centre of the horrible pit; never to see redemption thence, or the face of Him in mercy, whom I had sought with all my soul. But in the midst of this confusion and amazement, where no thought could be formed nor any idea retained save eternal death possessing my whole man, a voice was formed and uttered in me, ' Thy will, O God ! be done; if this be thy act alone, and not my own, I yield my soul to Thee.' In conceiving these words, *from the Word of Life,* I quickly found relief: there was all-healing virtue in them, and the effect was so swift and powerful, that even in a moment all my fears vanished, as if they had never been, and my mind became calm and still, and simple as a little child; the day of the Lord dawned, and the Son of Righteousness arose *in me,* with divine healing and restoring virtue in his countenance, and He became the centre of my mind."

Thus experiencing forgiveness of past sins, and reconciliation with his heavenly Father, through the atonement and merits of his dear Son, Thomas Story was brought into the state of a little child, prepared to receive and learn other lessons in the school of Christ; and as he took up his daily cross and followed on to know the Lord, he became more and more perfectly instructed in the way and work of salvation. Up to this time he had attended Friends' meetings but two or three times, and it is noteworthy, that under the unfoldings of the Holy Spirit to his soul, he had been convinced of the doctrines and embraced the testimonies held by Friends, before he became associated with and joined in membership with them. In course of time he was entrusted with a gift in the ministry of the gospel, and labored abundantly for the salvation of souls, both in Great Britain and America.

Thomas Chalkley was another valuable instrument, raised up by the Head of the Church to advocate his cause, and labor in his vineyard. He was born in Southwark, London, in 1675, his parents being Friends. From very early life he was often brought under the contriting influence of heavenly love, warming his heart with earnest longings after the approbation of his heavenly Father; and strong convictions and sorrow when he gave way to temptation, and went counter to the manifestations of what was required of him. He says, "I very well remember the work of God upon my soul, when I was about ten years of age, and particularly at a certain time when I had been rebelling against God and my parents, in vanity and lightness: and as I had offended both, so I was corrected by both; for I had not only to feel the anger of my parents, but the Lord frowned upon me, insomuch that I trembled exceedingly, and was as though I heard a voice say to me, 'What will become of thee this night, if I should take thy life from thee?' At which I was amazed and in great fear. Then I covenanted with God that if He would be pleased to spare my life — for I thought God would have taken it from me that very moment — I would be more sober, and mind his fear more than I had done before."

Young as he was, he was preserved in much innocence, being enabled to walk circumspectly, and often to reprove his youthful companions, who gave way to improper conduct. Nevertheless, with his strong natural propensities and quick sensibility, he often found it hard work to take up the daily cross and deny himself. He remarks, "Thus I went on for several years, feeling that peace which passeth natural understanding, which many times accompanied my poor and needy soul; and being advanced to about fourteen or fifteen years of age, I remember that I used to shun the cross of speaking in the plain language,— which I always read in the Holy Scriptures,—to those whom I conversed with, except my father and mother, who would not allow me to speak otherwise." Convinced that it was a religious duty, and that avoiding its use was playing the hypocrite, he besought Divine help, and on an occasion soon after, when he had to speak to an officer of rank, he addressed him in plain language. At first the officer was offended, saying, "Thee! what dost thou thee me for?' Thomas remarked, he supposed that when he addressed the Almighty, he used *Thou* and *Thee* to Him, and queried whether he was too great to have the same language applied to him?—He appeared struck with a new thought, and ever after treated T. Chalkley with marked respect.

Continuing strictly obedient to duty, as manifested by the Holy Spirit in his soul, though young in years, he became grounded and built up in the unchangeable Truth, and was entrusted with a gift in the ministry, in the twentieth year of his age. Referring to the work of a minister, he says, " I did fervently pray that I might minister the gospel in the power of Jesus; for I clearly discerned in the Light of the Son of God, that all ministering out of Christ's power, was neither edifying, nor efficacious unto souls; therefore, I did earnestly beseech God for the continuance of the gift of his Spirit, that I might be enabled to preach the gospel in the power of Christ Jesus. The concern that was upon me on this account at that time, is hard to be expressed in words."

He was soon engaged in visiting the churches in different parts of England and Scotland; being concerned, while he felt restrained from entering largely into the pursuit of lawful things, to earn enough by the labor of his hands, not to make the gospel chargeable to any. In the twenty-third year of his age, with the approbation and unity of Friends, he paid a religious visit to Friends in America, where, some time after, he removed to reside, taking up his abode a little out of the city of Philadelphia.

Richard Claridge, Samuel Bownas and many others, might be mentioned, did space admit, who were raised up by the Head of the Church, to take the places of the faithful servants, who, having served their generation according to the will of God, had fallen asleep; and to proclaim the same blessed doctrines of primitive Christianity, and to illustrate their sanctifying effects in life and conversation.

In the notice of the sufferings of Friends in some of the West Indies, it has been mentioned, that much of it arose from the exactions of the insular governments, for the support of the military force. Representation of the loss and damage consequent on the levying and collection of fines, for failure to muster or to supply substitutes with arms, horses, &c., as also on account of refusing to take an oath, having been made to King William, he, in 1689, had the following order from Council issued to the Governor of Barbadoes; which was also applicable to other officers of the same grade in different Islands:

" Upon reading a petition of the people called Quakers, inhabiting the Island of Barbadoes, setting forth, that because the said Quakers could not bear arms, nor take an oath in any case, they have suffered much by virtue of an act made to settle the militia in the said Island; as in the petition hereunto annexed, is more at large expressed; his Majesty in Council is graciously pleased to refer the matter of the said petition to the examination of James Kendal, Esq., his Majesty's Governor of Barbadoes for the time being; who is to give the petitioners such relief in relation to the militia, as to him shall seem just and reasonable to answer their particular circumstances, and to make report thereof to his Majesty."

This order, in measure, abated the suffering of Friends on the several Islands; but in Barbadoes and other places, they were long prohibited by law from holding meetings for worship, and their ministers were forbidden to preach. They were also subjected to severe punishment, for teaching their negroes the truths of the Christian religion, or allowing them to attend their meetings for worship. Informers were encouraged, as in England, and Besse gives a long list of those employed in this business, who either came to an untimely end, or died in great poverty and wretchedness.

The tide of emigration from Great Britain to the Colonies on the American shore did not slacken for some years, the main stream being directed towards Pennsylvania, and the great body of emigrants to that Province being in religious profession with Friends. Others, of different religious professions, attracted by the widespread fame of the Colony, began to flock there, and were well satisfied to enjoy the rights and privileges secured to them under the mild government of the Quakers. Many Friends — ministers and others — who were noted in the Society in England and Wales, removed, with their families, to reside on the banks of the Delaware, or to establish themselves in the rich valleys or noble forests of the more interior counties. The various offices necessarily connected with the Provincial and municipal governments, were almost altogether filled by Friends. Many of the more eminent ministers were members of the Council, and of the Assembly. It was customary, in these bodies, before proceeding to the business of the day, to sit for a considerable time in reverential silence; seeking to receive some portion of that heavenly wisdom which is profitable to direct, in order rightly to perform the duties devolving upon them. Although the bulk of the early settlers were farmers and mechanics, with but ordinary education, there was a considerable number of Friends who were fairly entitled to the character of well-learned scholars; men who were proficient in the knowledge of the classics, Hebrew, and some of the modern languages, as well as in mathematics.

In 1683 a band of Germans, from Kreisheim in the German Palatinate, who had been convinced of the principles of the gospel as held by Friends, principally through the ministry of William Ames and Stephen Crisp, crossed the Atlantic, and on arriving in Pennsylvania, settled about six miles north of Philadelphia; and being joined by others, from different parts of Germany, they gave their home the name of Germantown. They were an humble, simple-hearted people; and the addition thus made to the meetings was felt to be a strength to the Society.

Upon the death of King Charles II., not long after the departure of William Penn. from the Colony, James II. was duly proclaimed King, and the proclamation, signed by Thomas Lloyd, a valuable minister, was transmitted to the Home Department in England. Thomas Lloyd was President of the "Commissioners of State," composed of five Friends, who, in the Governor's absence, acted in his place. But this arrangement proving inconvenient, after existing three years, it was changed, and a deputy-Governor appointed. The first deputy-Governor (Captain John Blackwell), not being a Friend, was anxious to raise a military force among the inhabitants; to which, of course, Friends would not consent; and with this introduction of discordant views and policy, it was soon found necessary to remove the deputy, The colonists, however, continued to prosper and increase, so that, by 1690, there were twelve thousand inhabitants.

War having broken out between England and France, in 1688, and the latter power having obtained. strong foothold among the Indians, not only in Canada, but along the lakes and throughout the western wilderness, the officers at different stations stirred up the Indians to make common cause with them, and engage in hostile incursions on the British colonies. Alarmed at the threatened destruction and suffering, the governments of New England and New York invited the government of Pennsylvania to make common cause with them, in measures of offence and defence. But Friends remained true to their principles, of war being inconsistent with Christianity, and steadily refused to contribute, in any way, to warlike measures; trusting to the protecting care of Him whose cause they desired to promote, and to the feelings of kindness and good will which they knew existed among the Indians towards them. They had seen other Colonies, with all their appliances for war, prepared under the belief that their formidable array would deter assault and secure peace, had, one by one, drawn upon themselves the horrors of the stealthy, ruthless warfare waged by the enraged savages, while no Friend had suffered violence from the red men, in Pennsylvania; and they were confirmed in the safe policy of relying on the protecting power of the Almighty Prince of Peace. This course was highly distasteful to those of the settlers who had not embraced the peaceable principles of the gospel, as Friends had. They blamed their refusal to co-operate with the proposed alliance, reproached them for neglect of duty, and predicted the direful consequences that would result from want of a military force to defend the settlement.

A rumor was got up, and industriously spread, that a band of five hundred Indians had assembled at a place bordering on the domain of the whites, where one of their principal chiefs had his wigwam; intending to make a descent on the peaceable Quakers, and destroy all before them. At the announcement that the unarmed inhabitants were about to be subjected to the tomahawk and scalping-knife of the savages, consternation prevailed among many of the people. The Council received glowing representations, made by these, of the alarming state of affairs; when one of them, Caleb Pusey, a Friend of well-known integrity and religious worth, offered, if five others were appointed to accompany him, to go, unarmed, and see those hostile Indians, if indeed they were to be found. The offer being accepted, the six Friends performed the journey on horseback, and, on arriving at the dwelling of the chief, found the old man resting at his ease, and surrounded by none but the women and children.

Friends kept to their testimony against war and all military measures, notwithstanding the pressure of the Home Government, and the dissatisfaction of their own militant fellow-citizens, for many years. Finally they were overborne, the policy of the government was changed, and in course of time, the power going into the hands of others, they were subjected to penalties — often severe — for adherence to their conscientious belief.

In 1688, the Friends at Germantown presented an address to their Monthly Meeting, upon the evils of buying and selling or holding slaves. The subject appears to have been considered of great importance, and the Monthly Meeting, after deliberating upon it, concluded to send the communication up to the Quarterly Meeting. The latter meeting, thinking the matter " of too great weight for them to determine," represented it to the Yearly Meeting. The Yearly Meeting, knowing that, as the legislative body, its decisions would assume the character of discipline, adopted the following minute: "A paper was presented by some German Friends concerning the lawfulness and unlawfulness of buying and keeping negroes. It was adjudged not to be so proper for this meeting to give a positive judgment in the case, it having so general a relation to many other parts, and therefore at present they forbear it."

As this remonstrance from the Friends at Germantown was the first official action, in the Society on the subject of slavery, and the disposal of it, at the time, exhibits the embarrassments felt in dealing with a subject affecting so many public and private relations, it is of much interest. It is also noteworthy as the initiatory step in a series of actions among Friends, which finally resulted in removing from them the reproach of holding their fellow-men in bondage; and probably as giving primary impulse to the wide-spread philanthropic efforts, successfully made in after years, for the emancipation of the cruelly oppressed blacks, in all professedly Christian countries. It is as follows:

"This is to the Monthly Meeting held at Richard Worrell's.

"These are the reasons why we are against the traffic of men-body, as followeth. Is there any that would be done or handled at this manner? viz., to be sold or made a slave for all the time of his life? How fearful and faint-hearted are many on sea, when they see a strange vessel, — being afraid it should be a Turk, and they should be taken, and sold for slaves into Turkey. Now what is *this* better done than Turks do? Yea, rather it is worse for them, which say they are Christian; for we hear that the most part of such negers are brought hither against their will and consent, and that many of them are stolen. Now, though they are black, we cannot conceive there is more liberty to have them slaves, as [than] it is to have other white ones. There is a saying, that we shall do to all men like as we will be done ourselves; making no difference of what generation, descent or color they are. And those who steal or robb men, and those who buy or purchase them, are they not all alike? Here is liberty of conscience, which is right and reasonable; here ought to be likewise liberty of the body, except of evil-doers, which is another case. But to bring men hither, or to rob and sell them against their will, we stand against. In Europe there are many oppressed for conscience sake; and here there are those oppressed which are of a black color. And we who know that men must not commit adultery,—some do commit adultery *in* others, separating wives from their husbands and giving them to others; and some sell the children of these poor creatures to other men. Ah! do consider well this thing, you who do it, if you would be done at this manner? and if it is done according to Christianity? You surpass Holland and Germany in this thing. This makes an ill report in all those countries of Europe, where they hear of [it], that the Quakers do here handle men as they handle there the cattle. And for that reason some have no mind or inclination to come hither. And who shall maintain this your cause, or plead for it? Truly we cannot do so, except you shall inform us better hereof, viz., that Christians have liberty to practise these things. Pray, what thing in the world can be done worse towards us, than if men should rob or steal us away, and sell us for slaves to strange countries; separating husbands from their wives and children. Being now this is not done in the manner we would be done at [by] therefore we contradict, and are against this traffic of men-body. And we who profess that it is not lawful to steal, must, likewise, avoid to purchase such things as are stolen, but rather help to stop this robbing and stealing if possible. And such men ought to be delivered out of the hands of the robbers, and set free as in Europe.* Then is Pennsylvania to have a good report, instead it hath now a bad one for this sake in other countries. Especially whereas the Europeans are desirous to know in what manner the Quakers do rule in their Province;—and most of them do look upon us with an envious eye. But if this is done well, what shall we say is done evil?"

"If once these slaves (which they say are so wicked and stubborn men) should join themselves,—fight for their freedom,—and handle their masters and mistresses as they did handle them before; will these masters and mistresses take the sword at hand and war against these poor slaves, like, we are able to believe, some will not refuse to do; or have these negers not as much right to fight for their freedom, as you have to keep them slaves?

"Now consider well this thing, if it is good or bad? And in case you find it to be good to handle these blacks at that manner, we desire and require you hereby lovingly, that you may inform us herein, which at this time never was done, viz., that Christians have such a liberty to do so. To the end we shall [may] be satisfied in this point, and satisfy likewise our good friends and acquaintances

* Alluding probably to the abolition of the old feudal system.

in our native country, to whom it is a terror, or fearful thing, that men should be handled so in Pennsylvania.

"This is from our meeting at Germantown, held y⁰ 18 of the 2 month, 1688, to be delivered to the Monthly Meeting at Richard Worrell's.

> Garret henderich
> derick up de graeff
> Francis daniell Pastorius
> Abraham jr. Den graef.

"At our Monthly Meeting at Dublin, y⁰ 30—2 mo., 1688, we having inspected y⁰ matter, above mentioned, and considered of it, we find it so weighty that we think it not expedient for us to meddle with it here, but do rather commit it to y⁰ consideration of y⁰ Quarterly Meeting; y⁰ tenor of it being nearly related to y⁰ Truth. On behalf of y⁰ Monthly Meeting.

> Signed   P.   JO. HART.

"This, above mentioned, was read in our Quarterly Meeting at Philadelphia, the 4 of y⁰ 4th mo. '88, and was from thence recommended to the Yearly Meeting, and the above said Derick, and the other two * mentioned therein, to present the same to y⁰ above said meeting, it being a thing of too great a weight for this meeting to determine.   Signed by order of y⁰ meeting.

> ANTHONY MORRIS."

Considering the bold and unequivocal manner in which Friends avowed the obligation to carry into practical effect the principles, precepts and mode of life enjoined in the New Testament; the suffering they had themselves meekly and patiently endured, for regulating their conduct and conversation to what they believed to be in accordance therewith, and the marked effect which this consistent course had had in curbing their passions, in softening their manners, and clothing their spirits with a measure of Christian love for all mankind, it seems hard to understand, in the present day, how they could have been betrayed into the toleration of slavery among themselves, for the length of time they did; mild as it was under their patronage, and relieved by the earnest efforts made to instruct their servants, young and old, and to give them a knowledge of the truths contained in the Holy Scriptures.

George Fox, and many of his co-laborers, who were brought into contact with slavery by their visits to the West Indian Islands, and

---

* There were three others signed it.

the North American Colonies, had earnestly exhorted their fellow-members who held slaves, to teach them the truths of Scripture, to endeavor to bring them into the fear of God, to allow no cruelty to be practised on them, and after they had served a term of years, to set them free. Many who joined the Society by convincement in the West Indies held slaves at the time, and continued to do so, under the belief that, inimical as were the rulers and inhabitants of the Islands to the negroes, it was a duty to take care of them. That the advice of George Fox, concerning the treatment they should receive, was duly appreciated and carried out, by Friends there, is amply attested by the laws passed, imposing severe penalties on Friends for instructing the negroes in the Christian religion, and having them to assemble with them for Divine worship. William Penn, as has been stated, gave the same advice as G. Fox to the colonists of Pennsylvania, and provided that the bondmen should have the option of freedom, after a designated number of years' service. There were many Friends in the Colonies who never were slaveholders; but the evil was allowed, and not a few were implicated in it.

No sooner were the English Colonies established on the shores of the Atlantic, than it became a practice to ship convicts to them,—more especially to Virginia and those south of it,—who were bound to serve for a term of years, if not for life: indented servants were also freely transported and sold to the highest bidder. When, therefore, a Dutch man-of-war entered the James River, in 1620, with some negroes on board, who were offered for sale, and *they* probably incapable of telling the story of their having being kidnapped, and cruelly torn from their native shores, the outrageous wrong committed by purchasing them for slaves, was lightly estimated, and the horrible system of chattel slavery thus inaugurated, altogether unforeseen. The Puritans of New England, not long after they had fixed their abode on the bleak shores of Massachusetts Bay, forbade the introduction of slaves into their Colony, and made importing or trading in them punishable by death. Roger Williams had a law passed in Rhode Island that " black mankind" should not be held in slavery more than ten years. In New Netherlands, however, slavery was encouraged so long as that Province was under the control of the Dutch, and New Amsterdam became a slave mart. The New England Colonies, including Rhode Island, notwithstanding their first righteous opposition to it, afterwards became implicated in the abominable traffic; and several of their ports obtained an infamous notoriety for the extent to which it was carried by their inhabitants.

In 1686, the Yearly Meeting held at Burlington had directed all the Quarterly Meetings within its jurisdiction, to send up representatives; and by the Minutes of 1688, it appears representatives were present from three Quarterly Meetings in Pennsylvania, viz., Philadelphia, Bucks, and Chester; and four from New Jersey, viz., Burlington, Salem, Gloucester, and Shrewsbury; and in 1689, from one in Delaware, in addition. The epistles sent by the Yearly Meeting to that of London, in different years, speak in strong terms of the love and unity prevailing among the members, the gracious owning and sensible presence of the adorable Head of the Church in their assemblies, and the growth of their meetings and members.

CHAPTER XXXII.

Account of the Heresy and Separation of G. Keith — Long-continued labor of Friends for his Restoration — Continued increase of Friends in the American Colonies — Friends in England seek relief from the imposition of Oaths — Declaration of Faith by Friends — "Primitive Christianity Revived" — Efforts of Friends to have an Affirmation substituted for an Oath finally successful.

THE harmonious condition of the Society within the limits of the Yearly Meeting of Pennsylvania, which has been spoken of, was not long after broken up, and disunity and dissension introduced and spread, through the instrumentality of one who, in former years, had been a noted champion in the defence of the doctrines and testimonies held by Friends; advocating and defending them, by his pen as well as by word of mouth. This person was the apostate, George Keith.

Notice has already been taken of this notorious man, who, born in Scotland, had been carefully educated among the Presbyterians, and graduated at the University in Edinburgh, where the degree of Master of Arts was bestowed upon him. With natural talents of high order, and well trained by the education received, he was well fitted for usefulness and influence in whatever position he might be placed. By what instrumental means, if any, he was convinced of the doctrines held by Friends, and brought to a willingness to embrace and live in accordance with them, is not known; the accounts preserved of his first appearance among them, merely stating that he came to Aberdeen from the southern part of Scotland, as a minister on a religious visit to his brethren. This was in 1664. He soon gained the affection and confidence of the little flock in that country, that stood as witnesses for the truths of the Gospel, amid the bitter scorn and persecution which for years were levelled against Friends; boldly promulgating their doctrines, and patiently and meekly partaking with others, of the barbarous treatment inflicted on them. Well informed in biblical and ecclesiastical lore, and disciplined in the logic of the schools, G. Keith was a ready disputant, and prepared to encounter his opponents with their own weapons. He joined Alexander Jaffray in exposing and refuting the malicious charges against the Quakers, publicly preached by G. Meldrum, of Aberdeen. He was engaged, with Robert Barclay, in defending the *theses* put forth by the latter, against the assaults of students of Aberdeen; and was associated with Stephen Crisp, Geo. Whitehead, and Wm. Penn, in the famous dispute with the Baptist ministers in London. For nearly thirty years he stood side by side with the noble band who showed their faith by their works; count ing nothing too near or too dear to be sacrificed, when duty called them to come up to the help of the Lord against the mighty, and, with spiritual weapons, cast down imaginations and every high thing that exalted itself against the knowledge of God; and its members were beloved for the work's sake.

In 1682, he left Scotland and removed to reside at Edmonton, in Middlesex, England, to take charge of a classical school, which, for several years had been conducted by Christopher Taylor, a minister among Friends, noted for his knowledge of languages, who was about to remove to Pennsylvania. Among other laws enacted to extend and secure the power of the "Church of England," was one which forbade any person teaching the classics, without first procuring a license from a Bishop. George Keith had not been long engaged in his new employment, before he was cited to appear before the Bishops' Court, for breaking this law, and, on his refusing to comply with the order of the Court, he was committed to jail. How long he was imprisoned does not appear; but in 1684 he had opened a similar school in London, and was again committed to Newgate for a like offence, where he was kept five months. Having, some time prior to these events, become acquainted with the celebrated doctor Von Helmont, who, while in professional attendance on Lady Conway, before and after she joined Friends, had become much interested in them, though not uniting in their religious principles, G. Keith had imbibed some of the strange notions of that learned man; and too much relying on the deductions of his reason in matters of faith, had become somewhat weakened in his hold on the Gospel principles, wherein he had once appeared to be firmly established.   The loss thus sustained had been manifest to some of his brethren, more deeply experienced in the religion of Christ than himself, and more quick in discerning the stratagems of Satan; and they had tenderly admonished him of his danger. ˙ It now was more fully shown, by the withdrawal of that sustaining power, which, in time past, had enabled him to endure cruel whippings and long imprisonments, for the cause of truth and righteousness, and to glory in tribulations.   He became impatient under suffering, and resolved to emigrate to America, rather than endure it any longer.   His first engagement after crossing the Atlantic, was to assist in running the boundary line between East and West Jersey, but he settled in Philadelphia in 1689.

The subject of sound literary education had, from their rise, received close attention from Friends.   George Fox, as has been noticed, had early recommended the establishment of boarding-schools, for both sexes, where they might be taught "in all things civil and useful in the creation;" and the reports to the Yearly Meeting in London, in 1691, show there were fifteen such schools, supported by Friends in different parts of England.   The early settlers of Pennsylvania, were equally alive to the importance of education, and a year had not passed over after their first landing, when a school was opened under the case of a Friend named Enoch Flowers.   In 1689, Friends in Philadelphia, anxious to secure more liberal education, founded a public school, where classical as well as English literature was to be taught, and in which the children of those not able to bear the expense, were to be instructed gratuitously.   This institution was incorporated in 1697, and a few years later, William Penn granted another charter, extending its privileges and powers.   The views of Friends, in relation to the importance of a sound and comprehensive education, are thus set forth in the preamble to this document: "Whereas the prosperity and welfare of any people depend, in great measure, upon the good education of youth, and their early introduction in the principles of true religion and virtue, and qualifying them to serve their country and themselves, by educating them in reading, writing and learning of languages, and useful arts and sciences, suitable to their age, sex and degree; which cannot be effected in any manner so well, as by public schools, for the purposes aforesaid," &c. Four years after the establishment of this school, the Assembly passed an Act making it obligatory that every child in the Province should be taught to read and write.

Friends by no means ignored the use of human reason and learning, in the knowledge and work of religion. But they rejected the opinion that man's reason, however developed by culture and aided by study of Divine truths in the Scriptures, is a light or power sufficient to guide, or to enable him to walk in the way of salvation. Christ is the alone Author and Finisher of the saints' faith, and his light communicated to the soul, by the measure of the Holy Spirit which He has purchased for every human being, must make manifest the things that belong to the soul's peace, guide, guard and strengthen him in the exercise of his intellectual faculties, as he enters, and takes step after step, in the strait and narrow way that leads to eternal life.

Of the public school opened in Philadelphia in 1689, on his arrival in that city, George Keith was made head master; with a fair compensation for the first year, and a more liberal one guaranteed for the second. He, however, had lost the staidness and weight which once attended him, and became unsettled and censorious. He gave up the school at the end of the first year, and soon after went on a professedly religious visit into New England; during which he challenged, at different times, several of other religious professions to dispute; but it was remarked, that this seemed rather to display his adroitness as a polemical disputant, than from a true religious concern to promulgate or defend the truth. He also wrote and published three tracts, rebutting charges publicly brought against the doctrines and practices of Friends, defending and advocating them. Becoming puffed up with the head knowledge he had attained, and, like Diotrephes of old, wishing to have the pre-eminence, he indulged in criticisms on the ministry of some of his less learned brethren, and found fault with the discipline, as well as the manner in which it was administered. Having prepared what he considered an improved code, he presented it to the meeting of ministers, in the city, for its approval. That body, not satisfied to sanction the essay, referred its consideration to the Yearly Meeting. The Yearly Meeting, equally uneasy with some of the proposed changes, declined to adopt it; but expressed its willingness that the whole matter should be submitted to the Yearly Meeting in London. This course George refused to have taken, and withdrew the document. But at this check to his assumption of superiority, he took deep offence; which soon manifested itself in watching for occasion to bring charges against Friends, especially those who, seeing the mistaken course he was pursuing, felt bound in Christian love to advise and warn him.

In 1691, he charged two approved ministers with having said, that " The Light of Christ was sufficient for salvation, without anything else;" which they denied; as they fully owned the offices and atonement of Christ when in the prepared body, as necessary to salvation. In the Yearly Meeting of ministers in that year, he accused one of those Friends of having said, that he [G. K.] " preached two Christs;" and he insisted on the meeting going into an investigation. This took place, and the meeting censured both,— the Friend charged, with having used expressions which admitted the meaning attached to them by G. Keith; and the latter, for not observing gospel order towards the Friend, and for using highly improper language to him.

It now became evident that George Keith had departed from the doctrine of the universality of Divine Grace, and its sufficiency to *bring* salvation, as ever held by Friends, and for which he had contended so many years. It was in vain that honest-hearted and religiously experienced Friends endeavored to show him the evils of the course he was pursuing, and besought him to change it, and seek to come once more into unity with the Society he had so long served, and which had cherished esteem and love for him. He began to make railing accusations against them, and finding that he was supported by a party, willing, like himself, to escape from the restraints of the self-denying principles held by Friends, and adopt some form of religion that would admit of more liberty to the natural man, and thus remove the offence of the cross, he determined to put himself at their head, set sound Friends at defiance, and build up a sect holding opinions like his own.

Friends in England, hearing of the charges and contentions which were agitating the church in Pennsylvania, were brought under much concern, and several of the more eminent and deeply experienced among them addressed an epistle to their brethren there, which abounds with religious instruction and pertinent advice. The following extract will give some idea of its character, and of the controversy they had to deal with.

After speaking of the obligation to guard against speculations about things which have not been revealed, and entering into disputes relative to them, but rather to show by conduct the efficacy of the religion professed, and to cultivate charity and brotherly kindness; they say, that though Friends have always believed the Gospel dispensation to be a spiritual dispensation; yet it was " In nowise to oppose, reject, or invalidate Jesus Christ's outward coming, suffering, death, resurrection, ascension, and glorified estate in the heavens; but to bring men to partake of the remission of sins, reconciliation and eternal redemption, which He hath obtained for us, and for all men, for whom He died and gave himself a ransom; both for Jews and Gentiles, for Indians, Turks and Pagans, without respect of person or people. And Christ is to be fully preached unto them, according to the Holy Scriptures, by them whom He may send unto them for that end: that as the benefit of His sufferings extends to all, even to them that have not the Scriptures or outward history thereof, they may be told who was and is their chief friend, that gave Himself a ransom for them, and hath enlightened them ; yet not excluding those from God's mercy or salvation by Christ, *who never had nor may have* the outward knowledge or history of Him, if they sincerely obey and live up to his Light; for his light and salvation reach to the ends of the earth. Yet still we that have the Holy Scriptures, and those plain, outward confirmed testimonies concerning our blessed Lord and Saviour Jesus Christ, both as to his coming in the flesh and in the Spirit, have cause to be thankful to God for the peculiar favor, and that the Scriptures are so well preserved to posterity ; and we beseech you let us keep to the plainness and simplicity of Scripture language, in all our discourses about matters of faith, divinity and doctrine ; and sincerely believe, own and confess our blessed Lord and Saviour Jesus Christ, the Son of the living God, in all his comings, appearances, properties, offices and works, both for us and in us."

This document, which breathes throughout the spirit of Christian love, was signed by nine well known and highly esteemed Friends, and was well fitted to command serious consideration, and soothe any angry feeling that might have sprung up ; while it clearly held forth the faith of Friends on the points in dispute. But it had no better effect on George Keith, than the labors of his friends where he lived, had produced. He became more irascible, and more bent on widening the breach that separated himself and party from the Society. Having proposed that the time for holding the meetings for worship in Philadelphia should be changed, with which Friends did not unite, he took great offence, and, determined to have his own way, set up a separate meeting; claiming the character of Friends, under the assumed title of " Christian Quakers." He now resorted to the press, and published several baseless charges against Friends; endeavoring to criminate them as unbelievers in Christian truths. In the Quarterly Meeting of Philadelphia, held in the First month of 1692, he accused the whole assembly of having come together " to cloak heresies and deceit," and finally declared, " There were more damnable heresies and doctrines of devils among the Quakers, than among any profession of Protestants."

This sad lapse and schism had now come to a crisis. The Church had sincerely sought, in meekness and restoring love, to win George Keith back to the position from which he had fallen; but he told them that " He trampled upon the judgment of the meeting as dirt under his feet." In order to clear the cause of Truth from the reproach he had brought upon it, and, as much as it was in their power, to protect the Society from further harm, the Quarterly Meeting of Ministers, in the Fourth month of 1692, after hearing the report of two of its members who had been appointed to deal with him, came to a judgment to issue an address " To the several Monthly and Quarterly Meetings in Pennsylvania, East and West Jersey, and elsewhere, as there may be occasion;" in which they give a plain statement of the origin and development of the schism, the unjustifiable acts of George Keith, his departure from sound doctrine, the labor of Friends for his restoration, his setting up a separate meeting, and his rejection of their brotherly counsel and efforts to heal the breach. The meeting therefore declares it can no longer own him as a member, acknowledge him as a minister, nor give countenance to those who are siding with or supporting him in his course; and it earnestly advises the latter to give up their separate meetings, and return into fellowship with their brethren. This address was signed by twenty-eight ministers.

Before issuing this testimony, it was submitted to the inspection of George Keith, with the view that, if there was any part to which he could make valid objection, it might be duly reconsidered. He declined the offer; but his separate meeting, soon after, published two documents, disowning all those concerned in the testimony against him, and charging them with a violation of all gospel order and Christian kindness. He was now disowned, as a member, by the Monthly Meeting of Friends of Philadelphia.

Some robbers having stolen a small sloop from the wharf at Philadelphia, and escaping with it down the river, committed several robberies. Three of the Magistrates in the city issued a warrant for their capture; and they were overtaken and apprehended. This was effected without using any military force. Bent on bringing whatever odium he could on Friends, Keith published a scurrilous attack on the Magistrates who signed the warrant, and who were Friends, charging them with having violated their professed peaceable principles; and also casting severe personal reflections on the Deputy-Governor, Lloyd. Apprehending that, by this and other similar means, which he was industriously pursuing, he might produce so much disaffection towards the government, as finally to subvert it, the Magistrates had Keith indicted and brought to trial. He was found guilty, and fined £5; which fine, however, was never collected; the object of the trial being merely to vindicate Friends as conscientious supporters of civil government; and stop the spread of distrust and fear among the inhabitants. Keith did not fail to misrepresent this proceeding as persecution, on account of his religion.

This troubler of the Church now gave public notice of his intention to appeal to the Yearly Meeting, and his reasons for so doing. When that body assembled, at Burlington [1692], instead of prosecuting his appeal before it, he and his partisans met separately, and sent a message to the meeting, requiring that the appeal should be heard before them; claiming to be the Yearly Meeting. This summons not being regarded, the Keith party gave judgment in favor of their leader; and put forth also a confession of faith, drawn up in terms calculated to deceive the unwary.

The Yearly Meeting of Friends reviewed the proceedings of the subordinate meetings, confirmed them, and gave forth its condemnation of George Keith and his adherents; which was signed by two hundred and fourteen Friends. Other Yearly Meetings in America felt the deplorable consequences of this grievous inroad upon the peace and harmony of the Society, and, after taking the necessary means for obtaining a knowledge of the merits of the case, those of New England, Long Island, Maryland, and other General Meetings, including that in Barbadoes, where he had had his publications disseminated, declared their disunity with George Keith, and those associated with him.

Professing that though thus disowned by Friends in America, he was in unity with the Society in Great Britain, he resolved to carry his cause there, and seek from London Yearly Meeting sanction of his course and his principles. Accordingly, with Thomas Budd, who had been his active partisan throughout his contentions, he went over to England. In order to secure a fair exhibit of the circumstances of the case, Friends of Burlington Yearly Meeting appointed Samuel Jennings and Thomas Ducket to attend in London as respondents; who carried with them a statement of the causes and reasons of G. Keith's disownment, and an epistle. Finding on his arrival in England that some Friends were shy of him, Keith at once entered complaint against them, to the Six Weeks' Meeting in London; but that body, ascertaining that the subject involved transactions which had taken place in Pennsylvania, declined entering into the matter, but referred it to the Yearly Meeting.

London Yearly Meeting had no jurisdiction over any of the meetings of Friends in America; but as this was a case involving points of faith as well as discipline, attended with the destructive effects of a separation in a Yearly Meeting, where Friends were a large and influential body; and as the Burlington meeting had implied its willingness to have its proceedings reviewed by London Yearly Meeting, by sending over respondents, the latter Meeting concluded to consider the whole subject. Therefore, on the day when the epistles from the different corresponding meetings in America were read [1694], all of which referred to the defection, George Keith was invited to attend. He, at the same time, presented to the meeting his statement and defence, which, at his request, was also read, and the meeting decided to enter upon the examination of the merits of the case, when its other business was finished.

During the investigation, which lasted six days, all the documents, epistles and other papers in the case, issued by Friends, were read; as were also the different pamphlets and other documents published by George Keith; and both parties were fully heard in their oral pleadings. The members of the meeting then gave their opinions, and the judgment was given, " That the separation lay at George Keith's door; and that his printing and publishing the differences as he had done, was wrong, and out of the wisdom and counsel of God;" and the meeting required him either to call in those publications, or to put forth his condemnation of them, and make public something that would clear Friends in America from the gross errors charged on some few there, and to retract the bitter language he had used in those publications, and use all his influence to remove the separation he had caused, and " Help forward a reuniting and amicable composure, for the holy truth's sake, the glory of God, and the peace of his people." The meeting disapproved of the Magistrates, who were Friends, suing him at law. Here, it says, " There appears to have been too much height of spirit on both sides, and both had need to be deeply humbled; both provokers and provoked."

This advice being rejected by Keith, and he continuing to make unjustifiable and unfounded charges against Friends, at the next Yearly Meeting, he was allowed to be present, and have read before it, another statement of his cause,— in which, however, he charged Friends with holding unsound doctrines, and declared he had many to support him,— the meeting then " Proceeded weightily, in the fear of God and sense of his eternal power," to give its sense of George Keith's paper and his spirit. He was permitted to be present the next day, to hear the judgment arrived at, and on its being communicated, he broke out into violent and offensive language towards Friends, and went away in anger. The meeting, after having thus exhausted the means for his recovery and reconciliation, unanimously agreed to issue a testimony of disownment, which contains the following. " It is the sense and judgment of this meeting that the said George Keith is gone from the blessed unity of the peaceable Spirit of our Lord Jesus Christ, and hath thereby separated himself from the holy fellowship of the Church of Christ; and that while he is in an unreconciled and uncharitable state, he ought not to preach or pray in any of Friends' meetings, nor be owned or received as one of us, until by a public and hearty acknowledgment of the great offence he has given, and hurt he hath done, and condemnation of himself therefor, he gives proof of his unfeigned repentance, and does his endeavour to remove and take off the reproach he hath brought upon Truth and Friends; which, in the love of God, we heartily desire for his soul's sake."

Disowned by the whole Society, Keith commenced holding meetings at Turner's Hall, London [1695]; where, as he retained the garb and language of a Friend, he was joined by some who had left the Society with Wilkinson and Story, and by others attracted by curiosity. He continued to publish accusations and invectives against Friends, and challenged George Whitehead, William Penn and others to publicly dispute with him. But to them he was " as a heathen man and a publican," and they declined meeting him, making their reasons public. Thomas Ellwood, George Whitehead and one or two others, published replies to his printed attacks, ex-

posing their untruthfulness, and quoting largely from his published
works, issued in former days, to show how he misrepresented Friends
and their doctrines, and using his own words to confute his present
charges.

Thus the following is taken from his published reply to Cotton
Mather, who had brought charges against Friends similar to those
now preferred by him. " Our principles do mostly agree with the
fundamental articles of the Christian Protestant faith. According to my best knowledge of the people called Quakers, and those
owned by them as preachers and publishers of their belief, being of
an unquestionable esteem among them, and worthy of double honor,
as there are many such, I know none of them that are guilty of such
heresies and blasphemies as they are charged with. And I think
I should know, and do know those called Quakers, having been
conversant with them in public meetings as well as in private discourses, with the most noted and esteemed among them, for about
twenty-eight years past, and that in many places of the world, both
in Europe and America."

It was not long before he grew tired of the miserable position in
which he had placed himself, and having now no fixed religious
principles, he sought a change. He threw off the dress, language
and manners of a Friend, and courted the patronage of the " Established Church," and as much was hoped from him as a bitter
enemy to the Quakers, he was erelong ordained a minister in it, by
the Bishop of London. Under the auspices of " The Society for
the Propagation of the Gospel in Foreign Parts," he went again to
America, making large promises of the success he should have in
gathering Quakers back to the mother church. While there he was
instrumental in having Samuel Bownas — who at that time was
travelling in the Colonies, on a religious visit — shut up illegally
and unjustly in jail, for nearly a year, and in frequently disturbing
Friends in their meetings by his indecorous intrusions ; but his
efforts at refolding those he pretended to consider lost sheep, were
a failure. In little more than two years he went back, and was
given a "living," at Elburton, in Sussex. He became noted for
the severity with which he exacted tithes, and closed his career in
1714, saying, in the honest hour of death, " He wished he had died
when he was a Quaker ; and he did believe if God had taken him
out of the world when he went among the Quakers, and in that
profession, it had been well with him."

Bishop Burnet's account of G. Keith and his course, based on the statements of Keith, is very erroneous.   He, however, thus confirms his joining the Episcopal Church.   " He continued these meetings [at Turner's Hall], *being still in outward appearance a Quaker,* for some years, till having prevailed so far as he saw any probability of success, he *laid aside their exterior,* and was reconciled to the Church, and is now in holy orders among us, and likely to do good service in undeceiving and reclaiming some of those misled enthusiasts."

Those in Pennsylvania, who followed Keith into separation, though they had set up meetings of their own in Philadelphia, Burlington, Bucks, and other places, and continued, for a few years, to trouble Friends by intruding on their meetings, yet they soon quarrelled among themselves; a few saw their error, and acknowledged it, and were received back into the Society; some joined other religious Societies,—principally the Baptists,—others gave up all profession of religion, and by the end of that century, they had almost disappeared.

Friends continued to increase in Pennsylvania and New Jersey, not only by the arrival of new immigrants of their own religious belief, but also from numerous convincements of the correctness of their Christian doctrines and testimonies, among people willing to take up the cross and join in membership with them.   A considerable body of Welsh came over and settled in Pennsylvania, giving the name of North Wales to the part of the country where they lived.   Many of these became worthy, consistent Friends, some being convinced under the ministry of Ellis Pugh, their fellow countryman, who had come into the country some time before. They established a meeting in 1698, which they called Gwynedd. Not only was it by ministry that many were added to the Society, but the guarded, consistent conduct and otherwise exemplary lives of members, were effectual, in many instances, to arrest the attention of honest inquirers after Truth, and lead them to embrace a religion producing such fruits.

Colonel Fletcher, who, when the government of Pennsylvania was joined to that of New York, held the reins of power there, came on to Philadelphia to have the affairs of the Province regulated according to his own ideas of what was required.   He entered the city accompanied by a military escort, and soon summoned the Assembly to meet him.   He demanded of the latter money and supplies, to aid in defending the frontiers.   Friends were largely in the majority, and instead of complying with his requisition, they resolved, that their laws were not affected by the change in the government, and they called on him at once to recognize their validity. He claimed that he was not bound by what had been done before he was clothed with power, under the great seal of the kingdom ; with which their laws could not come in competition. The Assembly, however, resolved, that the charter granted by Charles II., had never been revoked, and unless that was done, the rights and privileges of the Colonists could not be legally invaded.

Fletcher was finally obliged to yield to the determined stand taken by the Assembly, to acknowledge the form of government already instituted, and the binding authority of the laws it had passed. Afterwards the Assembly voted a tax of one penny on the pound, to be paid to the home Government, with the stipulation, that " it should not be dipped in blood." Fletcher was greatly dissatisfied, and wrote home, advising that Penn's charter should be broken, and Pennsylvania and New Jersey be both united in one Province with New York, so that the Quakers might be outvoted. But after William Penn had been cleared of any complicity with treason, he applied for the restoration of all the rights granted him in the charter of Pennsylvania, and upon a full examination and the removal of objections, a patent was issued, reinvesting him with his original power and functions. This was in the latter part of 1694.

Preachers from other Colonies, where Friends had established themselves, and from across the Atlantic, frequently visited their brethren ; watering the heritage with streams of gospel ministry, and laboring to keep the camp clear of defilement ; and during the years under review, their religious concern, and that of residents equally engaged in the Lord's work, were blessed. The same may be said of Friends in other Provinces ; though in them the increase of the Society was much more slow, in consequence of comparatively few members from distant countries settling among them. All acknowledging the same faith, and generally maintaining the same testimonies, the stream of unity and harmony flowed uninterruptedly ; while the respective meetings were on the watch to prevent the introduction of unsound doctrine, or any evil that would create disunity, and mar their peace and prosperity.

Friends in England, though freed from the action of most of the unjust laws, by which they had been made to suffer so long and so terribly, were yet subjected to great inconveniences, to imposition and loss, on account of being conscientiously restrained from taking an oath. Encouraged by the more liberal feeling in relation to religious belief, apparently prevailing, they presented a petition to Parliament in 1693, that relief might be granted them, by the passage of a law substituting a solemn affirmation in all cases where an oath was then required. This petition being read, was referred to a committee; which reported after examination, that "Upon the whole, it is the opinion of this committee, that the Quakers ought to be relieved, according to the prayer of their petition."

Those who were opposed to Friends were, however, numerous and influential enough in Parliament, to prevent action being taken on the report; and it was passed over for that session.

Sensible that the misrepresentations and perversions of the doctrines held by Friends, which had been persistently asserted and industriously circulated by George Keith and his abettors, had prejudiced the minds of many against them, and alive to the duty of clearly informing the public of the faith held and ever promulgated by them, Friends in England published, and had widely spread, an exposition of their faith on several fundamental points, as they had done repeatedly before. This document was entitled "The Christian Doctrine and the Society of the people called Quakers, cleared," &c. Owing to the same cause, Friends in Pennsylvania had felt called to issue a Declaration of Faith, similar, so far as it goes, to that issued by Friends in England; but as the latter includes the substance of the former, and treats on some points not noticed in it, the Declaration put forth by Friends in England will be given at the conclusion of this work.

William Penn published "Primitive Christianity Revived;" in which he gives the objections made to the doctrines of Friends, and answers them; showing the common misrepresentation, and the truth of the doctrines held. The following touches on points that have been before noticed:

"SEC. VIII., OBJ. 1. Though there be many good things said, how Christ appears and works in a soul, to awaken, convince and convert it; yet you seem not particular enough about the death and sufferings of Christ; and it is generally rumored and charged upon you by your adversaries, that you have little reverence to the doctrine of Christ's satisfaction to God for our sins, and that you do not believe, that the active and passive obedience of Christ, when He was in the world, is the alone ground of a sinner's justification before God.

" ANS. The doctrines of satisfaction and justification, truly understood, are placed in so strict an union, that the one is a necessary

consequence of the other; and what we say of them, is what agrees
with the suffrage of Scripture, and, for the most part, in the terms
of it; always believing, that in points where there arises any difficulty, be it from the obscurity of expression, mis-translation, or the
dust raised by the heats of partial writers, or nice critics, it is ever
best to keep close to the text, and maintain charity in the rest. I
shall first speak negatively, what we do not own; which, perhaps,
hath given occasion to those who have been more hasty than wise,
to judge us defective in our belief of the efficacy of the death and
sufferings of Christ to justification:

"2. First, We cannot believe that Christ is the cause, but the
effect of God's love, according to the testimony of the beloved disciple, John, chap. iii. 16: 'God so loved the world, that he gave his
only begotten Son into the world, that whosoever believeth in him
should not perish, but have everlasting life.'

"Secondly, We cannot say God could not have taken another
way to save sinners, than by the death and sufferings of his Son, to
satisfy his justice, or that Christ's death and sufferings were a strict
and rigid satisfaction for that eternal death and misery due to man
for sin and transgression; for such a notion were to make God's
mercy little concerned in man's salvation; and, indeed, we are at
too great a distance from his infinite wisdom and power, to judge
of the liberty or necessity of his actings.

"Thirdly, We cannot say Jesus Christ was the greatest sinner in
the world (because he bore our sins on his cross, or because he was
made sin for us, who knew no sin), an expression of great levity
and unsoundness, yet often said by great preachers and professors
of religion.

"Fourthly, We cannot believe that Christ's death and sufferings
so satisfy God, or justify men, as that they are thereby accepted of
God. They are indeed thereby put into a state capable of being
accepted of God, and, through the obedience of faith and sanctification of the spirit, are in a state of acceptance. We can never think
a man justified before God, while self-condemned; or that any man
can be in Christ who is not a new creature; or that God looks
upon men otherwise than they are. We think it a state of presump-
tion and not of salvation to call Jesus Lord, and not by the work
of the Holy Ghost; Master, and he not yet master of their affections;
Saviour, and they not saved by him from their sins; Redeemer, and
yet they not redeemed by him from their passions, pride, covetousness, wantonness, vanity, vain honors, friendships, and glory of this

world; which is to deceive themselves; for God will not be mocked; such as men sow, such they must reap. And though Christ did die for us, yet we must, by the assistance of his grace, work out our salvation with fear and trembling: as He died for sin, so we must die to sin, or we cannot be said to be saved by the death and sufferings of Christ, or thoroughly justified and accepted with God. Thus far negatively. Now positively what we own as to justification.

" 3. We do believe that Jesus Christ was our holy sacrifice, atonement, and propitiation; that he bore our iniquities, and that by his stripes we were healed of the wounds Adam gave us in his fall; and that God is just in forgiving true penitents upon the credit of that holy offering which Christ made of himself to God for us; and that what he did and suffered, satisfied and pleased God, and was for the sake of fallen man, who had displeased God; and that through the offering up of himself once for all, through the eternal Spirit, He hath forever perfected those (in all times) that were sanctified, who walked not after the flesh, but after the spirit. Rom. viii. 1. Mark that.

" 4. In short, justification consists of two parts, or hath a twofold consideration, viz., justification from the guilt of sin, and justification from the power and pollution of sin; and in this sense justification gives a man a full and clear acceptance before God. For want of this latter part it is, that so many souls, religiously inclined, are often under doubts, scruples, and despondencies, notwithstanding all that their teachers tell them of the extent and efficacy of the first part of justification. And it is too general an unhappiness among the professors of Christianity, that they are apt to cloak their own active and passive disobedience with the active and passive obedience of Christ.

" The first part of justification, we do reverently and humbly acknowledge, is only for the sake of the death and sufferings of Christ; nothing we can do, though by the operation of the Holy Spirit, being able to cancel old debts, or wipe out old scores; it is the power and efficacy of that propitiatory offering, upon faith and repentance, that justifies us from the sins that are past; and it is the power of Christ's spirit in our hearts, that purifies and makes us acceptable before God. For until the heart of man is purged from sin, God will never accept of it. He reproves, rebukes, and condemns those that entertain sin there, and therefore such cannot be said to be in a justified state; condemnation and justification being contraries. So that they that hold themselves in a justified state by the active and passive obedience of Christ, while they are not actively and passively obedient to the Spirit of Christ Jesus, are under a strong and dangerous delusion; and for crying out against this sin-pleasing imagination, not to say doctrine, we are staged and reproached as deniers and despisers of the death and sufferings of our Lord Jesus Christ. But be it known to such, they add to Christ's sufferings, and crucify to themselves afresh the Son of God, and trample the blood of the covenant under their feet, who walk unholily under a profession of justification; for God will not acquit the guilty, nor justify the disobedient and unfaithful. Such deceive themselves; and at the great and final judgment, their sentence will not be, 'Come, ye blessed;' because it cannot be said to them, ' Well done, good and faithful;' for they cannot be so esteemed who live and die in a reprovable and condemnable state; but, 'Go, ye cursed,' &c."

"Sec. IX.—1. And lest any should say we are equivocal in our expressions, and allegorize away Christ's appearance in the flesh; meaning only thereby our own flesh; and that as often as we mention Him, we mean only a mystery, or a mystical sense of Him, be it as to his coming, birth, miracles, sufferings, death, resurrection, ascension, mediation and judgment; I would yet add, to preserve the well disposed from being staggered by such suggestions, and to inform and reclaim such as are under the power and prejudice of them,

"That we do, we bless God, religiously believe and confess, to the glory of God the Father, and the honor of his dear and beloved Son, that Jesus Christ took our nature upon him, and was like unto us in all things, sin excepted: that He was born of the Virgin Mary, suffered under Pontius Pilate, the Roman Governor, was crucified, dead, and buried in the sepulchre of Joseph of Arimathea; rose again the third day, and ascended into heaven, and sits on the right hand of God, in' the power and majesty of his Father; who will one day judge the world by him, even that blessed Man, Christ Jesus, according to their works.

"2. But because we so believe, must we not believe what Christ said, 'He that is with you shall be in you.' 'I in them, and they in me,' &c. 'When it pleased God to reveal his Son in me.' 'The mystery hid from ages, is Christ in the Gentiles, the hope of glory.' 'Unless Christ be in you, ye are reprobates!' Or must we be industriously represented as deniers of Christ's coming in the flesh, and the holy ends of it, in all the parts and branches of his doing and suffering, only because we believe and press the necessity of believing, receiving and obeying his inward and spiritual appearance and manifestation of himself, through his light, grace and Spirit, in the hearts and consciences of men and women, to reprove, convict, convert and change them? This we esteem hard and unrighteous measure; nor would our warm and sharp adversaries be so dealt with by others: but to do as they would be done to, is too often no part of their practice, whatever it be of their profession.

"3. Yet we are very ready to declare to the whole world, that we cannot think men and women can be saved by their belief of the one, without the sense and experience of the other; and that is what we oppose, and not his blessed manifestation in the flesh. We say that He then overcame our common enemy, foiled him in the open field, and in our nature triumphed over him, that had overcome and triumphed over it in our forefather Adam, and his posterity: and that as truly as Christ overcame him in our nature, in his own person, so by his Divine Grace, being received and obeyed by us, He overcomes him in us: that is, He detects the enemy by his light in the conscience, and enables the creature to resist him, and all his fiery darts; and finally, so to fight the good fight of faith, as to overcome him, and lay hold on eternal life.

"4. And this is the dispensation of Grace, which we declare has appeared to all, more or less; teaching those who will receive it, 'to deny ungodliness and worldly lusts, and to live soberly, righteously, and godly in this present world; looking for (which none else can justly do) the blessed hope and glorious appearing of the great God, and our Saviour Jesus Christ,' &c. And as from the teachings, experience and motion of this grace we minister to others, so the very drift of our ministry is to turn people's minds to this grace in themselves, that all of them may be up and doing, even the good and acceptable will of God, and work out their salvation with fear and trembling, and make their high and heavenly calling and election sure; which none else can do, whatever be their profession, church or character; for such as men sow they must reap; and his servants we are whom we obey. Regeneration we must know, or we cannot be children of God, and heirs of eternal glory. To be born again, another Spirit must prevail, leaven, season, and govern us, than either the spirit of the world, or our own depraved spirits; and this can be no other Spirit than that which dwelt in Christ; for unless that dwell in us, we can be none of his, Rom. viii. 9. And this Spirit begins in conviction, and ends in conversion and perseverance; and the one follows the other.

Conversion being the consequence of convictions obeyed, and perseverance a natural fruit of conversion, and being born of God;
'For such sin not, because the Seed of God abides in them.' But
such, through faithfulness, continue to the end, and obtain the
promise, even everlasting life.

"5. But let my reader take this along with him, that we do acknowledge that Christ, through his holy doing and suffering, for
being a Son he learned obedience, has obtained mercy of God his
Father for mankind, and that his obedience has an influence to our
salvation, in all the parts and branches of it; since thereby He became a conqueror, and led captivity captive, and obtained gifts for
men, with divers great and precious promises; that thereby we
might be partakers of the Divine nature, having escaped the corruption that is in the world, through lust. I say, we do believe
and confess, that the active and passive obedience of Christ Jesus
affects our salvation throughout, as well from the power and pollution of sin, as from the guilt, He being a conqueror as well as a
sacrifice, and both through suffering. Yet they that reject his
Divine gift, so obtained, and which He has given to them, by which
to see their sin and the sinfulness of it, and to repent and turn away
from it, and do so no more; and to wait upon God for daily strength
to resist the fiery darts of the enemy, and to be comforted through
the obedience of faith in and to this Divine grace of the Son of
God, such do not please God, do not believe truly in God, nor are
they in a state of true Christianity and salvation. 'Woman,' said
Christ, to the Samaritan at the well, 'hadst thou known the gift of
God, and who it is that speaketh to thee,' &c. People know not
Christ and God, 'whom to know is life eternal,' because they are
ignorant of the gift of God, viz.: 'A manifestation of the Spirit of
God is given to every man to profit withal;' which reveals Christ
and God to the soul. Flesh and blood cannot do it, Oxford and
Cambridge cannot do it, tongues and philosophy cannot do it: for
they who by wisdom knew not God, had these things for their
wisdom. They were strong, deep and accurate in them; but, alas!
they were clouded, puffed up, and set further off from the inward
and saving knowledge of God, because they sought for it in them,
and thought to find God there. But the key of David is another
thing, which shuts and no man opens, and opens and no man
shuts; and this key have all they that receive the gift of God into
their hearts, and it opens to them the knowledge of God and
themselves, and gives them quite another sight, taste and judgment

of things than their educational or traditional knowledge afforded them. This is the beginning of the new creation of God, and thus it is we come to be new creatures.

"And we are bold to declare, there is no other way like this, by which people can come into Christ, or be true Christians, or receive the advantage that comes by the death and sufferings of the Lord Jesus Christ." *

* That views on these important points of Christian doctrine, closely approximating, if not identical with those held by Friends, were entertained by some of the more enlightened theologians of that day, is shown by the following extracts from a work entitled "Rational Theology and Christian Philosophy in England in the Seventeenth Century," by John Tulloch, published in 1872. First from Benjamin Whichcote, who appears to have been for some time in fellowship with Puritans, and afterwards, being connected with the "Church," was made Provost of King's College, Cambridge. Speaking of the necessity of Christ's work within man, as well as his work without, he says: "For God's acts are not false, overly, imperfect. God cannot make a vain show; God, being perfectly under the power of goodness, cannot deny Himself — because if He should, He would depart from goodness, which is impossible to God. Therefore *we* must yield; be subdued to the rules of goodness, receiving stamps and impressions from God, and God cannot be further pleased *than when goodness takes place.* They therefore deceive and flatter themselves extremely who think of reconciliation with God by means of a Saviour acting upon God on their behalf, and not also working *in and upon them to make them God-like.*"— Vol. 2d, pages 64, 65.

Second from John Smith, also a teacher at Cambridge, and who is spoken of as "a Christian inwardly and in good earnest;" "Divinely given, evangelical righteousness never merely lies alongside the soul, formally imputed to it as an *addendum,* securing its acceptance with God; but it spreads itself over all the powers of the soul, quickening it into a divine life. It is not a doctrine wrapped up in ink and paper, but a *vitalis scientia,* a living impression made upon the soul and spirit." "The Gospel does not so much consist *in verbis* as *in vertute;* neither doth the evangelical dispensation therefore please God so much more than the legal did, because as [being] a finer contrivance of His infinite understanding, it more clearly discovers the way of salvation to the souls of men; but chiefly because it is *a more powerful efflux of His divine goodness upon them,* as being the true seed of a happy mortality, continually thriving and growing on to perfection. It does not hold forth such a transcendent privilege and advantage above what the law did, *only because it acquaints us that Christ, our true High Priest, is ascended up into the holy of holies,* and there, instead of the blood of bulls and goats, hath sprinkled the Ark and Mercy Seat above with His own blood; *but also because it conveys that blood of sprinkling into our defiled consciences, to purge them from dead works.* Far be it from me to disparage in the least the merit of Christ's blood, His becoming obedient unto death, whereby we are justified. But I doubt some-

In 1694, Friends again petitioned Parliament on the subject of oaths, stating more specifically the evils they suffered, and entering more elaborately into argument to show the disadvantage resulting to the community as well as to themselves, by thus depriving them of the rights of freemen, and of giving evidence in courts of judicature. The presentation and advocacy of this petition was willingly undertaken by the poet Waller, then a member of the house. A more favorable disposition was manifest than the preceding year, but no bill was passed.

In this year Queen Mary died, and not long after a plot was discovered against King William, and renewed efforts appeared likely to be made for the return of James Stuart to the throne. This induced both Houses of Parliament to draw up and sign what was called an " Association ; " wherein they pledged themselves to support and defend the King, to revenge his death should he be killed, and to resist James and his assistants. This being presented to the King, the example was followed by the different corporations in the Kingdom. As the peaceable principles of Friends forbade their entering into any such league, they had published a statement, setting forth their views as to the setting up or pulling down kings or governments, the religious principles that restrained them from signing the " Association " as they had been requested, and their loyal feelings towards King William.

During the sitting of Parliament in 1695, there was an evident inclination to give relief to Friends, by passing the desired law to accept their affirmation instead of an oath. But there were not a few of the members deeply prejudiced against them, and bitterly opposed to doing any thing in their favor. Among the most influential of these were several of the Bishops in the upper House, and the Bishop of London was the most active of them. They repeatedly moved for amendments to the bill, which made the affirmation required, virtually an oath, and exerted themselves so adroitly and successfully, that it looked probable the whole attempt at relief would fail. King William, however, becoming interested in the matter, gave

times some of our dogmata and notions about justification *may puff us in far higher and goodlier conceits of ourselves, than God hath of us ;* and that we profanely make *the unspotted righteousness of Christ to serve only as a covering wherein to wrap up our foul deformities and filthy vices ;* and when we have done so, think ourselves in as good credit and repute with God as we are with ourselves, and that we are become heaven's darlings as much as we are our own."— Vol. 2d, p. 182.

his influence in favor of Friends so effectually, that in the forepart of 1696, a bill was passed by both Houses, and being signed by the King, became the law of the land. The Bishops and their party, however, succeeded in limiting the law to seven years, and in tacking to it an article for making the collection of tithes more prompt and secure. Some Friends, tenderly scrupulous, thinking that the wording of the required affirmation, brought it too near to the character of an oath, refused to avail themselves of it. In compliance with the petition of such, some years after, it was modified.

Several conscientious Friends in Ireland, learning that their brethren in England were seeking relief from the difficulties and losses attending the maintenance of their testimony against oaths, and that an affirmation was proposed as a substitute, became jealous, lest the cause of truth might suffer; and in the freedom of Christian fellowship, they addressed an epistle to the Meeting for Sufferings in London; desiring that Christ's command of using yea and nay might be adhered to, and the exercise of patience, until the Lord opened the way for relief in such manner as there would be no snare or doubtfulness, to those of tender consciences. The principal objection to the Affirmation was, that the sacred name was introduced into the form of words.

CHAPTER XXXIII.

Efforts to obtain some relief from Tithes — Attempt to have the Laws for collecting Tithes made more Stringent — Frustrated by the action of Friends — Renewed efforts to subject Friends to Persecution — End of Legal Persecution — Death of C. Marshall — Death of J. Crook — Visit of W. Penn, T. Story and John Everet to Ireland — Testimony respecting Friends in Ireland — T. Story and R. Gill in Philadelphia — Death of Thomas Lloyd — Some Account of R. Barrow — Second visit of W. Penn to Pennsylvania — Some Observations on Friends; their Faith; Discipline; Suffering, &c. — Declaration of Faith.

AS several Friends had long been and still were under grievous suffering for their testimony against hireling ministry; many of the clergy taking advantage of the law which allowed suits to be entered in Ecclesiastical Courts, for the collection of tithes, church dues, &c., where the defendants were liable to exorbitant charges

and protracted imprisonments; and some of them, using this power
to the uttermost; the Meeting for Sufferings in this year, (1695),
drew up a statement of the respective cases; and having obtained
an audience of the King, laid it before him, and gave him full information, not only as to the cases mentioned, but also the reasons
why Friends could not pay or compound for tithes. He heard
them respectfully, made many inquiries respecting their principles,
and expressed his approval of liberty of conscience. Shortly after
an act of grace was passed, by which about forty Friends, imprisoned for tithes and other ecclesiastical demands, were liberated.

Under the prompting of the inveterate bigotry and intolerance
that had inflicted persecution on Friends from their beginning, a
bill was now presented to the House of Lords to extend the severe
provisions and penalties of an Act of Henry VIII. for the collection
of the larger revenues of the "church," to the collection of small
tithes and church rates. The Bishop of London, who was a principal promoter of the measure, was made chairman of the committee
to which it was referred.

Having obtained a copy of this bill, Friends at once saw the
object had in view by its advocates, and that, if passed into a law,
it would be, in the hands of their implacable enemies, an instrument for renewing the practice of enormous oppression and suffering, similar to what had been borne by them prior to the passage
of the Toleration Act. The Meeting for Sufferings therefore prepared a statement of their objections to the bill, and four of its
members appeared before the committee having it in charge. Upon
the Bishop of London asking, what were their objections to the
bill? G. Whitehead replied, the same as were given by Parliament
for abolishing the Star Chamber, and High Commission Courts in
the reign of Charles I. That this bill, if it became a law, would
place Friends under an absolute power of the clergy and their
Courts, without appeal or redress; even where the amount claimed
was not over sixpence. The Bishop asking whether they had
reduced their exceptions to writing, they produced the statement
prepared. The civil lords treated Friends with kindness, and the
bill was never reported. 1696.

But the expiring struggles of hatred to Non-conformists, and especially to Quakers, for more power, was not yet over. An apostate
Quaker, named Leslie, a co-laborer with Keith, having published an
untruthful and scurrilous book entitled, "The Snake in the Grass,"

in which he had compacted all the false charges of Friends being blasphemers and traitors, so freely brought against them before, it was made use of by some priests at Norfolk to publish what they styled " Some few of the Quakers' many horrid Blasphemies." This was answered by G. Whitehead ; and W. Penn wrote and presented to the members of Parliament, a brief remonstrance against such malicious slanders being credited. Under the influence of F. Leslie, the priests and their abettors at Norfolk, the Justices and grand jurors signed a petition to Parliament for the censure or suppression of the Quakers; and two of the priests in 1698, waited on the members with it; urging that it might be presented and acted on. A few of the first sentences will give an insight of the character of the petition, and the spirit of its instigators. " We cannot, without resentment, take notice of the great growth and daily increase of the Quakers, and the mischiefs and dangers from thence threatening this nation. If is observable with what restless zeal their deluded teachers and — as we suspect — many *Romish emissaries* under *their* disguise, ramble into all parts of these Kingdoms, and boldly spread their *venomous* doctrines everywhere," &c. Friends had interviews with a number of the members, and the petition was withheld from presentation.

A similar petition was brought up in the same year from the Magistrates, &c., of Bury St. Edmunds, who had been notorious for the persecution of Friends while they had the power—charging that " the principles [held by Friends] of faith, were anti-Christian ; of government, anti-monarchical ; in point of doctrine, anti-scriptural ; and in practice, illegal," &c. This was also suppressed by those to whom it was entrusted.

The spirit of persecution, though it survived these public rebukes from the National Council, ceased to make itself felt by process of law or petitions against Friends; except that many of the Episcopal clergy, made use of the power put into their hands, to harass and oppress them for tithes and their "church dues ; " for the non-payment of which, on demand, they continued to extort large sums in the shape of fines, and by occasionally seizing property of three or four times the value of the original charge.

King William gave his support to the spirit and letter of the " Toleration Act," discouraging all attempts to oppress Non-conformists. When the seven years had expired, to which the Act for accepting the Affirmation of a Friend instead of an Oath was limited, he gave his influence to have it prolonged ; and although some of the

" High Church party " opposed it, Parliament extended its action for eleven years more.

In 1698, died Charles Marshall, who had long stood as a pillar in the Church, having been an approved and laborious minister for nearly thirty years. He was a native of Bristol, and had received a good education in his youth. His parents had been religiously concerned to train him in a knowledge of the principles of the Independents, with whom they were in membership, and to guard him from evil company, and cherish in him an abhorrence of all immoralities. As he grew into manhood, participating in the restless, inquiring spirit then prevailing, he went from one noted preacher to another, and from one profession to another, but failed to find the rest or satisfaction he longed for. He therefore deserted them all, and betook himself, with a few others, to retirement and self-examination, devoting one day out of seven to fasting and prayer.

At the time John Camm and John Audland visited Bristol, in 1654, they felt drawn to have a religious opportunity with the few associated with Charles Marshall; and the latter, by the powerful ministry of John Audland, was fully convinced of the doctrines he taught; and coming to understand the revelations of Divine Grace to his soul, he submitted to its requirements and teachings, and was thus brought out of darkness into the marvellous light of God's salvation. He joined in membership with the then small Society, faithfully maintaining its doctrines and testimonies. In 1670, or about sixteen years after his convincement, he was put in trust of a gift in the ministry; and in the course of years he travelled largely throughout Great Britain, preaching the Gospel, and aiding and encouraging his brethren in their many exercises and sufferings. He took an active and efficient part in the controversy with Wilkinson and Story, giving earnest support to the cause of discipline and order; and when he found the affectionate labor of Friends was unavailing to reclaim the anarchists, he bore an unequivocal testimony against them and their course. His friends testify, that notwithstanding the many trials, sickness and sufferings he had to pass through, he retained his mental vigor and spiritual ability to the last, and was favored with a foresight of his last illness before it came on; being, through the abounding mercy of his Saviour, prepared to meet the pale messenger when sent to his house; closing his eyes with his own hand, and resigning up his soul to his Redeemer, with entire composure.

John Crook, another faithful soldier in the Lamb's army, finished

his course in the year 1699. Some account of his unjust imprisonment and trial, at the old Bailey, in 1662, has been given. Notwithstanding the manner in which he was then treated, and the
almost certain exposure to the same kind of cruel punishment, to
which continuance in the straight and narrow way which he had
chosen, would expose him, he did not shrink from the path of duty,
and cheerfully submitted to be imprisoned, again and again, and to
suffer the reproach and ignominy heaped upon the despised servants
of Christ. He stood nobly for the truth, through good report and
evil report; ever ready to help those who were in bonds or under
suffering, and laboring that the camp should be kept clean, so that
it should be as a city set upon a hill, bringing glory to our Father
who is in heaven.

As old age came upon him, he endured great suffering from
internal disease, which at times was as much as his frame could
bear, and he remarked, "That if he did not feel an inward power
from the Lord, he could not subsist under his violent pain." He
also observed, "That the furnace of affliction was of good use, to
purge away the dross and earthly part in us." When bodily
strength admitted, he continued faithful in attending meetings for
worship, and mingling with his friends in religious engagements.

Longing to depart and be with Christ, he pleasantly remarked
how the ancients were gone or being taken away: "They step away
before me; and I, that would go, cannot. Well! it will soon be
my turn." His turn came in the Second month of 1699; when he
quietly and peacefully departed, in the eighty-second year of his
age.

In 1698, William Penn, John Everet, and Thomas Story, paid a
religious visit to Friends in Ireland. They appear to have kept
very much together; and their meetings were resorted to by such
crowds, of all ranks and professions, including some of the "clergy,"
that it excited the jealousy and anger of some of the higher dignitaries. There being a law at that time in Ireland, that no Papist
should own a horse worth more than £5 5s., and that if found
with one of greater worth, it might be seized and become the property of whoever would pay to the Magistrate £5 5s. for it; two
officers, coveting the horses on which the Friends rode, obtained a
warrant from a Magistrate, charging the Friends with being Papists,
and had their horses seized, intending to give the Magistrate the
£5 5s. But two Friends obtained a writ of replevin, and gave bond
to stand trial. William Penn at once wrote to the Lords Justices,

stating the circumstances of the case. The Justices, knowing that
Friends were not Papists, directly ordered the whole case stopped,
and the officers to be confined to their chambers. The latter, finding
they had involved themselves in a business that might bring serious
consequence on themselves, applied to William Penn, to intercede
on their behalf; which, when he thought they were sufficiently
penitent, he did; and they were forgiven and released; for which
they expressed much thankfulness.

The three Friends named, after being at the Half-Year's Meeting
held in Dublin, addressed an epistle to the Yearly Meeting in London, in which the following account of the state of things among
Friends in that nation, is interesting. "So that, dear brethren, we
have good tidings to give you of Truth's prosperity at large, and
more especially in the Churches; having had the comfort, in the
General Meeting of this nation, consisting of many weighty brethren and sisters, from all parts thereof, which was held in the city of
Dublin, in much love, peace, and unity, for several days; wherein
we had occasion to observe their commendable care for the prosperity of the blessed Truth, in all the branches of its holy testimony,
both in the general and in the particular; improving the good order
practised among the Churches of Christ in our nation."

" Indeed their simplicity, gravity and coolness, in managing their
Church affairs; their diligence in meetings, both for worship and
business; their despatch in ending differences, and expedients to
prevent them; but especially, their zeal against covetousness and
indifferency to Truth's service, and their exemplary care to discourage an immoderate concern in the pursuit of things of this life, and
to incite Friends to do good with what they have, very greatly
comforted us; and in the sweet and blessed power of Christ Jesus
the meeting ended and Friends departed." 1698.

Near the beginning of 1699, Thomas Story and Roger Gill went
over to America on religious service, and landing in Virginia,
after visiting Friends in that Province and in North Carolina, they
arrived in Philadelphia. Passing on into New York and New
England, they heard of the prevalence of an infectious disease in
Philadelphia; and after getting through with their labors in those
parts, they returned to the stricken city. Speaking of the awful-
ness of the visitation, Thomas Story says, " Great was the majesty
and hand of the Lord; great was the fear that fell upon all flesh. I
saw no lofty, airy countenance, nor heard any vain jesting to move
men to laughter, nor witty repartee to raise mirth; nor extravagant

feasting, to excite the lusts and desires of the flesh above measure; but every face gathered paleness, and many hearts were humbled, and countenances fallen and sunk, as such that waited every moment to be summoned to the bar, and numbered to the grave."

Roger Gill, who was deeply affected with witnessing the effects of this sore visitation, in one of his supplications to the Almighty in a public meeting, earnestly and solemnly petitioned, that the Lord " would be pleased to accept of his life, as a sacrifice for his people, that a stop might be put to the contagion." Some time after he was taken ill of the disease. He said he remembered " The free-will offering of himself to the Lord, and it is not in my heart to repent of the offer I have made." The disease was violent in its effects on his system, but he observed, " The Lord hath sanctified my afflictions to me, and has made my sickness as a bed of down." He died after seven days' illness, passing away peacefully, bidding farewell to those about him. The disease that had proved so fatal, ceasing almost immediately after the death of Roger Gill, and his remarkable prayer being well known, the occurrence was noted and much commented on.

While speaking of Philadelphia, it may be mentioned that Thomas Lloyd, who had been a noted minister and the Deputy-Governor of Pennsylvania, died in 1694. He was a native of Wales, his family ranking among the gentry of the country. He completed his education at the University of Oxford, where he obtained distinction among the students as a scholar. Early in life he was favored with the visitations of Divine Grace, and giving heed to its teachings, a willingness was wrought to reject the vanities and honors of the world — to obtain which he had a fair opportunity — and adopting, from heart-felt conviction, the religious principles of Friends, to join with them in membership, and faithfully maintain the testimonies of Truth that distinguished them. Dwelling under the sanctifying power of the anointing, which is truth and no lie, he found it to open to him the mysteries of Christ's kingdom, and to prepare him for the reception of a gift for the ministry, and in time to become an able minister of the gospel. While in his native country, he was imprisoned several years for refusing to take an oath, and his friends there bear testimony to the meekness, patience and love that adorned his highly intellectual character. He emigrated to Pennsylvania in 1682, crossing the ocean in the same ship that carried William Penn.

When William Penn returned to England, he made T. Lloyd,

with four others, "Council of State," and afterwards he held the office of Deputy-Governor; in which offices he served with fidèlity to his superior, and to the peace and prosperity of the people. As a minister, he labored abundantly, and his labors were blessed to the edification of the Church.

On the arrival of George Keith in Pennsylvania, Thomas Lloyd was instrumental in promoting his interest, and having him employed; so that his talents and learning might inure to the benefit of the community. But when he discovered that George had given heed to unsound opinions, and an unhallowed desire for pre-eminence, which were prompting him to violate the order of the Church and promote schism, he found it his duty to withstand him, and endeavor by affectionate labor and entreaty, to bring him to a sense of his error, and win him back to the fold. But finding that the Christian care and travail of the Church were unavailing, and that G. Keith had become an enemy to Friends, he used all his experience and influence to thwart his insidious and open attacks upon the Society; and when it became necessary, he joined with his brethren in issuing a public testimony against him. For this, he was greatly reviled and traduced by G. Keith and his party; but his meekness and patience were exemplary, and he was preserved from acting inconsistently with the pure religion he professed.

He was taken ill of a malignant fever that prevailed in Philadelphia at that time, Seventh month, 1694, and finished his course in six days after the disease first affected him. Near the close he said to some Friends who were with him, "I love you all, and am going from you. I die in unity and love with faithful Friends. I have fought a good fight, and have kept the faith; which stands not in the wisdom of words, but in the power of God. I have not sought for strife and contention, but for the Grace of our Lord Jesus Christ, and the simplicity of the Gospel. I lay down my head in peace, and I desire you may all do so." He died in the fifty-fourth year of his age.

Robert Barrow had been convinced of the truth of the Christian principles held by Friends, soon after they began to be promulgated by George Fox; and in the course of time he became an eminent minister in the Society. He travelled much throughout Great Britain, Ireland, the West Indies, and America. He suffered imprisonment repeatedly, and was often stripped of property by priests, who sued him for tithes. On one occasion he had a valuable horse, hay, and household goods, taken from him, on the suit of two daughter: of a priest. Their father had kept Robert's wife's father in jail until he died, for not paying him a small tithe. The daughters after the death of their father — the priest — had striven in various ways to harass the two daughters of the deceased Friend, in order to force them to pay the tithe for which their father had been kept in prison until released by death; but in vain. At length one of them was married to Robert Barrow, and the bridegroom's property was at once distrained, and sold to satisfy the greed of the persevering persecutors.

In 1694, in company with Robert Wardel, he travelled through the Provinces in America, where there were Friends, and in 1695, they embarked for the West Indies. They were both aged men, and the heat of the climate in Jamaica affected them unfavorably, and after being engaged in religious service there a short time, R. Wardel died. After finishing the work he found required of him on the Islands, R. Barrow, accompanied by Jonathan Dickenson and wife, embarked to return to America. The vessel was wrecked on the coast of Florida. Here he and his companions suffered almost incredible hardships and cruelty from the savages; who stripped them, and were several times deliberating about murdering them. They started to travel along the coast to St. Augustine, sometimes using a canoe to transport some on the water, while others travelled through the sands on foot. . The supply of food was so scanty and disgusting that they were nearly starved; and several of the party perished under the accumulated sufferings they underwent, before they reached the city. They were nearly two months on the route. At St. Augustine they were kindly cared for, and R. Barrow, J. Dickenson and wife, were sent to Charleston, South Carolina. Though suffering from dysentery, brought on by his exposure, and the unwholesome food he had been obliged to eat, Robert, after staying four weeks at Charleston, embarked for Philadelphia. He lived but a few days after his arrival at the latter city, but was greatly refreshed by the company of Friends there. He was fully aware of his condition, and entirely resigned to die. He dictated a letter to his wife, in which he told her the Lord was with him: and to his friends he said, "All things were well with him, and he had nothing to do but to die." An interesting account of the shipwreck, and the perils and sufferings of the ship's company, was published.

William Penn was married to his second wife in 1696. She was Hannah, the daughter of Thomas Callowhill, of Bristol. He had been absent from his Province for many years, though longing to return there, and oversee the working of the government he had instituted, and the growth of the prosperous Colony he had been a principal means of planting on the shores of the Delaware. But the various troubles in which he had been involved, and the great loss of pecuniary means that had resulted from his outlay for the Province, and the dishonesty of his agent in Ireland, had so crippled and embarrassed him, that he had been unable to carry out his strong desire to cross the Atlantic, and spend the remainder of life amid the Friends and scenes he pictured eminently propitious to secure comfort and peace. But in 1699, having settled his affairs in England and Ireland, so as not to require his personal oversight, in the Seventh month he embarked with his wife and family for Philadelphia, expecting to end his days in the Province. The voyage, providentially, was a long one, occupying three months; by which delay on the ocean they did not arrive in the city, until after the malignant fever, of which many had died, had passed away.

William Penn brought with him certificates from three meetings of Friends in England: one from "The Second Day's Meeting of Ministering Friends" in London; one from the "Men's Meeting of Friends" in Bristol, where he had resided for some years, and another from "A Monthly Meeting held at Horsham;" all expressing their full unity with and love for him as a member and minister. The reception of these certificates is recorded on the minutes of the Monthly Meeting of Friends, of Philadelphia.

The arrival of the Proprietor, after an absence of fifteen years, was hailed with joy by the people generally, and doubtless he supposed that he could now pass his days in usefulness and tranquillity. But Wm. Penn soon found that troubles beset him on every hand, and that his wise counsels, and cherished plans of improvement, were thwarted and opposed by a faction bent upon promoting their own selfish schemes and interests. This is not the place to enter into a narrative of the events that characterize the history of Pennsylvania at that time; suffice to say, such was the untoward course of affairs, that in little more than a year, William Penn was obliged to return to England, to use his personal influence and address, once more to preserve the charter that had cost him so dearly, in his possession. He never visited America again.

When the Seventeenth Century closed there were yet a few Friends left on the stage of action, who had early been brought to ·embrace the doctrines held by the Society, either through the immediate teaching of the Holy Spirit, or had been among the first converts to them, through the preaching of George Fox or his earliest co-laborers. These had witnessed those doctrines, as set forth by the numerous anointed ministers raised up by the Head of the Church, listened to and embraced by multitudes, as glad tidings of great joy; and they had seen the Society, though under ignorant or malevolent misrepresentation, and active, hard-hearted persecution, go on increasing, until after little more than fifty years from its beginning, it numbered, if a modern computation is correct— between seventy and eighty thousand members in Great Britain and Ireland, besides the thousands in America and elsewhere.

Its faith, which was clearly defined and unalterably fixed, had been again and again published to the world. It was full and scriptural; agreeing, in most fundamental points, with that professed by what was called the "Established Church;" stripped however of its ceremonies, its sacerdotalism, its man-made ministry, and its will worship; and invested with force and adaptation for practical influence on life, and the work of salvation, by the full recognition of the immediate guidance and operation of the Holy Spirit; a measure of which, it believed, is bestowed on every one that cometh into the world, for the purpose of leading out of error and sin, and bringing into a knowledge of the truth as it is in Jesus.* This faith had not been made up by mere study of the Scriptures; nor was it dependent on the incongruous opinions of commentators, in their critical renderings of the original text; but it had been learned in the school of Christ, under the immediate influence of his Spirit; by which their minds had been enlightened to understand the spiritual truths recorded in Holy Writ, and to know their faith to accord therewith.

* "Because we are separated from the public communion and worship, it is too generally concluded that we deny the doctrines received by the church, and consequently introduce a new religion. Whereas we differ least, where we are thought to differ most. For setting aside some school terms, we hold the substance of those doctrines believed by the Church of England as to God, Christ, Spirit, Scripture, repentance, sanctification, remission of sin, holy living, and the resurrection of the just and unjust, to eternal rewards and punishment. But that wherein we differ most, is about worship and conversation, and the inward qualification of the soul, by the work of God's Spirit thereon, in pursuance of these good and generally received doctrines.' —A Testimony to the Truth. Penn's Works, Folio, page 813.

This was in accordance with the declaration of Christ, "My doctrine is not mine, but his that sent me. If any man will do his will,
he shall know of the doctrine, whether it be of God or whether I·
speak of myself."

That they considered holding this faith, which they believed the
Society to have been raised up to republish and illustrate, was the outward bond of fellowship, and therefore essential to membership in
the Society, is amply proved ; not only by their repeated declarations, but by the abundant labor bestowed on those who, having
professed to be Friends, afterwards gave open evidence they had
departed from that faith ; in order, if possible, to' win them back to
sound doctrine ; and when they found their efforts unavailing ; by
firmly disowning them, and bearing testimony against their errors.*
They claimed no right to impose their understanding of the Scriptures—which they asserted were the only outward test and standard
of Christian doctrine—upon others, and thus prescribe their faith as
authoritative on other men's consciences ; but believing that the religious principles and practices into which they were led as a body
of Christian professors, were in accordance with the mind of Christ
and his apostles, as revealed in the New Testament, they could not
admit that the opinions and deductions drawn by others from the
Scriptures, opposed to or invalidating those principles or practices,
were likewise in accordance with the same mind, or that those holding such, could be Friends.

They rejected not the assistance of sound learning and criticism
to correct errors of' translation ; but they accepted the truths of the
gospel as being clearly revealed and expressed in the New Testament, and that they are as immutable as they are unequivocal. All,
therefore, who were rightly led to join in fellowship with them, they
believed would be convinced of the truths in the Scriptures, as Friends
understood them, and conform to the same principles and practices
that they had fully proved accorded therewith.†

---

* See accounts of treatment of J. Perrot and his followers ; of J. Naylor ; of
Wilkinson and Story and their followers ; of Jeffrey Bullock and of George
Keith and his followers ; given in the preceding pages.

† To the query, " Whether the Church of Christ hath power in any cases
that are matters of conscience to give a positive sentence and decision which
may be obligatory on believers ?" R. Barclay replies affirmatively, and in
the course of his argument, after stating that " all principles and articles of
faith which are held doctrinally are in respect to those that believe them
matters of conscience," he speaks thus in reference to the Society of Friends :
" Now, I say, we being gathered together into the belief of certain principles

The excellency of the church organization of the Society, had been tested by experience; and its discipline, designed to guard and preserve the members from conduct or conversation, inconsistent with the pure and self-denying religion they professed, was well fitted to promote their religious growth, and to keep the camp clean; when executed in the spirit and manner intended, and as enjoined by Christ, where He says, "If thy brother shall trespass against thee, go and tell him of his fault between thee and him alone; if he shall hear thee, thou hast gained thy brother. But if he will not hear thee, then take with thee one or two more, that in the mouth of two or three witnesses every word may be established. And if he shall neglect to hear them, tell it unto the Church; but if he neglect to hear the church, let him be unto thee as a heathen man, and a publican." They believed the apostle sets forth the spirit in which this labor is to be extended, where he exhorts, "Brethren, if a man be overtaken with a fault, ye which are *spiritual*, restore such an one, in the spirit of meekness; considering thyself, lest thou also be tempted."

As has been seen, Friends were raised up at a time, when the whole nation was embroiled in a sanguinary civil war; the rival parties, notwithstanding their bitter animosity and murderous intent, claiming to be disciples of the Prince of Peace, and to be fighting to defend or support his Church and kingdom. Yet, amid the jarring passions and heated party feeling that surrounded them, by submission to the transforming power of Divine Grace, they were brought to see and to feel the truth of the declaration of the Apostle, that all carnal contentions spring from the lusts that war in the members of unregenerate men, and are, therefore, contrary to the

and doctrines, without any constraint or worldly respect, but by the mere force of truth upon our understandings, and its power and influence upon our hearts, these *principles and doctrines* and *the practices necessarily depending upon them* are, as it were, the *terms* that have drawn us together, and the [outward] *bond* by which we became centred into one body and fellowship, and distinguished from others. Now if any one or more so engaged with us, should arise to teach any other doctrine or doctrines, contrary to *these* which were the *ground of our being one*, who can deny but that the body hath power in such a case to declare: This is not according to the truth we profess, and therefore we pronounce such and such doctrines to be wrong, with which we cannot have unity, nor yet any more spiritual fellowship *with those that hold them*, and [who] so cut themselves off *from being members*, by dissolving the very *bond* by which they were *linked* to the body."—Treatise on Church Government, Phila. edition, page 66.

commands of Christ and the precepts of his gospel; which breathe
"Glory to God in the highest, peace on earth, good-will to men."
They therefore bore an unwavering testimony against war, in all
its varied phases; and those — and there were many of them — who
were in the army when convinced of the truths of the gospel as
held by Friends, put up the sword into the sheath, and, seeking a
kingdom not of this world, could no longer fight.

The polemic strife, then fiercely waged, was little less bitter than
the military contest; and the uncharitable and intemperate feelings, fostered by excited discussions on controverted points of doctrine, led men to judge each other, and the opinions they respectively advocated, under the impulse of prejudice and sectarian
predilection, rather than by the standard of revealed truth, and the
dictates of a sound mind. The spirit of intolerance manifested
itself, not only in active persecution, where the power was possessed,
but in the coarse and indecorous language often used in the controversial writings of the day; and it is not to be denied, that occasionally some Friends were affected, more or less, by the contagion
which surrounded them, so far as to retort in harsh and unguarded
expressions, when addressing or speaking of their vilifying opponents.

Misunderstood and misrepresented, because of their frequently
speaking of Christ within, the hope of glory, and because of their
emphatic declaration that no one could be in a state of justification
before God, while still subservient to the law of sin and death, they
were charged with disbelief in the Deity and manhood of Christ;
in his atoning sacrifice for sin, and in justification through his sufferings, death and merits. But they always boldly and explicitly
denied the accusation, and unequivocally avowed their full belief in
Jesus Christ of Nazareth, as the Saviour of men; that they owned
Him in all his offices, and that He was to them all in all. They
owned Him as the Son of Man, born of the Virgin Mary, offering
Himself up as an atonement for sin, as the Mediator, and as God over
all, blessed forever; without whose preparation and divine assistance,
no step could be taken in the way and work of salvation. But
while believing these fundamental truths of the gospel, as professed
by the orthodox " churches " of the day, they were called to hold
up pre-eminently the all-important offices and indispensable need of
the Holy Spirit, or Grace of God, in the work of man's salvation.
They were commissioned to call on all to give heed to this Grace
of God, this Light wherewith Christ has enlightened every man that

cometh into the world; an unspeakable gift, purchased for man by his death on the cross.* They unhesitatingly declared, that it was only by the enlightening of his understanding through this manifestation of the Holy Spirit, that man could obtain a just estimate of his lapsed condition as a child of fallen Adam, or the exceeding sinfulness of his own sin; and by obedience thereto, come to experience that godly sorrow which worketh repentance unto salvation, not to be repented of; and be furnished with living, availing faith in Jesus Christ, as the Lamb of God that taketh away the sin of the world. That it was thus man experienced the benefits flowing from that most acceptable sacrifice, when Christ bore our sins in his own body on the tree, and through the Eternal Spirit offered Himself without spot to God, on Mount Calvary; and that as obedience to this Divine Grace was continued, he came to experience what it is to be washed, to be sanctified, to be justified, in the name of the Lord Jesus and by the Spirit of our God.

This work of regeneration and sanctification, they knew from experience, was no easy or superficial change from a state of nature; but that it was a crucifying and progressive transformation; in which they put off, concerning their former conversation, the old man, which is corrupt according to the deceitful lusts, and were renewed in the spirit of the mind; and put on the new man, which

---

* "That which God hath given us the experience of — after our great loss in literal knowledge of things — *and that which he hath given us to testify of*, is the mystery, the hidden life, the inward and spiritual appearance of our Lord and Saviour Jesus Christ, revealing his power inwardly, destroying enemies inwardly, and working his work inwardly in the heart. Oh! this was the joyful sound to our souls, even the tidings of the arising of that inward life and power which could do this. Now this spiritual appearance of his was after his appearance in the flesh, and is the standing and lasting dispensation of the gospel, even the appearance of Christ in his spirit and power inwardly in the hearts of his; so that in minding this, and being faithful in this respect, we mind our peculiar work, and are faithful in that which God hath peculiarly called us to, and requireth of us.

"There is not that need of publishing the other [the outward manifestation, atonement, resurrection, &c., of Christ] as formerly was. The historical relation concerning Christ is generally believed and received by all sorts that pretend to Christianity. His miracles, his death, his rising, his ascending, his interceding, &c., are generally believed by all people; but the mystery they miss of; the hidden life they are not acquainted with, but [are] alienated from the life of God, in the midst of their owning and acknowledging of these things." — Works of I. Penington, Phila. edition, Vol. 3d, page 386–87. See also the repeated declarations of G. Fox and other of the primitive Friends.

after God is created in righteousness and true holiness. They had practical knowledge, and they so declared, that this new creation is effected only as man allows God to work in him, by his Spirit, to will and to do of his good pleasure; and therefore that salvation is to be wrought out with fear and trembling.* Under a sense of the frailty of human nature and its proneness to sin, as also of the greatness and awful importance of this inward work, they taught the necessity of it being entered on in sincerity and uprightness towards the great Searcher of the thoughts and intents of the heart, and continued in close watchfulness, and faithfulness to his inspeaking word of Divine Grace.

To witness its continued progress, and prevent it being marred, they found it requisite, not only to refrain from what was generally deemed corrupt, but to come out from the vain fashions and customs of the world, to deny its friendships, and to bear testimony against all, however esteemed by men, that originated from or ministered to the deceitful lusts of the unregenerate heart. Hence it was, that adhering to the garb of the more religious professors, worn at the time they arose, stripped of all ornament, and feeling forbidden to change with the varying fashions, they soon became distinguished by the plainness of their dress, as well as by the use of the pronouns *Thou* and *Thee* to a single person, and refusing to give flattering titles, or to use complimentary phrases.† Beside being religiously restrained from indulgence in this corrupt language, they were in like manner withheld from the use of music,

---

* See the accounts of their religious conversion and growth given by G. Fox, G. Whitehead, S. Crisp, E. Burrough, W. Edmundson, John Burnyeat, F. Howgil, T. Ellwood and others, abbreviated in the present work.

† "We dare not give worldly honor, or use the frequent and modish salutations of the times, seeing plainly that vanity, pride, and ostentation belong to them. . . . It is not to distinguish ourselves as a party, or out of pride, ill-breeding or humor, but in obedience to the sight and sense we have received from the Spirit of Christ, of the evil rise and tendency thereof. For the same reason we have returned to the first plainness of speech, viz., *thee* and *thou* to a single person; which though men give no other to God, they will hardly endure it from us. It has been a great test upon *pride*, and shown the blind and weak inside of many."—Penn's Works, Folio, page 805.

"Plainness in apparel and furniture is another testimony peculiar to us, in the degree we have borne it to the world. . . . . Likewise temperance in *food*, and abstinence from the recreations and pastimes of the world, all which we have been taught by the Spirit of our Lord Jesus Christ to be according to Godliness." — "Primitive Christianity Revived," Penn's Works, Folio, page 806.

and other vain amusements; from gratifying pride in the furniture of their houses; and thus to bear practical witness in their daily lives and conversation, to the duty imperative on the Christian, to take up the daily cross, and in humble obedience to the Grace of God, to deny all ungodliness and worldly lusts, and to live soberly, righteously, and godly in this present world.*

Because they scrupled to bestow the title of "The Word," used by the evangelist John to designate Christ, on any inferior object, they were unjustly stigmatized as slighting or undervaluing the Holy Scriptures. They, however, invariably confessed undoubting belief in their divine origin; that they were the *words* of God, and able to make wise unto salvation, *through faith that is in Christ Jesus.* They enjoined on all in communion with them, to be diligent in reading and observing their contents, as being profitable for doctrine, for reproof, for correction, for instruction in righteousness, that the *man of God* may be perfect, thoroughly furnished unto all good works. But with the belief that a measure of the Holy Spirit, which dictated the Scriptures, is given to every man to profit withal, and that it is intended to lead into all truth, they saw that it must necessarily be the *primary* rule of faith and practice. Therefore they taught that the right interpretation and application of those parts of the Scriptures, that relate to spiritual things, can be come at only through the enlightening influence of this Spirit, which inspired their respective writers.† And as it is evident this

---

* "Seeing the chief end of all religion is to redeem men from the spirit and vain conversation of this world, and to lead into inward communion with God, before whom if we fear always we are accounted happy; therefore all the vain customs and habits thereof, both in word and deed, are to be rejected and forsaken by those who come to this fear; such as taking off the hat to a man, the bowing and cringing of the body, and such other salutations of that kind, with all the foolish and superstitious formalities attending them, all which man hath invented in his degenerate state, to feed his pride in the vain pomp and glory of this world; as also the unprofitable plays, frivolous recreations, sportings and gamings, which are invented to pass away the precious time, and divert the mind from the Witness of God in the heart and from the living sense of His fear, and from that evangelical Spirit wherewith Christians ought to be leavened, and which leads into sobriety, gravity and godly fear: in which, as we abide, the blessing of the Lord is felt to attend us in those actions in which we are necessarily engaged, in order to the taking care of the outward man."—Barclay's Apology, Proposition XV.

† And yet as the word of God may in some sense signify the *command* of God, referring to the thing or matter commanded, as the mind of God, it may be called the word of the Lord or word of God; as on particular occasions,

Holy Spirit cannot contradict itself, they believed that while it furnished the light to guide reason to the right understanding of what is contained in the sacred records, its subsequent revelations to individuals could not contradict those records, so comprehended.

Costly as was the price they paid, and terrible the fight of affliction through which they passed, while promulgating and practically exemplifying these doctrines and testimonies of the gospel as well as insisting on the Headship of Christ in his Church; that all spiritual gifts were to be received direct from Him, and exercised under his immediate prompting, without money and without price; nevertheless, under the overruling providence of their Captain and Leader, their sufferings probably enabled them to produce a much greater effect, than if they had been permitted to propagate their faith, by pen or word of mouth, unopposed or unmolested. The deep afflictions through which they passed with marvellous Christian patience and meekness, did much, with their consistency and straightforwardness, to commend them and their religion to every man's conscience in the sight of God, and when the eighteenth century dawned upon the world, not only they, but other religious professors, were reaping many benefits springing from them.*

the prophets had the word of the Lord to persons and places; that is to say, the mind or will of God, or that which was commanded them of the Lord to declare or do. So Christ uses it, when He tells the Pharisees that they had made the word (or command) of God of none effect by their traditions. But because people are so apt to think if they have the Scriptures they have all, for that they account them the only Word of God, and so look no further, that is, to no other Word from whence these good words came; therefore this people have been constrained, and they believe by God's good Spirit, once and again to point them to the great Word of words, Christ Jesus, in whom is Life, and the Life, the Light of men; that they might feel something nearer to them than the Scriptures, to wit, the Word in the heart, whence all holy Scripture came, which is Christ within them, the hope of glory. He is the only right Expounder, as well as the Author of Holy Scripture, without whose Light, Spirit or Grace they cannot be profitably read.—Penn's Works.

* William Penn, than whom there is no more competent and reliable witness, bears this testimony concerning them : "They were changed men themselves before they went about to change others. Their hearts were rent as well as their garments changed, and they knew the power and work of God upon them. This was seen by the great alteration it made and their stricter course of life and more godly conversation that immediately followed upon it. They went not forth or preached in their own time and will, but in the will of God; and spoke not their own studied matter, but as they were opened and moved of his Spirit, with which they were well acquainted in their own

They left a rich legacy to, and a serious responsibility on, those who should come after them, professing to believe in and uphold the same faith as they did. A legacy not to be rightly estimated or enjoyed by assuming their distinctive name — speaking highly of them as good men and Christians, and taking advantage of the character and privileges their noble conduct purchased — merely building the tombs of the prophets, and garnishing the sepulchres of the righteous — but by walking by the same rule, and minding the same thing that they did, and thus necessarily bringing forth the same fruits: and a responsibility thus to maintain the doctrines and testimonies that the blessed Head of the Church raised up the Society to witness to, as connected with the gospel in its purity and spirituality.

The following is the Declaration of Faith, mentioned on page 605. It is entitled "The Christian Doctrine, and Society of the People called Quakers cleared, &c."

After referring to the many misrepresentations put forth respecting the Doctrines held by Friends, it proceeds:

" We are, therefore, tenderly concerned for truth's sake, in behalf of the said people, (as to the body of them, and for all of them who are sincere to God, and faithful to their Christian principle and profession,) to use our just endeavors to remove the reproach, and all causeless jealousies concerning us, touching those doctrines of Christianity, or any of them pretended, or supposed, to be in question in the said division; in relation whereunto we do in the fear of God, and in simplicity and plainness of his truth received, solemnly

conversion; which cannot be expressed to carnal men so as to give them any intelligible account, for to such it is, as Christ said, 'Like the blowing of the wind, which no man knows whence it cometh or whither it goeth.' Yet this proof and seal went along with their ministry — that many were turned from their lifeless professions and the evil of their ways to the knowledge of God and an holy life, as thousands can witness. And as they freely received what they had to say from the Lord, so they freely administered it to others. . . . They came forth low, and despised, and hated, as the primitive Christians did, and not by the help of worldly wisdom or power, as former reformations in part have done; but in all things it may be said, this people were brought forth in the cross; in a contradiction to the ways, worship, fashion and customs of the world; yea, against wind and tide, that so no flesh might glory before God."

and sincerely declare what our Christian belief and profession has been, and still is, in respect to Jesus Christ the only begotten Son of God, his suffering, death, resurrection, glory, light, power, great day of judgment, &c.

"We sincerely profess faith in God by his only begotten Son Jesus Christ, as being our light and life, our only way to the Father, and also our only Mediator and Advocate with the Father.(a)

"That God created all things, He made the worlds, by his Son Jesus Christ, He being that powerful and living Word of God by whom all things were made;(b) and that the Father, the Word, and the Holy Spirit are one, in Divine Being inseparable; one true, living and eternal God, blessed for ever.(c)

"Yet that this Word, or Son of God, in the fulness of time, took flesh, became perfect man, according to the flesh, descended and came of the seed of Abraham and David,(d) but was miraculously conceived by the Holy Ghost, and born of the Virgin Mary.(e) And also further, declared powerfully to be the Son of God, according to the Spirit of sanctification, by the resurrection from the dead.(f)

"That in the Word, (or Son of God,) was life, and the same life was the light of men; and that He was that true light which enlightens every man coming into the world;(g) and therefore that men are to believe in the light, that they may become children of the light; (h) hereby we believe in Christ the Son of God, as He is the light and life within us; and wherein we must needs have sincere respect and honor to, and belief in Christ, as in his own unapproachable and incomprehensible glory and fulness: (i) as He is the Fountain of life and light, and Giver thereof unto us; Christ, as in himself, and as in us, being not divided. And that as man, Christ died for our sins, rose again, and was received up into glory in the heavens.(k) He having, in his dying for all, been that one great universal offering, and sacrifice for peace, atonement and reconciliation between God and man;(l) and He is the propitiation not for our sins only, but for the sins of the whole world.(m) We were reconciled by his death, but saved by his life.

"That Jesus Christ, who sitteth at the right hand of the throne

(a) Hebrew xii. 2. 1 Peter i. 21. John xiv. 6. 1 Tim. ii. 5. (b) Eph. iii. 9. John i. 1, 2, 3. Heb. i. 2. (c) 1 John v. 7. (d) Rom. i. 3, 4. (e) Matt. i. 23. (f) Rom. i. 3, 4. (g) John i. 4, 9. (h) John xii. 36. Isa. ii. 5. (i) 1 Tim. vi. 16. (k) 1 Pet. iii. 18. 1 Tim. iii. 16. Matt. xix. 28, and xxv. 31. Luke ix. 26, and xxiv. 26. (l) Rom. v. 10, 11. Heb. ii. 17, 18. Eph. ii. 16, 17. Col. i. 20, 21, 22. (m) 1 John ii. 2. 2 Cor. v. 14, 15. Heb. ii. 9.

of the majesty in the heavens, yet is He our king, high-priest, and prophet, (n) in his church, a minister of the sanctuary, and of the true tabernacle which the Lord pitched, and not man. (o)   He is Intercessor and Advocate with the Father in heaven, and there appearing in the presence of God for us, (p) being touched with the feeling of our infirmities, sufferings and sorrows.   And also by his spirit in our hearts, He maketh intercession according to the will of God, crying, Abba, Father. (q)

"For any whom God hath gifted, (r) and called sincerely to preach faith in the same Christ, both as within and without us, cannot be to preach two Christs, but one and the same Lord Jesus Christ, (s) having respect to those degrees of our spiritual knowledge of Christ Jesus in us, (t) and to his own unspeakable fulness and glory, (u) as in Himself, in his own entire being, wherein Christ himself and the least measure of his light or life, as in us or in mankind, are not divided nor separable, no more than the sun is from its light.   And as He ascended far above all heavens, that He might fill all things, (x) his fulness cannot be comprehended, or contained in any finite creature; (y) but in some measure known and experienced in us, as we are capable to receive the same, as of his fulness we have received grace for grace.   Christ our Mediator, received the Spirit, not by measure, (z) but in fulness; but to every one of us is given grace, according to the measure of his gift. (a)

"That the gospel of the grace of God should be preached in the name of the Father, Son and Holy Ghost, (b) being one (c) in power, wisdom, and goodness, and indivisible, or not to be divided, in the great work of man's salvation.

"We sincerely confess and believe in Jesus Christ, both as He is true God and perfect man, (d) and that He is the author of our living faith in the power and goodness of God, as manifested in his Son Jesus Christ, and by his own blessed Spirit, or divine unction, revealed in us, (e) whereby we inwardly feel and taste of his goodness, (f) life and virtue; so as our souls live and prosper by and in Him; and the inward sense of this divine power of Christ, and faith

(n) Zech. ix. 9.   Luke xix. 38.   John xii. 15.   Heb. iii. 1.   Deut. xviii. 15, 18.   Acts iii. 22, and vii. 37.   (o) Heb. viii. 1, 2.   (p) Heb. vii. 25.   Heb. ix. 24.   (q) Rom. viii. 26, 27, 34.   Gal. iv. 6.   (r) Eph. iii. 7.   1 Pet. iv. 10. (s) 1 Cor. viii. 6.   (t) John xv. 26, and xvi. 13, 14, 15.   (u) John i. 16. (x) Eph. iv. 10.   (y) Col. i. 19, and ii. 9.   (z) John iii. 34.   (a) Eph. iv. 7. (b) Matt. xxviii. 19.   (c) John i. 1, 2, 3, 4.   (d) John i. 1, 2.   Rom. ix. 5.   1 John v. 20.   1 Tim. ii. 5.   (e) 1 John ii. 20, 27.   (f) 1 Pet. ii. 3.   John vi. 33, 35, 51, 57, 58.

in the same, and this inward experience, is absolutely necessary to make a true, sincere, and perfect Christian, in spirit and life.

"That divine honor and worship are due to the Son of God:(g) and that He is, in true faith, to be prayed unto, and the name of the Lord Jesus Christ called upon, as the primitive Christians did,(h) because of the glorious union or oneness of the Father and the Son;(i) and that we cannot acceptably offer up prayers and praises to God, nor receive a gracious answer or blessing from God, but in and through his dear Son Christ.

"That Christ's body that was crucified was not the Godhead, yet by the power of God was raised from the dead; and that the same Christ that was therein crucified, ascended into heaven and glory,(k) is not questioned by us. His flesh saw no corruption,(l) it did not corrupt; but yet doubtless his body was changed into a more glorious(m) and heavenly condition than it was in when subject to divers sufferings on earth; but how and what manner of change it met withal after it was raised from the dead, so as to become such a glorious body, as it is declared to be, is too wonderful for mortals to conceive, apprehend or pry into, and more meet for angels to see: the scripture is silent therein, as to the manner thereof, and we are not curious to inquire or dispute it; nor do we esteem it necessary to make ourselves wise above(n) what is written as to the manner or condition of Christ's glorious body, as in heaven; no more than to inquire how Christ appeared in divers manners or forms;(o) or how He came in among his disciples, the doors being shut;(p) or how He vanished out of their sight after He was risen. However, we have cause to believe his body, as in heaven, is changed into a most glorious condition, far transcending what it was in on earth, otherwise how could our low body be changed, so as to be made like unto his glorious body;(q) for when He was on earth, and attended with sufferings, He was said to be like unto us in all things, sin only excepted;(r) which may not be so said of Him, as now in a state of glory, as He prayed for;(s) otherwise where would be the change both in him and in us?

"True and living faith in Christ Jesus the Son of the living God,(t) has respect to his entire being and fulness, to Him entirely

(g) John v. 23. Heb. i. 6.   (h) 1 Cor. i. 2. Acts vii. 59.   (i) John x. 30. 1 John v.   (k) Luke xxiv. 26.   (l) Psal. xvi. 10.   Acts ii. 31, and xiii. 35, 37.   (m) Phil. iii. 21.   (n) 1 Cor. iv. 6.   (o) John xx. 15.   (p) John xx. 19. Luke xxiv. 36, 37, and xxiv. 31.   (q) Phil. iii. 21.   (r) Heb. ii. 17, and iv. 15. (s) John xxii. 5.   (t) John xiv. 1.

as in himself, and as all power in heaven and earth is given unto ·
Him; (*u*) and also an eye and respect to the same Son of God (*x*) as
inwardly making himself known in the soul, in every degree of his
light, life, spirit, grace, and truth; and as He is both the word of
faith, and a quickening spirit in us;(*y*) whereby He is the immediate cause, author, object and strength of our living faith in his
name and power; and of the work of our salvation from sin and
bondage of corruption: and the Son of God cannot be divided from
the least or lowest appearance of his own divine light, or life in us
or in mankind, no more than the sun from its own light: nor is the
sufficiency of his light within, by us set up in opposition to Him the
man Christ, or his fulness, considered as in Himself, or without
us; nor can any measure or degree of light, received from Christ, as
such, be properly called the fulness of Christ, or Christ as in fulness,
nor exclude Him, so considered, from being our complete Saviour;
for Christ himself to be our light, our life, and Saviour, (*z*) is so
consistent, that without his light we could not know life, nor Him
to save us from sin or deliver us from darkness, condemnation or
wrath to come: and where the least degree or measure of this ligh*t*
and life of Christ within is sincerely waited in, followed and obeyed;
there is a blessed increase of light and grace known and felt; as the
path of the just it shines more and more, until the perfect day; (*a*)
and thereby a growing in grace, and in the knowledge of God, and
of our Lord and Saviour Jesus Christ, hath been, and is truly experienced. And this light, life, or Spirit of Christ within, (for they
are one divine principle,) is sufficient to lead unto all truth; having
in it the divers ministrations both of judgment and mercy, both of
law and gospel, even that gospel which is preached in every intelligent creature under heaven. It does not only, as in its first ministration, manifest sin, and reprove and condemn for sin; but also
excites and leads them that believe in it to true repentance; and
thereupon to receive that mercy, pardon, and redemption in Christ
Jesus, which He hath obtained for mankind in those gospel terms
of faith in his name, true repentance and conversion to Christ,
thereby required.

" So that the light and life of the Son of God within, truly obeyed
and followed, as being the principle of the second or new covenant,

(*u*) Matt. xxviii. 18, and xi. 27. John xvii. 2. Heb. i. 2, 3. (*x*) John xiv.
23, and xvii. 21, 22, 23, 24; 26. (*y*) 1 Cor. xv. 45. Rom. x. 7, 8. (*z*) John i.
4, 9, and iii. 19, 20, and xii. 35, 36, 46, and viii. 12. (*a*) Prov. iv. 18. Psal.
xxxvi. 9.

'as Christ the Light is confessed to be, even as He is the seed or word of faith in all men, this does not leave men or women, who believe in the light, under the first covenant, nor as the sons of the bond-woman; as the literal Jews were, when gone from the Spirit of God, and his Christ in them; but it naturally leads them into the new covenant, in the new and living way, and to the adoption of sons, to' be children and sons of the free-woman, of Jerusalem from above.

" It is true, that we ought not to lay aside, nor any way to under-value, but highly to esteem, true preaching and the holy scriptures; and the sincere belief and faith of Christ, as He died for our sins, and rose again for our justification; together with Christ's inward and spiritual appearance, and work of grace in the soul; livingly to open the mystery of his death, and perfectly to effect our recon-ciliation, sanctification, and justification; and wherever Christ qualifies and calls any to preach and demonstrate the mystery of his coming, death, and resurrection, &c., even among the Gentiles, Christ ought accordingly to be both preached, believed, and received.

" Yet supposing there have been, or are such pious and conscien-tious Gentiles, in whom Christ was and is as the Seed, or principle of the second or new covenant, the light, the word of faith, as is granted; and that such live uprightly and faithfully to that light they have, or to what is made known of God in them, and who therefore in that state cannot perish, but shall be saved, as is also confessed; and supposing these have not the outward advantage of preaching, scripture, or thence the knowledge of Christ's outward coming, being outwardly crucified and risen from the dead; can such, thus con-sidered be justly excluded Christianity, or the covenant of grace, as to the virtue, life, and nature thereof; or truly deemed no Christians, or void of any Christian faith in the life and power of the Son of God within, or be only sons of the first covenant, and bond-woman, like the literal outside Jews; or must all be excluded any true knowledge of faith of Christ within them, unless they have the knowledge of Christ as without them? No sure! for that would imply insufficiency in Christ and his light, as within them, and to frustrate God's good end and promise of Christ, and his free and universal love and grace to mankind, in sending his Son. We charitably believe the contrary, that they must have some true faith and interest in Christ and his mediation; because of God's free love in Christ to all mankind, and Christ's dying for all men, (b) and

(b) 2 Cor. v. 14, 15.

being given for a light of the Gentiles, and for salvation to the ends of the earth ; (c) and because of their living up sincerely and faithfully to his light in them—their being pious, conscientious, accepted, and saved, as is granted. We cannot reasonably think a sincere, pious, or godly man, wholly void of Christianity, of what nation soever he be, because none can come to God or godliness but by Christ (d) by his light and grace in them : yet we grant if there be such pious, sincere men or women, as have not the Scripture or knowledge of Christ, as outwardly crucified, &c., they are not perfect Christians in all perfections, as in all knowledge and understanding, all points of doctrine, outward profession of Christ ; so that they are better than they profess or pretend to be ; they are more Jews inward, and Christians inward than in outward show or profession. There are Christians sincere and perfect in kind or nature, in life and substance, though not in knowledge and understanding. A man or woman having the life and fruits of true Christianity, the fruits of the Spirit of Christ in them, that can talk little thereof, or of creeds, points, or articles of faith, yea, many that cannot read letters, yet may be true Christians in spirit and life ; and some could die for Christ, that could not dispute for him : and even infants that die in innocency, are not excluded the grace of God, or salvation in and by Christ Jesus ; the image and nature of the Son of God, being in some measure in them, and they under God's care and special providence. See Matt. xviii. 2, 10.

"And though we had the Holy Scriptures of the Old and New Testament, and a belief of Christ crucified and risen, &c., we never truly knew the mystery thereof, until we were turned to the light of his Grace and Spirit within us : we knew not what it was to be reconciled by his death, and saved by his life ; or what it was to know the fellowship of his sufferings, the power of his resurrection, or to be made conformable unto his death ; we knew not, until He opened our eyes, and turned our minds from darkness unto his own divine life and light within us.

"Notwithstanding, we do sincerely and greatly esteem and value the Holy Scriptures, preaching and teaching of faithful, divinely inspired, gifted, and qualified persons, and ministers of Jesus Christ, as being great outward helps, and instrumental in his hand, and by his Spirit, for conversion, where God is pleased to afford those outward helps and means ; as that we neither do nor may oppose the

(c) Isa. xlix. 6. Luke ii. 32. Acts xiii. 47. (d) John xiv. 6.

sufficiency of the light or Spirit of Christ within, to such outward helps or means, so as to reject, disesteem, or undervalue them; for they all proceed from the same light and Spirit, and tend to turn men's minds thereunto, and all centre therein.

"Nor can the Holy Scriptures or true preaching without, be justly set in opposition to the light or Spirit of God or Christ within; for his faithful messengers are ministers thereof, being sent to turn people to the same light and Spirit in them. Acts xxvi. 18; Rom. xiii. 2; 2 Cor. iv. 6; 1 Pet. ii. 9; 1 John ii. 8.

"It is certain, that great is the mystery of godliness in itself, in its own being and excellency: namely, that God should be and was manifest in the flesh, justified in the Spirit, seen of angels, preached unto the Gentiles, believed on in the world, and received up into glory.

"And it is a great and precious mystery of godliness and Christianity also, that Christ should be spiritually and effectually in men's hearts, to save and deliver them from sin, Satan, and bondage of corruption; Christ being thus revealed in true believers, and dwelling in their hearts by faith, Christ within the hope of glory, our light and life, who of God is made unto us wisdom, righteousness, sanctification, and redemption. 1 Cor. i. 30. And therefore this mystery of godliness, both as in its own being and glory, and also as in men (in many hid, and in some revealed), hath been and must be testified, preached, and believed; where God is pleased to give commission, and prepare people's hearts for the same, and not in man's will.

"Concerning the resurrection of the dead, and the great day of judgment yet to come, beyond the grave, or after death, and Christ's coming without us, to judge the quick and the dead (as divers questions are put in such terms), what the Holy Scriptures plainly declare and testify in these matters, we have great reason to credit, and not to question, and have been always ready to embrace, with respect to Christ and his apostles' own testimony and prophecies.

"1. For the doctrine of the resurrection:

"If in this life only we have hope in Christ, we are of all men the most miserable. 1 Cor. xv. 19. We sincerely believe, not only a resurrection in Christ from the fallen sinful state here, but a rising and ascending into glory with Him hereafter; that when He at last appears, we may appear with Him in glory. Col. iii. 4; 1 John iii. 2.

" But that all the wicked who lived in rebellion against the light of grace, and die finally impenitent, shall come forth to the resurrection of condemnation.

" And that the soul or spirit of every man and woman shall be reserved in its own distinct and proper being (so as there shall be as many souls in the world to come as in this), and every seed, yea, every soul, shall have its proper body, as God is pleased to give it. 1 Cor. xv. A natural body is sown, a spiritual body is raised; that' being first which is natural, and afterward that which is spiritual. And though it is said, this corruptible shall put on incorruption, and this mortal shall put on immortality; the change shall be such as flesh and blood cannot inherit the kingdom of God, neither doth corruption inherit incorruption. 1 Cor. xv. We shall be raised out of all corruption and corruptibility, out of all mortality; and the children of God and of the resurrection, shall be equal to the angels of God in heaven.(e)

" And as the celestial bodies do far excel terrestrial, so we expect our spiritual bodies in the resurrection, shall far excel what our bodies now are; and we hope that none can justly blame us for thus expecting better bodies than now they are. Howbeit, we esteem it very unnecessary to dispute or question how the dead are raised, or with what body they come; but rather submit that to the wisdom and pleasure of the Almighty God.

" 2. For the doctrine of eternal judgment:

" God hath committed all judgment unto his son Jesus Christ; and He is both judge of quick and dead, and of the states and ends of all mankind, John v. 22, 27; Acts x. 42; 2 Tim. iv. 1; 1 Pet. iv. 5.

" That there shall be hereafter a great harvest, which is the end of the world, a great day of judgment, and the judgment of that great day, the Holy Scripture is clear, Matt. xiii. 39, 40, 41; ch. x. 15; and xi. 24; Jude 6. 'When the Son of Man cometh in his glory, and all the holy angels with him, then shall he sit upon the throne of his glory, and before him shall be gathered all nations,' &c. Matt. xxv. 31, 32, to the end, compared with ch. xxii. 31; Mark viii. 38; Luke ix. 26; and 1 Cor. xv. 52; 2 Thess. i. 7, 8, to the end, and 1 Thess. iv. 16; Rev. xx. 12, 13, 14, 15.

(e) Matt. xxii. 30. Mark xii. 25. Luke xx. 36.

"That this blessed heavenly man, this Son of Man, who hath so deeply suffered and endured so many great indignities and persecutions from his adversaries, both to himself and his members and brethren, should at last, even in the last and great day, signally and manifestly appear in glory and triumph, attended with all his glorious heavenly host and retinue before all nations, before all his enemies, and those that have denied him; this will be to their great terror and amazement, that this most glorious heavenly Man, and his brethren, that have been so much contemned and set at naught, should be thus exalted over their enemies and persecutors, in glory and triumph, is a righteous thing with God; and that they that suffer with him, should appear with him in glory and dignity when He thus appears at last. Christ was judge of the world, and prince thereof, when on earth, John ix. 39, and xii. 31. He is still judge of the world, the wickedness, and prince thereof, by his light, spirit, and gospel in men's hearts and consciences, John xvi. 8, 11; Matt. xii. 20; Isa. xlii. 1; Rom. ii. 16; 1 Pet. iv. 6. And He will be the judge and final determiner thereof in that great day appointed; God having appointed a day wherein He will judge the world in righteousness by that man whom he hath ordained. Christ foretold it shall be more tolerable for them of the land of Sodom and Gomorrah in the day of judgment, than for that city or people that would not receive his messengers or ministers, &c., Matt. x. 15, and see chap. xi. 24, and Mark vi. 11; Luke x. 12, 14. It is certain that God knows how to deliver the godly out of all their trials, and afflictions, and at last to bring them forth, and raise them up into glory with Christ; so He knoweth also how to reserve the unjust and finally impenitent unto the day of judgment to be punished, 2 Pet. ii. 9. He will bring them forth unto the day of destruction, Job xxi. 30. The Lord can and will reserve such impenitent, presumptuous and rebellious criminals, as bound under chains of darkness, as were the fallen angels, unto the judgment of the great day, Jude 6; Matt. xxv. 30. It is not for us to determine or dispute the manner how they shall be so reserved; but leave it to God; He knows how."

"A Postscript relating to the Doctrine of the Resurrection and Eternal Judgment.

"At the last trump of God, and the voice of the archangel, the dead shall be raised incorruptible, the dead in Christ shall rise first, 1 Cor. xv. 52. 1 Thess. iv. 16 compared with Matt. xxiv. 31.

"Many are often alarmed in conscience here by the word and voice of God, who stop their ears and slight those warnings, but the great and final alarm of the last trumpet, they cannot stop their ears against, nor escape; it will unavoidably seize upon, and further awaken them finally to judgment. They that will not be alarmed in their consciences, unto repentance, nor out of their sins here, must certainly be alarmed to judgment hereafter.

"Whosoever do now wilfully shut their eyes, hate, contemn, or shun the light of Christ, or his appearance within, shall at last be made to see, and not be able to shun or hide themselves from his glorious and dreadful appearance from heaven with his mighty angels, as with lightning and in flaming fire, to render vengeance on all them that know not God, and obey not the gospel of our Lord Jesus Christ, 1 Thess. iv. 17; Matt. xxiv. 27; Luke xvii. 24; Dan. x. 6; Job xxxvii. 3.

"And though many now evade and reject the inward convictions and judgments of the light, and shut up the records or books thereof in their own consciences, they shall be at last opened, and every one judged of these things recorded therein, according to their works, Rev. xx. 12, 13, 14, 15.

"Signed in behalf of our Christian profession and people aforesaid,

GEORGE WHITEHEAD, CHARLES MARSHALL,
AMBROSE RIGGE,   JOHN BOWATER,
WILLIAM FALLOWFIELD, JOHN VAUGHTON,
JAMES PARKE,   WILLIAM BINGLEY."

INDEX.

PAGE

Ministers, Power of the, among the New England Puritans, . . 186
   "   Influence the Council to banish on pain of death, . . 186
Monk, General, March of, on London, ... 197
Monmouth, Duke of, Attempt of the, on the British throne, . . 542
Musgrave, Christopher, Speech of, respecting Friends, . . . 529

NAMES, Origin of, originally given to Friends, ... 38
   Naylor, James, joins Friends in 1651, ... 41
Naylor, James, Cruel treatment of, at Walney Island, . . . 67
   "   "   First visit of to London, Dispute of, with some
           Baptists, ... 124, 125
   "   "   Some account of 134
   "   "   Examination of, on charge of blasphemy, cleared,
           but imprisoned, ... 135
   "   "   Personal appearance, and fluency of, . . . 136
   "   "   Fall of, Trial, Punishment, Repentance, Restora-
           tion and Death of 136–144
Neal, Account by, of the course of the Dissenters generally, . . 264
   "   Further testimony of 460
Nicholson, Joseph, and wife, Banishment of, on Pain of Death, . 195
Norton, Humphrey, Sufferings of, at New Haven, ... 164
Norton, Priest, Apology of, for the cruelty of the Jailer at Boston, 178
Norton, Catharine, Visit of, in Ireland, ... 521

OATHS, Folly of—Testimony of Friends against . . . 212
   Oath, Condemnation for taking an, by E. Clifton, . . . 213
Observations relative to the early Friends and their religious
   faith, ... 623–631
Opinion, Religious, State of, in England in the beginning of the
   seventeenth century, ... 24
Opinion, change of, respecting Dissenters, ... 502
Orange, Prince and Princess of, Notice of, ... 553
Ordinance by Cromwell, forbidding enforcing conformity, . . 66

PARKER, HENRY, Persecution of G. Fox by . . . 474–490
   Parker, Alexander, Death of 562
Parliament, Long, Convening of the 19
   "   Religion degraded by, to exclude Dissenters, . . 214
   "   Enactment by, of a law against Quakers, . . . 217
   "   Refusal of, to sanction the King's Proclamation for
           relief of Dissenters, ... 310
   "   Convened at Oxford, ... 364
   "   Obliges the King to withdraw his second Proclama-
           tion of toleration, ... 474

THE END.

Featured Titles from Westphalia Press

Issues in Maritime Cyber Security Edited by Nicole K. Drumhiller, Fred S. Roberts, Joseph DiRenzo III and Fred S. Roberts

While there is literature about the maritime transportation system, and about cyber security, to date there is very little literature on this converging area. This pioneering book is beneficial to a variety of audiences looking at risk analysis, national security, cyber threats, or maritime policy.

The Rise of the Book Plate: An Exemplative of the Art by W. G. Bowdoin, Introduction by Henry Blackwel

Bookplates were made to denote ownership and hopefully steer the volume back to the rightful shelf if borrowed. They often contained highly stylized writing, drawings, coat of arms, badges or other images of interest to the owner.

The Great Indian Religions by G. T. Bettany

G. T. (George Thomas) Bettany (1850-1891) was born and educated in England, attending Gonville and Caius College in Cambridge University, studying medicine and the natural sciences. This book is his account of Brahmanism, Hinduism, Buddhism, and Zoroastrianism

Unworkable Conservatism: Small Government, Freemarkets, and Impracticality by Max J. Skidmore

Unworkable Conservatism looks at what passes these days for "conservative" principles—small government, low taxes, minimal regulation—and demonstrates that they are not feasible under modern conditions.

A Place in the Lodge: Dr. Rob Morris, Freemasonry and the Order of the Eastern Star by Nancy Stearns Theiss PhD

Ridiculed as "petticoat masonry," critics of the Order of the Eastern Star did not deter Rob Morris' goal to establish a Masonic organization that included women as members. As Rob Morris (1818-1888) came "into the light," he donned his Masonic apron and carried the ideals of Freemasonry through a despairing time of American history.

Demand the Impossible: Essays in History as Activism
Edited by Nathan Wuertenberg and William Horne

Demand the Impossible asks scholars what they can do to help solve present-day crises. The twelve essays in this volume draw inspiration from present-day activists. They examine the role of history in shaping ongoing debates over monuments, racism, clean energy, health care, poverty, and the Democratic Party.

International or Local Ownership?: Security Sector Development in Post-Independent Kosovo
by Dr. Florian Qehaja

International or Local Ownership? contributes to the debate on the concept of local ownership in post-conflict settings, and discussions on international relations, peacebuilding, security and development studies.

The Bahai Movement: A Series of Nineteen Papers
by Charles Mason Remey

Charles Mason Remey (1874-1974) was the son of Admiral George Collier Remey and grew up in Washington DC. He studied to be an architect at Cornell (1893-1896) and the Ecole des Beaux Arts in Paris (1896-1903), where he learned about the Baha'i faith, and quickly adopted it.

Ongoing Issues in Georgian Policy and Public Administration
Edited by Bonnie Stabile and Nino Ghonghadze

Thriving democracy and representative government depend upon a well functioning civil service, rich civic life and economic success. Georgia has been considered a top performer among countries in South Eastern Europe seeking to establish themselves in the post-Soviet era.

Poverty in America: Urban and Rural Inequality and
Deprivation in the 21st Century
Edited by Max J. Skidmore

Poverty in America too often goes unnoticed, and disregarded. This perhaps results from America's general level of prosperity along with a fairly widespread notion that conditions inevitably are better in the USA than elsewhere. Political rhetoric frequently enforces such an erroneous notion.

westphaliapress.org

Made in the USA
Coppell, TX
26 April 2021